ISBN 978-0-428-62505-4
PIBN 10805194

THE

MONTHLY REVIEW,

FROM

MAY TO AUGUST INCLUSIVE.

1838.

VOL. II.

NEW AND IMPROVED SERIES.

LONDON:

E. HENDERSON, 2, OLD BAILEY,

LUDGATE HILL.

1838.

CONTENTS

OF THE

MONTHLY REVIEW FOR MAY.

Vol. II. (1838) No. I.

CONTENTS

CONTENTS

OF THE

MONTHLY REVIEW FOR JUNE.

Vol. II. (1838) No. II.

CONTENTS.

CONTENTS

OF THE

MONTHLY REVIEW FOR JULY.

Vol. II. (1838.) No. III.

CONTENTS.

CONTENTS

OF THE

MONTHLY REVIEW FOR AUGUST.

Vol. II. (1838.) No. IV.

CONTENTS.

THE

MONTHLY REVIEW.

MAY, 1838.

Art. I.—*Arts and Artists in England.* By G. F. Waagen, Director of the Royal Gallery at Berlin. 3 Vols. 12mo. London: Murray. 1838.

The title in full of these volumes states that their contents consist of " Letters written during a Season in London, and Visits to the Seats of the Nobility and Gentry in the Country; with Descriptions of the Public and Private Collections of Works of Art, Sketches of Society," &c., being a translation from the German.

It cannot be necessary to use any argument to show that the opinions of the Director of the Royal Gallery at Berlin, on every thing connected with the arts of design, are entitled to much deference, or that the observations of an intelligent and highly cultivated foreigner have always a double value; for they not only detect peculiarities in our manners and modes of thinking, whether praiseworthy or otherwise, but they mirror the habits and sentiments of another, it may be highly, civilized community. Looking to these volumes, however, as they bear upon the Arts, and remembering at the same time some of the criticisms which have been advanced by artists of eminence not only regarding modern but the ancient masters, we cannot but become impressed with the notion, that there is a vast deal of individual taste, and, so to speak, mannerism of scanning a fine picture, evinced in much that is put forward as criticism by connoisseurs. It seems to us that the reverence paid to authority, or to the dictum of some Sir Joshua, and that sort of indefinite conceptions conveyed by a jargon of technical eloquence, have very often taken the place of sound canons on the Fine Arts, instead of any fixed and intelligible principles. Is it not the case also, that the observance of all ascertained principles and established rules will never produce an exquisite specimen, and on the other hand that the violation of some of these laws may pass unheeded amid the force of some prevailing excellence? If these views be correct, it is not an unlimited reliance that is to be reposed in the criticisms of any professed judge ; nor, indeed, should we be astonished to find a man of equal attainments and experience with our author—another director of some continental celebrated academy, traversing the same ground and inspecting the same galleries, writing, on his return home, a work as peremptory and feasibly reasoned as the present, yet differing widely in his conclusions. Painting, as it appears to us, labours under the sort of ambiguity and discrepancies alluded to in a particular degree; from which, however, it is to be hoped a variety of publications like the one before us is likely to rescue the art; for Dr. Waagen is assuredly no ordinary authority; nor could he have visited any other country where pictorial treasures are so abundant and multifarious, thanks to the untold gold of Englishmen.

Whatever hesitation we may entertain to the pinning of our faith to the director's sleeve, far be it from us to object to any of his criticisms. For us, who do not know an expertly painted copy from an original in any case, to indulge in the technical slang of amateurs would be worse than ludicrous, although not more presumptuous than the manner of multitudes who utter astonishingly clever things in this way. We therefore are content to follow our author, taking all that he utters as law, not to be gainsaid; believing at the same time that he will open the eyes of our artists and of our possessors of large collections of pictures to many defects and mistakes, so as to lead to correction.

It is pleasing and creditable to find him in the preface saying, " I must praise, and most gratefully acknowledge, the extreme liberality with which so many possessors of collections of works of art allowed me free access to them." But it is more hopeful still to hear him add, " The assent which many of them gave to my very free judgment on works which they highly valued, proved to me that they have the truth more at heart than the gratification of petty vanity as collectors; a fact which indicates a degree of intellectual culture as elevated as it is rare."

We shall begin, however, with some of our author's notices concerning the English school of painting, and the masters of whose works, he says, he, previously to visiting this country, hardly knew anything except from engravings; which is as much as to attest a circumstance that need not be doubted, viz., that very few of our pictures reach a foreign market. Ours is an importing rather an exporting country in respect of the fine, whatever may be said of the industrial arts. English money is still more abundant than English paintings.

In the passage now to be quoted, the writer is speaking of the National Gallery particularly, which contains some of the most celebrated English works, from an examination of which he formed the groundwork of the criticism now to be quoted.

" The origin of original painting in England, is in the eighteenth century, that is, at a time when both the original schools of the whole of modern times, of Italy, the Netherlands, and Germany, and their branches in France and Spain, had long lost their peculiar character, and in their stead there had succeeded all over Europe a manufacture of cold, monotonous spiritless pictures, founded on the general rules and precepts of art, which were communicated in the various celebrated academies. The demands of religion, the broad foundation on which, in other schools, historical painting had gradually grown up, from its first infancy to vigorous maturity, no longer existed. This highest branch of art was now only occasionally in request, for the decoration of palaces and other public buildings; all other demands on living artists were confined to portraits. Even the tradition of the technical part of painting, which had been conscientiously handed down in the old schools of living art as the most indispensable fundamental condition, even of the highest performances, had been gradually forgotten, as of inferior importance, amid all those dead rules of pure taste, and ideal beauty of form. When, therefore, men of decided genius for painting, such as Hogarth, and afterwards Reynolds, appeared in England, they found neither a foundation of technical knowledge, nor a more elevated and animated intellectual direction of art. Under this twofold deficiency English painting appears to me to labour, though in a lessening degree, even to our time. That hollow and empty idealism, at variance with all nature, which was then advocated as the only safe road for historical painting, necessarily offended every genuine talent for the arts, the first condition of which is a lively feeling for nature, and, as always happens, leads to a prejudiced opposition. This was the case with Hogarth. He had an eminent talent for catching what was characteristic in nature, and applying it to dramatic representations. If a painter, with the mind of Hogarth, had appeared in Florence in the fifteenth century, he would doubtless have treated with great applause, from the circle of the religious notions of those times, many highly dramatic scenes of monastic life, in which his turn for humour would have found its account, in many burlesque traits of the mode of life in the convents, which many painters of that time did not suffer to escape them. But as his age afforded him no general form in which he might have displayed his talents, he invented, in order to express himself in his own way, a new species of painting, namely, the *moral-humorous*, which holds in the general domain of painting nearly the same rank as the drama of ordinary life in poetry; so that Hogarth is to Raphael as Molière to Sophocles. The former show us man, dependent on his animal nature and on his passions, and, according to the manner and the degree in which these are opposed to his higher intellectual nature, excite laughter, compassion, contempt, abhorrence, disgust. The other show us the predominance of the divine nature in man, whether in combating that animal nature, and the passions, in honourable defeat, or in dignified composure after victory, and fill us with admiration, astonishment, veneration, rapture.

"This moral-humorous department is the only one in which the English have enlarged the domain of painting in general; for, with the exception of a few pictures by Jan Steen, I know nothing similar of an earlier period. In all other branches they are more or less excelled by the other schools. Portrait painting is the branch which they have cultivated with the most success, and the best portraits of Sir Joshua Reynolds take a high rank, even when compared with the performances of other schools. Next to this are the painters of what the French call *pièces de genre*, scenes of every-day life and still life, and especially their animal painters. Their landscapes are far lower in the scale, in such a comparison. But they are weakest of all in history painting, where inventive and creative fancy is the most called for. Having thus viewed the intellectual region of the art, let us briefly consider their progress in the scientific parts. Their drawing is, on the whole, indifferent; the forms often suffer from incorrectness, and still more by want of precision; on the other hand, most English painters have great brilliancy, fulness, and depth of colour, which makes much show and charms the eye; often, it is true, at the expense of fidelity to nature, and of delicately balanced harmony. For the mode of execution, it is a misfortune for the English school, that it at once began where other schools nearly leave off. From the most scrupulous execution of the details, which seeks to bring every object as near as possible to the reality, even for close inspection, the older schools but very gradually acquired the conviction that the same effect might be produced, at a moderate distance, with fewer strokes of the pencil, and thus attained a broader handling. But the English school began at once with a very great freedom and breadth of handling, where, in the works of Hogarth and Reynolds, indeed, every touch is seen in nature, and expresses something positive; but, in most of the later painters, degenerated into a flimsiness and negligence, so that but a very superficial and general image is given of every object, and many pictures have the glaring effect of scene-painting, while others are lost in misty indistinctness. As no good technical rules had been handed down to them by tradition, the English painters endeavoured to establish some for themselves, but with such ill success, that many pictures have very much changed, many are so faded that they have quite the appearance of corpses, others have turned black; the colour has broad cracks in it, nay, in some cases, it has become fluid, and then, from the excessively thick impasto, has run down in single drops."

Hence it will be seen that the Berlin Gallery Director does not entertain any immoderate degree of admiration of our older English masters. He concludes that Sir Joshua was not qualified to be an historical painter. "The characters and expressions," for example, in his "Holy Family," he says are "poor and unmeaning, the forms not rounded, the execution slight, the colouring warm, indeed, but false, and besides, in places faded and washed out." The connoisseur appears to have felt a greater admiration for Hogarth's genius, and bestows the phrase "eminent merit" upon the "Marriage à-la-Mode." West, however, comes off shabbily enough; for of him it is declared that "partly at his instigation, the infant plant of the English school of painting was shut up in the hot-house of an academy; and his works in this gallery prove that he was the real model of the president of such an institution, who, by his example and teaching, clipt betimes with his academical shears, according to prescribed rules, the wild luxuriant growth of the young plants. The truth of the words, 'The letter kills, the spirit gives life,' is rendered manifest to the eye by these pictures." Gainsborough and Wilson also get it over the knuckles; but to show that the Doctor's free judgments are not without discrimination, we need only quote a few sentences which are bestowed on Wilkie.

"If I might compare Hogarth with Swift, in his biting satire, with which he contemplates mankind only on the dark side, and takes special delight in representing them in a state of the most profound corruption, of the most frightful misery. I find in Wilkie a close affinity with his celebrated countryman, Sir Walter Scott. Both have in common that genuine refined delineation of character which extends to the minutest particulars. In the soul of both there is more love than contempt of man; both afford us the most soothing views of the quiet, genial happiness which is sometimes found in the narrow circle of domestic life, and understand how, with masterly skill, by the mixture of delicate traits of good-natured humour, to heighten the charm of such scenes; and if, as poets should be able to do both in language and colours, they show us man in his manifold weaknesses, errors, afflictions, and distresses, yet their humour is of such a kind that it never revolts our feelings. Wilkie is especially to be commended, that in such scenes as the Distress for Rent, he never falls into caricature, as has often happened to Hogarth, but with all the energy of expression remains within the bounds of truth. It is affirmed that the deeply impressive and touching character of this picture caused an extraordinary sensation in England when it first appeared. Here we first learn duly to prize another feature of his pictures, namely, their genuine national character. They are in all their parts the most spirited, animated, and faithful representations of the peculiarities and modes of life of the English. In many other respects, Wilkie reminds me of the great Dutch painters of common life of the seventeenth century, and likewise in the choice of many subjects—for instance, the Blind Man's Buff, but particularly by the careful and complete making-out of the details, in which he is one of the rare exceptions among his countrymen. If he does not go so far in this respect as Douw and Franz Mieris, he is nearly on an equality with the more carefully-executed paintings of Teniers and Jan Steen. His touch, too, often approaches the former in spirit and freedom, especially in his earlier pictures."

The predominance in this country of portraits, the Director holds to be a proof that the real value of the art is not properly understood; for that is not love of art, but merely love of self or of near relations is thereby manifested; and upon the whole he appears to think that the English school of painting is on the decline. He has still a lower idea of our sculpture. To Chantrey he accords the character of possessing "eminent talents in the natural style, so that all those who require nothing more of sculpture than that it shall represent every object precisely as it appears in nature, must often be highly gratified by his works." The higher requisites of an art, where owing to the peculiar qualities of the material to be worked into effect, modifications not necessary in the case where colours are employed must be adopted, he refuses to our most celebrated sculptor. Let us see what it is that the Doctor would have as explained, when enumerating the things which he considers to be the causes most inimical to the art in question in this country. These causes, he says, are to be looked for, partly in the public, and partly in the artists themselves.

" It requires a much more refined and elevated taste to enjoy a work of sculpture than of painting, and hence we find a taste for painting much more diffused also among the other civilized nations of Europe. In most of them, too, the want of opulence contributes to render the execution of important works of sculpture now rare, as they are always very expensive. In England, where the great mass of extraordinary wealth would very well admit of it, the execution is impeded by another cause. Sculpture, whose business is with the form, can attain a high degree of perfection only where frequent opportunities are granted it of representing the forms of the human body in unveiled beauty, as they come from the creative hand of divine nature. But the majority of the English, from a mistaken prudery, are decidedly averse from every representation of the naked figure, by which the sphere in which the artist moves, is very greatly narrowed. I must call that feeling mistaken, because the pure and noble spirit in which the genuine artist views natural forms, and employs them for the higher objects of art, for the representation of that beauty which proclaims its origin from the hand of the Deity, for the expression of intellectual relations, wholly excludes all reference to the difference of sex, and does not suffer them to occur to unprejudiced spectators, who are truly impressed with the real purport of a work of art. It is this hallowing of the naked form which properly constitutes the sublime innocence of art. Goëthe expresses himself to the same effect in his admirable Essay, ' *Der Sammler, und die Scinigen.*' Under these circumstances, we must not wonder that perhaps nine-tenths of the sculpture executed in England, consist of busts and portrait statues. But it is certainly the fault of the artists themselves that even these, to say nothing of the works of freer art, do not, for the most part, answer the higher demands of a cultivated taste for the arts. The want of feeling for beauty of form and leading lines with which I have already charged the English painters, has here a much more prejudicial effect, because these are the qualities on which the sculptor chiefly depends, whereas painting has besides a great and advantageous resource in colour. It is equally fatal in its consequences, that the relation between sculpture and its prototype nature is seldom rightly understood. Some sculptors are fettered by considering these subjects too much in the light of portraits, like scenes of familiar life, so that they imitate all the fortuitous details of the dress; another aims at an empty and false ideal, and degenerates into an indefinite and swollen softness."

The " much more refined and elevated taste" indicated, is more likely to find disciples amongst the mystics of Germany than in this country of shopkeepers and prosaic decencies. But to proceed;— Westmacott, the Director says, is the most eminent sculptor in England, being a "great admirer and thorough judge of the antique." But E. H. Baily, a much less known artist, " is, however, distinguished above them, (Chantrey and Westmacott,) in his later works, by a more correct feeling for arrangement and graceful outline."

Having thus glanced at our author's opinions concerning the English schools of art in the departments of painting and sculpture, we shall, before accompanying him on his tour to the seats of some of our nobility and gentry, afford our readers a treat by quoting some passages of a comprehensive nature ; first on the Drawings of the Ancient Masters, and secondly on the general decline of art in modern times.

" The drawings of the great masters have a peculiar charm. By them, more than by works of any other kind, you are introduced into the secret laboratory of art, so that you may follow a painting from the first germs, through its various stages and changes, till it attains its perfect form. Mr. von Rumohr, with his usual refined sense of art, directs our attention to the sure mechanical taste with which these old masters always employed, in their drawings, the material which was best adapted to the object they had in view. If they wanted to sketch upon the paper a first thought just as it arose in the fancy, they usually chose the red Italian chalk, with which sketching is so easy, or the soft Italian black chalk. The breadth and soft-ness of the strokes immediately give to such a first sketch something pic-turesque and massy ; and, at the same time, the material allowed of further finishing, in a high degree, if it were desired. But if they wished to arrest a rapidly passing effect in nature, as it was fresh in their fancy, to seize an accidental, happy, quickly changing cast of drapery, or to mark, sharply and distinctly, the main features of some character, they preferred the pen, which allowed them to unite the easy flowing line with the sure and dis-tinct indication of the forms. If they desired in the portrait, in a study, in the composition, to express the most delicate movement of the form, the fine play of the surfaces lying within the outlines, they generally took a rounded silver pencil. On paper covered with a mixture of white-lead and pale yellow ochre, verdigris, or some red, such a pencil marks but lightly and softly, and therefore allows of changing and improving *ad infinitum*, and by leaning harder, at length to mark decidedly, among all the others, the design in favour of which the artist has determined. If they wished to decide on the main distribution of light and shade, the full camel's hair pencil dipped in sepia or Indian ink, with its elastic point, its bold fulness, led the most rapidly and surely to their object. In such drawings, the outlines of the forms are often not marked, but result only from the limits of the shadows : when it was required, at the same time, to mark the form, the use of the pen was added. Lastly, for a more detailed marking of light and shade, coloured paper afforded them a middle tint, by the help of which they pro-duced, with black chalk in the shadows, and white in the lights, a very delicate gradation, and a great relief of the parts. On account of these many advantages, this mode of drawing has been very commonly used. It is not till after having seen, from a great number of such drawings, in how many sides a picture has been conscientiously prepared, that we can under-stand the great perfection and extraordinary composition of so many pic-tures of the times of Raphael ; and it is not till we have learnt to consider such pictures as the final result of a long series of studies of the most highly gifted minds that we are penetrated with a due sense of their great value."

When on the subject of Drawings by the Great Masters, we may with propriety refer to the Lawrence Collection, which has lately been dispersed, many of the most valuable specimens, we regret, having passed into foreign hands, the Prince of Orange alone having selected pieces at the first picking for which he paid 12,000*l*., while our Government in the exercise of a mistaken economy offered no more for the whole collection. The Prince's choice fell chiefly upon the Sketches and Drawings of Raphael, Michael Angelo, Corregio, Leonardo da Vinci, and Andrea del Sarto. There is still, however, a considerable number of the vast and precious store remaining in this country, and specimens by Rubens and Vandyke are at the moment we write exposed to sale. But although the whole collection might have been kept together and preserved for the benefit of the public, had Government shown the wisdom and taste of advancing 25,000*l*., the complete dispersion of the treasure, whether finding its way into foreign hands or those of private individuals at home, must for ever render it in a great measure valueless to the students of Art. We regard the loss as being the more provoking, seeing that it was during Sir Robert Peel's administration that the whole might have been secured to the nation, and seeing that he in the capacity of a collector has not scrupled to expend upwards of a thousand pounds in the purchase of the Drawings of one of the Masters alone whose works formed a portion of the mass. But it is some consolation to learn that fac-similes of a selection of Raphaels have been taken for publication, we believe under the patronage of the Queen.

Dr. Waagen's opinions with regard to the decline of Art, a fact that has been attempted by various hypotheses to be accounted for, are striking and in some measure original. It has been a very usual thing to charge the Reformation as the principal cause of falling off; but as he thinks very unjustly. He says,

" If, in the countries where the Reformation was generally received, the demand for pictures must naturally have much declined, this was by no means the case, where, as in Italy, it had little or no success; at least, it might be difficult to show, up to the year 1550, any considerable influence of the Reformation on the religious feelings of the people and artists in Italy. And yet the decline of the art from 1530 to 1550 is more striking there than anywhere else. Nor did this decline by any means extend to the religious treatment of subjects only, but to the conception, and the scientific and mechanical parts of painting in general. The main ground of this charge may, therefore, be rather sought in the total and general alteration of the mode of thinking, which took place from that time among the nations of Europe, in consequence of the more general diffusion of the art of printing. Greek Antiquity agrees in this with the middle ages, that intellectual education and instruction were diffused in the larger circles, chiefly through the medium of the senses, by works of art; and which also, on account of the expense and trouble of multiplying them by copies, had a very great influence on the proportionably small number of persons to whom books were accessible as a means of acquiring knowledge. This situation of art gave artists the calm and elevating consciousness of their

necessity in human society, since it was their part to provide for the gratification of so important and universal an intellectual want. Precisely
because art was necessary to education and instruction, the artists had at
the same time the correct feeling that they were to satisfy it, by the greatest
possible perspicuity and beauty, in the treatment of the subject they had
in hand, since otherwise the object would have been missed. Through
this happy circumstance, art among the Greeks, as in the middle ages, rose
to so extraordinary a height, and preserved for so long a time its vitality
and its purity. But when, from the beginning of the sixteenth century
the imparting of knowledge by books became so infinitely easy and general,
by the great diffusion of the art of printing, books soon became the principal means of all intellectual education, in the room of the arts. Hitherto
the picture, as the organ of contemplation, had exercised, by means of the
fancy and the sense of beauty, an indirect influence upon the understanding; henceforward language, as the organ of comprehension, acted directly
upon the understanding. This kind of influence is far more sharp, decided,
and extensive, but likewise more partial. With the unlimited dominion
which it gradually acquired, the want of intellectual instruction by means
of the senses by degrees disappeared, and the consequence was that, in the
end, even the faculty of rightly understanding a work of art was also lost.
But after historical painting had thus lost the position which that elevated
intellectual importance had given it, it lost likewise its ancient simplicity;
nay, degenerated into the rank of a handmaid of all the oblique intellectual
tendencies of the times, and thus gradually became an ordinary article of
luxury, a flat, unmeaning parade, with a certain boldness in its scientific
and mechanical part."

There is a great deal in this mode of accounting for the decline of
art since the middle ages which, was carried to its highest pitch by
Raphael, but which has never since his time been able to maintain the
elevation, for it has gradually been sinking. Neither is it probable
that any great revival will ever take place. The time has fled when
minds of the highest order can find any strong temptation to devote
themselves to the arts of design. The universal use of the invention
of printing, and the universal taste for literature, as well as the easy
access to all its finest stores, not only are circumstances which have
produced new modes of thinking, but have made the study of legislation, of jurisprudence, of ecclesiastical history and divinity, of
science, and even of mechanics, together with the admired accessories and handmaidens of these engrossing and important pursuits,
viz. scholarship and oratory, the surest roads to fame, emolument,
and rank. But in the days of Leo the Tenth and down to the beginning of the sixteenth century, the machinery of government was
simple, jurisprudence had no forum for the orator's display, the
church was neither the school of eloquence nor controversy which it
afterwards became, the sciences did not engage men of first-rate
genius, or the industrial arts the most active of our race; and, in
fact, the highest favour of courts as well as the acclaim of popular
applause were then lavished on successful Painters. Raphael was

pressed by Cardinal Bibiena to espouse his niece Maria Babiena, and at another period it was proposed to confer upon him a Cardinal's hat.

It is to be borne in mind also that genius will not now-a-days consent to be dependent on the patronage of the great. It will not be content with less than the commanding of homage, the homage of the whole community. That community does not as a body set a high value upon the arts of design. It is the works produced by the Press that are studied, while painting only is regarded as something ornamental, and second to what is directly and manifestly useful.

Besides, the Press is not the only cause of lowering the estimation and rank which once were accorded to art, but its professors and students have been more and more embarrassed down to the latest times, since the reign of the Great Masters, by another circumstance, which is thus explained by Dr. Waagen :—

"Among the Greeks, art and life went hand in hand. All the external circumstances of life, especially the costume, were of such a nature, that they fulfilled, as they were, the laws of beauty and taste, which the highest aims of the art require. The artist, therefore, was involuntarily impressed with his studies, in the living world around him, which is an immense advantage. He enjoyed the same opportunity for the study of the human figure by the public exercises in the Palæstra.. If the outward forms of life had not in the middle ages this purely plastic character, yet the feeling for the picturesque found nourishment in very many respects; in the architecture, in the various customes, in the richness and variety of the materials used for clothing. But such ugliness, deformity, and tastelessness has gradually arisen in the whole external world, that the historical painter is compelled to begin his work by total abstraction from the reality with which he is surrounded, in which he can find nothing corresponding with his object. He must create out of his fancy alone, and complete the details with the dead, wretched aid of models, and draperies artificially thrown over lay figures. If we consider what is required, under such circumstances, to create a work of art which shall produce in every part the impression of the intellectual, animated, and transitory, we ought in reason to be filled with the greatest admiration for an artist who produces such a performance, and look with indulgence on single imperfections."

Dr. Waagen's visits to the seats of our nobility and gentry in the country were numerous and extended. He went as far north as Howard Castle, where Lord Carlisle has a noble collection, and of which, a letter from the Duke of Sutherland to the housekeeper, " a respectable, elderly person," insured the critic a full examination. The chief strength of the paintings (for at Howard Castle there are rich exhibitions in other departments of art and *virtù*) is in capital works of the Carracci and their scholars, as well as in Flemish pictures of the time of Reubens. Two or three of the learned connoisseur's notices of the collection in question, will afford our readers an idea of his manner and closeness.

" *Giovanni Bellini.*—' The Circumcision.' The real original, marked with the artist's name, of the many copies made at a remote period, of the middle time of the artist. The characters of the old heads are very severe, and of astonishing glow in the colouring; the treatment admirably fused. From the Orleans Gallery. It is unfortunately damaged in some places.

" *Joan Gassaert, called Mabuse.*—' The Wise Men's Offering.' A rich composition, in which there are thirty principal figures. About six feet high and five feet wide. This picture, from the Orleans Gallery, is a most splendid conformation of my conjecture, that this artist, before he went to Italy, must have executed important works in the pure Flemish style of the school of Van Eyck; whereas people are used to judge of him by the mannered pictures in the Italian taste, which he painted during and after that journey. In this picture he is by no means inferior to the two most celebrated contemporary painters in the Netherlands, Rogier Van der Weyde, and Quintin Matsys. In the nobleness, refinement, and variety of the characters, he is superior, and in gravity and energy equal to them. The proportions of the figures are slender, the hands delicate, but rather long and lean. With the flowing and soft general cast of the draperies, there are some sharper breaks. All the parts are very decidedly marked; the flesh is mostly, in the shadows, of a deep brownish, in the lights, of a warm yellowish tone, and less clear than in the two other masters. The execution is, throughout, wonderfully solid and conscientious. The crown of the Wise Man kneeling, and the lid of the vessel, on which, according to the later manner of the master, we read IASPAR, &c., is executed in the old fashion in gold yellow. On the other hand, the gold brocade of the draperies is in the later and not so good manner, in which the whole surface is painted with a brown colour; the patterns drawn with black, the lights put in with yellow ochre. The combination of the colours, which are partially broken, has a very harmonious effect. In this, as in all the principal parts, it entirely agrees with the Crucifixion in the Berlin Museum, which has hitherto been erroneously ascribed to Memling; only that the latter, by forming cleaning, has lost its warm tone, and its old distinctness, whereas this picture, at Castle Howard, is in as fine a state of preservation as if it had been finished but yesterday. A small head with a hat and feathers, at a window, may, perhaps, be the portrait of Mabuse. It is erroneously believed that those of Albert Durer and Lucas Van Leyden are to be distinguished there. In the middle distances the Shepherds are devoutedly worshipping. The architecture of the building, in which the Child is visited by the Wise Men, is not Gothic, but already shews the influence of Italy. This picture is not only the capital work of those that remain of Mabuse, but is also one of the best of the whole ancient Flemish school.

" *François Clouet, called Janet.*—A collection of eighty-eight portraits of the most eminent persons at the courts of Henry II., Francis II., Charles IX., and Henry III., executed with much spirit and animation, in black and white chalk, in the manner of Holbein. These interesting portraits carry the spectator back to that age which Vitet has described with such characteristic individuality in his historical dramas. The names are written by a contemporary hand. It is very singular that the men are almost all handsome, the women, with few exceptions, ugly."

But we must not detain our readers with numerous criticisms of the above kind, because, however just and minute they may be, it is hardly possible thereby to convey any distinct ideas unless to persons who are already familiar with the specimens described. Still, merely to show some of the Director's corrections, and how frequently pictures have been in this country ascribed apparently at random by incompetent critics to celebrated artists, let us have a glance at the Liverpool Institution ; for towns as well as castles attracted our German guest.

" ' The Coronation of the Virgin ;' half figures. 1 ft. 5 in. high, 1 ft. 9 in. wide; a very good work of the Sienna school of the fourteenth century. It is here erroneously called Byzantine.

" *Filippino Lippi.*—' The Birth of the Virgin,' 6 in. high, 14 in. wide. One of the most beautiful and deeply felt pictures of this great master, of his earlier and best period. Here erroneously called Fiesole.

" *L. Krug.*—' The Nativity.' The Virgin kneeling, worships the Infant, which is lying on the ground; Joseph stands by, with a lantern. 11 in. high, 9 in. wide. This masterly picture, executed in the style of the German school, exactly agrees, in the essentials, with the well-known engraving by this master. (Bartsch, Vol. VIII. p. 536.) It is here most unaccountably called Anessio Baldovinetti."

Dr. Waagen did not confine his observation and criticism to Painting and Sculpture, but scanned external scenery and the manners of society with the eye of a poet and a philosopher. Like other German erudite and polished travellers, he looked for the reasons of things and was ever anxious to reduce effects to first principles. We need not depart from Howard Castle without presenting a specimen of the use which he made of his vision and his taste the moment he came in sight of the splendid locality. He says,

" On entering the park, you see at the end of a steep avenue a lofty obelisk, which was erected by Henry, Earl of Carlisle, in honour of the great Duke of Marlborough. Two double rows of ash-trees on the sides of the road, and, further on, two large meadows of a regular form, surrounded on three sides by wood, make a very fine appearance. The castle itself forcibly reminded me of Blenheim, and is by the same architect, Van Brugh; but it is less broken, and, though not of equal extent, has a grander and more massy appearance. In the whole arrangement of the palace and the garden, the architect evidently had Versailles in his mind, as the *ne plus ultra* of this style. In the grounds are colossal stone basons, to which the flowers planted in them give the appearance of flower-baskets. The principal ornaments, however, are numerous copies of the most celebrated antiques, the dazzling whiteness of which is contrasted with the bright green of the turf. The northern and rude climate has unfortunately made it necessary to paint them with oil colour : only the ancient large Boar of Florence still stands unpainted in a very good copy of the finest Carrara marble. On two sides are pieces of water, over one of which is a large stone bridge. All this, as well as a square building, which on every side has a portico of four pillars of the Composite order, and an elegant Mosaic floor ; a pyramid of considerable size ; and, lastly, a very large circular building, surrounded with pillars and crowned with a cupola, which contains the family vaults, give to the whole a rich and truly princely appearance. The high cupola with a lantern, which strikes you immediately on entering the house, is in the same character. According to the tasteless fashion of that age, Antonio Pellegrini, one of the late mannerists of the Venetian school, has painted in the cupola the Fall of Phaëton ; so that a person standing under it feels as if the four horses of the sun were going to fall upon his head. The corners are adorned with the four elements. More noble and important than all this show are the manifold works of art of various kinds which the spacious apartments of the palace contain, and which give it the appearance of a museum."

Chatworth (Duke of Devonshire's), Bowood (Marquis of Lansdowne's), Alton Tower (Lord Shrewsbury's), Keddleston Hall (Lord Scarsdale's), and other magnificent repositories of art, as well as truly English scenes obtain like notice and description. Having said that towns as well as castles attracted our traveller's attention, we quote a sample of his treatment of these large and crowded scenes.

" Bath is the queen of all the spas in the world, for there are certainly very few which can compare with it for beauty of situation, and none for magnificence of buildings. The city arises in terraces from the banks of the Avon, which winds through the valley to the top of the Lansdowne, a pretty steep eminence, about 800 feet high. The vast masses of architecture rising one above the other have a highly picturesque and striking effect, when seen from the valley. The eye is chiefly attracted by the Royal Crescent, situated about half way up the hill, and Lansdowne Crescent, which towers above all. This is the name given in England to large masses of building, the facades of which gradually recede from the ends to the centre, so as to form a curve more or less near to a semicircle ; a mode of building which is certainly very objectionable in its principle : they contain a larger or smaller number of dwellings for single families. The impression of grandeur and solidity is enhanced by the material, which is a stone found in the neighbourhood. Yet the various views from the several points of elevation, particularly Lansdowne Terrace and King's Terrace, are almost more beautiful and worth seeing. From the first you have a view over the whole rich valley, with the finely wooded eminences that rise on the other bank of the Avon, and the whole world of buildings, more or less elevated above the plain. The Gothic abbey which, with its tower, rises peacefully quite down in the valley, near the banks of the Avon, has, in every point of view, a most picturesque effect. The whole, too, has such a southern character, the air is so deliciously mild, that one fancies oneself in Italy, and cannot wonder that even the piratical Romans appreciated the advantages of this situation with the warm baths. It would therefore be incomprehensible to me, why this paradise, which unites in the most extraordinary degree the advantages of a great city with those of a romantic country residence, had I not already become acquainted with the power of the only absolute sovereign in this constitutional country, namely, *fashion.*"

While at Bath Mr. Beckford's treasures of art, of course, became an object of the Director's curiosity; and although he intimates that neither at that princely gentleman's house in the city, nor at his Tower in the vicinity, was he allowed sufficient time for examination, yet the sketch of what the traveller saw leaves an impression on the reader's mind of vast and various beauty, grandeur and gorgeousness. In the Tower besides pictures are rooms richly ornamented with select works of another kind. Of the earthenware called *majolica*, adorned with paintings and coated with varnish, there is a most enviable collection. There are enamelled vessels of striking beauty among these specimens, which belong to the sixteenth century, having been manufactured and ornamented by distinguished foreign artists. Our author speaks also in terms of high admiration of vessels of agate and nephrite, of Japan and Chinese porcelain, of glass, of gold, all several centuries old. He describes the furniture as corresponding in magnificence and costliness with the objects of *virtù*; such as tables of giallo and verde antico, and other rare marbles. There is a cabinet adorned with fine Florentine mosaic, while cedar and other expensive kinds of wood abound. The imagination absolutely reels amid such descriptions; then what must be the effect when the whole is present to the senses? But we must stop, after letting the Director be heard in his descant upon one apartment in Mr. Beckford's mansion in Bath.

" I shall never forget the dining-room, which, taken all in all, is perhaps one of the most beautiful in the world. Conceive a moderate apartment of agreeable proportions, whose walls are adorned with cabinet pictures, the noblest productions of Italian art of the time of Raphael, from the windows of which you overlook the whole paradisaical valley of the Avon, with the city of Bath, which was now steeped in sunshine. Conceive in it a company of men of genius and talent, between the number of the Graces and Muses, whose spirits are duly raised by the choicest viands, in the preparation of which the refined culinary art of our days has displayed its utmost skill, by a selection of wines, such as nature and human care can produce only on the most favoured spots of the earth, in the most favourable years, and you will agree with me that many things here meet in a culminating point, which, even singly, are calculated to rejoice the heart of man."

The result after reading Dr. Waagen's present work is, that England is wonderfully rich in respect of treasures of art, and that such travellers as Passavant and himself have done more to enlighten the public on the subject than any native artists or connoisseurs have ever done. The beauty of English scenery too, the perfection of English Landscape Gardening, and the warmth of English hospitality, come strikingly out. We have only to add, that the translation of the work betokens not only a ripe German and English scholar, but a writer intimately acquainted with the fine arts, otherwise he could not have conveyed in our language the point and perspicuity of the original.

ART. II.—*Memoirs of the Life of Sir Walter Scott, Bart.* Volume the Seventh and last. London: Murray and Whittaker. 1838.

IT has been with feelings in some measure akin to those which we have experienced at the commencement of the last act in a magnificent drama, or when opening the last volume of an all-absorbing romance, the catastrophe of which was already known, that we have received the present portion of the life of one of the most engaging and lofty characters that ever appeared on earth. Again and again we have said that never, excepting on the eve of publication of some of Scott's tales, have we so anxiously waited for the issuing from the press of any work as the several volumes of his life. To be sure the piece-meal manner of publication here adopted has been sufficiently tantalizing, and has repeatedly left us with provoking abruptness just at the moment when curiosity and interest were at the highest pitch. The complaint, however, cannot now be longer preferred; the mighty minstrel has been exhibited, bereft of all that ever distinguished him among men; his tongue is mute for ever; and, after the long and eager contemplation that held us in amazement, we are at last enabled to breathe freely, and to allow the pantings of the heart gradually to subside.

Having alluded to Scott's novels we may just observe, that since his death, and especially since perusing portions of the work before us, never have we looked into any of those inimitable productions, in which such vivid pictures are to be found of the magician himself, without experiencing the pressure of certain emotions that required the applause of philosophy and religious truths to keep under. Having for years had almost daily opportunities of scanning his features, of beholding the remarkable serenity of his bearing, and frequently of listening to his matchless discourse, and thence comparing and identifying him with himself, such a habit has been established, that whatever appears peculiarly characteristic in any of his tales sends the mind on painful excursions, and forces from us the irrational wish that such a man had never have grown old, or at least the selfish desire that he had lived beyond our time, were it but for the sake of sustaining the most delightful sympathies in regard to him, which his writings never, while he lived, failed to awaken. It requires an effort to believe that the tongue, which was so rich and various, should now be dumb for ever; that the judgment which was so masculine, the moral energies which were so active and exalted, should have been, ere animal existence ceased, prostrated and all but obliterated. How ready are we mentally to

exclaim, His like we shall never again see! How nearly inclined to
fret and lament that one who had so long ministered unceasingly to
our delight, and served to reconcile us to the world in spite of its
many evils, should be withdrawn never more to charm but by those
efforts which bring along with them a host of painful associations.

It is fortunate, however, that though the charmer be mute, though
his visage never more will attract the complacency of the world,
there is preserved of him one of the fullest and most transparent
pictures that ever has been bequeathed by the great and good.   In
the work before us, the hero of the story is to be heard and seen
with a distinctness that is all but real, almost even to the tones of
voice, and the contour of countenance; while, though a veil inter-
venes between the reader and these realities, the heart of the man is
palpable, the spirit breathes, and soul holds communion with soul.
In this ethereal respect, we are here actually led into the presence of
the departed; for Mr. Lockhart from overflowing stores, and by the
exercise of great literary skill, · has allowed his hero to speak most
pleasantly and variously for himself.

Independent of the peculiar value and interest belonging to Scott's
Life, considering him merely as a man of great genius and worth,
independent of the lessons which this history affords to mankind,
there is, as the biographer notices in the preface, a distinct point of
importance in which the present work is to be viewed.   It is possible that a difference of opinion may exist with regard to the precise value of Scott's character, but no doubt has ever arisen concerning the fidelity of his portraitures of Scottish life and manners,
both in past and contemporary periods.   The national character of
Scotland, however, is rapidly passing away; and but for the magician whose wand arrested the fleeting realities and fixed them in imperishable records, when standing " a Borderer between two ages,"
the pictures would not have been drawn and the images must have
been for ever lost.

We have more than once expressed our almost unqualified approbation of the present work, in so far as the biographer's task is concerned; and one of the most apparent excellences of the performance
consists in the unreserved spirit of fidelity evinced by the author.
Scott is not made to appear a faultless monster. We are perfectly
satisfied that Mr. Lockhart is sincere and honest when he declares
that he despises the notion of painting a great and masculine character unfaithfully, of leaving out anything essential to the preservation of the man as he was, which it was in his power to produce
and represent.   There are in the present volume, for example,
instances of a fearless openness, which it must have required considerable nerve to exhibit, and which, perhaps justly, must expose
the biographer to charges of a severe nature.

It can hardly be necessary to state to our readers that one of the
most striking and affecting exhibitions in the present volume must

be that of the gradual breaking up of Scott's constitution, physical and mental, till he became a complete but noble ruin. This exhibition acquires additional weight and pathos when it is observed that its subject was conscious of its progress, and that he struggled manfully against its inroads, and yet maintained a lofty serenity and cherished a habitual resignation, even amid the most alarming symptoms. To a man who had so long enjoyed the sunshine of intellect, not to speak of the physical energies of an athletic frame, the approach of that night in which his light was to set, and when oblivion and stupor were to possess him, offers a theme for consideration that is melancholy in proportion to the contrasts involved. It will be to the declension referred to that the majority of our extracts will have respect.

This last volume has an ominous opening as regards Scott's health, for it states that his constitution was, from successive attacks of the rheumatism, beginning to shake, and every aliment ended in aggravating his lameness. The period in question was winter 1826-7. To make things worse instead of reserving his evenings as formerly to light reading, or the enjoyment of his family and friends, he now regarded every minute not spent at the desk as lost. We find that his Diary contains the following entry for December 16.

" Another bad night. I remember I used to think a slight illness was a luxurious thing. My pillow was then softened by the hand of affection, and the little cares put in exercise to soothe the languor or pain, were more flattering and pleasing than the consequences of the illness were disagreeable. It was a new scene to be watched and attended, and I used to think that the *malade imaginaire* gained something by his humour. It is different in the latter stages—the old post-chaise gets more shattered and out of order at every turn; windows will not be pulled up, doors refuse to open, or being open will not shut again—which last is rather my case. There is some new subject of complaint every moment—your sicknesses come thicker and thicker—your comforting and sympathizing friends fewer and fewer—for why should they sorrow for the course of nature? The recollection of youth, health, and uninterrupted powers of activity, neither improved nor enjoyed, is a poor strain of comfort. The best is, the long halt will arrive at last, and cure all. This was a day of labour, agreeably varied by a pain which rendered it scarce possible to sit upright. My journal is getting a vile chirurgical aspect. I begin to be afraid of the odd consequences complaints in the *post equitem* are said to produce. I shall tire of my journal. In my better days I had stories to tell; but death has closed the long dark avenue upon loves and friendships, and I look at them as through the grated door of a burial-place filled with monuments of those who were once dear to me, with no insincere wish that it may open for me at no distant period, provided such be the will of God. My pains were those of the heart, and had something flattering in their character ; if in the head, it was from the blow of a bludgeon gallantly received, and well paid back. I think I shall not live to the usual verge of human existence; I shall never see the threescore and ten, and shall be summed up at a discount. No help for it, and no matter either."

We find, for instance, from a letter addressed to the biographer by a young man who was employed by Scott, about the period above mentioned, to copy papers connected with the Life of Buonaparte, that they commenced their several labours in the same apartment at six o'clock in the morning, and continued without intermission, excepting to take breakfast and dinner, which were served in the room beside them, till six o'clock in the evening; and all this Herculean labour to pay off the enormous debt which was over the poet's head.

There is a very characteristic letter of Scott's to William Clerk, in anticipation of a personal quarrel which General Gourgand was likely to fasten on him in consequence of certain documents which appeared in the Life of Napoleon. I will not baulk him, Jackie, says Sir Walter; for although he might have marched off upon the privileges of literature, he was resolved, should the affair come to hostile arbitriment, that Scotland should not be dishonoured through his sides. The Frenchman's wrath, however, burst forth in a very distant clap of thunder.

Literary toil and the quarrel alluded to, were not the only inconveniences which Scott had to bear up against; for it appears that between December 1826 and November 1827, the threatenings of severe treatment by certain Jewish brokers had caused him to make preparations for taking shelter in the sanctuary at Holyrood-house. But extreme measures were not after all adopted, so that he was allowed to have the free use of his time for the benefit of his creditors. It could not, however, have been greatly regretted had the Israelites made good their threats; for in that case Scott must have had recourse to the usual legal measures for the sake of obtaining his liberation; so that after resigning all his assets on the usual terms of sequestration, he would have been at perfect freedom to employ his time and pen for his own benefit, and as his taste and pleasure dictated. To the prospect of a sojourn in the sanctuary of Holyrood, it seems that the world is indebted for much that occurs in the first series of the Chronicles of the Canongate, and what pertains to the domicile of Chrystal Chroftangry. But the way in which to form anything like an adequate idea of Scott's labours and sacrifices, is to take into consideration this statement,—that between January 1826 and January 1828, the sale of his copyright and of his new works paid off very nearly 40,000*l.* of the enormous debt he had blindly incurred,—a marvel assuredly in the history of literature, and an achievement which richly deserved the vote of thanks which his creditors passed. Who could withhold his sympathy and admiration from such a hero after reading this statement, or who would not have shed tears of delight had the writer of the following notices been observed when they were entered in his Diary?

" ' My reflections in entering my own gate to day were of a very different and more pleasing cast, than those with which I left this place about six weeks ago. I was then in doubt whether I should fly my country, or become avowedly bankrupt, and surrender up my library and household furniture, with the liferent of my estate, to sale. A man of the world will say I had better done so. No doubt, had I taken this course at once, I might have employed the money I have made since the insolvency of Constable and Robinson's houses in compounding my debts. But I could not have slept sound as I now can, under the comfortable impression of receiving the thanks of my creditors, and the conscious feeling of discharging my duty as a man of honour and honesty. I see before me a long, tedious, and dark path, but it leads to stainless reputation. If I die in the harrows, as is very likely, I shall die with honour; if I achieve my task, I shall have the thanks of all concerned, and the approbation of my own conscience. And so I think I can fairly face the return of Christmasday.'

" And again, on the 31st December, he says:—

" ' Looking back to the conclusion of 1826, I observe that the last year ended in trouble and sickness, with pressures for the present and gloomy propects for the future. The sense of a great privation so lately sustained, together with the very doubtful and clouded nature of my private affairs, pressed hard upon my mind. I am now restored in constitution; and though I am still on troubled waters, yet I am rowing with the tide, and less than the continuation of my exertions of 1827 may, with God's blessing, carry me successfully through 1828, when we may gain a more open sea, if not exactly a safe port. Above all, my children are well. Sophia's situation excites some natural anxiety; but it is only the accomplishment of the burden imposed on her sex. Walter is happy in the view of his majority, on which matter we have favourable hopes from the Horse-Guards. Anne is well and happy. Charles's entry on life under the highest patronage, and in a line for which, I hope, he is qualified, is about to take place presently.

" ' For all these great blessings it becomes me well to be thankful to God, who in his good time and good pleasure, sends us good as well as evil.' "

Scott was in the habit of characterizing the uniform reprint of the Novels, with illustrations and notes, as the *Opus magnum*,—a designation which the prodigious sale of the edition has fully warranted; but this great undertaking, every one knows, only went *pari passu* with many other literary enterprizes, which it is not necessary for us particularly to enumerate. Nor was there any lack of tempting offers had he even doubled himself.

" ' Mr. Charles Heath, the engraver, invites me to take charge of a yearly publication called the Keepsake, of which the plates are beyond comparison beautiful, but the letter-press indifferent enough. He proposes

L. 800 a-year if I would become editor, and L. 400 if I would contribute
from seventy to one hundred pages. I declined both, but told him I might
give him some trifling thing or other.   To become the stipendiary editor
of a New-Year's-Gift Book is not to be thought of, nor could I agree to
work regularly, for any quantity of supply, at such a publication.   Even
the pecuniary view is not flattering, though Mr. Heath meant it should
be so.   One hundred of his close-printed pages, for which he offers L. 400,
are nearly equal to one volume of a novel.   Each novel of three volumes
brings L. 4000, and I remain proprietor of the mine after the first ore is
scooped out.'   The result of this negotiation with Mr. Heath was, that
he received, for L. 500, the liberty of printing in his Keepsake the long
forgotten juvenile drama of the House of Aspen, with My Aunt Margaret's
Mirror, and two other little tales, which had been omitted, at Ballantyne's
entreaty, from the second Chronicles of Croftangry.   But Sir Walter
regretted having meddled in any way with the toyshop of literature, and
would never do so again, though repeatedly offered very large sums—nor
even when the motive of private regard was added, upon Mr. Allen
Cunningham's lending his name to one of these painted bladders.

    " In the same week that Mr. Heath made his proposition, Sir Walter
received another which he thus disposes of in his Diary :—' I have an
invitation from Messrs. Saunders and Ottley, booksellers, offering me from
L. 1500 to L. 2000 annually to conduct a journal ; but I am their humble
servant.   I am too indolent to stand to that sort of work, and I must preserve the undisturbed use of my leisure, and possess my soul in quiet.   A
large income is not my object ; I must clear my debts ; and that is to be
done by writing things of which I can retain the property.   Made my
excuses accordingly."

    Think of a man considering 400*l.* as not worth his while for one
hundred close-printed pages of the Keepsake !   Is there a living
author who would not jump at the offer ?   We believe not one.   The
fact is, that since Scott's time a gradual depreciation has attended
the wages of literary labour, and that his enormous gains have operated in some measure both to swell the host of *litterateurs* and to
bring the calling of the writers of light works into contempt,—the
tinselled Annuals having a like tendency.   But while Mr. Lockhart sneers at these " painted bladders," he ought to remember that
he has contributed to them himself, at least in one instance which
we can point out.   He ought to bear in mind that an Edinburgh
publication, *Janus* by name, was indebted to his pen, although, it
never saw a second year.

    In the spring of 1828, Sir Walter spent some weeks in London.
We find him on the 19th of May dining with the Duchess of Kent,
and recording as follows :—

    " Dined by command with the Duchess of Kent.   I was very kindly
recognised by Prince Leopold—and presented to the little Princess Victoria
—I hope they will change her name—the heir-apparent to the crown as
things now stand.   How strange that so large and fine a family as that of
his late Majesty should have died off, or decayed into old age, with so few

descendants. Prince George of Cumberland is, they say, a fine boy about nine years old—a bit of a Pickle. This little lady is educating with much care, and watched so closely that no busy maid has a moment to whisper ' You are heir of England.' I suspect if we could dissect the little heart, we should find that some pigeon or other bird of the air had carried the matter. She is fair, like the Royal family—the Duchess herself very pleasing and affable in her manners. I sat by Mr. Spring Rice, a very agreeable man. There were also Charles Wynn and his lady—and the evening, for a court evening, went agreeably off. I am commanded for two days by Prince Leopold, but will send excuses."

In 1829, we find Scott multifariously engaged in writing; but we also find that by this time he had become subject to certain hæmorrhages which were relieved by copious cupping. The breaking up of his constitution was making sure progress. We read that on the 15th of February 1830,

" About two o'clock in the afternoon, he returned from the Parliament House apparently in his usual state, and found an old acquaintance, Miss Young of Hawick, waiting to show him some MS. memoirs of her father (a dissenting minister of great worth and talents), which he had undertaken to revise and correct for the press. The old lady sat by him for half an hour while he seemed to be occupied with her papers; at length he rose, as if to dismiss her, but sunk down again—a slight convulsion agitating his features. After a few minutes he got up and staggered to the drawing-room, where Anne Scott and my sister Violet Lockhart were sitting. They rushed to meet him, but he fell at all his length on the floor ere they could reach him. He remained speechless for about ten minutes, by which time a surgeon had arrived and bled him. He was cupped again in the evening, and gradually recovered possession of speech and of all his faculties in so far that, the occurrence being kept quiet, when he appeared abroad again after a short interval, people in general did not seem to have observed any serious change. He submitted to the utmost severity of regimen, tasting nothing but pulse and water for some weeks, and the alarm of his family and intimate friends subsided. By and by he again mingled in society much as usual, and seems to have *almost* persuaded himself that the attack had proceeded merely from the stomach, though his letters continued ever and anon to drop hints that the symptoms resembled apoplexy or paralysis. When we recollect that both his father and his elder brother died of paralysis, and consider the terrible violences of agitation and exertion to which Sir Walter had been subjected during the four preceding years, the only wonder is that this blow (which had, I suspect, several indistinct harbingers) was deferred so long; there can be none that it was soon followed by others of the same description."

Still he struggled manfully against his malady, and covered, says his biographer, during 1830, almost as many sheets with his MS. as in 1829. Letters on Demonology and Witchcraft for Murray's Family Library, being one of the works in hand, and also a Fourth Series of the Tales of a Grandfather—the subject being French

history. In both of these works, however, Mr. Lockhart remarks
there is a cloudiness of words and arrangement. Yet we find that
a lady, described as a person of rank, had so far mistaken his attentions, as to suppose him only prevented by modesty from offering
her his hand, about the very time when this cloudiness was dis-
closing itself.

Coming down to the autumn of 1830, the inroads of nervous disease had been making still more visible progress to the apprehension of Scott's family circle ; and the deep interest which he always
took in politics, seems to have been awakened to a distressing and
exhausting pitch by the question of Reform that was absorbing the
public mind, but in no quarter of the empire more decidedly than in
Scotland. The French revolution too, and the fear of the doctrines likely thence to be wafted to our shores, were at the time an-
noying him. He attended country and public meetings, and there
spoke boldly against the popular party, receiving for his reward
the strongest expressions of dislike, and not being entirely safe
from personal violence. Sir Walter's high Conservatism, his contempt of the unwashed artificers, and the danger to which he was
consequently exposed, will be gathered from the passages we now
extract.

" The first of these meetings was one of the freeholders of Roxburgh,
held at Jedburgh on the 21st of March, and there, to the distress and
alarm of his daughter, he insisted on being present, and proposing one of
the Tory resolutions,—which he did in a speech of some length, but delivered in a tone so low, and with such hesitation in utterance, that only a
few detached passages were intelligible to the bulk of the audience.

" ' We are told' (said he) ' on high authority, that France is the model
for us,—that we and all the other nations ought to put ourselves to school
there,—and endeavour to take out our degrees at *the University of Paris.*
—The French are a very ingenious people; they have often tried to
borrow from us, and now we should repay the obligation by borrowing a
leaf from them. But I fear there is an incompatibility between the tastes
and habits of France and Britain, and that we may succeed as ill in copying them, as they have hitherto done in copying us. We in this district
are proud, and with reason, that the first chain-bridge was the work of a
Scotchman. It still hangs were he erected it, a pretty long time ago.
The French heard of our invention, and determined to introduce it, but
with great improvements and embellishments. A friend of my own saw
the thing tried. It was on the Seine, at Marly. The French chain-bridge
looked lighter and airier than the prototype. Every Englishman present
was disposed to confess that we had been beat at our own trade. But by
and by the gates were opened, and the multitude were to pass over. It
began to swing rather formidably beneath the pressure of the good company ; and by the time the architect, who led the procession in great pomp
and glory, reached the middle, the whole gave way, and he, worthy,
patriotic artist, was the first who got a ducking. They had forgot the
great middle bolt,—or rather, this ingenious person had conceived that to

be a clumsy looking feature, which might safely be dispensed with, while he put some invisible gimcrack of his own to supply its place.'——Here Sir Walter was interrupted by violent hissing and hooting from the populace, who had flocked in and occupied the greater part of the Court-House. He stood calmly till the storm subsided, and resumed ; but the friend, whose notes are before me, could not catch what he said, until his voice rose with another illustration of the old style. ' My friends,' he said, ' I am old and failing, and you think me full of very silly prejudices; but I have seen a good deal of public men, and thought a good deal of public affairs in my day, and I can't help suspecting, that the manufacturers of this new constitution, are like a parcel of schoolboys taking to pieces a watch which used to go tolerably well for all practical purposes, in the conceit that they can put it together again far better than the old watchmaker. I fear they will fail when they come to the reconstruction, and I should not, I confess, be much surprised if it were to turn out that their first step had been to break the main-spring.'—Here he was again stopped by a confused Babel of contemptuous sounds, which seemed likely to render further attempts ineffectual. He, abruptly and unheard, proposed his Resolution, and then turning to the riotous artisans, exclaimed, ' I regard your gabble no more than the geese on the green.' His countenance glowed with indignation, as he resumed his seat on the bench. But when, a few moments afterwards, the business being over, he rose to withdraw, every trace of passion was gone. He turned round at the door, and bowed to the assembly. Two or three, not more, renewed their hissing ; he bowed again, and took leave in the words of the doomed gladiator, which I hope none who had joined in the insults understood—' MORITURUS VOS SALUTO.' "

On the 18th of May, 1831, says Mr. Lockhart,—

" I witnessed a scene which must dwell painfully upon many memories besides mine. The rumours of brick-bat and bludgeon work at the hustings of this month were so prevalent, that Sir Walter's family, and not less zealously the Tory candidate for Roxburghshire himself, tried every means to dissuade him from attending the election for that country. We thought over night that we had succeeded, and, indeed, as the result of the vote was not at all doubtful, there was not the shadow of a reason for his appearing on this occasion. About seven in the morning, however, when I came down stairs intending to ride over to Jedburgh, I found he had countermanded my horse, ordered the carriage to the door, and was already impatient to be off for the scene of action. We found the town in a most tempestuous state : in fact it was almost wholly in the hands of a disciplined rabble, chiefly weavers from Hawick, who marched up and down with drums and banners, and then, after filling the Court-hall, lined the streets, grossly insulting every one who did not wear the reforming colours. Sir Walter's carriage, as it advanced towards the house of the Shortreed family, was pelted with stones ; one or two fell into it, but none touched him. He breakfasted with the widow and children of his old friend, and then walked to the Hall between me and one of the young Shortreeds. He was saluted with groans and blasphemies all the way— and I blush to add that a woman spat upon him from a window ; but this

last contumely I think he did not observe. The scene within was much
what has been described under the date of March 21st, except that though
he attempted to speak from the Bench, not a word was audible, such was
the frenzy. Young Harden was returned by a great majority, 40 to 19,
and we then with difficulty gained the inn where the carriage had been
put up. But the aspect of the street was by that time such, that several
of the gentlemen on the Whig side came and entreated us not to attempt
starting from the front of our inn. One of them, Lieutenant R. Elliot of
the Royal Navy, lived in the town, or rather in a villa adjoining it, to the
rear of the Spread Eagle. Sir Walter was at last persuaded to accept
this courteous adversary's invitation, and accompanied him through some
winding lanes to his residence. Peter Mathieson by and by brought the
carriage thither, in the same clandestine method, and we escaped from
Jedburgh—with one shower more of stones at the Bridge. I believe there
would have been a determined onset at that spot, but for the zeal of three
or four sturdy Darnickers (Joseph Shillinglaw, carpenter, being their
Coryphæus), who had, unobserved by us, clustered themselves beside the
footman in the rumble."

Scenes of a nature like these must have proved injurious to Scott,
breaking down as he was, both in spirit and body, by an accumulation of complaints. We find him about the same date declaring
that the "task of pumping my brains becomes inevitably harder,"
when

> ' Both chain pumps are choked below.' "

He was engaged upon Count Robert of Paris and Castle Dangerous, but his efforts ceased to give satisfaction to James Ballantyne,—the latter circumstance being the source of much annoyance.
Apoplectic paralysis had affected his nerves and speech; doctors were
in frequent attendance; a limited diet was strictly enforced; and yet
he worked on. Lockhart says that one distressing symptom became quite apparent, viz. a constant setting tasks to the memory,
arising obviously from the fear that this prodigious engine had lost
or was losing its tenacity. But we must hasten forward and meet
him at Malta on his way to Naples, whither he had been persuaded
to proceed in hopes that the voyage and a warm climate might renovate his constitution. The following passages are from the Memoranda of a Scotch lady, Mrs. Davy, whom he had the pleasure to
meet at that island.

" *Sunday Morning, December* 5, Sir Walter spent chiefly in St John's
Church, the beautiful temple and burying-place of the knights, and
there he was much pleased and interested. On Monday the 6th he
dined at the Chief-Justice, Sir John Stoddart's, when I believe he par-
took too freely of porter and champagne for one in his invalid state.
On Tuesday morning (the 7th), on looking from one of our windows
across the street I observed him sitting in an easy-chair in the parlour
of his hotel, a book in his hand, and apparently reading attentively :—
his window was wide open, and I remember wishing much for the

power of making a picture of him just as he sat. But about 11 o'clock Miss Scott came over to me, looking much frightened, and saying that she feared he was about to have another paralytic attack. He had, she said, been rather confused in mind the day before, and the dinner-party had been too much for him. She had observed that on trying to answer a note from the Admiral that morning, he had not been able to form a letter on the paper, and she thought he was now sitting in a sort of stupor. She begged that Dr. Davy would visit him as soon as possible, and that I would accompany him, so that he might not suppose it a *medical* visit, for to all such he had an utter objection. I sent for Dr. D. instantly, and the moment he returned we went together to the hotel. We found Sir Walter sitting near a fire, dressed, as I had seen him just before, in a large silk dressing-gown, his face a good deal flushed, and his eyes heavy. He rose, however, as I went up to him, and, addressing me by my mother's name, ' Mrs. Fletcher,' asked kindly whether I was quite recovered from a little illness I had complained of the day before, and then walked to a table on the other side of the room, to look at some views of the new Volcano in the Mediterranean, which, by way of apology for our early visit, we had carried with us. With these he seemed pleased ; but there was great indistinctness in his manner of speaking. He soon after sat down, and began, of his own accord, to converse with Dr. Davy on the work he was then engaged in—the Life of Sir Humphry—saying that he was truly glad he was thus engaged, as he did not think justice had been done to the character of his friend by Dr. Paris. In speaking of the scientific distinction attained by Sir Humphry, he said, ' I hope, Dr. Davy, your mother lived to see it. There must have been such great pleasure in that to her.' We both remember with much interest this kindly little observation; and it was but one of many that dropt from him as naturally at the different times we met, showing that, ' fallen' as ' the mighty' was, and ' his weapons of war perished,' the springs of fancy dried up, and memory on most subjects much impaired, his sense of the value of home-bred worth and affection was in full force."

While at Naples, Sir Walter received great attention from a number of distinguished individuals, foreign as well as native. Among these the celebrated Sir William Gell deserves particular notice, one of the best of Cicerones that could anywhere be found to Pæstum, Pompeii, &c. We quote from Sir William's Memoranda a few particulars.

" When Sir Walter was presented at Court, the King received him with marked attention, and insisted on his being seated, on account of his infirmity. They both spoke, and the by-standers observed that His Majesty mentioned the pleasure he had received from reading the works of his visiter. Sir Walter answered in French, but not in a clear tone of voice ; and he afterwards observed, that he and the King parted mutually pleased with the interview, considering that neither had heard one word of what was uttered by the other.

" On the 17th of January I took Sir Walter to dine with the venerable Archbishop of Tarentum, a prelate in his 90th year, but yet retaining his faculties unimpaired, and the warmer feelings of youth, with well-known hospitality. The two elders seemed mutually pleased with the interview, but the difficulties of language were opposed to any very agreeable conversation.

" On the 26th of January I attended Sir Walter in a boat, with several friends, to the ruins of a Roman villa, supposed by Mr. Hamilton and others to have been that of Pollio, and situated upon a rock in the sea at the extremity of the promontory of Posilipo. It was by no means the recollection of Pollio that induced Sir Walter to make this excursion. A story existed that out of an opening in the floor of one of the rooms in this villa, a spectre robed in white occasionally appeared, whence the place had acquired the name of La Casa degli Spiriti, and none had presumed to inhabit it. The fact was, that a third story had been built upon the Roman ruins, and this being only inhabited by paupers, had fallen into decay, so as to endanger one angle of the fabric, and the police, for fear of accident, had ordered that it should remain untenanted. The house is situated upon a rock projecting into the sea, but attached on one side to the mainland. An entrance for a boat has been left in the basement story, and it is probable that a sort of open court, into which the sea enters at the back of the house, and in which is the staircase, was constructed for the purpose of cooling the apartments in the heat of summer, by means of the perpetual heaving and sinking of the ocean which takes place even in the calmest weather. The staircase was too much ruined for Sir Walter to ascend with safety, but he appeared satisfied with what he saw, and took some interest in the proofs which the appearance of the opus reticulatum, high up in the external walls, afforded of the antiquity of the place.

" On the 9th of February Sir Walter went to Pompeii, where, with several ladies and gentlemen at that time resident in Naples, I accompanied him. I did not go in the same carriage, but, arriving at the street of the Tombs, found him already almost tired before he had advanced 100 yards. With great difficulty I forced him to accept the chair in which I was carried, supplying its place with another for myself, tied together with cords and handkerchiefs. He thus was enabled to pass through the city without more fatigue, and I was sometimes enabled to call his attention to such objects as were the most worthy of remark. To these observations, however, he seemed generally nearly insensible, viewing the whole and not the parts, with the eye, not of an antiquary, but a poet, and exclaiming frequently ' The city of the Dead,' without any other remark. An excavation had been ordered for him, but it produced nothing more than a few bells, hinges, and other objects of brass, which are found every day. Sir Walter seemed to view, however, the splendid mosaic, representing a combat of the Greeks and Persians, with more interest, and, seated upon a table whence he could look down upon it, he remained some time to examine it. We dined at a large table spread in the Forum, and Sir Walter was cheerful and pleased. In the evening he was a little tired, but felt no bad effects from the excursion to the City of the Dead."

Scott had wished to return to England by the route of the Tyrol and Germany, having in contemplation an interview with Goëthe at Weimar. That poet's death, however, prevented the fulfilment of this design, and acted powerfully on the traveller. His impatience to get home became extreme, for all his fine dreams of recovery seemed to vanish at once. " Alas !" he exclaims, " but he at least died at home. Let us to Abbotsford." From this date the great Minstrel's history is one that touches the feelings in an extraordinary manner. It is pathetic and awakening in a remarkable degree.

" The last jotting," says Mr. Lockhart, " of Sir Walter's Diary, perhaps the last specimen of his handwriting records his starting from Naples on the 16th of April." We find, however, some notices from Sir William Gell's pen of the illustrious invalid's stay in Rome, in which there is a glimpse or two of sunshine, only to be rendered the more affecting by the general melancholy of the remaining narrative. Could admiration and assiduous attentions on the part of the great have banished solicitude and ailments Scott's must have been a happy and flattering journey. Sir William Gell writes,

" Soon after his arrival I took Sir Walter to St. Peter's, which he had resolved to visit, that he might see the tomb of the last of the Stuarts. I took him to one of the side doors, in order to shorten the walk, and by great good fortune met with Colonel Blair and Mr. Phillips, under whose protection he accomplished his purpose. We contrived to tie a glove round the point of his stick, to prevent his slipping in some degree, but to conduct him was really a source of danger and alarm, owing to his infirmity and total want of caution. He has been censured for not having frequently visited the treasures of the Vatican—but by those only who were unacquainted with the difficulty with which he moved. Days and weeks must have been passed in this immense museum, in order to have given him any idea of its value, nor do I know that it would have been possible for him to have ascended the rugged stairs, or to have traced its corridors and interminable galleries, in the state of reduced strength and dislike to being assisted under which he then laboured.

" On the 8th of May we all dined at the Palace of the Duchess Torlonia with a very large company. The dinner was very late and very splendid, and from the known hospitality of the family it was probable that Sir Walter, in the heat of conversation, and with servants on all sides pressing him to eat and drink, as is their custom at Rome, might be induced to eat more than was safe for his malady. Colonel Blair, who sat next him, was requested to take care that this should not happen. Whenever I observed him, however, Sir Walter appeared always to be eating ; while the Duchess, who had discovered the nature of the office imposed on the Colonel, was by no means satisfied, and after dinner observed that it was an odd sort of friendship which consisted in starving one's neighbour to death when he had a good appetite, and there was dinner enough.

" It was at this entertainment that Sir Walter met with the Duke and Duchess of Corchiano, who were both well read in his works, and delighted to have been in company with him. This acquaintance might have led to some agreeable consequences had Sir Walter's life been spared, for the Duke told him he was possessed of a vast collection of papers, giving true accounts of all the murders, poisonings, intrigues, and curious adventures of all the great Roman families during many centuries, all which were at his service to copy and publish in his own way as historical romances, only disguising the names, so as not to compromise the credit of the existing descendants of the families in question. Sir Walter listened to the Duke for the remainder of the evening, and was so captivated with all he heard from that amiable and accomplished personage, that at one moment he thought of remaining for a time at Rome, and at another he vowed he would return there in the ensuing winter. Whoever has read any of these memoirs of Italian families, of which many are published and very many exist in manuscript, will acknowledge how they abound in strange events and romantic stories, and may form some idea of the delight with which Sir Walter imagined himself on the point of pouncing upon a treasure after his own heart."

Had the magician of the north recovered his health and lived a few years longer, how splendid might have been the fruits of his visit to Malta and Italy! And yet it will be generally admitted that no work of his, whether scenery or character be considered, ever reached that pre-eminence which distinguishes those that belong to his native country, a thing to be expected of a writer who entertained an inextinguishable yearning of love for the land of his forefathers, as some of our few remaining extracts poignantly illustrate. After the 11th of May we read,

" The irritation of impatience, which had for a moment been suspended by the aspect and society of Rome, returned the moment he found himself on the road, and seemed to increase hourly. His companions could with difficulty prevail on him to see even the Falls of Terni, or the Church of Santa Croce at Florence. On the 17th, a cold and dreary day, they passed the Apennines, and dined on the top of the mountains. The snow and the pines recalled Scotland, and he expressed pleasure at the sight of them. That night they reached Bologna, but he would see none of the interesting objects there—and next day, hurrying in like manner through Ferrara, he proceeded as far as Monselice. On the 19th he arrived at Venice ; and he remained there till the 23rd ; but showed no curiosity about any thing except the Bridge of Sighs and the adjoining dungeons—down into which he would scramble, though the exertion was exceedingly painful to him. On the other historical features of that place—one so sure in other days to have inexhaustible attractions for him—he would not even look ; and it was the same with all that he came within reach of—even with the fondly anticipated chapel at Inspruck—as they proceeded through the Tyrol, and so onwards, by Munich, Ulm, and Heidelberg, to Frankfort. Here (June 5) he entered a bookseller's shop; and the people seeing an English party, brought out among the first things a lithographed print of Abbotsford. He said, ' I know that already, sir,' and hastened back to the inn without being recognised. Though in some parts of the journey they had very severe weather, he repeatedly wished to travel all the night as well as all the day ; and the symptoms of an approaching fit were so obvious, that he was more than once bled, ere they reached Mayence, by the hand of his affectionate domestic.

" At this town they embarked on the 8th June in the Rhine steam-boat; and while they descended the famous river through its most picturesque region, he seemed to enjoy, though he said nothing, the perhaps unrivalled scenery it presented to him. His eye was fixed on the successive crags and castles, and ruined monasteries, each of which had been celebrated in some German ballad familiar to his ear, and all of them blended in the immortal panorama of Childe Harold. But so soon as he resumed his carriage at Cologne, and nothing but flat shores, and here and there a grove of poplars and a village spire were offered to the vision, the weight of misery sunk down again upon him. It was near Nimeguen, on the evening of the 9th, that he sustained another serious attack of apoplexy, combined with paralysis. Nicolson's lancet restored, after the lapse of some minutes, the signs of animation; but this was the crowning blow. Next day he insisted on resuming his journey, and on the 11th was lifted from the carriage into a steam-boat at Rotterdam."

Scott lay in London for some weeks, when an universal interest and sympathy was manifested in his behalf. His condition during this period was generally that of stupor. We quote from the memorandum of Dr. Ferguson :

" ' When I saw Sir Walter he was lying in the second floor back-room of the St. James's Hotel, in Jermyn Street, in a state of stupor, from which, however, he could be roused for a moment by being addressed, and then he recognised those about him, but immediately relapsed. I think I never saw anything more magnificent than the symmetry of his colossal bust, as he lay on the pillow with his chest and neck exposed. During the time he was in Jermyn Street he was calm but never collected, and in general either in absolute stupor or in a waking dream. He never seemed to know where he was, but imagined himself to be still in the steam-boat. The rattling of carriages, and the noises of the street sometimes disturbed this illusion, and then he fancied himself at the polling booth of Jedburgh, where he had been insulted and stoned.

" ' During the whole of this period of apparent helplessness, the great features of his character could not be mistaken. He always exhibited great self-possession, and acted his part with wonderful power whenever visited, though he relapsed the next moment into the stupor from which strange voices had roused him. A gentleman stumbled over a chair in his dark room;—he immediately started up, and though unconscious that it was a friend, expressed as much concern and feeling as if he had never been labouring under the irritability of disease. It was impossible even for those who most constantly saw and waited on him in his then deplorable condition, to relax from the habitual deference which he had always inspired. He expressed his will as determinedly as ever, and enforced it with the same apt and good-natured irony as he was wont to use.

" ' At length his constant yearning to return to Abbotsford induced his physicians to consent to his removal, and the moment this was notified to him it seemed to infuse new vigour into his frame. It was on a calm, clear afternoon of the 7th July, that every preparation was made for his embarkation on board the steam-boat. He was placed on a chair by his faithful servant Nicolson, half-dressed, and loosely wrapt in a quilted dressing-gown. He requested Lockhart and myself to wheel him towards the light of the open window, and we both remarked the vigorous lustre of his eye. He sat there silently gazing on space for more than half an hour, apparently wholly occupied with his own thoughts, and having no distinct perception of where he was or how he came there. He suffered himself to be lifted into his carriage, which was surrounded by a crowd, among whom were many gentlemen on horseback, who had loitered about to gaze on the scene."

In the journey both on sea and land from London to Abbotsford, Sir Walter's prostration was rarely interrupted. But when he came near to Tweedside and to his home, the charm of familiar and strongly-beloved scenes operated with wonderful power upon him.

" As we descended the vale of the Gala he began to gaze about him, and by degrees it was obvious that he was recognising the features of that familiar landscape. Presently he murmured a name or two—' Gala Water, surely—Buckholm—Torwoodlee.' As we rounded the hill at Ladhope, and the outline of the Eildons burst on him, he became greatly excited, and when turning himself on the couch his eye caught at length his own towers, at the distance of a mile, he sprang up with a cry of delight. The river being in flood we had to go round a few miles by Melrose bridge, and during the time this occupied, his woods and house being within prospect, it required occasionally both Dr. Watson's strength and mine, in addition to Nicolson's, to keep him in the carriage. After passing the bridge the road for a couple of miles loses sight of Abbotsford, and he relapsed into his stupor; but on gaining the bank immediately above it, his excitement became again ungovernable.

" Mr. Laidlaw was waiting at the porch, and assisted us in lifting him into the dining-room, where his bed had been prepared. He sat bewildered for a few moments, and then resting his eye on Laidlaw, said, ' Ha ! Willie Laidlaw ! O man, how often have I thought of you !' By this time his dogs had assembled about his chair—they began to fawn upon him and lick his hands, and he alternately sobbed and smiled over them, until sleep oppressed him."

We think these sentences will fill many an eye with tears. The morning after his arrival at his own hall, he awoke quite conscious where he was. He desired to be wheeled through his rooms. " I have seen much," he said, " but nothing like my ain house." He was gentle as an infant, continues his biographer. Next morning he was still better, and enjoyed the open air for a couple of hours. He then desired to be placed in his library so as that he might look down upon the Tweed. These are touching little incidents, that are far more affecting in narrative than any theatrical display, in the form of fine speeches and dramatic effect, could be. But the crystal Tweed did not absorb the whole of Sir Walter's remaining consciousness, for he expressed a wish that his son-in-law would read to him ; and when asked from what book, he said, " Need you ask? There is but one." And after listening to the 14th chapter of St. John's Gospel, he added, " Well, this is a great comfort."

He sometimes called for a little of Crabbe's poetry, and evinced more or less, though a gradually declining power, of memory and judgment. We read that on the 17th of July,

" He appeared revived somewhat, and was again wheeled about on the turf. Presently he fell asleep in his chair, and after dozing for perhaps half an hour, started awake, and shaking the plaids we had put about him from off his shoulders, said, ' This is sad idleness. I shall forget what I have been thinking of, if I don't set it down now. Take me into my own room, and fetch the keys of my desk.' He repeated this so earnestly that we could not refuse ; his daughters went into his study, opened his writing-desk, and laid paper and pens in the usual order, and I then moved him through the hall and into the spot where he had always been accustomed to work. When the chair was placed at the desk, and he found himself in the old position, he smiled and thanked us, and said, ' Now give me my pen and leave me for a little to myself.' Sophia put the pen into his hand, and he endeavoured to close his fingers upon it, but they refused their office—it dropped on the paper. He sank back among his pillows, silent tears rolling down his cheeks ; but composing himself by and by, motioned to me to wheel him out of doors again. Laidlaw met us at the porch, and took his turn of the chair. Sir Walter, after a little while, again dropt into slumber. When he was awaking, Laidlaw said to me ' Sir Walter has had a little repose.' ' No, Willie,' said he—' no repose for Sir Walter but in the grave.' The tears again rushed from his eyes. ' Friends,' said he, ' don't let me expose myself—get me to bed—that's the only place.' "

One scene more,—

" Perceiving, towards the close of August, that the end was near, and thinking it very likely that Abbotsford might soon undergo many changes, and myself, at all events, never see it again, I felt a desire to have some image preserved of the interior apartments as occupied by their founder, and invited from Edinburgh for that purpose Sir Walter's dear friend, William Allan—whose presence, I well knew, would even under the circumstances of that time be nowise troublesome to any of the family, but the contrary in all respects. Mr. Allan willingly complied, and executed a series of beautiful drawings, which may probably be engraved hereafter. He also shared our watchings, and witnessed all but the last moments. Sir Walter's cousins, the ladies of Ashestiel, came down frequently, for a day or two at a time ; and did whatever sisterly affections could prompt, both for the sufferer and his daughters. Miss Barbara Scott (daughter of his uncle Thomas), and Mrs. Scott of Harden, did the like.

" As I was dressing on the morning of Monday the 17th of September, Nicolson came into my room, and told me that his master had awoke in a state of composure and consciousness, and wished to see me immediately. I found him entirely himself, though in the last extreme of feebleness. His eye was clear and calm—every trace of the wild fire of delirium extinguished. ' Lockhart,' he said, ' I may have but a minute to speak to you. My dear, be a good man—be virtuous—be religious—be a good man. Nothing else will give you any comfort when you come to lie here.'—He paused, and I said, ' Shall I send for Sophia and Anne?'—' No,' said he, ' don't disturb them. Poor souls ! I know they were up all night—God bless you all.'— With this he sunk into a very tranquil sleep, and, indeed, he scarcely afterwards gave any sign of consciousness, except for an instant on the arrival of his sons. They, on learning that the scene was about to close, obtained anew leave of absence from their posts, and both reached Abbotsford on the 19th. About half-past one P.M., on the 21st of September, Sir Walter breathed his last, in the presence of all his children. It was a beautiful day—so warm that every window was wide open—and so perfectly still, that the sound of all others most delicious to his ear, the gentle ripple of the Tweed over its pebbles, was distinctly audible as we knelt around the bed, and his eldest son kissed and closed his eyes."

Such was the termination of a great and good man's career, hastened, no doubt, by a dangerous and inordinate ambition, which in the face of prudence and open dealing landed him in a labyrinth of difficulties from which it cost him his life to extricate himself. In his speculation about the mystery which Scott kept up in regard to his fictions and his business-concerns, the biographer's sagacity and impartiality may be discovered, and the value of the work shortly tested. The extract at any rate about to be introduced, saves us the labour of seeking for any other theory, and from the attempt particularly to characterize the life as a literary effort, which would necessarily be unsatisfactory.

" The whole system of conceptions and aspirations, of which his early active life was the exponent, resolves itself into a romantic idealization of Scottish aristocracy. He desired to secure for his descendants (for himself he had very soon acquired something infinitely more flattering to self-love and vanity) a decent and honourable middle station—in a scheme of life so constituted originally, and which his fancy pictured as capable of being so revived, so as to admit of the kindliest personal contact between (almost) the peasant at the plough, and the magnate with revenues rivalling the monarch's. It was the patriarchal—the clan system that he thought of; one that never prevailed even in Scotland, within the historical period, that is to say, except in the Highlands, and in his own dear Borderland. This system knew nothing of commerce—as little certainly of literature beyond the raid-ballad of the wandering harper—
                ' High placed in hall—a welcome guest.'
His filial reverence of imagination shrunk from marring the antique, if barbarous, simplicity. I suspect that at the highest elevation of his literary renown—when princes bowed to his name, and nations thrilled at it—he would have considered losing all that at a change of the wind as nothing, compared to parting with his place as the Cadet of Harden and Clansman of Buccleuch, who had, no matter by what means, reached such a position, that when a notion arose of embodying ' a Buccleuch legion,' not a Scott in the Forest would have thought it otherwise than natural for *Abbotsford* to be one of the field-officers. I can, therefore, understand that he may have

from the very first, exerted the dispensing power of imagination very liberally, in virtually absolving himself from dwelling on the wood of which his ladder was to be constructed. Enough was said in a preceding chapter of the obvious fact, that the author of such a series of romances as his must have, to all intents and purposes, lived more than half his life in worlds purely fantastic. In one of the last obscure and faltering pages of his Diary he says, that if any one asked him how much of his thought was occupied by the novel then in hand, the answer would have been, that in one sense it never occupied him except when the amanuensis sat before him, but that in another it was never five minutes out of his head. Such, I have no doubt, the case had always been. But I must be excused from doubting whether, when the substantive fiction actually in process of manufacture was absent from his mind, the space was often or voluntarily occupied (no positive external duty interposing) upon the real practical worldly position and business of the Clerk of Session, of the Sheriff—least of all of the printer or the bookseller.

" The sum is, if I read him aright, that he was always willing, in his ruminative moods, to veil, if possible, from his own optics the kind of machinery by which alone he had found the means of attaining his darling objects. Having acquired a perhaps unparalleled power over the direction of scarcely paralleled faculties, he chose to exert his power in this manner. On no other supposition can I find his history intelligible;—I mean, of course, the great obvious and marking facts of his history; for I hope I have sufficiently disclaimed all pretension to a thorough-going analysis. He appears to have studiously escaped from whatever could have interfered with his own enjoyment—to have revelled in the fair results, and waved the wand of obliterating magic over all besides; and persisted so long, that (like the sorcerer he celebrates) he became the dupe of his own delusions.

" It is thus that (not forgetting the subsidiary influence of professional Edinburgh prejudices) I am inclined, on the whole, to account for his initiation in the practice of mystery—a thing, at first sight, so alien from the frank, open, generous nature of a man, than whom none ever had or deserved to have more real friends.

" The indulgence cost him very dear. It ruined his fortunes—but I can have no doubt that it did worse than that. I cannot suppose that a nature like his was fettered and shut up in this way without suffering very severely from the ' cold obstruction.' There must have been a continual ' insurrection' in his ' state of man ;' and, above all, I doubt not that what gave him the bitterest pain in the hour of his calamities, was the feeling of compunction with which he then found himself obliged to stand before those with whom he had, through life, cultivated brotherlike friendship, convicted of having kept his heart closed to them on what they could not but suppose to have been the chief subjects of his thought and anxiety, in times when they withheld nothing from him. These, perhaps, were the ' written troubles' that had been cut deepest into his brain. I think they were, and believe it the more, because it was never acknowledged.

" If he had erred in the primary indulgence out of which this sprang, he at least made noble atonement.

" During the most energetic years of manhood he laboured with one prize in view; and he had just grasped it, as he fancied, securely, when all at once the vision was dissipated : he found himself naked and desolate as Job.

How he nerved himself against the storm—how he felt and how he resisted
it—how soberly, steadily, and resolvedly he contemplated the possibility of
yet, by redoubled exertions, in so far retrieving his fortunes, as that no man
should lose by having trusted those for whom he had been pledged—how
well he kept his vow, and what price it cost him to do so—all this the
reader, I doubt not, appreciates fully. It seems to me that strength of character was never put to a severer test than when, for labours of love, such
as his had hitherto almost always been—the pleasant exertion of genius for
the attainment of ends that owed all their dignity and beauty to a poetical
fancy—there came to be substituted the iron pertinacity of daily and nightly
toil in the discharge of a duty, which there was nothing but the sense of
chivalrous honour to make stringent."

ART. III.

1.—*Alice, or the Mysteries; a Sequel to " Ernest Maltravers."* By the
   Author of " Pelham," " Rienzi," " The Student," &c. &c.   3 Vols.
   London : Saunders and Ottley. 1838.

2.—*Count Cagliostro: or, the Charlatan. A Tale of the Reign of Louis
   XVI.* 3 Vols. London : E. Bull. 1838.

WE rose from the perusal of Ernest Maltravers with so profound a
feeling of admiration and delight, that we looked forward with impatience for the appearance of the promised sequel to that powerful work.
Nor have our anticipations of a fresh intellectual banquet been in
the slightest degree disappointed. The same measured dignity of
composition, the same lofty sentiment and refined philosophy, the
same easy and closely-wrought style which make that work the *facile
princeps* of Mr. Bulwer's writings—the highest step he has yet attained in his ascent to that perfection towards which he strains—
are carried on with undiminished excellence through the present
volumes. There is no falling off, no flagging on the wing, no uneven-
ness in the onward course of the narrative. The same characters,
varied indeed by time and circumstances, hold the same relative
position to each other which was decreed by the principle of their
original formation, and conformable to that formation they modify the
events that bear them onward to the goal.

A deep study of the great volume of human life has enabled Mr.
Bulwer to conceive with judgment what his long practice has enabled
him to execute with ability. There is a completeness, a certainty
in his pictures, which at once strike our admiration and challenge
our scrutiny. The incidents are woven from every-day life ; the political intrigues which are still rife in our recollections, the new
interests, the passions, the follies of the passing hour, are skilfully
made available to the purposes of fiction, and over all is flung the
solemn hues of a high and mystic philosophy, which invest them
with the shadowy grandeur and religious gloom of the Greek
drama.

We have seen in the first part of the work, Maltravers driven from his high career and native soil by the machinations of successful villany ; Lumley Ferrers, the man who acted " upon system," a peer, and affianced to the heiress of his uncle's immense wealth ; the peerless Florence Lascelles in the tomb—Cæsarini in a madhouse. Maltravers was resolved the world should not hear him groan, he wrestled with his spirit like the patriarch of old. He wandered from clime to clime, through deserts and wastes, and barbarous hordes, but the barbarous state restored him to the civilized. He returned to his hereditary hall, purposed to be an actor in the strife no more, but to be a calm spectator of the turbulent scene. The changes which time and travel had wrought in his character are thus pourtrayed.

"Ernest Maltravers, never a faultless or completed character. falling short in practice of his own capacities, moral and intellectual, from his very desire to overpass the limits of the Great and Good, was seemingly as far as heretofore from the grand secret of life. It was not so in reality—his mind had acquired what before it wanted—*hardness ;* and we are nearer to true virtue, and true happiness, when we demand too little from men, than when we exact too much.

"Nevertheless, partly from the strange life that had thrown him amongst men whom safety itself made it necessary to command despotically—partly from the habit of power, and disdain of the world, his nature was incrusted with a stern imperiousness of manner, often approaching to the harsh and morose, though beneath it lurked generosity and benevolence.

" Many of his younger feelings, more amiable and complex, had settled into one predominant quality, which more or less had always characterized him—Pride ! Self-esteem made inactive, and Ambition made discontented, usually engender haughtiness. In Maltravers this quality, which properly controlled, and duly softened, is the essence and life of honour, was carried to a vice. He was perfectly conscious of its excess, but he cherished it as a virtue. Pride had served to console him in sorrow, and, therefore, it was a friend—it had supported him when disgusted with fraud, or in resistance to violence ; and, therefore, it was a champion and a fortress. It was a pride of a peculiar sort—it attached itself to no one point in especial—not to talent, knowledge, mental gifts—still less to the vulgar common-places of birth and fortune ;—it rather resulted from a supreme and wholesale contempt of all other men, and all their objects—of ambition—of glory—of the hardness of life. His favourite virtue was fortitude—it was on this that he now mainly valued himself. He was proud of his struggles against others —prouder still of conquests over his own passions. He looked upon FATE as the arch enemy against whose attacks we should ever prepare. He fancied that against fate he had thoroughly schooled himself. In the arrogance of his heart, he said, ' I can defy the future.' He believed in the boast of the vain old sage—' I am a world to myself ! ' In the wild career through which his later manhood had passed, it is true that he had not carried his philosophy into a rejection of the ordinary world. The shock occasioned by the death of Florence yielded gradually to time and change ; and he had passed from the deserts of Africa and the East, to the brilliant cities

of Europe. But neither his heart nor his reason had ever been enslaved by
his passions. He had never again known the softness of affection. Had
he done so, the ice had been thawed, and the fountain had flowed again into
the great deeps. He had returned to England; he scarce knew wherefore,
or with what intent; certainly not with any idea of entering again upon the
occupations of active life;—it was, perhaps, only the weariness of foreign
scenes and unfamiliar tongues, and the vague, unsettled desire of change,
that brought him back to the father-land. But he did not allow so unphilo-
sophical a cause to himself; and, what was strange, he would not allow one
much more amiable, and which was, perhaps, the truer cause—the increasing
age and infirmities of his old guardian Cleveland, who prayed him affectionately to return. Maltravers did not like to believe that his heart was still
so kind. Singular form of pride! No, he rather sought to persuade himself, that he intended to sell Burleigh, to arrange his affairs finally, and then
quit for ever his native land. To prove to himself that this was the case, he
had intended at Dover to hurry at once to Burleigh, and merely write to
Cleveland that he was returned to England. But his heart would not suffer
him to enjoy this cruel luxury of self-mortification, and his horses' heads were
turned to Richmond, when within a stage of London. He had spent two
days with the good old man, and those two days had so warmed and softened
his feelings, that he was quite appalled at his own dereliction from fixed
principles. However, he went before Cleveland had time to discover that
he was changed; and the old man had promised to visit him shortly."

He abandons his literary pursuits, takes the management of his
estate into his hands and becomes an active magistrate. It happens by a very natural train of circumstances, that Evelyn Cameron,
the beautiful and wealthy heiress of Mr. Templeton, alias Lord
Vargrave, is domesticated at the Rectory, the seat of Mr. Merton,
in the neighbourhood of Burleigh; her mother, Lady Vargrave,
ci-devant Alice Darvil, never quitting her cottage in Devonshire.
Maltravers is at once smitten with the enchanting girl, whom as
a pretty child he once remembered lifting in his arms on the road
at Fulham. Her smiles thawed the ice in which he had enveloped
his heart, and Maltravers once more loved—ardently loved.

" It is not to be wondered at, that the daily presence—the delicate flattery
of attention from a man like Maltravers—should strongly impress the
imagination, if not the heart, of a susceptible girl. Already prepossessed in
his favour, and wholly unaccustomed to a society which combined so many
attractions—Evelyn regarded him with unspeakable veneration; to the
darker shades in his character she was blind—to her, indeed, they did not
appear. True, that once or twice in mixed society, his disdainful and imperious temper broke hastily and harshly forth. To folly—to pretension—
to presumption—he showed but slight forbearance. The impatient smile—
the biting sarcasm—the cold repulse—that might gall, yet could scarce be
openly resented—betrayed that he was one who affected to free himself from
the polished restraints of social intercourse. He had once been too scrupulous in not wounding vanity—he was now too indifferent to it. But if
sometimes this unamiable trait of character, as displayed to others, chilled

or startled Evelyn, the contrast of his manner towards herself was a flattery too delicious not to efface all other recollections. To her ear his voice always softened its tone—to her capacity his mind ever bent as by sympathy —not condescension ;—to her—the young—the timid—the half-informed —to her alone he did not disdain to exhibit all the stores of his knowledge —all the best and brightest colours of his mind. She modestly wondered at so strange a preference. Perhaps a sudden and blunt compliment that Maltravers once addressed to her may explain it : one day, when she had conversed more freely and more fully than usual, he broke in upon her with this abrupt exclamation—

" ' Miss Cameron, you must have associated from your childhood with beautiful minds. I see already, that from the world, vile as it is, you have nothing of contagion to fear. I have heard you talk on the most various matters—on many of which your knowledge is imperfect ; but you have never uttered one mean idea, or one false sentiment. Truth seems intuitive to you.'

"It was, indeed, this singular purity of heart, that made to the world-wearied man the chief charm in Evelyn Cameron. From this purity came, as from the heart of a poet, a thousand new and heaven-taught thoughts, which had in them a wisdom of their own—thoughts that often brought the stern listener back to youth, and reconciled him with life. The wise Maltravers learned more from Evelyn, than Evelyn did from Maltravers."

"From the date of his accession to the peerage, the rise of Lumley Ferrers had been less rapid and progressive than he himself could have foreseen. At first, all was sunshine before him : he had contrived to make himself useful to his party—he had also made himself personally popular."

All this time Maltravers is quite unconscious of having once heard that by the will of the deceased Lord Vargrave, Lumley Ferrers was affianced to Evelyn Cameron; and in case of her refusal to marry him at eighteen, she was to forfeit thirty thousand pounds of her fortune. The position of Lord Vargrave rendered the fulfilment of the engagement indispensable ; but let us see what that position was.

" Perpetually absorbed in intrigues and schemes, he was too much engaged in cheating others on a large scale, to have time to prevent being cheated himself on a small one. He never looked into bills till he was compelled to pay them ; and he never calculated the amount of an expense that seemed the least necessary to his purposes. But still Lord Vargrave relied upon his marriage with the wealthy Evelyn to relieve him from all his embarrassments ; and if a doubt of the realization of that vision ever occurred to him, still public life had splendid prizes. Nay, should he fail with Miss Cameron, he even thought, that, by good management, he might ultimately make it worth while to his colleagues to purchase his absence with the gorgeous bribe of the Governor-Generalship of India."

Add to this, that his lordship had by practice become a nervous and formidable debater, was a special favourite with the then powerful female diplomatists, and personally liked by his royal master.

With this combination of advantages, his scheming spirit was busy in an attempt to carry the premiership by a *coup de finesse*, identically similar to that supposed to have been adopted by a talented ex-chancellor immediately previous to the breaking up of the Grey administration ; so that this political sketch becomes peculiarly interesting from bearing the stamp of historical verity. The cabinet are divided, the weaker party trying to out-trick the stronger.

But an indiscreet ebullition of independence in the House of Lords was so ill received as to convince Vargrave that he must postpone his views on the premiership for the present, and in the meantime his duns remind him that he must be doubly vigilant in prosecuting those on the heiress. He flies from the harassments of office to push his suit at the Rectory, and the rivals for the love of Lady Florence Lascelles are once more rivals for that of the far different Evelyn Cameron. Though Maltravers had never loved as he loved Evelyn, yet when he heard of her engagement to Vargrave, his stubborn and reflective principles of justice which had grown out of the chivalrous spirit of honour which he had worshipped in youth, he had resolved to conquer his attachment, and he entrenched himself in a rigid and almost chilling formality. But the acute mind of Vargrave was not slow to perceive the progress he had made.

A new and most dangerous candidate for the fair heiress appeared at this time in the person of a Colonel Legard. He was just the style to turn a romantic girl's head—a mixture of the wild and thorough-bred ; black curls, superb eyes, and the softest voice and manners in the world. Vargrave, in alarm, forces him into a place in the Ordnance—promotes a marriage between a rich Lord Doltimore and Miss Merton, whose affections he has engaged in order that she may aid him in the prosecution of his schemes upon the reluctant Evelyn.

All this time Lady Vargrave is not once seen by Maltravers, but continues in her seclusion in Devonshire, cherishing in her heart the painful remembrance of a bitter past, and consuming her years in silent sorrow over the grave of joy.

It looks rather improbable that no happy accident, no impulse of curiosity, should have helped the lover of the daughter to catch a glimpse of the mother. However, we must be indulgent towards the point upon which the whole structure of the story stands.

Maltravers overhears Evelyn declare that where she gives her hand she will give her heart, and interprets it as meaning that she loved her betrothed. His anguish for himself was lost in compassion for her, and the following interesting dialogue ensues :

" ' Miss Cameron,' said Maltravers, ' let me for one moment detain you ; I will not trespass long. May I once, and for the last time, assume the austere rights of friendship ? I have seen much of life, Miss Cameron, and my experience has been purchased dearly: and, harsh and hermit-like as I may have grown, I have not outlived such feelings as you are well formed to excite. Nay,'—(and Maltravers smiled sadly)—' I am not about to compliment or flatter—I speak not to you as the young to the young; the difference of our years that takes away sweetness from flattery, leaves still sincerity to friendship. You have inspired me with a deep interest;—deeper than I thought that living beauty could ever rouse in me again! It may be, that something in the tone of your voice, your manner, a nameless grace that I cannot define—reminds me of one whom I knew in youth;—one who had not your advantages of education, wealth, birth; but to whom Nature was more kind than Fortune.'

"He paused a moment; and, without looking towards Evelyn, thus renewed:—

"'You are entering life under brilliant auspices.—Ah! let me hope that the noonday will keep the promise of the dawn! You are suscepti-ble—imaginative; do not demand too much, or dream too fondly. When you are wedded, do not imagine that wedded life is exempt from its trials and its cares: if you know yourself beloved—and beloved you must be—do not ask from the busy and anxious spirit of man, all which Romance promises, and Life but rarely yields. And oh!' continued Maltravers, with an absorbing and earnest passion, that poured forth its language with almost breathless rapidity;—' if ever your heart rebels—if ever it be dissatisfied—fly the false sentiment as a sin!—Thrown, as from your rank you must be, on a world of a thousand perils, with no guide so con-stant, and so safe, as your own innocence—make not that world too dear a friend! Were it possible that your own home ever could be lonely or unhappy, reflect that to woman the unhappiest home is happier than all excitement abroad. You will have a thousand suitors, hereafter:—be-lieve that the asp lurks under the flatterer's tongue—and resolve, come what may, to be contented with your lot. How many have I known, lovely and pure as you, who have suffered the very affections—the very beauty of their nature to destroy them! Listen to me as a warner—as a brother—as a pilot who has passed the seas on which your vessel is about to launch. And ever—ever let me know, in whatever lands your name may reach me, that one who has brought back to me all my faith in human excellence, while the idol of our sex is the glory of her own. Forgive me this strange impertinence; my heart is full, and has overflowed. And now, Miss Cameron—Evelyn Cameron—this is my last offence, and my last farewell!'

"He held out his hand, and involuntarily, unknowingly, she clasped it, as if to detain him till she could summon words to reply. Suddenly he heard Lord Vargrave's voice behind—the spell was broken—the next moment Evelyn was alone, and the throng swept into the room towards the banquet, and laughter and gay voices were heard—and Lord Vargrave was again by Evelyn's side!"

As a means of dethroning the image at his heart, Maltravers flies from Burleigh to Paris; but in the gloomy Faubourg St. Germain pursued; haunted him; came upon him unawares; in solitude; in crowds. He meets once more Valere de St. Ventadour, much im-proved by the flight of time.

Of how many myriads of volumes has not love been the subject. We find in every work of fiction, of whatever class, elaborate descriptions of the birth, growth, and expansion of the tender passion. The theories of the tides of sentiment are unnumbered, and there is scarce a breath that moves above the gentle surface that has not found a local habitation and a name in the page of some work of genius. Sir Walter Scott sighed for the invention of a steam engine that might be safely applied to the descriptions of a heroine's person and dress, and an occasional apostrophe to love.

What pen but that of a most consummate writer could attempt anything on the subject, even slightly approaching to originality, on which the multitude of readers would not skip. Yet here is a passage so forcible, so clear, and so deep, without deviating into transcendentalism that we cannot refrain from extracting it.

" Love, in its first dim and imperfect shape, is but imagination concentrated on one object. It is a genius of the heart, resembling that of the intellect; it appeals to, it stirs up, it evokes the sentiments and sympathies that lie most latent in our nature. Its sigh is the spirit that moves over the ocean, and rouses the Anadyomene into life. Therefore is it, that MIND produces affections deeper than those of external form; therefore it is, that women are worshippers of glory, which is the palpable and visible representative of a genius whose operations they cannot always comprehend. Genius has so much in common with love—the imagination that animates one is so much the property of the other—that there is not a surer sign of the existence of genius than the love that it creates and bequeaths. It penetrates deeper than the reason—it binds a nobler captive than the fancy. As the sun upon the dial, it gives to the human heart both its shadow and its light. Nations are its worshippers and wooers; and Posterity learns from its oracles to dream—to aspire—to adore !"

Evelyn is at a loss to understand the conduct of Maltravers. If he loved her. why should he fly her? However she is determined to break off her engagement with Vargrave. Before returning to her mother's cottage, her preceptor and friend, the curate of the village, is charged to make the disclosure to his Lordship.

Lord Vargrave is now a desperate man, and *coute qui coute* he must possess himself of the fortune on which he had built his schemes, and which alone can save him from irretrievable ruin. His subtle spirit has soon matured a scheme for realizing his wishes, and the consummate adroitness with which he forces those around him to become his tools is forcibly pourtrayed in an interview he has with Lady Doltimore immediately after her marriage.

Evelyn is now transferred to Paris with the Doltimores, whither she is followed by the handsome Colonel Legard, whose congeniality of mental and personal qualities seemed as if nature intended him for the position to which he aspires. But Maltravers appears, and his ascendancy is at once acknowledged, and Legard magnanimously gives way to a rival who had saved his life, and whom gratitude forbade him to encounter.

" Meanwhile, what was the effect that the presence, the attentions, of Maltravers produced on Evelyn? Perhaps it was of that kind which most flatters us and most deceives. She never dreamt of comparing him with others. To her thoughts, he stood aloof and alone from all his kind. It may seem a paradox, but it might be that she admired and venerated him almost too much for love. Still her pleasure in his society was so evident and unequivocal, her deference to his opinion so marked—she sympathised in so many of his objects—she had so much blindness or forbearance for his faults (and he never sought to mask them), that the most diffident of men might have drawn from so many symptoms hopes the most auspicious. Since the departure of Legard, the gaieties of Paris lost their charm for Evelyn, and more than ever she could appreciate the society of her friend. He thus gradually lost his earlier fears of her forming too keen an attachment to the great world ; and as nothing could be more apparent than Evelyn's indifference to the crowd of flatterers and suitors that hovered round her, Maltravers no longer dreaded a rival. He began to feel assured that they had both gone through the ordeal ; and that he might ask for love without a doubt of its immutability and faith. At this period, they were both invited, with the Doltimores, to spend a few days at the villa of de Montaigne, near St. Cloud. And there it was that Maltravers determined to know his fate !"

In a solitary ramble in the neighbourhood of De Montaigne's villa, Maltravers is in the act of making his declaration, and is receiving the best assurance, which at length teaches him how beautiful is life, when—

" At that instant they were once more on the terrace where he had first joined Teresa—facing the wood—which was divided by a slight and low palisade from the spot where they stood. He ceased abruptly—for his eyes encountered a terrible and ominous opposition—a form connected with dreary associations of fate and woe. The figure had raised itself upon a pile of firewood on the other side the fence, and hence it seemed almost gigantic in its stature. It gazed upon the pair with eyes that burned with a preternatural blaze, and a voice which Maltravers too well remembered, shrieked out—' Love—love ! What *thou* love again ? Where is the Dead ? Ha !—ha ! Where is the dead ?'

" Evelyn, startled by the words, looked up, and clung in speechless terror to Maltravers. He remained rooted to the spot.

" ' Unhappy man,' said he, at length, and soothingly, ' how came you hither ? Fly not, you are with friends.'

" ' Friends !' said the maniac, with a scornful laugh. ' I know thee, Ernest Maltravers—I know thee ;—but it is not thou who hast locked me up in darkness and in hell, side by side with the mocking fiend ! Friends ! —ah, but no friends shall catch me now ! I am free—I am free !—air and wave are not more free !' and the madman laughed with horrible glee. ' She is fair—fair,' he said, abruptly checking himself, and with a changed voice, ' but not so fair as the Dead. Faithless that thou art—and yet she loved *thee!* Woe to thee!—woe—Maltravers, the perfidious! Woe to thee—and remorse—and shame!'

"'Fear not, Evelyn, fear not,' whispered Maltravers, gently, and placing her behind him, 'support your courage—nothing shall harm you.'

"Evelyn, though very pale, and trembling from head to foot, retained her senses. Maltravers advanced towards the madman. But no sooner did the quick eye of the last perceive the movement, than—with the fear that belongs to that dread disease—the fear of losing liberty—he turned, and, with a loud cry, fled into the wood. Maltravers leapt over the fence, and pursued him some way in vain. The thick copses of the wood snatched every trace of the fugitive from his eye.

"Breathless and exhausted, Maltravers returned to the spot where he had left Evelyn. As he reached it, he saw Teresa and her husband approaching towards him, and Teresa's merry laugh sounded clear and musical in the racy air. The sound appalled him—he hastened his steps to Evelyn.

"'Say nothing of what we have seen to Madame de Montaigne, I beseech you,' said he; 'I will explain why hereafter.'

"Evelyn, too overcome to speak, nodded her acquiescence. They joined the De Montaignes, and Maltravers took the Frenchman aside.

"But before he could address him, De Montaigne said—

"'Hush! do not alarm my wife—she knows nothing—but I have just heard, at Paris, that—that he has escaped—you know whom I mean?'

"'I do—he is at hand—send in search of him—I have seen him!—once more I have seen Castruccio Cæsarini!'"

Evelyn is within a few months of eighteen. Maltravers communicates the acceptance of his suit to Lord Vargrave, and the intriguing minister and the high-souled and haughty student once more stood face to face. But Vargrave has, with infinite pains and aided by some happy accident, wormed out the secret of the identity of Lady Vargrave with Alice Darvil—and of Maltravers with Mr. Butler of Dale Cottage. Evelyn may still be his. He flies to Paris with the secret; the interview between the rivals is fine and intensely interesting. After mutual criminations and defences on their estrangement from each other:—

"'Stay!' said Lord Vargrave (who, plunged in a gloomy reverie, had scarcely seemed to hear the last few sentences of his rival); 'Stay, Maltravers. Speak not of love to Evelyn!—a horrible foreboding tells me that, a few hours hence, you would rather pluck out your tongue by the roots, than couple the words of love with the thought of that unfortunate girl. Oh, if I were vindictive, what awful triumph would await me now! What retaliation on your harsh judgment—your cold contempt—your momentary and wretched victory over me!—Heaven is my witness, that my only sentiment is that of terror and woe! Maltravers, in your earliest youth, did you form connexion with one whom they called Alice Darvil?'

"'Alice—merciful Heaven! what of her?'

"'Did you never know that the Christian name of Evelyn's mother is Alice?'

" ' I never asked—I never knew—but it is a common name,' faltered Maltravers.

" ' Listen to me,' resumed Vargrave : ' with Alice Darvil you lived in the neighbourhood of ——, did you not ?'

" ' Go on—go on !'

" ' You took the name of Butler—by that name Alice Darvil was afterwards known in the town in which my uncle resided—(there are gaps in the history that I cannot of my own knowledge fill up)—she taught music—my uncle became enamoured of her—but he was vain and worldly. She removed into Devonshire, and he married her there, under the name of Cameron, by which name he hoped to conceal from the world the lowness of her origin, and the humble calling she had followed—— Hold ! do not interrupt me. Alice had one daughter, as was supposed, by a former marriage—that daughter was the offspring of him whose name she bore—yes, of the false Butler !—that daughter is Evelyn Cameron !'

" ' Liar—Devil !' cried Maltravers, springing to his feet, as if a shot had pierced his heart. ' Proofs—proofs !'

" ' Will these suffice ?' said Vargrave ; and he placed the letters of Winsley and Lady Vargrave before Maltravers. He caught them up; but for some moments he could not dare to read them. He supported himself with difficulty from falling to the ground ; there was a gurgle in his throat, like the sound of the death-rattle :—at last he read, and dropped the letters from his hand.

" ' Wait me here,' he said very faintly, and moved mechanically to the door.

" ' Hold !' said Lord Vargrave, laying his hand upon Ernest's arm. ' Listen to me for Evelyn's sake—for her mother's. You are about to seek Evelyn—be it so ! I know that you possess the godlike gift of self-control. You will not suffer her to learn that her mother has done that which dishonours alike mother and child ? You will not consummate your wrong to Alice Darvil, by robbing her of the fruit of a life of penitence and remorse ? You will not unveil her shame to her own daughter ? Convince yourself, and master yourself while you do so !'

" ' Fear me not,' said Maltravers, with a terrible smile ; ' I will not afflict my conscience with a double curse. As I have sowed, so must I reap.—Wait me here !' "

An interview with Evelyn satisfies Maltravers of the horror of his position.. Vargrave proffers his fales sympathy, but—

" Maltravers did not listen to these vain and hollow consolations. With his head drooping on his bosom, his whole form unnerved, the large tears rolling unheeded down his cheeks, he seemed the very picture of the broken-hearted man, whom Fate never again could raise from despair. He—who had, for years, so cased himself in pride, on whose very front was engraved the victory over passion and misfortune, whose step had trod the earth in the royalty of a kingly nature—the veriest slave that crawls bore not a spirit more humbled, fallen, and subdued ! He who had looked with haughty eyes on the infirmities of others, who had disdained to serve his race, because of their human follies and partial frailties—*he*, even *he*—the

Pharisee of Genius—had but escaped by a chance, and by the hand of the man he suspected and despised, from a crime at which Nature herself recoils,—which all law, social and divine, stigmatises as inexpiable,—which the sternest imagination of the very heathen, had invented as the gloomiest catastrophe that can befall the wisdom and the pride of mortals! But one step more, and the fabulous Œdipus had not been more accursed!

" Such thoughts as these, unformed, confused, but strong enough to bow him to the dust, passed through the mind of this wretched man. He had been familiar with grief, he had been dull to enjoyment; sad and bitter memories had consumed his manhood; but pride had been left him still! and he had dared in his secret heart to say, ' I can defy Fate!' Now the bolt had fallen—Pride was shattered into fragments—Self-abasement was his companion—Shame sate upon his prostrate soul. The future had no hope left in store. Nothing was left for him but to die!"

After writing to Evelyn that he renounced her love—that he would not reappear in the world until she was wedded to another—and that till then he was an exile and a wanderer with the brand of Cain on his brow, which her hand alone could efface—the agonized Maltravers flies once more to wrestle with himself in solitude. He selected the swamps about the castle of de Retz as congenial with the gloom of his soul, but the spirit of his mother appears to him in a dream.

" Return," it said, " to thine own land, and to thy native home, leave not the last relic of her who bore, and yet watches over, thee to stranger hands. Thy good angel shall meet thee at thy hearth." Maltravers once more returns to Burleigh. The weight is soon removed from his soul. From the foster-mother of Evelyn, whom an accident had settled in the village, he learns that she is the child of Mr. Templeton by a previous private marriage with a village beauty whom he had seduced, and who died in childbirth; that his own child had died shortly after the union of Alice to the sanctimonious banker. This is confirmed by Lady Vargrave and the curate Aubrey.

Lord Vargrave was well aware that Evelyn was not the daughter of Maltravers, for his uncle had confided to him on his death-bed the secret of her birth. But he so contrived the evidence as to deceive and remove Maltravers, and, by the threatened exposure of her mother's early errors, wrung a painful consent from Evelyn to their immediate union. Maltravers and Aubrey fly to rescue her from his snares.

" The sight of the Curate, in company with Maltravers, explained all at once to Vargrave. He saw that the mask was torn from his face—the prize snatched from his grasp—his falsehood known—his plot counterworked—his villany baffled! He struggled in vain for self-composure— all his resources of courage and craft seemed drained and exhausted. Livid, speechless, almost trembling,—he cowered beneath the eyes of Maltravers.

" Evelyn, not as yet aware of the presence of her former lover, was the first to break the silence. She lifted her face in alarm from the bosom of the good Curate—' My mother—she is well—she lives—what brings you hither ?'

" ' Your mother is well, my child. I have come hither at her earnest request, to save you from a marriage with that unworthy man !'

" Lord Vargrave smiled a ghastly smile, but made no answer.

" ' Lord Vargrave,' said Maltravers, ' you will feel at once that you have no farther business under this roof. Let us withdraw—I have much to thank you for.'

" ' I will not stir !' exclaimed Vargrave passionately, and stamping on the floor. ' Miss Cameron, the guest of Lady Doltimore whose house and presence you thus rudely profane, is my affianced bride—affianced with her own consent. Evelyn—beloved Evelyn ! mine you are yet—you alone can cancel the bond. Sir, I know not what you have to say—what mystery in your immaculate life to disclose; but unless Lady Doltimore, whom your violence appals and terrifies, orders me to quit her roof, it is not I— it is yourself, who are the intruder ! Lady Doltimore, with your permission, I will direct your servant to conduct this gentleman to his carriage !'

" ' Lady Doltimore, pardon me,' said Maltravers coldly ; ' I will not be urged to any failure of respect to you. My Lord, if the most abject cowardice be not added to your other vices—you will not make this room the theatre for our altercation. I invite you, in those terms which no gentleman ever yet refused, to withdraw with me.'

" The tone and manner of Maltravers exercised a strange control over Vargrave ; he endeavoured in vain to keep alive the passion into which he had sought to work himself—his voice faltered, his head sunk upon his breast. It was a most extraordinary picture, that group !—Caroline, turning her eyes from one to the other in wonder and dismay ; Evelyn, believing all a dream, yet alive only to the thought that, by some merciful interposition of Providence, she should escape the consequences of her own rashness—clinging to Aubrey, with her gaze rivetted on Maltravers ; and Aubrey, whose gentle character was borne down and silenced by the powerful and tempestuous passions that now met in collision and conflict, withheld by his abhorrence of Vargrave's treachery from interfering as a mediator, and yet urged by the apprehension of bloodshed, that for the first time crossed him, to interpose—almost to conciliate.

" There was a moment of dead silence—in which Vargrave seemed to be nerving and collecting himself for such course as might be best to pursue, when again the door opened, and the name of Mr. Howard was announced.

" Hurried and agitated, the young Secretary, scarcely noticing the rest of the party, rushed to Lord Vargrave.

" ' My Lord !—a thousand pardons for interrupting you—business of such importance !—I am so fortunate to find you !'

" ' What is the matter, Sir ?'

" ' These letters, my Lord,—I have so much to say !'—

" Any interruption, even an earthquake, at that moment must have been welcome to Vargrave. He bent his head with a polite smile to the party, linked his arm into his Secretary's, and withdrew to the recess of the farthest window. Not a minute elapsed, before he turned away with a look of scornful exultation. ' Mr. Howard,' said he ; ' go and refresh yourself, and come to me at twelve o'clock to night ; I shall be at home then.' The Secretary bowed, and withdrew.

" ' Now, Sir,' said Vargrave to Maltravers, ' I am willing to leave you in possession of the field. Miss Cameron, it will be, I fear, impossible for me to entertain any longer the bright hopes I had once formed; my cruel fate compels me to seek fortune in any matrimonial engagement. I regret to inform you, that you are no longer the great heiress: the whole of your capital was placed in the hands of Mr. Douce for the completion of the purchase of Lisle-Court. Mr. Douce is a bankrupt; he has fled to America. This letter is an express from my lawyer; the House has closed its payments!—Perhaps we may hope to obtain sixpence in the pound. I am a loser also; the forfeit money bequeathed to me is gone. I know not whether, as your trustee, I am not accountable for the loss of your fortune (drawn out on my responsibility); probably so. But as I have not now a shilling in the world, I doubt whether Mr. Maltravers will advise you to institute proceedings. Mr. Maltravers, to-morrow, at nine o'clock, I will listen to what you have to say. I wish you all good night.' He bowed—seized his hat—and vanished.

" ' Evelyn,' said Aubrey; ' can you require to learn more—to feel that you are released from union with a man without heart and honour ?'

" ' No, no; I am so happy !' cried Evelyn, bursting into tears. ' This hated wealth—I feel not its loss—I am released from all duty to my benefactor. Oh God, I am free !' "

Before the hour of meeting Vargrave had time to peruse his other letters, his party had been dismissed as imbeciles ; but Lord Vargrave, in the prime of life, versatile, accomplished, vigorous, bitter, unscrupulous, was of another mould—he was to be dreaded, and therefore, if possible, retained ; his power of mischief being further increased by his reported union with an heiress of immense wealth. Had he a spot of honest ground to stand upon, he might have shrunk from stepping into the very post of which he, and he alone, had been the cause of depriving his patron and relative, but the pennyless adventurer had no other refuge from utter ruin. The vice-royalty of India was a nice straw for a sinking man to catch at. During this interval the madman, Cæsarini, burst into the apartments of Maltravers, and detailed to him the cool villany practised against him by Lumley Ferrers to break off his marriage with Florence Lascelles. Thus we have the three chief characters of the tale mysteriously brought together and confronting each other, before the *justitiæ vindex* interposes to remove two of them from the scene.

" ' You wished an interview—an explanation,' said Lumley ; ' I shrink from neither. Let me forestall inquiry and complaint. I deceived you knowingly and deliberately, it is quite true—all stratagems are fair in love and war. The prize was vast! I believed my career depended on it —I could not resist the temptation. I knew that before long you would learn that Evelyn was not your daughter—that the first communication between yourself and Lady Vargrave would betray me; but it was worth trying a *coup de main.* You have foiled me, and conquered :—be it so ;

I congratulate you. You are tolerably rich, and the loss of Evelyn's fortune will not vex you as it would have done me.'

" 'Lord Vargrave—it is but poor affectation to treat thus lightly the dark falsehood you conceived—the awful curse you inflicted upon me! Your sight is now so painful to me—it so stirs the passions that I would seek to suppress—that the sooner our interview is terminated the better. I have to charge you, also, with a crime—not, perhaps, baser than the one you so calmly own—but the consequences of which were more fatal—you understand me?'

" 'I do not.'

" 'Do not tempt me—do not lie!' said Maltravers, still in a calm voice, though his passions, naturally so strong, shook his whole frame. ' To your arts I owe the exile of years that should have been better spent ; —to those arts, Cæsarini owes the wreck of his reason, and Florence Lascelles her early grave! Ah! you are pale now—your tongue cleaves to your mouth! And think you these crimes will go for ever unrequited— think you that there is no justice in the thunderbolts of God?' "

Lord Vargrave is strangled on the same night by Cæsarini, who concealed himself in his apartment, and made his escape without suspicion. Cæsarini himself is found in the Seine, and recognized at the morgue a few days after.

Maltravers resigns his pretensions to the hand of Evelyn in favour of Colonel Legard, and once more clasps to his bosom the long-lost Alice, whose heart, never even in thought, had swerved from its early worship.

" Maltravers once more entered upon the career so long suspended. He entered with an energy more practical and steadfast, than the fitful enthusiasm of former years. And it was noticeable amongst those who knew him well, that while the firmness of his mind was not impaired, the haughtiness of his temper was subdued. No longer despising Man as he is, and no longer exacting from all things the ideal of a visionary standard, he was more fitted to mix in the living World, and to minister usefully to the great objects that refine and elevate our race. His sentiments were perhaps less lofty, but his actions were infinitely more excellent, and his theories infinitely more wise."

Such is a faint outline of a work that, in vigour and justness of expression, loftiness of sentiment, and closely woven narration, may bear a comparison with the very best models of the modern novel. The struggle of genius with adverse fate, its long, and for a time unequal, combat with the repressive influences called circumstances, which bind it to earth and prevent it from soaring into the regions of its lofty aspirations, and the victory which ultimately rewards a bold and persevering resistance, and thus solve the mysteries of life, presented a fine subject for the novelist. We do not think that Mr. Bulwer has succeeded in placing it very forcibly before us. The character of Maltravers is not suited to engage our enthusiastic affection or esteem ; there is too great a parade of lofty qualities.

We admire but we do not love. Then the incidents are a tissue of
improbabilities, though nothing can be finer than their execution.
It requires considerable facility of credence to become persuaded
that a young peasant girl, whose mind was, as Mr. Locke says, a
tabula rasæ, could, in the short space of a few months, attain to
such a degree of intellectual developement, even admitting the miraculous or magnetizing powers of Maltravers. A similar incident
has been employed by Madame Dudevant in her clever little novel
of *Rose et Blanche,* where an idiot girl, Denise Lazare, bursts
suddenly from the crysalis state of imbecility into the butterfly
existence of a first-rate actress, retaining all the while an ardent
and a constant passion for the man she had first loved. But we
always thought it was rather a severe tax upon our credulity, although
the change is wrought by medical rather than sentimental means.
Then the improbability of Alice remaining so long in the neighbourhood of London, as Lady Vargrave, without once catching a glimpse
of Maltravers, and that he should be so long in the company of Miss
Cameron without ever having had the luck to see her mother—the
complication of circumstances arising from two secret marriages on
the part of Templeton—the preternatural means by which Maltravers
is guided to the discovery of the real birth of Evelyn, and the fact
of Lumley Ferrers sticking to him like an evil genius, thwarting all
his designs for the greater part of his life—all challenge our scepticism at the first glance. Maltravers is, in fact, the common hero
of romance; a little sublimated, who, after enduring manifold annoy-
ances from the wicked possessor of those qualities which are the
antagonists of his own, at length prostrates his tormentor and keeps
the stage to himself. As to the moral we cannot say that it is not
still liable to be questioned. A character of a highly virtuous and
lofty stamp is degraded rather than exalted by an attempt to reward
virtue with temporal prosperity. It is a dangerous doctrine to teach
young people that rectitude of conduct or principle are naturally
allied or adequately rewarded by the gratification of our passions or
the attainment of our wishes, though we are ready to concede the
morality of atonement, and permit to error the right to hope as
the reward of submission to its sufferings. We now dismiss "Alice,
or the Mysteries" with a conviction that it will be as popular as
its predecessor.

Cagliastro is one of those productions which, to use the words of
Voltaire, are written *en depit de l'encre et du papier.* It is just
the sort of work which we can imagine some "monstrous clever
young man" to indite in his leisure moments, instead of playing at
billiards or lounging in Regent Street. A perspicuous style is the
only praiseworthy quality we have been able to discover. The incidents are trite and commonplace, the plot unskilfully woven, and
the reflections and moral sentiments the veriest drivelling. Who
but a very young or very imbecile writer would publish such sentiments as these:

. " Throughout the whole progress of this detested journey—this accursed pilgrimage called life, there is but one god-like joy, which any mind of sense and spirit would wish to repeat. It is—away with the paltry delicacy of shuffling phrases, and ambiguous expressions—it is the full, free, unrestrained, entire, and perfect, moral and physical possession of the being we love."

The following defence of inconstancy is equally novel and interesting.

" How ridiculous, then, to abuse men for their want of constancy. Could we command our affections, who would cease to love ? who would throw away the treasure which constitutes his happiness, and which he values more than all the riches of the world? It is in spite of ourselves—in spite of our utmost efforts to recall our first enthusiasm, that we gradually begin to view the once loved face with indifference, and to feel that her society has no longer a spell for our disenchanted minds. To love is to be blest, and who, that found himself in Eden, would voluntarily leave it? It is customary to talk, as if the inconstant man made a selfish gain by his change of sentiment; but what can he profit by the decay of the sweetest sentiment of our nature ? As well rail at the capitalist, because he gets rid of his depreciated securities. Alas ! it is with a heavy heart that he parts with bonds, once the representatives of thousands, for a fraction of their original value. But it is with a far profounder sentiment of despair, that the man of reflection perceives his warmest and most cherished feelings will not abide the withering touch of time and custom ; and that the love he fondly deemed eternal, has hardly the durability of an Autumn flower."

The plot of the story is contrived to exhibit the wonderful attainments of the Count Cagliostro, who acquired considerable reputation by his success in victimizing the Parisians before the breaking out of the revolution. In the memoirs of the Abbé Georgel he is described as "an enthusiastic empiric, a new apostle of the religion of nature, who created converts in the most despotic manner and subjected them entirely to his influence. Some speedy cures effected in cases that were pronounced incurable spread the fame of Cagliostro far and wide, and raised his renown to that of a truly miraculous physician. His attention towards the poor, and his contempt for the rich, gave his character an air of superiority, and which excited the greatest enthusiasm. Those whom he chose to honour with his familiarity, left his society in ecstasy at his transcendant qualities." Our author has sought to dramatise this extract, to place before our eyes the great conjuror in the midst of his incantations, but we question whether he has added to the force of the impression produced by these few sentences.

The first exploit of the charlatan is the seduction of the niece of the Cardinal Jomelli. This he affects, passing himself off on the nuns of the convent where she is confined, by personating no less a personage than Saint John the Baptist. The offspring of this miraculous amour, the heroine of our tale, is conveyed away to some distant mountain, and at six years old is purchased from a blacksmith by the Duke de Fronsac, who intends to rear her to be his chief mistress. She grows up a miracle of beauty in his grace's establishment. The Marquis is so enraptured that he lays a wager on her charms with an Englishman of fortune. To see her and fall in love with her was one and the same thing to Mr. Cleveland. Like Moore's " Epicurean," this latter gentleman feels a complete satiety of all the enjoyments of life, and is proceeding to rid himself of the burden by throwing himself into the Seine, when he meets the Duke's beauty intent on adopting the same expedient to get rid of the Duke. An explanation ensues, and the would-be suicides plunge into love instead of plunging into the Seine. The Duke de Fronsac employs Cagliostro to discover the retreat of his Dulcinea, no difficult task to that man of mystery. It happens that her mother has kept her reputation and married a marquis. The marchioness is most anxious to find her lost daughter, and also employs Cagliostro to find her. The latter succeeds in inducing the fair Antonia, who is his own daughter, to leave Cleveland and go to live with the marchioness under the title of her niece. But the Duke de Fronsac discovers the imposture—the affair gets wind—the marchioness and her daughter are sent to the bastile. The revolution breaks out—the bastile is attacked—Cleveland and Cagliostro deliver the ladies from the murderous assault of the mob, and carry them away in a hackney coach. Such is the plot. We shall conclude with a short specimen of the execution. The extract details some of the conjurations of the charlatan.

" ' Seat yourself again on yonder mystic couch,' replied Cagliostro. ' This time you will lose your consciousness ; and will not recollect anything you may see, hear, or say. But when brought under the magneto-electric influence, you will readily answer all questions that are proposed to you respecting your own destiny.'

" ' And how shall I ascertain the correctness of your report ? ' asked the Duke.

" ' Count D'Ostalis shall witness the process. Yet bethink you, it was not without good reason that Dame Nature hid the future from our prying eyes. The foreknowledge of your fate will not enable you to avoid it. The anticipation may affect your mind with terror—may inspire you with the profoundest caution, but all in vain. The anticipation, and the terror, and the caution, will constitute links in the immense chain of pre-ordained events —nay, perhaps, they may be made the very means of fulfilling your destiny.'

" ' I should have thought,' answered the Duke, ' that a fatalism so complete as yours, would not have left me the choice of knowing my fate or remaining in ignorance : but be that as it may,' (and his haughty lip curled as he spoke) ' be assured that terror forms no part of my composition. I would rather know the worst, and be satisfied.'

" ' That is your deliberate resolution ? ' demanded Cagliostro.

" ' It is,' replied the Duke firmly.

" ' Be it so. Your desire shall be gratified. It is a pity,' muttered Cagliostro, as the Duke walked boldly up to the couch, and seated himself on it, ' It is a pity so much moral courage and such indomitable resolution never found a fitting sphere of action.'

" ' Cagliostro gave him as before a preparatory draught, and then set his machinery in motion. The Duke speedily sunk into deep slumber. His eyes still remained open, but their sense was shut; and there was something in the fixed stare of his vacant pupils that made his companions feel that he did not perceive them. Cagliostro, having accurately marked the time by his watch, at last said in a forced and unnaturally low tone of voice, ' Duke de Fronsac, enact the last scene of thine own career.'

" The sleeping nobleman seemed immediately agitated by the most frightful convulsions. He struggled fiercely, like one contending with a crowd of assailants. The big drops of perspiration broke out on his brow; his eyes rolled with ghastly force and rapidity, and his whole appearance assumed the aspect of a victim resisting his murderers, with desperate but ineffectual efforts. At length words found their way in broken gasps from his labouring bosom. ' Drive on—who stops my carriage—over the canaille, if they will not give way—ha! what means this? Weapons!—We are beset! Pierre! Jacques, use your pistols.—Back caitiff! on your life back! —Nay, if you will—ha! ha! ha! I have still the other ball!—Ah! take, take your fingers from my throat—ruffians I defy you all—spit at you— Cagliostro! demon! What dost thou here!'

" ' This is dreadful! damnable!' exclaimed Count D'Ostalis, exasperated beyond all endurance by the horrible exhibition : ' Stop this scene instantly—or I will drag him off the sofa—I will by Heavens—' "

ART. IV.—*The Despatches and Correspondence of the Marquess Wellesley, K. G., during His Lordship's Mission to Spain as Ambassador Extraordinary to the Supreme Junta in* 1809. Edited by MONTGOMERY MARTIN. London: Murray. 1838.

THE extraordinary interest which has been excited by the publication of the Despatches, Minutes and Correspondence of the Marquess of Wellesley, written during his Administration in India, might well induce the editor of them to collect and arrange in chronological order those now before us ; for though these documents are much more limited in number and extent, and relate not only to a much shorter period of time and a much narrower scope of subject, yet they are valuable both as models of diplomatic wisdom and correspondence, and as giving the clearest of all possible views of an eventful era in history. Not only have we here the statesmanship and patriotism of the Marquess in the purest and most eloquent language of which the occasions admitted, but other men of celebrity figure in these pages, foreign and British, so as to convey a plain and pointed view both of national and individual character. Here we have not only Spain and the Spaniard exhibited for times past, and, we fear, for times to come, but Canning and Wellington are prominent, particu-

larly the latter.   Our endeavour therefore will be to let the Marquess
be seen in his wonted style of being sagacious and firm, yet temperate amid circumstances of great delicacy, to let Spain and her countrymen in respect of chivalrous auxiliaries, be beheld—and, not least
in importance, to let the great Captain of the age be duly appreciated, going so far back in the history of the late war as 1809, when
he was merely Sir Arthur Wellesley.

It must be perfectly unnecessary for us to glance either at the
state of the continent previous to 1809, or to the share which the
British had in the Peninsular war down to that time.   It is sufficient to remind our readers that the Marquess of Wellesley's Mission to the Supreme Junta in Spain, as Ambassador Extraordinary,
took place when England commenced her more active interference in
that country.   This was on the expulsion of Ferdinand the VII.,
and when a great part of the kingdom was occupied by the French.
Mr. Canning, then Secretary of State for the Foreign Department,
was the originator of the embassy ; and its design was, that while a
large armament was to be sent to Spain, under the command of Sir
Arthur, the Marquess was to maintain an efficient negociation with
the Supreme Junta, in order that the operations of the British army
might be the means of securing solid benefit to the cause of the
allied powers.

The appointment of the Marquess as ambassador to Spain took
place in April 1809, but a sudden and severe illness detained him in
this country until the 24th of July, so that it was the 31st of the
same month before he arrived off Cadiz.   He was received in Spain
with every demonstration of welcome and honour.   He lost not a
moment to make himself master of the relation of parties, the condition of the British army which had distinguished itself so triumphantly at Talavera two or three days before his landing, and the
situation of Spanish affairs in general.   Don Martin de Garay, the
Secretary of State acting under the Supreme Junta at Seville, was
the principal of the Spanish correspondents.   By this time, however, the complaints of Sir Arthur Wellesley were loud and
frequent on account of the necessary supplies being withheld from
his army.   To be sure, to the Marquess and to himself the promises of support were equally numerous and precise ; but partly from
the prevalence of Spanish intrigue and insincerity, partly from the
disorganization and want of general and great arrangements which
prevailed, and partly from the want of an efficient authority on
the part of the Supreme Junta, the consequence was that Sir Arthur
Wellesley was at length obliged, for the preservation of his troops,
to fall back on the Portuguese frontier, in order to have access to a
regular provisioning of the army, to procure the means of conveyance for ammunition, &c., and to obtain for his wounded hospital
accommodation.   This decided step, which was taken after weeks
and weeks of great privation, filled the Junta and the Spaniards with

dismay. They complained, misrepresented, and entreated. But Sir Arthur and the Marquess stuck to their points, demanding the necessary provisions for sustaining the vigour of their country-men, and hearty co-operation on the part of those whom they were willing and eager immediately to serve. And such are the topics, such the burden of the Despatches and Correspondence now before us, furnishing, we think, a useful lesson to Colonel Evans and all other foreigners who would chivalrously engage themselves as auxiliaries or allies in behalf of Spain on her own soil. Here is a letter which appears pretty early in the volume, and which, while characteristic of the writer in more particulars than one, explains in some measure the exigencies of his troops.

" Sir Arthur Wellesley to the Marquess Wellesley.
"MY LORD, Jaraicejo, August 13th, 1809.
" I have the honour to enclose an answer which I have received from General Cuesta to the letter which I addressed to him on the 11th instant, with my reply of this date. The plan which he proposes, of dividing between the two armies, in proportion to their numbers, all the provisions received at Truxillo, however specious in appearance, would be fallacious in practice, and would probably starve the British army.

" It would not be difficult to forbid the convoys of provisions coming from Seville, from going to Truxillo; and it is probable that the supplies of provisions from Seville do not amount to one fourth of the consumption of both armies; the remainder being supplied by the country, in which of course the Spanish army has the preference. An arrangement of this description is impracticable of execution, even if the commissaries of the two armies would act fairly by each other; but this is not to be expected : every commissary will do the best he can for the troops to which he is attached; and many articles must be procured in the country, which will not be brought to account in the magazine of Truxillo.

" In short, my Lord, it comes to this; either the British army must be fed with the necessaries which it requires, or I will march it back into Portugal, whether that kingdom is invaded or not by the French corps which have moved within these few days towards Placencia.
"ARTHUR WELLESLEY.

" P.S. I beg to mention to your Excellency that the troops have received, this day and yesterday, only half an allowance of bread; and the calvalry no forage except what they can pick up in the fields. The troops suffer considerably for the want of salt; and neither officers or soldiers have had any wine for the last fortnight. In case I should move, I must leave behind me two thirds of the small quantity of ammunition I have got; having been obliged to give all the Portuguese carts (which had carried the ammunition hitherto) to move the wounded; and not having been able to procure means of transport for any thing in this country.

" Surely, my Lord, the Junta have had time since the 19th of last month to supply the wants of the army, with which they were then made acquainted ?"

Two days later Sir Arthur again writes thus :—

" I consider the answer of the Junta to the note of your Excellency, in
respect to supplies of provisions for the army and to the means of transport required, to be entirely unsatisfactory.   The army cannot exist in the
shape of an army, unless these supplies and means are provided; and the
Junta has already been informed by me, that if Spain, or rather that part
of Spain which is under their government, which in fact now comprizes
the whole kingdom, excepting that part of Estremadura and of Castile
and Arragon occupied by the enemy's troops, cannot, or is unwilling to
make the exertion which is necessary in order to provide the supplies and
means, Spain must do without the British army."

General Cuesta, the commander of the Spanish army, was an
old, obstinate, intractable man, whom the Junta would fain have got
rid of, although, like other untoward circumstances in Spanish life
and affairs, the government was afraid of giving him offence; while
in accordance with the weakness of the same government, it seems
to have been wished that the removal of the Spanish general should
be at the instance of the British ambassador, he insisting for such a
strong step, which the Marquess however prudently avoided.   At
last the stubborn old fellow resigned, alleging increasing infirmities
and a necessity for the use of baths as the reason for the much-
longed-for change, General Eguia taking the command.

We must insert, before going farther, one communication more
from Sir Arthur Wellesley to the Marquess.   Like all the other
letters by either of these correspondents one string is harped upon
with painful uniformity ; how much more painful and provoking the
reality than the reading !   The collection of such documents, indeed,
as only appear in the present thin volume, impresses upon the mind
more strongly than the ordinary current of historical works the mag-.
nitude and multifarious concerns which the general of a mighty army
has to superintend and direct. But it is to the Peninsula, to the campaigns in which Moore, Wellington, Evans, and others have distinguished themselves, to disorganized Portugal and Spain that we
must look for some of the most harassing duties that modern generalship has encountered.

" Sir Arthur Wellesley to the Marquess Wellesley.
"MY LORD,   Jaraicejo, 18th August, 1809.
" I have the honour to enclose different reports, which I received yesterday, of the measures taken by the Spanish officers and troops to prevent
the British army from foraging.   The foraging parties, to which the
reports relate, were necessarily obliged to go to a distance of four or five
leagues (from sixteen to twenty miles) in order to procure the forage they
required ; which, with the distance they would have to return, appears to
be sufficient work for the parties and their horses.   But, when having
performed this work, they are deprived of the forage by the Spanish
cavalry, it must be obvious that the equipment of the army must be
ruined.   I understand that similiar outrages were committed on the
foraging parties yesterday ; but I have not yet had the official reports of
them.

" General Eguia did me the honour of calling on me yesterday, when I communicated to him these reports, and he promised that the evils complained of should be redressed. I desired him, however, to prepare to occupy, in the course of this night, the posts in the neighbourhood of the bridge of Almaraz, as it was impossible for me to remain any longer in this part of the country, suffering, as the army does, wants of every description.

" In my last letter I apprized your Excellency of the wants of the cavalry, and of my having been obliged to remove them to the neighbourhood of Caceres to look for food. In my conversation with General Eguia yesterday, I found that the Spanish cavalry had on every day received some barley, although not an entire ration. The enclosed reports will shew your Excellency in what manner this same cavalry, which occupies every village in the neighbourhood of this army, supplies itself with straw. The British army has no bread for this day; the troops receiving in lieu of that necessary, half a pound of flour, or one-third of their ration for each man; notwithstanding that General Eguia told me yesterday, that on this day, and always in future, provision would be made to supply both infantry and cavalry with their full rations of provisions and forage.

" More than a month has now elapsed since I informed General Cuesta, that if the British army were not supplied with means of transport and with provisions, not only I would not co-operate in any forward movement beyond the Alberché, but that I could not remain at all in Spain; and the General informed me that he sent a copy of my letter to the Supreme Central Junta; and indeed I sent a copy of it to Mr. Frere. In the course of this month, if proper measure, or indeed if any measure had been adopted, supplies might have been forwarded to us from the most distant parts of Andalusia; but instead of that, we have not received a mule or a cart, or an article of provision of any description, under any order given or arrangement made by the Government: so that when I shall march, I shall be obliged to leave behind me my ammunition, and six, and probably twelve pieces of cannon; and I assure your Excellency most solemnly, that since the 22nd of last month the horses of the cavalry and artillery have not received three deliveries of barley, and the infantry have not received ten days bread.

" Under these circumstances, I can remain in Spain no longer; and I request you to give notice to the Government that I am about to withdraw into Portugal. I have no doubt that the Government have given orders that we should be provided as we ought to be; but orders, I have to observe, are not sufficient. In order to carry on the contest with France to any good purpose, the labour and services of every man, and of every beast in the country, should be employed in the support of the armies; and these should be so classed and arranged, as not only to secure obedience to the orders of the Government, but regularity and efficiency in the performance of the services required from them. Magazines might then with ease be formed and transported wherever circumstances might require that armies should be stationed. But as we are now situated, 50,000 men are collected upon a spot which cannot afford subsistence for 10,000 men, and there are no means of sending to a distance to make good the deficiency. The Junta have issued their orders to supply the deficiencies of means of transport as well as of provision ; but for want of arrangement, there are no persons to obey these orders, and this army would perish here, if I would remain, before the supplies would arrive.

" I hope your Excellency and the Government will believe, that I have not determined to go till it has become absolutely necessary. I assure you that there is not a general officer of this army who is not convinced of the necessity of my immediate departure."

On August 31st, the same correspondent writes from Merida, that the Spanish government have lately sent forward a large number of shirts and sheets for the use of the hospitals ; but that the persons who brought them immediately decamped with their mules, so that for want of means of conveyance, Sir Arthur was apprehensive that he would be obliged to leave such acceptable supplies behind him. To uphold the British name, however, he offers to pay the Spanish government for the articles. He was glad about the same period to avail himself of nine carts which had arrived at his position with biscuits from Seville, for the removal of the sick to the hospital at Elvas, which is in Portugal. And yet amid all this scarcity of the means of conveyance of baggage, ammunition, and the sick, the Spanish army had such abundance of assistance as not only to take with it the guns captured at the battle of Talavera, and a bridge of boats which had been on the Tagus, but to lay hold of and carry along the ammunition which the British had laid down on account of the wants complained of.

Frequent are the notices that the British are not half fed, that they are unfit for active service from want of the necessaries of life, and that the horses have either to exist on what they pick up at random, or on unwholesome food, so that, as respects these indispensable agents in war, 1500 of them were lost in the short period of five weeks, exclusive of the loss by engaging with the enemy. To be sure, M. de Garay, the Secretary of State, expresses astonishment that the British army should have entered Spain unprovided with the means of transport, and he also, in the face of Sir Arthur's oft-repeated representations to the contrary, alleges that our countrymen have suffered no distress of an unusual nature, during the campaign in question. General Eguia, too, asserted that Sir Arthur made use of the want of provisions as a pretext for withdrawing from Spain, and that it was a false one, for that there was abundance for the army. "Until this assertion was withdrawn," says our great Captain, " it was impossible for me to continue correspondence with General Eguia, after I should have replied to his letter, I hope with the temper which became my situation and character."

But let us see what was the tone in which the Marquess addressed the Spanish government and its ministers.

" The Marquess Wellesley to Don Martin de Garay.

"SIR,   Seville, August 21, 1809.

" In my note of the 12th instant, I submitted to your Excellency my desire to be permitted to state to you the plan which it might be necessary to adopt for providing the British army in Spain with the means of supply and of movement.

" Before I could attempt to suggest such a plan, it was requisite that I should know, with some degree of precision, the arrangements which had already been made by the government of Spain for these important objects, and the result of those arrangements. This knowledge alone could enable me to determine the measures from which success might be expected, or those from which failure was to be apprehended.

" The documents which I have received this day from your Excellency, compared with Sir Arthur Wellesley's letters, have afforded me a clear view of the real causes of distress, which has checked the operations of the British army in the full career of its glory, and has at length compelled it to fall back on the supplies provided in Portugal.

" From these papers it appears, that the government, at considerable intervals of time, has issued orders to different officers and public authorities to provide supplies for the army : but it does not appear that the necessary means have been employed to enforce and to secure the execution of those orders, or to ascertain, in due season, to what extent they had been executed, in what respects they had failed, or what were the causes either of their total failure or of their partial success.

" No magazines or regular depôts of provisions have been established, under persons properly qualified to superintend the collection and distribution of provisions, and to make regular returns of their proceedings to their British general, as well as to the Spanish Government. No regular and stated means of transport and movement have been attached to the army or to magazines, for the purpose of moving supplies from place to place ; nor have any persons been regularly appointed to conduct and superintend convoys, under the direction of the general commanding the army.

" No system of sufficient efficiency has been adopted for drawing forth from the rich and abundant provinces the resources which might have been applied, by a connected chain of magazines under due regulation, to relieve the local deficiency of those countries in which the army might be compelled to act.

" Accordingly, the result of the well-intentioned but inefficient zeal of the officers of government has been totally inadequate to the exigencies of the occasion.

" The supply of the various articles enumerated in the returns, which your Excellency has done me the honour to communicate to me, is very unequal to the wants of the army, especially in those articles which include the means of movement.

" But I must observe to your Excellency, that even these inadequate supplies have not reached the object of their stated destination ; and that the British army in point of fact has derived no benefit whatever from any of the orders described in the papers which I have had the honour of receiving from your Excellency. The failure of these orders, issued with so sincere a desire of aiding the efforts of the British army in the general cause, precludes all rational hope of better success under the same defective system.

" Your Excellency will therefore understand the considerations which
prevented Sir Arthur Wellesley from confiding the safety of his gallant
troops to the result of measures, which however amicable and sincere in
their principle, had been proved, by fatal experience, to be entirely fruitless
in their consequences, and therefore utterly insufficient to secure to his
army the means of continuing beyond the reach of those supplies which he
had provided in Portugal.

" I have the honour, &c."

Here, although greater nerve and distinctness cannot exist than
appear in Sir Arthur's correspondence, a species of firm, high-
minded statesmanship is so beautifully and eloquently maintained,
as strikes us to be the very model of diplomacy, both in a literary
and historical sense. If, along with the observance of these excellences, the reader of the present volume will mark the definite
scope which the Marquess apprehended for his line of conduct in
his mission, the integrity, clearness, and urbanity with which he
addressed himself to his purpose, and the honour resulting to his
country from the spirit and acts of his negotiations, the publication
before us will be regarded as not only a model of patriotic and
enlightened negotiation, but as an elegant episode in the annals of
nations.

The Despatches and Correspondence before us, at the same time,
must have the effect of pressing upon the reader's mind a fact
necessary to be remembered by our rulers and statesmen now and
hereafter. It is this, that if with the powerful backing of the British government, with the countenance and concurrence of the British nation, a mighty British army, led on and negotiated for by the
Wellesleys, had such untoward difficulties as above noticed to
struggle against in Spain, when the whole legitimacy, too, of Europe
was enlisted on the same side, is it reasonable to withhold from the
late fractional and sneered-at attempt, by ill-disciplined, ill-assorted,
badly supported, and cruelly betrayed troops against Don Carlos, a
share of that honour which was at last so lavishly showered upon
the armies of Wellington ? But we must eschew interfering with
questions which have lately provoked much party feeling, and after
one extract more from Sir Arthur's Correspondence, published in
the volume before us, and some passages of a document by the
Marquess, close the article.

Sir Arthur, on the 24th of August, writes to the ambassador ;
and, amongst other things, not only estimates the value of Spanish
co-operation, but refers to what, by treaty and tacit understanding,
must have been meant and expected of the British when passing
over to Spain. He says :—

" In the battle at Talavera, in which the Spanish army, with very trifling
exceptions, was not engaged, whole corps threw away their arms, and ran
off in my presence, when they were neither attacked nor threatened with

an attack, but frightened I believe by their own fire. I refer your Excellency for evidence upon this subject to General Cuesta's orders, in which, after extolling the gallantry of his army in general, he declares his intention to decimate the runaways; an intention which he afterwards carried into execution. When these dastardly soldiers ran away, they plunder every thing they meet; and in their flight from Talavera, they plundered the baggage of the British army, which was at the moment bravely engaged in their cause.

"I have found, upon inquiry and from experience, the instances of the misbehaviour of the Spanish troops to be so numerous, and those of their good behaviour so few, that I must conclude that they are troops by no means to be depended upon; and then the question arises again, whether, being at liberty to join in co-operation with those troops or not, I ought again to risk the King's army. There is no doubt whatever that every thing that is to be done, must be done by us; and certainly the British army cannot be deemed sufficiently strong to be the only acting efficient military body to be opposed to a French army, not consisting of less than 70,000 men.

"Upon every ground, therefore, of objects, means and risks, it is my opinion that I ought to avoid entering into any further co-operation with the Spanish armies, and that at all events your Excellency should avoid holding out to the Government any hope that I would consent to remain within the Spanish frontier with any intention of co-operating with the Spanish troops in future.

"At the same time I see the difficulty in which the Government may be placed. Their army may be seized with one of those panic terrors to which they are so liable, and may run off and leave every thing exposed to instant loss. To which I answer, that I am in no hurry to withdraw from Spain. I want to give my troops food and refreshment; and I shall not withdraw into Portugal, at all events, till I shall have received your Excellency's sentiments upon what I have submitted to your judgment.

"If I should withdraw into Portugal, I shall go no further than the frontier (but for this I should not wish to engage), and I shall be so near that the enemy will not like to venture across the Guadiana, unless he comes in very large force indeed, leaving me upon his flank and his rear; I shall therefore, in effect, be as useful to the Spanish Government within the Portuguese frontier as I should be in the position which has been proposed to your Excellency, and indeed more useful, as I expect that the nearer I shall move to Portugal, the more efficient I shall become; at the same time, that by going within the Portuguese frontier, I clear myself entirely from the Spanish army, and should have an opportunity hereafter of deciding whether I will co-operate with them at all, in what manner, and to what extent, and under what conditions, according to the circumstances of the moment.   "I have the honour to be, &c.

"ARTHUR WELLESLEY."

Both Sir Arthur and the Marquess were decidedly of opinion that no engagement existed either in the treaty between the British and the Spanish Government, or in the spirit of the alliance, to entitle the latter to demand the aid of the army of the former in Spain.

Sir Arthur also became convinced that the Junta exhibited by their conduct, and in the distribution of their forces, not so much the consideration of military defence and military operations, as "political intrigue, and the attainment of trifling political objects." To be sure, Don Martin de Garay, in the name of his Government, laboured strenuously, and particularly in one long document, to show that England, or at least England's hero, had not kept good faith with Spain, in removing his troops. In one sentence he says, "but whatever may be the plans of that military chief, he can never say that the inaction or the small degree of zeal in the Spanish Government has forced him to vary those which that Government expected from so generous an ally." Why, the British General repeatedly complains of the weakness of the Spanish Government of the time, and re-asserts again and again that whatever its zeal might be to afford his army necessary sustenance and aids, it was frustrated by some means or another, chargeable on the nation.

To M. de Garay's long letter of complaint and vindication, Marquess Wellesley replied, addressing himself to Don Francisco de Saavedra. The letter is the last in the volume, and is dated 8th November, Cadiz; shortly after which the writer of it returned to England, having been nominated to the office of Secretary of State for the Foreign Department, on the change of administration which ensued upon the death of the Duke of Portland. We extract the larger portion of the document in question.

"Sir,

"The note from M. de Garay, under date the 3rd of October, containing his Excellency's reply to my note of the 8th of September, has been communicated to Lord Viscount Wellington, of whose observations I have the honour to enclose a copy.

"From the remarks of the Commander-in-Chief of the British army, it will appear that the exertions of the Spanish Government, described by M. de Garay, however active and sincere, have been entirely fruitless.

"Whatever orders may have been issued at Seville for the supply of provisions to the British army, for the security of its means of transport, or for the co-operation of the Spanish general and armies, the fact is, that the British troops neither received adequate means of subsistence nor of movement, nor sufficient aid of any description, in the course of the last campaign.

"The detailed statements, contained in the enclosed letter from Lord Wellington, leave no doubt of this fact. It is for Spain to judge, whether the cause of this calamity is to be found in her Government, in its officers, or in the state of the country.

"It is neither my duty nor my inclination to exhibit criminal charges against any civil or military officer in the service of Spain. If the facts stated by the British Commander-in-Chief should appear to demand enquiry into the conduct of any individual, it is to be supposed, that the Government of Spain will institute the necessary process, without requiring the British Ambassador to undertake the invidious office of criminal accusation.

"It is sufficient for me to have ascertained the existence of the evils, which I have repeatedly submitted to the consideration of the Spanish Government, and when the active operation of the British army in Spain is again solicited by the Spanish Government, I am compelled to require the correction of those evils, before I can consent to recommend any such operation to the British Commander-in-Chief.

" M. de Garay has attempted to insinuate, that the British Commander-in-Chief was actuated, in his retirement towards the frontier of Portugal, by some motives different from those which had been publicly declared.

"M. de Garay charges me with a deliberate determination to urge the retreat of the British army from Spain. These insinuations are entirely void of foundation.

" M. de Garay also states, that the British army has abandoned Spain. This assertion is grossly and manifestly erroneous. Your Excellency is sufficiently informed of the anxious solicitude manifested by Lord Wellington and myself to maintain such a position in Spain, as might effectually protect the Southern Provinces and the City of Seville; and your Excellency knows, that the British army, for upwards of two months, has actually occupied a position upon the river Guadiana, nearly the same as that earnestly recommended by M. de Garay himself.

" It is unnecessary to remind your Excellency, that ever since the 31st of August, the British army has been stationed from Badajoz to Merida, and, occupying that station, has accomplished the defensive purposes originally intended. It will remain for M. de Garay to explain by what argument he can now justify the assertion, that the British army has abandoned Spain.

" The discussion which has lately arisen respecting the difficulty of furnishing provisions for the British army at Badajoz, has sufficiently proved the anxiety of the Commander-in-Chief to make every reasonable sacrifice to the security of Spain. On the other hand, your Excellency must recollect the recent attempts which have been made at Badajoz, to compel our army to retire from that position.

" If the distress of our army, and the want of provisions, or the necessity of defending Portugal, had compelled Lord Wellington to retire within the Portuguese frontier, I trust that the justice and liberality of the Spanish character would still have vindicated the British Commander-in-Chief from the imputations which are insinuated in M. de Garay's note."

The few extracts which we have presented, will, we feel confident, illustrate and enforce certain points stated by us in our preliminary remarks,—we mean the value of Spanish co-operation with auxiliaries and allies, who may serve in Spain,—the elegant and superior statesmanship of the Marquess of Wellesley, and the firmness as well as straightforward generalship of the Captain of the age. Mr. Montgomery Martin is at home as editor of such documents, as well as when acting the Statistician. We have only to add, that by the publication prefixed to the Despatches and Correspondence of a long Speech delivered by the Marquess of Wellesley (then Earl of Mornington) in the House of Commons in 1794, as illustrative of the opinions which he then entertained relative to the general prin-

ciples, designs, and power of France, afterwards so strongly exemplified in the invasion of Spain, the editor has contributed to extend
the noble orator's fame both for eloquence and as a politician.

ART. V.—*Essays on Natural History, chiefly Ornithology.* By CHARLES
WATERTON, ESQ. Author of "Wanderings in South America." With
an Autobiography of the Author. London: Longman & Co. 1838.

THESE Essays have already appeared in Mr. Loudon's Magazine of
Natural History, and are now published in a collected form by the
same indefatigable labourer in the cause of science and rural economy.
They treat of the habits of birds, and of some of our quadrupeds and
insects, the author's object being not only to correct certain erroneous opinions entertained by other Naturalists, and to enforce those
formerly advanced by himself in his curious and singularly interesting "Wanderings," but to do away the many accusations which
ignorance and prejudice have brought forward to injure the character
of various species of the lower animals—one of the most important
benefits resulting from the study of natural history, and one to which
Mr. Waterton, like Mr. Jesse in his "Gleanings," has largely
contributed.

Our author has little patience for mere closet, theoretic, or literary
students of natural history. The results of observation, of traversing
the woods, the wilds, the solitudes, and the bogs, instead of studying
books, are alone satisfactory to him, and we may add, the only things
he puts forth. To be sure some most extraordinary statements and
adventures characterise his "Wanderings," which brought down
upon his head suspicions of his being allied to the Munchausen family.
But these charges were preferred merely by persons who had nothing
but their own ignorance and want of experience to adduce in opposition, and who were unaware of the ardour, the nerve, the romantic
devotion of Mr. Waterton in his favourite pursuit. For our part we
place unlimited confidence in any narrative of facts which he has
ever published; while we know also, that competent and unprejudiced
persons who have visited Walton Hall, inspected Mr. Waterton's
valuable collections, and had the pleasure and benefit of conversing
with him, have come away fully impressed not only with the conviction that none of his wonderful accounts are exaggerations, but that
the exploits referred to were perfectly within the power of an adventurous and enthusiastic personage like our author. If, however, any
scepticism on the subject has remained in the minds of individuals
who have not enjoyed the advantages of a visit to the most hospitable and delightful residence of our Naturalist, they are bound to
accept the invitation and challenge he puts forward in the spirited and
amusing "Autobiography" prefixed to these Essays, when, in
allusion to his accounts of encounters with wild beasts, he says, "I
particularly request those readers of the 'Wanderings' who may

still doubt my word to meet me in person, and then show me any
passage in the book which they may suspect to deviate from the
truth. It will give me pleasure," continues he, "to enter fully into
the point in question; and I shall not have the slightest doubt of
being able to convince them that they are wrong in their surmises."
Whoever refuses to comply with this most reasonable request, does
not deserve to be listened to; while it would be unbecoming the
character and station of Mr. Waterton to treat such a one with any
of his pearls.

We do not say that there is any thing unfair in a good-natured
joke at Mr. Waterton's expense, when he comes to discourse of his
exploits and triumphs about the cayman and the like, were it for
nothing else than the deliberation and the coolness with which he
threw himself upon the most formidable and ferocious animals,
whether in cave, marsh, or lake. Indeed, his "Wanderings," as
well as the "Autobiography" now before us, provoke jocularity and
are intended to do so as well as to inform. But we need not expend
any light artillery of our own upon the present occasion, seeing that
there is ready for our hand sufficiency of the kind by an able volunteer to satisfy the most cheerful and the most eager.

We commence by following at a rapid rate our author in the
sketch he gives of his life, which as already stated is both spirited
and amusing. In fact we question if the Squire of Walton Hall be
capable of writing anything which will not partake so much of his own
extraordinary—we shall not say eccentric—character, (seeing that
the term has already been complained of by him,) as necessarily to
engage the ear, the fancy, and the hilarity of his readers. The only
occasions on which he fails to do so, are when religious creeds and
religious contests with their political consequences engage him; and
then, if he does not exhibit the spirit of a fanatic, he at least evinces
an illiberality which is totally at variance with his practice; for the
moment he comes to refer to or mention individuals of the vast number with whom his talents, worth, and rank in society have brought
him into contact, a heart of great generosity, kindliness, and com-
panionship displays itself, most pleasurable to behold. Of course,
we express no opinion about the merits of Roman Catholicism,
the doctrines of the Reformation, or the policy and practices of the
disciples of either; but we must be allowed to state, that had our
author more carefully observed a similar abstinence, the present
volume would have been more generally acceptable, and more generally read than we fear it will be. The "Autobiography," however,
is worth dipping into, and though for the most part intentionally
light as to matter and manner, it will suggest some important hints,
as well as be found amusing.

Mr. Waterton says that he was born at Walton Hall, which is
near Wakefield, in the county of York, some five and fifty years
ago; and since he has a great repugnance to have a portrait

taken by the pencil, he volunteers one by the pen, to the following effect :—

" I feel as though I were not more than thirty years old.   I am quite free from all rheumatism pains; and am so supple in the joints, that I can climb a tree with the utmost facility.   I stand six feet high, all but half an inch.   On looking at myself in the glass, I can see at once that my face is any thing but comely : continual exposure to the sun, and to the rains of the tropics, has furrowed it in places, and given it a tint, which neither Rowland's Kalydor, nor all the cosmetics on Belinda's toilette, would ever be able to remove.   My hair, which I wear very short, was once of a shade betwixt brown and black : it has now the appearance as though it had passed the night exposed to a November hoarfrost.   I cannot boast of any great strength of arm; but my legs, probably by much walking, and by frequently ascending trees, have acquired vast muscular power : so that, on taking a view of me from top to toe, you would say that the upper part of Tithonus has been placed upon the lower part of Ajax.   Or, to speak zoologically, were I exhibited for show at a horse fair, some learned jockey would exclaim, he is half Rosinante, half Bucephalus."

This vigour of leg, suppleness of joint, and general constitutional soundness, has not been preserved, as we shall see, without encountering various and formidable assaults.   In the meanwhile, not to forget his birth and pedigree, we learn that he ought to be pretty well off, as far as breeding goes, if it be true that the good qualities of man and of cattle descend to their offspring ; for, continues he, " I come in a direct line from Sir Thomas More, through my grandmother; whilst by the mother's side I am akin to the Bedingfelds of Oxburgh, to the Charltons of Hazleside, and to the Swinburnes of Capheaton."   We also learn that his ancestors (the family has been in possession of Walton Hall for some centuries) were sufficiently notorious to have had their names handed down to posterity, and that up to the reign of Henry VIII. things went on swimmingly with the Watertons.   After this, conscience and political as well as territorial advancement were at odds, excepting, says our naturalist, " in good Queen Mary's days," when " there was a short tide of flood in our favour."

We pass over our hero's boyhood and education, merely citing that though sent to a school of repute when nine years old, he made more proficiency in finding birds' nests than in literature,—that he one day rashly adventured on a large horse-pond in an oblong tub, and was upset,—that after returning home from the said school, the family chaplain one night prevented him from closing accounts here below, by saving him from going out at a window, three stories high, when fast asleep, a crow's nest in a neighbouring wood having charmed the somnambulist,—and that he completed his course of education at Stonyhurst in Lancashire, under certain Fathers of the Society of Jesus, whom the French Revolution had driven from Liège.

At Stonyhurst, Charles seems to have made laudable progress in the various branches of a polite education, and at the same time not to have neglected his bird-nesting and other propensities character-istic of a naturalist, to the violation, sometimes, of the regulations of the establishment. The fathers, however, seeing the great aim of his disposition, indulged it as far as possible, one of them even pre-dicting that the youth would travel into distant countries, and be exposed to many dangers—accompanying the prophecy with these words,—" There is only one way for you to escape them (the many dangers). Promise me that, from this day forward, you will never put your lips to wine, or to spirituous liquors." The promise was given, and, adds the author, it has been faithfully observed. In the course of his " Autobiography" he tells us that he also formed and kept the same resolution in regard to malt liquors, so that he fore-stalled and outstripped the obligations of the strictest Temperance Societies of which we have yet heard.

Hunting and other field-sports, as well, of course, as bird-nesting, ferretting, and other kindred pursuits, succeeded the schooling o f our naturalist. His favourite occupations were also, no doubt, extended in Spain, whither he went on a visit to two of his maternal uncles. There, after a delightful sojourn, a contagious disease assailed him, and brought him to the gates of death. He recovered, while thou-sands upon thousands sunk around him under the pestilence. But to balance the suffering of a dreadful vomiting and fever, red par-tridges abounded in the neighbourhood of Malaga, where his uncles resided. Goldfinches, also, appeared to be much more common than sparrows. Quails and bee-eaters arrived in vast numbers, and once, " when I was rambling on the sea-shore, a flock of a dozen flamingoes passed nearly within gunshot of me." Nay, at Gibraltar he counted from fifty to sixty apes, it being " a well-known fact, that apes are found in no other part of Europe except in Gibraltar." These may seem to be trifling facts to record, and assuredly not one traveller in ten thousand would insert them long after in any short autobiography. But what does all this prove, excepting that had it not been for the love and enthusiasm thus evinced the world never would have been put in possession of the " Wanderings," nor even of the present less ambitious volume ? It is also characteristic of our author when he states, " I brought over with me from Spain, a superbly mounted Spanish gun, and a beautiful ivory crucifix : they had been a present from the Duchess of Alva to my deceased uncle."

A paternal uncle having owned certain estates in Demerara, Mr. Waterton, when still a very young man, petitioned and was allowed to superintend them ; which, while there was no safe travelling in Europe on account of the war, was a good opening for one who longed to see something of the world beyond what his native country afforded, and especially to an enthusiastic student of natural science.

Indeed he declares that while in Guiana he enjoyed the finest opportunities in the world of examining the habits of water fowl, and other circumstances and points in nature precious to the ornithologist. While in that country, too, he had several adventures, the history of which he narrates. For example, when, in the year 1808, Admiral Collingwood sent despatches to Demarara to be forwarded to the Spanish government in the Orinoco, Mr. Waterton was requested by Governor Ross to be the bearer of them.

"I sailed from Demerara in the Levina flag of truce. After we had doubled Point Barima, we found the current rushing down with astonishing rapidity, and carrying with it enormous fragments of trees into the Atlantic Ocean. We soon found it necessary to get the vessel into the eddy water, close to the bank ; and at all the points where the stream met us, we carried out a hawser in the small boat, and lashed it to the branches of the trees which overhung the river. By means of this perpetual warping, we worked our slow and tedious way up to Sacopan, and thence to the fort at Barrancas, where the Spanish officers provided us with a craft of their own. It was a long boat, schooner rigged, and admirably adapted to the service for which it was intended. During the whole of the passage up the river, there was a grand feast for the eyes and ears of an ornithologist. In the swampy parts of the wooded islands, which abound in this mighty river, we saw water fowl innumerable ; and when we had reached the higher ground, it was quite charming to observe the immense quantities of parrots and scarlet aras which passed over our heads. The loud, harsh screams of the bird called the horned-screamer, were heard far and near ; and I could frequently get a sight of this extraordinary bird, as we passed along ; but I never managed to bring one down with the gun, on account of the difficulty of approaching it. John Edmonstone, who is now in Edinburgh, will remember well this expedition.

"Whilst we were wending our way up the river, an accident happened of a somewhat singular nature. There was a large labarri snake coiled up in a bush, which was close to us. I fired at it, and wounded it so severely that it could not escape. Being wishful to dissect it, I reached over into the bush, with the intention to seize it by the throat, and convey it aboard. The Spaniard at the tiller, on seeing this, took the alarm, and immediately put his helm aport. This forced the vessel's head to the stream, and I was left hanging to the bush with the snake close to me, not having been able to recover my balance as the vessel veered from the land. I kept firm hold of the branch to which I was clinging, and was three times over-head in the water below, presenting an easy prey to any alligator that might have been on the look-out for a meal. Luckily, a man who was standing near the pilot, on seeing what had happened, rushed to the helm, seized hold of it, and put it hard a-starboard, in time to bring the head of the vessel back again. As they were pulling me up, I saw that the snake was evidently too far gone to do mischief ; and so I laid hold of it, and brought it aboard with me, to the horror and surprise of the crew. It measured eight feet in length. As soon as I had got a change of clothes, I killed it, and made a dissection of the head.

" I would sometimes go ashore in the swamps to shoot maroudies, which
are somewhat related to the pheasant; but they were very shy, and it required considerable address to get within shot of them. In these little
excursions, I now and then smarted for my pains. More than once, I got
amongst some hungry leeches, which made pretty free with my legs. The
morning after I had had the adventure with the labarri snake, a cayman
slowly passed our vessel. All on board agreed that this tyrant of the fresh
waters could not be less than thirty feet long."

Mr. Waterton's incidents of travel, his adventures, escapes, and
mishaps, while numerous, have much of variety in them, owing in a
great measure to his fearless and confident nature in situations where
most men would have trembled and lost themselves. The generous
features of his character on several occasions come out prominently;
and, at other times, his hearty appreciation of noble qualities wherever found is no less illustrative. For example, we find him warmly
applauding General Carmichael who was governor of Demerara in
1812, and with whom our author's first interview had a singular
origin. The General is represented as having had one of the most
difficult tempers to manage in the world. He was exceedingly
generous, but at the same time fiery; but then his placability was
no less remarkable. It so happened that an English gentleman had
been outlawed on account of some bill transaction; and when he
was in the greatest danger of being caught by the officers of justice,
Mr. Waterton came to his assistance and foiled the attempt. For
this contempt of authority he was cited to appear before the Governor.
The following scene then took place—

" On my name being announced he came into the hall. Whilst looking at me full in the face, he exclaimed in a voice too severe to last long:
'And so, Sir, you have dared to thwart the law, and to put my late proclamation at defiance?' 'General,' said I, 'you have judged rightly; and
I throw myself on your well-known generosity. I had eaten the fugitive's
bread of hospitality, when fortune smiled upon him; and I could not find
in my heart to refuse him help in his hour of need. Pity to the unfortunate prevailed over obedience to your edict; and had General Carmichael
himself stood in the shoes of the deserted outlaw, I would have stepped
forward in his defence, and have dealt many a sturdy blow around me,
before foreign bloodhounds should have fixed their crooked fangs in the
British uniform.' 'That's brave,' said he; and then he advanced to me,
and shook me by the hand."

It may be gathered from the above scene that the General was a
man of a very peremptory disposition. A proof to this effect is
given which is sufficiently characteristic.

" I was one day conversing with him concerning the interior of the
country, when an English gentleman came to lodge a complaint against
a Dutch lawyer, for detaining in his possession certain monies which he
ought to have delivered up. 'Are you quite right, Sir, in your story?'

said the governor to the English gentleman. 'I am, an't please your Excellency,' answered he. ' Then go and bring him hither,' rejoined the governor. He .returned with the lawyer in about half an hour. 'Did you recover the money for this gentleman ? ' asked the governor. ' I did,' answered the lawyer. ' Then why do you not give it to him ? ' ' Because —because'—and here he stammered in great agitation ; when the governor sternly asked him, ' Do you see that lamp-post in front of the window ?' ' I do.' ' Then,' remarked the governor, ' I 'll have you hanged on it, by Saturday night, if you do not refund the money.' The lawyer paid the money on the following day."

Mr. Waterton has been an extensive and frequent traveller both on the continent of Europe and in America ; and though his pur- suits after wild beasts exposed him to unusual dangers in the latter quarter of the globe, he did not always escape alarming accidents in the former. An instance may be quoted.

" As Captain Alexander and myself were returning over Mount Cenis, I fancied that the baggage had broken loose on the top of the carriage ; so I immediately mounted on the wheel to see what was the matter. As bad luck would have it, I came in contact with the window, and smashed the glass: two pieces of the pane, an inch long, penetrated a little above the cap of the left knee, on the inner side, and broke short off. This was at ten o'clock of the night. I put my thumb firmly on the wound, until the captain had brought one of the lamps to bear on it. On seeing the blood flow in a continued stream, and not by jerks, I knew that the artery was safe. Having succeeded in getting out the two pieces of glass with my finger and thumb, I bound the wound up with my cravat. Then, cutting off my coat pocket, I gave it to the captain, and directed him to get it filled with medicine, in a house where he saw a light at a distance. The next day a strong fever came on; so we stopped until it had abated, and then we went on again; and stopped again on account of the fever ; and again proceeded, until at last we reached Paris; the wound being in a deplorable state. Here Doctor Marshall, a friend from Demerara, took me under his care until I was in a state to proceed to England. He showed exquisite skill in his treat- ment of the wound, and would have done wonders for it had I stayed a sufficient length of time with him.

" On my arrival in London, Father Scott, of the Society of Jesus, came immediately to my assistance. Having inspected the wound, he took his departure without loss of time, and he brought back with him the cele- brated Mr. Carpue ; to whose consummate knowledge and incessant atten- tion I owe the preservation of the limb, and probably of life too. The knee continued stiff for nearly two years; but, by constant exercise, and by re- fusing the aid of a walking stick, it lost all rigidity, and is now as sound as though it had never been injured. I have often thought since, that I should have laid my bones in France, but for the unwearied exertions of my friend Captain Alexander."

We gather from the narrative before us, that our naturalist is no indifferent physician, and that his surgical powers are eminent, which his habits of dissecting specimens for his valuable collections must have greatly promoted. Having had on one occasion a ramrod, armed with brass at both ends, shot through his fore-finger, betwixt the knuckle and the first joint, the paper and ignited powder following the more substantial article, without delay he repaired to a house, and, having poured warm water plentifully upon the blackened wound, collected the ruptured tendons, which were hanging down, replacing them carefully, binding up the whole, "not forgetting to give to the finger its original shape as nearly as possible." He then proceeds to explain his medical system, which we extract for the benefit of the faculty and all others who may feel inclined, or be obliged, to prescribe for themselves. After having disposed of the finger as already stated, he says—

"I opened a vein with the other hand, and took away to the extent of two and twenty ounces of blood. Whilst I am on phlebotomy, I may remark, that I consider inflammation to be the root and origin of almost all diseases. To subdue this at its earliest stage has been my constant care. Since my four and twentieth year, I have been blooded above one hundred and ten times, in eighty of which I have performed the operation on myself with my own hand. This, with calomel and jalap mixed together, as a purgative, with the use of rhubarb in occasional cases of dysentery, and with vast and often repeated potations of powdered Peruvian bark, as a restorative, has enabled me to grapple successfully with sickness when I was far away from medical aid. In cases where laudanum was *absolutely* necessary, I was always extremely cautious, having seen far too many instances in other people of the distressing effects produced by the frequent use of this insidious drug. My severest trials of sickness were those when I had to contend with internal inflammation at the very time that I was labouring under tertian ague. In those cases, the ague had to bear all the burden, for I knew that it was not a mortal complaint; whereas internal inflammation was not to be trifled with for one moment. Under this impression, I would fearlessly open a vein, and would trust to Peruvian bark, at a later period, to counteract the additional encouragement which I had been forced to give to the ague, through the medium of the lancet. I am now, I think, in as perfect health as man can be. But let me finish the account of my accident. On reaching home, I applied a very large poultice, which was renewed twice every day. The inflammation never extended beyond the knuckles; and I recovered the full use of the finger in due course of time."

It is to his "Wanderings," however, that the reader must recur for the most extraordinary events in the course of our author's favourite researches in the wilds of America; and before passing on to notice a few portions of the Essays, it is proper to let him be re-heard in reference to some opinions that have been entertained respecting the former publication.

"Unenviable is the lot of him whose narratives are disbelieved merely for want of sufficient faith in him who reads them. If those who have called my veracity in question would only have the manliness to meet me and point out any passage in the book which they consider contradictory, or false, I would no longer complain of unfair treatment. If they can show that I have deviated from the line of truth in one single solitary instance, I will consent to be called an impostor; and then may the *Wanderings* be trodden under foot, and be forgotten for ever.

"Some people imagine that I have been guilty of a deception in placing the nondescript as a frontispiece to the book. Let me assure these worthies that they labour under a gross mistake. I never had the slightest intention to act so dishonourable a part. I purposely involved the frontispiece in mystery, on account of the illiberality which I experienced from the Treasury on my return from Guiana.

"I had spent many years in trying to improve the very defective process universally followed in preparing specimens for museums. The reader will see by the letter signed Lushington that I was sentenced to pay pretty handsomely for my exertions.

"'Treasury Chambers, May 18th.

"'Gentlemen,

"'The Lords Commissioners of His Majesty's Treasury, having had under their consideration your report of the 10th, on the application of Mr. Charles Waterton, for the delivery, duty free, of some birds, quadrupeds, reptiles, and insects, collected by him in Guiana, and recently imported from Demerara, I have it in command to acquaint you that my Lords have informed Mr. Waterton that, if he will specify the articles which he intends to give to public institutions, my Lords will not object to their being delivered duty free; but that, with regard to the specimens intended for his own or any private collection, they can only be delivered on payment of the *ad valorem* duty of 20 per cent.; and I am to desire you will give the necessary directions to your officers at Liverpool, in conformity thereto.

"'I am, &c.
"'(Signed)   J. R. LUSHINGTON.

"'Commissioners of Customs.'

"Stung with vexation at the unexpected contents of that peremptory letter, and annoyed at the detention of my collection, I determined not to communicate to the public the discovery which I had made of preparing specimens upon scientific principles; but, in order to show what I had done, I placed the nondescript in the *Wanderings*; hoping that its appearance would stimulate to investigation those who are interested in museums. Should there be any expression in the *Wanderings*, by which the reader may be led to imagine that I wish to pass off this extraordinary thing either for the head and shoulders of a man, 'os homini sublime;' or for those of an ape, 'Simia,—quam similis, turpissima bestia nobis;' it is my earnest desire that the said expression may be considered null and void. I have no wish whatever that the nondescript should pass for any other thing than that which the reader himself should wish it to pass for. Not considering myself pledged to tell its story, I leave it to the reader to say what it is or what it is not."

While there appears to be whim in the employment of the mystery alluded to, hardly becoming a zealous son of science, the blindness and mistaken economy of the government in the treasury resolution quoted above is deserving of exposure and reproach. Had the collection been made by a man of less opulence than Mr. Waterton, probably a foreign country might at this moment have been in possession of it, and the crowds of all ranks that are annually welcomed and most hospitably treated at Walton Hall would have been denied an intellectual feast, and an opportunity of appreciating a character of great worth belonging to the aristocracy of our country.

In the controversies which natural history has elicited, it is matter of regret that prejudice and irritating feelings have sometimes been substituted for truth and a pure desire to advance the interests of science. One of the points, which has given rise within these few late years to an unwarrantable keenness of temper, regards the means by which the Vulture discovers carrion and putrid animal matter ; Audubon and several of the American Ornithologists maintaining that it is by sight, while our author adopts the old-fashioned doctrine that it is by scent. We pretend not to decide where doctors differ ; but quote a few paragraphs of the Essay on the subject before us.

> "ON THE FACULTY OF SCENT IN THE VULTURE.
>
> "'Et truncas inhonesto vulnere nares.'" *Æneid.* lib. vi.
>
> "I never thought that I should have lived to see this bird deprived of its nose. But in the third number of *Jameson's Journal*, a modern writer has actually given 'An account of the habits of the Turkey Buzzard (Vultur Aura), with a view of exploding the opinion generally entertained of its extraordinary power of smelling ;' and I see that a gentleman in the *Magazine of Natural History*, vol. iii. p. 449, gives to this writer the honour of being the first man who, by his 'interesting treatise,' caused the explosion to take place.
>
> "I grieve from my heart that the vulture's nose has received such a tremendous blow ; because the world at large will sustain a great loss by this sudden and unexpected attack upon it. Moreover, I have a kind of fellow-feeling, if I may say so, for this noble bird. We have been for years together in the same country ; we have passed many nights amongst the same trees ; and though we did not frequent the same mess, (for 'de gustibus non est disputandum,'— and I could not eat rotten venison, as our English epicures do,) still we saw a great deal of each other's company.
>
> "Sancho Panza remarks, that there is a remedy for every thing but death. Now, as the vulture has not been killed by the artillery of this modern writer in *Jameson's Journal*, but has only had its nose carried away by an explosion, I will carefully gather up the shattered olfactory parts, and do my best to restore them to their original shape and beautiful proportions. In repairing the vulture's nose, I shall not imitate old Taliacotius, who, in times long past and gone, did
>
> ————'from
>
> The brawny part of porter's bum
> Cut supplemental noses, which
> Would last as long as parent breech !'

but I will set to work upon my own resources, and then the reader shall decide whether the vulture is to have a nose or remain without one.

" We all know what innumerable instances there are, in every country, of the astonishing powers of scent in quadrupeds. Thus, the blood-hound will follow the line of the deer-stealer hours after he has left the park ; and a common dog will ferret out his master in a room, be it ever so crowded. He is enabled to do this by means of the well-known effluvium which, proceeding from his master's person, comes in contact with his olfactory nerves. A man even, whose powers of scent are by no means remarkable, will sometimes smell you a putrid carcass at a great distance. Now, as the air produced by putrefaction is lighter than common air, it will ascend in the atmosphere, and be carried to and fro through the expanse of heaven by every gust of wind. The vulture, soaring above, and coming in contact with this tainted current, will instinctively follow it down to its source, and there find that which is destined by an all-wise Providence to be its support and nourishment."

We do not see that Mr. Waterton sufficiently accounts for what we think we remember to have been stated in Jameson's Journal, viz., that the Vulture traces its food, even when the wind must be driving the scent the contrary way to that which would bring it in contact with the olfactory nerves of the aerial wanderer. Let us listen, however, to a few of Mr. Waterton's facts on the subject.

" Let us here examine the actions of this vulture a little more minutely. If the Vultur Aura, which, as I have said above, I have never seen to prey upon living animals, be directed by its eye alone to the object of its food, by what means can it distinguish a dead animal from an animal asleep ? or how is it to know a newly dead lizard or a snake from a lizard or a snake basking quite motionless in the sun ? If its eye be the director to its food, what blunders must it not make in the negro-yards in Demerara, where broods of ducks and fowls are always to be found the day through, either sleeping or basking in the open air. Still the negro, whom habit has taught to know the Vultur Aura from a hawk, does not consider him an enemy. But let a hawk approach the negro-yard, all will be in commotion, and the yells of the old women will be tremendous. Were you to kill a fowl and place it in the yard with the live ones it would remain there un-noticed by the vulture as long as it was sweet ; but, as soon as it became offensive, you would see the Vultur Aura approach it, and begin to feed upon it, or carry it away, without showing any inclination to molest the other fowls which might be basking in the neighbourhood. When I carried Lord Collingwood's despatches up the Orinoco, to the city of Angustura, I there saw the common vultures of Guiana nearly as tame as turkeys. The Spaniards protected them, and considered them in the light of useful scavengers. Though they were flying about the city in all directions, and at times perching upon the tops of the houses, still many of the people, young and old, took their siesta in the open air, ' their custom always of the afternoon,' and had no fear of being ripped up and devoured by the surrounding vultures. If the vulture has no extraordinary powers of smelling, which faculty, I am told, is now supposed to be exploded since the appearance of the article in *Jameson's Journal*, I marvel to learn how these birds in Angustura got their information that the seemingly lifeless bodies of the Spaniards were merely asleep,—

> 'Dulcis et alta quies, placidæque similima morti,'

and were by no means proper food for them.

"Some years after this, being alongside of a wood, I saw a negro on the ground, and, as I looked at him from a distance, it struck me that all was not right with him. On going up to him I found him apparently dead. Life was barely within him, and that was all. He was a total stranger to me, and I conjectured that he had probably been seized with sickness as he was journeying on, and that he had fallen down there to rise no more. He must have lain in that forlorn and I hope insensible state for many hours ; because, upon a nearer inspection, I saw swarms of red ants near him, and they had eaten deeply into his flesh. I could see no marks that the vultures had been upon him. Indeed, their not being here caused me no surprise, as I had long been satisfied, from the innumerable observations which I had made, that the vulture is attracted to its food by the putrid exhalations which arise from it, when it has arrived at that state of decomposition which renders it fit, and no doubt delicious, food for this interesting tribe of birds. While I was standing near the negro, I could see here and there a Vultur Aura sweeping majestically through the ethereal expanse, in alternate rises and falls, as these birds are wont to do when in search of carrion ; but they showed no inclination to come and perch on the trees near the prostrate body of this poor unknown sable son of Africa

"Vultures, as far as I have been able to observe, do not keep together in a large flock, when they are soaring up and down apparently in quest of a tainted current. Now, suppose a mule has just expired behind a high wall, under the dense foliage of evergreen tropical trees; fifty vultures, we will say, roost on a tree a mile from this dead mule ; when morning comes, off they go in quest of food. Ten fly by mere chance to the wood where the mule lies, and manage to spy it out through the trees ; the rest go quite in a different direction. How are the last-mentioned birds to find the mule? Every minute carries them farther from it. Now, reverse the statement : and instead of a mule newly dead, let us suppose a mule in an offensive state of decomposition. I would stake my life upon it, that not only the fifty vultures would be at the carcass next morning, but also that every vulture in the adjacent forest would manage to get there in time to partake of the repast.."

To students of natural history our author's remarks on the preservation of Egg-shells must be valuable. He says—

"I have been blundering at this work for some years, 'seeking for something I could not find,' and always dissatisfied with myself on account of the failure. The object of my search was, to try to find out how I could properly dispose of the thin white membrane next the shell of the egg. When left in it is apt to corrupt ; in which case, the colour of the shell will sometimes fade, and an offensive smell is produced, which a lapse of years will not subdue. Last spring I thought I had succeeded ; but it turned out to be a very partial success. I, first, by blowing, discharged the contents of five swans' eggs, and then immersed the shells in a tub of water for a month. This enabled me to pull out the thin membrane by means of a piece of wire bent at the end. But I found that the colour of the shell had faded considerably. Moreover, the process required too much time; and I saw that there would be great difficulty in doing small eggs.

" About three weeks ago, a bright thought (a *rara avis* with me) struck me, just as I was in the act of climbing up to a hawk's nest. I felt certain that every difficulty had vanished, and I began to blame myself on the score of former dulness.

" In selecting eggs for your cabinet, always choose those which are newly laid. Make a moderately sized hole at the sharp end with a pointed instrument proportioned to the egg. Thus, for a swan's egg, use the point of your penknife; for a robin's, take a small pin. Having made the hole at the sharp end, make one at the blunt end; and let this last hole be as small as possible. This done, apply your mouth to the blunt end, and blow the contents of the egg through the sharp end, where the hole is larger. If the yolk will not come out freely, run a pin or a wire up into the egg, and stir the yolk well about. Now get a cupful of water; and, immersing the sharp end of the shell into it, apply your mouth to the blunt end, and suck up some of the water into the empty shell. Then put your finger and thumb upon the two holes, and shake the water well within, and after this blow it out. The water will clear your egg of any remnant of yolk or of white which may stay in after the blowing. If one sucking up of water will not suffice, make a second or a third.

" An egg, immediately after it is produced, is very clean and pure ; but by staying in the nest, and by coming in contact with the feet of the bird, it soon assumes a soiled appearance. To remedy this, wash it well in soap and water; and use a nail-brush to get the dirt off. Your egg-shell is now as it ought to be; and nothing remains to be done but to prevent the thin white membrane (which is still inside) from corrupting.

" Take a wine-glass, and fill it with the solution of corrosive sublimate in alcohol. Then immerse the sharp end of the egg-shell into it, keeping your finger and thumb, as you hold it, just clear of the solution. Apply your mouth to the little hole at the blunt end, and suck up some of the solution into the shell. You need not be fearful of getting the liquor into your mouth ; for, as soon as it rises in the shell, the cold will strike your finger and thumb, and then you cease sucking. Shake the shell just as you did when the water was in it, and then blow the solution back into the glass. Your egg-shell is now beyond the reach of corruption ; the membrane retains for ever its pristine whiteness; and no insect, for the time to come, will ever venture to prey upon it. If you wish your egg to appear extremely brilliant, give it a coat of mastic varnish, put on very sparingly with a camel-hair pencil. Green or blue eggs must be done with gum arabic, because the mastic varnish is apt to injure the colour."

Companion directions to the last, on preserving Insects selected for Cabinets, deserve to be cited.

" I only know of two methods to guard prepared insects from the depredations of living ones. The first is, by poisoning the atmosphere; the second is, by poisoning the preserved specimens themselves, so effectually, that they are no longer food for the depredator. But there are some objections to both these modes. A poisoned atmosphere will evaporate in time, if not attended to, or if neglected to be renewed ; and there is great difficulty in poisoning some specimens, on account of their delicacy and minuteness. If you keep spirits of turpentine in the boxes which contain your preserved specimens, I am of opinion that those specimens will be safe as long as the odour of turpentine remains in the box ; for it is said to be the most pernicious of all scents to insects. But it requires attention to keep up an atmosphere of spirit of turpentine. If it be allowed to evaporate entirely, then there is a clear and undisputed path open to the inroads of the enemy : he will take advantage of your absence or neglect ; and, when you return to view your treasure, you will find it in ruins. Spirits of turpentine poured into a common glass inkstand in which there is a piece of sponge, and placed in a corner of your box, will create a poisoned atmosphere, and kill every insect there. The poisoning of your specimens by means of corrosive sublimate in alcohol is a most effectual method. As soon as the operation is properly performed, the depredating insect perceives that the prepared insect is no longer food for it, and will for ever cease to attack it. But, then, every part must have received the poison ; otherwise those parts where the poison has not reached will still be exposed to the enemy ; and he will pass unhurt over the poisoned p arts, till he arrive at that part of your specimen which is still wholesome food for him. Now, the difficulty lies in applying the solution to very minute specimens, without injuring their appearance ; and all that can be said is, to recommend unwearied exertion, which is sure to be attended with great skill ; and great skill will insure surprising success. I myself have attended to the preservation of insects with the assiduity which Horace recommends to poets :—' Nocturnâ versate manu, versate diurnâ.' The result has been astonishing success, and a perfect conviction that there is no absolute and lasting safety for prepared specimens, in zoology, from the depredations of insects, except by poisoning every part of them with a solution of corrosive sublimate in alcohol. I put a good large teaspoonful of well pounded corrosive sublimate into a wine bottle full of alcohol. I let it stand over night, and the next morning draw it off into a clean bottle. When I apply it to black substances, and perceive that it leaves little white particles on them, I then make it weaker by adding alcohol. A black feather dipped into the solution, and then dried, will be a very good test of the state of the solution. If it be too strong, it will leave a whiteness upon the feather.

" A preparation of arsenic is frequently used ; but it is very dangerous, and sometimes attended with lamentable consequences. I knew a naturalist, by name Howe, in Cayenne, in French Guiana, who had lost sixteen of his teeth. He kept them in a box, and showed them to me. On opening the lid—' These fine teeth,' said he, ' once belonged to my jaws: they all dropped out by my making use of the *savon arsenetique* for preserving the skins of animals.' I take this opportunity of remarking that it is my firm conviction, that the *arsenetical soap* can never be used with any success, if you wish to restore the true form and figure to a skin."

The last Essay in the volume is on Museums, and ought to be

carefully studied by every director of these establishments. **Mr.
Waterton** has experience for his guide, as well as great ingenuity
and zeal for his pioneers.   We can find room only for an introductory
passage to the Essay in question.

" Some years ago, curiosity led me to stray into a very spacious museum.
As I passed through a kind of antechamber, I observed a huge mass of out-
stretched skin, which once had evidently been an elephant. I turned round
to gaze at the ' monstrum horrendum informe,' when a person came up,
and asked me what I thought of their elephant. ' If,' said I, ' you will give
me two cow-skins, with that of a calf in addition to them, I will engage to
make you a better elephant.' This unlucky and off-hand proposal was
within an ace of getting me into trouble. The sages of the establishment
took cognisance of it at one of their meetings ; and somebody proposed
that a written reprimand should be sent to me. However, a prudent voice
in the assembly caused their wrath to subside, and smiles played once more
over their hitherto benign countenances.

" I have occasionally noticed the defective manner in which birds are
stuffed for museums. At present, I will confine myself solely to quadrupeds ;
and in my remarks on the very inferior way in which they are preserved, I
beg to declare that I make no allusions whatever to any one museum in
particular.

" It may be said with great truth that, from Rome to Russia, and from
Orkney to Africa, there is not to be found, in any cabinet of natural history,
one single quadruped which has been stuffed, or prepared, or mounted (as
the French term it), upon scientific principles. Hence, every specimen
throughout the whole of them must be wrong at every point."

The ardour with which our author advocates the cause of animals
which have got a bad name may be judged of from one specimen.
He is treating of the habits of the Barn Owl, and showing the
benefits it confers on Man.

" This pretty aerial wanderer of the night often comes into my room ;
and, after flitting to and fro, on wing so soft and silent that he is scarcely
heard, he takes his departure from the same window at which he entered.

" I own I have a great liking for this bird ; and I have offered it hospitality and protection on account of its persecutions, and for its many services to me,—I say services, as you will see in the sequel. I wish that
any little thing I could write or say might cause it to stand better with the
world at large than it has hitherto done ; but I have slender hopes on this
score ; because old and deep-rooted prejudices are seldom overcome ; and
when I look back into the annals of remote antiquity, I see too clearly that
defamation has done its worst to ruin the whole family, in all its branches,
of this poor, harmless, useful friend of mine.

" Up to the year 1813, the barn-owl had a sad time of it at Walton Hall.
Its supposed mournful notes alarmed the aged housekeeper. She knew
full well what sorrow it had brought into other houses when she was a
young woman ; and there was enough of mischief in the midnight wintry
blast, without having it increased by the dismal screams of something which
people knew very little about, and which everybody said was far too busy

in the churchyard at night-time. Nay, it was a well-known fact, that if any person were sick in the neighbourhood, it would be for ever looking in at the window, and holding a conversation outside with somebody, they did not know whom. The gamekeeper agreed with her in everything she said on this important subject; and he always stood better in her books when he had managed to shoot a bird of this bad and mischievous family. However, in 1813, on my return from the wilds of Guiana, having suffered myself, and learned mercy, I broke in pieces the code of penal laws which the knavery of the gamekeeper and the lamentable ignorance of the other servants had hitherto put in force, far too successfully, to thin the numbers of this poor, harmless, unsuspecting tribe. On the ruin of the old gateway, against which, tradition says, the waves of the lake have dashed for the better part of a thousand years, I made a place with stone and mortar, about 4 ft. square, and fixed a thick oaken stick firmly into it. Huge masses of ivy now quite cover it. In about a month or so after it was finished, a pair of barn owls came and took up their abode in it. I threatened to strangle the keeper if ever, after this, he molested either the old birds or their young ones; and I assured the housekeeper that I would take upon myself the whole responsibility of all the sickness, woe, and sorrow, that the new tenants might bring into the Hall. She made a low courtesy; as much as to say, ' Sir, I fall into your will and pleasure ;' but I saw in her eye that she had made up her mind to have to do with things of fearful and portentous shape, and to hear many a midnight wailing in the surrounding woods. I do not think that up to the day of this old lady's death, which took place in her eighty-fourth year, she ever looked with pleasure or contentment on the barn owl, as it flew round the large sycamore trees which grow near the old ruined gateway.

" When I found that this first settlement on the gateway had succeeded so well, I set about forming other establishments. This year I have had four broods, and I trust that next season I can calculate on having nine. This will be a pretty increase, and it will help to supply the place of those which in this neighbourhood are still unfortunately doomed to death, by the hand of cruelty or superstition. We can now have a peep at the owls, in their habitation on the old ruined gateway, whenever we choose. Confident of protection, these pretty birds betray no fear when the stranger mounts up to their place of abode. I would here venture a surmise, that the barn owl sleeps standing. Whenever we go to look at it, we invariably see it upon the perch, bolt upright; and often with its eyes closed, apparently fast asleep. Buffon and Bewick err (no doubt unintentionally) when they say that the barn owl snores during its repose. What they took for snoring was the cry of the young birds for food. I had fully satisfied myself on this score some years ago. However, in December 1823, I was much astonished to hear this same snoring kind of noise, which had been so common in the month of July. On ascending the ruin, I found a brood of young owls in the apartment.

" Upon this ruin is placed a perch, about a foot from the hole at which the owls enter. Sometimes, at mid-day, when the weather is gloomy, you may see an owl upon it, apparently enjoying the refreshing diurnal breeze. This year (1831) a pair of barn owls hatched their young, on the 7th of September, in a sycamore tree, near the old ruined gateway.

"If this useful bird caught its food by day, instead of hunting for it by night, mankind would have ocular demonstration of its utility in thinning the country of mice; and it would be protected and encouraged everywhere. It would be with us what the ibis was with the Egyptians. When it has young, it will bring a mouse to the nest about every twelve or fifteen minutes. But, in order to have a proper idea of the enormous quantity of mice which this bird destroys, we must examine the pellets which it ejects from its stomach in the place of its retreat. Every pellet contains from four to seven skeletons of mice. In sixteen months from the time that the apartment of the owl on the old gateway was cleaned out, there has been a deposit of above a bushel of pellets.

"The barn-owl sometimes carries off rats. One evening I was sitting under a shed, and killed a very large rat, as it was coming out of a hole, about ten yards from where I was watching it. I did not go to take it up, hoping to get another shot. As it lay there, a barn-owl pounced upon it, and flew away with it."

This is a long extract and more than we can well afford room for; but it is so characteristic of the writer and so agreeable that we are sure none of our readers will think it misplaced. Altogether one rises from the perusal of the volume, not only with high and warm notions in regard to Mr. Waterton's head and heart, but with the conviction that the real disciple of Natural Science is a lover of his species and a friend to all sentient creatures.

ART. VI.—*A Dissertation on the Causes and Effects of Disease, considered in Reference to the Moral Constitution of Man.* By HENRY CLARK BARLOW, M.D. London: Longman and Co. 1838.

IT is not alone, nor indeed chiefly, the physical causes and effects of disease which Dr. Barlow in this Inaugural Dissertation has undertaken to indicate, but rather the relations which these things hold in the moral history of our species; for he justly thinks that without a constant consideration of the adaptation of disease to the moral and mental constitution of man, both in reference to this life and that which is to come, no true or complete philosophical notions or system can be arrived at on the subject of the physical ills to which the human body is exposed, and of which it is the frequent martyr. Our author's aim, in fact, is, to show that disease is not an enemy, if all its bearings, tendencies, and uses in the economy of man's nature and destinies, be duly regarded; but that, on the contrary, it is an appointed cure for much greater evils, both because it is the means of suggesting preventives and remedies for vaster and more inveterate maladies, and because when it is endured its purpose and its capacity are to elevate and purify the noblest qualities of man and thereby secure for him the highest enjoyments. In the development of his views and the enforcement of his doctrine, Dr. Barlow displays the results of enlightened reflection and of enlarged philosophy; although we could have wished in a short essay on such an extensive field as he has chosen, that there had been fewer repetitions of his main drift and conclusions, and more progressive and expanding power to the manifest and more compact establishment of his principal ideas. Still, however, as regards medical science, morals, and religion, the production is one of merit; not merely because it sets in a clearer light than has generally been done the intimate connexion, or the unity, that subsists in all the exhibitions of God's will and providence with regard to man's best interests, but because the author's earnestness, philanthropy, and piety take a strong hold of the reader's sympathies, producing by means of a gracious and gratifying infection feelings as well as convictions akin to those cherished by the essayist. A glance at the leading doctrines and arguments of the work, will enable our readers in some measure to appreciate its merits and importance.

When interpreting the phenomena of matter, still more the phenomena of mind, but still more the united phenomena of both as these most strikingly develop themselves under the reign of disease, a comprehensive observation and knowledge of nature in a variety of aspects and relations become absolutely necessary before any one can arrive at satisfactory or agreeable conclusions. If wounds, fevers, pestilence, mental derangement, and the like, were merely to be viewed in a nosological manner, and only abstractedly under an enumeration of symptoms and sufferings, human existence in this world might well be pronounced a curse to which an Almighty being had subjected us, as if he delighted in the pain and misery of his passive creatures. If, however, a wider scope of particulars is embraced, if the complex history of man, the wonderfully subtle ramifications and the unlimited capacities of his nature be studied, it then will appear even to human reason that disease is not a wanton infliction, and if Revelation with all its truths and hopes be admitted, then such inflictions like all other understood phenomena will stand forth as witnesses of the wisdom and goodness of the Creator.

On referring disease to the interpretation of Scripture, our author's conclusion is only such as every Christian will readily assent to; but the evidence and the arguments which go to prove that the ailments and maladies to which man is heir to, considering him as a mortal, and merely in relation to this world, are not circumstances of unmixed evil, but are adapted to further and exalt his moral nature, and consequently to enlarge his capacity as well as taste for earthly enjoyment, may not be so manifestly clear or cogent. Therefore it will chiefly be to the illustrations made use of on this view of the subject that we shall direct attention.

Does any one think that man, constituted in body and mind as he is, would have been benefited even in this world had he been invulnerable to disease? Hear what Dr. Johnson says;—" If the senses were feasted with perpetual pleasures, they would always keep

the mind in subjection." He also asserts that " we should pass on
from crime to crime, heedless and remorseless, if misery did not.
stand in our way, and our pains admonish us of our folly." Paley
also declares, that " A world furnished with advantages on one side,
and beset with difficulties, wants, and inconveniences on the other,
is the proper abode of free, rational, and active natures, being the
fittest to stimulate and exercise their faculties : the very refractori-
ness of the objects they have to deal with, contributes to the purpose." He adds, " A world in which nothing depended upon ourselves, however it might have suited an imaginary race of beings,
would not have suited mankind ;" while, as our author clearly
shows, such an imaginary race could neither have entertained the
same exalting motives, the same purifying sympathies, nor have
reached the same high intellectual development and capacity of enjoyment which have ample scope and inducements in the present state
of our existence.

But even the amount and virulence of disease are to a great extent dependent upon ourselves either as individuals, or as a community ; while, if we consider suffering as lending an opportunity
for studying not only the most effectual human means of removing
it, but of preventing its continuance, return, and propagation, the
evil of its occurrence on any occasion decreases and assumes a moderated aspect. Then as to the moral effects of disease, these are
also much in our own power and under our own controul.

To see that the prevention and amelioration of suffering under
endemical diseases, for example, depends much upon man, just attend to the influence of draining unhealthy marshes, of cleanliness,
of agriculture, of the planting of trees for the purpose of intercepting
the progress of malaria. Think also of the benefits of a free current
of air in houses and streets to neutralize any noxious qualities that
may mingle in the atmosphere. Then the lessons as to diet, modes
of life, habits of exercise, and above all, the regulation of the mind,
necessarily come in for their share of importance, to the modification
·of prevailing maladies that cannot from local or periodical circumstances be wholly avoided.

Our author quotes Dr. John Hunter's authority, who even says,
" If a disease arise from contagion, there are sure remedies against
it, which are so well ascertained, that while the plague, the most
contagious and fatal of all diseases commits its greatest ravages in
large cities, individuals remain in the midst of them in perfect security, trusting to a careful seclusion under proper regulations." Dr.
Barlow follows up this opinion in the following manner :

" When the plague is at Constantinople, the Frank residents live in perfect security within the suburb of Pera; and it is well known that the disease does not even cross the confined streets of the city, though not more
than ten feet wide. During a residence at Aleppo, at the time of the plague,

Dr. Russell found himself quite safe at a distance of four or five feet from the sick. The contagion of small pox ' was believed by Dr. Haygarth, not only from his own experience, but also from a series of experiments conducted by Dr. O'Ryan of Lyons, not to extend beyond half a yard from the patient; and the contagion of typhus to be at least as limited.' That the morbific effluvia, therefore, are confined to a very small space around the sufferer, we may fairly conclude ; and if we ask, Why is this ?—why does not the matter of contagion extend its influence or treble this distance ?— the obvious reply is, Because the laws of Nature have been framed with a benevolent purpose, and herein is this purpose apparent, in that, as Dr. Henry remarks, ' it admits of all those soothing and beneficial ministrations, which do not require a very near approach to the sick, with little or no danger to the friends and attendants.'

" It is a happy circumstance for mankind, that by shutting themselves up, they may shut out this formidable malady. But absolute seclusion does not appear to be required. Dr. Russel, during his residence at Aleppo, although he confined himself to the house, used to prescribe for the numerous patients who came to consult him, from a window raised a few feet above the ground, and yet escaped the disease. Bonaparte also, during his Egyptian expedition, in order to inspire confidence, did not hesitate to shake hands with the sick, though he carefully avoided inhaling their breaths. Indeed, so long as the breaths of the patients are avoided, and as much as possible all personal contact, the medical attendants seem to run little risk, and may inhale, for a limited time, the atmosphere of a pest house without taking the disease.' "

Though our author states that contagious diseases are more under human controul than some others, yet he admits that none have perhaps been so destructive, from the utter diregard shown to the causes which combine to occasion them. It is to be hoped, however, that some of these causes have become better understood, and that in the course of civilization they will be unknown, such as war, which Dr. Barlow in a very interesting chapter shows to be one of the most conspicuous.

" Though it may be difficult to determine *in what manner* a contagious poison is generated in the living system, yet it is very easy to point out *under what circumstances* this takes place, and to specify the conditions favourable to its production ; for these are matters of experience so notorious, that both ancient and modern history afford abundant instances of their reality and confirmation. The crowding together of considerable numbers of men in camps and besieged cities, where, to all the horrors of war, fatigue, famine, and despair are added ;—the privations and sufferings consequent upon military operations in general, especially when these are associated with defeat and mental depression—are causes which have been known so frequently to give rise to malignant contagious diseases, and to be the occasions of their spreading, that the connexion has become proverbial ; and the appearance of the pestilence has justly been regarded as an almost necessary consequence of drawing the sword. There is scarcely any instance, says Sir John Pringle, of a town being long invested without some

malady of this kind breaking out. In this way arose the plague at Athens,
as described by Thucydides. In a similar state of things appears to have
originated that fearful disease, which has been traced to the troops of
Charles VIII. engaged in the siege of Naples in 1494, and from thence
spread so rapidly over Europe, and with such dreadful devastation, that to
use the words of Dr. Traill, ' it seemed to threaten the extirpation of the
whole civilized world, and was by many attributed to the hand of heaven
inflicting punishment for the enormous flagitiousness of mankind.' "

Small-pox is said to have first appeared in the Abyssinian army,
besieging Mecca, two months before the birth of Mahomet. Epi-
demics are also pointed out as arising during the wars that succeeded
the French Revolution, such as typhus. Our author thus closes
this branch of his subject—

" The most formidable epidemic that ever occurred in England, the
' Sudor Anglicanus,' was of similar origin. Scarcely had the destructive
wars waged by the rival houses of York and Lancaster ceased, ere the distracted country was again plunged into similar scenes by the hostile intentions of the Earl of Richmond, among whose troops, on their landing at
Milford Haven in 1485, this desolating pestilence first appeared, and in a
short time is said to have swept off one third of the population. The late
epidemic Cholera also was nursed in the lap of war. So obvious, indeed,
was the connexion and progress of this disease with military operations,
that, to use the words of a medical officer, it looked ' as if the hand of
Providence would thus signally mark his aversion to the calling of a
soldier.' ' How often,' remarks the same writer, ' have we seen the ex-
piring embers of the disease by this means fanned into a flame in a body of
men, and again dispersed by it with fatal effect over a whole line of
country ? These are facts for our rulers to weigh and to act upon, they
clothe war with additional horrors, and exhibit its destructive influence extending far beyond its immediate sphere of action.' War not only gives
rise to disease, but wherever a tendency to disease exists, increases its force,
and augments its fatality. This was proved by sad experience during the
turmoil of colonial warfare, and has been severely felt by British troops in
European countries subject to endemic diseases. Indirectly, war leads to
disease by causing a scarcity of food—the crops being destroyed, or the land
left uncultivated ; and not unfrequently by occasioning national poverty, the
resources of a country being lavishly squandered in reckless disregard of its
best and truest interests. Hence, war produces famine, and famine produces
pestilence ; and thus these three—War, Famine, and Pestilence—the triple
source of the most severe of human sufferings, acknowledge one common
origin, and equally exhibit, in the conditions of the physical world, the consequences of neglecting moral laws ; thereby illustrating, in a marked
manner, the intimate relation that exists between them, and the unity of
design which characterises both."

Dr. Barlow feelingly observes, that although the origin and principles of many diseases be still hid from us, although an epidemic
be still to us " the pestilence that walketh in darkness," yet the

modus operandi of several such has been ascertained ; while, as to remedies and ameliorating efforts, it is most gratifying to know, that whatever tends to improve the condition of the poor and wretched, to increase the comforts and multiply the enjoyments of life, to promote morality and the principles of virtue ; whatever, in short, adds to the amount of human happiness, uniformly prolongs the period of human existence, removes the most deadly distempers, and renders all other diseases fewer and less fatal.   Let us attend to some of the moral influences of a pestilence as they operate upon society, set forth in the present pages.

" In the event of an epidemic, such as the cholera, for instance, every one feels a personal interest in providing against the common enemy, and self-love may, for a time, act the part of universal charity; but it is not improbable, that what was first prompted by interested motives may afterwards be continued from motives of real benevolence : the opportunity having once been given for such kindly exercise, it may for its own sake be continued ever after, to the great advantage both of the giver and receiver. In this way, a prevalent epidemic may become a felt benefit to many, as was the case with the poor in Edinburgh during the late cholera.   At the same time, it cannot be denied that the physical and moral sufferings attending such a disease are great, very great, yet not so great as are the existing evils it is calculated to remedy, by bringing to light states of abject wretchedness and misery, which, hid in the dark abodes of guilt and poverty, were hitherto unnoticed or unknown, and thus leading to the removal of those sources of vice and immorality, of disease and infamy, which, like *foci* of perpetual *fomites*, from time to time spread their infection around. Moral motives, when allowed their proper scope, may go far to the removal of much that is amiss, both in our social relations and individual capacities; but higher motives than these are necessary to remedy many consequences of evil habits, which have accumulated around us.   These motives we happily now possess, and all that seems necessary to their complete development is a more serious consideration of their importance.   I need scarcely say that ' Christian philanthropy' is here meant, for the exercise of which the sufferings of frail humanity afford so ample and appropriate a field.   The fear of an epidemic, however, may do more than prompt to the exercise of benevolence ; it may be truly said to ' bring down the high looks of the proud,' as well as ' to rise up the poor out of the dust :' "

But there is a long list both of bodily and mental complaints, the frequent causes of which are obvious to every one.   It can hardly be necessary to name intemperance, irregular and immoral habits of all sorts, as being detrimental to health and happiness.   Negligence and carelessness, even the indulgence of an indolent harmless life, are injurious to man who is formed for activity, and from whom something better than negative virtues are required.   How much more certainly then must the positive, enormous, and continuous violations of those physical and moral laws necessary to the well

G 2

being of each, and all as a whole, prove disastrous! Hear what our author says regarding certain prevalent vices.

" The frequent dependence of mental disease on depraved moral habits is too obvious to need a lenthened illustration. When we find that fatuity, and mania in all its forms, often take their rise from the unchecked recurrence of improper thoughts, from the licentious workings of unhallowed passions, from profligacy and open profaneness,—that the repeated railings of an unruly tongue may pass into the ravings of a maddened spirit,—or that the stifled whispers of the ' still small voice,' may end at length in frenzy or despair,—we cannot but recognise the importance of those moral motives which have been neglected, and must acknowledge the justice of that law, which punishes with such seeming severity a course of conduct long and wilfully persisted in.

" But if we were required to point out any one particular vice which more than another crowds the cells of our lunatic asylums with incurable inmates, we should instance that by which human nature is despoiled of its supremacy, and the intellectual lords of the creation degraded to the level of the brutes. It is from indulgence in spirituous liquors, that by far the greater number of confirmed insanities arise, and exhibit that particular character of religious horror, which has led superficial observers to mistake the disease for that of true religious mania, and has caused the abettors of infidelity unblushingly to affirm that it is religion which drives men mad. The true *monomania religiosa* is a very rare disease ; not so, however, that religious horror often mistaken for it, and arising, as Dr. Traill has well remarked, not from the cultivation of religion, but from the neglect of it."

What can be more manifest than that every one has much in his power in regard to the infliction of such dreadful maladies as have just been mentioned? And is it not also obvious, that had not these been appointed as a natural result of the violation of wise laws, these laws must have been a dead letter, and the power of the lawgiver proved not to be equal to his wisdom and benevolence? While, however, every person who has arrived at the years of discretion has his own health and happiness greatly under his controul, according as he uses and values his opportunities, still his personal and immediate welfare constitutes not all the motives to obedience of the universal laws of nature as established by God; for diseases are transmissible; they may so affect the system as to become constitutional : therefore think of the inducements which have been set before man to obey those enactments, the violation of which transmits a taint to his posterity, thus poisoning the innocent and rendering them the monuments of a reckless, unfeeling pest to kindred and society !

If what Dr. Johnson has said about the pleasures of sense be true, then pain is sometimes preferable ; and especially must this be the case when pain comes as the natural effect of vicious pleasures, for then it must act as a monitor to avoid similar infractions of wise and benevolent laws. But even in a therapeutic point of view, our author is of opinion that pain often acts as an auxiliary in restoring healthy action. He continues—

" Nor should its influence on the mind be overlooked, if Dr. Gregory was right in supposing, that it contributes ' ad claritatem et acumen ingenii.' But however this may be, it is very certain, that pain is capable of shedding a satisfaction over intervals of ease, which few enjoyments exceed : the general cheerfulness observed in the wards of a surgical hospital, among those patients who are comparatively free from pain, is, I think, an evidence of this. The degree of suffering which pain occasions depends very much on the state of the mind, and the fortitude with which it is borne. The stoics could so reason on this subject, as to convert it into an occasion of triumph ; but though a moral courage, capable of enduring pain, and of profiting by it, is greatly to be wished, yet indifference to pain is neither desirable nor enviable, and may defeat the very object of its dispensation. Upon the whole, pain seems appointed to take place only where and when it may be useful, and not to occasion unnecessary suffering ;—by its variety it informs us of its seat, and of the kind of morbid action which produces it. ' The sense of pain is in proportion to the magnitude of the disease, only within certain limits. The extremity of disease may abate or even obliterate the sense of pain altogether.'—' Surely,' concluded Dr. Latham, ' there is a benevolent intention conspicuous in all this.' "

The advantages of disease in a religious point of view, and as calculated to stimulate man to a cultivation of his noblest faculties, preparatory to their glorious exercise in a future state of existence, as well as to prompt him to the performance of those duties, the reward of which awaits him during eternity, fall under our author's enlarged view of his subject. Upon these points, however, we do not particularly enter, although whatever conduces to our real welfare on earth cannot be disjoined from the far more lasting results alluded to. Disease, even when considered as the forerunner of the King of Terrors, is a merciful dispensation ; for it takes away the horror which is entertained of death when health abounds. And, to conclude, see what disease has been the means of suggesting and effecting towards the promotion of those arts and sciences which give the highest relish and dignity even to healthful existence.

" A desire to recover means for the removal of disease would appear to have been the first serious inducement to the scientific study of nature. Thus arose botany, once cultivated only by the physician, whose researches in the vegetable kingdom have been richly rewarded by the profusion of remedies submitted to his choice. Chemistry and mineralogy, though possibly dating from other designs, have been greatly promoted by the same praiseworthy motive, and increased importance has thereby been given to the study of natural history generally. But perhaps the most important achievement of human industry, urged onward to discover and provide for the occasions of disease, is the knowledge we have acquired of the structure and functions of our own bodies. Anatomy and physiology have thus become sciences not only of great and permanent importance in themselves, but possessing a still higher interest, in that they have made known to us the most admirable contrivances of creative wisdom, and have furnished a most convincing evidence of the benevolent intentions of the Deity. They show, as Sir Charles Bell has well said, ' that the care of the most tender parent is in nothing to be compared with those provisions for our enjoyment and safety, which it is not only beyond the ingenuity of man to supply to himself, but which he can hardly comprehend, while he profits by them.' To the same source may be ascribed the progress of comparative anatomy. with the assistance thence derived to other sciences, and the illustration it has afforded of the ancient history of the globe we inhabit. Mechanical science has also participated in the same, by the application of its principles to the most humane purposes, the removal of pain and mitigation of suffering. Nor has literature passed unnoticed. The attention here bestowed by medicine, while it has helped to raise the one, has conferred honour upon the other. To the influence of disease, in drawing attention to its occasional causes, and enforcing the means of prevention, are no doubt owing many of the improvements in building and ventilating houses ; the formation of sewers and drains, and other matters tending to the increased comfort and convenience of the population generally, whereby many sources of physical depression and moral depravity have been done away : health and cheerfulness have been promoted, where sickness and suffering pre-, viously prevailed ; improved habits and manners have been introduced ; the tone of moral feeling has been raised, and human happiness considerably augmented. In short, could we trace this influential agent, disease, through all its workings, we should probably find, that in drawing forth the energies of the human mind, in developing its faculties, and promoting our welfare. it has a far wider sphere of operation, and performs a much more important part than we could *à priori* have suspected ; and though there be some things about disease, to us at present inscrutable, it ought to satisfy us, that we see and know enough of its uses and tendency, to be fully persuaded that it acts for our good. ' The further advances have been made in the knowledge of nature, and the more open it has been laid to our view, the more glorious it has appeared, and the stronger proofs have been discovered of the perfections of its author.' So that if we were able to discover the connexions and dependencies of all its parts, seeming discrepancies would disappear, and the whole scheme be viewed in all its just proportions—a work of wisdom and of marvellous skill.''

Art. VII.—*Memoirs of Sir William Knighton, Bart. G.C.H., Keeper of the Privy Purse during the Reign of his Majesty George IV. Including his Correspondence with many distinguished Personages.* By Lady Knighton. 2 vols. London: Bentley. 1838.

Those who anxiously looked forward to the publication of these volumes, expecting to have a greedy appetite for court-scandal gratified, will be disappointed ; for Lady Knighton has evidently sup-.

pressed every document that has directly borne upon the secret, personal, and political intrigues that must have been disclosed to her husband, in the course of an era when these arts were understood to be particularly rife. Any person, however, who carefully reads the great mass of letters here published, these coming as they do from all classes of persons, and very many of them from individuals who have been much before the public, can experience no difficulty in detecting a number of most significant and instructive particulars ; and in this way the work throws valuable light not only upon human nature, but upon an important period in our national history. The lessons, too, which Sir William's own life affords, have an individual distinctness and force that every reflecting mind will feel to be suggestive and important to the greatest and the humblest in the land.

But though the publication may be thus generally estimated, we must object to it in a certain degree, on account of this very questionable fact and practice, viz., that the majority of these letters were confidential communications, many of the writers being still alive, while the relatives and families of all of them may have reason to feel that they in some measure have been compromised for the sake of one man's fame, the widow of that one man having it in her power to suppress or to circulate exactly so much as suited her natural partialities. Having said this much as becomes us as journalists, bound to guard our literature against every base infusion, since the tendencies both of those who possess secret correspondence and of the scandal-loving multitude are in favour of every breach of confidence of the kind mentioned—although in the present instance affection for the departed, instead of any grosser selfish purpose prompted the publication—we proceed to give some account of the work, extract some of its contents, and to blend these with such observations as may be suggested.

In two points of view these volumes may be advantageously and usefully studied ; first, as they exhibit the character and history of Sir William Knighton himself, and, secondly, as they picture the higher classes of mankind, even royalty itself, especially George the Fourth, in his private and confidential moments : and the result of the whole, both as respects the Keeper of the Privy Purse and the monarch whom he served, is engaging and complimentary.

Every young man may profitably read these Memoirs, because they offer a striking instance of what perseverance, zeal, and probity may accomplish, though unaided by great wealth, high birth, or political interest. Every head of a family also may here gather valuable lessons, because while we see a man whom one of the most lavish and haughty kings that ever reigned delighted to honour,— a man who was that king's irresponsible adviser and to a great extent *de facto* king himself, it is in his social circles, and especially at his domestic hearth, that his chief delight was experienced. Every

courtier, too, should be instructed by the purity and honesty of him
who was the mediator between the sovereign and all others who
sought the sovereign's smiles.

William Knighton first saw the light in the year 1776; and
although his family was respectable, a father's irregularities had so
reduced the condition of those who immediately depended upon him,
that our hero and an infant sister had nigh been committed to the
care of the parish. We here quote a letter which, while honourable
to the writer, throws considerable light upon his early condition.

"To the question of your friend relating to me, '*Do you know his history?*'
I answer, Few do, I believe, and scarcely he himself. He is indebted to
Providence for what he possesses, and to industry and application for what
he may else have obtained. At one time he was in a measure deserted by
the world, and a consultation was held whether he and his infant sister
should be committed to the care of the parish. Before the sun had shone
two years on one, and one year on the other, they were left orphans; and
the father that was thus deprived of life had spent in irregularity and
intemperance a comfortable independence, and died at the age of twenty-
nine. *Reflection* was the inheritance of those he left behind,—probably of
more value than gold. My grandfather, whose death immediately followed
my father's, died, possessed of much wealth, but in misery, because his fancy
suggested that he had done nothing for us orphans: but it proved otherwise. To him I am indebted for the fortune I possess, which educated me,
and brought me to that which I now attempt to profess. A part of this
fortune was attempted to be kept from me by my father's younger brother;
but it has been happily recovered since I have been in this place.

"The stories that have been told of me have been beyond everything
wonderful. 'Tis but of little consequence. The mother of Euripides sold
greens for her livelihood, and the father of Demosthenes sold knives for the
same purpose; but does it lessen the worth of the men? Yet, as Johnson
observes, 'there is no pleasure in relating stories of poverty; and when I
tell them that my father was an old bookseller, let them be content without
further inquiry.' What man, now he is dead, did not rejoice at the honour
of his acquaintance? Many would be as proud to handle the pencil of
Titian as the sceptre of the emperor he painted. And now, perhaps you
will say, what necessity was there for all this? To which I reply, Not to
satisfy public curiosity, nor to be told again; but you will perceive that as
I write you creep into my confidence, and that when I converse or write to
you, I appear to be prating about myself. It will be the better way, when
you have read this letter, to burn and forget it, with this reflection on me,
—that *I* from my childhood have been obliged to think."

His father having died, and his grandfather having left five hundred pounds to forward and support the boy's education, he was at
length apprenticed to a surgeon apothecary at Tavistock. Here he
steadily and industriously conducted himself; and, indeed, as was
the case throughout the whole of his history, displayed an amiabi-
lity of temper and an anxiety to distinguish himself that ought to
be a model for every youth; though at no period and under no cir-

circumstances do we discover evidences in him of superior intellectual powers. Common sense not genius was his guardian.

Having served his time as an apprentice, he repaired to London to attend lectures and hospitals in the ordinary fashion. He afterwards commenced practice in Devonport, having obtained a doctor's degree from Aberdeen. He seems to have been prosperous in business while in the country, and to have there found his ambition for a higher sphere of action fostered ; for in 1803 he settled in London. But here the College of Physicians would not honour his Aberdeen degree. In entire good keeping, however, with the whole of his life, he was not to be beaten even by that exclusive and powerful body ; for, though he had been in respectable practice, earning an enviable income, and was now a married man, he determined to equip himself with whatever the strictest formality demanded. Accordingly he repaired to Edinburgh where he studied for three years, after which he returned to the metropolis, duly qualified.

It is needless to trace his future career very closely. Suffice it to say that he accompanied the Marquess of Wellesley to Spain, during his mission in 1809, and that some time after his return, he was introduced to the Prince Regent, who declared that " he was the best-mannered medical man" he had ever met. It would seem, therefore, that elegant insinuating manners, not altogether separated from the sweet incense of a flattering tongue, we suspect, went a great way in favour of the speedy elevation of our physician. At any rate he became one of the Regent's physicians ; a few years later he was made Auditor of the Duchy of Lancaster, and at last Keeper of the Privy Purse.

But it was not without exciting the jealousy of the faculty that the Regent was known to have declared Knighton the best mannered medical man he had ever seen ; and indeed the misrepresentations that reached the royal ear, threatened to have for ever marred the fortunes of our hero. Unwearied perseverance, probity, and prudence, however, were an over-match for professional enmity, which we believe is in no other liberal calling so bitter and prevalent as in that to which reference is made. We shall afterwards see how complete was his triumph over all obstacles, and how entirely George the Fourth trusted and even loved him,—relying constantly upon him for advice and comfort, and plainly showing that among all the worshippers of royalty, no one had ever so completely won the confidence of the singularly fastidious personage alluded to. In fact Sir William became not only Keeper of the King's Privy Purse but of his conscience.

We have said that these Memoirs lend much and favourable light as regards the private feelings of George the Fourth. They at the same time afford such an insight into human nature, into the hollowness and unsatisfying qualities of mere worldly pomp and greatness, as is exceedingly instructive. The monarch's life of which we speak, it is universally known, was not one even of domestic quiet, or at any time of enviable pleasure. The embarrassment of his pecuniary affairs, which is frequently exhibited in a striking manner in these Memoirs, of itself was sufficient to embitter life; nor can one fail to remark how wonderfully powerless the monarch was to do that which he pleased with his own. The sovereign of England, after all, is the greatest slave in the empire. It will be easy to give proofs of the several points above mentioned, and of others not less important.

The extravagance of George the Fourth was not the only source of his embarrassment. He seems until the appointment of Sir William to the keepership to have been most painfully at the mercy of others whose follies were perhaps greater, but whose irresponsibility shielded them from exposure, the whole disgrace of their conduct falling upon their unfortunate master. There is no slight degree of significance in the following letter, written by Sir William, not long after his accession to his principal office.

" ' Sir,—I yesterday received from Lord F. C. a message that it was your majesty's desire to see me at the Lodge this morning. My first duty and impression was, of course, to obey your majesty's most gracious commands; but circumstances have arisen, connected with your majesty's interests, which oblige me to remain in town, and to forego that pleasure which is always so acceptable to my feelings, namely, that of throwing myself at your majesty's feet. I am so surrounded with cares on your majesty's account, so separated from every kind of support but what I derive from my own intellectual efforts, that, when I say happiness and myself are strangers, I do not mention it in the language of complaint, but only to hope that when I venture to oppose any of your majesty's commands, your majesty will believe it always arises from those feelings of devotion and honesty which are the true characteristics of my nature towards your majesty. I am aware it often happens, humble as I am, that it alone falls on me to raise the voice of opposition towards some of your majesty's schemes. This, I fear, must gradually tend to separate your majesty's mind, as far as agreeableness of feeling is concerned, from me: nevertheless, I do hope that your majesty will believe I am on every occasion influenced with the purest affection and most unsullied attachment towards your majesty's person.— I have the honour to be, sir, your majesty's most dutiful subject and attached servant,　　　　　　　　　　　　　　　　　　　　　　W. K.

" ' 10th June, 1822.' "

It would appear that there were occasions when Sir William in spite of his vigilance and economy was taken all-a-back by some sudden announcement of new difficulties for which he was not prepared. Mr. Dickie, a clerk in Coutts's bank declares, that the keeper has more than once, " in my presence, most respectfully but firmly remonstrated with his Majesty upon the impossibility of managing his affairs with any satisfaction, or indeed propriety of conduct, if such unforeseen expenditure occurred." And it would seem also that this freedom and firmness sometimes excited temporally the royal displeasure. We quote a letter from the King, which refers to some such slight and transient frowns.

" ' You may easily imagine, warm and sincere as my affections are towards you, I have had but little rest since we separated last night. The feeling that I may possibly and unfortunately, in a hurried moment, when my mind and my heart were torn in fifty different ways from fifty different causes, have let an unjust or a hasty expression escape me to any one, but most especially to you, whom I so truly love, and who are so invaluable to me as my friend, is to me a sensation much too painful to be endured ? therefore let me implore you to come to me, be it but for a moment, the very first thing you do this morning; for I shall hate myself until I have the opportunity of expressing personally to you those pure and genuine feelings of affection which will never cease to live in my heart so long as that heart itself continues to beat. I am much too unhappy to say more, but that I am ever your affectionate friend, G. R.' "

George the Fourth has not generally obtained much credit for possessing a forgiving nature ; yet the last quoted letter evinces a placable as well as a tender spirit. There is also reason to believe that Sir William gradually ascended in the royal confidence and friendship ; and, indeed, the keeper had not long held the privy purse without overcoming the King's irritability. His Majesty was a sensible as well as a proud man, and finding his servant faithful and trustworthy beyond most or all of those who had enjoyed access to the back-stairs, a singular and peremptory resolution was at length carried into force, as our next extract testifies, which among other things evinces a full sense of that trustworthiness. The document is dated Royal Lodge, October 26th, 1822.

" I hereby authorise and direct Sir William Knighton, bart., keeper of my privy purse, to give notice to our several tradesmen, that they are not to receive orders, or to furnish any articles of furniture, &c. &c. &c., or to incur any expense whatsoever from their different trades, where such expense is to be provided for by my said privy purse, without receiving a specific order, in writing, for that purpose, from the said Sir William Knighton, bart. ; and I do also give my authority to the said Sir William Knighton, bart., and order and direct him, during our will and pleasure, to undertake the entire management of my private affairs, with a view to the observance of the most strict and rigid economy, that we may have the opportunity of relieving ourselves from certain embarrassments, which it is not necessary to mention further in detail. We do, therefore, rely with confidence on the said Sir William Knighton for the strict performance and fulfilment of all our wishes on this head.
" George R.".

The Civil List of George the Fourth amounted, if we recollect aright, to the enormous sum of 385,000*l. per annum*; and yet so numerous were the demands upon this income, and so difficult was retrenchment in the great offices of the household, not to speak of his

Majesty's own extravagant taste, that the above remarkable species of protection was resorted to, which cannot but convince every candid mind that had honester servants and less selfish courtiers always surrounded the throne, this monarch's name might have descended to posterity in a fairer light than some of his acts and habits have stamped upon his history. It requires but to read the present volumes to arrive at the conviction that his career and reign encountered a multiplicity of harassing occurrences. We find him, for example, writing to Sir William, while the latter was at Vienna in 1825, on one of the many important missions in which he served, in the terms we now copy.

"My Dear Friend.—I have so little to say since your departure from hence, that it is scarce worth while troubling you with a line even now, especially as in the course of a few days I look for your reappearance, except to acknowledge and thank you for the short epistle I received from you, dated Frankfort. Tranquillity, I am sure you will be pleased to learn, has, in general, been the order of the day since you left us. However, there have been, and I am fearful they are still existing, some difficulties and misunderstandings in the final arrangement of that business which has caused you so much trouble and anxiety, and which at present do, and which I fear, will still procrastinate the final adjustment until your return. It is impossible to detail to you what cavillings there have been, and what strange crotchets have started up, and sometimes seemingly upon the merest trifles among the lawyers, and indeed, pretty much all the parties concerned : such immensity of talking backwards and forwards, here and there,—the mistake of a sentence, and even of a single world,—all which creates delay; and even if there be the possibility of correcting it and setting it to rights again afterwards, I think but little progress has yet been made; and I see the impracticability, and next to the impossibility, of its being brought to any final issue until the moment of your return, when by your good and kind advice, it may in all likelihood be ultimately settled."

Yet this letter it seems was written during a period of comparative tranquillity. Ere its conclusion, the writer says, "As to the bodily health, I am certainly not as well as I ought to be, although I complain but little." He afterwards, however, again refers to the state of his mind and his feelings as being the chief seat of his troubles.

Having quoted an allusion to health, a letter under the same royal hand will satisfy the reader that his Majesty had sometimes a complication of troubles to combat.

"Royal Lodge, June 18th, 1827.

"As to myself, I am pretty well bodily ; but I have little or no use of my poor limbs, for I can neither walk up nor down stairs, and am obliged to be carried, and in general to be wheeled about every where; for my powers of walking, and even of crawling about with crutches, or with the aid of a strong stick, are not in the smallest respect improved since you last saw me,—at the same time that my knees, legs, ankles, and feet, swell more formidably and terribly than ever. This, I am sure, you will agree with me, ought now to be seriously attended to without delay, by some plan devised and steadily acted upon, in order to stop the further progress, and to remedy it effectually and finally; for there is no question it is an increasing and progressive evil (at least so I fear), unless steps be found, and that speedily too, of averting it. You must now have had enough of my epistolary quality; I shall, therefore, dear friend, hasten to a conclusion, with the assurance that I am always your sincere and affectionate friend, G. R."

Does any one suppose that the sovereign of England's life is one of uninterrupted luxury and ease? Let such peruse the short epistle we next cite, written during an interruption of Sir William Knighton's activities in consequence of illness.

" ' Dear friend,—For God's sake, for all our sakes, pray, pray take care of yourself; and do not think, upon any account, of stirring until to-morrow morning. It is true, I am jaded and quite worn out, and writing from my bed, where I have laid down for a little rest; but to-morrow will be quite time enough. Little or no advance, I regret to say, has as yet been made, amidst, perhaps, almost unravelable perplexities.

" ' Yours affectionately,
" ' G. R.

"'St. James's Palace, Friday, April 6, 1827.'"

The two letters which follow exhibit the King in an amiable, a benevolent, and considerate light.

" A little charitable impulse induces me to desire you to inquire into the distressed circumstances of poor old O'Keeffe, now ninety years of age and stone-blind, whom I knew a little of formerly, having occasionally met him at parties of my juvenile recreation and hilarity, to which he then contributed not a little. Should you really find him so low in the world, and so divested of all comfort, as he is represented to be, then I do conceive that there can be no objection to your offering him, from me, such immediate relief, or such a moderate annual stipend, as will enable him to close his hitherto long life in comfort, at any rate free from want and absolute beggary, which I greatly fear at present is but too truly his actual condition and situation. Perhaps, on many accounts and reasons, which I am sure I need not mention to you, this had best be effectuated by an immediate application through you to our lively little friend, G. Colman, whose good heart will, I am certain, lead him to give us all the assistance he can, especially as it is for the preservation of one of his oldest invalided brothers and worshippers of the Thespian muse.

"G. R."

His Majesty's estimate of domestic and wedded felicity evinced in the next communication, could not be formed from his own experience.

" It was fully my intention to have written you a few lines on Christmas-day, but I was then, and had been confined ever since this day se'ennight, to my room, with a general cold and feverish attack, attended with great tightness and oppression upon the chest, and for which, by Sir Henry's advice, we were obliged to have recourse to the lancet, which produced the expected relief, but not such entire relief as to set me free from my chamber, but from which, thank God, I am to emerge this day, by going down to dinner for the first time. My affection for you made me feel that, however I might be suffering myself, it would be both cruel and unjust in me, knowing how very little time you ever allow yourself to pass in comfort with your family (especially at this season of the year), were I to write that to you which, from your affection to me, might have induced you generously to break up your domestic board by coming away to me suddenly, or, at any rate, have cast a damper over those happy, cheerful, and enviable hours, which you cannot fail to enjoy when surrounded by your happy domestic circle ; and that long may this be your case, dear friend, my best prayers are, and ever will be offered up. Now, good bye to you. I look forward with impatience to Wednesday next, the 2nd, when I rely and depend upon seeing you. Till then, God bless you !—Yours affectionately,   G. R."

As already intimated the correspondents in these volumes are very numerous and various. Princes of the blood royal, lords, lawyers, authors, artists, statesmen, and petitioners of sundry grades figure in them. None of the letters are more characteristic than those of Canning, who exhibits statesmanship throughout. Here is one which lets us into some little of the writer's habits.

"F. O. March 3rd, 1826.

"My dear Sir—The only ill effect of my attendance in the House of Commons on Thursday was a sleepless night ; a grievance which I do not remember ever to have experienced to the same degree before. I was not feverish ; I was not exhausted ; I was not even tired ; and I can generally get to sleep, putting aside whatever is upon my mind ; but Thursday night I could not. I felt as if every limb from top to toe was alive, like an eel ; and I lay all night, not tossing or tumbling, but as broad awake as if it were mid-day. The consequence was, that I kept quietly at home (by Holland's advice) all yesterday, and did not go to the House of Commons ; for which reason, I have not written to his Majesty—perhaps you will have the kindness to explain why. There was indeed nothing to report, except the second reading of the Duke of Clarence's Bill, by a majority of 128 to 39, almost without debate. All the rest of the sitting was occupied with petitions. Here is Lushington's report of it.

"I am quite well this morning ; having (by order) dined more liberally yesterday, and drunk a little wine, and afterwards slept like a top from eleven to seven. I rejoice in your good accounts of his Majesty, and am greatly relieved by what you say of yourself.

"Ever most sincerely yours,
"GEORGE CANNING."

Do the heads of the Foreign or Colonial Offices at the present day expedite business in the manner indicated below ?

"F. O. March 28th, 1826.

"My dear Sir—With this letter goes the paper which the king desired to be copied for his majesty's private use. I am just setting off for Bath, with a good conscience, having so cleared off the arrears accruing during parliament time, that I believe I do not owe a despatch in any part of the world; and, if I did, I have not a messenger left by whom to send one. I am assured, however, that the well, though now pumped dry, will fill again by the time of my return to town on Friday. I propose being at the Castle, at Salt Hill, on Thursday evening. Very sincerely yours,

"GEO. CANNING."

"P.S. As his majesty has found his hand, could you not submit for his majesty's signature some of the treasury warrants? This is not my business, otherwise than as the whole race of office-men look to the 5th of April, and will look in vain unless there be a royal signature before that day to some one of the papers or parchments, I do not rightly know which.

"G. C."

Now for a sample of friendship and policy combined.

"F. O. November 11th, 1826.

"My dear Sir—Sir Walter Scott is returned to England, as I learn from a note of Mr. Croker's, inviting me to meet Sir Walter at dinner next Friday.

"Is it possible that Sir Walter may take that opportunity of speaking to me about his son? If so, would it not be advisable that I should be apprized of his Majesty's gracious interest in the young man's favour beforehand?

"*I will, of course, make it a point of finding the means to do what his Majesty wishes.* But although Sir Walter Scott and I are old friends, and though his reputation and his misfortunes entitle him to every possible attention, *as a member of the Government, I shall be glad to have the protection of the King's commands in doing an act of kindness by Malachi Malagrowther.*

"Ever, my dear Sir, most sincerely yours,

"GEO. CANNING."

Scott, like many more statesmen as well as authors, was glad to have recourse to Sir William's good offices; nor from the several letters of his here published, do we ever find him losing sight of the mainchance, or betraying any qualities so plainly as an admiration of the King approaching to servile adulation, together with a sharp look-out for the furtherance of the interests of those most dear to him; natural and likely enough features in the character of a man of so much shrewdness and devotion to the privileged, but a little too obtrusive to suit our ideas of true magnanimity and independence. One of Sir William's letters may be quoted in reference to the poet.

"Dalkeith Palace, August 16th, 1822.

"Here I am in Dalkeith Palace, a place most beautifully and romantically situated, well wooded, and quite delightful. Tell dearest D. that

I am again in a haunted room, for I heard strange sounds all the night through. Yesterday was the day of our arrival. The weather continued wet, stormy, and uncomfortable during the whole night at Leith Roads; the yacht at anchor had an uncomfortable motion. I saw, for the first time, Walter Scott, who came on board immediately on our coming to anchor. He has no trace in his countenance of such superior genius and softness [loftiness?] of mind as the beauty of his writings displays; but the moment he speaks, you discover a correctness of understanding and a display of intellect, marked by the utmost accuracy of thought. Speaking of the incessant rain, he said, in his Scotch phraseology, 'All I can say is, I am perfectly ashamed of it.' The king then desired him to take a glass of cherry brandy, which he graciously handed to him himself. Walter Scott, when he had drunk it, craved a great favour from his majesty, that he might be permitted to put the glass in his pocket to keep it as a relic, to his feelings above all value."

In a note it is added that Scott's flattery was extremely well applied; and that when his Majesty left Edinburgh, he writes,—" This is a vile day : but it is right Scotland should weep when parting with her good King."

When speaking of our poet and author, we may diversify our extracts by quoting an anecdote of another.

" 'I was,' says Sir W. 'Lord Byron's medical attendant for some time previously to his marriage. One morning, on making him my accustomed visit, I found the table at which he was writing covered with printer's proof-sheets, scraps of manuscript verses, &c. On my being announced, he neither raised his head nor the *pencil* from the paper he was rapidly scribbling, but said, ' Be so kind as to take a book, and be silent for two minutes.' A longer time had scarcely elapsed, when he threw down the pencil with an air of satisfaction, exclaiming, 'I have done it at last! ' He apologised for claiming a poet's indulgence, saying, that the last four lines of that stanza had given him more trouble than the whole of the poem besides; adding, ' The right words came into my head just as your carriage drove up.' His lordship then rose, and, with a smile, said abruptly, 'Knighton, what do you think I am going to do? I am going to marry.' I replied, ' I am sorry to hear it, my lord.' ' The d—l you are! And why should I not ? ' ' Because I do not think you are constituted to be happy in married life.' He looked grave, and after a pause, said, ' I believe you are right; but the ladies think otherwise,' (alluding to his sister, Mrs. L.) ' However, the die is cast; for I have presented myself in due form to the lady's papa. I had an amicable reception. The only personal question put to me was when I was mounting my horse : Sir Ralph called after me, ' Pray, my Lord, how do you pronounce your name? Birron or By-ron ? I replied, ' BY, sir, spells *by*, all the world over.' "

We have left ourselves room for only one extract more. It contains an account of a visit to the Royal Vault to choose a resting-place for the body of the Duke of York.

"Royal Lodge, 20th January, 1827.

"It may make you comfortable to know that I do not attend the funeral of his late Royal Highness the Duke of York; but I remain with his Majesty in the silence of his chamber.

"Two nights since, the King sent me to Saint George's Chapel at Windsor, for the purpose of descending into the vault which contains the Royal Family who have died within these few years. One man preceded me down the ladder that leads to this gloomy abode, whilst another held the ladder above: the first man carried a lighted torch We then traversed a subterraneous passage of about one hundred yards in length, at the end of which, looking to the east, was the coffin of King George the Third, elevated a little on a block of marble; on one side was the late Queen Charlotte; on the other, his Majesty's daughter the Princess Amelia; next to the Princess, Prince Edward, who died early; and on the other side of the Queen, another prince who died young. Then, by turning round, and looking in a different direction, on the right, in a niche, was the Princess Elizabeth, at whose birth I was present; in the next niche, the Princess Charlotte and her baby, her heart in an urn: next to the Princess Charlotte, the old Duchess of Brunswick; and farther on in the vault, the late Duke of Kent. The object of this melancholy and memorable visit was to fix on a desirable spot to place the remains of the Duke of York, that his Majesty might know, through my affectionate feelings to fulfil his wishes, that the Duke was placed in a situation to be as near the late King as possible.

"It is quite out of my power to describe to you the imposing and solemn situation in which I found myself,—in the dead of night, with a single torch in my hand, in the bowels of the earth, with my late King and Queen and their dead family, all of whom I believed had at that moment a spiritual existence. I felt as if the Almighty was present, and almost imagined that the spirits of the departed were also before me. I never shall forget this visit!

"I remained in the vault above a quarter of an hour. The hour at which I now write is four o'clock; the minute-guns are firing. The remains of the Duke of York will reach Windsor about eight. I am obliged to write in a great hurry.   "Yours ever, &c.

"W. K."

This last is a fitting letter to close our extracts from the memoirs and correspondence of one, who not only the more he saw of grandeur and state became the more enamoured of domestic life, and the more attached to his family, but who never was ashamed of his old friendships. Indeed, an account of a visit to the scenes of his childhood, after he had long mingled with the first and most exclusive personages of the land, forms one of the most touching portions of the publication. It must not be forgotten that Sir William always revered religion, and professed a heart-felt sense of the importance of its ordinances. Towards the close of his life his piety assumed a deeper and an engrossing character, every thing appearing to him of trifling importance when compared with the concerns of an immortal existence. He was a liberal, considerate, amiable, and good, if not a great man.

ART. VIII.

1.—*Hood's Own; or Laughter from Year to Year.* Nos. I. II. III.
London: Baily & Co. 1838.

2.—*The Life and Adventures of Nicholas Nickleby.* No. I. By "Boz."
London: Chapman & Hall. 1838.

3.—*Jorrocks' Jaunts and Jollities, with Twelve Illustrations by "Phiz."*
London: Spiers. 1838.

HERE we have a goodly trio, each of whom has been, and is sure to continue, a favourite of John Bull. This said John, as all the world knows, is a person made up of strange contradictions. One of these consists in his being a great grumbler, and that the slighter the real or pretended annoyance, whether in state, municipality, parish, club, or domicile, his grumbling is the gruffer. In fact he is not content, he would be unhappy had he nothing to complain of; and so far does he carry the propensity, that he is ready to boast of his grumbling as essential to his nationality, really thinking it part and parcel of the country's constitution. It is by this species of small-fire and pop-gun warfare that his spleen evaporates. A safety valve is thus opened to him, which, if long shut, nothing less than conspiracies and wars would be bred to the imminent danger of King, Lords, and Commons. To prove how proud John is of his failings, which, as described, only amount to foibles that upon the whole operate wholesomely, preserving his temper from becoming stagnant and muddy, just let any stranger, foreigner, or alien, assail his country and its institutions, its people and its manners, on the very points which have for a lifetime, perhaps, been the theme of his own grumbling, and you will instantly find that he is prepared for action in their defence, and that his voice, though not now loud, is deep and determined that no change, no innovation, shall come within his sphere. John, in reality, is a stubborn conservative, though he goes a round-about way to work.

Mr. Bull's anomalous nature exhibits itself in another though after all a kindred contradiction to the one above noticed. He is perfectly aware of his foibles, and will, in good set terms, affect seriously to lament them; but let any clever humorist or caricaturist good-naturedly expose or laugh at him on their account, and who but John himself will more heartily join in the sentiment? Let the grumbler and confessor of national frailties or eccentricities be ever so staid or devoted to the shop and the counting-house; let him be in the worst possible humour with himself or those about him; let him be speeding his way to Bank or Lawyer, and depend upon it, if, in passing a print-shop, his eye alights upon one like his present self shown up to the life, he will not only be for the time cured, but will be like to burst his sides with laughter, congratulating himself also that he is one of the most direct descendants of the

ancient and true Bull family. Perhaps a more apt and complete
evidence of this national peculiarity cannot be offered than that
which the Metropolis, the centre of all that is characteristic of the
English people, daily, constantly, and in every quarter, furnishes.
The peculiarities, the vulgarities, if you will, of the natives of Cock-
neyland, are proverbial; but who does not know that none so much
as Cockneys enjoy caricatures of themselves, be it by the pencil or
by the pen? How else can it be that such humorists as those
whose works are now before us are in such repute and have such an
extensive sale within the sound of Bow Bells.

Hood, for example, has by various productions long kept Town
and Country in the best terms with themselves and him, by raising
innocent laughter from " Year to Year," were the "Comic Annual"
alone to be taken into account. In " An Inaugural Discourse,"
prefixed to the earliest Number of his " Own," now before us, he
asks, " How many years is it, think you, 'since we were first ac-
quent?'" And the answer is, "' By the deep *nine*,' sings out the
old bald *Count Fathom* with the lead line; no great lapse in the
world's chronology, but a space of infinite importance in individual
history." After this he proceeds to inform his readers that sad
inroads have been made of late upon his health, but that his " Practical Philosophy" consists in converting " a serious illness into a
comic wellness." He then asks, " by what other agency could I
have transported myself, as a Cockney would say, from *Dull*age to
*Grin*nage?" Such has been and is to be " Hood's Own" system,
a theory and practice which he recommends to all, and which many
regularly adopt at his suggestion, as the vendors of this merry periodical can well attest. May he grow fat when thus pleasantly cater-
ing for many appetites!—for we are concerned to learn that,

" In the absence of a certain thin ' blue-and-yellow' visage, and attenuated figure,—whose effigies may one day be affixed to the present work,—
you will not be prepared to learn that some of the merriest effusions in the
forthcoming numbers have been the relaxations of a gentleman literally
enjoying bad health. The very fingers so aristocratically slender, that now
hold the pen, hint plainly of the ' *ills* that *flesh* is heir to:'—my coats have
become great coats, my pantaloons are turned into trowsers, and by a worse
bargain than Peter Schlemihl's, I seem to have retained my shadow, and
sold my substance. In short, as happens to prematurely old port wine, I
am of a bad colour, with very little body. But what then? That emaciated
hand still lends a hand to embody in words and sketches, the creations or
recreations of a Merry Fancy: those gaunt sides yet shake heartily as ever
at the Grotesques and Arabesques, and droll Picturesques that my Good
Genius (a Pantagruelian Familiar) charitably conjures up to divert me from
more sombre realities."

We need not at this time of day strain our vocabulary to describe
Mr. Hood's peculiar vein of humour. Indeed it requires no more

H 2

than an acquaintance with a single effusion of his, whether it be
prose or verse, to discover his marvellous fecundity of frolicsome
thought, and oddity of fancy.   His very wordiness and everlasting
ringing the changes upon words affords a curious theme of study;
while the harmlessness of his jokes, the healthy and sound sentiments which are breathed throughout them, infect the reader's heart,
and put him in such good terms with the author that it is impossible
to be otherwise than bettered by an intercourse with him.

In the present publication, Mr. Hood not only dresses up and
sets before us some of his choicest standard pieces, but treats us to
numerous novelties, these frequently being appropriate to the season.
Two specimens from the third Number will suffice to show that
there is no falling off in these later efforts, and that Laughter from
Ear to Ear promises to last from Year to Year, excited by the fertile
wit of our old acquaintance.   The first specimen consists merely of
a few observations on a female meeting which has been convoked
to abuse and oppose the poor law.   He says,

" When the Steam washing Company was first established, there was a
loud and shrill outcry against what was facetiously called the cock laun-
dresses, who was roundly accused of a shameful invasion of woman's provinces, and favoured with many sneering recommendations to wear mob
caps, and go in stuff petticoats and pattens. But if Hercules with the distaff
be but a sorry spectacle, surely Omphale with the club cuts scarcely a
better figure.   The he creatures may now fairly retort, that it is as consistent with manhood to go out washing, as for womanhood to do chairing
at the public meeting. If it be out of character for a fellow in a coat and
continuations to be firsting and seconding linen, it is equally anomalous for
a creature in petticoats to be firsting and seconding political resolutions ;
and for my own part, as a matter of taste, I would rather see a gentleman
blowing up a copper flue, than a lady blowing up the foulness of the poor
law."

Mr. Murphy, and his late contemporary weather-prophet, deservedly come in for a share of Mr. Hood's laughable sarcasm.   Who
but Francis Moore's spirit should be the loquitor in such a case ?

" *The Apparition.*
In the dead of the night, when, from beds that are turfy,
    The spirits rise up on old cronies to call,
Came a shade from the Shades on a visit to Murphy,
    Who had not forseen such a visit at all.
' Don't shiver and shake,' said the mild Apparition
    ' I'm come to your bed with no evil design ;
I'm the Spirit of Moore, Francis Moore the Physician,
    Once great like yourself in the Almanack line.'
Like you I was once a great prophet on weather,
    And deem'd to possess a more prescient knack
Than dogs, frogs, pigs, cattle, or cats, all together,
    The donkeys that bray, and the dillics that quack.

With joy, then, as ashes retain former passion,
  I saw my old mantle lugg'd out from the shelf,
Turn'd, trimm'd, and brush'd up, and again brought in fashion,
  I seem'd to be almost reviving myself!
But oh! from my joys there was soon a sad cantle—
  As too many cooks make a mull of the broth—
To find that two Prophets were under my mantle,
  And pulling two ways at the risk of the cloth.
Unless you would meet with an awkwardish tumble,
  Oh! join like the Siamese twins in your jumps;
Just fancy if Faith on her Prophets should stumble,
  The one in his clogs, and the other in pumps!
But, think how the people would worship and wonder,
  To find you ' hail fellows, well met,' in your hail,
In one tune with your rain, and your wind and your thunder,
  ' 'Fore God,' they would cry, ' they are both in a tale!' "

The Illustrations are as whimsical and droll as the letter-press, the one, for instance, wedded to the Apparition being entitled the " Moon on the Wain ;" a good round luminary, to be sure, resting on as majestic a waggon as ever eight horses dragged up Holborn Hill.

One of the most extraordinary events in the history of modern periodical literature, has been the success that has attended the " Pickwick" and " Oliver Twist " papers by Mr. Dickens. It is not easy to account entirely for this popularity. True it is that his humour is often exquisite ; but its very slyness and the apparent sincerity of the author, who writes as a person who never laughed at his own jokes and pictures, one would think must have hid from the crowd, who admire broad grins, the accuracy of the whole. And yet the frequenters of tap-rooms, equally with parlour customers, and West End exclusives, are in raptures with Boz ; a fact which must, at least, be held conclusive as to the real merits of his writings. We are inclined to attribute his celebrity, indeed, chiefly to two or three leading circumstances, each of them flattering to his genius. First, his creations are truly human. They breathe and speak not only characteristically, but are plain and manifest representatives of distinct varieties in the species, possessing as regards their separate classes a perfection of truthfulness. Thus there is a universality of humanity about each of his characters that is warm and attractive ; while the clear classification of the *dramatis personæ*, and the individuality of each, complete the dramatic effect which brings the reader into actual contact with the whole. Joined to the truthfulness of his characters and the artistic skill with which he groups them, Boz introduces familiar scenic accompaniments, while he constitutes practical truths and ordinary occurrences, the things and the occasions on which his accurate observation and active fancy work.

Secondly, our author has a great command of appropriate sentiments, with which to enrich and enforce the point aimed at in the
narrative. While that narrative is plain, he intersperses it with
such a multitude and variety of reflections, either fully expressed or
slightly suggested, that the utmost liveliness is the result, each
reader having enough and to spare of that seasoning which is most
congenial to his taste. There is matter for the most vulgar, even
to the slang of the day; there is pathos for the more refined; and
there is elevated moral lessons for the sages of society; while each
class can derive pleasure from what is suited especially to their
neighbours, were it merely from the fact that they know its suita-
bleness.

And lastly, the whole contains just so much of caricature as to
convey a humorous and good-natured setting off of the truthful
picture, and to relieve it from the dull and naked reality of every-
day life. It ought to be added that Boz's readers are never rendered conscious of having their turbulent passions awakened, and
that they are uniformly allowed to enjoy the quiet which arises from
harmless amusement, and not unfrequently the satisfaction of being
made more akin to their fellow-creatures, though probably far removed
by exterior or conventional circumstances.

The first number of Nicholas Nickleby being all that has yet
reached us, it is impossible to speak with any certainty of its comparative merits in relation to "Pickwick" and "Oliver Twist."
There appears to have been, if possible, a greater degree of care
and labour in the outset here, than on the former occasions; a
policy which is to be approved of when an author has his own great
fame to rival and maintain. We suspect, however, that Boz will
not be able to do much more than transpose his old matter, and
that when he leaves London completely, he will be out of his element. There is already brought upon the stage a usurer, Ralph
Nickleby of Golden Square. Newman Noggs, the clerk of the
foregoing—the nephew of the same, Nicholas Nickleby, a youth of
spirit—and Wackford Squeers, a cheap, one-eyed Yorkshire schoolmaster, are also introduced, and promise us much good laughter.
The principal incidents are a public meeting held at Bishopsgate
Street, got up to puff off a joint stock speculation, called "The
United Metropolitan Improved Hot Muffin and Crumpet Baking
and Punctual Delivery Company;" and the appearance of Mr.
Wackford Squeers at the Saracen's Head, to receive pupils. A
sketch of Golden Square, destined from hence to become classic
ground, and of Mr. Squeers arranging terms with a stepfather, will
favourably introduce Boz in his new undertaking.

"Although a few members of the graver professions live about Golden
Square, it is not exactly in anybody's way to or from anywhere. It is one
of the squares that have been—a quarter of the town that has gone down in

the world, and taken to letting lodgings. Many of its first and second floors are let furnished to single gentleman, and it takes boarders besides. It is a great resort of foreigners. The dark-complexioned men who wear large rings and heavy watch-guards and bushy whiskers, and who congregate under the Opera colonnade and about the box-office in the season, between four and five in the afternoon, when Mr. Seguin gives away the orders— all live in Golden Square, or within a street of it. Two or three violins and a wind instrument from the Opera band reside within its precincts. Its boarding-houses are musical, and the notes of pianos and harps float in the evening time round the head of the mournful statue, the guardian genius of a little wilderness of shrubs, in the centre of the square. On a summer's night, windows are thrown open, and groups of swarthy mustachioed men are seen by the passer-by lounging at the casements, and smoking fearfully. Sounds of gruff voices practising vocal music invade the evening's silence, and the fumes of choice tobacco scent the air. There, snuff and cigars, and German pipes and flutes, and violins and violoncellos, divide the supremacy between them. It is the region of song and smoke. Street bands are on their mettle in Golden Square, and itinerant glee-singers quaver involuntarily as they rise their voices within its boundaries."

Now for the dominie, to whom Nicholas Nickleby is engaged as usher, and the stepfather with his tender charge.

"The stranger continued. 'I have been thinking, Mr. Squeers, of placing my two boys at your school.'

"'It is not for me to say so, Sir,' replied Mr. Squeers, 'but I don't think you could possibly do a better thing.'

"'Hem!' said the other. 'Twenty pounds per annewum, I believe, Mr. Squeers?'

"'Guineas,' rejoined the schoolmaster, with a persuasive smile.

"'Pounds for two, I think, Mr. Squeers,' said Mr. Snawley, solemnly.

"'I don't think it could be done, Sir,' replied Squeers, as if he had never considered the proposition before. 'Let me see; four fives is twenty, double that, and deduct the—well, a pound either way shall not stand betwixt us. You must recommend me to your connexion, Sir, and make it up that way.'

"'They are not great eaters,' said Mr. Snawley.

"'Oh! that doesn't matter at all,' replied Squeers. 'We don't consider the boys' appetites at our establishment.' This was strictly true: they did not.

"'Every wholesome luxury, Sir, that Yorkshire can afford,' continued Squeers; 'every beautiful moral that Mrs. Squeers can instil; every—in short, every comfort of a home that a boy could wish for, will be theirs, Mr. Snawley.'

"'I should wish their morals to be particularly attended to,' said Mr. Snawley.

"'I am glad of that, Sir,' replied the schoolmaster, drawing himself up. 'They have come to the right shop for morals, Sir.'

"'You are a moral man yourself,' said Mr. Snawley.

"'I rather believe I am, Sir,' replied Squeers.

"'I have the satisfaction to know you are, Sir,' said Mr, Snawley. 'I asked one of your references, and he said you were pious.'

"'Well, Sir, I hope I am a little in that way,' replied Squeers.

"'I hope I am also,' rejoined the other. 'Could I say a few words with you in the next box?'

"'By all means,' rejoined Squeers, with a grin. 'My dears, will you speak to your new playfellow a minute or two? That is one of my boys, Sir. Belling his name is; a Taunton boy that, Sir.'

"'Is he, indeed?' rejoined Mr. Snawley, looking at the poor little urchin, as if he were some extraordinary natural curiosity.

"'He goes down with me to-morrow, Sir,' said Squeers. 'That's his luggage that he is sitting upon now. Each boy is required to bring, Sir, two suits of clothes, six shirts, six pair of stockings, two nightcaps, two pocket handkerchiefs, two pair of shoes, two hats, and a razor.'

"'A razor!' exclaimed Mr. Snawley, as they walked into the next box. 'What for?'

"'To shave with,' replied Squeers, in a slow and measured tone.

" There was not much in these three words, but there must have been something in the manner in which they were said to attract attention, for the schoolmaster and his companion looked steadily at each other for a few seconds, and then exchanged a very meaning smile. Snawley was a sleek, flat-nosed man, clad in sombre garments and long black gaiters, and bearing in his countenance an expression of much mortification and sanctity, so that his smiling without any obvious reason was the more remarkable.

"'Up to what age do you keep boys at your school, then?' he asked at length.

"'Just as long as their friends make the quarterly payments to my agent in town, or until such time as they run away,' replied Squeers. 'Let us understand each other; I see we may safely do so. What are these boys—natural children?'

"'No,' rejoined Snawley, meeting the gaze of the schoolmaster's one eye. 'They an't.'

"'I thought they might be,' said Squeers, coolly. 'We have a good many of them; that boy's one.'

"'Him in the next box?' said Snawley.

"Squeers nodded in the affirmative, and his companion took another peep at the little boy on the trunk, and turning round again, looked as if he were quite disappointed to see him so much like other boys, and said he should hardly have thought it.

"'He is,' cried Squeers. 'But about these boys of yours; you wanted to speak to me?'

"'Yes,' replied Snawley. 'The fact is, I am not their father, Mr. Squeers; I'm only their father-in-law.'

"'Oh! is that it?' said the schoolmaster. 'That explains it at once. I was wondering what the devil you were going to send them to Yorkshire for. Ha, ha! oh, I understand now.'

"'You see I have married the mother,' pursued Snawley; 'it's expensive keeping boys at home, and as she has a little money in her own right,

I am afraid (women are so very foolish, Mr. Squeers) that she might be led to squander it on them, which would be their ruin, you know.'

" ' *I* see,' returned Squeers, throwing himself back in his chair, and waving his hand.

" ' And this,' resumed Snawley, ' has made me anxious to put the of some school a good distance off, where there are no holidays—none as those ill-judged comings home twice a year that unsettle children's min so—and where they may rough it a little—you comprehend ?'

" ' The payments regular, and no questions asked,' said Squeers, nodding his head.

" ' That's it exactly,' rejoined the other. ' Morals strictly attended to, though.'

" ' Strictly,' said Squeers.

" ' Not too much writing home allowed, I suppose ?' said the father-in-law, hesitating.'

" ' None, except a circular at Christmas, to say that they never were so happy, and hope they may never be sent for,' rejoined Squeers.

" ' Nothing could be better,' said the father-in-law, rubbing his hands.' "

We augur from the above that Mr. Dickens is about to defend the oppressed against the oppressor ; and, indeed, from the portion of the work before us, that his indefatigable and influential pen will take a very decided stand in behalf of the weak, whether chicanery, fraud, heartlessness, or violence be the engines wielded by the strong.

" The Hunting, Shooting, Racing, Driving, Sailing, Eating, Eccentric and Extravagant Exploits of that Renowned Sporting Citizen, Mr. John Jorrocks, of St. Botolph Lane and Great Coram Street," have occupied certain papers which originally appeared in the " New Sporting Magazine ;" and the favour with which they were received by the readers of that journal has led to their reprint in the present collected and uniform style. The writer is manifestly a sportsman, and also a person well acquainted with the various scenes and characters which he portrays. Besides, his sketches are those of a close and accurate observer. He writes cleverly and smartly ; he can strike off a picture with ease and a happy rapidity, and is no copyist. His humour is not so sly as that of Boz, his caricatures being broader and coarser. He seems, however, to be equally much at home in Modern Babylon, while his disportings in the provincial haunts of citizens and swells display a thorough knowledge of these resorts of the idle and the wealthy.

Mr. Jorrocks is a Cockney out and out. He conducts a large business in the grocery line, and distinguishes himself oft and greatly at the Surrey Hunt. He dashes down to Newmarket, and other places of modern resort, and breaks English with the fearlessness of a coiner.

Our first specimen is that of a swell at a Surrey Hunt.

" At this interesting period, a ' regular swell' from Melton Mowbray, unknown to every one except his tailor, to whom he owes a long tick, makes his appearance, and affords abundance of merriment for our sportsmen.   He is just turned out of the hands of his valet, and presents the very *beau idéal* of his caste—' quite the lady,' in fact, His hat is stuck on one side, displaying a profusion of well-waxed ringlets ; a corresponding infinity of whisker, terminating at the chin, there joins an enormous pair of moustaches, which give him the appearance of having caught the fox' himself, and stuck its brush below his nose.   His neck is very stiff ; and the exact Jacksonlike fit of his coat (which almost nips him in two at the waist), and his superlative well-cleaned leather Andersons, together with the perfume and the general puppyism of his appearance, proclaim that he is a ' swell ' of the very first water, and one that a Surrey sportsman would like to buy at his own price, and sell at the other's.   In addition to this, his boots, which his ' fellow' has just denuded from a pair of wash-leather covers, are of the finest, brightest, blackest, patent leather imaginable ; the left one being the identical boot by which Warren's monkey shaved himself, while the right is the one at which the game-cock pecked, mistaking its own shadow for an opponent, the mark of its bill being still visible above the instep ; and the tops—whose pampered appetites have been fed on champagne—are of the most delicate cream-colour, the whole devoid of mud or speck.   The animal he bestrides is no less calculated than himself to excite the risible faculties of the field, being a sort of mouse colour, with a dun mane and tail, got by Nicolo, out of the Flibbertygibbet mare, and he stands seventeen hands and an inch.   His head is small and bloodlike, his girth a mere trifle, and his legs, very long and spidery, of course without any hair at the pasterns to protect them from the flints ; his whole appearance bespeaking him fitter to run for half-mile hunters' stakes at Croxton Park or Leicester, than contend for foxes' brushes in such a splendid country as the Surrey.   There he stands, with his tail stuck tight between his legs, shivering and shaking for all the world as if troubled with a fit of ague.   And well he may, poor beast, for—oh, men of Surrey, London, Kent, and Middlesex, hearken to my word—on closer inspection he proves to have been shaved ! ! ! "

A dinner party at Jorrocks' in Great Coram Street requires a minute indoor knowledge of how such festivities are conducted, and an elaborate description.   Let us find the master of the house driven from his duties as butler, drawing corks *in prospectu*, though " dressed in nankeen shorts, white gauze silk stockings, white neckcloth, and white waistcoat, with a frill as large as a hand saw,"— the smart new blue piece of Saxony, with velvet collar and metal buttons, had to do homage while bottle and corkscrew were in hand.   A capacious yellow hackney-coach having arrived, and been emptied of its contents, " Come, gentlemen," says Mr. Jorrocks,—

" Let's be after going up stairs.—Benjamin, announce the gentlemen as your missis taught you.—Open the door with your left hand, and stretch the right towards her, to let the company see the point to make up to.'

The party ascend the stairs, one at a time, for the flight is narrow, and rather abrupt; and Benjamin, obeying his worthy master's injunctions, threw open the front drawing-room door, and discovered Mrs. Jorrocks sitting in state at a round table, with annuals and albums spread at orthodox distances around. The possession of this room had long been a bone of contention between Mr. Jorrocks and his spouse; but at length they had accommodated matters, by Mr. Jorrocks gaining undivided possession of the back drawing-room (communicating by folding doors), with the run of the front one, equally with Mrs. Jorrocks on non-company days. A glance, however, shewed which was the master's, and which the mistress's room. The front one was papered with weeping willows, bending under the weight of ripe cherries on a white ground, and the chair-cushions were covered with pea-green cotton velvet with yellow worsted bindings. The round table was made of rose-wood, and there was a ' what not' on the right of the fire-place of similar material, containing a handsomely bound collection of Sir Walter Scott's works, in wood. The carpet-pattern consisted of most dashing bouquets of many coloured flowers, in winding French horns on a very light drab ground—so light indeed, that Mr. Jorrocks was never allowed to tread upon it except in pumps or slippers. The bell-pulls were made of foxes' brushes; and in the frame of the looking glass, above the white marble mantel-piece, were stuck visiting cards, notes of invitation, thanks for ' obliging inquiries,' &c., &c. The hearth-rug exhibited a bright yellow tiger, with pink eyes, on a blue ground. with a flossy green border; and the fender and fire-irons were of shining brass. On the wall, immediately opposite the fire-place, was a portrait of Mrs. Jorrocks before she was married, so unlike her present self that no one would have taken it for her. The back drawing-room, which looked out upon the gravel walk and house-backs beyond, was papered with broad scarlet and green stripes, in honour of the Surrey-hunt uniform, and was set out with a green-covered library table in the centre, with a red morocco hunting chair between it and the window, and several good strong hair-bottomed mahogany chairs around the walls. The table had a very literary air, being strewed with sporting magazines, odd numbers of ' Bell's Life,' pamphlets, and papers of various descriptions; while on a sheet of foolscap on the portfolio were ten lines of an elegy on a giblet pie which had been broken in coming from the baker's, at which Mr. Jorrocks had been hammering for some time. On the side opposite the fire-place, on a hanging range of mahogany shelves, were ten volumes of ' Bell's Life in London,' ' The New Sporting Magazine,' bound gilt and lettered, ' The Memoirs of Harriette Wilson,' ' Boxiana,' ' Taplin's Farriery,' ' Nimrod's Life of Mytton,' and a backgammon board that Mr. Jorrocks had bought by mistake for a History of England.''

An addition is about to be made to the party, who obtains a sketch of pedigree, which Jorrocks may be supposed to excel at, on account of habits acquired in the connoisseurship of horses.

" Presently, a loud long-protracted ' *rat-tat-tat-tat-tan, rat-tat-tat-tat-tan,*' at the street door, sounded through the house; and Jorrocks, with a slap on his thigh, exclaimed, ' By jingo! there's Green. No man knocks with such wiggorous wiolence as he does. All Great Coram Street and parts adjacent know when he comes. Julius Cæsar himself couldn't kick

up a greater row.' ' What Green is it—Green of Rollestone ?' inquired
Nimrod, thinking of his Leicestershire friend. ' No,' said Mr. Jorrocks,
' Green of Tooley Street. You'll have heard of the Greens in the Borough,
'emp, 'op, and 'ide (hemp, hop, and hide) merchants—numerous family,
numerous as the 'airs in my vig. This is James Green, jun., whose father,
old James Green, jun., *verd antique* as I calls him, is the son of James
Green, sen., who is in the 'emp line, and James is own cousin to young old
James Green sen., whose father is in the 'ide line.' The remainder of the
pedigree was lost by Benjamin throwing open the door and announcing
Mr. Green; and Jemmy, who had been exchanging his cloth boots for
patent-leather pumps, came bounding up stairs like a racket-ball."

But according to our taste and opportunities of observation the
description which we last of all copy evinces a finer and steadier
hand. We think the picture which it conveys of an inn and its
hangers on, where coaches stop for dinner, is true to the life.

" As they reach the foot of the hill, the guard commences a solo on his
bugle, to give notice to the innkeeper to have the coach dinner on the table.
All huddled together, inside and out, long passengers and short ones, they
cut across the bridge, rattle along the narrow street, spanking the mud from
the newly-watered streets on the shop windows and passengers on each side,
and pull up at the Pig and Cross-bow, with a jerk and a dash as though they
had been travelling at the rate of twelve miles an hour. Two other coaches
are ' dining,' while some few passengers, whose ' hour is not yet come,' sit
patiently on the roof, or pace up and down the street with short and hurried
turns, anxious to see the horses brought out that are to forward them on
their journey. And what a commotion this new arrival creates ! From
the arched doorway of the inn issue two chamber-maids, one in curls, the
other in a cap; boots, with both curls and a cap, and a ladder in his hand;
a knock-kneed waiter, with a dirty duster, to count noses ; while the neat
landlady, in a spruce black silk gown and clean white apron, stands smirking,
smiling, and rubbing her hands down her sides, inveigling the passengers
into the house, where she will turn them over to the waiters to take their
chance the instant she gets them in. About the door the usual idlers are
assembled—A coachman out of place, a beggar out at the elbows, a sergeant
in uniform, and three recruits with ribbons in their hats ; a captain with his
boots cut for corns, the coachman that is to drive to Dover, a youth in a
straw hat and a rowing shirt, the little inquisitive old man of the place—
who sees all the mid-day coaches change horses, speculates on the passengers, and sees who the parcels are for—and, though last not least,
Mr. Bangup, the ' varmint' man, the height of whose ambition is to be
taken for a coachman. As the coach pulled up, he was in the bar
taking a glass of cold sherry ' without' and a cigar, which latter he
brings out lighted in his mouth, with his shaved white hat stuck knowingly on one side, and the thumbs of his brown hands thrust into the
arms-holes of his waistcoat, throwing back his single-breasted fancy-
buttoned green coat, and showing a cream-coloured cravat, fastened
with a gold coach-and-four pin, which, with a buff waistcoat and tight drab
trousers buttoning over the boot, complete his ' toggery,' as he would call
it. His whiskers are large and riotous in the extreme, while his hair is

dipped as close as a charity-school boy's. The coachman and he are on the best of terms, as the outward twist of their elbows and jerks of the head on meeting testify. His conversation is short and slangy, accompanied with the correct nasal twang."

Our funny trio have thus, for one month at least, supplied us with matter that is entirely free from any deleterious ingredient. But we believe there is no other country in the world which could boast a similar variety of harmless description and humour,—gross indelicacy or outrageous extravagance beyond the caricaturists of England, for the most part usurping the place of innocence and truthful sentiment,—London alone being an exhaustless field for the cultivation and exercise of the same.

ART. IX.—*Regal Records ; or a Chronicle of the Coronations of the Queens Regnant of England.* By J. R. PLANCHE, F. S. A. London : Chapman and Hall. 1838.

MANY persons may affect to treat state pageants as child's play, and to regard them, especially in our age, when economy, matters of obvious utility, and intelligence directed to practical purposes, are in highest repute, as an affront offered to civilization and an encroachment upon the national purse that ought no longer to be tolerated. We believe, however, that mankind and the English people in a particular degree, are much more affected and influenced by forms and ancient customs than individuals will readily confess for themselves; nor do we think that it would be difficult to show that the ceremonials observed at coronations have both immediate and indirect and remote consequences of real, practical, and extended importance. It can require, for instance, a very moderate degree of reflection to perceive how much the stability of monarchy depends upon the halo which artificial pomp and pageantry, tinselled and theatric ingenuities if you will, throw around the sovereign ; or to discover in the nature of the human mind how operative is a vista imposingly emblazoned in creating and upholding the veneration essential to loyalty. But it is needless at the present moment of unmingled and universal love and admiration of our youthful Queen to attempt to weave any fine theory or exposition concerning the association of moral sentiments on the points referred to ; nor do we suppose that among the most economical, the most practical and matter-of-fact subject in the British empire, there is one who, in anticipation of her Majesty's coronation, will not be glad to learn how these ceremonial pageants have heretofore been conducted, and to be informed of the novelties recommended by any such competent person as our author, or of those which are likely to be introduced. There is not a native of England at this moment, we dare to affirm, who would be a party to such a transaction as is recorded of some of the Puritans in the

disposal and mockery of the ceremonial paraphernalia of Edward the
Confessor, as described in the following passage :—

"In an iron chest in Westminster Abbey, the Parliament Commissioners found—

One crimson taffety robe, very old, valued at £0 10 0
One robe, laced with gold lace, valued at 0 10 0
One liver cull^d (coloured) silk robe, very old, and worth
    nothing.
One robe of crimson taffety sarcenett, valued at 0 5 0
One pair of buskins, cloth of silver, and silver stockings,
    very old, valued at 0 2 6
One pair of shoes of cloth of gould, at................. 0 1 0
One pair of gloves, embroidered with gould, at 0 1 0

The whole wardrobe of the sainted monarch estimated at the sum of
thirty shillings and sixpence.

"On the 3rd of June 1643, Henry Marten, afterwards the notorious
regicide, had forced open the chest, and taken out the crown, sceptres,
robes, &c. of Edward the Confessor, and invested the Puritan poet and
satirist George Withers; who, says Wood (in his *Ath. Oxon.* vol. iii.,)
'being crowned and royally arrayed, did march about the room with a
stately garb, and afterwards, with a thousand apish and ridiculous actions,
exposed those sacred ornaments to contempt and laughter.' They were
a second time dragged out by some soldiers of Westbourne's company in
July the same year, and finally sold or destroyed in 1649, as before mentioned."

Mr. Planché is deeply learned in those antiquarian branches to
which his present compact, neatly illustrated and embellished volume
is devoted. He is well known as the author of a succinct and accurate work on the "History of British Costume;" and his "Regal Records" are not only at this moment opportune and calculated
to excite a temporary interest, but they form a suitable companion
to the earlier publication mentioned. Besides, though the coronation
ceremonials of our Kings have found not only chroniclers but recent
historians, a remarkable want of gallantry has been evinced in regard
to our Queens Regnant, none of them until now having obtained a
popular describer. At last, however, the pleasant duty has fallen
into excellent hands; for while Mr. Planché has bestowed praiseworthy industry in gathering from by-gone records and ephemeral
documents every thing that could throw light upon the subjects under
his consideration, he has with good effect brought his previous studies
and individual knowledge to help himself out, the result being, as
already intimated, a volume of no ordinary interest, in an antiquarian or temporary point of view.

Our author has been able to produce a minute account of Mary's
coronation, derived from contemporary writers as well as from official
documents. And yet there is an extraordinary discrepancy among

these authorities upon certain points of the ceremonial in regard to this sovereign of unpopular memory. For example, Stryps, in speaking of her progress through the city, says that she sat " in a chariot of cloth tissue drawn with six horses all trapped with the like cloth of tissue;" the French Ambassador, M. De Noailles, however, describes the vehicle as " a litter covered with a canopy of gold, and borne by *two mules*." Elizabeth's coronation has been detailed in various publications, from which Mr. Planché has drawn his abridged account; while Anne's, which at present becomes particularly curious as forming, most probably, the precedent to be chiefly observed on the approaching heraldic solemnity, has been gathered from the Herald's College, from the London Gazette, a Harleian MS., and a MS. presented by Miss Banks. It is to the particulars of this latter ceremonial display that we naturally have recourse for extracts, the parade and formalities observed in Westminster Hall claiming our earliest attention.

In the description of the entrance scene, an enumeration of the great officers of state being given, we are then told that —

" The Queen's Majesty with a circle of gold on her head set with diamonds, her train borne by the Duchess of Somerset, assisted by four ladies of the bed-chamber, and the Lord Chamberlain, proceeded through the court, and passed directly to the throne at the upper end of the hall, where her Majesty seated herself in her chair of state under the canopy on the side of the table, where was provided a chair, cushion, and footstool, and a long table covered with a rich carpet; some of the great officers placed themselves on her Majesty's right and left hand, and the Lord Great Chamberlain, Lord High Constable, and Earl Marshal, stood on the outside of the table opposite to the Queen. The Queen being seated on her throne, and the great officers standing on each side her Majesty (except the Earl Marshal, the Lord Great Chamberlain, and the Lord High Constable, who placed themselves on the outside of the table before her Majesty to receive the regalia). The Master of the Jewel House, attending with the other officers there, with the regalia in his custody, first presents the sword of state in a rich scabbard, with girdle and hangers, to the Lord High Constable, and he to the Lord Great Chamberlain, who laid it on the table before the Queen; next the sword called curtana; then the pointed sword; and lastly, the third sword; which three last being presented in like manner as the sword of state, one after another, were drawn out of the scabbard by the Lord Great Chamberlain, and laid, also, on the table. In like manner, the Master of the Jewel House presented the gold spurs to the Lord High Constable, and he to the Lord Great Chamberlain, and laid, also, on the table."

It is probable that this part of the ceremony will be dispensed with; nor, if it should take place, can we perceive the propriety of exhibiting so many swords as glittered before Anne. We shall afterwards see that such weapons of war and offence constituted grotesquely enough a portion of a female sovereign's baubles. One

formality observed on Anne's coronation is sure to be left out, viz.,
the introduction of the Dukes of Aquitaine and Normandy as
feudatories to the English crown. It must not however be supposed
that these identical personages did homage for any provinces in
France even at the period mentioned; but this vain and boastful
part of the heraldic and feudal ceremony, was performed we doubt
not, with sufficient gravity, by " Sir Jas. Clark and Jonathan
Andrews, gentlemen of the Privy Chamber, to represent them,"
(the Dukes); still these state worthies were dressed " in crimson
velvet mantles, lined with miniver, powdered with ermine; each of
them his cap in his hand of cloth of gold, furred and powdered with
ermine."

We must now go to the Abbey from the Hall, the procession
being " through the New Palace Yard into King Street," and
afterwards—

" Along the broad sanctuary into the west door of the Abbey Church,
all the way being covered from the steps of the throne into the Hall to the
steps of the theatre in the church with two breadths of blue broad cloth
spread upon boards railed in on both sides, and strewed with sweet herbs
and flowers, and guarded by several parties of her majesty's horse and foot
guards; the drums beat a march, the trumpets sounded, and the choir of
Westminster sung an anthem from the Hall to the church."

Many were and many have been ever since on similar occasions,
the ceremonies performed in the Abbey. The sermon preached
was by the Archbishop of York upon these remarkable words from
Isaiah, " kings shall be thy nursing fathers, and queens thy nursing
mothers." In the declaration and oath which followed occurred this
question and answer :—

" *Archbishop.* Will you to the utmost of your power maintain the laws of
God, the true profession of the gospel, and the Protestant reformed religion,
established by law; and will you preserve unto the bishops and clergy of
this realm, and to the churches committed to their charge, all such rights and
privileges as by law do or shall appertain to them or any of them ?—*Queen.*
All this I promise to do."

A number of symbolic forms we pass over ; but as we promised
something more about swords, let us see how they were handled and
applied on the solemnity described. Having been informed that
" the lord who carries the sword of state, returning the said sword
to ye Officers of the Jewel House, which is thereupon deposited in
the traverse in King Edward's Chapel ; he receiveth thence, in lieu
thereof, another sword, in a scabbard of purple velvet, provided for
the Queen,"—we are afterwards told how the weapon comes to be
used—

" The queen standing up, the sword is girt about her by the Lord Great

Chamberlain, or some other peer thereto by her appointed; and then the queen sitting down, the archbishop saith :—' Remember him of whom the royal Psalmist did prophesy, saying, Gird thee with thy sword upon thy thigh, O thou most mighty! Good luck have thou with thine honour. Ride on prosperously because of truth, meekness, and righteousness. Be thou follower of him. With this sword do justice. Stop the growth of iniquity, protect the holy church of God, help and defend widows and orphans, restore the things that are gone to decay, maintain the things that are restored, punish and reform what is amiss, and confirm what is in good order, that doing these things you may be glorious in all virtues, and so represent our Lord Jesus Christ in this life, that you may reign for ever with him in the life to come: Amen.' Then the queen, rising up, ungirds her sword, and going to the altar offers it there in the scabbard, and then returns and sits down in her chair; and the chief peer, or he to whom her majesty shall vouchsafe that honour, offereth the price of it (silicet 100 shillings), and having thus redeemed it, receiveth it from the altar by the Dean of Westminster, draweth it out of the scabbard and carrieth it naked before her majesty during the rest of the solemnity."

Anne's ministers had the delicacy not to put on the spurs, but the dignitaries of the church and the peers did homage, some according to privilege saluting the cheek, others the hand. We understand there has been considerable discussion about the manner and propriety of one form of this part of the ceremany, so symbolic of affection and devotion, in regard to the approaching solemnity. The Marquess of Londonderry, we presume, will for one stand up for the ancient privileges in their most endearing shape, and who can blame him?

One portion of the ceremony in Anne's case is worthy of being followed in all time coming, and must ever meet with favour in the eyes of John Bull; we mean the right sumptuous banquet which took place in the Hall.

"Her majesty, having washed, seated herself in her chair of state at the table, and then the hot meat was brought up in this manner, two of her majesty's women sitting at her feet. The lord the sewer, with the lord his assistant, went to the dresser of the kitchen, where the master of the horse to her majesty, as sergeant of the silver scullery, called for a dish of meat, wiped the bottom of the dish. and likewise the cover within and without, took assay of that dish, and covered it, then delivered that dish and the rest of the hot meat to the gentlemen pensioners, who carried it to the queen's table."

Before sitting down to the feast her Majesty underwent a considerable change in regard to her vestments, for she was " within her traverse disrobed by the Great Chamberlain, &c. of her royal robes of state, which were forthwith delivered to the Dean of Westminster," they being, we presume, a most cumbrous load ; and " again she was arrayed with her robes of purple velvet furred

with ermine, which were worn the rest of that day." Certain forms
having been gone through,

"Then the dishes of hot meat were carried up by the gentlemen pensioners,
bareheaded, and placed on the table by the lord carver, with the help of the
lord the sewer and his assistant. Then the mess of dillygrout was brought
up to the queen's table by Mr. Leigh, in right of his claim as lord of the
manor of Addington, in Surrey, who was knighted that day. Then the
two clerks of the kitchen, in black-figured satin gowns and black velvet
caps."

Prince George of Denmark dined at the queen's table, and, as
Parliament was sitting, the Commons were entertained in the
Exchequer Chamber ; but we need not enumerate the number, the
quality, and the disposal of the guests. Suffice it to say, that all
things were " performed with great splendour and magnificence
(not greater it may be surmised than at the coronation of George
IV.) ; about half an hour past eight in the evening, her Majesty
returned to St. James's," having come from the same place so early
as eleven o'clock in the morning, privately however. The day concluded with bonfires, illuminations, and " other demonstrations of a
general satisfaction and joy."

Mr. Planché's account of the crown, the coronation-chair, and other
items of the regalia is curious and minutely precise. The figures
introduced help to complete the picture of these things ; and from
these figures we should say, that of all the various forms of the
crown the more modern are the most clumsy and tasteless.

The suggestions which our author throws out with regard to the
alterations and innovations which might judiciously be adopted in
Victoria's case, we think are in good keeping with the circumstances
of the present reign, some of them having precedents for their
authority. We learn, for instance, that Mary and her sister
Elizabeth both made a progress through the city from the Tower to
the Palace at Westminster, having lodged in the Tower on the
night preceding. It seems that the occupation of the Tower is
deemed a testimony of sovereignty. Yet how many royal persons
have found the fortress a prison, and the immediate stage to the
scaffold ! Charles the Second also followed the same course on his
coronation, having restored this part of the pageant after it had been
discontinued by his immediate predecessors, with the view of adding
pomp and celebrity to the restoration. Since his time, however, the
formality has again been neglected ; but Mr. Planché appears to
think that it ought to be re-introduced, and, as our youthful Queen
is an enthusiastic and expert horsewoman, that the progress, instead
of being in a " chariot" or a " litter," like her's of *bloody* notoriety,
a cavalcade would be greatly relished by the people and beautifully
picturesque.

Another suggestion is, that the arms of the principality of Wales, instead of the repetition of those of England, in the fourth quarter, would not only improve the appearance of the shield, but be a gratifying compliment to a most loyal and deserving nation. Mr. Planché proceeds,—

"Another word whilst upon the subject of Wales. The Guelphic order being an Hanoverian decoration, and, consequently, no longer at the disposal of the sovereign of Great Britain, it has been rumoured that her majesty will probably institute some new order of knighthood in its place. In such a case we would most humbly recommend to her majesty's gracious consideration the claims of a British saint and champion, who has been sadly overlooked. Here have we Saint George and ' the most noble order of the Garter' for England ; St. Andrew and ' the most ancient order of the Thistle' for Scotland ; and St. Patrick with his ' most illustrious order' for Ireland : but Wales, the fourth gem of the British crown—that gives a title to its heir—that gave a title to the Black Prince—the land of Arthur and Lewellyn, the country of the bards, the soil of the royal tree of Tudor —has not only been excluded from representation in the arms of every British sovereign save Elizabeth, but her patron saint has been denied the honours of chivalric fellowship, which have been lavished on every other holy and renowned champion of Christendom."

Supposing it probable or possible that her Majesty may be advised to create a new order upon her coronation, and to institute a new decoration,— a species of legion of honour,—our author seems also to contemplate, that, instead of the burden and expense of knighthood, some symbol and rank might be conferred on persons who may distinguish themselves greatly, and which would be highly prized. Thus, whether in science, art, or literature, eminence might be honourably marked, and a cheap method of rewarding merit effectually sustained. But whatever may be the measures adopted to add *éclat* to the approaching coronation, there can be no doubt of its being a gorgeous and splendid pageant, and, what is better, of its affording to an empire a day for testifying the height of unalloyed joy and congratulation.

ART. X.—*Narrative of a Voyage round the World.* By W. S. W. RUSCHENBERGER, M.D. London : Bentley. 1838.

A VOYAGE round the world is not such a formidable enterprize now-a-days as it was a century or three-quarters of a century ago. But what may we expect it to be, some ten or twenty-five years hence, when steam-power by high pressure, or by other improvements and refinements, is carried so far beyond all which railroad and paddle-machinery has yet accomplished, as even to outstrip the prophetic vision of a Watt ! Steam-power ! What of that ? Do we not find that Mr. Monck Mason has lately in his " Aeronautica, or Sketches Illustrative of the Theory and Practice of Aerostation," drawing his arguments in a great measure from his excursion to Germany in the monster balloon, promulgated the doctrine that three days might suffice to effect the passage of the Atlantic? " The very circumference of the globe," says he, " is not beyond the scope of his expectations ; in fifteen days and fifteen nights, transported by the trade-winds, he does not despair to accomplish in his progress the great circle of the earth itself." It is not for us, after the extraordinary experience of the conjecturalist to utter a word about any old-fashioned understanding of physical laws, but merely to turn to that which has been done, and to extract from the experience of experimentalists some of the results which appear most novel or most deserving of notice. In accordance with this principle, we now call the attention of our readers to a circumnavigatory work by brother Jonathan, who, in a variety of respects, proves himself to be a legitimate descendant of the Anglo-Saxon family.

Of the Anglo-Saxon family, we say; and if we are not greatly mistaken, the Yankees are, we are sure they ought to be, proud of our progenitorship in maritime as well as naval enterprize and exploits. No doubt there has been much boasting about the *build* of their ships, the beauty of their sea-faring architectural materials, and their far-sightedness, their energy, and dexterity in enlarging and maintaining mercantile activity with the most civilized and the most remote nations of the world. And who dare deny their right to self-gratulation on this point, unless when it is urged in disparagement or in despite of Old England ?—for then the boast comparatively is far more theoretical and presumptive than real ; and when brought to the test of experience and fact is found to be reduced to this, that the Americans of the United States are no more than legitimate and worthy descendants of the greatest maritime people which the world ever saw.

It is true that the author of the present volume, exhibiting a good deal of the acuteness, and cherishing the opinionativeness of his countrymen, would have his readers to believe that no race can cope with the Americans as sagacious adventurers, and successful diplomatists, where half-civilized or savage nations are to be negotiated with. We find, for instance, that he says, that the commerce of Zanzibar is very considerable, and that it is destined to increase. That " the Americans obtain here gum copal, ivory, and hides, for which they give American cottons and specie. The American cotton manufactures have taken precedence of the English, not only at this place and in many parts of the East, but on the Pacific Coast of America." He continues,—" The English endeavour to imitate our fabric, by stamping their own with American marks, and by other means assimilating it ; but the people say the strength and wear of the American goods are so superior, that, lest they be deceived, they will no longer even purchase from Englishmen."

How much truth there may be in this particular instance and

statement, it is not for us to say. But taking the facts to be as described, it is worthy of remark, that, while Great Britain is assuredly extending by a steady progress her commerce, her merchants look to established outlets, rather than risk their vast capitals and high-minded intercourse rashly with new and unsystematized correspondents; whereas the disposition and the necessity on the part of our transatlantic brethren lead them to enter, generally speaking, upon a cheaper, a less secure, and latterly a less profitable intercourse, with all their showy advantages and numerical triumphs; the fact is, that America cannot, upon the whole, compete as a mercantile nation with Great Britain.

Then as to science, Dr. Ruschenberger must not measure lines with the generality of European or English navigators; no, not even with the functionaries who act under the conductors of maritime, commercial, or diplomatic expeditions. What is to be thought of an M. D. as a natural philosopher, who could swallow such a fanciful story as the following?

"On this occasion, Commodore Kennedy stated he had been once, for ten days, in so complete a calm, that the animalculæ died, and the ocean exhaled from its bosom on all sides a most insufferable stench. Instances of this kind illustrate the utility and necessity of winds and the agitation of the seas: absolute calms, continued for any considerable period, in the wind or waves, would prove equally fatal to all manner of animal life. The respiration of all animals, whether this function be carried on by lungs or gills, or other organs, is essential to their being. Those living on land breathe the atmosphere, and rob it, at each inspiration, of a portion of oxygen, which principle is necessary to existence; those inhabiting the deep derive the same principle from the waters, though by different means; and in both cases, the air, or water, thus deprived of its vital principle, must be replaced by fresh supplies, or in a very short time all the oxygen in their vicinity is exhausted, and the animals, whether of sea or land, must perish."

Is there nothing else to preserve the great deep from corruption, but the winds which ruffle its face? We have always understood that salt is an excellent means for doing so. And does our author think, that if the breeze never stirred and the waves were imperceptible to human vision there would be no tidal motion, no currents, no chemical depositions and decompositions to preserve the ocean from completely stagnating and becoming putrid, so as to poison the animalculæ whose element it is? And certainly this is the first time that we ever heard that there was any danger in the air or the water being robbed of their vital principle by the number of breathers that exist, except for the winds. Our author falls into other mistakes by going beyond his depth, which we need not anxiously ferret out; our desire being to set before our readers some of the most curious and novel particulars in the work, which, upon the whole, contains a plain and straight-forward narrative, bearing marks everywhere, too, of shrewdness as well as of keen observation.

The full title of these volumes states that they contain the Narrative of a Voyage which took place " during the years 1835, 1836, 1837 ; including a Narrative of an Embassy to the Sultan of Muskat and the King of Siam," the author being surgeon to the expedition.   He thus enjoyed opportunities and facilities of observation, which in ordinary cases are not within the reach of navigators.   The purpose of the mission was to negotiate commercial treaties with the Sultan above mentioned, and also with the courts of Siam and Cochin-China.   Success has attended the American negotiations with the two former ; but the Envoy's bad state of health, the jealousies of the Cochin-Chinese, and some other unforeseen circumstances, prevented the completion of any treaty with them in the meantime.

It was the *Peacock* sloop of war to which our surgeon was attached, which proceeded directly to Arabia, to Zanzibar, where it was conjectured the Sultan of Muskat was residing at the time, a place which is acquiring no inconsiderable importance in a commercial and political point of view, and which is likely to become the capital of its present ruler's dominions.   We must refer our readers, however, who are curious about diplomacy and the mercantile relations of this country as well as of America with the Sultan and his subjects, to the Narrative itself ; counselling them, at the same time, not to take the Doctor's view of every point as correct, and also to bear in mind that the administrators of British affairs in India are not likely to submit to any treaty with their allies and friendly neighbours in the eastern seas, that is disadvantageous to themselves. We hasten forward to Siam, and, stopping at Bankok, quote an extraordinary account of a human fish.

" The better sort of sampan is a light canoe, moved by half a dozen or more short paddles, with a covered cabin in the centre, upon the floor of which the passenger reclines, and, by drawing the curtains, may be entirely concealed.   Some are so small, that we are astonished they are capable of floating under the weight of a man, and others again are propelled like the Venetian gondola by a single oar, managed in a row-lock three feet high.   The sampan of this description is usually sculled by a woman standing on the stern, without any other garment than a pair of drawers, with the occasional addition of a piece of black crape cast over the shoulders.   The body is gently bent forward over the oar, and, to obtain a firm footing, one foot is placed in advance of the other, while the arms, in easy motion, impart speed to the vessel.   The attitude and movement of these figures are eminently graceful, as they are seen threading their way through the mazes of junks and sampans of all sizes, which are all day gliding along from point to point, in every direction, and always occupying a very small space.   The sampans are admirably adapted to the navigation of the canals and river, as we soon discovered, when one of our long-oared boats moved among them. They were often upset by us; but the Siamese always took the mishap in gentleness of spirit, and very quietly swam either to the shore, or to regain the sampan. Living so constantly on the water, they may be said to be a swimming people, though I am told they have a great dread of the sea. They are seen bathing at all times of the day, either swimming, or squatted on the veranda in front of the houses, dipping water out of the river with a basin, and pouring it over themselves. Not along ago, Bankok presented the singular phenomenon of an amphibious infant, that forsook the mother's breast, and betook itself to the water on all occasions. Luck-loi-nam, literally the child of the waters, swam when she was but one year old; and, in 1832, when she had attained three years of age, was frequently seen swimming in the river. Her motions were not like those of other swimmers; she floated without any apparent exertion, turning round and round. When not in the water, she was cross and discontented, and, when taken out, cried, and strove to return; if indulged, she tumbled and rolled about, seemingly with unalloyed pleasure. Luck-loi-nam, though well-formed, could neither walk nor speak, but uttered a gurgling, choking sound in the throat. Her vision was imperfect; and, up to the time mentioned, she had never eaten any thing but her mother's milk."

It is farther stated that the child usually applied to the breast, on being taken out of the river, of her own consent; that the mother was a fine-looking woman, and that a sister of the child, a girl of eight or nine years of age, was always seen swimming in company to protect the infant of the waters against accidents.

The account of the royal family of Siam, and some of their customs, is curious and in no slight degree amusing. We select some particulars from this part of the book.

" The morning after our arrival, we visited his Highness the Prince Momfanoi, literally, ' Prince of Heaven, junior.' He is also called Chawfanoi, the ultimate syllable signifying the younger. He is half brother to the king, and in truth, rightful heir to the throne, which, on the late king's death, his present magnificent majesty usurped, and afterwards proposed to create Chawfaya, the elder brother of the prince and legitimate successor, second king. This proposal, however, was scorned by him; and declaring that he would never bend to, nor do homage to the usurper, he assumed the yellow robe of the Talapoins for life. By this means he is enabled to keep his word, because they are excused from all the slavish ceremonies of Siamese etiquette, and, in the presence of the higher grades, the king himself appears upon his elbows and knees. On the refusal of Chawfaya, an uncle of the reigning monarch was appointed second king; but since his death, which occurred about three years since, no successor has been named to this office, and it is asserted that his majesty will not make another second king, because he is entitled, according to Siamese custom, to one-third of the revenue of the empire. Chawfaya leads a very holy life, measured by the Siamese criterion of sanctity, and enjoys a rank equal to that of a bishop. His assumption of the yellow robe a second time, makes Momfanoi the legitimate heir; but his accession to the throne

is not absolutely certain. The king has the power of naming his successor
from among his lawful heirs. The reigning monarch, though he possesses
more than three hundred wives, has no children living legitimate enough
to wear the crown; and since the death of his lawful son, Prince Momfanoi, has ' crept into favour,' and rumour states that he is about being
affianced to his magnificent majesty's favourite daughter, notwithstanding
.that he has already nine wives."

  · If this alliance takes place, no doubt is entertained of his succeeding to the throne. Besides, he is extremely popular, and full
of enterprize and military spirit. He is not only, according to the
present account, one of nature's princes, but he seems to be a jack
of all trades, as well as a master in his own country of a variety of
refined arts.

  The Americans, after having been visited by the Prince, returned
the compliment on board of his own barque, and their welcome was
hearty. The size of the vessel is about two hundred tons, and somewhat after the European fashion. The Prince was fitting her out with
the aid of three English sailors. The strangers found him upon this
occasion wearing nothing but a sort of heavy silk waist-cloth. He
offered tea and cigars. His attendants, who appeared to be on a familiar footing with him, were resting on their elbows and knees around
him. Every thing was going on actively in the vessel, the workmen
being generally seated on the deck. Momfanoi himself took the gouge
from the hands of a mechanic, and, squatting down, began to apply
it with skill. In the meanwhile a shout as if from a hundred voices
was heard, raised in a long canoe-like boat, and where a hundred
oars were plied, the rowers standing behind the oars, loudly marking
time with the right foot, " while one stood in the bows, striking
two pieces of bamboo, as a guide to their simultaneous efforts."
The boat and crew belonged to the Prince, who thus exercised them
daily, several thousands, besides, being thus regularly trained.

  Though Momfanoi is thus shown to delight in warlike affairs, he
loses no opportunity of acquiring general knowledge. On one occasion he was very particular in having explained to him the object of
lightning-rods in ships, and the day afterwards his armourer was
busy at work making one for his vessel. The name of his barque
is " Royal Adelaide ;" and with his own hand, he has painted the
words, in English characters, on a rack for small arms, at the after-
hatch. His taste for painting is displayed frequently. In fact he
exercises himself in the art of drawing. The account of a visit to
the Prince's palace must not be curtailed.

  " The walls are snowy white and surmounted by embrasures for guns.
We accompanied the prince on shore, and, as we walked to the palace gate,
every native we met fell on his face till Momfanoi had passed. Within
the walls we found, every where, evidence of the master's tastes. A number of people, male and female, were at work, some twisting, or 'laying-

up,' rope, and others at various other occupations. Several of both sexes had chains on the arms and legs, and their naked backs bore recent marks of bamboo. It was the first time I had seen women in chains, and I felt a sudden recoil of mind at the sight of mingled disgust and pity, and perhaps a desire that they should be at once free; but, on reflection, I suppose it was correct, for they are not of the same comparative feebleness of body as in Christian lands. Before entering his dwelling, Momfanoi led us to see his pets; a large baboon, half a dozen beautiful deer, a pair of large black bears from Borneo, with a white stripe over the fore part of each shoulder; these were tame and playful: a large cassowary from New Holland, so tame as to eat from one's hand, was running about at liberty. He now called our attention to a variety of parrots and krokotoas, in the corridor or veranda, surrounding the house; and then led us to his stables to see his fine stud of horses, and thence, to look at several storks, jungle fowls in cages, and half a dozen asses and monkeys. He had ordered three or four alligators to be brought from beneath the stable, in the mean time, and their jaws to be secured, that we might examine them without risk. In another part of the court, or area, were field-pieces, and guns of various kinds and calibre, ships, spars, &c., neatly arranged beneath a shed. He had numerous questions to ask about every thing he exhibited, and was never satisfied till he felt sure that he clearly understood the answers which were given to him. He now led us into the house, saying, ' Gentlemen, you are welcome—I am glad to see you.' The interior is lofty, though but of one story, and is divided into three apartments by two screens, which do not reach the ceiling. The centre apartment was furnished in the Anglo-Asiatic style, and as neatly as any house I have seen in India. On a table near a sofa, at one end of this drawing-room, were violins, flutes, and a flageolet, upon which instruments his highness performs. The adjoining apartment was fitted as a study, furnished with a small collection of English books, a fine barometer, &c. A small room, communicating with it, is arranged as a private museum; in which there are many fine specimens of natural history—quadrupeds, birds, reptiles, &c., all preserved and set up by himself."

Truly Momfanoi is the prince of princes, and gains prodigiously on the reader as the author proceeds. Let us see him at table, and have a sample of barbaric display and etiquette. After some music, says the author—

" When we took leave, he detained some of us to dinner; and, in the mean time, entertained the company by shewing them several Siamese curiosities, and conversing on all subjects. About three o'clock P.M., the table was spread in the Anglo-Asiatic style,—a mixture of English comfort and Eastern display; the dinner was remarkable for the variety and exquisite flavour of the curries. Among them was one consisting of ants' eggs, a costly and much-esteemed luxury of Siam. They are not larger than grains of sand, and, to a palate unaccustomed to them, are not particularly savoury—they are almost tasteless. Besides being curried they are brought to table rolled in green leaves, mingled with shreds or very fine slices of fat pork. Here was to be seen an ever-to-be-remembered luxury of the East. Two slaves stood waving fans behind the Prince's chair, and many other attendants were crouched upon elbows and knees around the room, to whom he occasionally translated such parts of the conversation as he thought would interest them. While he thus sat conversing cheerfully, circulating his choice wines, accurately cooled, and entertaining his guests, a slave was crouched beneath the tables busily occupied in scratching his highness's naked shins."

In the event of Momfanoi ascending the throne, it will naturally be expected from the above notices that great reforms will take place in Siam, industrial, mercantile, and educational. Our author anticipates beneficial results in regard to Christianity, and that the American Missionaries will experience them. Indeed, though there should be nothing more done than the impulse which the Prince's example will lend, the hope is not too sanguine which looks forward to important changes for the better. Even at present, however, in as far as regards Missionary labours, Siam furnishes a deeply interesting field. We know not what the disciples of Phrenology, depending upon the light of their so-called science, will read concerning futurity from the Doctor's account of the Siamese skulls and organs ; but novices and enthusiasts as regards this modern doctrine will find him an earnest manipulator, whose discoveries may perhaps afford grounds for important speculations. It is stated that their skulls are small and of a vertical shape in the occipital region, resembling some of the ancient Peruvians from Pachacamac. In both also, it would appear, that the lateral halves of the cranium violate, to a singular extent, the laws of symmetrical proportion. This is not the first circumstance which we have heard mentioned to disprove the doctrine that separate species of the human family inhabit different and widely divided parts of the earth.

The Siamese, like all rude and uncivilized nations, are superstitious, but in a characteristic manner. Without referring to a belief in ghosts, witchcraft, lucky and unlucky days, their credulity takes the shape of a reliance upon conjuration. For instance, in the case of theft, the potent wielder of charms and the dictator of ordeals is summoned for the detection of the offender. A person having lost from his apartment two bars of gold, the following method of trial was adopted.

" Immediately on missing them, all those persons suspected of the theft were called together, and a conjuror summoned to declare who was the guilty individual. He came provided with several square bars of a metallic appearance, six or seven inches long. and thick as the little finger, which on examination proved to be of a species of clay. He charged each person with the theft, and asked individually whether any among them knew any thing of the gold, and was answered in the negative. He then lighted a small wax candle, and stuck upon each side of it a tical, obtained from the man who had lost the gold, and muttering an invocation or spell, took a piece of clay, and three times very ceremoniously raised it above his head. Then, measuring it very carefully by the little finger, he broke it into pieces an inch and a half long, and gave to each suspected person three of them, which they were directed to chew as fast as possible, and prove their innocence by spitting, when the mastication was complete. All set to work chewing, and soon all were trying to spit; and, as upon the success of the effort depends the innocence or guilt of the accused, in the opinion of the Siamese, the scene may be readily imagined. In this case there were ten attempting to spit: and, at last, after much labour, all succeded, except a girl of fifteen, who was finally pronounced guilty; and the conjuror, with the candle and ticâls, walked off in triumph. The test by clay is so much in favour, that, upon this ordeal alone, persons are often heavily ironed, and daily flogged, until they confess, or the stolen property be returned. In the present instance, the poor girl received only a promise of such treatment, and probably owes her escape altogether to the proverbial faithlessness of the Siamese to their words."

It is not to be expected that the drama in Siam can have many attractions for civilized and educated spectators. Much of the performance, according to Dr. Ruschenberger's account, consists in dancing, knocking of heads against one another, and other Grimaldi-like gestures. One half of the actors, in the piece witnessed by our author, appeared to be females; yet, as once was the case in countries of greater pretensions, the whole were males. Long nails must be fashionable and regarded as a beauty among the Siamese if their stage offers an index of national taste; for those of the *actresses* on the occasion described, " were elongated and turned backwards, by metal appendages, at least three inches in length." Theatricals at any rate are in great repute, for most of the wealthy nobles entertain a company of players and have a stage in their private dwellings.

Take the account of a grand procession.

" A band of a dozen men, in red and green uniforms, their cheeks swelled by their efforts, marched onward, closely followed by seven elephants. First came a huge black, fourteen feet high, then a large white, followed by another much smaller, and four spotted elephants of ordinary size. By the side of each walked a keeper, and several slaves bearing silver salvers, loaded with peeled sugar-cane and luscious bananas. The driver sat on the neck of each, in front of the houdah, or saddle-cloth, which was gold. Broad hoops of gold embraced each lusty leg, and jewelled rings glittered on the tusks of the white elephants; and from the ears of all of them were suspended tails of beautifully white hair. The pageant wheeled round and halted on one side of the hall of justice. The slaves now set down their salvers before their respective elephants, and we were invited to admire and feed the animals, the possession of which, in the opinion of the Siamese, gives their king pre-eminence above every other monarch in the East. The small elephant is the beauty of her race. She has a soft white skin, a beautiful chestnut-coloured eye, and a most complaisant manner of disposing of sugar-cane and bananas from the hand of the stranger. The other white elephant is a very much larger animal; but the skin is of a yellowish hue. Both are supposed to be animated by the transmigrated souls of Siamese monarchs. The spotted elephants are all large. With the exception of the ears and shoulders, which are speckled rather than spotted, their colour is dark and uniform. The forehead of each animal is painted black, the outline of which is white, and traces the form of a headcloth. The careful keeping and strict attention bestowed on these elephants shew how highly they are prized. The minute examination and admiration of our party gave visible satisfaction to the keepers, as well as to the crouching multitude around."

How different are the modes of estimating or displaying rank and wealth? Some regard simplicity, others imposing forms, as the surest tests of greatness. Luxuries, too, are interpreted precisely as taste fancies. We have seen that scratching the shins was alone enjoyed by one and the head of a party while feasting themselves. And we are farther informed, that, instead of looking at the dress of a Siamese to ascertain his eminence in general society, it is necessary to scan the slave who follows him, who bears upon a tray the badge or symbol of his master's rank. " Tea-kettles of gold and silver, plain or ornamented, are patents of the highest grades of nobility, and are presented by the king as commissions of office." But if the dress of a native of Siam does not indicate his status in the community, the king's majesty appears to be maintained by much more formality of speech, than can always be convenient. When he chooses to put any questions, it is stated that—

" The secretary makes three salams, and mentions the king's titles before he repeats to the second, and he goes through the same ceremony to the third. The answer begins with three salams from the interpreter, who repeats a string of titles, 'P'hra, Putie, Chucka, Ka, Rap, Si, Klau, Si, Kla, Mom, Kà P'rah Putie Chow,' Mr. Roberts, ' Ka P'hra Râchâ, Tau, Krap, Thun, Hie, Sap, Thi, Fa, La, Ong, Thule, P'hra, Bat;' then follows the answer and three salams."

When we accompany the Doctor to Cochin-China, we find that other *criteria* of superiority, and other methods of exhibiting eminent rank, exist. The Doctor says—

" On the 17th, Cochin-Chinese officers, who visited us on the day of our arrival, came on board in a long canoe, pulling forty oars. They were seated in the bows, the place of honour with these people, under the shade of an umbrella; and on this occasion were accompanied by an individual who, besides Cochin-Chinese, spoke Malay. We had on board a Dutch passenger from Batavia, who spoke French and Malay ; and, thus armed, we held a much more satisfactory intercourse than we had done hitherto.

" They were received in the cabin, where they disposed of themselves as they did on their first visit. They inquired the respective rank of the officers present; but were unwilling to believe that Mr. Roberts was the Envoy, because he did not, like the Commodore and Captain, wear epaulettes. To this subject they frequently recurred, and did not appear to be satisfied in the end. This should be a hint to future diplomatists to Cochin-China, to adorn themselves with some glittering badge of distinction."

Mr. Roberts was the citizen who had charmed the American government with accounts and prospects of the vast field opened for enterprize in the Indian Archipelago, and was the Envoy empowered to carry into effect the objects of the Mission upon which the *Peacock* was engaged. From the following anecdote we gather, that he was worthy of being trusted with such important negotiations, at least if plausible expertness and off-hand readiness in the forms of foreign diplomacy may be regarded as a test. Having mentioned that the Cochin-Chinese are a polite people, and punctilious observers of etiquette, our author adds—

"At Vungham, the chief Mandarin questioned the propriety of one of his rank and numerous titles holding intercourse with Mr. Roberts, who came from a country where he understood there were no titles and all men were equal. Mr. Roberts, perceiving that, unless this objection were removed, all negotiation would be at an end, replied that the Mandarin had been in some measure misinformed. He told him if his Chinese secretary would take a piece of paper, he would enumerate his own titles, and convince him of his error. The secretary selected a half sheet of paper, but Mr. Roberts requested him to take a whole one, as that even would be scarcely large enough. The American officers present were of course at a loss to imagine how Mr. Roberts would extricate himself from this seeming difficulty. But not so Mr. Roberts. He dictated as follows:—' Edmund Roberts, Esquire, Special Envoy from the President of the United States to the Emperor of Cochin-China, Citizen of the United States, Citizen of Maine, Citizen of New Hampshire,' and continued enumerating himself citizen of each of the twenty-four States; for being citizen of all, he was so of them severally. Before the sheet was half full, the Mandarin exclaimed, it was unnecessary to go further, as his titles already exceeded his own. Had he not been satisfied, Mr. Roberts intended to enumerate as many of the cities, towns, and villages as he could remember, not doubting the success of this *ruse diplomatique.*"

It were to be wished that old England, with her hereditary monarchy and aristocratic distinctions, had always representatives equally clever in the application of high-sounding and multitudinous titles of honour. Our author, in giving a specimen of the Chinese mode of close reasoning, relates an anecdote in relation to the late Lord Napier, who was termed by them an " Eye"—the only word, it would seem, that these ingenious and shrewd people could find in their language equivalent to the term Superintendent.

"The British merchants were anxious to impress upon the Chinese that Lord Napier was a man of exalted rank, and consequently could not submit to the indignity of communicating with the Government through the medium of the Hong merchants. They told them he was a lord, a nobleman; which the Chinese, having no hereditary nobility except in the family of the Emperor, could not clearly comprehend. They remarked, He is a nobleman in your country; how many men are there of the same rank?' and were told, ' a great many, perhaps a thousand.'

"' Are there any people of higher rank ?'
"' Yes, Viscounts.'
"' Well; how many Viscounts have got ?'
" ' A great many.'
" ' Well; any of higher rank than Viscounts ?'
" ' Yes, Earls.'
"' Well; any more ?'
"' Yes, Marquises.'
"' Well; any more ?'
"' Yes, Dukes.'
"' Well; any higher than Dukes ?'
"' None except the King and Royal Family.'
"' Well, then, now me know; this Eye, Lord Napier, all the same as one common Mandarin !' "

Allusion has already been made to Dr. Ruschenberger's phreno-logical notices, and, we now add, that he seems not only to be an outrageous believer in the doctrines of the science, but that some of his alleged discoveries, by the exercise of his manipulating skill, have staggered us not a little. On several occasions he astonishes the people of the East, even the sagacious and jealous Chinese, both by his discoveries of what those who submitted to his examinations confessed to be the truth in their past history, and by predicting what was in the womb of futurity. He tells us, that—

" One wished to know whether a young man, who had just submitted his head to examination, might be safely trusted if sent into the country to collect money. Another asked, in relation to his clerk, ' Can me trust that man go Nankin for pigeon—buy silk—suppose he no stop talk with gal, and no make he pigeon ?' Another inquired if I could determine positively, by examining a married lady's head, whether her issue would be ' one gal or one bull child.' Being very anxious for the latter, and having offered up many prayers to the goddess Kuan-yin for a son, he was much disappointed to learn that the practical application of phrenology did not extend quite so far."

We are perfectly ready to let the Doctor prophesy as long as he chooses, and to let others repose what confidence they please in his powers; but when he comes deliberately to tell us, that he made many Chinese converts to the phrenological system, by the practical demonstration of its truth, we must hesitate; or, if at all brought to credit him to the fullest extent of his statement, we must suppose that, as in the case of some persons suffering under disease, it is impossible to enumerate the symptoms of any complaint which will not be, more or less, appropriated and believed to hold true in the immediate case, so, among the Chinese merchants, the nature of whose dealings and habits it could not be very difficult to learn, our author has exhibited his confidence in phrenology, and the results of his study of character, in a manner perfectly amazing to the patients, extracting from them all he wished to know.

Art. XI.—*The Shajrat ul Atrak; or, Genealogical Tree of the Turks and Tatars.* Translated and abridged by Col. Miles. London: Wm. H. Allen and Co. 1838.

Few pieces of Eastern literature have ever been popular in Europe, and least of all in England. The floridity of its style, and the extravagance of its imagery, so far surpassing what the candour of sentiment seems to demand in the estimation of minds which regard truth and intellectual strength as the noblest exhibitions, are considered as being opposed both to sound taste and derogatory to the honour of human nature. It does not readily occur to those who have imbibed, and still less to those who are fully alive to the purity and power of that literature which has been formed on the Greek models, that Oriental rule and an Oriental climate have begotten habits of thought and modes of expression quite natural and intelligible to the people of the countries in question ; and that what seems in the West the most defective in taste, and the farthest from sober wisdom, is in the East, and to the imperfectly developed minds there predominating, the picture of truth and beauty embodied.

The monstrous fables too which abound in Eastern mythology, have deeply and thickly infused language with extravagances and absurdities, which are tiresome and ridiculous to Europeans ; and the general conviction that the facts contained in their histories, are few, slight, and uncertain, is such that none but an Orientalist, or an enthusiastic student of Oriental literature, can ever think it worth his while to separate the gold from the dross. It is therefore no wonder that the nations of the West have seldom manifested sympathy with those of the East, and that, except for the reports of their barbaric pearl and gold, infinitely less would have been known of them, and far less cared for them, than as the matter in reality stands.

The present volume does not prove an exception to the general character of Oriental histories ; and yet we think that Colonel Miles has contributed by his translation and abridgment of the original, a curious and in some points of view a valuable addition to literature and recorded truth. The work purports to contain the genealogy of the Moghool race, written by command of Alugh Beg Mirza. Its merit, says the Colonel, "is said to consist chiefly in the details it gives of the life and conquests of Chungeez and his descendants." He continues—" I shall not presume to decide, but I, perhaps, may be allowed to say, as my opinion, that it contains, besides, many valuable historical documents." Now, although from our own knowledge, we dare not pronounce concerning the accuracy of this last opinion, yet there need be no hesitation in coming to the conclusion, that the traditions here collected, going back as they do to the earliest times in the history of the human family, and the date of the fabrication of many of them being very distant, throw a light not only upon the origin and growth of languages and of nations, but corroborate or bear manifest relation to the simple and marvellous records of Scripture in many particulars and on many occasions. The candid and reflecting reader of this genealogical history cannot for a moment suppose, had the Holy Scriptures never existed, that the present traditions could ever have been framed and preserved from century to century ; he cannot for a moment believe that had the Scriptures not contained marvellous truths that the distortions here to be detected could ever have been invented. Two or three extracts will sufficiently exhibit the sort of relation subsisting between these traditions and the facts narrated in the Bible, monstrously overlaid as the latter frequently are. But we must first glance at the translator's notices concerning the Toorkish family.

Moghoolistan, or the territory of the Moghools, is described as a wide tract on the western frontier of China, extending, on a rough calculation, from the 30th degree of north latitude to about the 45th, and from the 100th degree of east longitude to the 128th. Now Zingis, or Chungeez Khan, as Colonel Miles has it, was a mighty conqueror in these and other regions ; and what is more, the existing dynasties reigning at Constantinople, Delhi, and Pekin, are descended from his tribe and family. Whence the confusion has arisen which occurs in the terms Tatar, Moghool, and Toork is not very clear ; " but it may be useful," says the Colonel, to state, that the Persian and European historians confound the two former, although by this history they are separate tribes, whereas, in their own country, they are all called Toork." Afterwards he says, " I believe, however, they will be found all Moghools, and, at the same time Toorks."

Having merely glanced at certain notices, which, coming from an Oriental scholar, and a keen researcher into Oriental antiquities, deserve consideration, we proceed to quote a few specimens of the book which he has placed before us in an abridged form ; nor can we do better than begin with the beginning.

" It has," says the historian of this Genealogical Tree, " reached us by tradition, that after the creation of the world, a period the length of which is only known to God and his prophets, God willed the creation from earth of Adam, and that he should be invested with the honorary dress of his lieutenancy : ' Of a truth I have appointed myself a lieutenant on the earth'—these words attest the verity of this ; and, consequently, the Angel Gabriel was sent to the earth, to collect a little moist mould, or clay, to form the pure body of Adam from that place on which the holy Kaaba now stands.

" When Gabriel arrived on the surface of the earth, and attempted to take a handful, the Earth adjured him, in the name of the Creator of the heavens and the angels, to desist ; for said the Earth, some unworthy creature may be formed of my clay, and, on his account, I may fall under the displeasure of the Almighty. Gabriel therefore returned and reported the adjuration and affliction of the Earth, and his pity on her, to the Almighty, who next appointed the angel Michael to this office. The

Earth, on his descent, renewed her complaints, and adjured him not to take any portion of her substance : he accordingly desisted and returned. God then directed the angel Israfeel to proceed ; but as the Earth still continued her adjurations, he also returned : and the fourth time Azrael* was sent. The Earth attempted to prevent Azrael from performing his office ; but he disregarded her adjurations, and said, the commands of the Most High are superior to thy oaths and imprecations. He then collected a handful of mould from every part of the earth, moist and dry, white and black, loose and bound, salt, sweet and sour. To the number of every individual of mankind he took a little earth ; and the grave of every one will be in the place whence he took the earth of which each was made."

As the historian proceeds we find the admixture of fable and revealed truth become more apparent. Thus, a handful of earth is said to have been taken to the garden of Eden by Azrael, and there moistened or kneaded with the waters of Tusnim. It serves a purpose no doubt to add, that " it was made known to all the angels and inhabitants of Paradise that the light of Mahummudanism was deposited with the waters of Tusnim in the clay of Adam, and also that the sole object in creating Adam was to provide for the future mission of Mahummud." After some conjectures about the derivation of the name of our great progenitor, the genealogist declares that all the angels acknowledged his intelligence and excellence, and bent the knee to him, except Iblis, " and he was of the genii." This invention has been considered necessary, we suppose, to account for the catastrophe that is next recorded in these words,

" God then placed Adam in the garden of Eden, and created Eve from his left side while he was between sleeping and waking. By many he is said to have been forbidden to eat wheat; by Abdalla, the son of Abas, grapes ; and by others figs. Iblis being cursed for refusing to kneel to Adam (' of a truth my curse shall be upon thee to the day of resurrection'), and seeing that for one crime he had forfeited all the merit of his former obedience, departed in mortal enmity to Adam, and determined to do him any injury in his power. Now Adam was in Paradise and Iblis could not enter there. At length, however, as is detailed in history and tradition, by art and the assistance of a peacock, stationed on the walls of Paradise as a sentinel, and a serpent, the guard at one of the gates, he did enter. After this, Iblis first deceived Eve, and made her eat of the forbidden fruit, and she induced Adam to eat also. As soon as they had done this, the heavenly covering fell from their bodies, and they became naked : they, therefore, took leaves of the figtree to hide their nakedness. These five individuals were then expelled Paradise by God's command. It is said that Adam and Eve were not suffered to remain more than three hours after their transgression ; also that, on Friday, the 5th or 9th of the month Nisau, at the seventh hour of the day, Adam descended or fell on a mountain of

---

* The angel of death.

Serindeep (Ceylon), in Hindostan: Eve descended at Judda, a town on the sea-side, near Mecca; the peacock fell in Hindostan; the serpent at Isfahan; and Iblis at Sumuan, or Sumnath. It is also related, that it was after Adam fell on the earth that his beard grew. He remained one hundred years in Serindeep, in prayer and great affliction; and from the tears he shed sprang up pepper, cardamums, cinnamon, &c., and those spices are benefits derived from him. After one hundred years had expired, on the Ashoora, or 10th Mohurrum, his repentance was accepted before God."

After Adam's fall, he was taught the blacksmith's trade, in order to forward his agricultural labours. He had forty-one children—twenty-one sons and twenty daughters. Seth was a weaver. From the whole sprang forty thousand families or tribes. But what of Cain and Abel, for it is not to be supposed that the genealogist's fables and mythos can pass over all mention of these brothers?

"When Cain and his twin-sister, Ikleema, were born, Cain, on account of her beauty, was desirous to possess her; Adam, however, gave her to Abel, and a quarrel arose between them in consequence. Adam, therefore, desired them to sacrifice to the Most High, and said he would give Ikleema to him whose sacrifice was accepted. They accordingly took each a goat to the top of a mountain, and fire from heaven consumed that of Abel; Adam, therefore, gave Ikleema to him. Cain, now entertaining a violent hatred to Abel, struck him on the head with a stone while he was asleep, and killed him. It is related that Cain, for a long time, not knowing what to do with the body of Abel, carried it about with him, till one day he arrived at a place where two ravens were fighting; and one being killed, the living one hid him beneath the earth—this taught Cain to bury his brother. Until this period Adam did not know what death was; but when he became aware of its nature he cried bitterly, and in his grief composed certain verses in the Syriac language; and the learned have translated them into the Arabic verses, 'Death will change and destroy cities and those governing them, and disfigure the face of the earth. It will change everything possessing colour or nourishment, and even the divine counte-nance is naught but corruption. Returned to me is my grief for my son Abel. He is slain, and is now enclosed in his narrow grave.'"

We do not notice any more of these distortions and inventions than that the Toorks or Moghools are all descended from a grand-son of Noah and son of Japhet.

That Chungeez Khan, of whom and his descendants this work purports chiefly to contain particulars, was a mighty warrior and terrible in battle, may be inferred from a tradition, among the Moghools, which is to this effect:—When a hundred thousand men are killed, one of the dead stands upright to denote that number; it is then mentioned that in a certain battle three men were found standing in this manner. The fables, however, which obscure to the ordinary reader even the details of comparatively modern history, are very abundant in the work before us; so that it would be imprudent were we to occupy much of our space with them. The death and sepulture of the dreadful monarch may be taken as an example.

Chungeez Khan, it is said, having addressed himself to his family, exhorting them to cherish brotherly love to one another—to keep his death secret—to put Shidurkoon to death whenever they might lay hold on him, closed his eyes and breathed his last. The narrative then proceeds thus :

" The family of Chungeez Khan observed his directions to keep his death secret so punctually, that, until the arrival of Shidurkoon to make his submission, no appearance whatever of mourning or sorrow was manifested in his court. When Shidurkoon left the city of Artakia, in the hope the assurances which had been given him by Chungeez Khan would be observed, the ameers and Noyauns who accompanied him treated him with every respect and attention, and pretended to escort him to meet Chungeez Khan ; when, however, they arrived at a small distance from the camp of the Moghools, a body of troops, which had been kept ready to put him and his adherents to death, arrived and massacred the whole of them, sending them, as the historian, with his usual liberality, says, to offer their homage to Chungeez Khan in the infernal regions : the Moghools after this immediately despatched a body of troops, and plundered the city of Artakia, and carried off the inhabitants to Moghoolistan as slaves. On the arrival of Chungeez Khan's family in Moghoolistan, they buried the body of Chungeez Khan at the foot of a favourite tree, under the shade of which he was accustomed to sit when out hunting, and which he had directed should be his place of burial. He also directed that a mausoleum of magnet, or loadstone, might be made, and that his body should be placed in it in a coffin of steel. It is related, that when his children had constructed the mausoleum and placed the coffin therein, as he directed, the latter became suddenly attracted on all sides, and remained suspended in the air. His family then caused the vicinity to be forbidden (*koork*), or laid waste ; and now the mausoleum is in the midst of a thick forest, through which there is only one narrow path. It is said that some *kafirs* (infidels) have taken up their abode in this place, and that a devil at times enters the coffin, and gives responses to such questions as are proposed to him. These the hearers look upon as oracles ; and the kafirs, who are the attendants or priests there, and who worship this coffin, conform to these pretended oracles, and increase infidelity by their promulgation : the infidels consider this tomb as the house of God. There is no other road than that described to this mausoleum, from the thickness of the forest surrounding it. Some modern historians say, that Chungeez Khan was born when the sun was in the sign Libra ; and as that sign is esteemed influential on the atmosphere, for that reason the learned in the religion of Mani (the Manicheans) directed that the body of Chungeez Khan should be suspended in the air on a cross. The sons of Chungeez Khan, however, refused to offer such an indignity to the body of their father ; and, therefore, to avoid such an exposure, the Manicheans formed the mausoleum of loadstone as above described. The sons of Chungeez Khan and the Noyauns were much pleased at the ingenuity of the undertaking, it being such as was never before attempted."

The only other piece of information which we think it necessary to copy for the use of persons who may ever be called on to decide on questions of legitimacy concerning the real or pretended descendants of kings and queens is this, that it is a proof and token of royalty to hide the visage when asleep.

ART. XII.—*Report from a Select Committee appointed to inquire into the Causes of Shipwrecks.* 1836.

THE rapid increase in the number of shipwrecks between the years 1800 and 1836, created considerable excitement some short time since, and led to the inquiry of a parliamentary committee on the subject. It is an ascertained fact, and one which merits the deep consideration of the British public, that shipwrecks have been very much upon the increase during the last ten years. By returns from the books at Lloyd's, it appears that for a period of three years, from 1814 to 1818, the number of ships wrecked and missing amounted to 1,203, while the number lost from 1833 to 1835 amount to 1,702. The loss of property occasioned by these wrecks is estimated at £6,015,000 for the first period, being an average of £2,005,000 per annum; and for the second period £8,510,000, being an average of £2,836,666 per annum. The loss of life, which to the shipping interest seems a secondary consideration to the loss of property, has been estimated for the first period at 2,228 or 763 per annum; and for the second period 2,682 or 864 lives per annum.

During a period of four years 272 vessels were lost from the port of Tyne alone, and assuming them to have been total losses, and the value of the whole to be £10 per ton, the loss of property from this single port would average £151,222 per annum. The number of lives lost in the above-mentioned period was 682, and the amount of money paid out of the Seamen's Association of Shields, for relief of members of that society, only amounted to £1935. 15s. 9d.

The entries in Lloyd's books are far from embracing the whole extent of loss of property by shipwreck in the united kingdom; but calculating from them, and allowing for the losses of which no record is preserved, it has been assumed that the annual loss of property in British shipping may be estimated at three millions sterling; while the annual loss of life has, on the same grounds, been very fairly estimated at one thousand souls. The public is the sufferer in both cases for the loss of property, and the loss of labour ultimately falls upon it. It must pay the underwriter a high rate of insurance in order to enable him to cover such losses, and it must support the wives and children of the drowned seamen.

This increase in the number of shipwrecks of late years has been traced to the operation of a variety of causes, more or less satisfactory; the principal of which it is our intention to lay before the public in the present article.

The first in order to which we shall refer, is the defective construction of ships. For nearly a century back, a systematic opposition has been offered to every attempt to improve the construction or increase the durability of British merchant vessels. While the Dutch possessed and encouraged Witzen; the French, Boguer, Duhamel, Claubois, Bordu, and Roume; the Spaniards, Inan; the Germans, Euler ; and the Swedes the celebrated Chapman ; the English neglected the only work they possess on the subject which can lay claim to any science, viz. the Treatise on Shipbuilding and Navigation, by Murray, published in 1754; and consigned both the book and the author to the same unmerited obscurity.

In 1737, Mr. Jackson, a practical chemist, fancied he had discovered a process, the application of which would add to the durability of timber used in shipbuilding; but so jealous were the workmen of anything that by increasing the durability of ships would curtail their own profits, that they raised an outcry against the method, stating that they ran the risk of being poisoned by working upon such materials, and succeeded in stopping the experiments until a certificate was obtained from the College of Physicians to the effect that the articles made use of were not injurious to the health. Previous to the year 1760 there was no registry of ships in existence, and Lloyd's was an obscure Public House. At this period a classification of mercantile shipping was found to be a desideratum, and efforts were made to complete one for the guidance of underwriters. This went on until 1778, when the arbitrary and overbearing conduct of some of its members gave such cause for dissatisfaction that several members seceded from the body and set up a book for themselves. In 1798 the committee for conducting the registry set up and acted on a new principle of classification, totally at variance with sound reasoning, and which prevailed without any modification until 1834. Instead of classing the ships of which they gave an account according to the actual state and condition ascertained by a careful surveyor, they stamped the character of a ship wholly by her age and the port at which she was built, without any regard to the manner in which she was built, the wear or damage she might have sustained, or the repairs she might from time to time have received, or even being new built, thereby lessening the inducement to build ships on principles of durability, obviating the necessity of surveying their hulls, and taking away the encouragement to keep them in the best state of repair. What mattered the strength of a vessel, it was sufficient if she were new. However slightly constructed she might be she was entitled to be registered in the first class for a given number of years varying from six to twelve, after which she was superannuated to be replaced by some hastily and cheaply built successor, expressly designed to last no longer than the allotted period of first class vessels. But the system was a flourishing one. The underwriter cheered on the shipowner, the shipowner

cried to the shipbuilder and he encouraged the men who smote with
the hammer and adze.   The lives of sailors and passengers went
for nothing in the account, or, if at all considered, the system might
be taken as a check upon population, a relief to the redundancy of
labour.   Many of these frail barks foundered on their first voyage,
few of the crews survived to give the melancholy account of their
disaster, and of those who did survive not one in a thousand was
capable of tracing it to its proper cause.

In 1814, Cadogan Williams submitted a plan to Lord Stanhope
and the East India Company to increase the safety of merchant
vessels by their construction, and in 1820, Sir Robert Seppings
opened out new principles of construction for the mercantile navy.
In 1829, Watson originated a similar improvement.   But no progress was made—overbuilt, capacious, burdensome vessels still continue in repute with British shipowners, which necessarily induces
shipbuilders to build them of that description and form.   They
build them to answer the rules of classification laid down at Lloyd's,
and if they were to build on a superior principle they would get no
credit for their pains.   In 1834 an alteration was made to a considerable extent, that the real state and condition of a ship, all things
considered, should enter into the classification as well as age ; ships
repaired were allowed to be restored to class of A. 1. for a limited
period, though they had passed the prescribed age and a certain
portion of the timbers of the framework were required to be bolted.
These were very important improvements, and if rigorously carried
into effect, would in a great measure have corrected the evil.   But
with the lax administration of the committee they had the effect of
lulling the disapprobation of the public, and promoting the system
of insurance.   The method as pursued in the navy of bolting all the
timbers, and making the framework of the vessels solid, would increase the expense by one-sixth of the whole cost, and therefore
prevent her from competing successfully with a foreign ship subject
to no restriction in a trade in which there was no protection given
to British ships.   Moreover, if ships were generally filled in in this
way, as the risk would be less the premiums of insurances would be
reduced in proportion.   So that it is neither the interest of the shipowner or underwriter that the principle of safety should be carried
to the utmost.   On these points the evidence of Mr. Ballingball,
manager of a Shipping Company, and a surveyor of shipping at
Kirkaldy, is curious and decisive.

" Chairman.] Do you think that the additional cost which this would
incur, the chief reason why the ship-owners do not adopt this plan ?—No,
I do not.   I apprehend if you put a safe ship and an unsafe ship in a shipowner's option at the same price, he will take the unsafe ship and insure it
in preference to taking the safe ship and insuring it.

" What induces you to think so ?—A very plain reason.   If I am proprietor of a vessel costing £1,000, and she is sent on a voyage—if she gets

exposed to danger on a rock or sand bank, and if she goes to pieces, I call on the underwriters, and I get the £1,000, the sum she is insured for; but if, instead of going to pieces, she be got off in a damaged state, she must be repaired, and the underwriter will only pay two-thirds of the amount of the repairs. So that if the repairs amount to £300, he will only pay £200, and the owner must pay the remaining £100 out of his own pocket. This is not all. During the time the vessel is undergoing repairs, the owner must pay the wages and provide the victuals of the master and crew, which may be reckoned at £50, making £150 which the owner will have to pay for his vessel being preserved instead of being lost."

He says this is a very simple abstract question.

" I am a shipowner for the purpose of making money ; am I to make £150 or lose it. I have stated £100 and £1,000 in these proportions, but it will hold good with other sums in the same proportions.

"For these reasons you think it is more the interest of a shipowner when his ship does get on shore that she should go to pieces and he should recover the whole value than that she should be saved, by which he is put to considerable expense ?—Decidedly.

" You think no ships are built sufficiently strong ?—Most decidedly, not one ship is built sufficiently strong in Britain."

The evidence of Mr. H. Woodroffe, secretary to the Seamen's Society of South Shields, is equally decisive as to the weakness of new vessels, and the instances he adduces of new ships foundering is absolutely appalling.

"There was the Princess Victoria in 1833. On her first voyage from Archangel, returning laden through the White Sea with grain, coming down on a very fine day, carrying royals, the ship absolutely burst to pieces. The mate and the boy were drowned, and the remaining part of the crew with great difficulty saved themselves.

" You think that occurred from the ship being badly built ?—Yes. There was also the Nathaniel Graham, on her first voyage, came to Shields, and there loaded with coals, grindstones, and the like. Last year she was put in dock, and found very defective. The shipwrights found it impossible to caulk her ; she was so lapped up and so bad.

" Where were they built ?—At Sunderland ; and the Nathaniel Graham went round to Scotland to take in passengers, and on the 20th of June last year, she struck on a rock, and literally fell to pieces. Forty-one persons were drowned."

The next cause of calamities at sea which seems to us most deserving of attention is the incompetency of masters and officers, to which may be appended the drunkenness of officers and men. The greater number of ships in the outports are held by tradesmen in shares, who are totally incapable of judging of the competency of their commanders or the finding of their ships. The instances of the gross ignorance of masters are too numerous to mention. There is no board or office at which any person is required to give proof of his capacity. Even certificates of apprenticeships and fidelity of service are dispensed with. In many instances neither the captain nor any of his crew had served a regular apprenticeship. The tradesmen who have become part-owners of ships send their sons to sea, and, after they have made a voyage or two, they give them charge of vessels as mates or captains. Mr. Woodroffe states it as a fact, that a young man was taken from a butcher's shop to be put in command of a vessel, when neither he nor his mate could make out a common day's work in navigation. Ships with such incompetent commanders are insured to a large amount, very often beyond their actual value. No inquiry is made by the Insurance office as to the character of the commanders ; no inquiry is made as to the cause of the loss of a ship by his ignorance or neglect. Some men have been known to lose three or four vessels in a short space of time. The ignorance and mismanagement of officers leads to the insubordination and carelessness of sailors. They lose all respect for the commander because they know he is not a seaman, and instead of moving with alacrity to the order from the quarter-deck, they stand thunderstruck to see the orders coming promiscuously contrary to the rules of nautical science, and most unquestionably no men have a better right to express their indignation than they have ; for, in case of wreck, they lose either their lives or their property without having any legal claim for wages, after the loss, on the owner, who walks off with the full value of his unseaworthy or mismanaged ship in his pocket. The evidence of Mr. Coleman, an officer of the East India Company's service, and a teacher of navigation, places the matter of incompetent commanders in a very striking point of view. After stating that there were many commanders within his experience who were deficient in a competent knowledge of seamanship, he is asked—

" Within your experience has it happened that you have known persons of very tender years for that capacity filling the office of commanders ?— I know a great many ships commanded by mere boys, some who have only been to sea three years; three years and a half is very common, and in that short space of time they would not have made themselves competent upon the subject of manœuvring a ship in any weather, especially with sudden shifting winds, in hard squalls, or during a gale of wind.

" To what do you attribute the appointment of persons of so early an age and so little experience ?—I know several persons who boast of having three or four young sons and nephews in command of ships, and stating that they were in command of ships at eighteen, as they had been themselves.

" Are you acquainted with any case in which a still younger person than that had the command of a vessel ?—Yes : I can mention a lad named Storey, who commanded a ship named the Headby's of 270 tons sailing from Belfast to Quebec who was but 14 years of age.

"He was nominally the commander, but the authority over the crew would be in some one inferior to himself?—Yes; he could not manage them. I can only account for it by supposing, probably, his father might have been the owner; that his father died, and he, coming to the property, possibly might say ' *I'll* be captain,' and as it was his own property nobody could turn him out of it: that he actually did command the ship there is no doubt.

"Is it mainly to the youth and incapacity of the commanders that you attribute these losses?—There is no doubt about it in my mind, having witnessed several hundred instances during the last 18 years."

Further, by the evidence of this highly intelligent witness, it appears that the officers of the East India Company's service are uniformly examined, and that during a period of two centuries there did not occur a single instance of the loss of a ship from bad equipment, want of skill in seamanship, or a deficiency in navigation, and that they did not lose one ship in ten thousand compared to the merchant service. This result he attributes to the efficiency of the officers and men, and the superiority of the ships which was a consequence of their being their own insurers. The house of Daniels and Co. of Mincing Lane, are equally careful in having their captains and mates examined in the various branches of professional knowledge, and during nineteen years they have lost but one ship, and that was in a hurricane. They attribute the safety of their ships to the precautions they take, and though they insure every ship they send out, those precautions procure them no abatement in the rate of premium. Cases of loss have also in numerous instances arisen from want of proper charts, chronometers, and other instruments. Many commanders cannot for want of funds purchase these things, and they are tempted to say they have them when they have not. Many captains go without chronometers, and many brought them to Mr. Coleman on the day previous to sailing, and requested to be informed of the use of them. When told that it was impossible to make them comprehend in an hour what would require several weeks of study and attention, the general reply was "Oh, never mind, the passengers will see I have a chronometer on board, which will satisfy them." As an instance of erroneous reckoning, consequent upon this ignorance, Mr. Coleman stated the following facts:

"A gentleman brought his son to me, and requested I would give him my candid opinion whether he was competent to command a ship or not; and I assured him that he was not. I declared, with much earnestness, that, in the first instance, he had not sufficient nautical knowledge or experience for such a serious trust; in the next place that he knew no more about navigation than one of my daughters. His father was exceedingly desirous of putting his son in command notwithstanding. I predicted the result, having frequently assured him that his son would lose the ship if he was trusted with the command of her. And so he did; and, at the same time, eleven or twelve lives were lost with her. It happened on one of the

islands to the eastward of New South Wales, from which he fancied he
was 300 miles distant, as afterwards appeared by the reckoning in his
journals. He was but eighteen or nineteen, and his father came to me and
stated his regret that he had not taken my advice."

Another instance is given of the commander of a vessel to
Bombay who did not know how to take out a logarithm or to use a
chronometer. Such commanders frequently take out boys with
them to make the necessary calculations. These lads are nurses to
the captains and actually navigate the vessels. The captain is
entirely dependent upon them, and must succumb to their humours.
As for lunar observations, they know nothing whatsoever about
them.

Captain E. Brenton, R. N., gives a pleasant account of the captain
of a merchant vessel whom he met at sea, who spoke to him and
asked him if he could send a man on board to take an observation
for him. The request set the whole ship's company in a roar of
laughter, and Captain Brenton said, " What has led you to come
to sea without a person who could take an observation for you :"
the worthy captain replied, " You can have no profits if you do not
run no *risks*."

Such then being the ascertained extent of this monstrous nuisance,
is it not surprising that some efforts are not made to remedy its evil
consequences,—consequences involving the lives of thousands of
British subjects. The law will not allow an apothecary to practise
until he has given proof of his skill. It requires him to put his
knowledge to the compounding of medicines to the test, before it
will suffer him to administer them to a patient. But it allows the
captains and officers of merchant vessels, to take charge of the lives
of a crew of seamen, and as many passengers as their false representations and showy advertisements can allure, without troubling
itself in the least as to the qualifications of such men to take upon
them a trust involving such responsibility. Of the many witnesses
who bore testimony to the existence of this evil, there was not one
who did not declare in favour of a board of examination for licensing
captains and mates in London and the outports. Has any effort
been made to carry such a suggestion into effect ? Has any effort
been made to raise the character of British seamen, by establishing
a registry of their services, conduct, qualifications &c. No! like
the unreformed government, the system works well and it is
impolitic to interfere with the management of private property.
Turn we now to the pendant of disasters by ignorance, disasters by
drunkenness. This is undoubtedly the greater and more general
evil of the two, for even in cases where officers are competent seamen, they render themselves unfit for the exercise of their knowledge
and the discharge of their duties by intemperance. This is the
chief cause of disasters at sea,—the great impediment to improving
the character of seamen.

The remission of duty on spirits shipped for the use of the crew of merchant vessels, and the practice of distributing allowances of spirits in the navy, tend in a very great degree to foster and encourage the system of intemperance. The practice as pursued in the navy is characterised by Captain Brenton and Sir Edward Codrington as " downright insanity," and to it and it alone, they attribute insubordinations, mutinies, neglects, losses and disasters of every description. With regard to the merchant vessels, whole crews are frequently shipped in a state of beastly intoxication, the vessel being worked out of port by substitutes technically termed " riggers :" many vessels have been run ashore by the mismanagement of these bad deputies of drunken seamen, and even on the voyage the actual strength of the ship's company,—so necessary in cases of emergency—is very much diminished in efficiency by the grogginess of a greater or less number of individuals. Captain Brenton considers spirits far more dangerous than gunpowder,— ships frequently taking fire from the drawing off of spirits which are always kept under hold—crews getting access to the spirit casks and becoming intoxicated—to which may be added, contradictory and improper orders from officers, mutiny and insubordination from seamen,—a bad look out,—ships running foul of each other, and all the variety of forms of shipwreck.

A pilot whom he took on board at Dungeness, stated to Mr. Purnell, dock-master of Liverpool, that he frequently boarded ships in the Channel, near, or at the pilot stations, and the first sight that attracted his notice was the captain drunk and stretched on the quarter deck, or some other convenient place, and totally unable to command his ship. This statement was further corroborated by a pilot he took in below the Ness.

The statements of this witness with regard to the baneful effects of the use of spirits, and the happy effects attending the temperance plan pursued by the American ships is so valuable, that we cannot refrain from laying a portion of it before our readers.

" Are those details at all in accordance with your experience as to what you have either seen, or known, or heard of vessels sailing to and from Liverpool ?—Yes; I believe nine-tenths of all the losses which occur are caused directly or indirectly through intemperance.

" Has this subject attracted very much attention at Liverpool among ship-owners and merchants and captains ?—It has ; so much so, that some ship-owners have determined on sending their vessels to sea without ardent spirits on board.

" Have any vessels returned or completed their voyage, having gone out without any spirits on board ?—Several.

" What has been the impression on the minds of the merchants who tried this experiment, whether it was advantageous or otherwise?—That it was advantageous.

" Have you had communication with captains or officers in Liverpool on this point ?—I have.

" Did they state that they had experienced any inconvenience from the want of spirits ?—On the contrary, they state that all their previous difficulties arose from the use of ardent spirits, and that they are now resolved on an entire disuse of them.

" In what did the advantages strike you as most apparent; was it in the greater efficiency of the men, or in the greater subordination and the greater prevalence of harmony?—All these combined; they are better conducted ; there is less risk of life and property when men are temperate and efficient.

" Is this system of sailing without spirituous liquors extensively practised by the Americans ?—To a very great extent.

" Have you any idea of the number of ships that sail on what are called temperance principles ?—Some say three-fourths, others nine-tenths of the American vessels are now sailing on temperance principles; I know it is a very rare thing to meet with an American vessel in Liverpool with ardent spirits on board for the use of the officers and crew.

" So general has the practice become in American vessels, that you more frequently find them without spirits than with ?—Yes, it is much more so.

" In America itself is the opinion prevalent of the superior state of the ships so sailing; have the insurance companies in that country made any difference in respect of vessels sailing without ardent spirits ?—It is the general opinion that the risk is considerably lessened, and consequently the underwriters have taken the subject into their very serious consideration. I am in possession of some facts relating to that point; I find in the ' Seaman's Magazine,' published in New-York for 1835, it is stated, ' The subject of temperance among seamen, as the opinion of merchants, ship-owners on this subject was elicited by means of a circular from the New-York State Temperance Society, was recently submitted to the consideration of the Board of Underwriters in the City of New-York, and the following resolution was unanimously adopted : ' Resolved, That the different marine insurance companies in the city of New-York will allow a deduction of five per cent. on the net premiums which may be taken after this date on all vessels, and on vessels together with their outfits if in whaling and sealing voyages, terminating without loss, provided the master and mate make affidavit, after the termination of the risk, that no ardent spirits had been drunk on board the vessel by the officers and crew during the voyage or term for which the vessel or outfits were insured.'

" You believe that resolution to have been acted on, in the insurance of vessels ?—Yes; shortly after that the Baltimore Insurance Company passed a similar resolution in this form : ' Resolved, That the Baltimore Insurance Company, in the City of Baltimore, will allow a deduction of five per cent. on the net premium which may be taken after this date, on vessels terminating their voyage without loss, provided the master and mate make affidavit after the termination of the risk, that no ardent spirits had been drunk on board the vessel by the officers and crew during the voyage or term for which the vessel was insured.' The Virginia Marine Insurance Company at Richmond have adopted the same rule, and it is believed that several of the insurance companies in Boston have acted on a similar plan for some years.

"American vessels now frequent the port of Liverpool in much larger proportion to English than in any other port of England?—They do.

"Speaking generally, what is the estimation in which American ships and American officers are held in Liverpool, as compared with English? —Generally speaking, the ships are esteemed as a class superior in construction and better governed than very many of our English ships, and consequently they have the preference of goods and passengers.

"Are goods shipped in American vessels more readily than in English vessels, supposing the tonnage and the voyage to be the same?—I have heard observations to this effect from American captains, 'I do not care how many English ships are put up in opposition to me, we only fear each other;' that is to say, they are only afraid of American ships opposing American ships, but are not apprehensive of loss from English ships being put in opposition to them, knowing a preference will be given to them both for passengers and goods.

"Is that consistent with your own experience?—Yes, I believe it to be perfectly true.

"Do you think the superiority of the American ships, in their nonliability to accidents from fire and wreck, and running foul of each other from the drunkenness of the officers and men, is one of the elements in the consideration of the men who prefer it?—I have no doubt of that, and I feel afraid that our commerce suffers considerably in consequence of it.

"Have you heard that assigned as a reason?—I have frequently.

"In point of fact, is the loss of American ships, sailing between America and Liverpool, equal to the loss of English ships?—I think not; it is a very rare occurence; I seldom hear of the loss of an American ship on the coast of England.

"Have the Government of America taken any steps to introduce this system of abstinence from spirits in her navy?—They have."

American captains it appears are more sober, steady, and better conducted men than English captains, though it may be that they are not better seamen, although some competent witnesses have held that they are. They hold a higher rank in their country, they are better paid and more respected than the masters of merchant vessels in England, nor is it in their masters alone that the superiority of American ships consists, they have the advantage in construction, equipment, and morality of their crews. The increase in their mercantile marine is estimated as high as $12\frac{1}{2}$ per cent. per annum, while the losses are very inconsiderable. A large proportion of the seamen shipped on board these vessels are British, and those invariably the best seamen. This is partly owing to the temptation of higher wages, and partly to the circumstance of American ships requiring more men upon their homeward than on their outward voyage, which causes a regular annual draught of British seamen who generally continue in the American service.

With regard to a registry of seamen, the Shipowners' Association of Liverpool established an office to effect one that would give a full account of the services, character, and conduct of officers and sea-

men of all ships arriving in that port ; but they failed from the want
of power to enforce the filling up of their documents, and from the
opposition of the seamen to such a regulation.   But even supposing
the power of enforcing those regulations is supplied, the difficulties
which lie in the way of the accomplishment of such an object are
still very great.   The time lost in consulting the registry and making
the necessary examinations would be more than the shipowners
or masters of vessels could or would spare, and the difficulty of
identifying the applicant as the person described in the registry
would be almost insurmountable.   Men would take a new character
with a new name, and be always provided with good certificates. In
addition to this, the majority of captains are not fitted for the exercise of the arbitrary power of stamping the characters of their officers
or men, prejudice would have its way, and hence would arise litiga-
tions without end.   So that a registry, though highly desirable,
would be attended with very great difficulties.

The proposition of Captain Brenton of having one or more training ships moored off Woolwich, in which a thousand boys might be
properly educated and trained in the duties of seamen, for the supply
of the navy and merchant service, is deserving of attention, as the
least objectionable mode of remedying the evils we have just noticed,
and if properly carried into effect would entirely supersede the necessity of impressment.   Each of the 15,000 parishes of England might
furnish one apprentice, and defray his expenses until he should be
fit for service.   Something similar has been attempted by the
Marine Society, but the training of the children is neither careful
nor extensive.   On the whole, we may conclude, that such a plan
as that recommended by Captain Brenton of training ships, together
with a registry for seamen in London and the outports, a board of
examination for licensing captains and masters, and the discon-
tinuance of shipping spirits (except in very moderate quantities
indeed), would be found the most effectual remedies for the last two
mentioned causes of shipwrecks, viz. incompetency of masters and
officers, and drunkenness of officers and crew.

With regard to the operation of the system of insurance tending to
produce losses there can be no question, but that the erroneous principle of classification which prevailed up to 1834, encouraged a system of cheap and careless building, careless equipment and careless
management, or to use the very strong expression of one of the
witnesses—of wholesale murder.   And notwithstanding the adoption
of a sounder and more perfect system since that period—a system
which purports to scrutinize with as much accuracy as is possible,
and ascertain with as much precision the real merits and defects of
ships wherever built, and to class them accordingly in the register—
the impression made by the exposure of the old system has not yet
been erased from the public mind.   Many men conversant with the
subject are most decided in connecting losses with insurances, Mr.

Ballinghall stated that it was the interest of the underwriter that numerous losses should occur, as premiums were thereby increased and consequently the capital of the underwriter. Mr. Willis an insurance broker and underwriter of Lloyd's stigmatises the idea as an absurdity, and declares that as the premiums is always in the rates of the risk—low premiums and small risks would be equally profitable and far preferable to the underwriter. In fact the new system originated with the underwriters, and was carried against the consent of the shipowners, whose opposition was ostensibly grounded on jealousy of interference, though the deterioration of their property might have had something to do with it. But to set the case of the underwriters in the clearest possible light we shall make an extract from the evidence of Mr. Willis.

" Do not you think that the active employment of shipping in the British service has greatly increased of late years ?—It has, certainly.

" Have you ever formed any idea of the proportion in which such increase has taken place, and the number of voyages made now as compared with the number made at any previous period ?—There is a decided increase in the number of voyages in many trades, particularly a vast increase more than there was during the war, from various causes, the delays of convoy and so on ; but there is more activity.

" The risks must be increased with an increase in the number of voyages made ?—Unquestionably, the risks of casualties.

" You would expect the losses to be greater, if, in the same number of ships, an increased number of voyages were made ?—Yes ; but I am of opinion there is a decrease in the losses.

" Then if there be a decrease in the losses, the decrease is proportionably greater, if simultaneously with the decrease of losses there has been an increased employment of the shipping ?—Yes.

" From your experience as an underwriter at Lloyd's have you found any general indisposition on the part of that body to promote objects by which the dangers of navigation would be diminished, in consequence of any supposed injurious effect upon their interest arising from such diminution of risk ?—I have found invariably the contrary ; a strong disposition on all occasions to promote anything that might lessen the hazards of navigation.

" Do you think that the profits of an underwriter must necessarily be increased by an increase of the hazards of navigation, attended by what may be considered a proportionate increase of premium ?—The idea appears to me to be absurd quite.

" Do prudent underwriters generally prefer risks involving small hazards at a low premium, to receiving very high premiums upon extremely hazardous insurances ?—Undoubtedly they do. I can speak from my experience, as an insurance broker, of the extreme difficulty, almost the impossibility, of insuring a really known indifferent vessel, at any premium ; I have repeatedly recommended my friends to get rid of a vessel, from the impossibility of insuring her. Underwriters will not lend themselves to the insurance of vessels of known inferior class.

" Then, if it has been stated in evidence before this Committee, that the underwriters of Lloyd's opposed the adoption of any means that may secure life and property, lest by diminishing the risk their profits should be diminished, your experience enables you to say that such evidence must be unfounded ?—I should say such evidence must have proceeded from parties wholly ignorant of the nature of the business at Lloyd's; it must be mere conjecture ; it certainly is the reverse of the fact. Many applications have been made to the committee at Lloyd's to encourage different inventions connected with maritime affairs; but the committee have no funds which they can apply to such purposes, for the funds that they have are wholly absorbed in donations to encourage merit, and donations for life-boats, and various liberal remunerations for saving of lives, and for getting together the immensely voluminous correspondence we have from various parts of the world, so that there is no fund for the encouragement of any object tending to improve navigation; but the committee have always felt desirous of giving them what countenance they could, and they have generally referred the parties to public boards, having themselves no means of holding out encouragement from their funds.

" If, then, they have in any instance not given direct pecuniary encouragement to inventions, that has not arisen from any indisposition to forward such inventions, but from the want of funds in their hands legitimately applicable to such a purpose ?—Decidedly from the want of funds only.

" Will not the number of persons carrying on the business of underwriters be always likely to be proportioned to the extent of business to be done ?—Clearly.

" And therefore it does not necessarily follow that a large increase of business must increase proportionably the profits of any individual carrying on that business ?—Decidedly an increase of profitable business would speedily produce an increase of underwriters.

" In other words, the business of underwriting may continue to be a profitable one to the individual carrying it on, although in the aggregate there may be less insurance to be effected throughout the community ?— It may, undoubtedly.

" Chairman.] You have spoken of the superior safety of American ships ; are you aware that it is becoming a general practice with American ships to sail without spirits on board ?—I believe it is.

" Are you aware that the house of Baring sent a vessel called the Alexander Baring from London to Canton, at the opening of the China trade ?—I am.

" Do you know that she went out, in imitation of the American ships, without any spirits on board ?—I believe many vessels go without spirits on board ; I believe the best results have proceeded from it. I have seen a letter from the captain of a vessel which I chartered from Dantzic to New South Wales. During the time his crew were at Dantzic there were some of them in gaol, in consequence of insubordination, from the facility of procuring spirits. The captain writes, that since they have arrived at the Sound they are in the best of health, and they are perfectly reconciled to the privation of spirits, and he did not anticipate any trouble from them.

" Do you know that the Alexander Baring performed a remarkably successful and harmonious voyage, in consequence of the absence of spirits from the ship?—I dare say she might; there is a great preference in favour of it.

"Did you ever hear of a ship at Hamburgh, belonging to the Barings, being unable to get freight, while American vessels, lying alongside, did procure freight; the only difference being, that in the one spirits were drunk and in the other spirits were not drunk?—No, I cannot suppose that; I think there must have been a stronger motive than that.

"Mr. Young.] Do not you imagine, that the fact of a commander of a ship having been able to procure a crew who would consent to abstain from ardent spirits is indicative of that crew having been men generally of good character and sober habits?—Probably that might have been the case, with some few exceptions, no doubt.

"Do you think, from what you know of the habits of sailors, that however desirable it may be to get rid of the habits of intoxication, it would be possible to man any considerable number of vessels with men who would voluntarily consent to abstain from ardent spirits during the voyage?—I think it would be difficult."

The sub-committees for the classification of ships consist of three persons, one selected from each class, one merchant, one shipowner, and one underwriter, and a chairman who is chosen by the whole committee. They are paid one pound each for their attendance from eleven till one o'clock. Their proceedings are founded on the reports of the surveyors of the society, who are stationed in all the principal ports of the kingdom. These surveyors are sixty in number, receiving salaries ranging from £30 to £500 a year. There are three for the port of London, and thirteen for the eight principal ports. The fitness of these latter functionaries is tested by a public examination before the committee. They are not permitted to engage in any business whatsoever, and receive from £150 to £500 a year. Their business is to watch the progress of the building of all ships which are to be registered, and to transmit a circumstantial report of the material points, which may enable the committee to form an accurate judgment as to the quality and condition of each particular ship when it comes under their consideration on an application to have her classified. Neither the name of the owner or builder is communicated to the committee before the decision, in order to exclude the possibility of bias; and when it is considered that the saleable value of a ship depends very much on the place she holds in the registry book, the diminution of a year on the higher classes lowering her value £2 or £3 a ton, this regulation cannot be too highly approved of. Of the 12,000 vessels, the whole mercantile force of Great Britain, (above 50 tons) there are 7000 surveyed and classed in this book, and it is almost impossible to insure any ship that has not been registered. The entry is made at the voluntary application of the shipowners, as the society have no charter to entitle them to enforce their regulations. The fees for entry are, for ships under 150 tons, 10s. 6d.; from 150 to 300 one guinea; from 300 to 500 two guineas; from 500 and upwards five guineas. These fees, together with the subscriptions of parties who take a book, for which the public companies pay ten guineas, and individuals three, form the funds to meet the expenses of the society, which amount to £7000 a year. When the committee have passed the survey, it is signed by the chairman and the secretary of the society; it is then open to the perusal and inspection of the owners, in order that they may see all that has been stated by the surveyor, and correct any errors that may have crept into his report, after this the vessel is registered, according to her class, for a period of years proportionate to the durability of the materials of which she is composed, and the manner in which she is constructed—the latter is always the governing principle. The operation of this system, it has been declared, must eventually take away from a ship-builder all inducement to build his ship weak intentionally in order that she might injure herself, and, certainly, as far as we can judge of it from the details here given, we must say that we can come to no other conclusion on the subject. What it may be in operation, we are unable to decide—opinions are contradictory on the subject. That the new system is not quite as perfect as its own functionaries would have us believe, is broadly asserted by Mr. Ballinghall, confirmed by Mr. Marshall, agent of the emigration committee.

" Previous to the formation of the new Society, were there not very many inferior and defective ships afloat and at sea?—Undoubtedly; up to the period when the investigation took place in the years 1823 and 1824, and subsequently, there were a very large portion of British shipping very inferior; it was proved that several of them were sent to sea in an insufficient state to perform the services on which they were employed.

" Do you conceive that to be the consequence of classification by age?—To a considerable extent I do.

" Since that period, age has formed only one of the elements of classification?—Since that period, up to within I think the last three years, that is up to the time when the committe was formed, from whom the new system emanated, there was no change of the principle which contitutes a first class vessel.

" It is only three years since that alteration took place?—I think about three years.

" Do you think many inferior ships defective in their construction, and in an inefficient state of repair, still continue in the service of the mercantile navy?—I should say there are several, but I am of opinion they are not so numerous as heretofore.

" They are gradually diminishing and going out of existence?—Yes, I think ships which have been latterly built are not so much subject to be termed slop-built ships; there are fewer of that description of vessels than formerly, though there are still no inconsiderable number.

" Do you consider that there are a larger proportion of ships wrecked than what you would call a fair proportion, according to the natural course of events ?—I have been surprised at the extent of wrecks, and have been long impressed with the feeling that they have grown to such a multitude as to call for Parliamentary legislation."

We have now glanced at the primary causes of casualties at sea, with the remedies most likely to obviate them. We regret that our limits will not allow us to notice the minor causes, as well as the extensive ameliorations proposed by the committee; their suggestions have done little more than swell the mass of parliamentary papers, and supply wrappers to the chandler : while their originator and compiler, Mr. Buckingham, is lecturing (perhaps on this very subject) in New York, or some other port of Yankee land.

NOTICES.

ART. XIII.—*The Normans in Sicily : being a Sequel to " an Architectural Tour in Normandy."* By HENRY GALLY KNIGHT, Esq., M.P. London : Murray. 1838.

A PRECEDING volume containing a view of the Architecture of the Normans in France and England, by our author, exhibited so much taste and antiquarian knowledge, that we might well expect a no less valuable work when the Island of Sicily, the third scene of Norman conquest and dominion, is the subject. And to confirm the reasonableness of this expectation, it can hardly be necessary to do more than mention that Mr. Knight repaired to the spots described, accompanied by an architect, that the guarantee of a professional eye might not be wanting to confirm the testimony of an amateur.

The volume, however, has other features and merits than those which are of a purely artistic character; for Mr. Knight has prefaced the architectural tour with a historical sketch of the train of events which led to the establishment of the Normans in the South of Europe, rightly judging that the annals of history will best account for the very peculiar features of the works of the Normans in the regions specified. And really the scenes and events described in this sketch, resemble rather what might be expected in a melodramatic theatre than those belonging to real life.

The Norman conquest of Sicily, unlike the terrible invasion of France by that people, had for its origin the reception merely of a few emigrants and stipendiaries, who, in the year 1003, landed at Salerno. They were in number only about forty, and under the direction of Drogo, on his return from a pilgrimage to Jerusalem. Other arrivals in the course of time took place, till at last a people at first heartily invited and welcomed, obtained the dominion over the ancient inhabitants, substituting their laws and institutions for those that had long been recognised.

By the year 1025, the footing which the Normans had obtained in Sicily was not only firm, but had been established by means of the most gallant exploits. Under the leadership of William, who was the very model of a knight, and who transfixed with his lance the Saracenic governor of Syracuse, such a panic was struck into his opponents as

gained him the surname of Bras de Fer. He was also saluted by his followers with the title of Count of Apulia. The form of government which
he selected, for the men of the North were remarkable in respect of an
inclination for institutions, was a purely military, and purely aristocrati-
cal council composed of twelve members, elected by the army amongst
their generals, and dignified with the appellation of counts. But we need
not trace the progress of the conquest more particularly than to announce
that it became complete in 1090, when the last stronghold of the Saracens fell into Norman hands, rewards being liberally distributed amongst
those by whom the great acquisition had been principally brought about,
by Roger, the Great Count, as he is usually called by the old writers.
He died in 1101, lamented by all his subjects, Normans, Lombards,
Greeks, and Saracens, over whom he had presided with strict impartiality.
All were contented, and it was not till afterwards that the Saracens discovered they were really a conquered people.

At the time of which we are now speaking, four languages were in use
in Sicily; the Greek, the Latin, the Arabic, and the Norman; and all
laws and deeds were published in three tongues. The conquest of a
whole nation in such circumstances must have been attended with peculiar
difficulties, and no doubt required an extraordinary extent of vigour and
prudence. Our author hints in the following passage at the astonishing
triumph, not only over the degenerate Greeks, but the victorious
Saracens.

" The chroniclers may have augmented the disproportion of numbers,
but making all due allowance for such exaggerations, the achievements of
the Normans still appear almost miraculous, and even their enemies testify
that the charge of their cavalry was irresistible. It was partly the armour
in which they were encased, partly the character of their antagonists, partly,
local jealousies. In Calabria, the enmity of the Lombards to the Greeks ;
in Sicily, the enmity of the Greeks to the Saracens. But the causes of
their uniform success, are chiefly to be found in the manly and martial
exercises to which the Normans were accustomed from their earliest years ;
in the chivalrous and adventurous spirit of the age, which excited their
minds ; and, above all, in that confidence in self which makes the soldier
invincible. Each individual Norman was, in effect, a legion."

It is natural to expect that where so many distinct races at one
time existed, as was the case in Sicily, a great variety of interesting
antiquities may be traced; but as these afford subjects for minute description for which we have not room, a specimen or two of more popular
matter will sufficiently display how adequate the author's acquirements
are to the performance of any task which requires clear and elegant delineation. Take from his historical sketch the portrait of the Emperor
Frederick the Second, who was the most remarkable man of the age in
which he lived.

" The warrior, the troubadour, the philosopher; who, inferior to none of
his predecessors in the field, took advantage of every interval of repose to
improve the laws and institutions of his kingdom, and to soften the nature,
and refine the manners, of his vassals by the cultivation of letters and the
encouragement of the arts.

" But in his external appearance, and in the character of his mind, he united cheerfulness with greatness. There was a radiance in his eye that inspired affection, and a majesty in the expression of his countenance that commanded respect.

" Fulfilling all the duties of his station, he was glad, when he could, to forget the burthens of empire; to enjoy as well as to reign. He was keenly alive to the charms of beauty; he delighted in the sports of the field; but literary pursuits were his chief relaxation.

" He spoke six languages with fluency; the Norman, the German, the Saracenic, the Greek, the Latin, and the Italian.

" His happiest hours were passed in the palace of Palermo, to adorn which he ransacked the East and the West. In its gardens were seen the plants, birds, and beasts of every clime; and in its neighbourhood he pursued his favourite amusement of hawking without restraint. It was in that palace that he collected around him a society of poets and men of letters—superintended the translation of learned works, and, by his own example, encouraged the bards of romance. It was in this academy, and under Frederick's fostering care, that the Sicilian language was reduced into form, and articulated the first accents of the Italian muse.

" To Frederick, Sicily owed an amended code, the germ of municipal bodies, and the more popular branch (il braccio Demaniale) of its national council.

" In Italy he instituted the public schools of Naples and Padua; built several towns and castles, and more than one mansion for the Teutonic knights. In Calabria, he built the town of San Stefano, and Aquila, in the Abruzzi. For his own occasional residence, principally with a view to the chase, he built the castle of Apricena on the heights of Monte Gargano in Apulia, and the Castel del Monte, on the lower range of the hills near Barletta. But his most singular foundation was at Nocera in Apulia. Having witnessed the courage and experienced the fidelity of the Saracens of Sicily, in his various wars, he removed 20,000 of those Mahomedans to Nocera, to be a check upon his enemies, and there established a colony which was seen by the Popes with the greatest aversion."

Mr. Knight's sketch and reflections drawn forth by a visit to Syracuse are striking in no ordinary degree.

" No spot which I ever beheld ever illustrated the transitory nature of earthly things more strongly than modern Syracuse. Historians have distinctly described the vast magnitude of the ancient city. Enough vestiges remain to confirm the truth of their statements. The harbour is still in existence, which originally made Syracuse the emporium of the world; but the harbour only contains a few fishing-boats and speronaras, and the Syracuse which now exists is but the wreck and mockery of departed greatness.

" You cast your eyes on the rising ground at the upper end of the harbour. Where is Neapolis? Where is Tyche? Where Achradina? There they assuredly stood; but what is *now* there?—Absolutely nothing!

" On the other side of the bay you distinguish the Doric shafts of the temple of Jupiter Olympicus : the very temple which contained the statue from which Dionysius the elder purloined the mantle of gold. How deep into the past do these remembrancers carry your thoughts!

" Modern Syracuse is confined to the small peninsula on which formely stood that portion of the ancient city which was called Ortygia—as if London were reduced to the Tower and Tower-hill, or Paris to the island in the middle of the Seine. The neck of land which unites the peninsula to the coast divides the larger from the smaller harbour.

" Rising with the sun, we got into a boat, and landed on that part of the shore which is nearest to the vestiges of Neapolis. The first thing we came to, in this desolate region, was a single column—itself recording the whereabouts of wealth and grandeur—a single column of Cipollino marble—the remnant of the once beautiful portico of the Temple of Ceres. From thence we proceeded to the theatre, and the amphitheatre, which has recently been cleared out, and then ascended to the vacant site of Neapolis by the very road which, in former times, was incessantly trod by busy thousands, of whom we were only reminded by their tombs, which we saw caverned in the rock on either side.

" At length we arrived at the ruins of the fortress which is known to have stood at the extreme point of ancient Syracuse, and which fortunately remains to place the real extent of the city beyond the possibility of a doubt. Of this building there are considerable remains; and in the wall of the city, which comes up to the fortress, you are able to discover the traces of the very gate through which Marcellus entered. This part of Syracuse was on elevated ground, from hence Ætna is again seen in the distance.

" From hence we had a long and wearisome ride back to the modern town. We traversed the entire length of what was Syracuse, as it might be setting out from Shoreditch to go by the Strand to Westminster, traversing a space that was once no less crowded with houses and thronged with men. The whole is now a rocky common, only frequented by a few sheep and goats—nothing to remind you of the past, except the grooves here and there worn by the chariot wheels in the rock, indented lines that trace the foundations of houses and the occasional gurgling of water, when you hit upon the course of the stream which is brought by the aqueduct. Here and there, in the wide extent, are a few patches of cultivation, and one or two modern farms, but nothing ancient; and you puzzle your brains to conceive what can have become of the temples and the palaces, the vast piles of marble and stone, the materials, the very dust, of the London of antiquity."

Among the results, in a strictly antiquarian sense, of our author's tour in Sicily. the following is important :—he finds that the Normans adopted a style of building and design in that island totally different, not only from that which they observed in France and England, but equally remote from what prevailed in Calabria, the Saracenic pointed style having been adopted by them. There are some difficulties and niceties to be encountered in pursuing this inquiry, which our author has disposed of with his usual candour and discrimination. But we can only afford room for adding that a Series of Thirty Drawings, folio, by his companion in travel, Mr. Moore, has been published to illustrate the text before us, thereby furnishing the fullest picture of the Saracenic and Norman remains in Sicily, for the benefit of artists and amateurs. Mr. Knight must therefore be regarded as an eminent contributor to architectural knowledge, and as an indefatigable promulgator of taste, by his discoveries and descriptions of some of the most curious facts that have engaged the speculations of the antiquary and the connoisseur.

Art. XIV.—*Hints to Professing Christians on Consistency.* By A Village Pastor. London: Wightman. 1838.

A sensible and pious work; though tiny in point of bulk, it contains much that is important and impressive. The inconsistencies detected by the writer are not more prevalent than they are clearly explained and sharply reproved by him. The little volume is calculated to correct many errors.

Art. XV.—*The Happy Transformation.* London: Wightman. 1838.

This small work is attested by W. H. Pearce, Missionary from Calcutta—who is its editor, and who has added a "Warning Voice to the Young"—to contain the authentic history of a London Apprentice. The Apprentice, it seems, from having been a thoughtless and erring youth has become pious and is reformed. To persons of a like age, the inhabitants of large towns, and otherwise placed in similar circumstances, more seasonable and useful lessons cannot be presented than what these earnest and touching Letters offer. They are written by the Apprentice himself and are creditable to his head and his literary taste, as well as strikingly illustrative of his religious feelings.

Art. XVI.—*Italy; a Poem.* By Samuel Rogers. A New Edition. London: Moxon. 1838.

A neat, nay a beautiful as well as cheap edition of a delightful and elegant work that has heretofore appeared in gorgeous and expensive costume. The woodcuts which embellish it, though by no means so elaborate and costly as the plates which illustrated the larger impression of the Poem, are sweet and appropriate gems.

Art. XVII.—*Memoirs of the Life and Correspondence of the Late Right Hon. Henry Flood, M. P. &c.* By Warden Flood, Esq. Dublin: Cumming. 1838.

Decidedly the most unsatisfactory Life we ever read, purporting to record the history of an eminent man, and a celebrated orator, who figured during one of the most interesting epochs in the annals of a nation. Neither of his hero nor of the period in which that hero flourished has this namesake of one of Erin's greatest Parliamentary Patriots given a clear or striking account. The style is turgid and bombast, according to the worst species of Irish verbosity; while the matter is poor and badly arranged; evils which are the more provoking, seeing that the author professes to entertain a high idea of the greatness of his theme; for he says in the only sentence which we think it necessary to quote of his work, when speaking of Flood's era, that "We begin when the dawn of freedom pierces the gloom of past centuries, and we advance as the morning of nationality breaks upon us, which promises so much for its meridian brightness."

Art. XVIII.—*Rufus, or the Red King: a Romance.* In 3 Vols. London: Saunders & Otley. 1838.

We hold it to be one of the most difficult things which an author can set himself to perform, when he undertakes to write a romance, particularly if

the era of the tale chosen be that of the olden time. In all such works great
inventive powers are not only required, but fidelity to nature, not literal, but
poetic and dignified, and fidelity also to facts, which nothing less than the
combined knowledge of the historian and antiquary can maintain. Their
characters must be individualized, scenes must be highly coloured, actions
must be dramatized, while, since every sort of talent and information may
be rendered available to the story, the whole, whether in the way of events,
descriptions, or actors must tend to one point and one consummation.
Every novel or romance ought to be a picture of life and nature in a great
variety of aspects, and under a great variety of light and shadow ; and if the
author goes far back he must so closely and warmly identify himself with
the spirit of the time and his characters, as to bring others under the same
spell and to sympathize with the same creations with himself, an intimate
acquaintance with the human heart and a correct observation of nature
(these two great objects are the same in essentials at all times) being manifested throughout. No person could have shown himself more perfectly
convinced of these and other requisites than the author, whose very meritorious work is now before us, has done in an able Preface. His Romance
going back to a period which requires knowledge of manners long departed
from us, evinces much care and study even to the minuteness of costume.
It is probable, that had Scott's tales of chivalry never appeared the present
work would not have been written—the Red King would never have been
cast in the shape that is now before us; and since the work cannot but
recal the remembrance of some of the Northern Magician's fictions, disadvantageous comparisons will be but too apt to suggest themselves. We
must, however, pronounce Rufus to be a production of no ordinary rank,
not merely on account of its own merits, but as affording great promise of
future achievements on the part of a young author ; for since he has laid
it down as a rule to be sedulously studied, not to trust " to forms of any
kind, or to any thing simply external," although we dare not say that he
has uniformly fulfilled the resolution, he, with the mind, the imagination,
and the earnestness which he possesses, is sure, being in the right way to
perfection, to produce better things than what he has yet done. By a habitual attention to the rule laid down he will lend more prominence, more
definiteness and individuality to his actors than he has here exhibited ; he
will, instead of long descriptions of dress, armour, and other exterior things,
and instead of being extremely anxious to ape the supposed phraseology of
the period of the story, throw himself upon character, fathoming its distinctive lineaments, and portraying the pressure of each of his individuals upon
the age, and the progress of the plot. As it is, however, the author's spirited
style, his skill in writing, the beauty of his language, and the variety as
well as abundance of his characters and incidents, are qualities that effectually prevent the reading of his Romance from ever becoming wearisome.
If not always with great power, the author holds on confidently and rapidly ;
if we have not always a clear view of the age attempted to be pictured, there
is always a stirring and engaging story.

THE
MONTHLY REVIEW.

JUNE, 1838.

ART. I.—*The Life of William Wilberforce.* By his Sons, R. I.
WILBERFORCE, M. A., Vicar of East Farleigh; and S. WILBERFORCE,
M. A., Rector of Brightstone. 5 Vols. 8vo. London: Murray. 1838.

IT would be difficult to name an individual belonging to recent times
whose history, carefully and deliberately compiled and written, can
be so fraught with interest and permanent value as that of him the
memoirs of whose life are now before us. William Wilberforce, whether
as a statesman, a philanthropist, or a private Christian, for about half
a century was much before the world; his talents, his accomplishments, his virtues, and his consistency throughout a career of extraordinary activity, presenting one of the most beautiful, intellectual,
and moral pictures that have ever been studied. To have been long
prominent in the political theatre, and to be treated by all parties as
trustworthy and independent, are rare coincidences; to have fought
many battles and waged protracted war without alienating the affections of opponents, is equally uncommon; to be religious yet cheerful,
strict yet charitable, and after all to be beloved by every one, are
certainly not less extraordinary combinations and attainments.
Such, however, may be pronounced to have been the reward and the
circumstances which distinguished Wilberforce's services and character while he lived, accompanying him to the very close of his race,
and with an ever-accruing distinctness and strength; and similar
but not diminished testimonies are assuredly in store towards his
memory.

The life and character of such a man as we have already intimated, admit of being profitably viewed in a variety of aspects. He
may, with the utmost propriety, be regarded as affording an attractive and instructive subject of private biography; or his efforts and
triumphs of a public nature, may be taken as forming lofty passages of national and universal history. Who can deny that his
influence and works will leave their impress on distant countries and
during future ages? But it does not appear to us necessary to
attempt a dissertation upon the character and entire achievements
of our hero. The world is aware what they are, and has fondly
acknowledged them. It seems to be sufficient, if abiding closely by

a few of the lights collected in the present volumes and classifying
them, we enable our readers to descry the great principles that
guided their possessor, and some of the steps taken in the course of
his mental formation.   In this way, although nothing like a complete
analysis of the voluminous and diversified matter in the life can be
furnished,—nothing, for instance, like an estimate of Wilberforce's
political creed or progress, yet we may obtain a deeply-interesting
conception of the importance of singleness of purpose, of the power
of individual perseverance in the paths of benevolence, and of the
excellence and happiness which accompany enlightened Christianity
in every position.   The anecdotes which may happen to strike us
particularly will serve to enliven our matter.   But first a few words
as to the sources whence the memoirs have been derived, and the
manner in which the great philanthropist's sons have performed
their task.

Wilberforce, it seems, had for a long time contemplated the probability or rather the certainty of his being made the subject of
biography.   He kept a diary for many years ; he extended memoranda on religious points ; he preserved numbers of letters ; he dictated notes for the information of others in regard to particulars of
of his history and experience of the world ; and when are joined to
all these, the reminiscences of his own family and others, there may
reasonably be expected to have been provided an abundant harvest
of materials for the biographers to arrange, publish, and comment
upon.

Still we suspect that a good deal has been suppressed that might
have ministered to the appetite of those who admire nothing so much
as the particular opinions of any eminent person concerning the
many individuals who must have come under his notice; especially
had these opinions embraced anecdotes derogatory to reputation.
Not that Mr. Wilberforce is to be presumed to have been capable
of invidiously or falsely seeking to cater for the pleasure of scandal-
mongers ; but how he could keep memoranda of his multifarious
transactions with the almost numberless host of personages with whom
he was constantly, coming in contact, and not have expressed more
racy things and detailed more pungent stories than we generally find
in these volumes, we cannot understand, especially as he was a
lively man and fond of social intercourse, but by supposing that the
pruning knife of his literary executors has been often-applied.   The
real value of the work, however, is not thereby injured; for the character and services of its hero are exhibited with sufficient clearness
and force to enable the reader completely to appreciate their nature
and value.

We expected, indeed, as Mr. Wilberforce was a religionist
of a strict and decided creed, one who was not ashamed to be pious
and the missionary of piety, in a form and with an earnestness which
the educated and higher orders generally reckon nearly allied to

vulgar methodism, that an exclusive class would almost alone
have found these volumes interesting; or at least, that, if a wider
circle of readers were engaged, that these would chiefly consist of
those merely humane persons who, apart from a zealous profession
of religion, had recently had their hearts awakened to the enormities
of slavery. But the fact is, that William Wilberforce's piety though
sincere was rational, and the farthest possible removed from noisy
fanaticism. Besides, he was fond of social intercourse as stated
above, and a master of social elegance, whether the flow of animal
spirits, of conversational eloquence, or of a benign nature be considered. And who with these qualities, under the regulation of a
sound judgment and with the weight of a nobly-earned character,
could be otherwise than courted and admired by the merely worldly
gallant and gay? But we must not longer linger on the threshold;
and must proceed to let the accomplished man, the eminent
Christian, and the benevolent champion, be beheld in a variety of
places and on a variety of occasions.

Mr. Wilberforce was born in 1759 at Hull, his father being a rich
merchant and the descendant of what is understood by the terms
good and ancient family. He was a delicate child, constitutionally
feeble, slender in appearance, and the subject of frequent ailments.
But his disposition was as sweet as it was lively, his very voice
being so melodious as to constitute a suitable organ of his fine soul.
The father died when the son was nine years old, which led to his
removal to an uncle's at Wimbleton. Here he remained about three
years, having imbibed during that period the strict and extreme
opinions from the relations alluded to, of the followers of Whitefield.
On his return to Hull, efforts were used to cure him of his methodism; and some readers may not expect to find such reflections from
him as the following in reference to these efforts, which happened to
prove successful. He says, " I think I have never before remarked
that my mother's taking me from my uncle's when about twelve or
thirteen, and then completely a methodist, has probably been the
means of my being connected with political men and becoming
useful in life. If I had stayed with my uncle I should probably have
been a bigoted-despised methodist; yet to come to what I am,
through so many years of folly as those which elapsed between my
last year at school and 1785, is wonderful."

Having returned to Hull as above mentioned, and having been
enticed to enter into the pleasures usually pursued by persons of
like years, he also was subjected to a regular system of education.
We also learn, that, while studying under the direction of the Rev.
K. Basket, and when only fourteen, he addressed a letter to the
editor of a York paper on " the odious traffic in human flesh;"
which shows at least that the frivolities and light-heartedness of
youth were rather those of a buoyant and lively spirit than such as
blunt the moral sensibilities. Indeed, while at St. John's College;

Cambridge, which he entered when seventeen, though gaiety still had great charms for him, he appears to have been a fair scholar, and at all times exempt from the gross vices which pollute the atmosphere of our ancient universities. We have not, however, many minute details of his academical career, nor of his genius for learning. But his readiness in the art of composition, and an apt memory for treasuring the gems of poetry, are circumstances sufficiently characteristic of an elegant and tasteful mind, and prepare us to hear that in society he was a choice ornament.

On leaving Cambridge, Mr. Wilberforce, whose fancy lay not in a mercantile line, had the ambition to think of entering parliament. He accordingly canvassed the borough of Hull, for which he was at length returned, the sacrifice in point of money not being less than eight or nine thousand pounds. In the metropolis, he was among the liveliest and the gayest. He became a member of several fashionable as well as extravagant clubs. He gambled, and seemed to be in as fair a way to ruin as thousands of those who flutter and spend their healths and incomes at the West End. Still all along evidences appear of tenderness of conscience, of unperverted principles, of energetic resolutions. He was completely weaned from play by having been the winner of 600*l*., and seeing the annoyance which his gain occasioned the losers. He was also a most assiduous attender on his parliamentary duties, having in the House and elsewhere laid a deep and lasting foundation of friendship and confidence with William Pitt. And to show how well he understood the way to acquire stability and be useful in parliament, we cite the counsel which he on one occasion offered a friend. "Attend," said he, "to business, and do not seek occasions of display; if you have a turn for speaking the proper time will come. Let speaking take care of itself. I never go out of my way to speak, but make myself acquainted with the business, and then, if the debate passes (pass) my door, I step out and join it." Before closing all references to his early gaiety and attractive qualities in what are called brilliant society, we may mention that the Prince of Wales was charmed by him at Devonshire House, his melodious singing and talent at mimicry being among the list of his fascinations.

But though Wilberforce not long after his entrance into public life was weaned from the seductions of frivolity and fashion, we are told that he was in equal danger from the severer temptations of ambition.

"With talents of the highest order, and eloquence surpassed by few, he entered upon public life possessed of the best personal connexions, in his intimate friendship with Pitt. Disinterested, generous, lively, fond of society, by which he was equally beloved, and overflowing with affection towards his numerous friends, he was, indeed, in little danger from the low and mercenary spirit of worldly policy. But ambition has inducements for men of every temper; and how far he was then safe from its fascinations, may be learned from the conduct of his brother 'Independents.'. They were a club of about forty members of the House of Commons, most of them opponents of the Coalition Ministry, whose principle of union was a resolution to take neither place, pension, nor peerage. Yet, in a few years, so far had the fierceness of their independence yielded to various temptations, that he and Mr. Bankes alone, of all the party, retained their early simplicity of station. He himself was the only county member who was not raised to the peerage. He, too, would no doubt have been entangled in the toils of Party, and have failed of those great triumphs he afterwards achieved, but for the entrance into his soul of higher principles. His later journals abound in expressions of thankfulness that he did not at this time enter an official life, and waste his days in the trappings of greatness."

Before arriving at that period when it is said higher principles than those of mere ambition took possession of him, a trip to France along with Mr. Pitt and Mr. Eliot affords some interesting and political anecdotes. They started in autumn 1783, having met at Canterbury, from which they were to proceed to Rheims, in order to acquire some facility in the French language before entering the capital. None of the three, however, were very provident; for each trusted to the others to procure letters of introduction; and when the neglect was discovered, they could only conveniently obtain from Mr. Peter Thelluson a recommendation to his correspondent in Rheims. This correspondent turned out to be a man of no higher consideration than a dealer in figs and raisins, and was unacquainted with any of the gentry of the place; so that after spending nine or ten days, the three *grands seigneurs* had made no farther progress in the language of our gay neighbours than was to be expected of persons who spoke to no human being but each other and their courier, who was an Irishman. Among the circumstances that at length brought the strangers into notice, we must quote those furnished by the Abbé de Lageard, who was secretary to the Conseil d'Etat. He states,—

"One morning, when the intendant of police brought me his daily report, he informed me there are three Englishmen here of very suspicious character. They are in a wretched lodging, they have no attendance, yet their courier says, that they are *grands seigneurs*, and that one of them is the son of the great Chatham; but it is impossible, they must be *des intrigants*. I had been in England, and knew that the younger sons of your noble families are not always wealthy, and I said to Mons. du Chatel, who wished to visit them officially and investigate their character, 'Let us be in no hurry; it may be perhaps as they represent; I will inquire about them myself.' I went to their lodgings the same evening and got their names from the courier, and true enough they were said to be Mr. W. Pitt, Mr. Wilberforce, and Mr. Eliot, all three members of the British Parliament, and one of them lately a leading member of the government. Amongst other things Mr. Pitt complained, 'Here we are in the middle of Champagne, and we cannot get any tolerable wine.' ' Dine with me to-morrow,' I replied, ' and you shall have the best wine the country can afford.' They came and dined with me, and instead of moving directly after dinner, as we do in France, we sat talking for five or six hours."

The Abbé de Lageard's considerateness and hospitality on this occasion did not pass unrewarded. A man of family and fortune and in office at the period mentioned, was not likely to escape the fury of the revolution. In fact he was stripped of every thing but his faith and his loyalty; and having become an emigrant in England, received from Mr. Wilberforce, we are told, a willing and ample return of kindness. But a few farther particulars of the three Englishmen's stay in Rheims will be acceptable.

"Nothing could exceed his (the Abbé's) kindness to them : for a fortnight he was their constant attendant; he made them acquainted with the noblesse who resided in the neighbourhood of Rheims : he gave them permission to sport over the domain of the archbishop; and, upon his return, introduced them to a familiar footing at the palace. In their many conversations with the Abbé, Mr. Pitt was the chief speaker. Although no master of the French vocabulary, his ear, quick for every sound but music, caught readily the intonations of the language ; and he soon spoke it with considerable accuracy. He inquired carefully into the political institutions of the French ; and the Abbé has stored up his concluding sentence—'Monsieur, vous n'avez point de liberté, mai spour la liberté civile vous en avez plus que vous ne croyez.' As he expressed in the strongest terms his admiration for the system which prevailed at home, the abbé was led to ask him, since all human things were perishable, in what part the British constitution might be first expected to decay ? Pitt, a parliamentary reformer, and speaking within three years of the time when the House of Commons had agreed to Mr. Dunning's motion, that the influence of the crown had increased, was increasing, and ought to be diminished, after musing for a moment, answered—' The part of our constitution which will first perish, is the prerogative of the king and the authority of the House of Peers.' ' I am greatly surprised,' said the abbe, ' that a country so moral as England can submit to be governed by a man so wanting in private character as Fox ; it seems to show you to be less moral than you appear.' ' C'est que vous n'avez pas été sous la baguette du Magicien,' was Pitt's reply ; ' but the remark,' he continued, ' is just.' Through the abbé's kindness, they mixed familiarly with different ranks, and saw much of the interior of French society."

The three Englishmen were no longer *nobodies* or *des intrigants*. We are told,—

"The position Mr. Pitt had occupied at home, attracted the observation of the French. An aged marechale at Rheims sought in him a purchaser for her most costly wines, and disclaimed earnestly his assurances of poverty. ' Le ministre doit avoir, sans doute, cinque ou six mille livres sterling de rente.' And at Paris, whither they removed upon the 9th of

September, it was hinted to him, through the intervention of Horace Walpole, that he would be an acceptable suitor for the daughter of the celebrated Neckar. Neckar is said to have offered to endow her with a fortune of 14,000*l.* per annum; but Mr. Pitt replied, ' I am already married to my country.' The story of their embarrassments at Rheims preceded them to Fontainbleau, where, by special invitation, they soon joined the gala festivities of the court, and Mr. Pitt was often rallied by the queen."

Very many notices occur in these volumes of Mr. Pitt, who was much beloved as well as admired by Wilberforce. Proofs of this will afterwards appear in our extracts ; but still it is but justice to state in behalf of the immediate subject of these memoirs that he was not a slavish admirer, a circumstance which must have operated to place him high in the estimation of the great minister. On one occasion Wilberforce says, " I well remember the pain I felt in being obliged to vote against Mr. Pitt, the second time he spoke in parliament ;" a striking combination of affection and independence.

In the spring of 1784, we find our hero distinguishing himself by an extraordinary display of eloquence at a meeting in York convoked to oppose the Coalition Ministry. It is stated that when the proposers of an address had spoken, and the whig lords had been heard in answer, the day by this time being far advanced, and the listeners growing weary of the contest, a revival of interest was most unexpectedly created.

" At this time Mr. Wilberforce mounted the table, from which, under a great wooden canopy before the high sheriff's chair, the various speakers· had addressed the meeting. The weather was so bad, ' that it seemed,' says an eye-witness, ' as if his slight frame would be unable to make head against its violence.' The castle yard, too, was so crowded, that men of the greatest physical powers had been scarcely audible. Yet such was the magic of his voice and the grace of his expression, that by his very first sentence he arrested, and for above an hour he continued to enchain, the attention of the surrounding multitude. The disadvantage under which his figure had at first appeared, from the scale and construction of the hustings, was soon forgotten in the force and animation of his manner.—' I saw,' said Boswell, describing the meeting to Dundas, ' what seemed a mere shrimp mount upon the table ; but, as I listened, he grew, and grew, until the shrimp became a whale.' "

It is added that he was distinctly heard to the utmost limits of the crowd, and interrupted only by an express from Mr. Pitt, which, without disconcerting him, enabled him with the greatest possible effect to announce to the assembled county, that, by dissolving parliament, the King had at that very moment appealed to the decision of the nation.

Notice has already been taken of the danger which the temptations of ambition held out to Wilberforce ; and the applause and fame that followed his eloquent and opportune display at York may

be supposed to have fanned the flame. Nor had he miscalculated
the extent of his popularity among the voters, for he was returned
by them a representative of their weighty and numerous interests.

But a change was about to be wrought in his views, and a permanent range of principles and duties to be established in his heart,
from which were to flow the mighty triumphs he was destined to be
the instrument of achieving. Mr. Wilberforce repeatedly visited the
continent about the era of which we have been speaking. One of
those visits was in company with Isaac Milner, afterwards Dean of
Carlisle; and to the intercourse and influence of this excellent
churchman, the revival of Mr. Wilberforce's religious impressions,
in a much milder and more cheerful form, however, than were those
experienced in his juvenile years, are in a great measure ascribed.
We are now in the year 1785, and shall quote one passage in
relation to the serious subject.

" Mr. W. took up casually a little volume (Doddridge's ' Rise and Progress of Religion'), which Mr. Unwin, Cowper's correspondent, had given
to the mother of one amongst his fellow-travellers; and, casting his eye
over it hastily, asked Milner what was its character. ' It is one of the
best books ever written,' was his answer; ' let us take it with us and read
it on our journey.' He easily consented, and they read it carefully
together, with thus much effect, that he determined at some future season
to examine the Scriptures for himself, and see if things were stated there
in the same manner. In this journey he was alone with Milner."

We cannot pass from a reference to the remarkable change which
came over Mr. Wilberforce's mind about the year 1785, and which,
it appears, cost him many conflicts, without quoting a paragraph of
a kindred nature to a singular but characteristic one which we cited
in a former part of our paper. He says,—

" That gracious Providence which all my life long has directed my
course with mercy and goodness, and which in so many instances known
only to myself has called forth my wonder and gratitude, was signally
manifested in the first formation of my Parliamentary connexion with the
county of York, and in its uninterrupted and long continuance. Had the
change in my religious principles taken place a year sooner, humanly
speaking I never could have become member for Yorkshire. The means
I took, and the exertions I made, in pursuing that object, were such as I
could not have used after my religious change : I should not have thought
it right to carve for myself so freely, if I may use the phrase, (to shape
my course for myself so confidently,) nor should I have adopted the
methods by which I ingratiated myself in the good will of some of my
chief supporters ; neither after having adopted the principles I now hold,
could I have conformed to the practices by which alone any man would
be elected for any of the places in which I had any natural influence or
connexion."

Before observing Mr. Wilberforce in some of his characteristic

phases at home, posterior to the *great change* of which we have
been hearing, or culling from his memoranda a few specimens in the
way of anecdotes and sketches, we shall diversify the interest of our
subject by taking a glimpse or two derived from his residences on
the continent.   Here is a notice of something which he witnessed at
Nice in 1784, that deserves to be read at the present day, when
similar infatuation to that described disgraces the metropolis of
England, as well as other communities more liable to be influenced
by mystic arts.   " The natives of Nice," says Mr. Wilberforce,

" Were in general a wretched set—several of them, however, poor
noblesse.   There were nightly card parties at the different houses, and a
great deal of gambling.   The most respectable person amongst them was
the Chevalier de Revel: he spoke English well, and was a great favourite
of Frederic North's, who was then at Nice in a very nervous state, and
giving entire credit to the animal magnetisers.   The chief operator, M.
Toalag, tried his skill on Milner and myself; but 'neither of us felt any
thing, owing, perhaps, to our incredulity.   North, on the contrary, would
fall down upon entering a room in which they practised on him; and he
even maintained to me, that they could affect the frame though in another
room, or at a distance, and you were ignorant of their proceedings. '

The famous physiognomist, Lavater, furnished the following particulars :—

" Saw Lavater—He says that the English are remarkable for smooth
foreheads, and strong-marked eye-brows.   We called upon him in the
evening—he could give us he said only half an hour, but we got him on
the *subject;* his supposed revelations—physiognomy he dismissed as not
serious enough to be mentioned in comparison—and he said, on our offering
to go, such a conversation as that ought not to be broken off—it would be
to go against Providence—strange stories—forty guineas—revelation—
his papers prevented being discovered.'   'I had been chosen treasurer,'
said Lavater, 'of a certain charitable institution, and had received the
funds subscribed for its conduct, when a friend came in great distress,
and begged me to advance him a sum of money to save him from bankruptcy.   You should have it at once, but I have no such sum.   ' You
have the charity fund in your power; lend me what I need from that :
long before the day comes on which you must pay it over, I shall be able to
replace it, and you will save me and mine from ruin.'   At last I reluctantly consented.   His hopes, as I had foreseen, were disappointed; he
could not repay me; and on the morrow I must give in my accounts.   In
an agony of feeling, I prayed earnestly that some way of escaping from
my difficulties might yet present itself, that I might be saved from dis-
gracing religion by such an apparent dishonesty.   I rose from my knees,
and in the nervous restlessness of a harassed mind, began to pull open
every draw I had, and ransack its contents.   Why I did it I know not,
but whilst I was thus engaged, my eye caught a small paper parcel, to the
appearance of which I was a stranger.   I opened it, I took it up, and found
that it contained money : I tore it open, and found in it the sum I needed

to settle my accounts. But how it came there, or where it came from, I could never learn.' ' Child spoke for whom he had prayed on christening. An excellent man in his whole conduct—kissed us with extreme affection, and said, if he received anything we should too. He and many others ardently look for the coming of some ' Elu,' who is to impart to them a large measure of grace. He will know the ' Elu ' the moment he sets eyes on him.' "*

We may as well, before returning from Switzerland, quote a letter written thence to Lord Muncaster as a specimen not only of Wilberforce's playful epistolary style, but as descriptive of his patriotic feelings and certain forebodings when the political horizon was, as at many other times, not quite clear.

" Berne, 14th Aug., 1785.

" Dear Muncaster,—That a man who has been for the last week environed by eternal snows, and hemmed in by the Shreckhorn, and the Wetterhorn, and the Jungfrau, should stoop to take notice of a grovelling being, who crawls along the level surface of the county of Cumberland, is an instance of genuine steadiness and equal serenity of temper which will not pass unobserved and unadmired before so accurate an observer as yourself. Yet I dare say you think yourself most magnificent, with your Hardknot and Wrynose, and discover in your Lilliput, risings and fallings invisible to the grosser organs of the inhabitant of Brobdignag.—If you read on thus far, I am sure your patience will hold out no longer, and my letter goes into the fire, which in your cold part of the world you will certainly be sitting over when my packet arrives, about the end of the month. You then go to Lady Muncaster, and with a glance on your sevenfold shield, on which the setting sun is gleaming with a brilliancy which would throw a stoic into raptures, you lament over me 'as a poor, infatuated, perverted renegade, ' false to my gods, my country, and my father.' The greatest punishment your old regard will suffer you to inflict on me, will be a perpetual condemnation to breathe the air of the House of Commons, and to have no other ideas of a country prospect, or a country life, than can be collected from a stare from Richmond Hill, or a dinner at the Star and Garter. No, Muncaster, I am no renegade. True to my first love, a long and intimate acquaintance has made me find out so many excellences and perfections, that my affections are not to be changed, though in the course of my travels I see a fairer face, or a more exquisite symmetry,

' 'Tis the dear, the blest effect of Celia altogether.'

If, therefore, you should hear of my taking a country house in one of the Swiss cantons, don't take it for granted that I have forgot the land of promise. Allow now and then a transient infidelity; my constancy shall be unshaken to my true Dulcinea. ' These are my visits, but she is my home.' But, to drop all metaphor, I have never been in any other part of the world, for which I could quit a residence in England with so little regret :

---

* " Milner subsequently endeavoured to reclaim Lavater from his mystical notions, by a Latin letter, in the composition of which he took vast pains. 'I am a poor man,' Lavater briefly replied, ' and the postage of long letters is inconvenient to me.' "

God grant that the public and private state of our own country may never reduce it to such a situation as to give this the preference in my esteem. At present I have the same unalterable affection for Old England, founded as I think in reason, or as foreigners would tell me, in prejudice; but I feel sometimes infected with a little of your own anxiety; I fancy I see storms arising, which already ' no bigger than a man's hand,' will by and by overspread and blacken the whole face of heaven. It is not the confusion of parties, and their quarrelling and battling in the House of Commons, which makes me despair of the republic (if I knew a word half way between ' apprehend for,' and ' despair,' that would best express my meaning), but it is the universal corruption and profligacy of the times, which taking its rise amongst the rich and luxurious, has now extended its baneful influence and spread its destructive poison through the whole body of the people. When the mass of blood is corrupt, there is no remedy but amputation. I beg my best remembrances to Lady Muncaster, and my little friends, Penny and Gam. Tell the latter, if he will meet me at Spa, I will turn him into a pancake as often as he will.—Believe me to be, ever yours most affectionately, W. WILBERFORCE."

It was in 1787 that Mr. Wilberforce became the leading and parliamentary champion of freedom to the slave. We need not dwell upon the vastness, the variety, or the perseverance of his exertions in this sacred and mighty cause, which to the end of his days he heroically and constantly promoted; nor enumerate the many fields in which he advocated the interests of humanity, of benevolence, and religion. His life for about half a century was one uninterrupted triumph by argument, example, and achievement over cruelty, ignorance, and prejudice. Instead, therefore, of dilating upon his philanthropical career, or tracing its progress, we shall extract an account of his daily life while in London:—

" His house was continually open to an influx of men of all conditions. Pitt and his Parliamentary friends might be found there at ' dinner before the House.' So constant was their resort, that it was asserted, not a little to his disadvantage in Yorkshire, that he received a pension for entertaining the partisans of the minister. Once every week the ' Slave Committee' dined with him. Messrs. Clarkson, Dickson, &c., jocosely named by Mr. Pitt his ' white negroes,' were his constant inmates, and were employed in classing, revising, and abridging evidence under his own eye. ' I cannot invite you here,' he writes to a friend who was about to visit London for advice, ' for, during the sitting of Parliament, my house is a mere hotel.' His breakfast table was thronged by those who came to him on business, or with whom, for any of his many plans of usefulness, he wished to become personally acquainted. * * * * His ante-room was thronged from an early hour; its first occupants being generally invited to his breakfast table; and its later tenants only quitting it when he himself went out on business. Like every other room in his house, it was well stored with books; and the experience of its necessity had led to the exchange of the smaller volumes, with which it was originally furnished, for cumbrous folios, ' which could not be carried off by accident in the pocket of a coat.'

Its group was often most amusing; and provoked the wit of Mrs. H. More to liken it to ' Noah's ark, full of beasts clean and unclean.' On one chair sat a Yorkshire constituent, manufacturing or agricultural; on another a petitioner for charity, or a House of Commons client; on another a Wesleyan preacher; while side by side with an African, a foreign missionary, or a Haytiean professor, sat perhaps some man of rank who sought a private interview, and whose name had accidentally escaped announcement. To these mornings succeeded commonly an afternoon of business, and an evening in the House of Commons."

Surely business and labours in the cause of charity and humanity must have been as meat and drink to such a delicate and fragile frame as that which Mr. Wilberforce wore. It was the ethereal principle within that upheld him, fed as it was by the very processes which exercised its powers.

The name of Clarkson having been mentioned, and whose life has been identified with the great subject of slavery, we have farther to notice that the authors of the present volumes offer some remarks on this philanthropist's " History of Abolition," which are not calculated to recommend that work, nor to enhance the character of its author for judgment and fairness. It is plainly stated that his book conveys an entirely erroneous idea of the abolition struggle,—that Mr. Clarkson's estimate of his own services is so exaggerated as to have led him to make many mistakes,—that the egotism is extravagant,—that Mr. Wilberforce in looking into the work soon saw enough to induce him to refuse to read it, lest he should be compelled to remark upon it,—and that though entirely pleased, according to his ready forgetfulness of himself, with what had been said of his services, he, Mr. W. declared that undoubtedly justice had not been done in the book to Mr. Stephen. Without pretending to be able to judge exactly between the relative merits of the several great advocates and promoters of abolition, and without feeling ourselves called upon to exempt the present authors from the partialities inseperable from human nature, we must say that the simple insertion of certain letters without comment, and the general straightforward current of the entire narrative wherever Mr. Wilberforce or Mr. Clarkson or others are concerned, have produced in our minds a thorough conviction that the " History of Abolition" is neither so full nor so fair on the great theme of which it professes to treat as the memoirs and testimonies before us ; and that the individual efforts of the two philanthropists named assume different positions when gathered from both works, from what they did when estimated alone by the author of the " History."

In connexion with Mr. Wilberforce's political career, his sagacity and energy, for instance, in the year 1795, when the state of France drove so many of his countrymen to despair, excited the most serious alarm of others, and stirred to madness and rebellion not a few enthusiasts or evil-disposed persons, we shall present some account of what took place at York, in consequence of a public meeting which had been called in opposition to the ministry. Tuesday, the 1st of December, was fixed on for the purpose, at a short notice, and secretly, that the requisitionists might be safe from any intrusion from the metropolis.

" ' When undressing at twelve o'clock on Saturday,' says Mr. Wilberforce, ' I received a note from Sir William Milner, saying that the York meeting was to be held upon Tuesday next; but I had given up all idea of going.' He thought it quite impossible that a general meeting could be gathered on so short a summons; and to attend a party council of his enemies would have been manifestly foolish. Yet his suspicions were perhaps aroused by the communication of a friend, who came to tell him that ' something extraordinary is certainly designed in Yorkshire, since —— was seen to set out on the north road this morning in a chaise and four.' Enough, however, was not known to show that his presence would be useful, still less that it was so far necessary as to justify his travelling upon the day which it was his chiefest privilege to give up to religious employments, until he was in his carriage on his way to church on Sunday morning. Just as he had got into it, an express arrived from Mr. Hey and Mr. Cookson, informing him of all that had been done, and urging him at all costs to be present at the meeting. ' I sent immediately to Eliot, and then went there. He and I, on consideration, determined that it would be right for me to go: the country's peace might be much benefited by it.'

" Sending back therefore his carriage to be fitted for the journey, he went himself to the neighbouring church of St. Margaret's—' Sir George Shuckburgh there—talking—sad sermon,'—and then called on Mr. Pitt. ' I saw Pitt—he clear—much disquieted.' Whilst they were still together, his servant brought word that his carriage could not be got ready so soon as was required. ' Mine,' said Mr. Pitt, ' is ready, set off in that.' "

It was suggested that if it was found out in whose carriage the member of Yorkshire rode, he would be murdered. However,—

" ' By half-past two,' he says, I was ' off in Pitt's carriage, and travelled to Alconbury Hill, four horses all the way,' two outriders preceding him; a provision then essential to a speedy journey, even on the great north road. After a few hours' rest, ' I was off early on the Monday morning, and got at night to Ferrybridge. Employed myself all the way in preparing for the meeting.' He had been supplied by Mr. Pitt with samples of the various works by which the fomenters of sedition were poisoning the public mind; and of such importance was his mission deemed, that an express was sent after him to Ferrybridge with further specimens. ' Almost the whole of Monday,' says his secretary, ' was spent in dictating; and between his own manuscripts and the pamphlets which had followed him, we were almost up to the knees in papers.' "

The state of the country at the time, the scene at York, and the dramatic share which our hero took in it, have now to be described.

" ' On Monday,' says a private letter of the day, ' there went through

Halton turnpike above three thousand horsemen.' These were principally clothiers, (Billy-men, as they were long called from the event of the next day,) riding on the ponies which carried commonly their cloths to the adjoining markets. Many came from Saddleworth, a distance of near sixty miles, spending a great part of the night upon their journey; and stormy as was the next morning, (Dec. 1.) they still crowded the road from Tadcaster to York. ' It was an alarming moment,' says an eye-witness, ' when these immense numbers began to pour in, while as yet we knew not what part they would take.' But by Monday evening the supporters of the government began to feel their strength. ' When we arrived at York,' says Mr. Atkinson, ' we were told that our adversaries were collected at the great inn in Lendal, and that our friends were to meet at seven, at the George in Coney Street. Thither we repaired without delay, and found a respectable body of gentlemen already assembled. The enemy, through the friendship of the corporation, had previously secured the Guildhall, where they could lay their plans at leisure. We sent a deputation to offer to meet them the next morning in the Castle Yard, according to their first announcement, where both parties could act freely, but they refused. They then proposed to admit our men and theirs into the Guildhall by forties; but this we declined, knowing that the hustings would be filled with the mere dregs of York, hired to drown with noise what they could not overcome by argument; but we offered to meet them on any fair and open ground they chose. In the morning we assembled at the York Tavern, which was about as near to the Guildhall as the tavern at which they met; and at half-past nine we spread our forces even to its gates. They sent out to reconnoitre, and found our strength treble theirs. We were in high spirits, and the enemy were exceedingly discouraged. As soon as the gates of the Guildhall were opened, our men rushed in with theirs; but by entering through the Mansion House they had previously possessed the hustings, and had chaired Sir Thomas Gascoigne. This unfairness stirred up the Leeds' spirit; our men pushed up to the hustings, and lifted several of their number into the midst of their opponents' crowd. These immediately called upon Sir Thomas to quit the chair, and wait till the freeholders had voted in a chairman. He refused to leave it, and they hoisted him out, and voted Mr. Bacon Frank into his place. Our party then proposed and carried by a majority of three to one an adjournment to the Castle Yard, the usual place of meeting, and where numbers had already gathered.'

" At this period of the business, the want of any leader of acknowledged power was deeply felt amongst the supporters of the constitution. The plans of the opposite party had been long matured, and their bands were marshalled under their appointed chiefs; but the friends of order had come suddenly together, and there was none to take the lead in their movements, or engage their general love of order in support of these necessary though obnoxious Bills. Just when this want was most acutely felt, Mr. Wilberforce's carriage turned the corner into Coney Street. His approach was not generally known. ' You may conceive our sensations,' says a Leeds gentleman, ' when he dashed by our party in his chariot and four a little before we reached York.' He was received with the same exultation by the assembled concourse. ' He arrived,' says Mr. Atkinson, ' at about a quarter to eleven, amidst the acclamations of thousands. The city resounded with shouts, and hats filled the air. 'What a row,' he said to his son, when quietly entering the city thirty-two years later by the same road, ' what a row did I make when I turned this corner in 1795; it seemed as if the whole place must come down together.' "

Mr. Wilberforce's political conduct throughout the whirlwind of the French revolution, and when the principles and practices which characterized that tremendous convulsion threatened to desolate England, was distinguished by the most praiseworthy independence. Though he was not an alarmist, yet he entertained serious fears in regard to his country. Still he stood up for peace against the minister, his admired friend, and hazarded his influence in those circles of society which it was his interest to conciliate, by a conscientious discharge of duty. In 1794 he moved an amendment to the King's Speech at the opening of parliament, and afterwards voted with the opposition on Mr. Grey's motion for peace. Some of the consequences were, that his Majesty afterwards *cut* him at a levée, and that Mr. Pitt became for a time estranged. But purity of motive, well-earned reputation, and his energetic procedure at the York meeting in 1795, won for him the " very highest wave of popular applause," and his seat was not endangered at the ensuing election.

One passage more ought to be cited illustrative of the great and good man's clear conception of his duty when strong temptations were held out to him. It refers to the year 1825, and may afford a lesson to some commoners at this moment who no doubt have been meditating on the several events that may distinguish the approaching coronation.

" In the course of this autumn, an arrangement was suggested to him by the friendly zeal of Sir John Sinclair, which would have removed him to the calmer atmosphere of the Upper House. ' To your friendly suggestion,' was his remarkable reply, ' respecting changing the field of my parliamentary labours, I must say a word or two, premising that I do not intend to continue in public life longer than the present parliament. I will not deny that there have been periods in my life, when on wordly principles the attainment of a permanent, easy, and quiet seat in the legislature would have been a pretty strong temptation to me. But, I thank God, I was strengthened against yielding to it. For (understand me rightly) as I had done nothing to make it naturally come to me, I must have endeavoured to go to it; and this would have been carving for myself, if I may use the expression, much more than a Christian ought to do.' "

Mr. Wilberforce seems after the permanent change which took place in his religious sentiments to have studied constantly the avoidance of all pharisaical rigidity and bitterness against the vices and frivolities of those among whom he mixed. Indeed it was not in his nature to be illiberal, dogmatic, or austere. Still he must have found it difficult on many occasions to reconcile his most serious

and absorbing príñciples with the laxities to which his social intercourse exposed him ; and the truth is, that the manner and extent
of his accommodations were sometimes the theme of ridicule and
animadversion.   The principle of " dining with such a one to do her
or him good," was on the part of some apt to be turned to the purposes of laughter.   But would it not have been far more becoming
to presume, that a man of Wilberforce's endowments, energies, and
unwavering designs, like an Evangelist among the rich, the fashionable, and the powerful, must have had constant scope for elevating
the tone of conversation, directing and purifying the current of feeling, and stimulating exalted motives, by allowing himself, consistent-
ly with his cheerful and active nature, to mingle where equally zealous
but coarser reprovers or guides must have done harm or been
defiled, than by a sweep of gratuitous wit or ridicule to judge of him
by the common standard of religious enthusiasts ?   Whatever good
among the higher ranks his excellent and appropriate work on
Practical Christianity may have done, and it is understood to be
signal, yet we feel convinced that his living and graceful example,
joined to his wide spread celebrity, must have been more operative.
The very fact that his charities amounted to several thousands a
year, without limitation to particular sects or parties, must have been
the means of fixing thousands of eyes upon him, and of decking him
with a beauty and authority to which grateful homage would be
done.

A few anecdotes, sentiments, and sketches must now complete
our review of these volumes.   Here are certain parliamentary portraits by Wilberforce of contemporaries.

" When Lord Londonderry was in his ordinary mood, he was very tiresome, so slow and heavy, his sentences only half formed, his matter so confined, like what is said of the French army in the Moscow retreat, when
horse, foot, and carriages of all sorts were huddled together, helter-skelter ;
yet when he was thoroughly warmed and excited, he was often very fine,
very statesman-like, and seemed to rise quite into another man.

" Our general impression of Sheridan was, that he came to the House
with his flashes prepared and ready to let off.   He avoided encountering
Pitt in unforeseen debating, but when forced to it usually came off well.

" Fox was often truly wonderful.   He would begin at full tear, and roll
on for hours together without tiring either himself or us.

" Pitt talked a great deal among his friends.   Fox in general society was
quiet and unassuming.   Sheridan was a jolly companion, and told good
stories, but has been overrated as a wit by Moore.

" Fox was truly amiable in private life, and great allowance ought to be
made for him : his father was a profligate politician, and allowed him as
much money to gamble with as ever he wished."

We quote an anecdote illustrative of the levity or light hearted-
ness of the French, as related to Wilberforce by the great man who
was witness of it.

" Shortly after the tragical death of Marie Antoinette, M. Perigord, an emigrant of some consequence, who had made Mr. Pitt's acquaintance at Versailles, took refuge in England, and on coming to London went to pay his respects in Downing Street. The conversation naturally turned upon the bloody scenes of the French Revolution ; on their fatal consequences to social order ; and in particular on the barbarity with which the unfortunate Queen had been treated. The Frenchman's feelings were quite overcome, and he exclaimed amidst violent sobbing, ' Ah Monsieur Pitt, la pauvre Reine ! la pauvre Reine !' These words had scarcely been uttered, when he jumped up as if a new idea suddenly possessed him, and looking towards a little dog which came with him, he exclaimed, ' Cependant, Monsieur Pitt, il faut vous faire voir mon petit chien danser.' Then pulling a small kit out of his pocket, he began dancing about the room to the sound of his little instrument, and calling to the dog, ' Fanchon, Fanchon, dansez, dansez ;' the little animal instantly obeyed, and they cut such capers together that the minister's gravity was quite overcome, and he burst into a loud laugh hardly knowing whether he was most amused or astonished."

Pitt as we intimated before often comes up.

" Oh how little justice was done to Pitt on Warren Hastings' business ! People were asking, what could make Pitt support him on this point and on that, as if he was acting from political motives ; whereas he was always weighing in every particular whether Hastings had exceeded the discretionary power lodged in him. I well remember, I could swear to it now, Pitt listening most attentively to some facts which were coming out either in the first or second case. He beckoned me over, and went with me behind the chair, and said, ' Does not this look very ill to you ?' ' Very bad indeed.' He then returned to his place and made his speech, giving up Hastings' case. He paid as much impartial attention to it as if he were a juryman."

Of Sir Sydney Smith, who is said to have been scandalously used, inasmuch that while others got ribands and peerages, he never had anything—

" At the time of the siege of Acre, he got from the old Pacha a ring, or some other emblem of authority, which gave him absolute command over all the gates ; and one of his first employments of it was, to go to the Pacha's dungeons and set all the captives free. The Pacha grumbled in vain, exclaiming pathetically, ' But, Sir Sydney, they owe me moneys."

Whitbread is described as having been a rough speaker ; as one that spoke " as if he had a pot of porter at his lips, and all his words came through it." We have after this the remembrance of tears which the great brewer drew from the Philanthropist upon the Lottery question. Then follow an anecdote of him and certain comparisons.

" After Canning's speech on Lord Bexley's Resolution about a pound note and a shilling being of equal value with a guinea, he said to me, ' Well, I do envy him the power of making that speech.' This was very curious to-

me, because I never could have guessed that it was at all the model to
which he aspired. Poor Canning! I knew him well, and he knew that I
knew him. He felt that I knew him before he became well acquainted
with Pitt. He had a mind susceptible of the forms of great ideas; as for
these men, they have not minds up to anything of the sort; their minds
would burst with the attempt. I have often talked openly with Canning,
and I cannot but hope that some good may have come from it. When I was
with him once, he was in bed, on a sort of sofa-bed, at Gloucester Lodge,
and Southey was mentioned. 'I did not know that he was in town.'
'Yes, he is, and dines with me to-morrow; but I am afraid you will not
come because it is Sunday.' Canning was not a first-rate speaker! Oh
he was as different as possible from Pitt, and from old Fox too, though he
was so rough; he had not that art, 'celare artem.' If effect is the criterion of good speaking, Canning was nothing to them, for he never drew
you to him in spite of yourself. You never lost sight of Canning; even in
that admirable speech of his about Sir John C. Hippesley, when your mus-
cles were so exercised by laughing, it was the same thing; yet he was a
more finished orator than Pitt."

The trial of Warren Hastings has furnished many anecdotes.
Mr. Wilberforce says, " One day while it was proceeding,

" An important point came on when only Burke and two or three more
were present—little Michael Angelo among them, very pompous. Ned
Law, who was to argue the case as Hastings' counsel, began, ' It is a pity,
sir, to raise a discussion on this matter. This is no doubtful question of
political expedience, it is a mere point of law, and my honourable friend
there,' pointing to little Michael, ' from his accurate knowledge of the law,
which he has practised with so much success, can confirm fully what I say.'
Michael puffed and swelled, and almost assented. Burke was quite furious,
and ran to him and shook him, saying, ' You little rogue, what do you
mean by assenting to this?' Michael is talked of for a peer. It is not
unlikely; he has no son. He was left a good fortune by his father, who
was a builder, and he got on by keeping a good cook and giving excellent
dinners. I remember Sheridan playing off on him one of his amusing
tricks. He did not know where to go for a dinner, so sitting down by
Michael Angelo he said, ' There is a law question likely to rise presently
on which from your legal knowledge you will be wanted to reply to Pitt,
so I hope you will not think of leaving the House.' Michael sat still with
no little pleasure, while Sheridan slipped out, walked over to Michael's
house, and ordered up dinner, saying to the servants, ' Your master is not
coming home this evening.' He made an excellent dinner, came back to
the House, and seeing Michael looking expectant, went to release him,
saying, ' I am sorry to have kept you, for after all I believe this matter will
not now come on to-night.' Michael immediately walked home, and
heard to his no little consternation, when he rang for dinner, ' Mr. Sheridan
had it, sir, about two hours ago.' "

Mr. Wilberforce's last interview with Burke at the time of the
Portsmouth mutiny obtains this notice :—

" Burke was lying on a sofa much emaciated ; and Wyndham, Laurence, and some other friends, were round him. The attention shewn to Burke by all that party was just like the treatment of Ahithophel of old. ' It was as if one went to inquire of the oracle of the Lord.' I reported to them the account I had received, and Burke being satisfied of its authority, we held a consultation on the proper course for government to follow. Wyndham set off for London the same night with the result of our deliberations."

Indefatigable lawyers.

" One of the most remarkable things about Romilly was, that though he had such an immense quantity of business, he always seemed an idle man. If you had not known who and what he was, you would have said —' he is a remarkably gentleman like, pleasant man ; I suppose, poor fe'low, he has no business'—for he would stand at the bar of the House, and chat with you, and talk over the last novel, with which he was as well acquainted as if he had nothing else to think about. Once indeed I remember coming to speak to him in court, and seeing him look fagged and with an immense pile of papers by him. This was at a time when Lord Eldon had been reproached for having left business undischarged, and had declared that he would get through all arrears by sitting on until the business was done. As I went up to Romilly, old Eldon saw me, and beckoned to me with as much cheerfulness and gaiety as possible. When I was alone with Romilly, and asked him how he was, he answered, ' I am worn to death ; here have we been sitting on in the vacation, from nine in the morning until four ; and when we leave this place, I have to read through all my papers, to be ready for to-morrow morning ; but the most extraordinary part of all is, that Eldon, who has not only mine, but all the other business to go through, is just as cheerful and untired as ever."

But we must hasten to a close and go forward to the last scene of all in our great Philanthropist's earthly career, having as we think presented a sufficient number of passages from the voluminous Life to afford an index to the character and achievements of its subject, and to the diversified contents of the work.

" The next morning his amendment seemed to continue. To an old servant, who drew him out in a wheel-chair, he talked with more than usual animation; and the fervency with which he offered up the family prayer was particularly noticed. But, in the evening, his weakness returned in a most distressing manner; and the next day he experienced a succession of fainting fits, to which he had been for two years subject, which were followed by much suffering, and which for a time suspended his powers of recollection. His physician pronounced, that if he survived this attack, it would be to suffer much pain, and probably, also, with an impaired understanding. During an interval, in the evening of Sunday, ' I am in a very distressed state,' he said, alluding apparently to his bodily condition. ' Yes,' it was answered, ' but you have your feet on the Rock.' ' I do not venture,' he replied, ' to speak so positively ; but

I hope I have.' And, after this expression of his humble trust, with but one groan, he entered into that world where pain and doubt are for ever at an end. He died at three o'clock in the morning of Monday, July 29th, aged 73 years and 11 months."

. Such are some glimpses of the life of a highly-gifted man, of whom it has been justly said that he lived at once as the inhabitant of the visible and invisible world. He furnishes, without doubt, a most attractive incentive to a Christian course; but there is the other view, just now hinted at, which these Memoirs forcibly press upon the reader's attention, and which, to human creatures, is only second to immortal interests, and, indeed, inseparable from them— we mean the gladdening aspect which Mr. Wilberforce's history lends to sublunary scenes, to the present world, to human experience, in the midst of the imperfections and evils which too frequently disfigure the fleeting hour. The Divinity and an immaculate existence were constantly in the thoughts and before the hopes of this great man; but then he was so alive to all that was beauteous and joyous on earth, that his happiness could not have been greater though he had believed that this world was all in all. Sir James Mackintosh said of him—" I never saw any one who touched life at so many points; and it is the more remarkable in a man who is supposed to live absorbed in the contemplation of a future state." The same delicate discriminator, speaking of the philanthropist in his advanced age, adds,—" He is quite as remarkable in this bright evening of his days, as when I saw him in his glory many years ago."

- Behold him in his retirement, as pictured in the work before us :—

" Who that ever joined him in his hour of daily exercise cannot see him now as he walked round his garden at Highwood, now in animated and even in playful conversation, and then drawing from his capacious pockets (to contain Dalrymple's State Papers was their standard measure) a Psalter, a Horace, a Shakspeare, or Cowper, and reading or reciting chosen passages, and then catching at long stored flower leaves, as the wind blew them from the pages, or standing by a favourite gumcistus to repair the loss? Then he would point out the harmony of the tints, the beauty of the pencilling, and the perfection of the colouring, and sum up all into those ascriptions of praise to the Almighty which were ever welling from his grateful heart."

The fact is, and it is a significant one, he loved flowers with all the simple delight of childhood; so that when we unite his innocency and playfulness with his habitual self-examination, with his intense sympathy for his kind, with his numberless benevolent exertions, with his acknowledged singleness of purpose and unswerving energy and perseverance in the great and holy causes which he espoused, we cannot wonder that in the senate and in domestic life he

attained a station that no man ever surmounted. All these and
other features of character, however, can alone be fully perceived and
appreciated from the innumerable single traits brought out in the
pages before us; of which we have only farther to state, that the
talent, the fidelity, and the affection which distinguish the performance of the biographers, are in due keeping with the sacredness of the
duty they had to perform both to their revered parent and the
world; and that the modesty of their manner in never putting themselves forward instead of their precious theme, or making it the
mere occasion of their own display, becomes its moral sublimity—
for morally sublime it is; since the humanities which Wilberforce
awoke, the Christianized spirit which his principles and practical
efforts instilled into society in behalf of the distressed and the
debased in every sphere, have not died with him, but continue and
will continue to shed a mellow lustre over Great Britain, enabling
her to hold on in the van of civilization and its Apostleship throughout the world.

Art. II.—*The Athenian Captive.* A Tragedy. In Five Acts. By
  Thomas Noon Talfourd. London: Moxon. 1838.

One cannot rise from reading " Ion," or the " Athenian Captive,"
without a strong affection for the author of them, begot by the
polished purity and fervent character of his muse. They are works
evidently emanating from a mind deeply sensible of the higher requisites of the drama, and making it a matter of consequence to
adhere to its strictest rules, as well as to bring to its support all that
study as well as individual genius can command to sustain and elevate its pretensions. The very fault which chiefly marks these pieces
arises from a prevailing desire and tendency to render them vehicles
of sentiment and lessons that are inseparable from the purest enjoyment and the noblest aspirations; hence his superabundance of
lovely images and predominance of beautiful descriptions, as well as
carefully chosen thoughts laboured most gracefully, rather than dramatic action or bursts of individualized passion. Mr. Talfourd
declares that he regards the drama's cause, meaning thereby its
legitimate models to be the cause " of humanity and of goodne s ;"
and that this is his prevailing belief and his earnest wish to i lus-
trate it is discoverable in every scene and passage of his two elegant
tragedies. Had every writer of plays looked upon the subject with
the same accuracy of taste, and an equally high sense of the influence
and capabilities of the drama, the disrepute into which the stage has
fallen, both as a source of refined amusement and a school of instruction and reproof, would probably have been confined to sects or
individuals whose austerity it would be neither wise to imitate nor
eulogize. In a preface, which is as beautifully expressed as it
is kindly conceived in regard to Mr. Macready, the author's anxiety

for the interests of the acted drama is forcibly shown. He says,
" More than contented with the unhoped-for association I had obtained with the living influences of scenic representation, in the
indulgence accorded to " Ion," I should have postponed all thought
of again venturing before the public, until years had brought leisure,
which might enable me to supply, by labour and by care, what I
knew to be wanting in the higher requisites of tragic style. But I
could not perceive a gentleman, whose friendship I had long enjoyed,
forsaking the certain rewards of his art, and the tranquil pleasures
of domestic life, to enage in the chivalrous endeavour to support a
cause, which I believe to be that of humanity and of goodness, and
which seemed almost desperate, without a feverish anxiety to render
him assistance, and perhaps a tendency to mistake the will for the
power. The position of the two great theatres, with a legal monopoly, which has been frittered away piecemeal without recompense, until nothing remains but the debts which were contracted
on the faith of its continuance, and the odium of its name ;—opposed to a competition with numerous establishments, dividing the
dramatic talent and dissipating the dramatic interest of the town ;—
rendered the determination of Mr. Macready to risk his property,
his time, and his energies in the management of one of them, a
subject of an interest almost painful. Impressed with this sentiment, at a time when it was unforeseen that one of the most distinguished of our authors would lend his aid, who, no tragic creation
of Knowles 'cast its shadow before,' with its assurance of power and
of beauty, when the noble revivals of Lear and of Coriolanus were
only to be guessed at from those of Hamlet and Macbeth,—I determined to make an attempt, marked, I fear, with more zeal than
wisdom. Having submitted the outline of this Drama to the friend
and artist most interested in the result, and having received his
encouragement to proceed, I devoted my little vacation of Christmas
to its composition ; and, with the exception of some alterations (for
the suggestion of the principal of which I am indebted to him),
succeeded so far as to finish it before the renewal of other (I can
hardly say) severer labours. Whether I may succeed in doing
more than thus gratifying my own feelings, and testifying their
strength by the effort is, at this time, doubtful ; but, in no event,
shall I regret having made it."

Comparing the " Athenian Captive" with " Ion," we should say
that the effort, though occupying much less time, we believe, than
did the former piece, as an acting play, will be more effective.
It contains a very considerable rapidity and variety of incident.
Many of the sentiments and situations are touching or arousing.
In the character of Ismene there is originality. The hero Thoas is
a rhapsodist so much under the controul of fate as to assume a tragic
eminence. The other *dramatis personæ* have numerous touches
of nature about them to awaken sympathy, while the author's pecu-

liar taste for poetic description finds opportunity for its indulgence. The plot is simple, and the time of action two days; the whole bearing a pretty close resemblance to the Greek models. The story, however, is deficient in respect of probability, and we are too soon put into possession of what must be its catastrophe, to admit of the utmost anxiety and interest which a perfectly constructed plot is capable of imparting.

Creon is king of Corinth, a fretful, unstable old man, of the Lear family. Ismene is his second wife, and more nearly allied to the Lady Macbeth race. Hyllus and Creusa are his twin-offspring by the former union; and Thoas, a warrior, who is taken captive in battle, in consequence of generously saving the life of Hyllus, the hostile King's son, effectually secures the attachment of the stripling and the gratitude and love of Creusa. But we must let the story be more clearly understood and more deeply felt by snatching passages from several of its scenes.

On the opening of the piece Iphitus priest of the temple of Jupiter, the Avenger at Corinth, in the capacity of an Augur, is watching the flight of birds to read what is to be the issue of the war with the Athenians which is at the moment waging; and Creon is complaining of the inroads made by age which prevents him from distinguishing the winged signs described by the priest. His anxiety is increased by learning that his youthful son has rashly hastened to the battle; nor is his perplexity and techiness subdued by hearing it added that some stinging speech of the Queen, who is an Athenian by birth, whose loveliness under basest vestments had enthralled his Majesty many years before, had roused the spirit of the stripling, and driven him to prove his valour against the people she vaunted of. Creon commands Iphitus to bid her, whose " sad and solemn words have power to thrill and madden," to his presence.

" *Re-enter Iphitus.*

" *Creon.* Comes the queen hither? Does she mock our bidding?
Iphitus. At stern Minerva's inmost shrine she kneels,
And, with an arm as rigid and as pale
As is the giant statue, clasps the foot
That seems as it would spurn her, yet were stay'd
By the firm suppliant's will. She looks attent
As one who caught some hint of distant sounds,
Yet none from living intercourse of man
Can pierce that marble solitude. Her face
Uprais'd, is motionless—yet while I mark'd it—
As from its fathomless abode a spring
Breaks on the bosom of a sullen lake
And in an instant grows as still—a hue
Of blackness trembled o'er it; her large eye
Kindled with frightful lustre;—but the shade
Pass'd instant thence; her face resum'd its look

Of stone, as death-like as the aspect pure
Of the great face divine to which it answered.
I durst not speak to her.
    Creon.   I see it plain ;
Her thoughts are with our foes, the blood of Athens
Mantles or freezes in her alien veins;
Let her alone."

We shall have other opportunities of observing how much vigour
the poet has shewn in the delineation of this revengeful woman.
But it may be as well here to forestall a speech in which the cause
of her deep and long cherished enmity is explained.

    " *Ismene.*   What shame !
Thou hast not heard it.   Listen ! I was pluck'd
From the small pressure of an only babe,
And in my frenzy sought the hall where Creon
Drain'd the frank goblet; fell upon my knees;
Embrac'd his footstool with my hungry arms,
And shriek'd aloud for liberty to seek
My infant's ashes, or to hear some news
Of how it perish'd :—Creon did not deign
To look upon me, but with reckless haste
Dash'd me to earth ;—yes; this disgrace he cast
On the proud daughter of a line which trac'd
Its skiey lineage to the gods, and bore
The impress of its origin—on me,
A woman, and a mother !"

Such is the manner of accounting for the vindictiveness of a
matron who traces her descent from Theseus, and who is raised by
force to the· bondage of a throne in a land hostile to that to which
all her loves cling.

Hyllus slightly wounded is conducted to his father's palace, for
the Corinthians have on that day been victorious, and Thoas is a
captive.

    " *Creon.*   Canst thou tell his name,
Who impious drew the blood of him who soon—
Too soon, alas !—shall reign in Corinth ?
    Hyllus.   One
I'm proud to claim my master in great war ;
With whom contesting, I have tasted first
The joy which animates the glorious game
Where fiercest opposition of brave hearts
Makes them to feel their kindred !—one who spar'd me
To grace another fight—the sudden smart
His sword inflicted, made me vainly rush
To grapple with him; from his fearful grasp
I sank to earth : as I lay prone in dust,
The broad steel shiv'ring in my eyes, that strove

To keep their steady gaze, I met his glance,
Where pity triumph'd ; quickly he return'd
His falchion to its sheath, and with a hand
Frank and sustaining as a brother's palm,
Uprais'd me ;—while he whisper'd in mine ear,
' Thou hast dar'd well, young soldier,' our hot troops
Environ'd him, and bore him from the plain
Our army's noblest captive.
  Creon.   He shall die ;
The gen'rous falsehood of thy speech is vain.
  Creusa. O no ! my brother's words were never false ;
The heroic picture proves his truth ;—they bring
A gallant prisoner towards us. Sure, 'tis he !''

Creon leaves it to the captive to choose between death or a life-
long portion with slaves ; and is resolved on encountering the former
till the melting words of the gentle Creusa, and the pleadings of the
grateful young prince, persuade him to submit to bondage and the
garb and labours of the slave ; every badge of the warrior being taken
from him except a dagger which Hyllus enables him to conceal in
his vest.

In Act II. we are introduced to a Court in the palace of Creon.
Games in honour of the late victory are commenced, and Thoas is
required to make sport for the entertainment of the court. In the
meanwhile a cry is heard that Hyllus is in danger.

  " Messenger.   As his chariot, far
Before all rivals, glitter'd to the goal,
The coursers plung'd as if some fearful thing
Unseen by human eyes had glar'd on theirs ;
Then with a speed like lightning flash'd along
The verge of the dark precipice which girds
The rock-supported plain, and round it still
In frightful circles whirl the youth ; no power
Of man can stay him.''

Thoas bounds to his rescue, and the preservation of the youth is
thus explained to the tender-hearted Creusa,—

    " Be calm ; thy brother is preserv'd ;
Urg'd by his furious steeds, his chariot hung
Scarce pois'd on the rock's margin, where the vale
Lies deepest under it ; an instant more,
And Hyllus, who serenely stood with eyes
Fix'd on the heavens, had perish'd ; when a form
With godlike swiftness clove the astonish'd crowd ;
Appear'd before the coursers, scarce upheld
By tottering marl ;—strain'd forward o'er the gulf
Of vacant ether ; caught the floating reins,
And drew them into safety with a touch

So fine, that sight scarce witness'd it.   The prince
Is in his father's arms.
   Creusa.   Thou dost not speak
The hero's name;—yet can I guess it well.
   Iphitus. Thoas.—He comes !
   Creusa.   Let me have leave to thank him."

After these vivid and beautiful passages, we have some very
pretty love-making between the young lady and the declamatory
Athenian. On his returning to his tasks from this interview,
Hyllus probes the secret of the guileless damsel's sudden and
incipient love, thus :

   " *Creusa.* He speaks of tasks. My brother, can'st endure
To see a hero who hath twice preserv'd
Thy life—upon whose forehead virtue sits
Enthron'd in regal majesty—thus held
In vilest thraldom ?
   Hyllus.   Ah ! my sweet Creusa,
Thy words breathe more than gratitude.
   Creusa.   My brother,
I pray thee, do not look into my face.
   Hyllus. Nay, raise thy head, and let thine eye meet mine;
It reads no anger there. Thy love is pure
And noble as thyself, and nobly plac'd ;
And one day shall be honor'd."

Next we are introduced to a banquet in the palace. At the
Queen's insiduous suggestion, Thoas is the slave who is appointed
to carry round the cup. The degrading task proves extremely
offensive to Creusa and Hyllus, as well as to the captive ; but Creon
at the instigation of Ismene will have it so.

        " [*Thoas takes the cup, and approaches Creusa.*]
   Creusa.   Nay, tremble not.
Think thou dost pay free courtesy to one
Who, in the fulness of a grateful heart,
Implores the gods to cherish thee with hope
For liberty and honour.
   Thoas.   Words so sweet
Reward and o'erpay all.
   Creon.   Corinthians, rise !
Before the gods, who have this day espoused
The cause of Corinth, I this votive cup
Pour with one glorious prayer—Ruin to Athens !
    [*Thoas dashes down the cup he is about to hand to the King.*]
   Thoas. Ruin to Athens ! who dares echo that ?
Who first repeats it dies ! These limbs are arm'd
With vigour from the gods that watch above
Their own immortal offspring. Do ye dream,

Because chance lends ye one insulting hour,
That ye can quench the purest flame the gods
Have lit from heaven's own fire?
   Hyllus. [*Trying to appease the guests*] 'Tis ecstasy—
Some phrensy shakes him !
   Thoas.   No ! I call the gods,
Who bend attentive from their azure thrones,
To witness to the truth of that which throbs
Within me now. 'Tis not a city crown'd
With olive and enrich'd with peerless fanes
Ye would dishonour, but an opening world
Diviner than the soul of man hath yet
Been gifted to imagine—truths serene,
Made visible in beauty, that shall glow
In everlasting freshness; unapproach'd
By mortal passion ; pure amidst the blood
And dust of conquests ; never waxing old;
But on the stream of time, from age to age,
Casting bright images of heavenly youth
To make the world less mournful. I behold them !
And ye, frail insects of a day, would quaff
' Ruin to Athens !'
   Creon.   Are ye stricken all
To statues, that ye hear these scornful boasts,
And do not seize the traitor? Bear him hence,
And let the executioner's keen steel
Prevent renewal of this outrage.
   Iphitus.   Hold !
Some god hath spoken through him.
   Ismene.   Priest ! we need
No counsel from thee.
   Hyllus.   Father, he will bend—
'Twas madness—was't not, Thoas ?—answer *me :*
Retract thy words !
   Thoas.   I've spoken, and I'll die."

We can in some measure conceive the wonderful effect which
Macready's acting will lend to this scene. Thoas, however, is not
instantly put to death, for the Queen, whose dark and solemn nature
can wield the peevish and passionate old King as she wills, suggests
that he be doomed to a horrid cell, deep in a rock, to await the
tortures which leisure may frame for him. Such is her ostensible
policy, but in reality that at midnight she may bring him to her
presence by one of her confidential servants. Hyllus earnestly
pleads for his twofold deliverer, but in vain; for at the suggestion of
Ismene that the prince is longing to mount the throne, the stripling
is banished beyond the bounds of the city. Before midnight arrives,
Creusa visits the Captive, having procured means to set him at
liberty. He is, however, too true to a promise to the Queen to
avail himself of the opportunity, for he has given her his word that

he will wait on her, when sent for.   The fatal appointment terrifies
Creusa, who thus farther explains the mysterious character of her
Majesty.

> " *Creusa.*   To the Queen ?
> What would she with thee ?   She is steel'd 'gainst nature ;
> I never knew her shed a tear, nor heard
> A sigh break from her—oft she seeks a glen
> Hard by the temple of avenging Jove,
> Which sinks 'mid blasted rocks, whose narrow gorge
> Scarce gives the bold explorer space ; its sides,
> Glistening in marble blackness, rise aloft
> From the scant margin of a pool, whose face
> No breeze e'er dimpled ; in its furthest shade
> A cavern yawns, where poisonous vapours rise
> That none may enter it and live ; they spread
> Their rolling films of ashy white like shrouds
> Around the fearful orifice, and kill
> The very lichens which the earthless stone
> Would nurture :—whether evil men, or things
> More terrible, meet this sad lady there,
> I know not—she will lead thee thither !''

Ismene's purpose in sending for the Captive, and indeed all her
schemes, have been to render him a ready tool of her revenge.   She
offers him liberty if he will slay Creon ; but, though a foe to Corinth,
he will not consent to act the traitor.   She labours to arouse his
Athenian nature by dwelling upon the wrongs which the King hath
done to her, an Athenian Matron ; and in the course of the interview she discovers, without, however, communicating the discovery
at the time, that Thoas is her son—that he was the babe from whom
she was so cruelly torn, turning her nature into that of a tigress.
He has agreed to fly, but her condition is that his escape must be
by passing through a particular chamber, and obeying her command;
that if an arm be raised to stay his course, if a voice be heard, or if
aught mortal meet his sight, the fugitive's knife is to quench its life.
It is very obvious that this is subjecting the judgment and foresight
of Thoas to a most arbitrary power of Fate ; for the dullest dolt
must have perceived that he is about to commit murder, and that
Creon was to be the victim.   And such is the fact ; whence remorse,
the trials of friendship and love, and a number of dramatic incidents
and situations, are evolved during the remainder of the drama.   These
we need not particularly trace ; it being sufficient for the purposes
of exhibiting the poetry, and the general drift of the plot, to add a
few unconnected extracts to those which have already been quoted,
with some regard to the course of the story.

Thoas having found his way to the Athenian camp, is chosen
General of the army on account of his warlike exploits ; and, in the
hurry and success which awaits him in chastising the Corinthians·

after their short triumph, the horror of his soul on account of murdering the old King is for a little while smothered. At last he enters Corinth, triumphantly, where he is joyously hailed by the Queen, who reigns for the time in spite of the rights of Hyllus.

" *Thoas [Alone.* Again I stand within this awful hall;
I found the entrance here, without the sense
Of vision ; for a foul and clinging mist,
Like the damp vapour of a long-closed vault,
Is round me. Now its objects start to sight
With terrible distinctness ! Crimson stains
Break sudden on the walls ! The fretted roof
Grows living ! Let me hear a human voice,
Or I shall play the madman !
                    Enter Ismene, richly dressed.
    Ismene.   Noble soldier,
I bid thee welcome, with the rapturous heart
Of one, for whom thy patriot arm hath wrought
Deliverance and revenge—but more for Athens
Than for myself, I hail thee ! why dost droop ?
Art thou oppressed with honours, as a weight
Thou wert not born to carry ? I will tell
That which shall show thee native to the load,
And will requite thee with a joy as great
As that thou hast conferr'd. Thy life was hid
Beneath inglorious accident, till force,
Of·its strong current urged it forth to day,
To glisten and expand in sun-light. Know
That it has issu'd from a fountain great
As is its destiny.—Thou sharest with me
The blood of Theseus.
    Thoas.   If thy speech is true,
And I have something in me which responds
To its high·tidings, I am doom'd to bear
A heavier woe than I believ'd the gods
Would ever lay on mortal ; I have stood
Unwittingly upon a skiey height,
By ponderous gloom encircled,—thou hast shown
The mountain-summit mournfully revers'd
In the black mirror of a lurid lake,
Whose waters soon shall cover me,—I've stain'd
A freeman's nature ; thou hast shown it sprung
From gods and heroes, and wouldst have me proud
Of the foul sacrilege.
    Ismene.   ·   If that just deed,
Which thus disturbs thy fancy, were a crime,
What is it in the range of glorious acts,
Past and to come, to which thou art allied,
But a faint speck, an atom, which no eye
But thine would dwell on ?

Thoas.   It infests them all,
Spreads out funereal blackness as they pass
In sad review before me.   Hadst thou pour'd
This greatness on my unpolluted heart,
How had it bounded! now it tortures me,
From thee, fell sorceress, who snar'd my soul
Here—in this very hall!—May the strong curse
Which breathes from out the ruins of a nature
Blasted by guilt—
   Ismene.   Hold! Parricide—forbear!
She whom thou hast aveng'd, she whom the death
Of Creon hath set free, whom thou wouldst curse,
Is she who bore thee!
    Thoas.   Thou!
    Ismene.   Dost doubt my word?
Is there no witness in thy mantling blood
Which tells thee whence 't was drawn?   Is nature silent?
If, from the mists of infancy, no form
Of her who, sunk in poverty, forgat
Its ills in tending thee, and made the hopes
Which glimmer'd in thy smiles her comfort,—gleams
Upon thee yet;—hast thou forgot the night
When foragers from Corinth toss'd a brand
Upon the roof that shelter'd thee; dragg'd out
The mother from the hearth-stone where she sat,
Resign'd to perish, shrieking for the babe
Whom for her bosom they had rent?   That child
Now listens.   As in rapid flight, I gazed
Backward upon the blazing ruin, shapes
Of furies, from amid the fire, look'd out
And grinn'd upon me.   Every weary night
While I have lain upon my wretched bed,
They have been with me, pointing to the hour
Of vengeance.   Thou hast wrought it for me, son!
Embrace thy mother.
   Thoas.   Would the solid earth
Would open, and enfold me in its strong
And stifling grasp, that I might be as though
I ne'er was born.
   Ismene.   Dost mock me?   I have clasp'd
Sorrow and shame as if they were my sons,
To keep my heart from hardening into stone;
The promis'd hour arriv'd; and when it came,
The furies, in repayment, sent an arm,
Moulded from mine, to strike the oppressor dead.
I triumph'd,—and I sent thee!
   Thoas.   Dost confess
That, conscious who I was, thou urg'd my knife
Against the king?

Ismene.   Confess!—I glory in it!—
Thy arm hath done the purpose of my will;
For which I bless it. Now I am thy suitor,
Victorious hero! Pay me for those cares
Long past, which man ne'er guesses at;—for years
Of daily, silent suffering, which young soldiers
Have not a word to body forth; for all,—
By filling for a moment these fond arms,
Which held thee first.
    Thoas. [*Shrinking from her.*] I cannot. I will kneel
To thank thee for thy love, ere thou didst kill
Honour and hope!—then grovel at thy feet,
And pray thee trample out the wretched life
Thou gav'st me.

Ismene accuses Hyllus of the crime which Thoas has committed,
and the youth, though informed by the real murderer of the truth, is
willing to die for the friendship he bears his deliverer in battle and
in the sports.   Some fine situations occur for the display of Creusa's
tender affections.   Thoas unravels the secret of the murder in a
highly dramatic scene by using his dagger against himself, and
telling the truth, and the Queen, seeing how fate has fooled her,
comes to the end so finely conceived in the following lines :

                                    " She rush'd,
With looks none dared to question, to the cave ;
Paused at its horrid portal ; toss'd her arms
Wildly abroad : then drew them to her breast,
As if she clasp'd a vision'd infant there ;
And as her eye, uplifted to the crag,
Met those who might prevent her course, withdrew
Her backward step amidst the deadly clouds
Which veil'd her—till the spectral shape was lost,
Where none dare ever tread to seek for that
Which was Ismene."

We shall only quote further a passage where the Captive gives
utterance to his attachment to the city of his birth, which doubtless
breathes the classic associations of the author—associations akin to
those, on the supposed part of Thoas, which Scott has so fondly and
naturally expressed in regard to his " own romantic town."

                                    " From Athens ;
Her groves ; her halls ; her temples ; nay, her streets
Have been my teachers. I had else been rude,
For I was left an orphan, in the charge
Of an old citizen, who gave my youth
Rough though kind nurture. Fatherless, I made
The city and her skies my home ; have watch'd
Her various aspects with a child's fond love ;

Hung in chill morning o'er the mountain's brow
And, as the dawn broke slowly, seen her grow
Majestic from the darkness, till she fill'd
The sight and soul alike ; enjoy'd the storm
Which wrapt her in the mantle of its cloud,
While every flash that shiver'd it reveal'd
Some exquisite proportion, pictur'd once
And ever to the gazer;—stood entranc'd
In rainy moonshine, as, one side, uprose
A column'd shadow, ponderous as the rock
Which held the Titan groaning with the sense
Of Jove's injustice ; on the other, shapes
Of dreamlike softness drew the fancy far
Into the glistening air ; but most I felt
. Her loveliness, when summer-evening tints
Gave to my lonely childhood sense of home."

Art. III.—*Danmarks og Hertugdommenes Statsret med stadigt Hensyn
til dens ældere horfatning ved* Joh. Fred. Wilhelm Schlegel, &c.
*The Present Public Law of Denmark, and of the Duchies, in Con-
nexion with its Past State.* By J. F. W. Schlegel, Counsellor of
Conferences, Doctor and Professor of Law in the Royal University of
Copenhagen, Assessor to the Supreme Court, Knight of Dannebrog,
&c. 2 Vols. Copenhagen. 1836.

The countries which compose the present dominions of the Danish
monarchy, are an interesting object of attention in many points of
view.   This is a part of the northern hive, from whence issued forth
those swarms of barbarians that subverted the Roman empire, and
·infused a fresh portion of vigour into the exhausted races of the
South.   Here are. emphatically *gentis cunabula nostræ.*   From
these regions came the Anglo-Saxons, the Danes, and the Normans,
by whom England was successively conquered, and repeopled after
the extirpation of the original inhabitants, and from whom we derive
our language, our laws, and whatever it is that peculiarly distinguishes
us from other races of men.

   The various fortunes of the different states of modern Europe
which were built up on the ruins of the Roman empire form a singularly attractive subject of speculation to the political inquirer.
They were all free in their primitive institutions and manners, and
it is a wonder how such brave men were gradually fashioned to bow
their necks to the double yoke of feudal and ecclesiastical tyranny.
But the various mutations through which they have passed, until
they have reached that condition of society in which we see the
present kingdoms of Europe, deserve a still more scrutinizing examination.   In some, the aristocracy triumphed over both the crown
and the people.   In others, the rights of every order were absorbed

in the dazzling brilliance of the crown ; whilst few had the wisdom or the good fortune to find refuge under the shadow of constitutional freedom. Take again that remarkable state which was founded, not by the rude invaders of the North, but by fugitives from the catastrophe of the falling Empire, on the sand-banks formed in the lagunes at the mouths of the Po, whence the proud mistress of the Adriatic raised her lofty turrets, and survived for so many ages every other dominion. For three centuries she retained her democratical form of goverment. The Doges, with almost sovereign authority, succeeded, and these again were stripped of almost all but nominal power, by an aristocracy the most jealous, crafty, cruel, and despotic that the world has yet seen.

The political revolutions of Denmark may be said to have taken an opposite direction. Like the other Scandinavian and Gothic kingdoms of Europe, the monarchy was originally elective, or rather the hereditary principle was so imperfectly established, that it may be said rather to have had reference to a dynasty, than to have indicated by any constant rule the individual who was to succeed to the vacant throne.* Four orders of the state were gradually formed, in the progress of society, with distinct political rights ; the clergy, the nobility, the burghers of the towns, and the peasantry. Each of these orders had a right to be represented in the States General of the kingdom. Written constitution there was none; but on the accession to the throne of Christopher the Second, whose despotic inclinations were suspected by his subjects, the first capitulation was drawn up in 1320, to the faithful observance of which his successors were compelled to take a solemn oath, before they were crowned, or acknowledged as kings. The last capitulation was that signed by Frederic the Third, in 1648, which provided that the crown should for ever be elective, and restrained the royal prerogative within still narrower bounds. As the clergy and the nobility, who possessed all the little learning of the age, drew up these capitulations, they were naturally more careful to insert such conditions as favoured their own pretensions, than mindful of the rights and privileges of the other orders. The Reformation came, and with it a correspondent depression of ecclesiastical influence. The Protestant religion was declared to be the established religion of the state, the clergy fell back into the second rank among the orders of the kingdom. The nobles, who now occupied the first, greedily seized

---

" * This elective quality of the crown, as well as its independence of the Papal See, is expressed with some energy by king Waldemar the Third, in his answer to the Pope's nuncio, who claimed an authority over him, according to the extravagant pretensions of the church of Rome in that age. ‘ Naturam habemus a Deo, regnum a subditis, religionem a Romanâ ecclesiâ; *quam si nobis invides, renuntiamus per præsentes.*’ "

upon the property of the church, which according to a resolution of the diet of Copenhagen ought to have been annexed to the domains of the crown. The peasants had already been deprived of their personal liberty in Zealand and the adjacent islands. The nobles compelled the greater part of those in Jutland and Fionia to surrender their proprietary interests, and consent to become their vassals and tenants. Thus they revenged upon this oppressed class the share it had taken in the insurrection in favour of the dethroned king Christian the Second, and abused for this purpose their power as intendents of the bailiwicks and administrators of the royal domains. The diets of the kingdom were rarely convoked, and the peasantry still more rarely summoned to attend them, though their right to be represented in these national assemblies was never formally questioned. Instead of the regular diets were substituted convocations of the senators and nobility, called *Herredage*. The calamitous wars of Frederic the Third had fully exposed those defects in the constitution of the government which the heroic character and splendid abilities of Christian the Fourth had, to a certain degree, concealed from view. In fact, the nobility gradually encroached both upon the crown and the commons, until the state became an unmitigated aristocracy, under the name of a kingdom, and with the forms of a monarchy, as Venice was under the name and with the forms of a republic. The resentment and despair of the clergy and the commons, which were aggravated by the refusal of the nobility to bear their due proportion of the burthen of the new taxes required by the necessities of the state, found no other resource than the extreme one of rendering the government hereditary, and of conferring on the king the absolute powers of sovereignty. Lord Molesworth reproaches the Danes with the levity which thus threw away, in a single day, the liberties of themselves and their posterity; and with that bitter spirit of sarcasm which pervades his work, he compares them to the Cappadocians of old. And the authors of the "Voyage de Deux Français," consider the *Lex Regia* as the very essence of despotism, and yet they very sagely conclude that the Danes have never had occasion to repent this surrender of their liberties! The truth is, they had no liberties to surrender; the burghers and the clergy were both oppressed by the nobles, and the peasantry were abject slaves, *glebæ adscripti*; it was only the feudal aristocracy who lost by the revolution of 1660.

Although the Danish literature is rich in treatises on the civil and criminal jurisprudence of the country, a work upon the public law of Denmark was still wanting. Foreign inquirers, who sought for information respecting the political institutions of this kingdom, had recourse to the work of Lord Molesworth, entitled "An Account of Denmark as it was in the Year 1692," which bears too many marks of prejudice and passion to be entitled to implicit confidence. Professor Schlegel has convicted his lordship of gross inadvertence, at least, in very generously conferring upon the crown of Denmark the sovereignty of the Shetland islands, although they had been in possession of the Scottish king about a century and a half before he wrote. It is true they did once belong to Norway, and were pledged to Scotland; and the Danish government has often sought in vain to redeem them.

Professor Schlegel, the author of the work now before us, is already known to the literary and political world by his controversy with Dr. Croke, relating to the celebrated judgment of Sir William Scott in 1799, on the case of the Swedish convoy. He is also the author of several treatises on the municipal law and legal antiquities of his own country, and on subjects of general legislation, which, as they were published in German and Danish, are comparatively unknown except in the north of Europe. He has rendered an essential service to the public by the present work, which contains a valuable body of information respecting the political law of Denmark, a subject very little understood in other countries. He has thrown upon it all the lights which could be derived from history, and has been careful to connect the present with the past by reverting to the primitive origin of institutions which have been gradually modified by time and circumstances, and which are much more complicated in their structure than is generally imagined.

The author shows that the political maxim of the unity and indivisibility of the monarchy had been adopted as a part of the fundamental laws of the kingdom, as early as the reign of Gorm the Old in the tenth century. He strongly maintains the doctrine of its perpetual independence of the empire. The territories now belonging to the Danish crown are, the kingdom of Denmark, and the Duchies of Sleswig, Holstein, and Lauenburg; Iceland, Greenland, and the Ferroe Isles; St. Croix and St. Thomas in the West Indies, and Tranquebar, with some other small possessions, in the East Indies. The *Duchies* are held in a different capacity from the crown of Denmark. They were fiefs of the empire, and each has its own peculiar constitution and system of internal administration. The Duchy of Lauenburg is a recent acquisition. It belonged to Hanover, by whom it was ceded to Prussia, in exchange for other territories on the left bank of the Elbe; and again ceded by Prussia to Denmark, in exchange for Swedish Pomerania, which Denmark had received from Sweden as a partial compensation for the loss of Norway. In his quality of Duke of Holstein, the king of Denmark had a seat in the college of princes of the empire, and in the assemblies of the circle of Lower Saxony; is a member of the present Germanic confederation; has one of the seventeen votes in the smaller chamber of the diet at Frankfort; and contributes a contingent of 3,600 troops to the army of the confederation.

The fourth chapter treats of the ancient form of government in Denmark, and contains a historical deduction, showing how it was

gradually modified by the increasing power and influence of the
superior orders of the state, the clergy and nobility; and by such
striking events as the introduction of Christianity, the organization
and endowment of the church, the union of the three crowns of the
North at Calmar in 1397, under Queen Margaret, and the Reformation in 1536. The kingdom was partly hereditary and partly
elective, as was shown at the accession of a new dynasty, when
Sveno, the son of a sister of Canute the Great, who as a collateral
had no hereditary right, mounted the throne by the free choice of
the people; and again when Christian the First was elected by the
diet in 1448, and commenced the present reigning dynasty of the
house of Oldenburg. Mr. Schlegel examines the circumstances of
the revolution of 1660-61, and shows that the government was rendered hereditary by an act of the diet of the thirteenth of October,
1660, and the king rendered absolute by another act of the tenth of
January, 1661; although those who have undertaken to write this
passage of history have confounded the two transactions. As there
were some partisans of the crown among the senators and the
nobility, the resistance of the aristocracy was much more feeble
than it would have been if they had not been thus divided. He
insists that the people were great gainers by this revolution, which
effectually bridled the aristocracy by whom they had been so long
oppressed. A council of state was formed, composed of the most
enlightened members of the community without regard to distinctions of birth, which was unfortunately abolished in 1670, in consequence of the jealousy of that all-powerful minister, Chancellor
Griffenfeld. The supreme tribunal and the administrative boards
were filled by an equal number of nobles and commoners. The
privileges which the *tiers état* secured by his change, by their being
rendered capable of holding public employments, by the impartial
and public administration of justice, and the establishment of a
more equal system of taxation, confirmed the stability of the new
order of things. He thinks that if this revolution had been, as some
pretend, the effect of a mere court intrigue, it would not have been
permanent. A similar change in the form of government which
took place in Sweden twenty years afterwards, under Charles the
Eleventh, did not cause the same astonishment, probably because
it was not so enduring, which may however be attributed to the
extravagant abuse of his absolute power by Charles the Twelfth,
and to the sudden demise of that monarch. The revolution under
Gustavus the Third was effected with great facility, and the change
of government might have become permanent had it not been for
the innumerable errors committed by his son. The author concludes that a people who regard their own interests will always prefer even an absolute monarch who may rule with moderation, to an
aristocracy which must inevitably be oppressive.

However this may be, it is certain that the Danish people be-

lieved themselves reduced at this period to the desperate alternative
of choosing between these two extremes. The aristocracy had acquired a complete ascendancy over the other classes of the nation.
They exercised their dominion with insolence and oppression.
They cast all the burthens of the state upon the other orders, and
monopolized to themselves all its privileges. They extorted from
Frederic the Third, on his accession to the throne, a capitulation,
in which he not only acknowledged that he held his crown from
their choice, but bound himself to act in subordination to the senate
in the administration of the government, and to appoint to office
from their recommendation. The peasantry were, as we have seen,
in the lowest state of vassalage. The depressed and despised
burghers had just saved the kingdom from foreign conquest, by
their courageous defence of Copenhagen against the attack of the
Swedes in the memorable siege of 1659. Under these circumstances,
the diet was assembled, consisting of the nobles, the delegates of
the clergy, and the deputies of the towns, the wretched peasantry
being entirely omitted in the convention. The finances of the
kingdom, exhausted by a disastrous war, required fresh supplies.
The nobles irritated the other orders by insisting upon their ancient
privilege of exemption from an equal participation in the burthens
of taxation. Scenes ensued similar to those which marked the first
meeting of the States General in France in 1789, but with actors
of another stamp, and with a far different result. In a more enlightened age, this opportunity might perhaps have been improved
to establish a limited monarchy with constitutional securities. But
the clergy and the burghers, irritated at the insolent pretensions of
the nobility, and aided by a party among the latter, released Frederic from the obligations of the capitulation which he had signed
on his accession to the throne, declared the government hereditary
in the house of Oldenburg, and summoned the deputies of the peasantry to attend the diet. The revolution was completed by the act
of the tenth of January, 1661, which conferred on the monarch the
absolute authority of the nation.

At this distance of time, and with the imperfect means which we
have of forming a judgment concerning a transaction which has
been so much discoloured by opposite passions and prejudices, it is
difficult to form an impartial estimate of the characters and conduct
of the authors of this revolution. Among the principal actors were
Svane, bishop of Zealand (afterwards archbishop), and a leader of
the ecclesiastical order; Annibal Schested of the nobility; and
Nansen, a burgomaster of Copenhagen, and prolocutor of the commons. The portrait of the first of these has been drawn by Professor Jens Möller in his biographical sketch of Archbishop Svane,
inserted in a Danish publication, called the Historical Calendar,
and seems to lend some verisimilitude to the sombre colouring of
Lord Molesworth's picture of this remarkable event. After all,

whatever might have been the secret wishes of the court, and the designs of the leaders who favoured its pretensions, it is not probable, even according to Lord Molesworth, that the revolution would have taken such a turn, had it not been for the folly and insolence of the nobility, who spurned the just claims of the other orders, and treated with contempt the sound and reasonable arguments by which they were maintained. To borrow his own words,—

" This manner of arguing was very displeasing to the nobles, and begat much heat, and many bitter replies on both sides. At length, a principal senator, called *Otto Craeg,* stood up, and in great anger told the president of the city, that the commons neither understood nor considered the privileges of the nobility, who at all times had been exempted from taxes, nor the true condition of themselves, who were no other than slaves (the word in the Danish is *unfree*) : so that their best way was to keep within their own bounds, and acquiesce in such measures as ancient practice has warranted, and which they were resolved to maintain. This word *slaves,* put all the burghers and clergy in disorder, causing a loud murmur in the hall ; which *Nansen,* the president of the city of *Copenhagen,* and speaker of the House of Commons, perceiving, and finding a fit occasion of putting in practice a design before concerted (though but weakly) between him and the bishop, in great choler rose out of his seat, and swore an oath, *that the Commons were no slaves, nor would from thenceforth be called so by the nobility, which they should soon prove to their cost.* And thereupon breaking up the assembly in disorder, and departing out of the hall, was followed by all the clergy and burghers. The nobles being left alone to consult among themselves at their leisure, after a little while adjourned to a private house near the court. In the mean time the commons, being provoked to the highest degree, and resolving to put their threats in execution, marched processionally by couples, a clergyman and a commoner, from the great hall or parliament-house to the Brewers' Hall, which was the convenientest place they could pitch upon to sit apart from the nobles, the bishop of Copenhagen and the president of the city leading them. It was there thought necessary to consider speedily of the most effectual means to' suppress the intolerable pride of the nobility, and how to mend their own condition ; after many debates, they concluded that they should immediately wait upon the king, and offer him their votes and assistance to be absolute monarch of the realm, as also that the crown should descend by inheritance to his family, which hitherto had gone by election. They promised themselves the king would have so great obligations to them for this piece of service, that he would grant and confirm such privileges, as should put them above the degree of slaves. They knew he had hitherto been curbed by the nobility to a great measure ; and now saw their own force, being able (since they had arms in their hands, and the concurrence of the soldiers) to perform what they undertook. At the worst, they supposed they should only change many masters for one, and could better bear hardships from a king, than from inferior persons. Or, if their case were not bettered, at least they thought it some comfort to have more company in it ; besides the satisfaction of revenge on those that had hitherto not only used them ill, but insulted over them so lately. They knew the

king, and had seen him bear with an admirable patience and constancy all
his calamities; were persuaded that he was a valiant prince, who had often
exposed his person for the sake of the public, and therefore thought they
never could do enough to show their gratitude; which is the usual temper
of the people upon any benefit received from their prince."

Professor Schlegel proceeds to explain the history of the *Lex
regia* of 1665, the causes which retarded its publication until the
reign of Frederic the Fourth, and the contents of this fundamental
law of the Danish monarchy. The edict, called the law of *Indi-
genat*, promulgated under the late king Christian the Seventh, on
the twenty-ninth of January, 1776, was also intended as a second
fundamental law. It excluded foreigners, with a few exceptions,
from public offices and employments. But the Danish publicists
consider it as a maxim, that the king cannot part with any portion
of the royal prerogative as fixed by the *Lex regia*. They therefore
regard the edict of 1776 as merely directory, and not as furnishing
a positive rule for the exercise of the royal prerogative. In fact it
has been departed from in several rescripts and ordinances. The
Lex regia regulates the succession to the throne, and confers on
the king the whole legislative and executive power. It gives him
the sole authority of making, repealing, amending, and interpreting
the laws; of appointing to all offices, civil and military; of commanding the forces and fortified places of the kingdom; of making
peace and war; of levying taxes and duties; of exercising supreme
jurisdiction over the ecclesiastics and ecclesiastical affairs. This is
a sufficiently compendious and comprehensive code of despotism.
But in order to estimate the real nature and constitution of the
government and its actual practice, it would be necessary to consider
how far it has been modified by manners, usages, and institutions
which have supervened, and which, though apparently inconsistent
with the letter of this fundamental law, have very much mitigated
its harsh and repulsive features. The increased and constantly
increasing force of public opinion, the example of neighbouring
countries, the growth of European civilization, and the general diffusion of knowledge, have all had their influence. Charters, parchments, seals, and other forms, are comparatively inefficacious; and
as in a free government, so in one which is arbitrary in theory, more
depends upon the general sense of mankind and the spirit of the
people, upon that law which is written upon the hearts of men, than
upon these mere instruments and conventional forms. Hence it
happens that there are many things which a king of Denmark cannot venture to do in this age, which he might have done with impunity in those unsettled and barbarous times when his nominal
authority was much less than it is now, and has been ever since the
the revolution to which we have adverted. Hence it happens, that
the government of Denmark, though in theory an unqualified des-

potism, has been of late years administered with mildness and forbearance.   Among the circumstances of improvement in the internal
administration which deserve to be noticed, is the entire emancipa-
·tion of the peasants, who were formerly in a state of the most abject
slavery, not only oppressed by their masters, but exposed to the
grossest abuses in the exercise of the prerogative of purveyance in
the royal progresses through the country.   Their complete liberation
was finally accomplished on the first of January, 1800, in consequence
of the provisions of an edict issued in 1788 under the administration
of the present king, then crown prince.   Count A. Bernstorff, the
celebrated prime minister of Denmark, who set the example by
freeing his own peasants, and Count Raventloz, late minister of state,
by their persevering efforts overcame the obstacles which this humane
and liberal measure encountered from a portion of the aristocracy.
This revolution is commemorated by a chaste monument erected by
public subscription, on the high road near the western gate of Copenhagen, in 1792.   It is a simple obelisk, of reddish freestone, standing on a pedestal of Norwegian marble, the base of which is adorned
with classic bas-reliefs, representing the Roman ceremonies of emancipation, and four statues of Italian marble standing around it,
emblematic of Fidelity, rural Industry, Courage, and Patriotism.
The crown Prince himself laid the corner stone of this monument,
the inscriptions on which (in Danish) express the public gratitude
to " the son of the king and friend of the people," and recite that :—

" The king, being aware that civil liberty, regulated by just and equal
laws, inspires the love of country, and courage in its defence, the desire of
knowledge, love of labour, and hope of happiness, has therefore ordained,
that servitude should henceforth cease; so that order and diligence may
preside in the execution of the rural code, and that the husbandman, free,
bold, enlightened, industrious, and good, may become an estimable and
worthy citizen."

This beneficent measure does great credit to the administration
under which it was conceived and executed.   It was very naturally
followed by an edict of the sixteenth of March, 1792, prohibiting
the African slave trade to be carried on by Danish subjects from
and after the beginning of the year 1803, and interdicting the importation of slaves into the Danish colonies after that period.   It
also established some regulations for the improvement of the mind,
morals, and general condition of the black slaves in the Danish
West India islands.   This law has not, like the interdictions of
some other countries, been suffered to remain a dead letter, but has
been executed with good faith and constant vigilance.
     Among the political institutions of Denmark, which, in addition
to the influence of other circumstances, have contributed to limit
and restrain the theoretical despotism of the government, is that of
the supreme tribunal, *Hoieste Rett.*   By the text of the *Lex regia,*

the faculty of interpreting the law is attributed to the monarch, and in fact justice is administered in his name in all the tribunals, but in general with great purity and independence. This is especially the case with the *Hoieste Rett*, which was instituted by Frederic the Third, in 1660, and ordinarily consists of fifteen judges, who hold their offices *quamdiu sese bene gesserint.* It is the court of the last resort in the kingdom, and the only one where the proceedings are entirely public, and the pleadings oral. In the inferior tribunals, the proceedings are private, and the pleadings in writing. An appeal lies to it from the highest tribunals in Iceland, the Ferroe Isles, and the Danish colonies in the East and West Indies. But the duchies of Sleswig, Holstein, and Lauenburg have their own peculiar systems of jurisprudence, and local tribunals of the last resort. The session of the supreme tribunal of the kingdom is opened on the first Thursday of March annually by the king in person, attended by the great officers of state, with great pomp and ceremony. It is held on that occasion in the palace of Rosenburg, a venerable building in the modern Gothic style, erected in 1604, by Christian the Fourth, from the designs of Inigo Jones. The great hall in which it assembles is peculiarly adapted to make a striking impression on such an occasion. It is hung with very beautiful old tapestries representing the wars and victories of Christian the Fifth, with appropriate inscriptions in German; the ceiling is enriched with historical paintings in oil, by the Danish artist Krogk; and the entablature filled with representations in stucco of several memorable events in the reign of Frederic the Fourth, in high relief, the whole of which produces an impression not unworthy of the temple of national justice. The king is seated on his throne, at the foot of which are three massive lions of silver; and a cause is pleaded and decided before him *pro formâ.* On all other occasions, he is addressed, as if he were actually present, by the advocates, who turn towards the vacant throne, which stands between two long tables, at which the judges are seated, clothed in a costume copied from that of the parliament of Paris.

A chapter of the author's first volume treats of the king's titles, and of the arms of the kingdom; and this subject is naturally connected with the history of the Danish orders of knighthood. These are only two, that of the *Elephant* and of *Dannebrog*. The former is said by some to have been founded by Canute the Sixth, who warred in the Holy Land, and restored Ptolemais, or St. Jean d'Acre, to the Christians. But others assign it a much more modern date. The legend respecting the order of Dannebrog is, that king Waldemar the Second made war against the Pagans in Livonia, and the Danes having lost their standard in battle, a panic seized them, which was dissipated by the descent of a new standard from the sky, marked with a cross, upon which they rallied and defeated the enemy with great slaughter. Whereupon the king instituted the order of the knights of Dannebrog, or the national standard. This *ori-flamme* was lost in battle in after ages, and the order itself fell into oblivion, until it was revived by Christian the Fifth in 1671.

Another part of Mr. Schlegel's work treats of a subject in which foreign nations have a deep interest ;—the superiority claimed by the king of Denmark over the neighbouring seas, and especially the Sound, and the two Belts, together with the consequent right of levying duties upon the commerce of other nations for the passage of these straits into the Baltic sea. It contains a very full historical deduction of the ancient Danish claim to an exclusive sovereignty over these seas, which was the origin of the Sound duties, and a detail of the different treaties and regulations now existing, by which they are levied and collected. The seventh chapter of the first volume treats of the *regalian* right of coining money, and, in con-nexion with that subject, of the bank of Copenhagen, and its paper currency. The notes of the bank, which became extremely depre-ciated during the late war with England, have been redeemed and taken out of circulation, and the paper is almost at par under the present excellent administration of the bank. The next chapter treats of the royal posts, and their present organization. The Danish posts were established by Christian the Fourth, a monarch of whom the Danes are justly proud. Christian the Fifth granted them to his illegitimate son, Count Christian de Gyldenlowe, in the form of a fief of the crown, and the Norwegian posts to another of his sons. But they were re-united to the royal domain under Fre-deric the Fourth, who appropriated their revenues to pension the retired servants of the crown, their widows and children. The con-cluding chapter of the first volume treats of the island of Bornholm, and the peculiar privileges enjoyed by its inhabitants. This island, which was ceded to Sweden by the treaty of Reeskilde in 1658, shook off the Swedish yoke by its own exertions in the following war, and surrendered itself to Frederic the Third, upon certain stipulated conditions, which are still observed. The inhabitants are enrolled in a local militia, well organized, and commanded by their own officers, and are exempt from the conscription for the army to which all other Danish subjects are liable.

The second volume of the work before us gives an account of the public law of the duchies of Sleswig, Holstein, and Lauenburg, and of the local organization of Iceland, the Ferroe Islands, and the Danish colonies in the East and West Indies. It contains also an account of the civil and criminal codes of Denmark, and of its judi-cial institutions. Although we cannot quite agree with Lord Moles-worth (who on this occasion seems determined to make amends for blackening the other features of the nation by painting every thing in respect to the Danish laws *en beau*), "that for justice, brevity, and perspicuity, they exceed all that I know in the world," yet there are doubtless some things in the legal institutions of this country which are worth examination. Among these are the Conciliation or Arbitration Courts (*Forligelses-Commission*), which did not exist in Lord Molesworth's time, but were established by the present reigning monarch, and which experience has shown to be very useful in checking the spirit of litigation. The science of the legal antiquities of the country has also been diligently cultivated, and these, it is well known, are connected with our own *fontes originis juris*. The laws of Canute the Great have been studied and commented on by Professors Nyerup, Schlegel, and Kolderup-Rosenvinge; and though we regard these inquiries into the barbarous and antiquated jurisprudence of our remote ancestors as rather valuable for a history of manners than of laws, yet they may not be wholly without their use in the latter point of view. Mr. N. Falck, one of the professors of jurisprudence in the university of Kiel, in Holstein, in the preface to a German translation of Blackstone's Commentaries, which he has recently published, has much insisted upon the importance of these analogical studies, as throwing light upon German jurisprudence; and it is possible that this may reflect some in return upon the history and principles of the common law of England.

ART. IV.—*A Revision of the Common or Received English Translation of The Gospel and of the Three Epistles of John, the Evangelist and Apostle of Jesus Christ.* London: Fellowes. 1837.

WHEN a man of learning, biblical knowledge, and devout principles undertakes and endeavours to present a new and improved translation of any portion of the Canon of Scripture, we hold that the design and the attempt manifest a spirit that ought to be cordially hailed and warmly encouraged not only by every lover of sacred truth but by every friend of literature. To be sure, and the present Reviser concedes the fact, the common and received English translation of the Old and New Testaments is deservedly held in high veneration as a whole. Its simplicity and propriety of language has never been equalled by any later attempts at an entirely new version. Besides, its style and diction by long usage and familiarity have acquired a sort of prescriptive authority, which the mind loves to identify with all that is purely Scriptural and classical in revealed truth. Endeared to us in this way, it is with reluctance that any change is tolerated, unless it be a manifest and important correction. And yet every one is aware that there is room for many such corrections in the Bible, although, considering the variety of writers who figure in it, the difference of style, of language, of dialect, of idiom, not to speak of the several ages in which they wrote, the errors are wonderfully few.

But though there should be no positive error in the translation as it at present stands, though a passage may be literally turned into

English from the original Hebrew and Greek, it is obvious to any one in the least conversant with idiomatic peculiarities that a translation may be verbally correct and yet not faithful or full. Besides a language, say our own, is subject to changes, such as require the watchful eye of the scholar to point them out to the ordinary reader ; so that between one age and another a word or phrase may come by usage to have very different meanings. The Reviser instances, Church, Atonement, Baptism, &c. as proofs. We must, however, guard ourselves against admitting this fact of the varying usage and modification of language and its concomitant ideas, as an argument for wholesale alterations in versional renderings of the Holy Scriptures, or as even authorizing a hasty or prompt adoption of modes of expression which may happen to begin to prevail among a people. No ; for besides the veneration which antiquity begets as before noticed in reference to our common and received translation, operating upon our religious associations, that very translation has been the best standard and bulwark of the English language that exists, preserving it from decay and degeneracy far more than any other literary treasure, imbued as it is with the simplicity, the racy and fresh power of Saxon phraseology. But the facts now stated on the one and on the other side of the subject only render this more manifest and impressively true, that judgment; delicacy, taste of the rarest order, and a mind fully aware of the sacredness and importance of the task are absolutely called for from him who would in any case and to any extent become the critical translator and expounder of the original languages in which the Scriptures were given to mankind.

In no division of the sacred volume is there such a necessity for the scrupulous skill insisted on by us as where the peculiar and divine doctrines of the Gospel are recorded, and especially when these doctrines are only accessible to the many who have no immediate appeal but to their own vernacular translation ; which, while literal and excellent, is confessedly in numerous instances ambiguous, sometimes erroneous, and very often idiomatically obscure. To the unlearned reader, the concise or elliptical modes of expression in the original become the source of much perplexity, and to the zealous of erroneous belief.

Of all the writers in the New Testament St. John is the most doctrinal and spiritual, at the same time the most simple and unadorned. But while he is simple almost to baldness, there is a peculiar sublimity in his style suitable to the wonderful themes of his inspiration, which requires the greatest circumspection in any one who would expound his meaning. His conciseness and elliptical forms look as if he feared to utter an expletive that would add the slightest gloss to the Gospel, tarnish its purity, enfeeble its power, or denude it of any portion of grandeur.

The Reviser, however, as is very plainly intimated in the title-page, where he calls his work " An attempt to render clear and intalligible to the unlearned English reader the more obscure or ambiguous expressions of the holy Evangelist," has endeavoured by a strict attention to the grammatical and the idiomatical construction and usage of the original, and also by a peculiar, and what seems to him, a well-authorised latitude of translation, to convey a satisfactory rendering of St. John's Sacred writings. This is a very serious and solemn undertaking; but we are happy to say that, according to our judgment, he has brought to it praiseworthy assiduity and earnestness, eminent scholarship, and devout appreciation. We like to see him quoting the words of Origen, who says, that " the first-fruits of the Holy Scriptures were the Gospels; and that the first-fruits of the Gospels was the Gospel according to St. John, the true sense or meaning of which no one can clearly comprehend unless he have, as it were, like the Evangelist himself, reclined on the bosom of Jesus."

The Reviser's design and mode of procedure in the present work, which may be called a faithful translation with a brief comment incorporated with the text, deserve some explanation before we offer specimens for the consideration of our readers.

In order that the original doctrines and sentiments of the Evangelist may be clearly understood by the mere English reader, he with careful circumspection introduces additional words into the text by way of amplification or illustration as the case may require, or, he sometimes substitutes a new translation, that may affect the meaning of the passage, but much more frequently that which in these days may be deemed a more appropriate though synonymous term for that which is used in the received version. Such additions and alterations, however, are carefully designated and printed in Italic letters (as in the few instances adopted in the common translation) to distinguish them as expletives, or as new readings of the Greek original; so that the reader is immediately apprized of the insertion and may consider it accordingly. Of these brief insertions, we may say, that though at first sight they appear to be too frequently introduced, yet on closer examination they will be found to illustrate on the authority only of the context and of parallel passages (to which reference ought to be made in the promised Appendix,) what there was doubtful or indefinite to the unlearned reader. At the same time we may probably be justified in classing the present Translator among those who do not wish to insist too rigorously on the merely literal sense of the present English renderings, but who consider that a due reference to the Apostolical times, persons, places, and phraseology is intimately connected with the just interpretation of the original Scripture terms. His references to certain learned and eminent writers dispose us to view and to welcome his Revision, as founded exclusively on the peculiar authority of the plain Scriptural documents under the circumstances in which they were originally committed to the care of the Christian world, before they became obscure and perverted by

the controversies of the dark ages, and contaminated by the
jealousies and the prejudices of vain and heretical men.   It is thus
that he wishes to place these sacred documents of the Christian faith,
on their truest and most secure basis—on the primitive rock and
not on secondary formations.

As we are highly pleased both with the scheme and the execution
of the work, believing that it is eminently calculated to render the
Gospel plain and clear to the poor, whether in point of learning or
the means to procure far more voluminous productions explanatory
and illustrative of revealed truth, we have further to notice that the
Reviser seems to be intimately acquainted with most of the treasures
of criticism and exposition, by the learned in ancient and modern
times bearing upon the Holy Scriptures.   Nor is it an unimportant
assistance which he has lent in the mere matter of reading the text
of St. John, that he distinguishes the more emphatical words, and has
them printed in Roman capitals.   It has frequently been said that
to read the sacred record well, is as good as half a commentary;
but without strict attention to emphasis which can only be properly
applied by a knowledge and feeling of the context, there can be no
good, no satisfactory reading.   In this respect alone the revision
offers valuable aid to the ordinary reader as well as to the student
of scripture.

We proceed now to offer some specimens of the work, and cannot
do better than begin with the first five verses of St. John's Gospel,
which, it has been said, a Heathen scholar declared ought to be
written in letters of gold.

. " * In the beginning* *of all things* was the *WORD or* *Wisdom of
God,* and the Word was with GOD, and the Word was GOD.

" 2 This *same Word or Wisdom of God* was in the beginning with
GOD.

" 3 By *IT* all things were * *made to exist,* and WITHOUT it not even
ONE thing was *made* which WAS *made.*

" 4 In IT was *the *fountain of eternal* Life, and *the *knowledge of*
that *eternal Life* was the **spiritual and *true *LIGHT* of mankind.

" 5 But THAT *spiritual* LIGHT *then* shone *as it were* in *darkness, and
the darkness did not comprehend it."

Here is a specimen not only of the amplifications but of the alterations in the rendering of the Greek text which the Reviser has, at his
own peril, introduced; and it demands some notice.   We are not,
however, going to enter upon the theological discussion which the
personification of the term Logos has excited, here rendered by the
terms " Word" or " Wisdom of God."   Theological controversy
is not for our journal; but the translation of the above-mentioned
term, and indeed the whole of the revision, admit of literary discussion to which we confine ourselves.

On comparing the above rendering with the received English

translation, it will be perceived, that, in the third verse, the pronoun used is " it," instead of " him ;" an alteration which we presume. will be explained in the forthcoming Appendix to the present volume. In the meantime we may observe, that the writer has either knowingly or unconsciously adopted the interpretation which Vitringa puts upon the term " Logos," as quoted by Lardner in his " History of the Apostles," and consequently in the third verse he uses the neuter pronoun " it," instead of the personal pronoun " him." Besides, the original Greek text will grammatically, at least, bear this rendering by the neuter English " it." Tyndale in the first English translation uses the same pronoun ; and in many of the translations into the modern languages, as the French, " la parole," and the Spanish " la palabra," &c., where the noun is feminine, the subsequent pronoun takes the corresponding gender ; and the personification of the term " Word," or " Wisdom of God," with Jesus Christ, does not in fact occur till it is afterwards fully announced in the fourteenth verse. Perhaps it may appear that the adoption of the masculine personal pronoun " He" or " Him," has been an arbitrary and unnecessary deviation from the original English rendering of Tyndale ; and that the truth as well as the sublimity of this proem may have suffered from the alteration.

The 14th verse runs thus in the revision :—

" 14 Moreover the Word *or Wisdom of God* became flesh, *or Man incarnate in the person of Jesus Christ*, and dwelt among us, and we ourselves beheld his glory, *even* the glory as of the only-born *or chosen* Son of *God* the Father, *he being manifestly* full of *divine* grace and truth."

According to the Reviser's interpretation, this becomes a most important verse, deciding as it does at once the divinity of Jesus Christ.

We have not in this last extract, nor shall we in those which are to follow, encumber ourselves with the numerous asterisks which the Reviser has introduced, since they only show the multitude of readings which we expect to see explained and defended in the promised Appendix.

In any new translations of the New Testament which are submitted to our criticism, we are in the habit of turning to certain passages in which we are convinced the received English translation is wrong. One of these is to be found in the 4th verse of the second chapter of St. John's Gospel, to which we beg to recal the Reviser's attention. It does not appear to us that, " Woman, what hast Thou *at this time* to do with Me ?" is a rendering that is agreeable to the gracious speaker's character, or borne out by the Greek. Something like the idea that " it is not an affair of thine or mine," appears to us to be nearer the meaning:

Going forward to the 8th chapter, we quote the first eleven verses.

" 1 AND Jesus went unto the Mount of Olives *near to Jerusalem.*

" 2 But early in the morning he was again present in the Temple, and all the *common* people came unto him : and sitting down *as was usual* he taught them *there.*

" 3 And the Scribes and the Pharisees bring unto him *into the court of the temple* a woman who *they say* had been *certainly* taken in adultery : and making her stand *up* in the middle *of the court,*

" 4 They say to him, ' Master, *(that is, Teacher,)* this woman hath been taken actually committing adultery ;'

" 5 ' Now in the Jewish Law, (Levit. xx. 10 ; Deut. xxii. 22,) Moses hath commanded us, that ' such *women* should be stoned *to death* :' what, however, dost THOU say ?'

" 6 And THIS they said, *artfully* tempting him, *in order* that they might have *whereof* to accuse him : but Jesus stooped downwards, with his finger wrote *as it seemed the commandment of Moses,* (Deut. xvii. 6, 7,) upon *the dust of* the ground.

" 7 As, however, they persisted *in* asking him *the question,* he, lifting himself up, said unto them *(nearly in the words of Moses,* Deut. xvii. 6. 7.) ' Let HIM who is without sin among you [or, *rather let him who is the chief among your witnesses*] first cast a stone at her.'

" 8 And *then* again stooping downwards he wrote *as before* upon the ground.

" 9 Whereupon they having heard *what he so said,* and *moreover* being convicted *of sin and of witness* by their *own* conscience, went out one by one, beginning from the *chief or* eldest *of them even* unto the last *of them :* and Jesus alone was left, and the woman *remained* standing in the middle *of the court of the Temple.*

" 10 Then Jesus lifting himself up *again,* and seeing no one but the woman, said to her, ' Woman, where are those *men who were* thy accusers ? hath none *of them* condemned thee, *according to the Law of Moses* ?'

" 11 And she said, ' No one, Lord.' Whereupon Jesus said to her, ' Neither do I *so* condemn thee *on their testimony.* Go thy way, and henceforth sin thou not.' "

The authenticity of this history, it is well known, has been much doubted of by some commentators, who have suspected that there are also many errors in the text itself. The attempt which the present Reviser has made to elucidate both the narrative and the text is a very bold one, and we are not quite aware of the authority on which he has presumed to introduce an interpretation of the original so new and different. It may be allowed, however, that the consistency of the history, and the lesson conveyed in it become more apparent by his rendering, provided he shows that it can be substantiated. The reader has a right to see the passage critically and satisfactorily defended in the Appendix, which is shortly to appear, and which we could have wished the author had found it convenient to present simultaneously with what is before us.

The nineteenth chapter affords the Reviser several opportunities for the exercise of skilful criticism. Take the 18th verse.

" 18 Where *about the ninth hour after midnight, or third hour after sunrise,* they crucified him, and together with HIM, *they crucified* two other *condemned* persons, *one* on THIS side and *one* on THAT, and JESUS in the middle."

It may here be observed, that, by admitting the correctness of the above insertions, the discrepancy between the " sixth hour" of St. John, as mentioned in the 14th verse (reckoning by Roman time from midnight), when Christ was delivered up by Pilate to the Jews, and the " third" hour of St. Mark (reckoning by Jewish time, from sun-rise to six o'clock in the morning,) when " preparations were made for the crucifixion," may be satisfactorily reconciled.

" 21 Then said the Chief Priests of the Jews to Pilate, ' Write not ' THE KING OF THE JEWS,' but *write,* ' THIS MAN SAID I AM KING OF THE JEWS.' "

The distinction here made in the proposed alteration of the superscription on the cross is evidently required by the sense and context of the passage ; but it has not been noticed, as far as we know, in any former translation.

" 25 Now there stood near to the cross of Jesus, MARY his *own* mother, and (*Salome*) the sister of his mother, *who was called also* MARY *the wife* of Cleopas, *or Alphæus,* and MARY the Magdalene."

The obscurity and difficulty attending the clear discrimination of the " three Maries," arising from the different mention made of their names by the several Evangelists, are well known. We shall be glad to see the Reviser remove the doubts on this point by his promised notes.

" 28 After this, Jesus well knowing that all things were NOW wholly finished and *accomplished,* in order that the SCRIPTURE *of the Prophet David* might *also* be accomplished (Ps. lxix. 21), *himself* saith, *what in the Syriac language was understood to signify,* ' I THIRST,' (*or Eli, Eli.*")

The bold conjecture in supposing that the words, " I thirst," are in any way synonymous with the words " Eli, Eli," requires ample support. There is acknowledged difficulty in the passage, arising in a great measure from the contradiction produced by the different records of the several Evangelists. The Reviser's illustration evidently points to the Syriac word " Hil" or " Hila," which signifies " Vinegar ;" but something more is necessary, we think, to authorize his version and interpretation.

Every chapter in St. John's Gospel receives such critical and expletive attention from the present writer that our notices might be extended to a great length. The foregoing extracts and remarks, however, are sufficient to convey a strong idea of the importance and value of such a revision, and to show that it is wonderfully far from being a crude or commonplace production. The sentiment and opinion will be anything but lessened when the Epistles are perused and studied under his guidance, whether by the common reader or biblical student; but especially will admiration and reverence be enhanced for this latter most pure and admirable concentration of the Gospel spirit and code.

If a treatise which combines the genuine doctrines of the immortality of the soul, a luminous appeal to the eternal attributes of God as graciously displayed towards man, together with the practical result of universal brotherly love, and consequent virtue and felicity on earth, be worthy of our most serious study and acceptation, then will the Epistles of St. John be duly appreciated; a result 'far more valuable, though wrought out by simplicity of style, single-minded aspirations, and precepts humbly but fervently urged, than all that ever was or can be produced by the eloquence or logic of Plato, who gathered sweets from every rhetorical flower.

The first three verses of the First Epistle will furnish us with a specimen of the revision of this part of the work.

" That *Word or Wisdom of God, that Law or doctrine of eternal Life and Truth,* which was from the beginning *of all things with God the Father,* THAT which we have *now actually* heard, THAT which we have seen with our eyes, THAT which we ourselves have looked upon, and, *which we may say,* our hands have *palpably* handled concerning the word, *that is to say, the wisdom of God, or doctrine* of *eternal* Life;

" 2 (For that *word of eternal* Life hath *now* been manifested *to us,* and we have *truly* seen or *known,* and bear witness to, and declare to YOU *Christians* that *same word or doctrine of* eternal Life, which was *from the beginning* with *God* the Father, and which hath *now* been manifested to us, *in the person and glory and ministry of Christ.*)

" 3 THAT *word or wisdom* of *God, I say again,* which we have *thus actually* seen and heard, *and known,* declare we *now* to YOU, so that YE also may have *spiritual* communion with us *the Apostles of Christ:* and truly OUR communion is with *God* the Father, and with his chosen Son Jesus Christ *our Lord.*"

It may be observed that the introductory verses of this chapter appear to be the best and most authoritative comment on the proem of the Gospel of John, and that as such they have a double value emanating from the same divine fountain of inspiration, and confirming the same truths. The words of the original are here very much amplified indeed ; but it may admit of a doubt, whether in the present use of language, greater compression would not have been attended with ambiguity or confusion in the apprehension of the merely literal and unlearned English reader, whose mind it is desirable to imbue with a clear conception of such momentous truths.

Here follows another instance of considerable amplification of verses which have been the subject of much controversy. We do not meddle with the theological subject, but the extract may be regarded as affording an opportunity for trying the Reviser's learning, judgment, and creed. We go to chapter five in the same Epistle.

" 6 This *Jesus, namely,* Jesus the Christ, is he who is *assuredly* come, *and hath cleansed us both* by *the* water *of the spiritual baptism of ' repentance for the remission of sins,'* and *hath redeemed us* by *the sanctifying* blood *of his own obedience even unto death upon the cross: I say again,* NOT through *the outwardly purifying* WATER ONLY, but *rather* through *the* WATER *of inward baptism, or spiritual regeneration ;* and *also* through *his sanctifying* BLOOD, *or obedient death upon the cross ; leaving to us an example, that we should faithfully follow his steps :* and *moreover* it is the ' Spirit *of God'* which *now* witnesseth, *by its holy operation and effects,* that ' the *same* spirit is *the spirit of* TRUTH.'

" 7 *Testifying also,* That there are three *sure* witnesses *to the truth of the gospel faith* [in HEAVEN, *namely, First,* GOD the *heavenly* FATHER ; *and secondly,* the WORD, *or Wisdom of God, made manifest in Christ on earth ;* and *thirdly,* the HOLY SPIRIT *of God, the Comforter, the Regenerator and Sanctifier :* and these three *witnesses* are *spiritually* ONE *and the same witness.*

" 8 And *moreover* there are three witnesses *to this gospel-truth* on earth, namely, *First,*] the *regenerating* SPIRIT *of gospel-truth ;* and *Secondly,* the *purifying* WATER *of gospel-baptism and repentance ;* and *Thirdly,* the *sanctifying* BLOOD, *or the exemplary obedience of Christ unto death upon the cross ;* and these three *witnesses also* are *spiritually united* in ONE *and the same witness.*"

One other specimen we quote, and then close the volume. It is the opening of the Second Epistle.

" *I,* THE *christian* Elder, *John, hereby send greeting* to the elect *Christian* Matron *or Church at Jerusalem,* and to her *spiritual* children *in Christ, all of* whom I *myself* love in truth, and *whom* not *I* only, but also ALL my *Christian brethren,* who have truly known the *gospel*-truth, *love in like manner.*"

In this introductory greeting, as well as in that of the following Epistle, there is adopted, differently from other translations, the first personal pronoun " I," instead of the third " he," (the Elder), &c. This alteration seems to be justified by the ensuing verb, which is expressed in the first person, viz., whom " I " love. The Reviser also confidently renders the Greek word κυρία by the term " Matron," or "Church," as if κυρία, like many other words, were an hellenized term from the Latin " curia," that is, a principal or acknowledged court, place of assembly, or congregation (whence

P 2

probably may be derived the English word "church"). On this and many other points, however, we must expect further illustration in the forthcoming Appendix ; for, considering the great importance which attaches itself to every long-established scriptural expression, and the deep interest which is excited in the minds of all classes of readers by the slightest alteration in such verbal forms, it is due to the Reviser himself, as well as to the public, that the fullest elucidation should be given. We hope that what we have on this occasion quoted and said will, to some considerable extent, lead to further inquiries by others,—all which, if honestly and earnestly pursued by competent persons, must tend to confirm the truth and evolve Gospel doctrine.

The present writer has set a high example. He has in one literary respect, not as yet pointedly mentioned, pleased us much ; we mean his prevailing mode of rendering many forms of Greek construction and phrases peculiar to St. John and the Gospel writings, successfully reconciling thereby the idiom of our language to that of the original, so as in this respect to make his translation more literal than the present received version. It would, we think, be a great service to religion, to the learned as well as the unlearned, if he should have time to go over the whole of the New Testament, after the manner of which the specimen before us constitutes such an able and excellent proof. The labour, no doubt, would be vast, but to such a scholar, and a person of such biblical learning, not half so much as to others, differently harnessed for its performance. Unless, however, the work is already far advanced, we almost despair of finding the same hand, that has so satisfactorily executed the part upon which we have been engaged, completing the much-needed effort ; for we are led to believe that the Reviser has resided nearly fifty years on his own Preferment in the Established Church, and that he has ever been not only an ornament of that church, but one who has assiduously discharged his pastoral duties. If we are not misinformed, too, so far back as January, 1796, the Monthly Review favourably noticed a political poem, entitled "The Antidote," by the same author. We may therefore claim him as an old acquaintance ; and though his "Antidote" may, like many precious effusions, be now forgotten, we are confident that the work of his more ripened years now before us will be accounted, when he and we are no more, a valuable contribution to the knowledge of Gospel doctrine, and consequently prove serviceable to the interests of permanent practical religion.

Art. V.—*Montrose and the Covenanters, their Characters and Conduct, illustrated from Private Letters and other Original Documents hitherto unpublished, embracing the Times of Charles the First, from the Rise of the Troubles in Scotland to the Death of Montrose.* By Mark Napier, Esq., Advocate. 2 Vols. London: Duncan. 1838.

Mr. Napier, as it would appear, while making researches preparatory to his Life of the Inventor of Logarithms, found in the Napier charter-chest a number of documents that have never before seen the light, which, together with some other discoveries among the voluminous manuscripts belonging to the Advocates' Library, he is of opinion, throw a great deal of new illustration upon the characters and the events which distinguished the period of national history that forms the subject of his two volumes. We are ready to admit that he has not over-estimated the value of some of these muniments relative to individual or personal illustration; but we cannot accord to him the high honour to which any one must be entitled who succeeds in completely overturning the generally received opinions entertained by moderate minds relative to the most distracted era in the annals of Great Britain. Mr. Napier, in fact, is a decided partisan, who can see nothing but brightness, amiable points, or subjects of commiseration on the one side, and nothing but darkness, deformity, and positive wickedness on the other. He is an ultra-royalist and conservative in principle. He is a lively special pleader, but neither a liberal nor judicious historian. He is clearly of opinion that all is next to the authority of Gospel which the Napier chest contains, and that whoever thought not and acted not with Montrose, especially after his going over to Charles, was a traitor, whose motives must have been as base as they were ungallant and vulgar. The Covenant and its adherents are such vile themes, that our vocabulary fails him in his eagerness and frequency of denouncement; so that he has to hammer away with a certain circle of abusive epithets that become somewhat tiresome from repetition.

We are not going to enter the field of controversy with our author on subjects that for two centuries have occupied innumerable volumes. We only wish it to be understood, that we think virtue and right did not wholly reside with one party in the State, and that the age embraced was one of great political profligacy as well as one of great political martyrdom; that both on the side of the monarchy and the people there was a mighty sum of faction on the part of many of the leaders, and that on the part of their followers or disciples there was a vast deal of patriotism, honesty, and religious principle. According to our views the opposition to the divine right of kings, the national antipathy in Scotland to episcopacy, and to Charles's arbitrary proceedings in support of the establishment of that communion in the country where Knox's Reformation had taken such deep root, was the reverse of wanton rebellion, and had

quite contrary results down to the present day of producing infidelity,
ignorance, or the opposites of enlightened peace. We cannot
believe that all the sincerity and piety of the period in question were
with Charles and his counsellors ; we cannot believe, that, had they
and their principles met with no resistance Great Britain would
have been what she now is ; nay, we cannot but think that were
Mr. Napier and those of his *clique* (one of his own favourite epithets
in reference to the promoters and adherents of the Covenant) at this
moment in power, neither would political nor religious freedom in
Scotland be long countenanced by them. But we must eschew
even the threshold that would lead us to controversy, especially of
an ecclesiastical character, and particularly on the present occasion,
when, to correct the views of Mr. Napier, as we think they are
capable of being done, a minuteness of detail and of criticism, not
much less in extent than his own, would be required. Instead of
encountering this labour, it may be sufficient for our readers, and
amply fair to the author, if we let him be seen in some of his own
colours, as also where he may have brought to light some points of
character, anecdotes, and the like, which, for their value or their
novelty, deserve attention.

It is proper in the outset to state that the connection between the
Napiers and Montrose commenced in this way :—Archibald the first
Lord Napier (eldest son of the inventor of Logarithms), married
Margaret Graham, second daughter of John, fourth Earl of
Montrose, and thus became brother-in-law to the great Marquis,
the hero of the present volumes. To this first lord of the house of
Merchiston, a man of learning and high accomplishments, the
Marquis seems to have been in a great measure indebted for the
treasures of mind which distinguished him through life, and even to
the hour of his death. That the Merchiston charter-chest should
contain documents illustrative of one of Scotland's most renowned
warriors is thus a natural circumstance, though it may be questioned
whether the service which their publication will do to national
history, can amount to the value set upon them in the following and
many other passages to be found in the work before us,—

" The name and actions of Montrose were too conspicuous, and influential, in his critical times, not to have become familiar even to such
as cannot, in a strict sense, be termed readers of history. The romantic
pages, and historic genius, of Sir Walter Scott, have made the hero as
well known to the general or luxurious reader, as he is to those who study,
more inquiringly and systematically, all the historical annals of their
country. Hence there is an impression, widely prevailing though very
erroneous, that no more need or can be recorded of Montrose and his
times. But, I venture to say, had the original materials now first brought
to light in the following pages, been in the possession of David Hume or
Sir Walter Scott, greatly would the acquisition have aided, enlightened,
and enriched, a deeply interesting and important chapter of their historical

compositions. Even the domestic facts, though few in number, which I have been enabled to add to a more minute illustration of the principles of Montrose's public conduct than had hitherto been afforded, would have been treasures in the hands of the 'Great Magician.' With such stores, new to the world, his exquisite, but unfortunately too meagre 'Legend of Montrose,' might have expanded in a work of yet greater interest and effect; combining, too, the truth and importance of historical discovery, with some domestic matters of unquestionable fact, that beggar even his powers of romantic fiction."

We can hardly wonder that an author of Mr. Napier's political and ecclesiastical creed should, after this, profess to labour under an incompetency to do justice to the materials which he has ferretted out; and that in reference to the great captain of our age, he should declare, had he been conscious of sufficient ability, " I might have aspired to dedicate the result to the best existing representative of those lofty, unimpassioned principles,—so conservative of good government and time-honoured institutions,—those attributes of untainted integrity in the senate, and matchless heroism in the field, which may they never cease to be the characteristics of the British nation."

It must be confessed, however, that Mr. Napier very often loses sight of his self-distrust in other parts of his work, even when he runs counter to opinions that have been espoused, fought, and bled for by some of Britain's most famous sons. Mr. Brodie, the present Historiographer for Scotland, and author of a " History of the British Empire," who is made to stand many attacks, has not yet been one of these martyrs, and may not be worthy of ranking among the champions of the covenant. But the Historiographer is a whig, and Mr. Napier is glad to adopt a phrase suggested by a correspondent and to call whiggery an " unclean thing," although, surely, some men have marshalled under its banners who have not been defiled by aught that stains the archives of Britain. Our author is tender and high-minded enough to wail over the misfortunes of Charles of Montrose, and other cavaliers; but where is his modesty or generosity in characterizing the covenanters in a wholesale manner as an insidious, malevolent, unprincipled faction, who, instead of being grateful and too happy in receiving what the King and his advisers judged best for them, trampled religion and liberty under foot? Such are the merciful assertions of a writer who has the most crude and vague ideas we ever met with regarding a people's right of resistance, of a writer who has not courage or self-estimation enough to approach the Duke of Wellington with his new illustrations and comments, but who has no reluctance to joke or be witty about the *lifting up*, the *exaltation*, and such like phrases, meaning thereby the gibbet's eminence and displays, when hundreds upon hundreds of the said despised covenanters died rather than belie their consciences, or recede from the principles which they had espoused.

It is quite clear, indeed, that Mr. Napier does not think that the religion of the covenanters was fit for gentlemen, or that its professors could be any thing better than fanatics or anarchists. So much for modesty and a true estimate of lofty attributes.

There can be no objection to our author or any other making use of authentic documents to illustrate individual characters or events, provided individuals are not made to stand for the whole of a numerous or national party, whether that party be moderate or ultra on either side. We therefore have derived far more satisfaction from some of his personal discoveries than from the whole of his general inferences. In truth Mr. Napier is essentially a good gossip, not a convincing logician. He would make a lively chronicler of passing events ; but is one of the feeblest historians of what is bygone, where candour and unimpassioned research and construction ought to handle mighty antagonist principles and prodigious sacrifices. He has, for instance, made himself amusing as well as convincing, were argument or illustration necessary, which we deny to have been the case, in his endeavours to hold up Bishop Burnet as a pedantic, self-complacent, and time-serving character ; who, while professing independence, sometimes in connection with humility, sometimes with boldness, was apt to be swayed by mean and deceitful motives. Burnet's letter, so illustrative of his character to which we now allude, was occasioned by the Rye-house plot, when, after the suicide of Essex, Lord Russell was under condemnation and about to ascend the scaffold. This document, which has never before been printed, was addressed to John Brisbane, Esq., Secretary of the Admiralty at the time.

" ' DEAR SIR,

" ' I have writ the inclosed paper with as much order as the confusion I am under can allow. I leave it to you to shew it to my Lord Halifax, or *the King*, as you think fit, only I beg you will do it as soon as may be, that in case my Lord Russel sends for me, *the King may not be provoked against me by that.* So, Dear Sir, adieu.

" ' Memorandum for Mr. Brisbane.

" ' To let my L. Privy Seal know that out of respect to him, I doe not come to him. That I look on it as a great favour, that when so many houses were searched mine was not, in which tho' nothing could have been found, yet it would have marked me as a suspected person. That I never was in my whole life under so terrible a surprise and so deep a melancholy as the dismall things these last two or three days has brought forth spreads over my mind ; for God knows I never *so much as suspected* any such thing ; all I fear'd was only some rising if the King should happen to die ; and that *I only collected out of the obvious things that every body sees as well as I doe,* and to prevent that took more pains than perhaps any man in England did, in particular with my unfortunate friends, to let them see that nothing brought in Popery so fast in Q. Marie's days as the business of L. Jane Grey, which gave it a greater advance in the first moneth of that reigne than otherwise it is likely it would have made during her whole life. So that I had *not the least suspition of this matter;* yet if my Lord Russell calls for my attendance now, *I cannot decline it,* but I shall doe my duty with that fidelity as if any Privy-Counsellour were to overhear all that shall passe between us.

" ' I am upon this occasion positively resolved never to have any thing to doe more with men of business, particularly with any *in opposition to the Court,* but will divide the rest of my life between my function and a very few friends, and my laboratory; and upon this *I passe my word and faith to you, and that being given under my hand to you I doe not doubt but you will make the like engagements to the King;* and I hope my L. Privy Seal will take occasion to doe the like, for I think he will believe me. I ask nor expect nothing but only to *stand clear in the King's thoughts;* for preferment, I am *resolved against it, tho' I could obtain it;* but I beg not to be more under hard thoughts, especially since in all this discovery there has not been so much occasion to name me as to give a rise for a search, and the friendship I had with these two, and their confidence in me in all other things, may show that they know I was *not to be spoke to in any thing against my duty to the King.* I doe beg of you that no discourse may be made of this, for it would look like a sneaking for somewhat, and you in particular know how farre that is from my heart; therefore I need not beg of you, nor of my Lord Halifax, to judge aright of this message; but if you can *make the King think well of it,* and *say nothing of it,* it will be the greatest kyndness you can possibly doe me. I would have done this sooner, but it might have lookt like fear or guilt, so I forbore hitherto, but now I thought it fit to doe it. I choose rather to write it than say it, both that you might have it under my hand, that you may see *how sincere* I am in it, as also because I am now so overcharged with melancholy that I can scarce endure any company, and for two nights have not been able to sleep an hour. One thing you may, as you think fit, tell the King, that tho' I am too inconsiderable to think I can ever serve him while I am alive, yet I hope I shall be able to doe it to some purpose after I am dead; this you understand, and I will doe it with zeal; so, my dear friend, pity your melancholy friend, who was never in his whole life under so deep an affliction, for I think I shall never enjoy myselfe after it, and God knows death would be now very welcome to me; doe not come near me for some time, for I cannot bear any company, only I goe oft to my Lady Essex and weep with her; and indeed the King's carriage to her has been so great and worthy, that it can never be too much admired, and I am sure, if ever I live to finish what you know I am about, it and all the other good things I can think of shall not want all the light I can give them Adieu, my dear friend, and keep this as a witnesse against me if I ever fail in the performance of it. I am, you know, with all the zeal and fidelity possible, your most faithful and most humble Servant,

" Sunday Morning,   "G BURNET."
17th July 1683.' "

In a note the author adds some further and curious proof of Burnet's character; but we have only room to intimate that the abject letter just quoted did not succeed, that its writer was disgraced, and forced to go abroad, till the Revolution in which he was

an active agent restored him ; when King William conferred on
him a mitre. Brisbane was married to one of the Napier family,
which accounts for the letter being found by our author.

Perhaps the most interesting and novel particulars brought to light
by Mr. Napier are to be found in the Introductory Chapter, where
the first Lord Napier is the principal figure, although King Charles,
and still more the contemporary statesmen of Scotland, are prominent characters. Lord Napier appears to have been a pure and
eloquent patriot, as well as a deeply-learned man, among a foully
cunning and grossly dishonest class of his countrymen,—the judges
of the land, the officers of state, and the leaders among the aristocracy. No wonder that Scot of Scotstarvet wrote a work about the
period and persons in question, which he significantly entitled the
" Staggering State of the Scots Statesmen." To show of what un-
manageable materials some of these magnates were made, take the
following particulars :—

" At length Charles effected that memorable progress in the month of
June 1633. On the night before his coronation, he was feasted in the
Castle of Edinburgh by the old Earl of Mar, whom he had beheld at his
feet, crutches and all, ' stirring pity to cause injustice.' On the morrow,
when seated in the great hall of the Castle, to receive the crown which
some would fain have filched from him, it was Hay, the crabbed Chancellor—he whose ' manner was to interrupt all men when he was disposed
to speak, and the King too '—that now, in the name of the estates of the
kingdom, ' spake to the King.' Among the six noblemen, whom his
Majesty selected to support the bearers of his canopy, was Lord Napier.
Rothes, the father of the future Covenant, carried the sceptre—and Lorn,
the deeper and more deadly promoter of the Rebellion, assisted to bear
the train.

" The factious insolency of his Scotch nobles which Charles had experienced in England, he now met with, in more dangerous and personal
collision, ' at home.' No sooner had he set his foot in Scotland than he
created the chancellor Earl of Kinnoul, a favour which had little effect in
molifying the temper of that statesman. Charles had always wished that
the primate of Scotland should have precedence of the chancellor ;
' which,' (says Sir James Balfour) ' the Lord Chancellor Hay, a gallant
stout man, would never condescend to, nor ever suffer him to have place
of him, do what he could, all the days of his lifetime.' Once again Charles
endeavoured to effect this. It was when arranging the pageantry of his
coronation with Sir James Balfour, the Lord Lyon, in whose own graphic
words we must give the anecdote. ' I remember that King Charles sent
me to the Lord Chancellor, being then Earl of Kinnoul, the day of his own
coronation, in the morning, to shew him that it was his will and pleasure,
but only for that day, that he would cede and give place to the Archbishop;
but he returned by me to his Majesty a very brusk answer, which was,
that since his Majesty had been pleased to continue him in that office of
chancellor, which, by his means, his worthy father, of happy memory, had
bestowed upon him, he was ready in all humility to lay it down at his

Majesty's feet; but since it was his royal will he should enjoy it with the known privileges of the same, never a stol'd priest in Scotland should set a foot before him so long as his blood was hot. When I had related his answer to the King, he said, "Weel, Lyon, let's go to business; I will not meddle further with that old cankered, gouty man, at whose hands there is nothing to be gained but sour words." ' Thus even the regal procession, which to the eyes of all Scotland betokened gaiety and gladness, was to the devoted monarch replete with vexation and bitterness. From that hollow pageantry he passed to his Parliament of Scotland, with a spirit lofty, and long chafed, but as placable as it was royal."

Our author quotes an epitaph, which is to be found in James Balfour's manuscript in the Advocates' Library, bearing upon the character of another nobleman of the period, Thomas Hamilton, first Lord Haddington. It runs thus in modern orthography.

> " Here lies a Lord, who, while he stood
> Had matchless been, had he been—
> His epitaph's a syllable short,
> And ye may add a syllable to it,
> But what that syllable doth import;
> My defunct Lord could never do it."

The first Lord Napier, of whom we have already more than once made honourable mention, is represented, indeed, by our author as an almost immaculate character, as well as great by learning and talents. He obtains this high honour in a great measure in the pages before us, because, though described as a rigid Protestant, he would not join the Covenanting or Puritan cause, and because Montrose and he came to entertain the same loyal or royalist opinions. We have found, however, in the documents obtained from the Napier chest, here published for the first time, some evidences of ambition that savour of what in the case of other persons our author would be apt to describe in terms scarcely consonant with pure motives or safe authority. Mr. Napier has been speaking of his Lordship's political sagacity and prophetic views, as handed down in certain papers ; and proceeds,—

" I find another very interesting paper, all in his own handwriting, which appears to have been addressed to the King himself, a few years before his progress to be crowned in Scotland. . Whether it was actually sent to his Majesty, or, if sent, ever suffered to reach him, and how far the scheme proposed was practicable, there is now no means of knowing. But it will be seen from the tenor of it how intensely the writer had felt on the subject of the fatal effect of those mists of ignorance and ' mistakings,' as to the affairs of Scotland, in which the King was continually enveloped, by those who, for the sake of petty and private interests, so treacherously practised upon the facilities of his disposition.

" ' *Offers of useful service to your Majesty, some few propositions being first premised whereby the use of that service may be better known.*

" ' That the state of business is oftimes disguised to princes, for private ends.

. " ' That the truth of business is hardly to be expected from the relations of great men, whose friendships and dependencies extend far,—or from men *factious*,—or from such servants as endeavour to build up their fortunes with their own hands, not leaving to their masters to do it upon their good deserving,—or from parties.

. " ' That from *misinformation*, all errors, incongruities in matters of estate, and mistaking of the true means, whereby the just and gracious purposes of princes come to be disappointed, do proceed.

" ' That it is not easy to distinguish truth from falsehood, seconded by friends, and supported by reasons probable.

" ' That it is impossible to do any thing conveniently or rightly, or to determine any thing *de jure*, if first it be not known how it is *de facto*.

" ' That the justest and wisest princes must err in their directions given upon sinister information of the state of the business in hand.

" ' That it is an easy matter to a just prince, by following only the bent of his own inclination, to give such directions and commands, upon matters perfectly known to him, as thereby he may reap honour, profit, the love of his subjects, and the reputation of wisdom and justice.

" ' The truth of these foresaid propositions being so well known to your Majesty, it would be impertinent to me to go about to prove. But to be a means and instrument whereby the *true state of business of Scotland*, a place remote, may be conveyed to your sacred ears, is the best and most useful service can fall within the compass of my power, the highest of whose endeavour is to be a faithful servant, and not to make an unjust claim to eminent abilities. If, therefore, your Majesty may be pleased to prefer some honest and well-deserving servant to the place I hold of your Majesty, and to give me some place of access to your Majesty's person. (*without which*, services of that kind are nearly unuseful,) and a reasonable means that I be not forced to undo my estate, and instead of a useful servant become a troublesome suitor, (whereby there shall be more by many degrees brought in, and saved in your Majesty's coffers,) then I do humbly offer and undertake,—

" ' To establish such correspondence in most parts of Scotland, and in all the courts and judicatures thereof, with men honest and judicious, not interested in affairs, and not knowing one of another, who shall give me sure intelligence of the state of every business which shall occur; and if any of them shall chance to be partially affected, the relation of the others shall controul what is amiss in his. Which relations shall be made known to your Majesty by me, without passion or affection, and without respect to any end of my own or of others, as I shall answer to God in conscience, to your Majesty upon my alledgeance, and under pain of your highest displeasure. Whereby your Majesty shall reap these commodities following, and many more.

" ' 1. As the clouds which obscure and darken the sun are dispersed by the heat of the same, so shall the cloud of factions, compacted to no other end but to misinform your Majesty for their private advantage, and to the prejudice of your Majesty's just and gracious designs, be dissolved by the knowledge of the true state of things, and your Majesty's resolutions and directions, proceeding from that knowledge, being constant and absolute, shall render their combinations vain and of no force, and your Majesty's affairs shall go more smoothly than hitherto they have gone."

We do not copy any more of the *commodities* promised to his Majesty ; nor do we think it necessary to dwell upon the *modesty*, the *non-assurance,* of this Napier document. Our readers may have heard of an *imperium in imperio,* and we leave it to them to judge how far the sagacious Scotchman wished to be removed from the custodiership of that dignity. Truly his lordship must have intensely felt about the ignorance and " mistakings," as to the affairs of Scotland, when he was ready to take upon his own shoulders the entire concern of removing them. No doubt he must have been prepared to employ spies and other reputable agents; but Charles was too blind or too wise to adopt the scheme.

Our author is most indignant and rancorous against the spirit and language of the covenant which the great majority of the people of Scotland zealously subscribed. He says, that it " came reeking from the hot-bed of faction." Montrose, all the world is aware, was one of its earliest and at first staunchest supporters, although he afterwards joined the King's standard, who had ordered the famous service book to be read in the church service, which was tantamount in the people's eyes to the establishment and preservation of episcopacy, so hateful to the Scotch nation. We quote some passages to show how Mr. Napier accounts for his hero's conversion to royalty.

" The incident to which historians have generally referred the departure of Montrose from the path of rebellion, is, as Malcolm Laing expresses it, 'the returning favour of his Sovereign at Berwick,'—a vague and ill-formed assertion, that has been generally, though much too hastily, admitted. Let us consider the circumstances under which Montrose then met the King.

" Had the revolt of Scotland ended with the treaty of Berwick, amply sufficient as the concessions upon that occasion were for the ' Religion and Liberties' of Scotland, the real objects of the faction would yet have been unfulfilled. Their unchristian enmity against the Bishops, their irrational and sweeping projects against Episcopacy, were all unsatisfied.

" But Montrose, though hitherto he had aided the Movement with thoughtless ardour, was not, as we have elsewhere observed, one of the faction. He had been ' brought in' as a great prize, but never almagamated with the Rothes' clique, and when in highest favour with the ' Prime Covenanters,' was always considered by them apart from the initiated, and simply as a ' noble and true-hearted cavalier,'—' that noble valiant youth,'—' that generous and noble youth,' whose ' discretion was but too great in sparing the enemies' houses.' It was impossible that such a character, attached so loosely to the faction, should not have been awakened into loyal feelings by the conduct of the Covenanters, after the King's concessions at the treaty of Berwick.

" Dr. Cook, in his History of the Church, has adopted, without sufficient

examination, the popular theory of Montrose's loyalty. Speaking of the
occasion, when Montrose was one of the three noblemen who dared to
trust themselves with the King, he remarks, ' but what renders this conference peculiarly memorable is the impression which was made upon
Montrose; hitherto he had been zealous for the Covenant, but he now
changed, and resolved to employ his talents for promoting the royal cause;
the other two remained firm to their party.' This, apparently, is recorded
in no complimentary sense, and the contrast with his companions would
seem to be unfavourable for Montrose, although there is no fact brought
out inconsistent with his complete justification. If, however, by the impression alleged, no more is to be understood than some reaction in the
generous mind of Montrose, occasioned by a gracious reception from the
King, which he had never experienced before, or an explanation of the
King's intentions with regard to Scotland, as to which Montrose had been
deceived, his keenest eulogist might leave that accusation unrefuted. But
that Montrose should have been suddenly gained over, and have ' now
changed,' merely in consequence of some contingency that touched his
avarice or ambition, (for it is certain that no immediate reward was held
out, as when Rothes fell,) is, under all the circumstances, any thing but
a probable theory. He appears indeed to have been proof against the
mere prospect of admission to Court, or the first signal of his ' Sovereign's
returning favour,' as we learn from Mr. Archibald Johnston himself, from
whom we accept the anecdote as he gives it. That distinguished Cove-
nanter is strenuously endeavouring, in a long and characteristic epistle,
dated 2nd January 1639, a few months before this conference at Berwick,
to seduce Lord Johnston, and persuade him not to go to Court; when he
uses the argument,—' rather do nobly, as my Lord of Montrose has done,
who having received a letter from *the King himself* to go up with diligence to his Court, convened some of the nobility, shewed unto them
both his particular affairs, and the King's command, and that according
to his covenant of following the common resolution, and eschewing all
appearances of divisive motion, *nobly* has resolved to follow their counsel,
and has gone home to his own house, and will not go to Court at all.' It
would, however, be a poor defence for Montrose to maintain that he was
unmoved by the interview at Berwick with Charles, whose kingly presence and noble aspect were never so imposing as when he was beset by
difficulties and danger. The monarch may indeed have particularly
desired to reclaim Montrose. Struck by his stately and heroic bearing,
contrasted with the irreverent levity of Rothes, and the repulsive democracy of Archibald Johnston, and, perhaps, favourably impressed by the
humane forbearance which, contrary to the wish of the covenanting
clergy, had characterized Montrose even in rebellion, it is not unlikely
that Charles, in the words of his favourite poet, may have inwardly exclaimed at the sight of him,

—— O, for a falconer's voice
To lure this tassel gentle back again !

and the accomplished King, who fascinated Presbyterianism itself, had
indeed a falconer's voice for such a ' tassel gentle.' We believe, then,
that Montrose had felt his heart yearn towards Charles the First, that
some scales had fallen from his eyes, and that he departed from that inter-

view a wiser and a better man. But the popular *calumny* is certainly not history, and, indeed, we may distinctly trace its origin in circumstances that suggest a more adequate cause of Montrose's growing opposition to the convenanting faction."

We observe in a note, that Mr. Napier regards the Bristol riot and burning which took place only a few years back, and " many other circumstances," as resembling the rise of the troubles in Scotland of which he treats, and of what is to be " the subsequent fate of the British Monarchy." We are not prophets, and but poor analogists we fear ; otherwise, surely, we could not but see as our author sees. If, however, the war of opinion, which is the shape that hostilities take in the present day, is to enlist the sword and the scaffold for the arbitrement of disputed questions of policy in church and state, before those which agitate the country can be decided, it can hardly be expected that a more enthusiastic reformer will join the *Movement* than was Montrose when he attached himself and for a time belonged to the Covenanters, or that a more meteorlike career is to await any one than attended the chivalric espousal of the royal cause by this proud and noble warrior. Equal romance will be looked for in vain, superior bravery and skill to his cannot find room in human nature. Mr. Napier's account and estimate of his hero's system of war affords a good sketch and a favourable specimen of the book.

" Montrose's system of tactics, and military capacities in general, have been criticised by some modern historians, anxious to depreciate his character at all points, without, apparently, considering that the art of war was nearly in its rudest state in Britain at the period, and especially so among the too independent marauders from whom he was to derive the desultory and faithless following that constituted his army. Moreover, these critics seem not to have observed, or are pleased to forget, that throughout the whole of his brilliant campaigns, Montrose's resources were so limited and uncertain, that his success seemed to be the result of magic. That magic was his genius. Contemporary writers characterize his unexpected appearance in arms by the romantic simile of the sudden irruption of a *speat*, or mountain torrent. This says more for his military capacity than perhaps these descriptive chroniclers themselves were aware of. Montrose's policy, repeatedly pressed by him in vain, throughout the whole of the year 1643, upon Charles and his consort, was,—instant, determined, and rapid action. ' Strike a blow at once,' he said, ' in Scotland—and let it be a hard one—ere the armies of the Covenant are fairly on foot—and then Scotland is your own.' Such was Montrose's counsel in the Cabinet, and such was his system in the field. To his modern depreciators, who still call it no system, but the rash proposition of overweening vanity, we reply, that it is comprehended indeed in few words,—and so is the tactic of Napoleon. It may be well doubted, if any one of the great military geniuses of modern times would have offered other counsel than Montrose did at York and Gloucester, or could have offered better under the circumstances.

Montrose himself has placed it beyond a question, that had his advice been
instantly and fully adopted by the King and the loyal noblemen, the result
must have been what he anticipated.　But, as if royalty and loyalty had
both combined to despite Montrose, at the expence of their own ruin, he
was suddenly left alone, to the tardy and perilous experiment of the system he recommended, when the tide, which it was that system to seize,
had already been suffered to turn.　Yet still he did all but redeem the
golden moments lost, and afforded the most brilliant demonstration of his
capacity for executing in the field what he had urged in council.　Between
the 18th and the 22nd of August, he achieved the no small adventure of
passing from Carlisle to the Grampians in disguise.　There he had not the
prospect of raising ten men in arms.　A few autumn nights he spent among
the mountains, wrapped in his Highland plaid, seeking his destiny in the
stars or communing with the unconscious shepherds..　A rumour and a
letter sufficed to make him be up and doing.　On the sixth day from his
solitary arrival at Inchbrakie's, he was at the head of about three thousand
ragged enthusiasts—ere the tenth was past he had fought a pitched battle
of his own seeking—gained, over an army complete in all itsparts, a victory
that shook the Covenant, and instantly he was master of Perth."

The question of political and practical consistency on the part of
the Marquis we must leave to the fancy, ingenuity and laboured
construction of our author as found in his lengthened details ; and
pass on towards the close of the warrior's career, where we shall find
many affecting circumstances which induce the heart to regard him,
his followers, and friends as martyrs in the cause of royalty.
Among these adherents and followers none was more conspicuous or
constant than the second Lord Napier, Montrose's nephew, who
was glad to betake himself to foreign parts for self-preservation.
The only letter which Mr. Napier has found in the family chest
from this young nobleman relating to the Marquis, conveys such a
favourable picture of that great, and we doubt not, oft calumniated
man, a picture so different too from what Mr. Brodie, Lord Nugent,
and others have at no very distant period given, that it deserves to
be liberally construed and fully weighed.　It is addressed to the
writer's lady, and part of it is as follows :—

" ' Montrose then (as you did hear) was in treaty with the French, who,
in my opinion, did offer him very honourable conditions, which were these :
First, that he should be General to the Scots in France, and Lieutenant-
General to the Royal Army, when he joined with them, commanding all
Mareschals of the field.　As likewise to be Captain of the Gens-d'armes,
with twelve thousand crowns a year of pension, besides his pay; and assurance the next year to be Mareschal of France, and Captain of the King's
own Guard, which is a place bought and sold at a hundred and fifty thousand crowns.　But these two last places were not insert amongst his other
conditions, only promised him by the Cardinal Mazarine; but the others
were all articles of their capitulation, which I did see in writing, and used
all the inducements and persuasion I could to make him embrace them.　He
seemed to hearken unto me, which caused me at that time to show you that

I hoped shortly to acquaint you with things of more certainty, and to better purpose, than I had done formerly. But while I was thus in hope and daily expectation of his present agreement with them, he did receive advertisements from Germany, that he would be welcome to the Emperor. Upon which he took occasion to send for me, and began to quarrel with the conditions were offered him, and (said) that any employment below a Mareschal of France was inferior to him, and that the French had become enemies to our King, and did labour still to foment the differences betwixt him and his subjects,—that he might not be capable to assist the Spaniard, whom they thought he was extremely inclined to favour, and that if he did engage with them he would be forced to connive and wink at his Prince's ruin: and for these reasons, he would let the treaty desert, and go into Germany, where he would be honourably appointed; which sudden resolution did extremely trouble and astonish me. I was very desirous he should settle in France, and did use again all the arguments I could to make him embrace such profitable conditions, for, if he had been once in charge, I am confident, in a very short time, he should have been one of the most considerable strangers in Europe; for, believe it, they had a huge esteem of him, for some eminent persons there came to see him, who refused to make the first visit to the Embassadors Extraordinary of Denmark and Sweden, —yet did not stand to salute him first, with all the respect that could be imagined.

" ' But to the purpose. He, seeing me a little ill satisfied with the course he was going to take, did begin to dispute the matter with me, and, I confess, convinced me so with reason, that I rested content, and was desirous he should execute his resolution with all imaginable speed ; and did agree that I should stay at my exercises in Paris, till the end of the month, and go often to Court, make visits, and ever in public places, at comedies, and such things, still letting the word go that my uncle was gone to the country for his health, which was always believed so long as they saw me, for it was ever said that Montrose and his nephew were like the Pope and the Church, who would be inseparable. Whereas if I had gone away with him, and left my exercises abruptly, in the middle of the month, his course would have been presently discovered ; for how soon I had been missed, they would instantly have judged me to be gone somewhere with him, then search had been made everywhere, and if he had been taken going to any of the House of Austria who were their enemies, you may think they would have staid him, which might have been dangerous both to his person, credit, and fortune. So there was no way to keep his course close, but to me to stay behind him at my exercises, (as I had done for a long time before,) till I should hear he were out of all hazard, which I did, according to all the instructions he gave me.

" ' The first letter I received from him was dated from Geneva. So when I perceived he was out of French ground, I resolved to come here to Flanders, where I might have freedom of correspondence with him, as also liberty to go to him when it pleased him to send for me, which I could not do conveniently in France. For I was afraid how soon his course should chance to be discovered, that they might seek assurance of me and others not to engage with their enemy, which is ordinary in such cases. Yet would I never have given them any, but thought best to prevene it. And beside I had been at so great a charge for a month after his way-going, with staying at Court, and keeping of a coach there, which I hired, and coming back to Paris, and living at a greater rate than I did formerly, (all which was his desire, yet did consume much moneys,) and fearing to be short, (I) did resolve rather to come here and live privately, than to live in a more inferior way in France than I had done formerly. So these gentlemen which belonged to my Lord, hearing of my intention, would, by any means, go along, and (we) went all together to Haver-de-grace, where we took ship for Middleburgh, and from thence came here, where we are daily expecting Montrose's commands; which, how soon I receive them, you shall be advertised by him who intreats you to believe that he shall study most carefully to conserve the quality, he has hitherto inviolably kept, of continuing,—My dearest life, only your's,

"*Bruxelles, June* 14, 1648.

"NAPIER."

The same affectionate young nobleman goes on to take notice of some personal and family concerns in a way much to his honour as a man, and certainly, as is the case with all the Napier papers in these volumes, highly to his credit as a writer. His lady, it would appear, had desired to know if he had incurred any debt since going into exile; and his answer states, " my fortune, nor no friend, shall ever be troubled with any charge of anything I did spend there," (France); that ere " I be very troublesome to you, I shall live upon one meal a-day;" that though handsomely treated by certain Jesuits who told him that the king of Spain was willing to maintain him, he answered, he " would not live by any king of Christendom's charity." The document towards its conclusion contains those touching words—" I pray you do not show this letter except to very confident friends, and that which is written after my subscription to none.—Lord be with you." Now part of the tender things which the love-portion expresses is, " Be pleased, dear heart, to let me have one thing which I did almost forget—your picture, in the breadth of a sixpence,—without a case, for they may be had better and handsomer here, and I will wear it upon a ribbon under my doublet, so long as it, or I, lasts." " Send your picture as I desire it,—the other is so big I cannot wear it about me. Montrose, at his way-going, gave me his picture, which I caused put in a gold case of the same bigness I desire yours."

Mr. Napier has been enabled to illustrate the imprisonment and the last scenes of the Montrose tragedy by some hitherto unpublished papers. From the manuscript journals of the Lord Lyon, who was present when he was condemned, the following scene in the Parliament House is taken.

" Monday, 20th May. The Parliament met about ten o'clock, and immediately after the down-sitting James Graham was brought before them by the magistrates of Edinburgh, and ascended the place of delinquents. After the Lord Chancellor had spoken to him, and in a large discourse declared the progress of all his rebellions, he showed him that the House gave him leave to speak for himself. Which he did in a long-discourse, with all reverence to the Parliament,—as he said. Since the King and their Commissioners were accorded, he pleaded his own innocency, by calling all his own depredations, murders, and bloodshed, only diversion of the Scots nation from interrupting the course of his Majesty's affairs in England; and as for his last invasion from Orkney,—from which, *said he,* he moved not one foot but by his Majesty's special direction and command,—that he called an accelerating of the treaty betwixt his Majesty and this nation. To him the Lord Chancellor replied, punctually proving him, *by his acts of hostility,* to be a person most infamous, perjured, treacherous, and, of all that ever this land brought forth, the most cruel and inhuman butcher of his country; and one whose boundless pride and ambition had lost the father, and by his wicked counsels had done what in him lay to destroy the son likewise. He made no reply, but was commanded to sit down on his knees, and receive his sentence, which he did. Archibald Johnston, the Clerk Register, read it, and the Dempster gave the doom,—and immediately arising from off his knees, without speaking one word, he was removed thence to the prison. He behaved himself all this time in the House with a great deal of courage and modesty,—unmoved and undaunted—*as appeared,*—only, he sighed two several times, and rolled his eyes alongst all the corners of the House, and at the reading of the sentence, *he lifted up his face,* without any word speaking. He presented himself in a suit of black cloth, and a scarlet coat to his knee, trimmed with silver galouns, lined with crimson tafta; on his head a beaver hat and silver band. He looked somewhat pale, lank-faced, and hairy."

This is the testimony of one that was far from being a partial friend. No wonder that Montrose " looked somewhat pale, lank-faced, 'and hairy :" he was suffering under severe wounds received in his last conflict with the Covenanters. It was even doubtful if these wounds were curable, especially since the aid of a surgeon is said to have been denied him; and as for his being " hairy," even the humble functionary who could speedily have dressed his beard and locks was forbidden to serve him. These and other mean indignities, together with the officiousness of the covenanting clergy who pestered him day and night, circumstances all so characteristic of the age and of the rancour of religious wars, was heaped upon the magnanimous and haughty Marquis, to his enemies' disgrace and the future lustre of his name.

Most of the particulars which we next quote have been frequently narrated; but as they are striking in no ordinary measure, and illustrative of Montrose's habitual regard to forms, dramatic effects, and of his intrepid nature, they will always repay a perusal.

" Early next morning, (Tuesday the 21st of May 1650,) Montrose asked this same Captain of the guard why drums and trumpets were resounding through the town ? Perhaps, his own verse recurred to him,—

I'll sound no trumpet as I wont,
Nor march by tuck of drum,—

but he betrayed no symptoms of such regret, and when told that it was to
call out the soldiers and citizens in arms, because the Parliament dreaded a
rising of the malignants (*i. e.* the people) in his favour, 'What,' he said,
' am I still a terror to them ?   Let them look to themselves, my ghost will
haunt them.'   And now, having taken his breakfast of a little bread dipt
in ale, he commenced his toilet for death, with the serenity that never forsook him.   Those long light-chestnut locks of which he was not a little
vain, dishevelled, and perhaps matted with the blood of his wounds, he was
in the act of combing out and arranging, when a sullen and moody man
broke in upon him with the impertinent reproof,—' Why is James Graham
so careful of his locks ?'   ' My head,' replied Montrose, ' is yet my own—I
will dress it and adorn it,—to-night, when it will be yours, you may treat
it as you please.'   The tormentor was Archibald Johnston.   Montrose
seems ever to have studied propriety or effect in costume.   When he first
led the Claymores to save the Throne, ' that day he went on foot himself
with his target and pike.'   But now, he meant to ' die like a gentleman.'
In the centre of the Grassmarket of Edinburgh his murderers had erected
an ample stage, from which arose a gallows, with its corresponding ladder,
of the extraordinary height of thirty feet.   To this place, from the Tolbooth, Montrose had to walk.   No friend or relation was permitted to
accompany him, or sustain his spirit by their presence on the scaffold.   But
he had been suffered to adorn himself as he pleased, for Argyle had no
objection to the visible demonstration that it was the most graceful nobleman in the land who, at his fiat, was to die the death of a dog.   At two
o'clock in the afternoon he was led forth.   The manuscript diary of an eye-
witness has preserved to us this portrait :—' In his down-going, from the
Tolbooth to the place of execution, he was very richly clad in fine scarlet,
laid over with rich silver-lace,—his hat in his hand,—his bands and cuffs
exceeding rich,—his delicate white gloves on his hands,—his stockings of
incarnate (flesh-coloured) silk,—and his shoes with their ribbands (roses)
on his feet,—and sarks, (embroidered linen,) provided for him, with pearling (lace) about, above ten pund the elne.   All these were provided for
him by his friends, and a pretty cassock put on upon him, upon the scaffold,
wherein he was hanged.   To be short, nothing was here deficient to honour
his poor carcase, more beseeming a bridegroom, nor (than) a criminal going
to the gallows."

The Marquis was hanged on a gibbet of extraordinary height.
He was then beheaded and quartered, the members of his body
being disposed of in different quarters of the country most conspicuous to numerous beholders.   But Mr. Napier has not yet done
with the Merchiston charter-chest ; for in it, he says, there are
some mysterious relics, which, of course, it is his endeavour to
explain.

  " There is a rich satin cap of a faded straw-colour, lined with very fine
linen turned up with lace, and of the costume that is to be seen in the
portraits of some dignitaries of the reign of Charles I.   There is moreover a sheet, or handkerchief, about three feet square, also of the very
finest linen, and trimmed on all sides, with tassels at the corners, like a

pall. The trimming is lace of the same description (though not so broad)
as that which forms the wreath round the cap, being, probably, what
Nicholl describes as ' pearling, above ten pund the elne.' Lastly, we find
a pair of stockings, knit, of glossy thread, not at all the worse for the
wear, and still retaining somewhat of the original gloss, yet with any
thing but the appearance of having been knit in the present century. The
invariable tradition in the Napier family has been, that these are the cap,
handkerchief, and stockings, worn by Montrose on the scaffold; and,
unless explained by some history of the kind, why such articles should
have been thus separately preserved, it is not easy to understand. The
appearance of the stockings especially confirms the tradition. The tops of
them, which must have reached above the knee, have been completely
saturated with something that has now the appearance of faded blood,
diminishing downwards to a point, and, in one of the stockings, extending
to the instep. This is pointed out as the blood of Montrose, and the fact
of hewing off the limbs, when the stockings were only shoved down below
the knees, would perfectly account for those appearances, which indeed
are not to be accounted for in any other way. Upon the satin of the cap
there is a single small stain of what may have been blood, and the lace
appears to have been sprinkled with the same. The handkerchief is the
most stained, being marked, towards the centre, with blotches of different
shades and hues, as if it had been gore and matter. The tradition is, that
this was the handkerchief he wore at the time of his execution, and that
it had been dipt in his blood. But Montrose used no handkerchief as a
signal to be cast off, and this has not the appearance of a piece of dress
at all."

Our author has his theory about the supposed handkerchief.
After mentioning that the ladies of the Napier family took an especial interest in the Marquis's fate, and conjecturing that they probably provided him with his last gay garments, he goes on to state
that there has been a constant tradition in the said family, that the
Lady Napier of the time did contrive to obtain the warrior's heart,
(from its grave under the gallows near Merchiston Castle,) which
she caused to be embalmed. Hence our author derives his explanation of the fine linen sheet in the charter-chest, doubting not but
this is the cloth in which the heart was bundled up, the fabric
having first been trimmed and tasselled for a dainty winding sheet;
and thus, continues Mr. Napier, " we have a tale of real life,
surpassing the beautiful romance of Flora Mac Ivor." There are
other particulars about the heart, the care bestowed upon it, the
reverence in which it was held, and the pilgrimages to which it was
subjected. The head of Montrose, too, is the theme of romantic
and affecting circumstances, all which are minutely detailed by our
author whose present work, in spite of its manifest one-sidedness,
will amply at any time repay a careful perusal. It contains an
earnest and spirited chronicle of public and private events, a hearty
and undisguised effort to appreciate the characters of many historical characters; but beyond all this it brings for the first time before

the world documents, which, while they are highly honourable to
the Napier family, and strongly palliative of the great Montrose,
showing him, besides, in the most brilliant light as a man of genius
and rare accomplishments, are also in no mean degree contributive to
the illustration of nice points in our national annals, even after vast
numbers of similar discoveries to those afforded by the Merchiston
papers have been made from multitudes of muniment chests, relative
to the same eventful period, by preceding miners and explorers.

ART. VI.—*Report of the Commissioners appointed to inquire into the
          Affairs of the Island of Malta.* 1837.

MALTA, says Lord Byron, is a little military hot-house. Malta,
says the Duke of Wellington, is a fortress, a sea-port, a great naval
arsenal in the Mediterranean, and only as a great and commanding
naval station is it or can it be the slightest use to England, consequently it should be governed like a fortress, and the idea of talking
of such a place as a colony is absurd and despicable in the extreme.
A free press is, quoad Malta, just the same as hourly Saturnalia in
a regiment or a ship of the line. The whole island must, from the
nature of things, be like an island under strict military discipline;
otherwise, says the noble Duke, we shall lose both our garrison and
our harbour. Now we are at all times ready to profess our profound
admiration of the broad and powerful sense of the noble Duke, and
the opinion of the great captain and great statesman has undoubtedly
carried with it great weight on such a subject, backed as it is by a
bold and startling prophecy. Happily we have lived long enough
to know the value of political prophecies; we have heard them substituted for arguments on every great question which has engaged
the attention of the legislature for the last ten years. We have not
forgotten the awful pictures of bloodshed, anarchy, and confusion
which were to represent the state of England after the passing of
the Reform Bill.—the national debt spunged out, grass growing
on the East and West India Docks, and the Birmingham Union
sitting as a recent parliament in St. Stephen's Chapel. With the
realization of those inspired predictions before our eyes, we cannot
but admire the hardihood of politicians in still adventuring upon the
unexplored sea of futurity, where they have foundered so often and
so ingloriously.

But what is this Malta which our Whig government has thought
worthy of the honour of a special commission, to examine into all
sorts of matters whereto it might be feasible to attach the name or
imputation of abuse? Has there been room or pretence for our
inquiry into such a place as this? Or has it originated in a morbid
appetite for miscalled economy or bastard reform? These are the
questions we proceeded to examine for our own special enlighten-

ment, and the results of which examination we now proceed to lay before our readers.

The commissioners, Mr. Austin and Mr. Lewis, are allowed on all hands to be men of high character and attainments. The first is justly estimated as a lawyer and a jurist, of integrity and moral character unimpeached ; the second has carried on statistical as well as practical investigations of a higher class than those which usually come under the denomination of statistics, on a more difficult theatre, namely, Ireland ; and exhibited the result of them in a work deserving of great praise for the patience, temper, and upright purpose exhibited throughout it by the learned gentleman. If the field for the exercise of their political and administrative faculties is barren, certain it is they have displayed no want of conscientious industry. They have reported upon a free press, upon import duties, particularly upon corn, upon other administrative duties in the treasury department, upon public charities, upon marine police, all which subjects they have treated with elaborate acuteness and impartiality. They have shown no desire to slur over the duties prescribed to them, or to convert their office into a sinecure. It is impossible, says Lord Glenelg, in his despatch to Sir Henry Bouverie, the present governor of Malta—it is impossible that all the material facts should have been brought together with greater brevity or clearness, or that the principles which should direct his Majesty's government should have been stated with greater force and perspicuity.

The revenue of the government of Malta amounts to 95,600*l.* The annual produce of the various sources from which this sum is derived, may be classed under the following heads :—

		£.
1. Rents of the crown lands		23,000
2. Small internal taxes, chiefly licences for exercising trades, a tax on the transfer of landed property, and an auction duty . . .		2,000
3. Fees of courts and government offices . .		5,200
Duties on imports, tonnage dues, and quarantine dues		65,000
	Total	95,600

Thus we find the government annually raises by taxation about 73,000*l.* ; of this sum 65,000*l.* is derived from duties on imports, and of this latter sum about 35,000*l.* arises from duties on grain. The large population, and the unproductiveness of a considerable portion of the surface of Malta, necessitate the importation of about 73,000 salms or quarters of grain every year.

Under the government of the Knights of St. John, the inhabitants of Malta were furnished with grain and other articles of food by a corporate body or universita, which had the monopoly of the commodities in which it dealt, and fixed the prices of them in the island. This system was continued by the British government with respect to the supply of grain until the year 1822, the only change being the transfer of the purchases and sales from the universita to the Commissioners of the Board of Supply.

In June, 1822, the Board of Supply in its turn gave way to a new branch of public service, called the Grain Department; one section of which managed the collection of the duties on imported grain, and the other managed the purchases and sales of wheat on the government account. The duties levied on this commodity are graduated on a scale varying inversely with the price, that is, as the price rose the duty fell, and the converse. The principle of this scale is to begin with a duty on wheat of 12s. when wheat is at or under 25s. per salm; then to remit one shilling for every increase of 5s. up to 60s.; then to remit 2s. between 60 and 65s.; and to levy a duty of 1s. when the price is above 68s. The operation of this graduated scale was a great cause of complaint, and both British and Maltaic merchants were anxious for the subtitution of a fixed duty; this is the amount of improvement recommended by the commissioners after a laborious investigation of the working of the system. They recommend the fixing of a single rate of duty, leaving to the discretion of government any reduction in it which may be necessitated by a considerable rise in the price.

The condition of the working classes on whom this tax falls heavily, is very far from prosperous. The working people are scarcely ever employed for hire, and during several months of the year not more than a tenth part of them are in the receipt of wages. The rate of wages is from four to five vari, or 6¼ to 8¼ a day, which certainly does not admit of laying by a stock for the seasons when employment is scarce; nor are the circumstances of the farmers in a more flourishing condition than those of their labourers. They usually agree to give a larger rent than they are able to pay, and thus, as is the case in Ireland, they are either in arrear with their landlord or they are ejected by him, hence the commissioners very sapiently conclude that any remission in the taxes on provisions would benefit the landlord, and not either the farmer or the labourer, as no matter what the reduction might be their relative situations would be the same. Besides, the reduction of 1s. per salm or quarter on imported wheat, would cause a loss to the government of 2,900l. a year, while the gain to the labourer would be but 1¼ a month, or 18 Maltese grani, or 1s. 6d. a year; moreover the poorest of the population consume very little wheaten bread.

The produce of the taxes upon luxuries is very inconsiderable. The recommendations of the commissioners for an alteration of the duties hitherto levied on those articles, by exempting from duty articles on transit, and striking out unproductive imports, met with the unanimous concurrence of the Maltese merchants, and were immediately carried into effect by the government.

The following scheme will serve to give a fair idea of the consumptive powers of Malta, as well as of the improvements of the commissioners.

" It is proposed to repeal all the laws of the island now in force with respect to the arrival and departure of merchant vessels, the mode of collecting duties on imports and importing vessels, the rates of the duties themselves, and the bonding of goods (with the exception of regulations relating to the quarantine department, and the dues paid by vessels in quarantine).

" It is further proposed to consolidate (with amendments) in one law all the provisions on these subjects which it is expedient to preserve; and to substitute, for all existing duties on articles imported for consumption, the following duties :

" Beer in hogsheads . . . . . 12s. per hogsh.
Ditto in bottles . . . . . . 1s. per doz.
Cattle, bullocks, horses, and mules . . 20s. per head.
(The quarantine dues to be abolished.)
Charcoal . . . . 6d. per salm.
Grain :
Wheat . . . . 10s. ditto.
Indian corn . . . . . . 6s. ditto.
Barley . . . . 4s. ditto.
Saggina . . . . 3s. ditto.
Manufactured grain . . . . . 6s. per cantar.
Oil (olive) . . . . . . 6d. per caffiso.
Pulse and Seeds :
Beans, canary seeds, caravances, chick peas, hemp
seed, kidney beans, lentils, linseed, lupins, peas
and vetches . . . . . 2s. per salm.
Carob-beans and cotton seeds . . . 6d. per cantar.
Spirits . . . . 22s. per barrel.
Vinegar . . . . 2s. ditto.
Wine (supeiorr) . . . . . 11s. ditto.
Wine (common) . . . . . 2s. ditto.
The strike measure to be used universally.
The tonnage dues to be as follows :
Vessels above 40 tons, for every ton, or any part thereof, 6d.
A small duty to be levied on spirits manufactured in the island.
The dues for store-rent, &c. to be fixed at moderate rates."

The import duties on manufactured goods produce only 1,297l. 10s. 6d., but perhaps the following despatch with the annexed paper will convey a clearer idea on this subject.

" Copy of a Despatch from the Commissioners to Lord *Glenelg.*
" My Lord, Malta, 5 May 1837.
" The annexed paper, containing suggestions for the exemption of certain articles produced in Malta from duty in England, has been trans-

mitted to us by the Governor, with reference to our plan of a new tariff. We confess that we are not satisfied of the expediency of commercial privileges of this kind ; but we have no hesitation in expressing our opinion, that if such exceptions are to be made in favour of any dependency of England, they ought to be made in favour of Malta, on account of the narrowness of its resources and the poverty of its population, and the very small proportion which Maltese imports would bear to the quantity of imports from other countries. We will likewise state that the principle has been already admitted, in the case of cotton-wool, by the English Government. On the 17th February 1826, the Lieutenant-governor issued a notice that His Majesty's Government, with a view to encourage the cultivation of cotton-wool in this island, permits the importation of cotton-wool into the United Kingdom of Great Britain and Ireland free of all duty whatever, upon the direct importation of that article from Malta, and upon proof that it is *bonâ fide* the growth of this island.

We have, &c.

(signed)   *John Austin.*

George C. Lewis.

" *P.S.* We beg leave to add, that we pronounce no opinion upon the correctness of the statements, or the soundness of the arguments, contained in the following

PAPER.

" It is proposed to abolish *in toto* the existing duties of consumption at Malta upon all articles the produce or manufacture of the United Kingdom and of the British Colonies ; also upon tea. The only exceptions are, beer, British spirits, and Colonial rum ; the amount of duty, however, which will probably be levied upon these articles is estimated to fall short of 1,000*l.* per annum.

" Every facility being thus given to the introduction of British and Colonial produce or manufactures, it is hoped that the British Government, taking into consideration local peculiarities, and influenced by the principal of reciprocity, will be induced to consent to the free admission into the United Kingdom of the hereinafter-mentioned articles, the produce or manufacture of these possessions, which, it is to be particularly remarked, are European.

" The remission of the existing duties on these articles, though absolutely nothing as affecting either the British revenue or British interests generally, would prove of substantial benefit to Malta. It would, moreover, manifest such a marked desire to improve the condition of its overgrown and indigent population as could not fail to be duly appreciated, and of producing the happiest influence on the public mind.

" It may be urged, that were the point conceded, it might be quoted in favour of other British possessions, with a view to their obtaining privileges of a similiar nature ; but the peculiarly distinctive character of Malta forbids any such comparison.

" An island so insignificant in size, and so poor in resources, as to be mainly indebted for its daily supplies of the first necessaries of life to the neighbouring countries, can never be an object of jealousy, in a commercial point of view, to any country whatsoever ; for nearly all the productions of its scanty soil and of the industry of its inhabitants are consumed on the spot, whilst the quantities of exportable produce or manufactures are so comparatively trifling, that they can never influence, much less prejudice, any market of the least note.

"Nor, should the desired privilege be granted, is the remotest apprehension to be entertained of its being abused; for the identity of the article to be exported may be most clearly established, and unimpeachable certificates of origin (signed by the competent authorities) given in all cases.

"1. Aniseed.
2. Bones of Cattle and other animals, and of fish.
3. Cummin seed.
4. Cotton-wool.
5. Cotton yarn of native cotton-wool, spun by hand.
6. Cotton manufactures.
7. Embroidered muslin or cambric.
8. Fruits, raw or preserved.
9. Gold and silver, wrought.
10. Glass, broken, paying the same excise duty as is levied in England.
11. Honey.
12. Hides, hoofs and horns of cattle, killed in the island.
13. Iron, old broken, or old cast-iron.
14. Lace, made by hand.
15. Marble, wrought or unwrought.
16. Maccaroni.
17. Oranges, lemons, and limes.
18. Roll brimstone, paying the same duty as is levied in England on unmanufactured brimstone.
19. Rags.
20. Squills, dried or otherwise.
21. Straw and reed hats.
22. Segars, paying the same duty as is levied in England on unmanufactured tobacco.
23. Soap, paying the same excise duty as is levied in England.
24. Stone, wrought or unwrought.
25. Vermicelli.
26. Silk, raw or manufactured."

Having now laid before our readers the revenue and the sources from which it is derived, it remains for us to notice its application.

The functions of the treasurer at Malta are very different from those of a Lord of the Treasury in England. He is nothing more than the receptacle of the government money, which he is to disburse as the governor shall direct. His salary is 900*l.* per annum, with a house rent-free, rated at 40*l.* per annum; the total expense of the establishment of the treasury is rather less than 1,800*l.* A heavy expense is further entailed on the government of Malta by the large amount of pensions formerly granted by it :—

	£.	*s.*
" Pensions connected with the order of St. John of Jerusalem .	2,130	9
Pensions granted on restriction of office . . .	1,843	15
Pensions on Superannuation	3,955	7
Pensions granted for military service . .	1,431	13
	9,361	4."

Thus more than one-eighth of the taxes levied on Malta is consumed in the payment of pensions. Nor does this sum represent the entire annual expense of pensions in Malta. The government have at different times made grants of houses rent-free in the way of pensions, the value of which has been estimated at 393*l*. 9*s*. 6*d*. a year. The government further disburses a sum of 4000*l*. a year, professedly applied to the relief of the poor, but really in grants of 12*l*. a year to widows of clerks in government offices and other persons not belonging to the working classes. Upon this subject the Commissioners observe,—

" We should have great difficulty in conveying an adequate sense of the vehement and universal dislike of taxation which exists in this island, and of the vigilance with which every increase of the public burdens is watched. Although there is but an imperfect liberty of printed discussion, the amount of public money received by each person and the duties he has performed or in performing are known with a precision and canvassed with an interest which are only possible in a small community, the salaries of the present and the pensions of the former servants of government are known with far greater accuracy, and are much more generally discussed in Malta than in England, notwithstanding the attempted secrecy of government in one country and the unbounded publicity of government in the other."

Of course it is in a very poor, a very idle, and a very discontented society. People in England have too much to think of in conducting those myriads of schemes for filling their own pockets to pay much attention to the expedients resorted to by the men in authority for filling theirs; besides, they have the liberty of grumbling, the Maltese have not.

For these reasons, continue the commissioners, we think that for carrying into effect the reductions in the civil establishments of Malta, which seem to us requisite, the changes should be made without necessitating the grant of fresh pensions where such an arrangement is practicable. They next proceed to reduce the public revenue taken from this small and poor community to the lowest amount consistent with the public service; and in order thereto to abolish every office appearing to be needless, and to diminish every salary appearing to be exorbitant, reconciling the accomplishment of that paramount object, as far as they possibly can, with the pecuniary interests of those employed by government. The merging of the office of treasurer in that of chief secretary, and the abolition of the offices of superintendent and broker in the government grain department, are the practical results of these suggestions.

To effect these alterations, it was only found necessary to have the government money paid into a chartered bank, of which one of the government functionaries is a director *virtutute officii*, and to transfer the care of the government wheat to the collector of customs, who shall sell it through the medium of a public broker. The

claims to compensation of the removed officers were supported by
the commissioners, and acceded to by the government. Mr. Cal-
vert, the superintendent, receiving 200*l*., and Mr. Ward, the broker,
250*l*., per annum, from the period of the reduction of their offices.

The public charities supported and administered, or merely administered by the government of Malta, next engaged the attention
of the commissioners. The expense of the medical charities.
amounted in 1836 to 6,701*l*. 3*s*. 7*d*. The civil hospital of Valetta generally contains about 403 patients.

Upwards of eighty of these are infirm persons, not in need of
medical treatment. To keep a hospital with an expensive medical
establishment, and to use it in part as a mere asylum for the poor,
was manifestly bad economy. There is also a small hospital at
Civita Vecchia, called the Ospizio dello Santo Spirito, and another
in Gozo. A dispensary is attached to that at Valetta, and there is a
small sum paid to medical men for visiting the poor. Then there
are a lunatic asylum, an asylum for old men and women. A house
of industry, a foundling hospital, and a monte di pieta, or a pawnbroking establishment. The whole cost of these institutions amounts
to 17,138*l*.

The foundling hospital seems to be most serviceable to the
Maltese, and their activity in supplying it with patients seems
truly admirable. It receives 400*l*. a year from government, and
contains 270 infants. But as the supply of infants greatly exceeds
the supply of nurses, as many as four are sometimes given in charge
to one woman, so that the mortality is very great, and 400*l*. a year is
found a very insufficient sum for sustaining the productiveness of
the gallant islanders, who resemble the Irish in another curious
characteristic ; and instead of attributing their poverty to their own
improvidence in multiplying their numbers beyond the demand for
their labour, they lay it down to the acts or omissions of the government : the recommendations of the commissioners relative to these
public charities are:—

1st. To place them all under the management of a board.

2nd. To discontinue the payment of government alms, to make
all destitute persons admissible into the government institutions, and
to empower the board of charities to make regulations for the
government of these institutions, the object being to relieve the most
necessitous part of the poor population.

3rd. To restrict admissions into the foundling hospitals to foundlings properly so called.

They further recommend that the trade of pawnbroking shall be
thrown open to any person who may be desirous to pursue it, under
such regulations, for the prevention of abuses, as may be established
by law. These recommendations are ordered to be carried into effect
in the following despatch :—

" 1. The Commissioners propose to place the various charitable institutions maintained at the public expense, under the administration of a single board, thus reverting to the policy of Sir Thomas Maitland, in the year 1816. To this scheme I can anticipate only one objection, namely, that the gentlemen who are performing the separate duties gratuitously, and the officers who are at present paid for assisting them, might find the increased labour greater than they would be willing to undertake, or might demand some additional remuneration. But the Commissioners have foreseen and answered this difficulty. They entertain no doubt that the honorary members of the proposed single board would cheerfully undertake, and effectually discharge, the whole of this service, and that no addition to the salaries already paid will be required. Upon this understanding, I have to authorize you to carry their advice into execution, by consolidating the two existing Boards, selecting from their members those whom you deem best qualified to form the new administration of these charities. I also concur in the propriety of appointing the purveyor of charitable institutions to hold the office of secretary to the new Board at his present rate of salary. Before the members shall meet for the despatch of business, you will prepare and communicate to them for their guidance, such instructions as may be necessary to secure method, punctuality, and economy in the discharge of their duties.

" 2. The Commissioners next recommend the adoption, as far as the circumstances of the case will admit, of those principles in the distribution of public alms, which have been established in England under the Poor Law Amendment Act. With that view they propose that the buildings, as an ospizio for the aged, and as a house of industry, should be placed under the control of the new Board, and used for the reception of the destitute generally ; that the Board, with the concurrence of the local Government, should make all necessary regulations for the admission, classification, feeding, and clothing of destitute persons, and for the maintenance of proper discipline in the house ; and that the principle pervading all such regulations should be, at once to make adequate provision for the physical wants of the paupers, and to deny them indulgences which might be attractive to those who have the means of supporting themselves, and even to some of the contributors to the fund from which this expenditure is to be defrayed.

" You will strictly act upon and enforce the observance of these principles ; not of course forgetting, that in carrying plans of this nature into effect, much caution is necessary in order to avoid not only the giving a reasonable cause of complaint, but also the affording any plausible ground for the misconception and mis-statements which must be expected from prejudiced or interested opponents.

" 3. In pursuance of the same general principle, the Commissioners propose to admit no new candidates for the receipt of monthly alms, but to apply whatever saving may be thus effected towards the maintenance of the inmates of the ospizio and house of industry, and the improvement of the means of receiving them into this institution. You will act upon this suggestion, unless some conclusive objection which has escaped the research of the Commissioners should occur to you.

" 4. It is next proposed, that no children, except those publicly exposed and deserted, should be admitted into the foundling hospital. The abuse of this charity, which the Report describes, urgently requires correction. Indeed it is difficult to suppose a more noxious institution than an asylum for infants, into which are brought the children of parents desirous to transfer their own parental obligations to society at large. In the present case the practice appears to have assumed a character not very remote from that of a systematic infanticide, because the hospital, being overburdened with more children than it is possible to supply with nurses, they appear to have perished in no inconsiderable number from the want of the only nutriment by which it is in general possible that human life should be sustained in the first stage of existence. The establishment of receptacles even for deserted children is perhaps an equivocal advantage. But as, on the one hand, the maternal instinct, even of the most depraved women, affords a very great security against the abandonment of their offspring, so, on the other hand, the natural and laudable feelings of society at large would be revolted by withholding from their helpless children the public succour to which they appear to have so powerful a claim. Such also appears to be the view of the Commissioners. I concur with them, that to such foundlings alone the charity should hereafter be restricted, but that from such it should not be withheld. You will instruct the future governors of this institution accordingly.

" 5. I have further to announce my assent to the advice of the Commissioners, that the trade of pawnbroking should be thrown open to any person who may be desirous to pursue it, under such regulations for the prevention of abuses as may be established by law. You will submit to the Legislative Council the project of an ordinance for that purpose. To maintain this trade as a monopoly for the support of a public charity, is in fact to throw the charge of that charity in a great extent upon a single class of society, and chiefly upon that class which is least able to sustain the burthen. I assume that the monopoly raises the price at which this business is transacted. If the assumption be erroneous, then, as the Commissioners have observed, the law will at least produce no practical ill consequence, while it would assert an important general principle.

" 6. You will of course avail yourself of the Commissioners' offer to submit to you all the details necessary for carrying their plans into execution.

" 7. You will further take the necessary measures for printing the Abstracts, mentioned in the Report, of the statistical information which the Commissioners have collected as to the state of the poor in Malta, as to the means of improving their condition, and as to the economical state of the island generally. Perhaps the work may be better and more cheaply executed in England than at Malta. If so, the manuscript may be transmitted to me for that purpose.

" You will, of course, obtain from the Commissioners a copy of this Report, and you will communicate to them a copy of my present despatch.

I have, &c.

(signed)   *Glenelg.*

But what the Maltese will hail as the greatest benefit derived from the appointment of the commission, is the liberty of printing and publishing which it has recommended to be conceded to them. The law which restrained printing in the island was as rigid and relenting as even the Duke of Wellington could wish it to be. No one was allowed to exercise the trade of printer, or even to use a printing press, without a licence from the chief secretary; and, as no such licence ever was granted, the printing of the island was monopolized by the government office. Every writing printed and published in the island was printed at the government press, with the previous permission of the chief secretary and published with his previous licence, which permission and licence he was authorized to refuse to private applications without assigning any cause. Although the government never granted a licence to any private person, it granted such an indulgence to the Commissariat department and to the Church Missionary Society. The Commissariat press is under the control of the Commissary-general, and is only used for the printing of forms and documents; that, of the Church Missionary Society, is used for the printing of religious tracts and school-books to be circulated on the coasts of the Mediterranean. The conditions of its establishment were, that every writing printed at it should be previously approved of by the chief secretary, and that no such writing should be circulated in the island without his previous permission. But no precautions were taken to enforce those conditions, although the control of the government press is exercised with the greatest possible strictness, so much so, indeed, as not only to prevent the publication of writings on party politics, but to suppress discussion of every description on politics, legislation, morals, and religion. This prohibitory rule gives to the assailants of Catholicism an unfair advantage over its defenders. With a press at their disposal, and with ample funds for importing writings from England, the Protestant Missionary Societies were enabled to circulate attacks on the Catholic religion, while, in consequence of their limited means, the Catholics were debarred from answering those attacks through the same circuitous and expensive channel. The Maltese being, without exception, members of the Catholic church and strongly attached to that religion, their church is deemed the established church of the island, though the members of other churches have complete legal protection in the exercise of their respective modes of worship. It is not to be wondered at, therefore, that a feeling of irritation universally prevailed among the Maltese clergy against the government, which openly permitted the publication of insulting attacks which it was not in their power to answer. Not that the enlightened portion of the clergy have any objection to argumentative discussion and decorous examination; their soreness of feeling arose from the coarse ribaldry and calumnious misrepresentation of the writings published by their opponents.

Another of the mischiefs done by the censorship is the suppression of all useful information concerning the politics, the statistics, and the proceedings in the courts of justice, on all which subjects the most lamentable ignorance prevails in the island. Add to this, that the Maltese, seeing the mystery in which the government has so completely shrouded itself, and observing its jealous anxiety to preserve its own acts and those of its subordinates from comment, very naturally presume that it is because they cannot endure investigation. The system of concealment naturally gave rise to a settled tendency to misconstruction, and so far is this carried that even the withholding of an annual statement of its revenues and disbursements has subjected it to many imputations of prodigality and extortion, which have not the slightest foundation in fact. As the government honourably observed the rules it imposed upon others, and abstained from all attacks upon its opponents and all self-commendation, and as the censorship did not extend to writings printed abroad and imported for circulation, pamphlets, impeaching generally its system and conduct, dealing in confident assertions, and written in an inflammatory style, have been imported and greedily devoured by the discontented Maltese. Of course the advocates for the system of military discipline would laugh such objections to scorn, and point to the bayonet or the cat as a sufficient antidote for all such evils. Our Whig commissioners, however, are of a different opinion, and recommend the concession of liberty of the press, accompanied by a restrictive enactment and law of libel, calculated to meet all the objections that have been urged against it. In conveying the instructions of the home government for the immediate adoptions of these suggestions, Lord Glenelg says,—

" In the consideration of this subject the peculiar circumstances in which this island is placed, in consequence of its geographical position, and the necessity of maintaining in it a strong military force, have not been overlooked by his majesty's government; but it appears to them that while the concession in question is calculated to instruct the minds and raise the character of the people of Malta, no serious apprehension ought to be entertained that it will in any degree injuriously affect those important interests which render Malta so valuable a portion of the British empire. At the same time, however, his majesty's government think it essential that, in the first instance, any law of this nature should be of limited duration. Experience alone can prove the actual results of its operation ; and, at all events, some revision of its details may probably become necessary at no distant period."

However, as the richer classes are too economical to purchase a newspaper, and the poorer classes too ignorant to read one (not more than 50 out of 3,743 inhabitants of the casels being so far enlightened), and as no purchasers are to be counted on beyond Malta itself, it will be some time before a liberal newspaper, however ably conducted, will yield an adequate return to its proprietors. In the printing line, however, a new branch of industry is thrown open to

the industrious classes, and the ill feeling which is always the consequence of a monopoly is removed.

We have now gone through the several matters which have engaged the attention of the commissioners, and pointed out the extensive changes they have caused to be adopted in the administration
of the domestic affairs of the island. Their views are stated with
the utmost clearness and perspicuity, but are overlaid with a mass
of laborious argumentation, not unlike the address of a lawyer speaking against time, who is determined that people shall not say he
has done nothing for his fee. The whole business seems like breaking a fly upon a wheel, and, looking at the results obtained, we feel
surprised they could not have been arrived at by an intelligent
governor without the employment of the machinery of a commission.

ART. VII.—*Minutes of Evidence taken before the Select Committee on
Postage.* Printed by order of the House of Commons.

MOST of our readers are aware that the subject of Post Office
Reform has lately attracted the attention of many persons both
within and beyond the walls of Parliament. To one individual,
Mr. Rowland Hill, the country is mainly indebted for the creation
of this anxiety and stir. The changes which he has pointed out in
this important branch of national policy are upon a large and sweeping scale; such, indeed, as, on the first appearance of his Pamphlet
on the subject, appeared to some, who did not bestow much reflection concerning the matter, visionary and extravagant. On the
motion, however, of Mr. Wallace in the House of Commons, a committee was appointed to sift the question. He moved that an
inquiry should be pursued " into the present rates and mode of
charging postage, with a view to such a reduction thereof as may be
made without injury to the revuene, and for this purpose to examine
into the mode recommended for charging and collecting postage, in
a pamphlet published by Mr. Rowland Hill." In consequence of
the appointment of this committee, a very considerable mass of evidence was elicited on the subject previous to Easter last, and portions of that evidence we shall proceed to lay before our readers.

We do not believe that any one can attend even to the limited
evidence about to be produced, without perceiving that the subject
has an extremely important bearing not only upon the commercial
intercourse of the country, but on the civilization and moral habits
of all classes; and if it should appear that the revenue, as well as
the convenience and satisfaction of individuals and numerous classes
of the community, cannot fail to be materially advanced by the proposed changes, then surely there can be no rational objection to their
speedy adoption,—surely there can be no political partisanship involved in it, no Conservative principle at stake which requires to be
sedulously guarded.

It is proper to observe, as the regular readers of newspapers well know, that the committee appointed on Mr. Wallace's motion is by no means the only body that have taken cognizance of post-office reform and discussed Mr. Hill's schemes. A number of reports indeed have already been published resulting from commissions, one of these particularly regards the two-penny and three-penny post deliveries in and around the metropolis; and to this branch of the inquiry, before entering on the subject of the conveyances and rates of general-post letters, we call attention for a few moments.

In the particular report alluded to the following words are to be found :—" We therefore propose to your lordships, that the distinction in the rates and districts which now applies to letters delivered by the two-penny and three-penny post, shall not in any way affect correspondence transmitted under stamped covers ; and that any letter not exceeding an ounce in weight shall be conveyed free within the metropolis, and the districts to which the town and country deliveries now extend, if inclosed in an envelope bearing a penny stamp." From what fell from a cabinet minister in May was a twelvemonth, in reference to this proposal, the public had reason to expect that it would be carried into effect. The contrary, however, has been the result ; nor are we without our suspicions that means may have been used by officials and other partial influences to drive the Chancellor of the Exchequer from his propriety on this matter.

Let us see what Mr. Parker, the extensive publisher, has said when examined by the committee in reference to the proposal above quoted.

" Does your house issue circulars ?—We do not now issue circulars by post, because of the expense of postage, but if we had a very small postage it would be the most beneficial means of doing business which could be devised ; and knowing what has been proposed with regard to stamped covers, or franks, I have taken the liberty of putting together a catalogue to show the way in which communications might be made with the smallest possible trouble (*producing a printed copy of a proposed new frank or cover, containing a catalogue printed on the inside, and addressed in print on the back to himself in London*). If we had franks of that kind we should print in them a list of the things in which we mostly deal ; and our correspondents, by putting a few lines upon them, would convert them into an order ; it would be well worth the while of any person in business, like myself, to supply our correspondents with those franks, and, having the name printed upon them, they could not go to any other person ; and I have no doubt this mode would be adopted to an extent that it would appear almost romancing to describe ; but I am satisfied that many would avail themselves of it, not only for dealers with whom they are in communication, but for large consumers also. If the committee will look at it, they will see the mode in which communications may be made ; there is a list of between 200 and 300 books in which I deal ; I have got my clerks to write on the margins such letters as I am sure the country

dealers would send back upon the receipt of such a list. Here is the same
thing in sheets, to show the great facility they will afford for simplifying
correspondence. I presume that the covers will be sent in sheets like that
(*producing a specimen containing four envelopes*) ; these are produced
for the purpose of showing what may be introduced in that single sheet of
paper; there are nearly 300 separate titles in one envelope or frank ; that
is applicable to the retail trade as well as the wholesale. I am not a bookseller; I only sell the books I publish. To me, this mode is of the greatest
possible importance ; I have endeavoured to apply this to our every-day
transactions in business. I am quite sure this is a sort of correspondence
we should have day by day, as soon as any plan of cheap postage could be
brought into operation.

" You are of opinion that a very large addition of correspondence would
take place ?—There is no question of that ; the reduction of postage to
1*d*. or 2*d*. which has been talked of, opens up the idea of such an extensive
correspondence that I really hesitate to say the extent to which I think it
might be carried ; but I estimate that our receipt of letters alone would
be six or eight times what they are, and that the number of letters we
should decline enclosing would amount to three to one of all we now
receive ; but I cannot estimate the number of communications in the way
of circulars and advertisements we should send in the course of a year ; I
do not think I overstate it when I say they would be 20,000 or 30,000 in
the year, where we do not now send one ; all advertisements are expensive; and when we knew persons likely to purchase the books I publish, and could apply directly to them, there would be no limit to the
number I should send in the course of a year ; I print yearly about 200,000
such bills as this (*producing one*) ; and when they are printed, there is
sometimes a difficulty in getting them properly circulated, so as to repay
the expense ; we insert them in the reviews and magazines, and we send
300 to one correspondent to issue in his connexion and 200 to another,
and leave it to them to dispose of them in their own way; but a great
many of them are wasted."

He afterwards says,—

" This very mode of franking by envelopes would make an addition to
the penny-post in London to an extent which can hardly be described ; I
am sure that shopkeepers of every description would furnish families with
a number of those franked covers with their own addresses printed on
them ; and I reason upon the enormous expense to which persons who
know the advantage of advertising go. There are certain houses who
now think it beneath them to advertise, but I am quite sure that even
those would avail themselves of a list like this, if it might be sent to them
by a penny-post. The increase in the penny-post of London would be
very enormous. I speak thus strongly on the circulation of large numbers of printed lists, seeing I have been all my life a printer, and know the
feelings of persons who would circulate those things, if they could calculate on their getting into the hands of those to whom they are addressed."

To be sure measures would have to be carefully and studiously
adopted to prevent the forgery of these envelopes, which would

operate like franks; and this brings us to notice the fact, that Mr. Dickinson, the paper manufacturer, has invented a peculiar paper with lines of thread or silk stretched through its substance, which some competent judges pronounce to be the best preventive of forgery that has yet been suggested. In speaking of this fabric, Mr. Dickinson himself states that it may be recommended " for stamps and other government purposes, on the ground of its entire novelty and peculiarity, the difficulty of its manufacture, and of counterfeiting it, and of its admitting of an easy and definite description : it is an article not required for any general purpose or manufacture ; and the prohibition of its fabrication, or of its being in possession of any person, unless with permission of government, would be no hardship or inconvenience to the public. The possibilty of diversifying the colour, arrangement, and material of the threads, renders it capable of endless variety, and suited for numerous important objects, if adopted as a government paper."

Having presented these suggestions and recommendations with regard to the present Metropolitan Two-penny and Three-penny Deliveries, we pass on to the subject of the General Post throughout the empire.

Mr. Hill insists in his plan that deliveries may be made by the mail coaches in any part of the country,—in Edinburgh or Aberdeen, for instance,—for about the thirty-sixth part of a penny for each letter. Regarding the Post-office charge as a tax on correspondence, he would have the postage of all general-post letters to be the same, no matter how different the distance of their carriage. He also argues that if the rates of postage were reduced to the extent of which it is possible to do so, there would be no defalcation in the revenue thence derived, while a stop would be put to an enormous and demoralizing system of smuggling, which at present exists. And farther, we may mention, that he maintains, were stamped covers used, to be issued by the Stamp Office for one penny each, together with other simple alterations that might be introduced, despatch, regularity, as well as cheapness to the wondrous increases of epistolary correspondence, and consequently of intelligence and friendly intercourse, would be the inevitable result.

Mr. Hill's calculation as to the rate at which letters may be conveyed to any part of the kingdom is borne out, not only by that of the London booksellers and publishers, a class of people whose correspondence and parcels are particularly important and numerous ; but even the Postmaster General and other officers belonging to his establishment, however hostile they may be to the reforms suggested by Mr. Hill, render it manifest that his calculations as to the rate at which all letters may be conveyed and delivered are not far from the mark. But his scheme is not like that which at present preposterously prevails, and which makes what are called chargeable letters pay for the immense loads of franked letters, of stamped parcels, of newspapers to a certain extent, of acts of parliament for country magistrates, &c. &c. And why should men of business or private individuals,—why should commerce, friendship, and intelligence bear the burden of an enormous tax for the benefit of these various official or public concerns? But this is not all the hardship and evil which attach to the question. From the evidence now to be quoted, national and personal morality is deeply involved in the question; and, indeed, government could not well have devised a greater and more prevalent reward for the encouragement of smuggling and clandestine practices, most injurious not only to the revenue, but to straightforward dealing, than has been held out by our Post-office establishment and laws. We believe that the pieces of evidence about to be extracted by us will astound the majority of our readers. It is evidence that admits of no comment which a child may not instantly apply.

" *Mr. G. H.*—You reside in a town in Scotland, do you not?—I do.

" You once were in the capacity of a traveller between that town and others?—I was so for many years.

" In the capacity of a carrier, had you occasion to convey letters for your customers?—Yes.

" What did you charge for those letters?—We had various rates of charge, principally from 1*d.* to 2*d.*

" Did you charge 2*d.* for single letters?—I never made inquiry whether they were single or double; if it was a small packet we took it the same.

" Have you any recollection of how many letters you carried in that way daily?—I have made some calculation of the thing, but how far it might approximate to the truth I do not know, but I keep within bounds when I say 500 daily, myself and the other carriers on the station.

" How many letters do you think you yourself carried daily?—It would be a difficult thing for me to state, but I have seen occasionally probably 150 and 200, that is including circulars; but there were other days that I had few or none; I compute the number that I carried myself at about 50; that is, every day through the whole year; that is the average.

" At the time you were a carrier how many mails with letter-bags went daily between those towns?—There were four arrivals and four departures.

" What is the rate of postage between those two places?—There are two rates; 6*d.* by the day-mail, the night-mail is charged ½*d.* more, for what reason I know not.

" Although four mails went each way daily, the number of letters you speak of also went daily, otherwise than by post?—Yes.

" Were any of those other carriers exclusively employed in carrying letters?—Yes, there was one exclusively employed.

" Does the practice exist now?—It does.

" Is their motive for sending letters by you, and other carriers and by private persons, to save the postage?—Solely for cheapness; there may be some cases where it is for convenience.

" Is the desire considerable amongst the class of society you belong to and the labouring classes generally, for correspondence?—Very great indeed.

" Does that class resort much to sending letters otherwise than by the post when opportunities offer?—Yes, and they frequently avail themselves of opportunities when they hear of persons going.

" Do you mean that when they are apprised of persons going from one place to another, they avail themselves of the opportunities of sending their letters to their friends?—Yes, and one goes and tells another if he has a communication to send to individuals that such a one will take it for him.

" Perhaps you can speak to the fact, was the knowledge of your coming here availed of by people sending letters?—I brought a good number of letters, but my leaving home for London was known only to a very few, and I believe I shall have to take returns home; I was astonished at the number of letters I got.

" Does the same practice prevail of sending letters in all directions, so far as you know?—It does.

" Have you had an opportunity of knowing that yourself to be the practice?—Yes; I was in the practice of delivering letters to the various carriers to be transmitted to the different country towns."

This witness goes on to say that it is customary to send letters by steam-boats, wherever this means of conveyance exists; and to the question, how he would propose to put a stop to sending letters otherwise than by post, he answers shrewdly, " I should just follow the example that was set in putting down illicit distillation in Scotland. I would reduce the duty, and that would put an end to it, by bringing it down to the expense of conveyance by carriers and others."

Mr. John Reid, formerly in trade in Glasgow, but now residing in London, must have amused as well as opened the eyes of the members of the Committee, as well as of the Post-office functionaries, who seem to have been marvellously ignorant of the tricks played upon their department, or, at least, strongly averse to avow their incapacity to correct the evil. Hear this plain out-spoken witness :—

" You formerly were in trade in Glasgow?—Yes.

" You were pretty extensively engaged in the publication of works and the sale of books, were you not?—We were one of the most extensive publishers and booksellers, the two trades combined, in Glasgow.

" Can you state to the Committee, the extent of your correspondence in a year?—I dare say, I sent on an average, including circulars, 20 a day, or from that to 25 a day throughout the year.

" Were the circulars sent to all parts?—We sent them all over Scotland, England, and Ireland; we had accounts all over the three kingdoms.

" Have you sent them by post?—No; we scarcely ever sent them through the post.

" Had you the means of sending them other ways than through the post?—Yes; and equally certain.

. " Were you subjected to a prosecution for having done so ?—Once, out of about 20,000 times of infringing the Post-office, I was caught.

" How did you deal with that prosecution ?—I denied the matter, and they could not prove it; the consequence was, I got off after the exposé made to the House of Commons. Their Solicitor wrote to me to say if I would pay the expenses they would abandon it; but I wrote in answer that I had no intention of paying the expenses, and I heard no more of it.

" Have you yourself been in the habit of having circulars sent to you for delivery ?—Yes, for the last eight years,

" To what extent have you sent circulars by other means than the Post-office ?—I am sure it must have been to the extent of 20,000; it was a very common thing to do it 1,000 at a time.

" Have you any recollection of the number of letters which you received on different matters connected with your trade, by post ?—On the average, perhaps, from one to one and a half per day.

" How many by other means per day ?—Rarely less than a dozen; frequently more.

" Does it consist with your knowledge that the practice of sending letters otherwise than by post is very general ?—I have practised it as a system for the last eight years, and I know there are hundreds of others who are doing the same.

" Do you mean that the system is quite common in the neighbourhood with which you are acquainted ?—Yes. I have a letter in my pocket received this morning, written on Sunday at Glasgow; I had it an hour and a half sooner than I could have had it by the general post, and it cost me only 2d. I know the means by which it came.

" Does the practice prevail of sending letters to a great extent from the interior into the city of Glasgow ?—Most unquestionably.

" How many letters should you state you have seen one carrier have at a time ?—I am certain I have seen a carrier have more than 300 letters for delivery in his possession at a time.

" Those were sent at 1d. a piece ?—Yes.

" Do those letters you allude to come from long distances ?—I have had them almost from every town in Scotland.

" Carriers must in that case deliver them one to the other to forward ? —It is as regular a system as exchanging the Post-office bags; there are many carriers who do not come to Glasgow at all; those exchange letters with others; they meet at a particular part of the road and exchange their letters for Glasgow, or Edinburgh, or whichever way it may be.

" Is there much attempt at concealment in the practice of private conveyances ?—I do not know; sometimes we are frightened and sometimes we laugh at proclamations, but I rarely hear of any persons being caught.

" When you have to send letters to carriers, how do you send them to them ?—We send our boys to the carriers' quarters; they will not give a receipt for letters unless there is money, then they give a receipt for the money: they give a receipt for all parcels; we never go ourselves as if to ask any favour; we send them by little boys as a matter of trade.

" Were you in the habit of sending a piece of paper or a string round them ?—I never sent them so in my life; I have received them in that way. Some carriers will not take them if they are sealed; there is a

belief, but I believe an erroneous belief, that unsealed letters can be com-
. mitted to private hand without risk.

" In your enumeration of the various modes in which letters come to
Glasgow other than through the general post, did you not state that the
very largest and most prominent were the booksellers' parcels ?—Yes.

" Do you consider that you, having the advantage of being a bookseller
with a very large connexion in business, are a fair test of the world in
general ?—I think pretty fair, for I do not do it only for myself, but for
my friends. If I had half-a-dozen friends in London, they enclosed through
my parcels; and if I had half-a-dozen friends in the country, I enclosed
for them in my parcels; I dare say I enclosed as many for my friends as I
did for myself.

" Supposing an individualy had not the advantage of knowing a person like youself, who had the advantage of franking to the extent you had,
what would he do ?—Just the simplest thing in the world ; only come
and buy a quire of paper, or a sixpenny pamphlet, and return the next
day and bring his letter. I have forwarded hundreds for people I never
knew.

" Suppose that he neither wanted the quire of paper, nor the sixpenny
pamphlet ?—He would soon want paper if he wrote letters.

'' You have stated, that you think the increase of letters would be 15
times ; are you prepared to say that, in your judgment, the general increase
of letters sent by post would amount to that ?—I do not think it would ;
I decidedly think it would not amount to 15 times. I should bring it
down one or two if I were to include the average of all the trades.

" At what should you put the general average increase ?—I should
think it very fair to say 13 times, because I am certain warehousemen
send out six times as many circulars as booksellers do.

" Are you presuming, in that, calculation, that the postage is to be
reduced to 1*d.* ?—I go entirely upon that; I conceive it is only by making
it not worth a man's while to evade it, that the certainty of the use of it
can be secured."

Mr. Reid is fully borne out by other highly respectable witnesses.
One states that there are private means of communicating by coach
parcels, or enclosing them to friends and acquaintance. Nay, he
declares that he has known the coachmen of the mail take letters
frequently ; and that the guards of the local coaches consider to form
a part of their perquisites the privilege of taking notes. In every
possible shape the legal method of transmitting letters is evaded.

" *Mr. E. F.*—You are a——, in the town of——?— I am.

" Have you, in the course of your business, reason to know of other
modes of conveying correspondence than by post ?—I adopt them to a
very great extent myself.

'' Be pleased to state the modes you resort to—The usual mode is by the
small carriers ; we send all our annual accounts and communications by
the carriers, and we rarely make use of the Post-office.

" To what distance do you send those letters ?—Our connexion is within
a circuit of 50 miles; it is a country trade.

" How do you manage to send to such distances by carriers ?—Our local carriers deliver them themselves ; but where we send circulars to a distant town, either announcing a fresh supply, or our annual accounts, we are in the habit of forwarding the letters in one parcel to a house in the town, who distributes them for us.

" How do you send those parcels ?—we send them by a coach or an ordinary carrier ; the same mode is carried on in the staple manufactures of our town. I know that it takes place to a very considerable extent.

" In what manner do the manufacturers send their correspondence ?—Chiefly in their parcels to London; their principal business is with London.

" Do the letters you allude to relate to the business of the buyers, or general correspondence ?—Many of them allude to business; but it is a constant habit of merchants to make use of that mode of conveyance for private correspondence. Another class of manufacturers have agencies in London, and their mode of communication is by means of what are in the trade termed free-packets, which are forwarded by the coach proprietors free of carriage, with the exception of a charge for booking, for which the charge is 4d.; 2d. in the country, and 2d. in London. These always consist of letters and of correspondence between the house and its branch, and also contain patterns.

" Will you explain what is meant by free-packets ?—It is a trade term ; I endeavoured to ascertain further particulars from the coach proprietors, but for obvious reasons they declined giving me the particulars ; they do not like to acknowledge the transmission of free-packets. Their reason for allowing it is the fact of the parties using them paying them a considerable amount of carriage for their ordinary traffic. The manufactures sometimes are sent by coach, and, in consequence of that, they allow that privilege.

" The free-packets come in consequence of their having to send large parcels ?—Yes ; none but the houses which do considerable in the carrying trade have that privilege."

This witness afterwards, declares, that

" Another mode of evading the postage among the travelling houses is by printing a number of circulars on one sheet, and having them cut into slips, and distributed in a town by some mutual friend ; that I have had from a printer who prints the circulars.

" Are those slips left open, or are they sealed ?—They are all printed on one sheet, sealed up, and sent by post, paying one postage ; and each is a distinct announcement of their traveller's appearing on a certain day.

" When they come to be delivered, they are delivered as a slip of paper, and not in the shape of a letter ?—Just so.

" Do you mean that the free-packets to which you allude contain many letters not specifically referring to the business of the firm ?—Most certainly.

" What is the object of parties in sending them ?—To save postage.

" Do you understand the cost of postage to be the reason for adopting this mode ?—there is no doubt it is so.

" Have you reason to believe that, if a large production of postage took place, the Post-office would be generally resorted to for the conveyance of letters ?—I have no doubt of that; I should prefer it myself, as being more convenient and as economical; I think we should prefer it, even if it were a little higher, on account of its certainty. * * I think the reduction to a sum that would embrace every description of correspondence would be to a penny postage.

" Do you consider it an easy matter to put an end to the present illicit modes of conveying letters ?—It would be impossible by any other means but by a reduction of postage; if we were to pay the regular postage, it would amount to a prohibition : we could not afford to forward the letters.

" The Committee are to understand that it would be felt as a great relief to many persons if the rate of postage were such as to allow of their sending their letters by post, instead of adopting other modes ?—Yes.

" Would it be a considerable advantage to trade ?—It would be an incalculable advantage to trade ; to every branch of business.

" Perhaps you have on this occasion made yourself the means of bringing letters ?—I certainly have brought them ; I find it the subject of annoyance. My wife is separated at a considerable distance from her friends, and she cannot correspond with them at a less expense than 1s.; we should correspond more frequently if it were not attended with so great an expense; that will of course apply to other families, particularly persons separated from their parents ; and it is a matter of prohibition to our poor. I have had conversation with some of our poor labouring classes ; the families are more separated now than they used to be; the same trade is carried on in distant parts of the country."

Thus it appears that not only are there many ways taken to evade the Post-office exorbitant charges, but that the evasion is not confined to one or two branches of business, nor to any order of correspondence, but that it pervades the whole country, and is practised by every rank.

We shall not go particularly into the other branches of the evidence before us, which consists of the testimony of forty-four witnesses, selected not only from the functionaries in the Post-office department, but from every other source whence light could be expected to be derivable. One most important fact is established by the above testimony, viz. that like all injudicious and exorbitant taxes, that of postage defeats its own intent and object.

To one point we beg simply again to allude, before closing our paper, and it is one which ought to be the theme of universal satisfaction ; we mean the facility and cheapness which steam power has introduced as regards the conveyance of letters. One witness says, that steam-boats " have become so regular and quick, they have attained almost the regularity of mail-coaches." Another witness declares that 6,000 letters, which weigh about one cwt., may be by such means conveyed to Scotland for 2s. 6d. Then why should not the rail-roads, that are to open in so many directions, also be taken advantage of by the Post-office ? To the manufacturing districts of England, and as offering facilities to Ireland, these channels might become of essential service. But to conclude, where can we find a better argument in favour of Mr. Hill's views, when he maintains that a small postage would bring in a revenue not less in amount than is at present realized, than in the fact that during the last five years the increase of ship letters has been immense. The rate of postage thereby having been much moderated; whereas inland correspondence, even although population and intelligence have been on the advance, has remained nearly stationary?

Art. VIII.— *Madame Tussaud's Memoirs and Reminiscences of France. Forming an abridged History of the French Revolution.* Edited by Francis Hervé, Esq., Author of " A Residence in Greece and Turkey," &c. &c. London: Saunders and Otley. 1838.

Mr. Hervé proved himself a lively and versatile writer by his " Residence in Greece and Turkey," and has really made the Memoirs and Reminiscences of Madame Tussaud the text of a good deal of spirited gossip about the French Revolution, and the actors and victims who were most conspicuous in the course of that dreadful national convulsion. To be sure the publication has somewhat the appearance of its editor being a partner in the Bazaar Exhibition concern near Portman-square, where the ancient lady has so long and prosperously, we believe, displayed her literal powers of personification in wax and modelling; and therefore a smile cannot be withheld when we hear our gay-hearted editor claiming for a book, which is much more indebted to his light reading than to the memory of the pretended informer, the honour of presenting in a moderate compass one of the most faithful pictures that has ever been produced of the era in question. The fact is, that the volume is not far short of a literary curiosity, even in an age when so many stratagems and schemes are adopted to secure a temporary notoriety, and a remunerating sale of that which in itself is not possessed of much intrinsic value. A glance at the preface and contents of the work will suffice to exhibit its character and merits.

Mr. Hervé flatters himself that the present publication will be found acceptable, as it rests on the Memoirs and Reminiscences of one who was an eye-witness of many of the scenes which other authors have generally written from the descriptions of previous writers. Now, is it not manifest that he stands in no more favourable predicament than those whose accuracy he would impugn? Then his informant, it is declared, was born in the year 1760, and must therefore at this hour be considerably beyond the age which the psalmist regards as the limit of human life. Why then should her Memoirs and Reminiscences, seeing they are so accurate and full, not have made an earlier appearance? The truth must be that never till now did such a willing and hopeful person offer himself as editor, enlarger, and compiler.

At the same time Madame Tussaud seems to have enjoyed special opportunities for lending precision to many of the facts here recorded, although in a historical sense almost every thing gathered from her or the editor's reading has been repeatedly detailed before. She is, we are told, the daughter of a gentleman, a military officer, of the name of Grosholtz, who was aide-de-camp to General Wurmser. She was born at Berne, in Switzerland, about two months after the decease of her father; but when six years of age, her mother's brother, M. Curtius, a medical Parisian practitioner, took the widow and her family to the French capital, in order that he might superintend their welfare.

It seems when M. Curtius had practised at Berne, the Prince de Conti, who was sojourning in that city, happened to notice some of the doctor's portraits and anatomical subjects modelled in wax; and having been struck with the exquisite delicacy and beauty of the performances, invited him to Paris, promising to procure for him in that gay capital the patronage and the employment which royalty and the great could afford. The house of M. Curtius, it is stated, became accordingly the resort of many of the most celebrated men in France at that period; such as Voltaire, Rousseau, Mirabeau, La Fayette, &c. &c. It is true Madame Tussaud was then very young; but we are informed, that not only is she mistress of a very retentive memory, but being at the time a prettily little dark-eyed girl, who met with a good deal of flattery from these visiters, especially as she very soon rivalled her uncle in the matter of wax-work, she has, female-like, retained a more than usually accurate portraiture of these distinguished individuals who patted her head. We must say, however, that this accuracy, in so far as novelty can be mentioned, consists rather in a nicety of measurement as regards the height, the rotundity, the size, &c. of her and her uncle's sitters, than in anything mental or historically important. And yet when we say so, it is with the feeling that this shop-like peculiarity and tendency are indicative of truth,—conferring upon the work a quality which is worth the price set upon the handsome volume in which these particulars are narrated. Mr. Hervé, for instance, says, that with regard to the personal descriptions of the different characters introduced throughout the work, it may be confidently asserted, that they are likely to be far more accurate than those generally given by other authors, because Madame, from her profession, naturally is a more accurate observer of physical appearance than others usually are. Yea, it is added, that most of the translators from the French have fallen into the error of calculating the inch of France the same as the English inch; whereas the French foot is twelve inches seven-eighths English. This is trying the heroes and victims of the awful revolution by a very nice intellectual standard, that has seldom or perhaps never been used before.

But, as before said, we have no objections to it, and in Mr. Hervé's hands it has a racy use.

As the manners of society when Madame was a girl were such as to bring into play much sooner than now the forms of genteel life, she was enabled to display her precocity to the best advantage. She seems, indeed, to have treasured with a sprightly vivacity some of those intellectual conversations which such literary gladiators as Voltaire and Rousseau held, so as to furnish interesting anecdotes for the present generation. It is said,—

"Full well she remembers the literary discussions which were sometimes conducted with much bitterness by the opposing partisans of the favourite authors of the day; observing, that she never could forget the acrimony displayed between Voltaire and Rousseau in their disputes in the support, perhaps, of some metaphysical theory, in which themselves alone could feel interested, while the reflecting Dr. Franklin would calmly regard them, merely a faint smile sometimes enlivening his countenance, as he coolly contemplated the infuriated disputants; but the young La Fayette was full of fire and animation, listening with eagerness to all that passed; and his features, expressive of his ardent temperament, formed a singular contrast to the philosophic doctor, at whose side he sat; whilst the eloquence of Mirabeau shed a lustre on their conversazioni, composed, as they were, of such a nucleus of talent as might justly entitle them to be styled ' the feast of reason and the flow of soul.'

"One grand source of complaint, which was preferred against Voltaire by Rousseau, was, that he had often advanced different ideas, which were purely original, at M. Curtius's table, and which were intended to form the foundation of a future work, Rousseau ever specifying that such was his object; yet had he the mortification to find that Voltaire would forestal him, by bringing out a volume containing those very opinions which his rival had expressed; and, in fact, the very thoughts and subjects on which he had dilated, and designed as the outlines and substance of his next production. Voltaire, perhaps, scarcely apparently listening to what was said, or taking up the opposite side of the question, would argue with vehemence against the very doctrine which he would soon after publish to the world as his own. Thus, whilst Rousseau was conceiving and projecting materials for his work, and in the simplicity of his heart was proclaiming all his inspirations to his friends, his subtle contemporary was digesting all he heard, and, as quick in execution as the former in imagination, he turned the fertility of his rival's brains to his own advantage.

"Bitter, indeed, was then the venom which was emitted by those two celebrated authors at each other; most rancorous were the reproaches which Rousseau would launch forth against Voltaire, whilst *his* replies were not less deficient in their portion of gall. The latter was far more biting in his sarcasms than his competitor, who sometimes felt so irritated that, losing his self-possession, the point of his satire often lost its keenness. Voltaire, also, was ever gay, whilst Rousseau was generally the reverse, and rather misanthropic.

" When Voltaire retired, then would Rousseau give free vent to all his rage against his arch rival, till he would exhaust all the abusive vocabulary of the French language in expressing his wrath, exclaiming, *Oh, le vieux singe, le scelerat, le coquin!* (Oh, the old monkey, the knave, the rascal!) until he was fatigued with the fury of his own eloquence."

. We are afterwards told, in perfect keeping with the Curtius and Tussaud school, that Voltaire was very tall and thin, with a very small face, which had a shrivelled appearance ; that he wore a large flowing wig, was mostly dressed in a brown coat with gold lace at the button-holes ; that he had a long thin neck, together with other particulars of his costume and person. Rousseau, on the contrary, is described as being below the middle height, and inclined to be stout, patronising a wig with curls, something like that worn by the coachmen at this day of old-fashioned families in England. These and many other more minute and lengthened details of outward appearance abound in the work before us, to which we would direct the attention of all those who may be inclined to say, Show me a man's coat and I will show you his mind.

Madame Tussaud's talents and residence in Paris were destined to bring her into such notice as connects her history in a very striking degree with the great and frightful catastrophes which at the Revolution distracted France and appalled the world. We are told that among the different members of the royal family, who were often accustomed to call upon M. Curtius, and to admire his works, was Madame Elizabeth, the King's sister ; and as she took a great fancy for the art of modelling in wax, she engaged Madame T. not only to teach her, but to reside with her at the palace of Versailles. It is almost funny to think of the use to which the Princess seems particularly to have devoted the wax-work of her hands.

" She was very fond of modelling in wax figures of Christ, the Virgin Mary, and other holy subjects, many of which she gave away to her friends, But one of her occupations strongly exemplifies the temper of the times. It was much the custom, if any person was afflicted in the arm or leg, to send a representation of the limb affected to some church ; which is still a frequent practice in France, particularly in the provinces, hoping that the saint to whom it might be dedicated would effect a cure, or intercede with a higher power to restore the member to its pristine vigour. Madame Elizabeth, therefore, with pious zeal, would often model in wax the legs and arms of decrepit persons, who desired it, which were afterwards suspended at the churches of St. Genevieve, St. Sulpice, and des Capucins du Marché des enfans rouge. What were the effects of these remedies, Madame Tussaud did not state, nor was it the business of the biographer to inquire."

Of this unfortunate Princess the present volume contains many favourable testimonies, in regard, not only to her religious observances, but her charitable doings. We should take her to have been a weak-minded, well-meaning person from all we have read,—a monument, in fact, of that degeneracy of intellect and fatuity of purpose which characterised the decrepitude of a family doomed to extinction and final forgetfulness, we believe. Think of scenes, personages, and performances as given in the following and faithful, but by no means novel representations, disfiguring and rendering imbecile the government of a mighty empire.

"Amongst the various descriptions of fêtes and entertainments which took place at Versailles, Madame Tussaud states, that none had a more beautiful effect than those which were given on fine summer evenings, when the gardens were illuminated, and the waters playing; the variegated lamps were so introduced about the marble fountains, that they appeared as if mingled with the waters, communicating to their bright silver sheets all the resplendence of the prismatic colours which everywhere sparkled, as they reflected thousands of rays, which were emitted from innumerable lights, shedding their lustre in as many tints as the rainbow could describe. The most beautiful echoes also filled the air, produced from silver horns, played by skilful musicians, who were judiciously placed in the numerous arbours, bowers, and grottos, with which the gardens abound; the melodious tones from one horn were scarcely suffered to melt in air, before its fading note was heard from an opposite grove, gradually swelling into its round and fullest force, then gently dying away, until lost in the breeze, or hushed by the sound of falling waters, till again the ear would catch the more powerful notes of horns, playing together in parts, and ending in a continued succession of the most harmonious strains. Hundreds of orange trees were placed at certain intervals throughout the gardens, scenting the air with most delicious perfumes. Is it, then, surprising, that as many as a hundred thousand persons have been present at the same time to witness such a spectacle, where, in fact, several senses at once were gratified?—the sight, which was completely dazzled by the number of brilliant objects which, on all sides, were presented to the view; the hearing, by the exquisite sounds which, without intermission, were ever filling the air with their melodious notes, whilst the scent was greeted by the exquisite odours arising from beds of flowers, and the blossoms of the orange and myrtle, which were distributed in profusion around: in fact, a stranger, on first entering these elysian gardens, appeared as it were bewildered with delight, and as if transported to some fairy scene of enchantment.

"During the interval of the dances, whilst the fair were reposing from the fatigue of pleasure, then was the moment for the accomplished courtier to display the powers of his art, in an age when compliment, wit, and repartee were considered as qualifications indispensable for those admitted within the precincts of the royal saloons; all essayed their utmost efforts to outshine each other in the delicacy of their flattery, and in every finesse of gallantry; thus, while the lady listened to her *soi disant* adorer, her countenance, glowing with delight, would bespeak the tale to which she lent an ear, ever calculated to raise her in her own estimation, whilst the attitude and gesticulation of her elegant admirer alone would proclaim the theme of his eloquence. Groups such as these then filled the drawing-rooms; and those who breathed the soft balm of adulation were themselves as gratified as could be their fair and susceptible auditors, whilst an expression of joyous feeling beamed from every feature, and ' all went merrily as a marriage bell.' Alas, poor deluded beings! how little did they think, that the splendid suite of apartments, with their gilded cornices and painted ceilings, filled with beings on whom every artificial aid had been lavished to endow them with grace and elegance, clothed in drapery, glittering with embroidery and jewels, in a few short months would be polluted by the vulgar tread of the lowest wretches which the dregs of Paris could disgorge, of ruffians of the coarsest mien, who, with bare and bloodstained arms, vociferating their hideous yells, bellowing from room to room, with horrid oaths and imprecations, calling for revenge upon the royal inmates of the palace, turned that which had so late been a scene of revelry and pleasure into one of brutal riot and slaughter: yet such was the fact; the burdens upon the people, and the bondage in which they were held by the nobles, became insufferable; the string was too tightly drawn, and at length it snapped, and no powers then could re-unite the rebel cords, once set free; anarchy followed, and, too late, the oppressors saw their error, and that they had carried their tyranny one point too far."

But what was the condition of the husbandman, the tradesman, the payer of taxes, in those days of court revelry and splendour? Why, the peasantry were, as Mr. Hervé has justly remarked, in the last stage of misery and deprivation. An English author, who travelled in France at that period, states, that he has seen a plough drawn by a wretched horse, a cow, an ass, and a goat, whilst a peasant, without shoes or stockings, guided it, as a half-naked urchin was endeavouring to whip his team forward. So much for strong contrasts and the seeds of revolution. But we mean not to be political but anecdotical. Let us see what Madame T. has to say of the Bastille and Robespierre.

"The sensation excited by the capture of a prison, with which were associated such ideas of horror, may be easily imagined, and all Paris were flocking to visit the dungeons, upon which, for ages, no one could reflect without shuddering at the thoughts of those who were there doomed to pass their lives, without the hope of ever again being permitted to enjoy the blessings of day. Amongst others who were induced to visit those melancholy mementos of despotism and tyranny, Madame Tussaud was prevailed upon to accompany her uncle and a few friends for that purpose; and whilst descending the narrow stairs, her foot slipped, and she was on the point of falling, when she was saved by Robespierre, who, catching hold of her, just prevented her from coming to the ground; in the language of compliment observing, that it would have been a great pity that so young and pretty a patriot should have broken her neck in such a horrid place. How little did Madame Tussaud then think that she should, in a few years after, have his severed head in her lap, in order to take a cast from it after his execution. He was accompanied by Collot-d'Herbois and Dupont, who had come upon the same errand. They afterwards visited many of the cells, which were all that was loathsome and disgusting, being about eight feet square, and extremely low. They then proceded to examine the small bedstead and straw mattrass, which had been left as they were found on the capture of the prison; one chair and table, on which stood a pitcher, formed the rest of the furniture; a damp fœtid smell prevailing, in every respect nauseous to the senses.

" After recognising M. Curtius, and exchanging a few words with him, Robespierre harangued the people, as nearly as Madame Tussaud can remember, to this effect: Alas! (*mes enfans*) how severe a lesson do we now receive from these gloomy dungeons by which we are surrounded, and in which so many of our fellow-creatures have been immured! That monarchical dominion needs for its support the misery and persecution of such individuals whose virtuous minds have dared to resist the current of oppression, has been, from time immemorial, but too evidently manifest. We are now treading that ground on which, for centuries, have perished the victims of despotism; then may these mansions of misery, these monuments of tyranny and injustice, act as incentives to every patriot to hurl down the banners of arbitrary power, whilst every man shall lend a hand in raising the standard of liberty and independence, and boldly assert his natural rights!

" After visiting many different cells, they arrived at that where the Comte de Lorge had been confined, when Robespierre again burst forth into an energetic declamation against kings, exclaiming, Let us for a while reflect on the wretched sufferer who has been just delivered from a living entombment, a miserable victim to the caprice of royalty; and can we calmly behold such scenes, and are we so pusillanimous as to suffer their repetition without exerting all our physical and moral strength for their repression? No, Frenchmen! the torch is kindled which shall light the minions of aristocracy to their earthly tomb, and the heart of every lover of his country is inspired with an ardent zeal to maintain the cause of freedom, or to perish in the contest. For what is the value of our lives, if they can only be sustained by the sacrifice of our liberties? The orator was followed by Collot-d'Herbois and Dupont who also displayed their eloquence to the same effect, and were highly applauded by their auditors."

The artistic sort of employment upon which Madame T. has been so often engaged, may be illustrated and accounted for by her narrative as given by Mr. Hervé concerning the death of the monster Marat.

" An heroic girl, named Charlotte Corday, travelled from Normandy to Paris to rid her country of the monster Marat. When arrived in the capital, she was not quite resolved which should be her victim: Robespierre and Danton were nearly as odious to her mind as Marat, but the latter and his atrocities were more known in the provinces, particularly in the struggle which had taken place in the suppression of the insurrection in Cavados, where the cruel effects of his suggestions had been most severely felt. Her first attempt to see Marat proved unsuccessful; but on the second, although his housekeeper, a young woman who had lived with him, refused to admit her, yet Marat, who was in his bath, hearing the voice of Charlotte Corday, and having had a letter from her stating she had intelligence of importance to communicate, ordered that she might be suffered to enter. She first amused him with an account of the deputies at Caen, when he said, 'They shall all go to the guillotine.' 'To the guillotine!' exclaimed she; and as he caught up a pencil to write the names of the offenders, Charlotte Corday plunged a knife into his heart. 'Help, my dear!' he cried, and his housekeeper obeyed the call, and a man, who was near, rushed in and knocked down the avenger of her country with a chair, whilst the female trampled upon her. A crowd was instantly attracted to the spot by the uproar, when Charlotte Corday rose, looking around her with a composed and dignified air; and some members of the section arriving, they prevented her from being torn to pieces by the mob. Her beauty, her courage, and her calm demeanour interested the authorities in her behalf, and they conducted her to prison, protecting her from insult.

"As has already been stated, Madam Tussaud was brought to the scene of action a short time after it had happened, and took the cast from the demon's features, some gens d'armes attending her to keep off the crowd. She visited Charlotte Corday in the Conciergerie Prison, and found her a most interesting personage; she was tall and finely formed; her countenance had quite a noble expression; she had a beautiful colour, and her complexion was remarkably clear; her manners were extremely pleasing, and her deportment particularly graceful. Her mind was rather of a masculine order; fond of history, she had made it much her study, and naturally became deeply interested in the politics of her country; was a great admirer of pure republican principles, and thought she perceived the same feelings in the Girondins, to which party she became enthusiastically attached, and imbibed a proportionate detestation for the Mountain; hence the success of that resolution which brought her to the scaffold. She had been affianced to Major Belsance, a remarkably fine-looking young man, who was in the royal guards, and assassinated in one of the popular commotions in 1789. She wrote a letter to her father, begging pardon for what she had done, and stating, she believed it to be her duty, bidding him remember, that Corneille observed that the crime, and not the scaffold constitutes the shame. She conversed freely with Madame Tussaud, and even cheerfully, and ever with a countenance of the purest serenity. During her trial she displayed the same self-possession, avowed every thing without reserve. When conveyed to the scaffold, some few of the rabble abused her, but far more pitied and admired her, and many women shed tears as she passed. The smile of happiness lighted her features all the way to the place of execution; and when the last preparations were performing, as the handkerchief was withdrawn, and discovered her bosom, the blush of modesty suffused her cheek, but she never once displayed the slightest emotion of fear. As soon as her head was severed, the executioner held it up and buffeted it, an action which was witnessed by the people with shuddering. The remains were conveyed to the Madeleine, where Madame Tussaud took a cast from her face. Charlotte Corday was of a highly respectable family, and descended from Corneille; some first cousins of hers were still living a few years since at Argentan, in Normandy. When Marat's effects were examined, an assignat for five francs was found to be all the money he possessed; his housekeeper, therefore, whom, as Chaumette expressed himself, 'Marat had taken to wife one fine day before the face of the sun,' was considered as his widow, and was maintained at the charge of the state. He appears to have been

always poor. In 1774, he lived at Edinburgh, and gained his livelihood
by teaching the French language; he then published a work called ' The
Chains of Slavery,' with an address to the electors of Great Britain. The
honours which were decreed to Marat proved the awfully demoralised
state of the times; he was buried in the garden of the Cordeliers—his
favourite den, from whence he poured out his iniquity by reading his inflammatory paper to the people.   One blasphemous fanatic, in a declamation eulogising the deceased monster, said, ' Oh Marat ! Jesus Christ was
an angel, but thou wert a God ! ' "

We learn that Madame Tussaud has been thirty-six years in
England, and that if her reminiscences of France be favourably
received, she will be emboldened to do that for her sitters in England
which she was in the habit of doing for the great or notorious ones
across the channel.   Perhaps some may think that this promise
comes late considering her very advanced age at this moment ; but
the expectants who have enjoyed the gossipping of the present
volume may take comfort to themselves, after we inform them that
she is descended from a family remarkable for their longevity, that
one of them lived to the age of ninety, another to that of a hundred
and four, and another to that of a hundred and eleven.   So, take
comfort ye readers of light and interesting chat ; Mr. Hervé and
Madame, wedded as they at present are, will not disappoint you, or
be found inferior to hundreds who advance even higher pretensions.

ART. IX.—*Six Years in Biscay : comprising a Personal Narrative of the
   Sieges in Bilbao, in June,* 1835, *and December,* 1836. By John Francis
   'Bacon.' London : Smith, Elder, & Co.   1838.

This is an impartial and cleverly-executed sketch of the most interesting period of the contest which is now desolating the Peninsula,
and which promises to be interminable.   Public curiosity has
ceased to be aroused by victories which end in nothing, and defeats
which allow the discomfited party to take the field the day after.
Each succeeding winter sees Don Carlos recruiting his forces in the
Basque provinces, to sally forth with returning spring to lay waste
the province of Castile, while in the interim small bands are
launched forth to ravish the country with the speed and cruelty of
a horde of Tartars, burning, plundering, collecting troops, and har-
rassing the Queen's forces with endless marching.   Scarcely can we
summon patience to continue to peruse the accounts of the exploits
of those leaders whom every day brings forth, and who are all equally
insignificant and ruthless.   The fact is, both parties seem to be
anxious to prolong the contest ; guerilla warfare, plunder, and
butchery, is too congenial to the taste of the people to be easily
laid aside, and nothing but the armed troops of the hostile invader,
or the famine which their devastations have rendered imminent,

will effectually part the combatants, or cause them to relax their gripes upon each other's throats.

The causes which have engendered and nurtured this fierce struggle have been. so often and so ably discussed by public writers of all parties and of every shade of opinion that it would be superfluous for us to recapitulate them here. Mr. Bacon has left none of them untouched, and he has treated them all with great acuteness and candour. His long residence in the provinces of Biscay gave him particular opportunities of becoming thoroughly acquainted with the fueros of the Basques, and he has given a clear exposition in what those privileges really consisted.

The ecclesiastical aristocracy of Spain rested on a broad and a solid foundation. The consolidation of its power was the work of centuries, and its influence was widely and beneficially exercised through the community. Its easy familiarity with the peasantry maintained a feeling of equality and flattered that pride which is the characteristic of a race who boast that they acknowledge no superior. " Sois vos el Rey di Castilla?" (Are ye the King of Castile?) said a Spanish farmer to King Ferdinand, standing with free and lofty carriage, covered head, and unembarrassed manner, in the presence of his sovereign. It may be easily imagined that the man, who could see nothing more than the public functionary in the monarch, would be more easily reconciled to the superiority of the ecclesiastical than the lay lord. The former was his neighbour, his familiar acquaintance, his adviser—he was a better landlord and a better man. If the convent was wealthy, its wealth was for the benefit of the people. The most exquisite pictures, the finest music, the richest plate, the most gorgeous ceremonials,—all the pomp and circumstance of glorious worship, were for them, for their gratification, for their benefit. In the church all met on equal terms. There were no barriers to hedge round a class, and separate the *profanum vulgus* from their wealthier neighbours, and remind them of their inferiority ; and not only could the peasant look upon wealth and power, thus employed, without envy, but he looked upon it as his own. On the other hand, the lay lord, is an absentee, spending his rents at Madrid, and leaving his estate in the hands of his agent : his sumptuous furniture, his paintings, his grounds, carefully screened from observation. Perhaps he is a spendthrift and inexorable : the ecclesiastical lord, easy of access, and yielding at once to a tale of a bad season, a missed crop, or any other of the many casualties that may befal his tenant. The economy of the convent renders a reduction no sacrifice. In addition to all this he dispenses the favours of heaven with a liberal hand. Can it then be a matter of wonder that the Spanish peasant sides with the clergy ? and is it not a matter of surpassing wonder that the Cortes, both in 1812 and subsequently in 1821, with this deeply-rooted and widely-diffused veneration of the Spanish people for their clergy before their eyes, demolish at one fell swoop all the monastic orders, and appropriate their revenues to the state? A more politic and less decisive course would have more speedily effected their design. Instead of sapping and mining, they proceeded to take the vast fabric by storm.· Instead of disarming their hostility or pitting them against each other, they converted the whole army of monks into bitter and irreconcileable foes, and furnished their enemies with the most formidable weapons against themselves. The fact was, the middle classes had for centuries borne the weight of spiritual oppression; they were more conversant with foreigners and more alive to their degradation; they were burning for revenge, and when their time, as they fancied, was come, they struck boldly and blindly at the Colossus,· but their blows recoiled upon themselves: they threw the whole mass into the arms of Don Carlos. Opposed by the higher and educated classes, the clergy fell back for support upon the lower orders; they anathematised their opponents as traitors in this world and rejected in the next: to destroy them was the most praiseworthy of human achievements. Thus the furious and fierce fanaticism of myriads of peasants led on with perfect unity of purpose, is more than a match for the disjointed wavering and unimpassioned force of the superior classes. Nor has the spo-· liation of the monasteries added much to the available capital of the state, nor will it retard its bankruptcy by a single hour.·

In conjunction with these spiritual influences in rousing the un-compromising hostility of the most compact and ancient race of the Spanish peninsula, may be noticed the no less important political influences of their fueros or privileges. These may be shortly stated as consisting of exemption from conscription—exemption from maintaining soldiers in time of peace—exemption from taxation, except of their own imposing, including freedom from customs duties on goods imported from foreign countries—the right possessed by the Basque who dwells beyond the Ebro, if accused of any offence, of bringing his case before the juez mayor at Valladolid, and the right of governing themselves according to their own usages and customs, the king nominating only one of their officers, the corregidor. These are the fueros of Biscay, Alava, and Guipuscoa, as contrasted with the rest of Spain. These exemptions threw an unjust burden on the other provinces, and the Madrid government was anxious at all times to do away with them. A measure of this kind was resolved upon in 1830, and a strong body of troops was collected under the command of General O'Donnell to enforce the act of abolition. Nor did Don Carlos, as has been erroneously asserted, offer any opposition to this measure: it is true, that, with his usual policy, he made a show of succumbing to it: he deplored the necessity of infringing the fueros, and recommended that it should be done gradually. It was to the revolution of July, and to the dread of French interference felt by Calomarde and the apostolicals that the Basques were indebted for the suspension of the execution of the abolition scheme, the merit of which has been claimed by Don Carlos, and loudly vaunted by his party.

To the influence of the clergy was added the powerful influence of the lawyers. The escribanos form a numerous class in the Basque provinces, and they espoused the Carlist interest to a man. Thus while the monk hurled damnation on the soul of a heretic landlord, the escribano denounced confiscation against his lands, and the military powers held the sword over his head. Arguments like these were irresistible, and the authority of the Carlists was widely and firmly established.

The organization of the army was rapidly and skilfully conducted by the *diputaciones* in Biscay and Alava between 1823 and 1833. In Guipuscoa, the arrangements were not so active, as the presence of the Captain General and the garrison of Saint Sebastian offered an effective check to their proceedings.

The volunteers of Navarre were numerous, but inferior in equipment to those of the other provinces. At the first outbreak, the organised Carlist militia amounted to 57,000, with a further stock of 80,000 able to bear arms as a reserve; and an annual corps of at least 7000 for several years to come. This excellent organization of the provinces was owing to the exertions of Verastegui and Valdespina. To provide for the troops the whole province was divided into districts, and a commissary appointed for each. The number of rations of meat and bread supplied daily by the province of Biscay amounted to 10,290 or 72,030 weekly, equal to about 180 oxen, 108,045 pounds of bread, and 3,700 gallons of wine. The clothing of the troops was not so effectually provided for: it was composed of cloth purchased in France or Bilbao, or stolen in marauding parties into Castile, and made up in the provinces. A certain quantity of cloth was sent to a town, with orders to have it converted into jackets and trowsers in a given time, and the authorities instantly set all hands in the town to work. In this manner, says Mr. Bacon, was clothed and fed, by a small country not containing the eighth part of its population, an army as numerous as that of Bavaria.

In the matter of the manufacture and repair of arms, the Carlists possessed advantages of a peculiar kind in the iron works of Biscay and Guipuscoa. The numerous hands employed in the manufacture of this metal are dispersed over the country: many towns, such as Eybar, Plasencia, Elgoybar, Elgueta, Durango, Ochandiano, Tolosa, Vergara, and Balmaseda, are entirely devoted to the manufacture of arms and ironmongery in general. Three thousand of the Carlist soldiers were enabled to repair and even make their own arms and accoutrements. In the manufacture of gunpowder they had advantages equally peculiar; their forests furnished inexhaustible supplies of charcoal, which the long practice of the charcoal-burners enabled them to make of a superior quality; sulphur and saltpetre were obtained from France, and the friars worked incessantly at the manufactories at Onate and Ereno. The amount of money raised on the provinces by confiscations, customs, and subsidies, has been estimated at five millions of dollars, to say nothing of provisions, clothing, effects, and stores of all kinds, which may be computed at a very considerable sum. Thus we may observe that four provinces with a population, not exceeding that of Kent and Surrey, maintained, out of their own children, an army of 24,000 men, paid, clothed, and equipped them, and kept them recruited through a bloody war of four years ; and now, when entering on the fifth campaign, the army is rather increased than otherwise.

. To oppose this formidable force, the Queen had a nominal army amounting to 100,000 men, one half of which was officered by Carlists who neutralized its efficacy. Her government was surrounded by functionaries in the interest of her rival, busy in crippling and embarrassing its measures ; and, most grievous of all the calamities, her exchequer was empty, and her government was burthened with an accumulated load of debt. Add to this the hollow conduct of Louis Phillipe, and it is not at all surprising that it should take four years of active warfare to test the materials of the military and civil services, and to purge them from concealed enemies.[1]

. The Carlists had contemplated a rising all over Spain. With dismay they heard that Queen Isabel had been recognized without opposition through all the provinces, and that forces were pouring into Burgos from every quarter to support her title. Then followed the defeat of the Alavese; the march of Sarsfield upon Vitoria, and his subsequent delivery of Bilbao. During the period of their occupation, the Carlists had mulcted the inhabitants at a fearful rate ; and now they retired in rage, disappointment, and despair, crying out they had been deceived. Had Sarsfield followed close upon their heels and chastised the villagers for their past, and taken hostages for their future conduct, it is probable he would have crushed the enemies of the Queen at once. But what does he do ? He publishes an indulto for 15 days, and then remains inactive. The Carlists laughed at his indulto, seized six gentlemen of Bilbao and put to death Muroaga, the treasurer of the province.

Sarsfield was replaced by Valdez in the command of the army of the north. This general had acquired a deservedly high reputation in Peru. He brought with him some new general officers, amongst others, Bedoya, Osma, Benedicto, and Espartero. The first three soon lost the little reputation they had ; the last raised himself from a brigadier-general, in three years, to the post he now occupies of commander-in-chief of the Spanish armies. His predominant failing is said to be indecision—but he is capable of acting with startling energy on occasions. Although his conduct has been sometimes prejudicial to the cause, no doubt can be entertained of his being a zealous and faithful adherent to the queen. At the juncture we speak of, he succeeded the Count Armildez in the government of Biscay with 3500 men, exclusive of the fine regiment of Compostela which was left in garrison at Bilbao. Valdez behaved with activity and met with considerable success in pursuing the Carlists, his plans were well combined and well executed. Espartero, too, scoured the country to the east of the Nervion, whilst Iriarte and Quintana overran the encartaciones, where they were kept briskly employed by the Carlist Chief Andachaga. But whether Valdez did too little, or whether, as is surmised, he did too much, so that both Republicans and Christinos began to fear the war would end too soon, he was recalled and replaced by Quesada with fuller powers than his predecessor had enjoyed. The contending parties might now be said to be evenly matched. Quesada was at the head of 30,000 effective men, one-half of whom were employed in garrisons; while the thousands of enthusiastic peasantry which formed the Carlist force, no longer dispersed into independent guerilla parties, were now consolidated and combined, acting with unity of design and steady system under the guidance of a chief, with energies equal to the task —Thomas Zumalacarreguy.

The instant he assumed the command he struck a blow that secured his ascendancy, and spread consternation through the ranks of the Queen's army. He rushed down upon Vitoria, and meeting with a severe repulse, he turned aside to the north-west and enveloped a body of Christinos at Heredia. One hundred and sixty prisoners were massacred in cold blood to convince both sides that the Carlist general would not stick at trifles. The Queenites were intimidated, and, from that moment, the Carlists gained a moral superiority over their opponents, which they never lost. In civil wars, and particularly Spanish wars, the most sanguinary are treated with the greatest respect and deference. The activity of Zumalacarreguy hurried him upon new enterprizes. While the Christino generals were busy with speculating in the funds, he was scouring the valley of the Borunda, and cutting off the straggling garrisons. To crown his success and to raise the enthusiasm of the Basques to the highest pitch, Don Carlos joined the army in person: the bloody drama deepened in interest and horror.

To reinforce Quesada, who, though unsuccessful, had fought bravely, Rodil advanced with ten thousand men from Portugal. His character for obstinacy and cruelty made him a fitting opponent for the Carlist chief. But the plan of operations laid down by the war department at Madrid—viz. to garrison all the towns of any importance and to support them by movable columns—was pregnant with disasters. These towns were mostly situated in the valleys and are bad military positions. The keys of those valleys being in the hands of the Carlists, they poured an overwhelming force upon the small garrisons and cut them to pieces in detail.

" If, says " Mr. Bacon," instead of placing small garrisons in every town, commanded in many instances by officers of doubtful fidelity, the queens generals had established regular military camps, entrenched on the knots of the mountains commanding the entrance of many valleys, each camp consisting of 3000 men at least, the tactics of the Carlists would have been, in a great measure, frustrated. Of course it would be necessary that the soldiery be well commanded, in order that they might derive all the benefit from their situation. Huts might have been built for the soldiers, and the inhabitants of the valleys would not refuse rations when they saw an avalanche constantly hanging over their heads; for the access being easy to so many valleys, if they attempted to blockade the camp, all their young men must have been recalled from the faction. But nothing of this was done : the officers of the army, anxious to live in as good quarters as they could get, were reluctant to leave the snug little towns of Biscay and Guipuscoa, and thus the queen of Spain's generals frittered away 7000 or 8000 men in petty garrisons of 200, 300, and 400 men. The folly of this plan was soon perceived by Zumalacarreguy, and these small detachments were blockaded by single companies. In this manner, Ochandiano has a garrison of 300 men,—it is blockaded by thirty. No provisions are allowed to enter unless protected by a large force. The garrison cannot spare above 100 men to make a sortie, and this the besiegers well know, consequently, if the troops march out, they are skirmished with incessantly ; obliged to keep together, not knowing the number of their assailants, the regulars usually lose two and perhaps three for one, and when the casualties amount to twenty, their leader generally retreats, having taken little by his motion. The Carlists celebrate their victory by screeching and various antics ; all this has the effect of disheartening the queenites, until at last they will not stir forth on any account, and thus the garrisons become a dead weight upon the attentions of the commander-in-chief instead of an assistance."

While the Infante at the head of a chosen band enticed Rodil's columns into a wild-goose chase, the Carlist chief hung upon his rear, cut off his straggling brigades, surprised his convoys, and pounced upon the unsupported garrisons. Having lost 5000 men in a few months, Rodil relinquished the struggle and the command, on the very day which witnessed the disgraceful defeat of General O'Doyle at Alegria en Alava. The successes of the Carlists were in a great measure owing to the accurate information they received from a partisan on the general's staff. It is even asserted that the power of their friends at Madrid was invariably successful in attaching a Carlist to the staff of every successive general. The Carlist mode of warfare, as described by Mr. Bacon, will afford an easy solution of the causes of the protraction of hostilities.

" The Carlists tactics, which at such length I have above explained, were carried into full effect against Espartero ; they danced him and his division round and round the province ; but they never could get him to divide his troops, and as only two of the Biscay garrisons were inland, he was little troubled by their claims, for the sea offered easy means of relief to the places on the coast. Thus, beyond tiring his men, nothing particularly occurred for some time, until Arana, an old Spanish colonel, and now commandment of Biscay for the Carlists, being anxious to come to blows, took up a position near Elorrio, on a mountain-side, which was intersected with stone walls, forming a post of amazing strength. Here Espartero attacked him, and had the Biscayans been Kentucky riflemen, they would have destroyed his division; but they had such an excessive dislike to lose a man, that after their front line behind the parapet had delivered its fire, the troops ran off right and left, and rallied behind the second line of walls, thence to a third, and so on. But these unsteady volleys did the queenites little harm, and Colonel Echaluce, with his cazadores, having turned their right flank, Arana's men abandoned their superb position, after sustaining a loss of above two hundred men, which was equal to, if not more than that of Espartero.

" A regular European army, after being completely driven from such a strong position as that of Elorrio, would lose its *morale*, the soldiery would become disheartened, and tacitly allow their antagonists to be better men. Such was not, nor is the case with the Basques; they run off in every direction, and the scattered cottages and hamlets, for miles round, are filled with their soldiery, as gay and unconcerned as if they had been victorious. Their very dispersion renders it impossible to know what loss they have sustained, and they are always ready to hope for the best. Next day they direct their steps to some village, where they are sure to learn the place of re-union. Thus, after a sharp fight, which has perhaps disabled the column from moving any farther, the Carlist Basques would be two days later, operating in the rear of the column or showing fight in front. It may also be remarked that the Navarrese or Biscayan, when they run off the field, rarely throw their musquets away; the queen's soldiers almost always do so. The reason is obvious enough. The Basque soldier sought safety in dispersion; out of reach of the musquetry of the column he was secure, nor was it difficult to carry a fusil that distance; but the Christino soldier, when his regiment was broken, usually saw no safety except in flying to the nearest garrison town, and so, to run the faster, threw down his arms and all incumbrances to flight."

The misfortunes of the general raised the clamour of the nation: the Camarilla party at Madrid trembled and recalled Mina. The appointment of the veteran chief to the command of the northern army, raised the hopes of the Queen's party at home and abroad; nor were these hopes altogther disappointed. With a badly organized and dispirited army, and broken by sickness and infirmities, the Navarrese chief brought victory once more to the standards of the Queen, and at Unsue and Asarte overthrew the Carlists with great slaughter. Three thousand Navarrese perished in these two actions; and the veteran chief taught his quondam secretary that he was still his master; but though defeated three times in twelve days, Zumalacarreguy did not relax in his activity. He took Echarri and Aranaz; these successes were chiefly owing to the treachery or misconduct of the Carlist officers in the provincial regiments of the

Queen's army, which paralyzed the effect of its able commander and
neutralized his victories. The infirmities of Mina compelling him
to retire, Valdez was once more placed at the head of the army.

The winter of 1834-35 passed away, and with it all hopes of
the termination of the struggle. The conduct of Espartero and
other officers was in fact better adapted to prolong than to terminate the contest; it was his custom to march out with his column
for a few days, and then return and stay a week or a fortnight at
Bilbao. As he seldom went out of the high road, the Carlists in
derision nicknamed him el Ordinario de Durango—the Durango
carrier. While his column was out upon these paseos, Eraso's
batallions, laughing to scorn the lumbering movements of the Christino brigadiers, descended like lightning, first upon the small garrisons, and then upon Bilbao itself. On the 7th of March he seized
upon the beautiful and extensive flour mills within half a mile of the
Durango gate, and butchered a detachment of 36 men, who were
left to defend them. Don Archevala, the governor of Bilbao, beheld the slaughter of his men—the destruction of the supplies of
bread and flour for the town, without striking a blow in their defence;
and when the national guard murmured at his inactivity, he sent a
detachment of 53 men of their number to drive back the enemy,
who mustered 2,000 strong. They had scarcely proceeded beyond
the gate, when they were assailed by a shower of musket balls, ten
of their number went down in an instant, and the rest fired a volley
and ran back to the town. Archevala saved himself from the
indignation of the town's people by a rapid change of residence,
until Espartero returned, when he resigned his command, which was
given to Colonel Solano.

Valdez now appointed Espartero commander-iu-chief of the
Basque provinces in the room of Carratala, who had been soundly
beaten by Zumalacarreguy at Ormaistegui, and Iriarte took the
command of the six divisions by which they was held. The Carlists
chief was at the head of thirty battalions of good troops, flushed with
triumph at their repeated successes, and the contest promised to be
fierce and sanguinary in the extreme.

At this juncture the British government, then in the hands of the
Tories, interposed to mitigate the cruelties practised on both sides.
The Eliot treaty is by no means relished by Mr. Bacon, his strictures
upon it are not without foundation, and they are delivered in a
style approaching to indignant remonstrance.

"I am not desirous to appear the advocate of a war of extermination,
and am aware that most of the furious Spanish liberals who have impugned
this treaty, have done so when sitting in safety in their coffee-houses,
where it is marvellously easy to talk about national honour and so forth.
It is, however, clear enough, that had the envoy of the Duke of Wellington been desirous of throwing his weight and influence into the queen's
scale, he would have enlarged upon the barbarous murders in Bilbao and

Heredia; and the repeated slaughter of prisoners by the Carlist generals. He might also have slightly and delicately alluded to the civility received by his majesty so lately in England and Portugal, and then asked how he could sanction such a mode of warfare? It was evident that Valdez would not have refused to give quarter, and thus the treaty might have been confined to one article, simply specifying that all classes of combatants, on both sides, should have quarter when they asked it.

" Had such been the case, foreigners in general, and Englishmen in particular, would have been spared the pain of seeing the Carlists infringe the treaty—nay, declare that it did not include,

" 1st. All the national guards.

" 2nd. All the soldiers and officers of the free corps or volunteers.

" 3rd. All foreigners in the queen of Spain's service.

" Gracious God! here is a treaty which carefully excludes the militia, the very pith of the popular cause; next the volunteers and foreigners, with whom the only difference is, that they *are* volunteers, but not Spaniards. Whom, then, may it be said that the famous Eliot or Gurwood treaty protects? Why, the regular army; that is, the force of which many of the generals and officers were strongly suspected of a half-and-half hostility against the infante. Possibly Colonel Gurwood, himself one of the regulars, could not find, in the plenitude of his humanity for them, room for any one else. But, were such the case, how came the commissioner to shut his eyes to the fact, that the very army of Don Carlos came more under the description of ' militia and volunteers' than anything else? Besides, talking of foreigners, did not Colonel Gurwood see Captain Henningsen? Did he see no Frenchmen? no German? or, is it, that in the gallant colonel's opinion, a few gentlemen may do that with impunity, which the mob of plebeians are righteously hung for?

" But although the charge of partiality may rest with the commissioners, nothing can ever wipe away the stain which this treaty inflicted upon the Spanish army. They, soldiers by trade, whose profession was the noble career of arms, bargained to save themselves at the expense of the unfortunate tradesman who took up arms to defend his town, and his family from rapine and murder. The miserable national was often (I have witnessed it) obliged to sleep on the bare ground with his wife and children, and to resign his only bed to the soldiery. Often has he been compelled to sell his scanty furniture to find money to buy them fuel and oil, and yet this wretched father of a family is obliged to take his turn of duty, without pay or rations! and, if taken prisoner by the enemy, is duly delivered over to the peasantry to be tortured to death, or else, harder still, is sent to the mines at Barambio, to languish for months, until kind death ends his sufferings.

" Neither with the volunteer or the foreigner is the case so cruel as with the national; *they* are fighting men by trade, and receive pay; but why should they be put out of the pale of the treaty, as if unworthy of a thought? Are not Don Carlos and his followers continually dinning in our ears that his army is composed of volunteers? Well, then, if his forces are volunteers, why can he object to those of his opponents being of the same description?—Ay, there is the rub! and the duke's commissioners well knew it. D. Carlos and his officers wanted their own followers to be represented as all pious and virtuous volunteers fighting *pro bono regis.* The queen's forces, of course, were all conscripts, obliged to serve, poor things!—and as for foreigners, the commissioners could not see the French, English, Portuguese, Germans, Italians, at the headquarters of D. Carlos or those of his generalissimo, neither could they in after times hear the cries of their countrymen, murdered at Arrigorriaga and Hernani, agreeably to the '*tratado Eliot.*'

"Thus much for the famous Eliot convention, which, apart from the spurious philanthropy with which it was ostensibly covered, was discreditable to the English commissioners, who displayed a want of ordinary attention or common humanity in leaving out all mention of the militia, free corps, and foreigners, and was dishonourable in the last degree to the Spanish generals, who ought to have spurned the mere idea of bargaining for their own safety at the cost of the families who fed, clothed, and paid them—besides fighting for their cause as well, if not better, than themselves. The British commissioners might plead ignorance; but for the Spanish generals there is not the shadow of excuse."

The tide of victory now rolled steadily in favour of the Carlists. Iriarte having attached the Carlist Chief Sarasa at Guernica, with a fine division of troops, though somewhat fatigued after a long march on very bad roads, was completely routed and compelled to retreat upon Lequeitio. Espartero advanced with ten thousand men to check the enemy and cover the retreat of the broken divisions to Bilbao. But the triumph of Espartero, in his superior good luck, was destined to be of short duration. Having marched to the relief of Villafranca de Guipuscoa, he was defeated by the Carlist chief and driven back upon Vergara, with the loss of 2,000 men, while his adversary did not lose more than twenty: and now having triumphed over all the obstacles in his path, the Carlist laid siege to Bilbao.

Mr. Bacon gives us a most minute and in many particulars a most interesting account of the siege; but as the newspapers have already treated us to it at the time *usque ad nauseam,* we shall forbear entering into details already so well known. The errors committed both by besiegers and besieged were gross and glaring enough and they have been very clearly exposed in the present work. The Carlists are censured for not relishing the idea of marching in a close column up to a breach with grape playing upon both flanks, while round shot and musketry are pounding the front. The prospect is certainly not very agreeable, but our English troops would have done it. The Basque soldier is excellent at a skirmish, steady behind defences, quick in surprising a batallion which has lost its way, but he is not suited for sheer hard fighting. "He would rather," says Mr. Bacon, "make war for two years than fight such a battle as the 57th regiment did at Albuera." After the death of Zumalacarreguy, Eraso conducted the siege with little vigour, frequently changing the point of attack and exhibiting symptoms of great vacillation; but the great error was, in not having commenced by reducing Portugalete and blockading the town on that side.

We have now come down to the appointment of Cordova and the arrival of the British Legion. The first affair in which that body was engaged, was in protecting Espartero's march at Arrigorriaga. The following is Mr. Bacon's account of the affair :—

" On the 11th September the divisions of Ezpeleta and Espartero, about 9,000 strong, marched from Bilbao by the Puente Nueva, and took the road to Orduna. To protect the left flank of their march, Count Mirasol, accompanied by General Evans, with six battalions of the legion, left the town with about 3,000 men belonging to the garrison. Scarcely had the leading files of Ezpeleta's column opened upon the spot where the road from Durango and Orduna unite, when a heavy fire was poured in on the column. Some confusion at first ensued ; but a battalion being sent forward in skirmishing order, dislodged the enemy, who retired fighting upon his main body. A brigade of the Christinos was now sent over the heights of Ollargan, towards Miravalles and Arrigorriaga, which had the effect of enabling the column to advance as far as the former place. Here a deep glen descends from Pagasarri, forming the south-east boundary of Ollargan ; in the bottom of this ravine flows a small rivulet, and over it, near its junction with the Nervion, is a bridge, across which passes the road to Vitoria and Orduna. This bridge was held by the Carlists, who, after some resistance, were dislodged, and the column advanced along the road, whilst the enemy still tenaciously held the upper part of the ravine just mentioned. It was now past twelve, and Ezpeleta, thinking that all farther resistance would be but trifling, sent word to Mirasol that he might return with his division. Accordingly the British Legion, with the two field-pieces, were marched into the town, where they had scarce arrived when orders came for their return ; and indeed it was time, for Ezpeleta, after passing Miravalles, finding the position of Arrigorriaga held by the Carlists in great force, and learning also that they had secured the passes at Orduna, determined to return to Bilbao ; and, in consequence, halted his troops, and gave orders for them to march back. The retrograde movement of the Christinos, of course, brought the Carlists headlong on, and the rear was speedily engaged. It is reported, that when the Christino general ordered a retreat, he never sent a fresh brigade to the rear, but allowed it to be composed of the same battalions which had formed the advance, and had already been roughly engaged, and sustained no trifling loss ; nor did his foresight extend so far as to suspend his retreat until he had secured the heights of Ollargan, around the flank and base of which was the line of march.

" The Carlists, who had never abandoned the upper part of the glen of Miravalles, now sent a large force in that direction, to seize the heights of Ollargan. It was done ; and while the rear of the Christino columns was furiously assailed, the eastern slope of Ollargan sparkled with fire, the effect of which was soon visible in the fearful confusion which ensued among the dense columns which now choked the road at its base. Now Ezpelata's bad generalship had to be atoned for by the blood of his soldiers. The error of withdrawing the English was apparent, for they might, at

various combustibles, again attacked and entered the church. As before, the Carlists fought with singular courage, but this time their efforts were vain; they were driven from the church, after a severe contest; piles of combustibles, heaped beneath the high altar, were kindled in an instant. Retreating to the cloisters, the besiegers tried their utmost to impede the progress of the queenites, but these gave them no respite; they spread the flames over the whole of the convent, and the most desperate of the Carlists, blinded by the smoke, or scorched by the eddying flames, fell down into the burning mass, which was at eight o'clock blazing like a volcano, and by its lurid light, the rival camps and the winding river were as distinct as day. Although the besiegers now beheld the long-disputed convent in flames, they had small grounds for triumph; taken by surprise, it was re-taken by main force, and its destruction by the besieged themselves denoted the vigour of their defence, and gave Eguia clearly to understand that thousands of his army must perish, ere he was master of the place so dearly coveted. The loss of the besieged during this hard-fought day was nearly three hundred, including prisoners; that of the assailants, in all probability, was equal, if not more considerable.".

On the whole we can safely recommend Mr. Bacon's book as containing the clearest and most interesting sketch of this second war of succession, that we have yet met with. By the bye he finds it necessary in many instances to correct the mistatements of Captain Henningsen in very important particulars. His style is clear and forcible, his arrangement of his subject excellent, and though he is no soldier, as he tells us, his descriptions of the game of war are uniformly correct and masterly. Spirited engravings place before our eyes the principal scenes of action, and contribute most essentially to the clear understanding of the movements of the belligerents.

ART. X.—*Report of the Commissioners appointed to inquire into the practicability and expediency of consolidating the different Departments connected with the Administration of the Army.* 1837.

THE machinery by which the military power of Great Britain is wielded, and the expenditure requisite for its maintenance regulated and controlled, present a subject of most interesting consideration. The zealous endeavours of the reformed government to carry the principle of retrenchment, as far as is practicable, into the various branches of the public service, to simplify their construction, and to advance them to as near a point of perfection as it is possible to attain, have caused every department to undergo a searching scrutiny, so that the minutest details of official management are laid before the public without reserve.

The orders of government as to the employment of the army are communicated to the military authorities by the Secretary of State for the Colonial or the Home department. These ministers in their respective departments communicate with the Commander-in-Chief and the Master-General of the Ordnance upon all points connected with the internal defence of the country and the protection of the foreign possessions of the crown, and it is by one of them that all the higher appointments, to which the sanction of government is required, are authorized. The Secretary of State for the Colonies has besides, as Secretary for the War Department, an authority in all matters relating generally to the army. He submits to the king the advice of ministers as to the whole amount of forces to be kept up, and he makes known to the Commander-in-Chief the establishment decided upon. He transmits the orders of government to officers on foreign stations, and originates warrants for regulating the terms on which soldiers are to be enlisted, and the pensions they are to receive.

In addition to this, all military commissions are technically issued under the authority of the Secretaries. The Commander-in-Chief, having obtained the king's sanction for promotions or appointments, forwards a memorandum of those which are approved to the War Office; the Secretary at War then transmits the lists to the office of the Home or Colonial Secretary, as the case may be; the commissions are prepared in either of those offices, submitted to the king for his signature, and completed by being countersigned by the Secretary on their return. If a supply of arms is wanted for the troops, application is made by the Commander-in-Chief to the Secretary at War, and by him to the Secretary of State, to signify his Majesty's pleasure to the Master-General and Board of Ordnance for the issue of the arms, and the letter written by the Secretary is the proper authority to this department for furnishing the required supply.

The duties of the Secretary at War chiefly consist in preparing and submitting to Parliament the army estimates, in checking the details of military expenditure, and in attending to the due execution of military law. He is also, under the authority of Parliament, charged with the protection of the civil subjects of the realms against oppression and misconduct on the part of the military, and for this purpose he communicates with the magistracy upon all complaints against officers and soldiers, over whom he exercises an independent authority in enforcing the provisions of the law. He prepares and brings in the mutiny bill, frames the articles of war, and issues routes for the movement of troops. Next in importance are the duties of the Master-General and the Board of Ordnance. The same authority which is exercised by the Commander-in-Chief over the army, the Master-General of the Ordnance exercises over the corps of Artillery and Engineers. He has also the general government and direction of the Military Academy at Woolwich. The Board of Ordnance is to the Artillery service what the Secretary at War is to the rest of the army. But besides their own particular branch of the service, the whole army, and even the navy, must be attended to by the Board. Arms, ammunition, and military stores of every description are supplied by them to both services. They furnish clothing to the police force of Ireland, and the same, with great coats, to the entire army. They are likewise charged with the issue of various supplies, as fuel, light, both in Great Britain and abroad, and with provisions and forage. The construction and repair of fortifications, military works, and barracks, is another branch of the business of the department, and they also furnish various descriptions of stores for the use of the convict establishment in the penal colonies. The Board is composed of three officers—the surveyor-general, the clerk of the ordnance, and the principal storekeeper. The authority of the Master-General is supreme in all cases, both civil and military, and he is considered responsible for the manner in which the department is generally conducted.

Then comes the Treasury Board, which manages the supply of forage and provisions to the troops on foreign stations, the Commissariat officers corresponding immediately with that Board. The Board of Audit act as the advisers in military business, besides auditing the accounts of a part of the expenditure incurred by the commissaries for the service of the army on foreign stations. The Commissioners of Chelsea Hospital are charged with the management of the hospital, and all matters relating to pensions. Their proceedings are governed by patent, and by instructions thereon received from the Secretary at War.

Such is a brief outline of the functions of the different departments of the administration of the army. The chief defect of this system is, that the distribution of the expenses among so many departments does not permit of the whole charge of the army being seen under one comprehensive view. In France every military department is subordinate to the War Minister, who prepares the whole army estimate, and is responsible for the whole of the military expenditure: whereas, under the system we have just noticed, the individual presiding over each department presents to parliament the estimate of the expenses of that department, and of the portion of the military expenditure under his control. By these means the charge of the military force is spread over several estimates, and being mixed up in some of them with naval or civil expenditure, it becomes difficult to make out from the parliamentary papers an aggregate of the charge purely applicable to the military service.

In addition to the fact of the system being calculated to throw difficulties in the way of parliamentary investigation, it has been objected to that it is contrary to the soundest principles of finance, and causes an inconvenient separation not merely of account, but of the management of different branches of the same service. The functionaries entrusted with the discharge of various duties, having reference to one common object, are mutually independent of each other, and only connected together by their common subordination to the supreme authority of government. The natural result of this absence of concentrated authority are conflicts of opinion, diversities of system and delays, involving a multiplication of correspondence, and of needless formalities in the transaction of business.

For instance, the Board of Ordnance supplies guns and gun carriages to the navy. For this purpose they have gun wharfs at all the principal ports. If a carriage happens not to suit the vessel, or even if there is a bolt wanting, the captain of the ship must notify his wants to the Admiralty, and the Admiralty to the Board of Ordnance, who transmit their directions thereupon to their officers at the gun wharf. This circuitous proceeding is very tedious and tiresome. Again, Deputy Commissary-general Filder has stated, in his evidence, that on foreign stations it sometimes happens that disagreements between the Commissariat and Ordnance departments take place, when there is a question of the former furnishing articles to the latter—it has been found productive of considerable difficulties. Commissaries-general with an army in the field are amenable to two authorities, for they receive their instructions both as to their establishments and money from the Lords Commissioners of the Treasury, and, at the same time, they are under the orders of the commander of the army to which they are attached. They account to the Auditors of Public Accounts at Somerset House for the expenditure of their cash, and to the Board of Ordnance for their stores. Another result of this complexity of departments is, that each one endeavours to exalt its own importance, and to have everything connected with it complete and perfect. Hence the desire to secure those objects, rather than the exigency of the public service, has had too much influence over a great part of the public expenditure. Another anomaly worthy of notice is, that, though the Secretary at War submits the estimates to Parliament, and sustains all the difficulties occasioned by the objections raised against their amount, he has neither had authority to take measures for reducing that amount, nor any responsibility for the efficiency of the force kept up, and thus he is not unfrequently placed in an embarrassing position with respect to the government and the Commander-in-Chief.

From a perception of these defects, and with a view to remedy them by consolidating the different departments, a commission passed the great seal, in December, 1835, appointing Lord Howick, Lord Palmerston, Lord John Russell, Lord Strafford, Sir John C. Hobhouse, and Mr. Spring Rice, commissioners to inquire into the public expenditure and the mode of conducting the public business under the Board of Ordnance, the Paymaster-General of the Forces, Commissariat and Treasury, and to report whether any improvement could be introduced in the mode of carrying on the public service in the said departments.

After much laborious investigation and searching inquiry into all the details of the various departments of the military administration, the first and primary recommendation by the commissioners is, that a complete alteration should take place in the form and appointment of the Secretary at War. He should, say the commissioners, be a member of the cabinet, and be invested with the greater part of the authority with reference to the army which at present belongs to the Secretaries of State. By him the advice of the cabinet, as to the amount of the military establishment, should be laid before the King, and he should be the person to communicate on all points with the Commander-in-Chief on behalf of the administration, and hold himself immediately responsible to parliament for all the measures of the government with reference to the army.

This transfer would include these formal duties, such as the preparing and countersigning of military commissions, and the issuing orders for the delivery of arms and stores to the troops. The Secretaries of State might still retain the duty of signifying the King's commands for the employment of the armed force for any specific object, but those commands should invariably pass through the medium of the Secretary of War to the Commander-in-Chief. In fine, they would make the Secretary at War a war minister, exercising a direct control over every department of the administration of the army, including those large branches which are now managed by the Board of Ordnance.

In the Ordnance department this transfer of authority is to be effected by the division of the civil from the military business, the latter remaining in the hands of the Master-general, while the former is vested in a board attached to the War-office and superintended by the Secretary at War. The opinion of the Duke of Wellington is strongly against this decision. While reading his Grace's evidence it is impossible not to be struck with the extent and precision of his knowledge, and the readiness and force with which it is delivered.

" Do you conceive that a distinction could practically be made between that part of the duties of the Master-general and Board of Ordnance which is of a civil and that which is of a military character ?—I conceive that you must have a military officer of high rank to perform the military duties of the Master-general of the Ordnance; I do not mean only the command of the artillery and engineers, but all that relates to the fortifications in different parts of the empire, both at home and abroad; all which relates to the building and location of the barracks. All those matters must be settled by a military officer. I do not see how the civil duties connected with those establishments could be carried on, excepting by the same person. He must see that the estimates are correct; he must be in communication with Government respecting the expense of all the buildings and works which he is carrying on; and he must be responsible for keeping those works within their estimates, and within the sum which the Government think proper to ask for, and Parliament think proper to grant for their execution. The Master-general of the Ordnance is one of the officers who, by his commission, is enabled to expend money on unexpected services, which have not been considered, and for which money has not been granted by Parliament. The reason is obvious. We will suppose that any accident destroys works at Gibraltar or elsewhere, a power must exist to apply a remedy immediately; and it is understood that the Master-general of the Ordnance has the power of expending money for such a purpose directly. Under recent directions, that is, directions of eight or ten years standing, from the Treasury, this power was restricted to the sum of £500. Without the permission of the Treasury he could not expend more than that amount; but before those directions from the Treasury it was understood that he had the power of diverting the supply in case of the occurrence of such a misfortune as I have stated. I do not think it would be wise to deprive his Majesty's Government of that power; and I don't know that you could rely upon the exercise of that power in a judicious manner by any except a military officer of high rank, whom it should be thought proper to intrust with the performance of the duties of the Master-general. I believe, and it is stated in the evidence, that a great part of the civil duty performed by the Ordnance is so closely connected with the military duties of the artillery and engineers that it would be absolutely impossible to separate them: for instance, the manufacture of stores that is carried on at Woolwich is necessarily connected with military duties, and I do not see how it would be possible to separate those duties from the duties of the Master-general. All that relates to the location of the magazines, whether abroad or at home, might be deemed civil duties; but they are so connected with the military duty of the Master-general, and with the military and naval affairs of the country, that I do not see how they can be separated from the office of the Master-general. I am aware of observations in the Report, and in the evidence, respecting the mode of performing those duties in one office and the military duties by the Commander-in-Chief; but it must not be lost sight of that, in the office of the Ordnance, there are duties to be performed connected with the Navy as well as with the Army, which extend all over the world; and I really should not know how it would be possible for any Board, not constituted upon military principles, and in which the persons carrying it on were not accustomed to the military duties of the country, to carry on those duties in a way satisfactory to themselves or beneficial to the public.

"Could the difficulties which your Grace has now stated be obviated by giving the mere military command of the corps of artillery and engineers to a Lieutenant-general, and by placing this officer under the orders of a Board, having one or two professional members, and which should be supreme in all matters, whether civil or military?—I should think not; the Master-general of the Ordnance stands towards the Board of Ordnance in a relation quite different from that in which the First Lord of the Admiralty ever stood towards the Board of Admiralty. The Master-general has all the power of the Ordnance in himself. The Board of Ordnance consists of a certain number of gentlemen at the head of several departments in the Ordnance. When I first went to the Ordnance it consisted of five departments. There was a Lieutenant-general of the Ordnance, who had more immediate charge of the artillery and engineers; there was the Surveyor-general, the Clerk of the Ordnance, the Storekeeper-general of the Ordnance, and the Clerk of Deliveries of the Ordnance. Each of these was at the head of a separate and distinct department in the Ordnance. According to the old system these officers were checks upon each other, and they assembled in Board to consult upon the general business of the department, or on any difficulty occurring in any of their several offices ; and they were required by Act of Parliament to sign certain papers. I believe as many as three members of the Board at that time—I see it is now reduced to two—were required to sign every order for money ; but the fact is, that the Master-general could give such orders as he pleased. The whole power of the Ordnance is, by his patent, vested in him, if he chooses to exercise it. The First Lord of the Admiralty was never more than one of a Board. I believe that even when his present Majesty was Lord High Admiral he stood, in respect of his commission, in the same relation towards the council of the Admiralty as the Master-general of the Ordnance did towards the Board of Ordnance. But an Act passed shortly after his Majesty was appointed Lord High Admiral, which required that every thing done should be signed by two members of the council ; so that he stood towards his council in a relation quite different from that in which the Master-general of the Ordnance stood towards the Board. Although this is the case, there is no doubt whatever that the Board of Ordnance do transact a great deal of the detail of the business. But when I was Master-general of the Ordnance—and I believe it is the same now—they sent to me regularly every day a minute of their proceedings ; that is to say, a minute of every letter and paper received, and of every answer which they gave ; and it very frequently happened that I differed in opinion from the Board upon those answers, and that I corrected the answers, and stated my opinion from them ; and if we continued to differ in opinion, I have gone frequently to the Board to discuss these questions, that they might be decided by common accord after discussion. I believe that the practice has been continued up to the present moment ; so that this system of the Ordnance has all the advantage of a board for publicity, and the discussion and a fair review of every transaction : at the same time it has the advantage of the decision of one person, in case such decision should be necessary ; and also that every transaction is reviewed in every stage of it. That was the practice when I was Master-general ; and I do not think that any alteration of the kind proposed could be made with any advantage to the service. I am certain that it is the best that can be adopted for the general transaction of the business. And I understand that when the Committee of Finance sat in the years 1828, 1829, and 1830, the mode of transacting business at the Ordnance was much approved of, and that that mode was recommended as an example for other Boards."

The opinion of the noble Duke as to the impolicy of transferring the Commissariat to the Board of Ordnance is equally decided. His Grace is asked,

" Is the opinion of your Grace previously expressed with respect to the disadvantage of uniting the Commissariat and the Ordnance at all varied by the circumstances now brought under your notice ; (*viz.* that the Board of Ordnance is now intrused with the duty of making contracts for the supply of the troops in England both with forage and meat,) and do you not think that it would be a more natural arrangement that the same authority should contract for the supply of these articles to the troops, whether at home or abroad?—My opinion is that what has been stated to me now makes but little difference in respect of my view of that question, because I speak of the supply by the Commissariat as referable principally to what is doing abroad. I will explain myself. The Board of Ordnance are perfectly equal to making a contract for the supply of bread, meat, or forage at home; and I believe that they have always been in the habit of contracting for the supply of forage for the horses of the artillery; they are perfectly equal to the making such contracts at home, and the contractors would deliver meat and forage under such contracts to the troops. There would be the same disputes and difficulties which I know take place in general. But I am speaking of the difficulties of performing these services abroad. I am not sure that there would not be the same difficulty in Ireland. But certainly abroad the difficulties will be very great. I have felt that if, for instance, a large store of provisions and forage was to be formed at Malta, not only for the supply of his Majesty's forces, but for the fleet, the gentleman of the Ordnance who is employed as storekeeper at Malta, however respectable, is not a person who ought to be employed to make a contract for the supply of such a magazine, or to keep in store that which should have been thus supplied in consequence of the contract; much less to perform the various duties of the Commissariat officer in drawing money and negotiating bills, and the other duties that must be performed by a person of that description. I do not think that the description of gentlemen who are the storekeepers of the Ordnance, who are generally not persons of much education, although very good and respectable men, are men that should be employed in the performance of that duty. It may be said we had better take a higher description of man, and place under him the whole of the two departments. That higher description of man would cost more money, and I do not know whether anything would be gained by the arrangement. After all, he must take charge of all these Ordnance stores; and must send to the Ordnance the detailed reports, journals, and returns. He must be under the control of the officers of that department at home. The persons to take care of and superintend the receipt and issue of these stores must be in general the same as those who perform these duties at present; and I do not think it would be found that there is any great convenience in the superintendence of the duties at such a place by one person. In time of war I am positively certain it could not be done. The Board of Ordnance are very capable of making contracts; they are very attentive in the transaction of that description of business, and the due performance of contracts is very closely watched, but I do not think that the system could be carried beyond Great Britain. It might be tried in Ireland.

" Your Grace has said that on service it is perfectly impracticable?—In time of war I should say absolutely out of the question.

" Does the impossibility your Grace anticipates arise from the nature of the duty or the amount of the duty that would be devolved?—From both: I conceive that the office of Commissary-general with the Army is not very well understood, and he really ought to be relieved from a great part of the responsibility in respect to the account at home, in order that he might attend better to the performance of the duties on the spot by

those under him, both in respect of the supply of the troops, and the
accounting of money and stores at home afterwards; that he ought to be
relieved from the responsibility for everything, excepting the payment of
money to an accountant, before an account should be rendered of sums
already advanced. I have never entertained any different opinion upon
the subject. I think that that gentleman should be under the Treasury,
and responsible to the Treasury alone. The authority over him should be
direct; he could not be put under any other Board without inconvenience.
The Commissary-general is overborne by a money responsibility, which
is, after all, absolutely nugatory. Sir Robert Kennedy was a public
accountant for fifty-five millions sterling: how can any one be an accountant for fifty-five millions sterling? The officer at the head of that
department, with his deputies and assistants, should be responsible only
for the payments he makes to those deputies and assistants, and for their
accounting for every shilling they receive, and for their supplying the
troops, and accounting for the stores which they receive. Each commissary may have a certain disbursement. The account is a very simple
one; it contains nothing but meat, drink, and forage for the troops, and
food for their horses, under no great number of heads, and the person
who receives the money, makes the purchases and issues, ought to account
every week or every month to the Commissary-general. The public
would have the account at an early period. The Commissary-general
might likewise insist upon that, which I am afraid is sadly in arrear under
existing regulations—that is, an account of the stores received and
expended. A commissary receives so much meat or bread, or forage, by
purchase or otherwise, and he should account for the disposal thereof.
That being done, the Commissary-general might be relieved from pecuniary responsibility; the gentleman who makes the expenditure would be
responsible for the amount. I have no doubt that all those accounts
could be very easily settled, and that those nugatory responsibilities might
be got rid of.

"How many years was Sir Robert Kennedy before he was relieved
from that responsibility to which your Grace has alluded?—I think 15 or
20 years.

"Your Grace is understood to say that the Commissariat should be in
time of peace, as well as during war, under the Treasury?—Yes."

Sir James Kempt and Sir Henry Hardinge coincide in the
opinion of the Duke of Wellington against the expediency of the
proposed separation.

Sir James Kempt allows that the plan is practicable, but denies
that it would promote efficiency or economy. His reasons are
stated in the following answers:—

"Is your objection to the plan of the separation of the civil and military duties now performed at the Ordnance Office?—That is the main
objection which I have to the proposed plan. I approve of the principle
of consolidating different apartments under one chief, when it can be
effected; and I conceive that the consolidations which have already taken
place in the Ordnance have been attended with the best effects. I am
not prepared to say that the best possible way of transacting public busi-

ness is by means of a board, but I think that the system pursued at the Ordnance is the best that a board could adopt. The business at the Admiralty is now transacted, I believe, nearly upon the same system, and the consolidations which have taken place in that department have been effected on the same principle, *viz.* placing the whole civil and military authority under one chief.

" Will you state generally your objections to the separation of the civil and military departments of the Ordnance?—The military and civil duties of the two ordnance corps (particularly of the Royal Engineers) are so mixed up and blended together, that they could not be separated in the manner proposed, in my opinion, without prejudice to the public service. They would be placed under two masters, and a divided authority would, I apprehend, give rise at times to great jarring and inconvenience to the Government, and prove disadvantageous to the public service.

" You say you think it would be objectionable to take the military part of the department and to place it under the Commander-in-Chief, and to leave the civil department under the Board, constituted as the Ordnance Board is at present? Do you think the same objection would apply, supposing that Board so left was merged in another general department of the State, such as the War Office or any other office, so contrived as the Admiralty Board is, to take in all departments connected with the Army?—The same objection would not, of course, apply to such an arrangement, if the supreme authority be vested in the professional branch, as is the case at the Admiralty.

" Will you have the goodness to state what you conceive is the advantage of the present arrangement with respect to the Ordnance?—In answering this question, I must beg permission to enter into some details. The great advantage of the present arrangement of the Ordnance department I conceive to be this,—that there is no division of authority, the Master-general being supreme in all matters, whether of a civil or of a military nature. All business of a purely military character is transacted by himself, as Commander-in-Chief of the two ordnance military corps; while all matters of a mixed nature, that is partly military and partly financial (of which a great portion of the Ordnance business consists), and also everything of a purely civil nature, goes direct to the Board in the first instance to be dealt with. But every subject of the least importance is submitted to the Master-general by special minutes of the Board; and he may either modify or confirm the same, or revise them, or give, in short, any orders upon the subject that he may deem proper, if they are not inconsistent with his Majesty's Instructions, or with special Acts of Parliament. Every transaction of the Board is recorded in minutes, and they are regularly sent to the Master-general for his perusal, so that he is, in fact, acquainted with everything that passes in the department. The public also, I conceive, derive great advantage from the Ordnance department being an office of account, and responsible to Parliament for the due and faithful application of all moneys voted for Ordnance services. The Master-general has a two-fold duty to perform; one to uphold the character and efficiency of the two military corps under his command, the other, to reduce the expense of the department, in conjunction with the Board, by every practicable means, in order that the estimates submitted to Parliament may be as low as the nature and extent of the services to be performed will possibly admit of. Thus, according to the present arrangement of the Ordnance department, great facility is afforded for carrying into effect measures of economy *without difficulty*, or *controversy* with any other department, and this I conceive to be a very great advantage. While I held the office of Master-general, the expense of the department was very considerably diminished; two Board officers were reduced, and the office of treasurer was rendered unnecessary by the measures adopted for making payments. All vacancies were filled up from the half-pay and unattached list, in order to reduce the dead weight; two or more barrack stations were placed, whenever practicable, under one barrack-master; the offices of storekeeper and barrack-master were in many instances united; several very extensive depôts were abolished. The offices of director-general and inspector-general of artillery were consolidated, and the entire salary of the director-general saved to the public. A variety of measures were also in progress for effecting gradual reductions in the Ordnance establishments, both at home and abroad, and for the general improvement of the department, following up the principles acted upon by my predecessors in the office. I have entered into these details to explain to the Commission the working of the Ordnance department according to the present system, and I am disposed to think that the plan proposed will not work so well or so advantageous for the public service.

" In short, it is your opinion, that if the professional duties on the one hand, and the responsibility for the amount of expense on the other, had been placed in separate and perfectly independent authorities, that would. necessarily have led to a considerable difficulty and clashing in the working of the system, and have prevented the accomplishment of those reductions?—I am decidedly of that opinion.

" You conceive that the probable effect of having a person intrusted with the military command of the Artillery and Engineers, not in any degree responsible for the amount of the expense, would have been, that there would have been a struggle between the two authorities; that sometimes perhaps improper reductions of expense would have taken place, and that at other times reductions that were practicable might not have taken place?—I think it very likely that jarring and difficulties might have occurred under a divided authority, the civil and military duties of the two Ordnance corps being (as I before stated) of a mixed character.

" Of whom is the Board composed besides the Master-general?—The Master-general may preside at the Board if he pleases, but his office is distinct from that of the Board. It is composed of three members, *viz.*, the Surveyor-general, the clerk of the Ordnance, and the principal storekeeper; the clerk is charged with the finance department and the presentation of the estimates in the House of Commons.

" Although the Board is executive, you consider the Master-general to be the sole responsible officer for the whole conduct of the affairs of the Ordnance?—The Board is only executive in conjunction with the Master-general; all letters and orders are issued in the names of ' The Master-general and Board;' and as the supreme power is placed in the Master-general's hands, I certainly considered myself responsible for the department. I was appointed to the office on the formation of Lord Grey's Government, and so completely did his lordship look to me as the responsible person, that he requested me to bring before him the name of any of the Board officers that might not give me satisfaction, with a view to his removal. I undertook to discharge the duties of Master-general without the assistance of a lieutenant-general, on condition of being totally unconnected with the political business of the country; and upon the understanding that the strictest economy was to be observed in the department in all its branches, compatible with the efficiency of the service.

" You are aware that one great branch of the Army is conducted quite upon a contrary system to that which you say is so much preferable, *viz.* that the military and civil duties are kept entirely distinct, with a responsible independent officer at the head of each ?—I am; and believing that difficulties and delays will always arise in conducting public business under two masters, I think that a divided authority ought always to be avoided whenever it is practicable to do so."

In the face of this array of military authority the commissioners do not hesitate to recommend, that the superior tending and controlling authority over the Board Officers should be vested in the Secretary at War instead of in the Master-general and the Board, leaving the whole internal arrangement of the subordinate branches of the office unaltered, to be incorporated with the business of the War Office. The advantages to be derived from this change may be briefly stated to be these : The civil duties of the Ordnance will thus be placed under the superintendence of an authority which will view them in connexion with the wants and interests of the general service. For instance, if a new barrack is to be built, to replace or enlarge the accommodation of an old one, the matter will by the new arrangement be submitted to the authority responsible for the expense of the new building, and the maintenance of a proper force at the place where it is proposed to erect it, a nice comparison of these two points being necessary for deciding the question; under the present system, one department is answerable for the expense of the new building, while another watches over the interests of the troops who are inconvenienced by the want of it. On the one side there is a reluctance to undertake improvements, and on the other an eagerness to press for their adoption. Hence arise faults of every description, and a controversial correspondence is carried on between the two departments before any decision is arrived at.

Another advantage of the proposed alteration would be, that under the transfer a single set of superintendents or clerks would discharge the functions which are now performed by two sets. The similarity of duties of the Ordnance and War Office, both consisting of examinations of pay-lists, and the decision upon all claims upon allowances or pensions given to officers of artillery or their widows, would render it very easy to effect this superintendence, without any material addition to the labours of the gentlemen of the War department. In addition to this, much useless formalities and circuitous correspondence would be got rid of, and a considerable reduction might gradually be accomplished. There are other beneficial results, which are thus clearly and forcibly stated :—

" 1st. The accounts of military expenditure would be improved by getting rid of the separate estimate for the Commissariat, and including this branch of the military expenditure in the general estimate of the Army.

" 2nd. In many of the Colonies, the double sets of stores now kept up by the Ordnance and by the Commissariat might be consolidated with a consequent reduction of establishment; for though it has been stated that this could not be accomplished, because the Ordnance Storekeepers are not in general competent to undertake the duties of the Commissariat, we conceive that, even if this were admitted, all difficulty might be obviated by employing Commissariat officers, where those of the Ordnance were not equal to the duty, and that it cannot possibly be necessary to have a double establishment of officers in the same place, each charged with the custody and issue of stores of similar kinds.

" 3rd. The whole charge of making contracts for the Army might be placed in the same hands, instead of having the same supplies furnished to the same regiments at one time by the Ordnance, and at another by the Treasury, according to the accident of those regiments being stationed in Great Britain or in the Colonies.

" 4th. But above all, by this change the Treasury would be relieved from business which we consider it wrong in principle that it should undertake, and this large branch of the military service would be placed under the superintendence of the department which ought to be responsible to Parliament on all subjects connected with the Army. This last consideration is of so much importance that we cannot pass it by without some additional observations. The Treasury being charged with the general superintendence of the finances of the country, and with the duty of controlling the expenditure of each separate department, it seems to us that, when that Board also takes upon itself the direct management of a service involving large expenditure, it leaves its proper sphere. Whatever be the department which immediately applies the public money in carrying on any branch of the service, the proceedings of that department ought to be subjected to the superintendence of some distinct and superior authority; but this can no longer be the case when the Treasury, to which this authority properly belongs, and over which there is in the Executive Government no higher power, assumes also those administrative functions which ought to be subordinate. This is an objection of principle to the existing arrangement, which in our opinion should be decisive; but beyond this, we have to observe that the Board of Treasury seems peculiarly unfitted by its constitution for the task now committed to it, of managing the supply of the Army. With the numerous avocations of the department, it is impossible that its officers can give their attention to a business of so much detail as that of watching over the supply of all that is necessary for the troops in the various climates, and in the different kinds of service in which the Army is engaged. The Board of Treasury has also the further disadvantage in dealing with this subject, that it has not those means of judging of the manner in which the service is carried on, which are afforded by a daily cognizance of all the difficulties and complaints which arise; the reports of the medical officers, which ought to be so carefully attended to with reference to the mode of provisioning the troops, are not submitted to the Treasury, and if they were so, such is the mass of business which is brought before that department, that they could not be accurately examined. It is true that the Lords of the Treasury can call for all the information which they may from time to time require from other departments; they can, for instance, consult the Secretary at War and the Commander-in-Chief, as to whether a proposed ration is suitable to the climate and circumstances of the Colony where it is intended to be issued; and in like manner, upon other points, they can apply for assistance or advice to any quarter in which it may be attainable; but we need hardly observe that there is a vast difference between the dependence to be placed upon a judgment founded upon a narrow and partial information which can thus be obtained with a view to a decision on a particular point, and that which is formed by those who are habitually conversant with the subject upon which a question has arisen."

It certainly does appear most incongruous and absurd to find the auditors of public accounts reporting their opinion to the Treasury, whether a proposed change in the rations of soldiers in a particular colony is advisable or not. The only concern of the auditors should be to ascertain that the public money is properly accounted for; they should have nothing whatsoever to do with its application. The functions at present discharged by the Commissariat Officers are much too large, and too expensive to be intrusted to any one set of officers. It has been already stated by the Duke of Wellington, that fifty-five millions passed through the hands of the Commissary-general during the Peninsular war; but in order to give our readers a clear idea of the variety and importance of the duties of the Commissariat department, and of the manifold opportunities which unprincipled men in that department may have for realizing a large private fortune at the expense of the public, we shall quote a portion of the evidence of Mr. Archer, the head of the department, detailing those particulars.

" Will you furnish the Commissioners with a general description of the constitution of that department, and the manner in which its business is transacted ?—The Commissariat officers act abroad under directions from the Treasury Board, and it is their duty to provide provisions, forage, fuel, and light, for the troops employed on the respective stations. In many cases the Commissariat are enabled to provide those articles at a much cheaper rate than they could be supplied from England; in other cases it is necessary for the benefit of the public, and for the security of the troops, so as to prevent disappointment in the receipt of provisions, that articles should be supplied from this country; in all cases of contracts made abroad the Commissariat report the particulars to the Treasury, sending copies of their contracts, and the particular details of their proceedings in forming them, in order that the Treasury Board may be satisfied that they have taken proper proceedings in obtaining such supplies. The funds necessary for the payment of these supplies are provided either by remittances of specie to the stations, by the direction of the Lords of the Treasury, or by the negotiation of bills upon the Treasury Board by

the commissary in charge. The funds thus provided are appropriated
not merely to the payment of such contracts, or to the payment of any
other articles they may be called upon to furnish for the troops, but are
also applied for the use of the other public departments employed on
those stations; for instance, for the pecuniary wants of the Ordnance,
the Navy, and other departments. The Commissariat officer is also, as it
may be termed, the banker of those several departments, inasmuch as he
not only supplies them with money, but receives, on account of their respective departments at home, such moneys as they may have occasion to
remit to this country. There are also various other sources from which
the military chest is occasionally furnished with money. The Commissariat officers also make contracts for providing all building materials
which are required by the Ordnance department, and stores of various
descriptions, which are to be procured on the spot. The Commissariat
officers in charge are required to keep up a constant communication with
the Treasury Board upon all points of service in which they are engaged,
and the Treasury Board exercises a vigilant superintendence over their
proceedings. If the Treasury have occasion to make any observations,
or to object to any of the proceedings which are so reported, they call for
further information until they are satisfied, or give such instructions
or further directions as the circumstances of the case may appear to
require.

"In what manner is the communication managed between the Commissariat officers abroad and the Treasury; do they communicate directly
with one of the secretaries of the Treasury, or other persons?—With the
Treasury Board, through their secretaries.

"All letters from the Commissariat officers are addressed to the secretary of the Treasury?—Yes.

"What is the course of business upon those letters; are they referred
to yourself, as head of the Commissariat branch?—The preparatory step
on receiving letters is, that they are all docketed, registered, and then
delivered to me; and it is my duty to bring them under the consideration
of the secretaries for the directions of the Board."

We are at a loss to see what connexion there necessarily exists
between provisioning the army and drawing bills on the Treasury.
Why should the officer, who goes into the market to select and buy
commodities, be the banker of the nation abroad? Either of these
two duties taken separately is quite sufficient in itself to furnish
occupation to the most active and intelligent officers? Why not
confine the financial operations to one set of officers appointed
immediately under the Treasury, and leave everything appertaining
to the purchase and transfer of provisions to the other?

By this arrangement they would exercise a most salutary check
upon each other. The Treasury Officer, with his establishment of
clerks and deputies, should have the custody of the military chest,
should negotiate bills on the Government at home, and keep the
voluminous accounts which they require; the Commissary to devote himself entirely to securing provisions for the troops, which he
should pay for by orders on the military chest.

Thus every temptation to abuse would be avoided, and we should hear no more of those colossal fortunes which it is well known have been raised by functionaries in the Commissariat Department.

With regard to the transfer to the Admiralty of the charge of all that relates to naval artillery which is now in the hands of the Master-general and Board of Ordnance, the arguments on both sides of the question are very nicely balanced, so much so, indeed, that the Commissioners offer no suggestion on the subject. There can be no doubt, we think, that it would be a great improvement to place the gun wharfs at the principal naval stations, and all that relates to the construction of gun carriages, under the control of the Admiralty and annexed to the dockyards.

We have now taken a cursory view of the operation of the administrative functions of the civil departments of the army, noticing the defects that have been detected in the practical details of each, and the measures suggested for removing them. We have purposely abstained from embarrassing the statement with financial details, which might prove heavy and uninteresting. Suffice it to say, that the expense of each establishment has undergone the most careful examination, and the salaries of all officers from the highest to the lowest have been fixed on as economical a scale as is consistent with the efficiency of the public service.

ART. XI.—*Random Recollections of the Lords and Commons.* By the Author of " The Great Metropolis," " The Bench and the Bar," &c. Second Series. 2 Vols. London : Colburn. 1838.

BOOK-MAKING is like mining. When an author to his infinite surprise and delight has hit upon a productive vein of intellectual ore, he never fails to keep digging at it until it is exhausted : what took once, will not take again. Publishers vie with each other in alluring to the embraces the man whose work has proved a hit ; and publisher and author mutually encourage each other in labouring at the vein until the accumulation of rubbish practically admonishes them that it is time to break fresh ground. Thus the author of the volumes before us, having found that the first series of what may be termed the anatomy of legislators turned out an exceedingly profitable work, has lost no time in putting forth another as soon as ever he had collected a sufficient number of new subjects to furnish materials for lecture.

The present work forms a very good companion to Hansard's Parliamentary Debates, or to the closely-printed columns of legislatorial eloquence in the morning papers. We have the looks, gestures, intonations, and all the attributes of the external man to assist our fancy in bodying forth the individual from whose lips the words we read are supposed to issue. In addition to this, the measure of his intellect is so nicely taken, and so accurately and

confidently stated, that we know the precise degree of importance
to be attached to every word he utters. To country folks and inhabitants of the colonies, who seldom see a legislator, except at an
election, it must prove highly gratifying to have the whole legislative corps passed in review before their eyes, or rather to be
themselves transported in imagination into the interior of St.
Stephen's, and made partakers of the pleasure or ennui which its
proceedings may inspire. A very great portion of these volumes is
made up of the matter which has already appeared in the newspapers,
with a seasoning of the gossip of the gallery of the House of Commons. The descriptions of what are emphatically called the Scenes,
are the best parts of it. They are pointed with all those accompaniments which the morning papers must pass over, and are
vigorously and dramatically sketched.

The Victoria parliament has been rich in " Scenes." Its vulgarities have been stronger and more decided than those so loudly
inveighed against by the Quarterly Review, (alias John Wilson
Croker,) as characteristic of that which sat after the passing of the
Reform Bill. Our transatlantic brethren may hail this description
of the proceedings of " the first gentlemen in Europe," as a set
off against Mrs. Trollope. View them, for instance, in the outset, and you will be at no loss to comprehend the sequel.

The opening of parliament was marked by two " events" recorded by the author. The one was the storming of the gallery
by a host of " the fairest of the fair," which, as the ex feminine
was in the ascendant, was not at all to be wondered at. Indeed,
our author is delighted with the feat, and although this " untoward
event" caused the forcible exclusion of the whole corps of reporters but three, who were fortunate enough to secure their places
before the charge, he is quite reconciled to it as long as he is permitted to gaze on the " forest of plumes, the sparkling jewels, and
the lustrous eyes of the lovely intruders." Nay, he chivalrously
breaks a lance in their homage and declares that it was most extraordinary how silent and well behaved they were—traits, which he was
not prepared to expect. The second was the rushing of her Majesty's Commons into her august presence ; the latter event is
thus described :—

" The summons was forthwith followed by a scene which strongly
contrasted with that to which I have been alluding. There is a proverb,
which is current in certain districts of the country, that some people are to
be heard when they are not to be seen. The adage received a remarkable
illustration in the case of the representatives of the people, on this occasion.
No sooner had the door been opened, in obedience of the mandate of the
Queen, which leads into the passage through which they had to pass on
their way to the bar of the House of Lords, than you heard a patting of
feet, as if it had been of the hoofs of some two or three score of quadrupeds.
This, however, was only one of the classes of sounds which broke on the

ears of all in the House of Lords, and even of those who were standing in the passages leading to it. There were loud exclamations of 'Ah! ah!' and a stentorian utterance of other sounds, which denoted that the parties from whom they proceeded had been suddenly subjected to some painful visitation. All eyes—not even excepting the eyes of her Majesty—were instantly turned towards the door of the passage whence the sounds proceeded. Out rushed, towards the bar of the House of Lords, a torrent of members of the Lower House, just as if the place which they had quitted had been on fire, and they had been escaping for their lives. The cause of the strange, if not alarming sounds which had been heard a moment or two before, was now sufficiently intelligible to all. They arose from what Mr. O'Connell would called the mighty struggle among the members, as to who should reach the House of Lords first, and by that means get the nearest to the bar, and thereby obtain the best place for seeing and hearing. In this mortal competition for a good place, the honourable gentlemen exhibited as little regard for each other's persons, as if they had been the principal performers in some exhibition of physical energy in Donnybrook Fair. They squeezed each other, jammed each other, trod on each other's gouty toes, and 'punished' each other, as the professors of the pugilistic art phrase it, in every variety of form, without the slightest compunctious visiting. Hence the exclamations—in some cases absolute roars—to which I have alluded. The most serious sufferer, so far as I have been able to learn, was one of the honourable members for Sheffield, who had his shoulder dislocated in the violent competition to be first at the bar. Even after the M.P.'s were fairly in the presence of their sovereign, there was a great deal of jostling and jamming of each other, which extorted sundry exclamations indicative of pain, though such exclamations were less loud than those before alluded to. The Irish members played the most prominent part in this unseemly exhibition; and next to them, the English ultra Radicals. The Tories cut but a sorry figure in the jostling match. The Liberals were, as the common saying is, 'too many for them.' I thought with myself at the time, what must the foreign ambassadors and their ladies who were present think of English manners, should they unhappily form their notions on the subject from the conduct on this occasion of the legislators in the Lower House? It was a rather awkward exhibition for a body of men arrogating to themselves the character of being 'the first assembly of gentlemen in Europe.' "

This was as Lord Liverpool would say, "too bad;" but as for the astonishment of foreigners, we hold it very lightly; for we recollect having read in the Memoirs of Madame Campan, that the moment Louis XV. had breathed his last, a sound like a sudden discharge of a piece of ordnance rolled along the galleries. The fair chronicler started up in alarm, and on inquiry she found it was caused by the sudden and simultaneous rush of the courtiers who had been kneeling in affected grief around the dying into the presence of the living monarch, who was waiting in an adjoining chamber. In this race to be the first to worship the rising sun, the courtiers were as regardless of etiquette as if they had been chimney sweepers: so that foreigners may look at home. Besides, the Commons are but

the representatives of the mob, and as mobility they will bear themselves.   We have no doubt it will be highly gratifying to the Commons, besides being flagellated in detail, to find themselves thus
pounded *en masse.*

" In my former work on the House of Lords, I had occasion to speak of
the singular decorum, as compared with the other House, with which their
Lordships conduct all their proceedings.   I have often wished that those
who are prejudiced against hereditary legislators, were present two or
three evenings to witness their conduct during the debates.   They might
after all—whether justly or not is not for me to say, as I do not wish to
appear in these pages in the character of a politician,—they might after
all cling to the conviction that hereditary legislators are not the wisest
legislators; but of this I am certain, that they would be forward to admit
that, in point of manners, there is no comparison between them and the
assemblage in the other House.   It must have been a member of the
House of Commons who characterised that body as an ' assembly of the
first gentlemen in Europe.'   So far from being the first in Europe in regard to gentlemanly conduct, there is an assembly within a few yards of
them, who in this respect throw them completely into the shade.   The
most unpopular man among them is always treated with the greatest
respect; at least in outward appearance.   No peer was ever known to
give a forced cough, or to offer any sort of interruption, with the view of
putting down an unpopular speaker, or marking his disapprobation of an
obnoxious sentiment.   Even the late Lord King, when assailing with the
utmost freedom of remark the bench of Bishops,—who are everything
short of being absolutely sacred in the eyes of noble lords—even he was
always heard with the utmost courtesy.   On the late occasion of Mr.
Roebuck's addressing their Lordships in favour of the claims of the
Canadians, a striking instance of the respectful way in which the Peers
conduct themselves was afforded.   Though Mr. Roebuck's previous exhibition of a similar kind in the Commons, was so much marked by the
bitterness of his manner and the violence of his matter, as to be calculated
to create a prejudice against him, and though many parts of the speech
he made to them must have grated in their ears, yet they not only
heard him throughout his three hours' address with the most respectful
attention, but they even quitted their usual seats, and crowded together
close to the bar, to be as near as possible to him.   How different was it in
the comparatively democratic Commons!   Not a ' people's representatives,' so far as I saw, moved an inch towards the bar for the purpose of
being nearer the Canadian advocate."

But if the Lords are very polite, it is no less true they are very
dull.   Upon occasions they look as grave as if they were assisting
at the obsequies of a friend, and speak with as little animation and
gesture as if they were automatons.   Indeed, so impressed are their
Lordships with the sense of this characteristic of their proceedings,
that they hailed with the most decided demonstrations of satisfaction
the return of Lord Brougham to his parliamentary duties, after an
absence of two sessions.   His lively sallies, his frequent raillery, and

his stirring eloquence, served to leaven the aggregate mass of dulness of their Lordships, and afford them and the public much amusement. By all accounts, Henry's "himself again." He is all that he ever was ; nay, this session he has surpassed himself. His Canadian speech was one of the most brilliant ever delivered in Parliament. To ministers it was a thunderbolt.

" The affair," proceeds the author, " altogether strongly reminded me of a cross-tempered remorseless pedagogue, unsparingly applying the birch—regardless alike of their piteous looks and whining cries—to the persons of some half-dozen of his urchins, who had had the misfortune either to merit punishment, or to incur his displeasure when in one of his more savage moods. What added to the effect of Lord Brougham's castigation of Ministers in this case was, that every one present saw clearly that Ministers themselves felt it in all its rigorous severity. If anything could have given additional effect to the heaviness of every successive blow, it would have been the appearance and manner of his lordship. It did not seem to require an effort. His heart was evidently in the work : there was no indications of a reluctant application of the rod; as in the case of a father who does violence to his parental feelings when he chastises his child, and is only induced to do so from a conviction of its necessity, with a view to the correction of errors. With Lord Brougham the thing was manifestly a labour of love. You saw in the leer of his eye, in the general expression of his features, in the exulting tones of his voice, that to behold Ministers writhing around him, was to him a positive luxury, and one of the highest order."

Then his displays on the Slavery question were absolutely astounding. They were efforts almost superhuman, and seemed like inspiration. Notwithstanding his attacks upon Ministers, he still continues to occupy his old seat a few yards to the right of Lord Melbourne on the Ministerial benches, and he is most regular in his attendance in it. His close proximity to his " noble friend," on the ever-memorable night of the celebrated conflict between them as to which was the greatest proficient in glossing, fawning, bending the knee, and playing the spaniel at Court, was not the least amusing part of the scene. As for Lord Melbourne, never was there a Prime Minister who bore the cares of his high office with greater ease and unconcern. Nor do years press more heavily on his Lordship than the burden of office. The " scene" between him and Lord Lyndhurst on the occasion of the attack of the latter on the occurrences in the Milbank Penitentiary is very dramatically told ; but as it has already been very much canvassed, we shall pass it over for one in which bishops are the belligerent parties—their large wigs and lawn sleeves serving to increase the ludicrous effect of a scolding match.

" A personal squabble between any two of the bench of bishops, worthy of the name of ' a scene,' is a circumstance which very rarely occurs in the house. It is a pity, for the sake of the Church as well as for themselves, that it ever should occur at all. The most animated quarrel I have ever witnessed between two right reverend prelates, took place on the 22nd of February, on the occasion of the Archbishop of Canterbury pronouncing a high eulogium on the late Bishop of Sodor and Man. His Grace having resumed his seat, the Bishop of Exeter rose and said, with much emphasis, that he lamented the constitution of the ecclesiastical commission, whose acts he must deplore, as fatal to the security and dignity of the Church.

" The Bishop of London, who is one of the ecclesiastical commissioners, said, with great warmth and much tartness of manner, that the commis-. sioners had no right to complain of the reverend prelate's remarks on the constitution of the ecclesiastical commission; but they certainly had to complain of the *gross misrepresentations* which had been made on the subject.

The Bishop of Exeter again started up, and with considerable vehemence of manner, as well as in a tone of indignant defiance of the Bishop of London, said—' I repel not the insinuations, but the charge which has been made by the right reverend prelate; for I have been guilty of no misrepresentation. In my opinion the Church never received such a severe blow as this ecclesiastical commission would prove.'

" The Bishop of London made some other observation which was not distinctly heard, when the Bishop of Exeter again started to his feet, and met it by some other remark, which, from the warmth and hastiness of his manner, I could not catch. The scene was of short duration, but it was a very extraordinary one for two spiritual lords to enact. No one would have before believed that either of the two prelates could have lost his temper to such an extent. I thought at the time, that had the late Lord King, whose dislike to bishops was as proverbial as it was inveterate, been alive and present, the scene would have been to him a luxury of the first magnitude.' "

Next to the " Scenes," come a batch or two of Conservative peers, served up and dressed according to the most approved principles. There is not much novel information to be gleaned from the compound; few of them are worth a moment's notice, as legislators : as peers and men of fortune *c'est différent.* The Duke of Rutland is a decided and consistent Conservative : he never makes a political speech, but he has always something to say upon particular subjects. His fort is agriculture and the landed interest, and when we have said this we have said enough. We believe the poet Crabbe was his tutor, and we have not forgotten the feelings with which we read of the disrespectful manner in which he was treated at the table of the lords of Belvoir Castle. The Marquis of Bute sometimes presents a petition to their Lordships, tells them the accurate number of signatures, assures them that the parties are respectable, and leaves it to weigh with their Lordships. This plan saves time and breath, argument and eloquence, and if his stock of these commodities is to be estimated by his sayings, the noble Marquis must have a very large one upon his hands.

The Marquis of Camden, as Teller of the Exchequer, receives a splendid salary for doing nothing, which he very conscientiously returns into the Treasury. The amount of money so returned is said to be £300,000, and the "liberality" of a Tory peer is highly extolled for the sacrifice. We have some reason to think the outcry against sinecures, and the shame of appropriating the national money under a mere pretext, has had a good deal to do with the "liberality" of the noble Marquis; at least, we never recollect a trait of this species of liberality of refunding in the good old Tory times, though we have had some few too many of their dexterity in funding. However, we are not disposed to cavil, and we will gladly yield the noble Marquis the right of standing on the most honourable motives. Like the Duke of Rutland, the Marquis is a man of one topic, viz., the defence of the University of Oxford, of which he is Chancellor, against the attacks of Lord Radnor. He speaks as he looks—plain and unpretending. He recreates on horseback, and in the neighbourhood of the Strand, instead of the parks. He is sixty-eight.

The Marquis of Westmeath is remarkable for elevating his hand perpendicularly above his head and flourishing it in the air when he speaks, and for having made one pretty fair speech in his life, viz. one in July last on the affairs of Ireland. On these he is pretty well informed, but his ultra-toryism was the effect of his information. As for his appearance being striking, we beg leave to differ with the Recollector.

The Earl of Shaftesbury has a handsome salary for his services as chairman of Committees, but he never utters a sentence upon any question, although there is not a more lively bustling personage in the House. He has an intimate acquaintance with the forms of the house, and goes through the formalities with great expedition. His chief peculiarity is the rapid motion of his spectacles from his eyes to the crown of his head, and then down again, according as he directs his looks from the bill to the peers, or from the peers to the bill, he would not be guilty of the disrespect of staring at their lordships through his glasses. In appearance and dress, he is like a churchman who has got a good living. We should not omit to state that his Lordship rejoices in an eccentric sort of daughter named Lady Caroline Neeld, whose persecutions of her husband afforded such rare amusement in fashionable circles some time since.

Earl Stanhope, the nephew of Pitt, is a man of great kindness of disposition, and devotes himself entirely to subjects connected with the amelioration of the poor. In his character of the poor man's friend, he is a jealous opponent of the New Poor Law Bill. There is rather an amusing anecdote told of his Lordship's gold snuff box being appropriated by some poor man, while its owner was denouncing the Poor Law Act. He had laid the box on the table while addressing the meeting, and its golden gleams having fascinated the eyes of the "tax collectors," they greeted every word that fell from the noble speaker with thunders of applause. Every hand within reach of the table was actively engaged in thumping it most lustily. Even the gold box began to exhibit symptoms of exultation at the success of its noble owner. In the excess of its joy, it responded to the repeated application of fists to the table by repeated leaps, until at last it danced over and fell on the floor. From thence it was transferred into the pocket of some dexterous picker-up of unconsidered trifles, and never again gladdened the eyes of the noble Earl.

Lord Stanhope is a mediocre speaker. He cannot pronounce the letter *r*, without a curious burring sound. His voice, too, is a guttural squeak; and though his matter is tolerable, his manner is very inferior. He is a great patron of the sciences, in which he is said to be extensively versed. He is good looking, and dresses like a Quaker.

The Earl of Falmouth is a nobleman of considerable influence among his party. He is not so remarkable for talent, as for being a smooth and graceful speaker. His delivery prepossesses his hearers at once in his favour. He is a fine-looking man into the bargain, and gifted with great moral courage.

The Earl of Devon exhibits in his person the only instance on record of a servant of the House of Lords succeeding to a peerage, and sitting as an equal amongst the men he was formerly obliged to look up to as his superiors.

Having been clerk of the House for several years, he is a decisive authority on all matters of form and at the details of business. This is the extent of his ability.

Lord Glengall is chiefly noted for a remarkably fine head of black hair, curled as carefully as that of Augustus Tomlinson, and his having been the author of the popular farce of the Irish Tutor. Since he ratted from the Whigs, he seldom attends the House.

Lord Redesdale is a man of sense, a good, though an unpretending speaker. According to the Earl of Devon, he will be unequalled as a business man in the House.

Lord Strangford is another nobleman of fair average talents. As for Lord Alvanley, he is chiefly known as a wit, a propensity to jesting, having nearly cut short his career. Turn we now to the Commons House of Parliament; ludicrous scenes and vulgarities are the leading topics; here and there we meet with some amusing gossip. The author is a bad story-teller.

Whenever he attempts conversation, he is sure to break down. The reason is obvious—it is out of his sphere—footmen and ladies' maids may give a good second-hand version of the familiar colloquy of lords and ladies; and we should be inclined to place more reliance on the verisimilitude of their dialogue than on that of those whose colloquial phraseology is redolent of the tavern. Take, for instance, the state of the " Hat." After a very well deserved censure on the shabby and slovenly appearance of several members, particularly of the Irish liberals *en masse*, the author proceeds thus :—

"In the course of last session, the dress of some of the Irish Liberal members led to one of the most amusing incidents which have occurred for some time in connexion with parliamentary matters. I shall narrate it as briefly as I can. A letter dated from the Irish office, and having the name of Lord Morpeth appended to it, was received by an Irish member, who has long been noted for having his head encircled by a ' shocking bad hat.' The letter set out by acknowledging, with great gratitude, both on the part of Lord Morpeth himself and his colleagues in office, the distinguished honour and undoubted advantage which Lord Melbourne's administration had derived from the cordial and uniform support which it had received from the Irish members. At the same time it was impossible to shut their eyes, or rather their ears, to the fact, that in regard to dress, the Irish members as a body were not always all that could be wished ; a circumstance of which the Conservatives, who were very particular and very tasteful in the article of apparel, took special care to turn to the worst possible account against the Liberal party. The letter proceeded to observe, that while it was to his Majesty's ministers, and to the writer individually as an humble member of the Cabinet, a most gratifying fact that the Liberal party were fully equal to the Conservatives in point of moral character, intellectual acquirements, and parliamentary ability, it was not to be denied that it was extremely desirable that they should, if possible, present at the same time as respectable a personal appearance. Under these circumstances, it was hoped that the gentleman to whom the letter was addressed would not take it amiss if it was hinted by the Irish Secretary (Lord Morpeth) that he should pay a little more attention to his personal appearance, and, above all, to discard the ' shocking bad hat' which he had worn for some time, and grace his head by one of a more becoming character."

His first impulse was to examine the condemned head-gear, and then to wreak his vengeance on it ; however, recollecting it would be of use to enable him to proceed to the hatters, he put it on his head and set forward to replace it by a new one of unexceptionable shape.

"Scarcely had the new hat been adjusted on his head, and the honourable gentleman had looked in the glass and been satisfied that he looked sufficiently smart, than he started for the Irish office.

" ' Is Lord Morpeth within ?' was his inquiry of one of the servants, as he presented himself at the door.

" ' He is, Sir.'

" ' And disengaged ?'

" ' I believe he is, Sir ; but I'll see presently.'

" The servant rushed into Lord Morpeth's presence, and returned, informing Mr. —— that his lordship was quite at leisure.

" ' Ah ! how do you do ?' the honourable gentleman exclaimed, as he entered, at the same time presenting his hand to the Irish Secretary.

" ' How are you ?' responded his lordship, receiving with much cordiality the extended hand of his parliamentary supporter. 'Pray take a seat, Mr. ——.'

" A few common-place observations were exchanged between the parties, during which the honourable member kept alternately twirling about his hat, and smoothing down the pile with the cuff of his coat. His lordship still taking no notice of the new chapeau, Mr. —— lost all patience, and broke out into a regular Irish question—' Pray, Lord Morpeth, what do you think of my hat?'

" His lordship was a good deal confounded by the nature of the question, but, wishing to be polite, replied, casting a momentary glance at the article, that he thought it was a very good hat.

" ' Why, I have just paid eight-and-twenty shillings for it,' observed the Irish member.

" ' Oh, indeed—that was the price, was it?' remarked his lordship carelessly.

" ' And I have bought it from one of the most fashionable hat-makers at the West-end,' added the honourable gentleman.

" The noble lord looked still more surprised at his Liberal supporter, but managed to murmur out an ' Oh, you did, did you?' without anything marked in his tone.

" ' What do you think of its shape?' inquired Mr. ——, almost thrusting the hat into his lordship's face, that he might the more closely inspect it.

" ' Oh, I think it's very good,' was the answer, delivered in a way which showed that the Irish Secretary's astonishment was still on the increase.

" ' How do you like the brim?' inquired the honourable member for ——, again holding up the hat to the gaze of his lordship.

" ' Oh, I think the hat is unexceptionable in every respect,' answered the latter, looking the honourable gentleman in the face with an expression of infinite amazement, instead of again inspecting the hat.

" ' I'm *so* glad you like it,' observed Mr. —— with much emphasis, and in a tone of marked gratification.

" Lord Morpeth's silence was understood by the honourable gentleman to signify his concurrence in the proposition.

" And you don't think the brim too broad?' said the Irish member, after a momentary pause.

" Lord Morpeth by this time had become so utterly confounded, that he uttered not a word in reply to the latter observation.

" ' I was duly honoured with your note, and you see how prompt I have been in complying with your request.'

" ' Really,' answered the noble lord, raising his eyes from a document which was lying before him, and gazing on the Irish M. P. with an expression of countenance equally indicative of surprise and indignation— ' really Mr. ——, I don't understand all this. Pray, may I beg an explanation. I have sent you no note, nor made any request.'

" ' Well, come now, but I *do* hold that to be decidedly good,' remarked the honourable gentleman, affecting a little jocularity.

" ' Really Mr. ——,' said the noble lord, in yet more decided tones, ' this *does* require an explanation. Do you mean to ——'

" His lordship was prevented finishing his observation by the honourable gentleman taking out of his pocket a letter, which he thrust into the noble lord's hands, observing—'See, look at that.'

" Lord Morpeth looked at the epistle, and slightly coloured. After a momentary pause, he observed—' Mr. ——, this, I assure you, is not my writing.'

" ' Oh, come, come, Lord Morpeth,' said the other smiling, thinking his lordship was in joke.

" ' I assure you, upon my honour, it is not,' repeated his lordship, with great emphasis.

" ' Not your hand writing !' said the honourable gentleman in faltering accents, and looking singularly foolish, as the idea flashed across his mind that some wag had hoaxed him.

" ' It is not,' reiterated Lord Morpeth; ' some of your friends have been enjoying their joke at your expense.'

" ' Why, I don't altogether like such jokes,' stammered the other, quite crest-fallen and leaving the Irish office immediately, vowing retribution on the party, should he ever discover him, whose waggery had placed him in such ridiculous circumstances.

" Who the wag was, has not been yet discovered, and there is every probability that he will be as careful to preserve his secret as if he were a second Junius."

We suspect this conversation is not so accurately reported as that of honourable gentlemen in the House.

The number of new members in the Victoria parliament is 158, many of them mere youths, who, one would think, were more in need of guardians themselves than to be made the guardians of the interests of a great community. Many of those new members are most undeliberative in their appearance ; they are to be seen laughing or talking, or both, lounging in dozens at the bar, preventing all ingress, egress, trampling out of the House, smoking their cigars, and making a loud noise as they proceed up Parliament-street, as if they were sparks on a spree.

On first entering the House, new members cut a very awkward figure. They generally lounge about the side galleries, whence they may observe the bearing of the old ones ; and when they venture on the floor, their timidity and awkwardness affords a great amusement to their experienced brethren. What amazes them most is the loud cheers with which the more popular speakers are greeted. But cheering is a senatorial qualification very soon learned;

" But the new M.P.'s, in many instances, improved upon their practice, and literally greeted particular passages of favourite speakers with ' hurrahs,' at the full stretch of their voice. Several of the old members were much amused by the vigour with which one of these new-made legislators cheered particular passages in Lord Stanley's speech, on the second night of the discussion on the Irish Election Petition Fund. He stationed himself in the side gallery, on the left hand of the reporters, nearly opposite the Speaker's chair. Wishing to enjoy his ease and the eloquence of the noble lord at the same time, the new M.P., who was a little man, with a brown coat, and a dark country-looking face, stretched himself on one of the benches in a horizontal position. One who knew no better would, in the first instance, have fancied that he was enjoying a sound nap. Nothing of the kind; as his lusty cheering of the more effective passages in his lordship's speech conclusively proved. Whenever about to express his approbation, he raised up his head so as to attain a slanting posture; and then making the most wry mouth I ever witnessed, shouted out, as if hailing some friend a quarter of a mile distant, ' Hurrah ! hurrah ! hurrah !—ah—ah—ah !' The word was drawled out the third time to as great a length as his breath would permit. The lusty applauder of Lord Stantley's eloquence then lay down again, as if about to address himself to sleep, and again started up and vociferated in the same way whenever any other passage struck his fancy, until the noble lord resumed his seat. Mr. Law, the Recorder for London, and Mr. Pemberton, the celebrated Chancery barrister, were among the honourable members whom I observed nearest to this newly chosen M.P., and heartily and repeatedly did they laugh at his singular conduct."

The chapter of scenes in the House is cleverly done ; that which is filled with anecdotes of Dick Martin, Wilson, and Fuller is very lame indeed. The speech put into the mouth of Richard Martin is borrowed of course from some wit at the Eccentrics, or some convivial club, and might sound admirably in the mouth of one of Mrs. Hall's Peasants, or Mr. Lover's Rory O'Moor. The scenes are so numerous, and given at such length, that we regret our limits will not allow us to notice them in detail. True it is they have all been the topics of public amusement and discussion when they first appeared in the newspapers ; but they acquire a freshness and vigour by being surrounded by all the adventitious circumstances of their enactment, which considerably heighten their effect. Never did St. Stephen's Chapel witness such displays of uproar and confusion as it has witnessed during the first session of the Victoria parliament. There was a memorable scene between Mr. O'Connell and the House in the affair of accusation of perjury, in which they mutually reprimanded each other. Mr. O'Connell coming off triumphant. Then there was the scene between General Evans and Sir H. Hardinge, and between Mr. O'Connell and Mr. Walter, and a variety of others, which our readers will recollect.

That in which Mr. Kearsley, late M.P. for Wigan, cut so ludicrous a figure, we look upon as the most amusing. The personal appearance of the honourable member was in perfect keeping with the buffoonery of his manners. He was in his element in a scene, and generally contrived to get one up after dinner.

" Never was man on better terms with himself than was the ex-member for Wigan. A most expressive look of self-complacency always irradiated his globularly-formed, country-complexioned countenance ; while his small bright eyes were ever peering triumphantly over his little cocked-up nose. Then there was his ample harvest of black, bushy air, with a pair of excellent whiskers to match, not forgetting his well-developed cheeks. He is a little thickset man, with an inclination to corpulency. Whether he stood on tiptoe, to add to his five-feet-six-inches stature, when he addressed the House, I have no means of knowing; but I have always thought that he looked at least an inch and a half higher when speaking, than at any other time.

" By far the richest scene in which the honourable gentleman ever performed a part, or which I had then witnessed in the house, occurred on the 20th of June, 1836, while the House was in committee on the Stamp Duties and Excise. Mr. Bernal, as chairman of committees, was in the chair on the occasion. Mr. Roebuck, in a long speech, had been showing that the apprehension of increased obscenity or immorality in the newspapers, in the event of the duty being entirely repealed, was groundless; and in the course of his observations he was repeatedly assailed with cries of ' Oh, oh !' from the Tory benches.

" As soon as he had sat down, Mr. Kearsley rose, amidst tremendous roars of laughter; for the moment he presented himself, as before remarked, the House was invariably thrown into a violent fit of laughter. ' I can assure the honourable and learned gentleman,' said he, ' that I was not one of those who cried ' Oh, oh !' [Shouts of laughter.] I merely rose when the honourable member for Lincolnshire sat down, to congratulate him on the quiet, easy, soapy way in which he got through his arguments. [Roars of laughter from all parts of the House, which lasted for some time.] And now let me ask the noble lord opposite, (Lord John Russel,) and the right honourable gentleman, (Mr. Spring Rice,) with what pleasure they have listened to the disgusting speech of the honourable and learned member for Bath.'

" It were difficult to say whether the laughter, or the shouts of ' Order, order !' and other marks of disapprobation, most prevailed, for about half a minute after Mr. Kearsley had resumed his seat.

" Some measure of order being at length restored, Mr. Bernal said— ' Surely the honourable member cannot be aware of the expression he has just used: I trust he will withdraw it.'

" Mr. Kearsley—' I may have spoken in language stronger than usual, but the cause is strong; and I say, Sir, that a more *disgusting* speech I never heard.'

" Another scene of confusion and noise, surpassing that which had just taken place, now ensued. The shouts of ' Oh, oh !' ' Order, order !' &c., in a great measure drowned the laughter which proceeded from some parts of the house. What added to the uproarious appearance of the house was the unusually great number of members who chanced to be in it at the time. The hour, too, was peculiarly fitted for a scene. It was about ten o'clock, just as the great majority of honourable members had returned from a good dinner, and the grateful liquids which follow it. Mr. Kearsley, on making the last-quoted observations, quitted his seat, which was near the middle of the house, and descending from his bench to the floor, walked across it in something like a semicircular line; making at the same time a low and most unusual bow to Mr. Bernal, accompanied by a most extraordinary wafture of his right hand, which firmly grasped the forepart of a ' shocking bad hat.' Having next described the figure 8. by his pedestrian motions on the floor, the honourable member endeavoured to force his way out of the house, but found it impossible to break through the dense mass of M.P.'s who choked up the passage. Having ineffectually made the attempt to effect his exit, first at one part of the bar and then at another, a wag whispered to him—' Mr. Kearsley, you had better take your seat again.'

"Mr. Kearsley, looking the other for a moment significantly in the face, said—' Sir, I think you're right—I *will* take my seat again.' And so saying, he forthwith returned to the place whence he came.

"The laughter which followed these extraordinary movements of the honourable gentleman was such as cannot be described. It burst from all parts of the house in deafening peals. And certainly any scene more provocative of laughter was never witnessed in the House of Commons, and very rarely, I should think, anywhere else.

"A long time elapsed before any member in the house could so far compose himself as to speak. Mr. Bernal was the first. He said—' I am sorry to be obliged to call on the honourable member again. If I am in error, the committee will correct me when I say that the term he has used is one which is not justified by any rule of this House.'

"On this Mr. Kearsley started to his feet again, admist renewed shouts of laughter. ' Sir,' said he, addressing himself to Mr. Bernal, ' I am sorry to find fault with the honourable and learned member for Bath, but on a former occasion he charged me with uttering a falsehood.'

"Mr. Kearsley again abdicated his seat, and after making some extraordinary movements on the floor, as if he were at a loss to know whether he should go to some other part of the house, or make a fresh attempt at forcing his way through the dense plantation of honourable gentleman who stood at the bar, he decided on the latter; but with no better success than before. His movements, first to one place and then to another, presented a striking resemblance to an animal in an iron cage, always trying, but in vain, to get out of its confinement. Mr. Kearsley again returned to his seat.

"This of course led to a renewal of the laughter. Honourable members were never known to be so unanimous in this respect before. All party feeling was laid aside for the moment; and cordial and universal roars of laughter proceeded from all present.

"As soon as the House had laughed itself out of breath, Mr. Roebuck rose and begged that it would not, on his (Mr. Roebuck's) account take any more notice of what had fallen from the honourable member; adding, that he considered it the result of an infirmity of the honourable gentleman.

"Mr. Paul Methuen next rose, and insisted that Mr. Bernal should compel Mr. Kearsley to give satisfaction to the House, not only for the improper language he had used, but for his extraordinary conduct in walking across the floor of the house in the way he had done, and making such singular bows to the Chair.

"Before Mr. Bernal had time to utter a word, Mr. Kearsley again jumped to his feet, and darting sundry most indignant glances of his little eyes at Mr. Paul Methuen, exclaimed in most emphatic tones—' Paul ! Paul ! why persecutest thou me ?'

"A simultaneous roar of laughter, not unlike, one would suppose, the noise caused by some secondary Niagara, followed. And although the use of the words constituted a profane application of the language of Scripture delivered on a most solemn occasion, yet so singularly felicitous, in other respects, was the quotation—Paul being Mr. Methuen's christian name,— and so extraordinary were the tones of voice and the manner altogether in which the words were uttered, that even the religious members could not help joining in the universal shout, as energetically as the others. I speak without exaggeration when I say, that within the memory of the oldest member of the House, shouts of laughter so loud, universal, or lasting, were never before heard in St. Stephen's. The laughter, it was calculated, lasted full two minutes without intermission, and then only ended when honourable gentlemen found themselves physically unfit for the further exercise of their risible faculties. It would have done the heart of the laughing philosopher of antiquity good, to have seen so many—about five hundred—of his disciples, all exemplifying his precepts at once,—unless, indeed, he had been mortified at seeing those disciples surpass himself in their laughing exploits."

Equally ludicrous is the exhibition of the good-natured Mr. Howard, member for Carlisle. He had gone down to the first row of Ministerial benches, to make a few remarks in vindication of the Carlisle corporation against an attack of Lord Stanley.

"But, before doing so, he rose and looked around him to see if any other honourable member was about to address the House. Observing no one on his legs to speak, though honourable gentlemen were walking about by dozens, he commenced in this way : ' Mr. Speaker, as I see nothing, nor anybody at this time before the House, may I be permitted——'

" The infinite good-nature with which he began, coupled with the circumstance of his looking around him, as if wishing to re-assure himself that he was right, caused a universal laugh, which drowned the remainder of the sentence. He was about to proceed amidst a good deal of merriment and confusion, when the Speaker, observing that two of the Masters of Chancery had just entered the house with a message from the Lords, shouted as loud as he could, ' Mr. Serjeant-at-Arms !' meaning that Mr. Serjeant-at-Arms should usher in the messengers with the usual ceremony,

" Mr. Howard fancying, in the confusion of the moment, that the Speaker was calling on the Serjeant-at-Arms to take him into custody for some unconscious violation of the rules of the house, looked towards the latter gentleman with unutterable surprise, mingled with some alarm. A universal roar of laughter, in which the Speaker joined, at once convinced Mr. Howard of his mistake; on which he heartily laughed at the fears which had so suddenly and ungroundedly taken possession of his mind. After the message from the Lords had been delivered, he again endeavoured to address the House, but had not proceeded far when it was found that, there being no question before it, he was out of order. He then resumed his seat; on which Lord Stanley, who had a reply to the anticipated speech, in justification of the attack he had made on the Carlisle corporation, went over to the Ministerial side of the house, and seating himself beside Mr. Howard, and stretching his left arm along the top of the back part of the bench against which the honourable gentleman reclined, he looked up most poetically in Mr. Howard's face—just as if he had been a lady into whose ear the noble lord was pouring a declaration of his love—and in that position continued for at least ten minutes, all the while endeavouring to justify his conduct in attacking the corporation of Carlisle. Mr. Howard thus had the speech exclusively addressed to himself which Lord Stanley had intended to deliver to the House, consisting, at the time, of about three hundred members."

In addition to a timid lady-like way of speaking, Mr. Howard lisps. In the discussion on Newspapers, Sir R. Peel chanced to use the expression Penny Newspapers, he was corrected by Mr. Wakley, who observed, there were no Penny Newspapers, on which

" Mr. Howard, taking off his hat, and starting to his feet as if he had made some important discovery, observed, ' There's a Penny Magazine,'— pronouncing the last word ' Magathine.' The odd way in which the sentence was lisped out, in conjunction with the circumstances under which the remark was made, upset the gravity of the honourable members as effectually as ever Liston did an audience in the Olympic Theatre. So contagious did the laugh prove, that I believe not even Mr. John Richards nor Mr. Arthur Trevor escaped."

Mr. H. is described as the very personification of good nature and good humour.

A curious circumstance connected with Mr. Brotherton, member for Salford, is his abstinence from animal food. He is herbivorous from principle, and for a series of years he has not tasted flesh. The members and friends with whom he occasionally dines, knowing his opinions on the matter, take care to provide him with some sort of pudding or vegetable dish in the first course, which he enjoys quite as much as they do their spiced ragouts. Notwithstanding this meagre fare, there is not a man in the house, whose good humoured expanse of countenance and corpulent figure seem to plead so eloquently in favour of the roast beef of Old England. His abstinence is the result of a conviction, that it is equally repugnant to the dictates of revealed religion and humanity to eat animal food. This conviction he has sustained in an essay prefixed to a treatise on cookery, and though we dissent from the doctrine, we must admire the firmness and moral courage which enables him to advocate by his practice so unpopular an idea. Mr. B. is a great favourite with both sides of the house, indeed, with a face like his beaming with benevolence and good humour, it is impossible he could be otherwise. His efforts to make the House keep proper hours are deserving of the highest commendation, and constitute in themselves a great public service. But it appears he displays more obstinacy in adhering to his vegetable philosophy than in the practical enforcement of the doctrine of early hours.

" His radical error, in all the instances in which he failed last session, was in listening at all to the entreaties of honourable members to desist from his purpose. I allow that it was no easy matter to resist their solicitations: for to say nothing of the ' Oh! ohs!' which proceeded from what Mr. O'Connel would call the ' leather lungs' of certain gentlemen, whenever he rose, I have seen him entreated by the hands as well as by the ' most sweet voices' of three or four other honourable members all at once. I have seen one look him most imploringly in the face, and heard him say in tones and with a manner as coaxing as if the party had been wooing his mistress—' O do not just yet, Mr. Brotherton: wait one other half hour until this matter be disposed of.' I have seen a second seize him by the right arm, while a third grasped him by the left, with the view of causing him to resume his seat; and when his sense of duty overcame all these efforts to seduce or force him from its path, I have seen a fourth honourable gentleman rush to the assistance of the others, and take hold of the tails of his coat, literally press him to his seat. I have seen Mr. Brotherton, with a perseverance beyond all praise in this righteous and most patriotic cause, suddenly start again to his feet in less than five minutes, and move a second time the adjournment of the House, and I have again had the misfortune to see physical force triumph over the best moral purposes. Five or six times have I witnessed the repetition of this in one night. On one occasion, I remember seeing an honourable member actually clap his hand on Mr. Brotherton's mouth, in order to prevent his moving the dreaded adjournment."

Mr. Brotherton, while advocating the claims of the factory children four years ago, emphatically declared he was once a poor factory boy himself, and though now a rich manufacturer he did not shrink from confirming his statements by a reference to his own actual experience. He is liberal, but not ultra radical, a man of excellent moral character, and a dissenter.

In the notice on Mr. Grantley Berkeley we find the following remarks on the admission of ladies to the gallery, of which Mr. B. is the well known advocate.

" I am surprised that in a house where such transcendant gallantry is professed as in the House of Commons, Mr. Grantley Berkeley's efforts to procure admission for the ladies into the gallery should always be defeated. And what may appear still more surprising is the fact, that in most cases the greatest dandies—those who profess to pay such extreme attention to their dress from their devotion to the fair sex—are the most strenuous in their efforts to continue the exclusion of the ladies. But to use a familiar expression, ' I see how it all is;' these coxcomb legislators are so vain of having their own persons admired, that they cannot bear the idea of having such a phalanx of female beauty in the house as would, of necessity, withdraw attention entirely from themselves. Some of these dandy legislators not only display a profusion of rings on their fingers, and sport ' splendid chains' on their breasts, and lace as tightly almost as the ladies themselves; but you may nose them at a distance of many yards, through means of the rich perfumes with which they scent the surrounding atmosphere."

The satire of this passage may be just, but the reasoning is very stupid. The coxcombs he speaks of would be the greatest gainers by the admission of ladies, for they would engross all the admiration of that dear delightful " phalanx of beauty," as they do wherever they meet their eyes ; and if by attention, is here meant the attention of the other members, better that it should continue to be directed towards the coxcombs, than towards more dangerous and deluding objects ; if the attention of the strangers and reporters, we feel very certain they never trouble their heads about it.

The true ground of the opposition of members to Mr. Grantley Berkeley's motion is, that the presence of ladies, besides distracting attention, would aggravate the bitterness of taunts, and sharp expressions, inflame animosities, and cause those scratches which are now scarcely felt or are healed as soon as inflicted, to fester and rankle into incurable wounds.

" Lord John Russell," says the author, " seemed quite fidgetty. How his mind was exercised, is a question I cannot pretend to answer." Certainly not, unless his great Master Lavater whom he is perpetually invoking, were to enable him to read people's thoughts by staring at their faces. " One thing," continues our author, " must have appeared sufficiently clear to every one who observed the noble Lord—that he must have been somewhat more sedate in his appearance when he wrote his Essay on the British Constitution, and his Tragedy of Don Carlos."

Now what conceivable connection is there between Lord John's being fidgetty while listening to a prosy speaker, and his having written an essay and a tragedy. The *genus irritabile vatum* are not at their ease while they are writing, far from it, especially dramatists. Moore gives us a most ludicrous enumeration of the various eccentricities exhibited by authors in the act of composing : the probability is that Lord John's fidgettiness did actually arise from the throes of mental labour, or the compression of the embryo ideas that were too eager to rush into the world. A more misplaced and paltry allusion could not have been hit upon. There can be no doubt it was highly unbecoming both in Lord John Russell, Lord Morpeth and Mr. Spring Rice—the latter gentleman actually carrying on a conversation in the gallery—to testify such open disrespect to the oration which poor Mr. Sanford was labouring to deliver at their instigation and purely to oblige them, with his legs embarrassed with a sword, and his wrists with lace ruffles, and it would appear that the vein of vulgarity extends through the house from the leader downwards.

The length to which our extracts have already run must necessarily prevent us from noticing the characters of members in the 2nd volume. However, we cannot pass over Sir W. Molesworth and Mr. Leader, as they form a party in themselves. They are both young men of talent, distinguished as literateurs, and for considerable powers of eloquence. They are a sort of political Siamese twins who hold in common the same extreme political opinions.

Indeed they think, speak, and act in harmony, that one could almost fancy there was but one mind equally divided between them. In order that this interchange of sentiment and feeling may be less liable to interruption, they live in the same house in Pimlico, where Mr. Roebuck generally spends his Sundays. The unity of purpose which distinguished the extreme Radicals last session, and which has since disappeared, is to be ascribed to the circumstance of Sir W. Molesworth and Mr. Leader having come to the resolution—and carried it into practice too—of giving a series of parliamentary dinners to their party. They commenced the week before the opening of the session, and were given at the Clarendon every Sunday. Sir W. Molesworth paid one week and Mr. Leader the other. The fear of exclusion from these Sunday festivals operated most powerfully in keeping the party together. The dinners were discontinued during the present session and the party fell to pieces—a very intelligible satire upon parties and politicians.

Both Sir William and Mr. Leader take the precaution of writing their speeches, and of speaking from memory. They are both good scholars, but Mr. Leader has the best delivery of the two. As radicals, they are both men of inflexible obstinacy of character.

The failure of Sir F. Pollock and Mr. B. D'Israeli, and the lamentable catastrophe of the entire breaking down of Mr. Gibson Craig, the seconder of the address, are too notorious to need a comment. In the case of Mr. D'Israeli, there was a display of most ungentlemanly conduct on the part of the ministerial side of the House. He has since spoken and with partial success.

We close these volumes of the second series of Random Recollections, highly satisfied with the entertainment and instruction they have afforded us. They are as well written, though they do not profess the interest of the first. There is a more palpable effort at book-making evident throughout, and in some places the style is coarse and exaggerated; however, to the curious in the gossip of the gallery of the House of Commons, the perusal of these volumes must afford a very agreeable relaxation.

NOTICES.

Art. XII.—*Guide to Switzerland, &c. &c.* By Francis Coghlan. London: Baily and Co. 1838.

Mr. Coghlan takes the best and surest method of equipping himself for writing such works as the one before us. He visits the scenes, pursues the routes described, and then communicates in singularly plain and compact form the results of his experience; that experience extending to every thing, even the minutest, upon which tourists can possibly require information. His long and constant practice of supplying the world with similar productions, gives him a manifest advantage over almost every

other Guide ; and we may safely add, that the present volume fully equals
its predecessors by the same author.

ART. XIII.—*Poems, for the most Part Occasional.* By JOHN KENYON,
formerly of St. Peter's College, Cambridge. London : Moxon. 1831.

REFINED taste, a mind highly cultured, an imagination which habitually
luxuriates among touching and gentle thoughts and lovely images, everywhere manifest themselves in these Occasional Pieces. Perhaps there is a
want of power and originality evinced ; but then it ought to be borne in
mind that the accuracy of Mr. Kenyon's versification, and the fine symmetrical proportions preserved in whatever he puts his hand to, conceal
the vigour and dignity of his productions from the careless reader. It
appears to us that he possesses in an eminent degree those enviable qualifications which enable him by the disportings of his muse to contribute to
those elegant and rich feasts, of which it is impossible to taste without
finding the heart to be thereby mended and feeling purified. He can
even strike the higher chords of our nature, and afford to the mind the
sense of having its noblest powers and attributes exalted and expanded ;
and these are results which must certainly be numbered amongst the
greatest and most precious triumphs of poetry. From one of the longer
poems, the first, indeed, in the volume, we cull a specimen. The theme
is one that has been wearifully drawn upon by every poetaster, till it
might be supposed another image, another sentiment, could not be appended
to it—the Queen of Night, we mean. But see part of what a true poet
can say about this fair and universally admired goddess.

> " And Queen thou art in this thy realm of midnight,
> And lovely as queen-like ; yet not lovely less
> When thou art lapsing on through either twilight,
> Companion of the evening or the dawn.
>   *   *   *   *   *
> And ne'er did dawn behold thee lovelier yet,
> Than when we saw thee, one remembered day,
> Thee and that brightest of all morning stars,
> Hang o'er the Adrian ; not in thy full lustre,
> But graceful with slim crescent ; such as, erst,
> Some Arab chief beheld in his own sky,
> Of purest deepest azure ; and so loved it,
> So loved it, that he chose it for his symbol ;
> A peaceful symbol in a warlike banner !
> And oft, I ween, in many a distant camp,
> 'Mid the sharp neigh of steeds, and clash of cymbals,
> And jingle of the nodding Moorish bells,
> When he hath caught that image o'er his tents,
> Hath he bethought him of the placid hours
> When thou wert whitening his night-feeding flocks
> On Yemen's happy hills ; and then, perchance,
> Hath sighed to think of war."

Lovelier lines of melodious verse, and lovelier thoughts, we think have
seldom greeted the ear and heart. From the shorter and slighter pieces
we might pluck not a few gems. One must suffice ; and indeed together

with the foregoing admirable specimen, it cannot fail to impress the poetic reader's mind with a very high opinion of Mr. Kenyon's muse. Its title is Freedom.

> " 'Tis not because fierce swords are flashing there
> With licence and a reckless scorn of life,
> When for some petty gaude upstarts a strife,
> That freedom there must harbour. Slavery's air
> Breeds many a liveried satrap, prompt to dare,
> And soldier-serfs are ready there and rife
> To march at summons of the jerking fife.
>
> But where swords—some—are turned to ploughshare—where
> Others, not rusted, o'er the household hearth,
> In peaceful pomp, near cradled babe are hung,
> And sires rest reverenced in holy earth,
> And marriage-bells with holy cheer are rung,
> There Freedom dwells, Constraint's sublime reward,
> And Peace must rear her, e'en if War must guard."

Art. XIV.—*The Young Lady's Book of Botany.* London: Tyas. 1838.

An elegant little volume as regards binding, typography, and illustrations, twelve of these being carefully coloured; there are besides many other accurate representations of a less laboured character. But exterior and immediately obvious beauties are not the only excellences of the Young Lady's Book of Botany, for as an Introduction to that popular science it possesses the merit of being plain, suitable, and comprehensive. It is not only calculated to excite as well as to sustain and advance a taste for the cultivation of the branch of knowledge of which it treats, but to contain no inconsiderable degree of the knowledge required.

Art. XV.—*Rebecca Wilson, the Cumberland Girl.* London: Green. 1838.

This is the first Number of a small work for young folks. It is intended —and the scheme and execution are worthy of the intention—to engage the minds and hearts of those for whom it has been written by means of a tale concerning the natural features of Cumberland, and the social condition of the people of that district, as also to teach by life-like example, some of the most important lessons which a young girl in Rebecca Wilson's situation and with her disposition can receive or need. A series of little works with a similar design by the same hand, in the course of time, will amount to a valuable juvenile library, and be influential towards advancing the culture of the head, feelings, and taste of its susceptible readers.

Art. XVI.—*Letters from the Levant during the Embassy to Constantinople,* 1716-18. By LADY MARY WORTLEY MONTAGUE. London: Rickerby. 1838.

This is one of the republications of some of the choicest literary gems of

England, which Mr. Rickerby is, *seriatim*, tastefully giving to the World, and which Mr. J. A. St. John so ably, and we may add, so enthusiastically illustrates by means of Preliminary Discourses and Notes. The editor appears not only to have made Lady Mary's writings and moral character his close study, in behalf of both of which, indeed, he chivalrously fights, but he places before us abundant evidence to shew that the East and the Ottomans, the turbaned, the veiled and the haremed in Oriental climes have much engaged his reading, and even his partialities. The present edition of these Letters ought to supersede every other that has been published prior to it; for independent of their well-known value, the Preliminary Discourse and the Notes have a spirit and charm about them, which, while they convey much that the present generation must desire and be delighted to learn, must also be felt to be happily wedded to the text.

Art. XVII.—*The Travels of Minna and Godfrey in Many Lands.* From the Journals of the Author. London: Smith, Elder, and Co. 1838.

Holland is the theatre of which this little book treats. The curiosity, the observation, and the improvement of two juvenile travellers call forth a great deal of engaging as well as useful information respecting that country. We should say indeed that its author has struck the happy key by which excitement will minister to valuable knowledge, and by which the present gratification of the mind of such young persons as Minna and Godfrey will abide in the memory and become productive of rational and permanent satisfaction. The work has the merit, while not soaring above the capacity of young people, of being calculated to draw out their powers and latent capacities—of, in fact, treating them in a manner which must be considered not unworthy of being relished by matured minds. The illustrations from the Old Dutch Masters which enrich the volume are numerous and of a superior description.

Art. XVIII.—*The Victim. A Tale of the " Lake of the Four Cantons."* By the Author of "A Traveller's Thoughts." London: Longman. 1838.

This tale of Switzerland relates, its author tells us, to some period posterior to the great struggle for liberty in which Tell gained his immortality, merely because, as it seems to us, certain passages, which relate to patriotism, may be the more appropriately dove-tailed into it. Its improbability as a story requires, however, that the date of its occurrence be thrown as far back as the affixed limit will allow. Of its versification and its poetry, we must request the reader to judge for himself, from the following portion of the catastrophe :

> " ' Constance! thou knowest my suit,' he said,
>   ' That suit, forsooth, was once denied,
>   This lake—this lake—thy bridal bed,
>   Or, Constance! swear to be my bride ! '
>   ' Never! oh never! Let me die ! '
>   She shrieked, in fearful agony—
>   ' Rash maid ! thou temptest me—dost thou ?   . .

Seest thou the yawning gulph below?
Aye—seest thou not that chilly wave?
That word revoke—or 'tis thy grave!'
Down knelt the maid, but steady eye,
To heaven she raised imploringly—
'Great God! my Meinard is not nigh—
Thy will be done—I die! I die!'
Incarnate fiend!—could man stand by,
That maid in all her purity,
In youth, in bloom, in loveliness,
Nor feel one pang at her distress?
Say, durst thou lift thy impious hand
    Though hell should blight thee with its curse;
Yes! blast thee with a withering hand,
    Like murderous Cain, for thou art worse?
Or, heaven's it was—a righteous will,
That thou shouldst fill thy meed of ill!
Ev'n as she weeping knelt in prayer,
Ruthless he seized her silken hair
Nor stayed that prayerful lip to mark,
But hurled her from the quivering bark!
One heavy plunge—one woman's shriek—
Her life's last ebbing struggles speak—
Her look still fixed on that fierce brow;
As o'er her lips the chill waves flow,
A gurgling voice, that ceased to live,
Still faintly muttered—'I forgive!'
Yet as she slowly sank, her eye
Still gazed on his reproachfully."

Though Scott's measure has been borrowed, assuredly his muse has not. We must also observe that though the situation of Constance, as above described, was sufficiently critical and desperate to account for rapid transitions on her part, yet this does not afford an excuse for the inconsistencies of the author, which in the course of a very few lines are bold and numerous. For example, he assures us that the maid knelt down, and that she raised her "steady eye to heaven" imploringly,—but it follows, that as she "weeping knelt in prayer," and the villain tossed her into the lake, "Her look" was "*still* fixed" on his "fierce brow;" and again, though like a good Christian she mutters—"I forgive," in reality it is only a lip forgiving, for she actually "gazed" on her destroyer "reproachfully,"

ART. XIX.—*Areopagitica Secunda: or Speech of the Shade of John Milton, on Mr. Serjeant Talfourd's Copyright Bill.* London: Moxon. 1838.

THE Shade of John Milton puts forward in strenuous and eloquent style the arguments which Serjeant Talfourd and others have both in and out of Parliament advanced in support of the Bill in question. We know of nothing new that can be said either for or against the measure, although we have every reason to believe that before it passes into a law, several modifications and alterations will be introduced upon the shape it assumes at the moment we write. We however quote a specimen from the declamation and reasoning before us that would not disgrace the old blind Commonwealth man were he upon earth.

"In that my former appeal to the wisdom and equity of the English Parliament, these words were spoken by me with boldness, and heard by them with patience—' The just retaining by each man his several copy, which God forbid should be gainsaid.' Such, I say, was my language, when, from the fetters which were placed upon the spirits of men at that time by that despotic law, (the law against the Liberty of Printing,) I pleaded before your predecessors, as it were in chains. But now, mark the difference. When these chains have been struck off, when the minds of men have been manumitted from this hard bondage, when in the title of his work, instead of the signature and *imprimatur* of a civil or ecclesiastical licenser, you have prefixed the prænomen of liberty to the name of every writer in England, when we authors no longer are compelled to travel through the World with signed and sealed passports, to be produced at every barrier and custom-house in our road, but have earth, sea, and air thrown open to our free course; when we no longer are escorted by a printed testimony that we are neither deceivers, nor fools, nor idiots, nor bad citizens, nor vicious men; behold at this very time, for nearly one hundred years, have we now been shorn of our property, in the creations of that part of ourselves which is most our own. * * * * We Poets are the only true *makers*, as all the most polite tongues do plainly testify. If, again, it is the *manner* of creation, and the *instruments* employed by me therein, which makes an object to be virtually, essentially, and inseparably mine, then I would fain inquire why that which I create by means of an instrument which is the *very essence of myself*, in which my own identity resides, to which I retreat and cling as the very central hearth and altar of my whole earthly tenement, and on which the flame of my intellectual being will burn *for ever*—why, I say, is that which I forge in this furnace less my own than what is moulded in the short lived fires of the smith, or melted in the crucible of the chemist? They may possess some mysterious secret in their art, by which they may produce *material* forms of peculiar symmetry, copies of which they may multiply for ever, and the arcanum of their combination they may hand down to their children's children, and no law will wrest it from them. Not that this their privilege is to be condemned : no, applauded rather let it be, as the grant of a wise and generous people; but let not this be praised at the same time as just, that an invention worked by the hand, and ending in the produce of material forms, and one barren of fruit, being locked up in the mind of the inventors or of their descendants, should remain the property of their heirs for ever, while the *intellectual* fruits which grow from the heart and soul of man, and which cast their prolific seed far and wide into other minds, and which never cease to live and to give life, should, when hardly ripe, be rudely plucked from the parent-tree, and thrown into the lap of those who have never toiled to produce them."

Art. XX.—*A word to Parents, Nurses, and Teachers on the Rearing and Management of Children.* By Esther Copley. London: Simpkins, Marshall and Co. 1838,

This little work is particularly intended for the working classes, and may with much advantage be consulted by them; for in a cheap form it lays down those just principles and practical directions which the best and latest writers on the physical, mental, and moral training of the young, have expounded and enforced.

Art. XXI.—*Astronomy Simplified, or, Distant Glimpses of the Celestial Bodies.* By Frances B. Burton. London: Simpkins Marshall and Co. 1838.

The purpose of the author of these distant glimpses is to set forth the power and goodness of the Creator through Astronomical facts. This she does in familiar and concise language, and with as much energy and warmth as the limited space chosen for the treatment of such a stupendous and magnificent subject can well allow. The work may be recommended as a good popular enumeration of the ascertained truths in the science of the heavenly bodies.

Art. XXII.—*Normal Schools; and the Principles of Government Interference with Education.* A Lecture by Th. S. Gowing. London: Wertheim.

Mr. Gowing delivered this Lecture at the Ipswich Mechanics' Institution; and in it he considers and advocates the expediency of establishing Normal Schools, for the purpose of efficiently providing duly educated teachers, of guaranteeing to them an honourable recognition of their qualifications, and of raising their character in the general estimation of the community. The Lecturer also briefly explains his views of the manner and extent of interference which the State should exert in behalf of education, his first proposition being, "that the Legislature ought to affirm the necessity of every child in the land receiving a certain minimum of secular education;" secondly, "that the Legislature should leave religious education free and unshackled, in the hands of the different recognised religious bodies;" thirdly, "that use should be made of the organization existing in the various religious bodies as a machinery to aid in carrying the views of the State, as to secular education, into effect;" and fourthly, "that the machinery of the State should be confined to mere superintendence, to see that its own views, in respect of secular education (carefully abstaining from the remotest interference with religious education), were carried into effect." Whatever may be thought of Mr. Gowing's sentiments as extended on the various points noticed by us, or however unlikely their immediate adoption may be by the Establishment, we must say that his Pamphlet is not only earnest, but evinces much reflection on the important subject of which he treats. Besides, it affords another evidence of the increasing interest which is felt concerning the necessity of some systematic plan of intellectual and moral training being introduced, and that the experiment cannot be much longer delayed.

. ART. XXIII.—*Stenographic Sound-Hand.* By ISAAC PITMAN. London:
              Bagster.

WE have noted especially two distinct passages in the explanatory matter
. of this four-penny tome, or *card*, as Mr. Pitman calls it, which we extract.
1st. " The writer is preparing a ' Manual of Stenography' including an
. analytical sketch of the English language, and the application of it to short
hand characters ; also a scheme of an alphabet according to nature ; which
shall be published another day if it is worthy of publication ; to ascertain which,
this card, containing the principles, is thrown as a *feeler*." 2ndly. " Convinced as the writer is of the unspeakable importance of the art of writing,
. and more especially of short-hand, to man, while an inhabitant of this mate-
, rial world ; ·convinced". &c. &c. " he thinks he is not too sanguine in expecting, that, ere long, short hand will be the common hand in which the
. imperishable Word of God will exist no larger than a *watch*, and be as constantly used for the discovery and regulation of man's spiritual state, with
· reference to eternity, as the pocket chronometer is for the discovery and
regulation of time with reference to the present life." Of these sober sentiments we have not a word to utter, excepting, only to add, that Mr. Pitman's Stenography, for any thing we know to the contrary, is just as likely
as any other that is in vogue, to bring to pass the mighty revolution in
writing and religion anticipated by him.

· ART. XXIV.—*A Series of Practical Discourses.* By the REV. JAMES
    MACLEAN, Minister of Urquhart, Morayshire. London: Smith,
    Elder, & Co. 1838.

THE author says in his short Preface that these Discourses " pretend to no
peculiar excellence, either of matter or of style," but that, " as they were
composed with much care, and with an anxious view to the religious improvement of those committed to his spiritual charge," they may, he hopes,
prove useful to others. If Mr. Maclean mean by peculiar excellence of
matter and style, originality of thought and bold appeals to the imagination
and feelings, why, he is quite correct, for he has made no effort of the kind ;
but if the excellence of the preacher consist in plain, practical, impressive,
and forcible illustration of revealed truths that concern every man every
moment of his life, expressed in language which is a model of neatness and
precision, then we say these Discourses are excellent both in matter and
style. They are, as they profess, essentially practical, not doctrinal or controversial ; so that every one who wishes to equip himself by the study of
sound and correct examples for pulpit oratory, or who has an eye rather to
the moral and religious improvement of his flocks than to sectarian distinctions, ought to make the Minister of Urquhart's sermons his study. We
know not either in the Established or Dissenting Churches of these Kingdoms of any communion which would be otherwise than pleased and
instructed by Discourses that are conceived in the purest spirit of Christian
warmth, enlightenment, and singleness of purpose.

ART. XXV.—*The State of the Science of Political Economy ·Investi-
   gated.* By. WILLIAM ATKINSON. London: Whittaker.

THIS essay appears in the form of a Report which has been approved of by
the Sub-committee of the Central Agricultural Society, in which Society

the subject of Political Economy has been taken up. It contains an able and searching examination of the arguments which have hitherto been advanced by the principle writers on the laws which regulate the formation of Wealth, Smith, Malthus, Malthus, M'Culloch and others; and arrives at a conclusion which amounts to this, that Science is a term arbitrarily and presumptuously applied to Political Economy as handled and elucidated by these writers. Having demolished or attempted to demolish the theories and illustrations of others in the present publication, Mr. Atkinson, whose essay has been approved of by the members of the sub-committee above mentioned, will with their countenance and assistance, in a future Report, endeavour to construct an affirmative proposition, demonstrating what are the correct principles of the Science, and what are the practical conclusions to be deduced from accurate premises; thus professing to have discovered the true foundation of a system of commercial action, and reciprocity. Among the names of the Members of the Sub-committe, we observe that of R. Montgomery Martin, and those of others which afford a strong presumptive argument in behalf of Mr. Atkinson's work; nor will a perusal falsify that argument.

ART. XXVI.—*The Confessions of Adalbert.* By FRANCIS THEREMIN, D. D. Translated from the German by SAMUEL JACKSON, ESQ. London: B. Wertheim. 1838.

DR. THEREMIN is Chaplain to his Majesty the King of Prussia, Member of the Supreme Consistory, &c. &c., and is one of those German divines who belong not to the School of Rationalists, or any other of what is generally understood by the term *unscriptural* schools, which have been so numerous and various in Protestant Germany. We still think, however, that there is, at least, in the Doctor's style a portion of that mysticism and transcendentalism which has extensively infected the mind of his countrymen. At the same time there is great warmth of piety, earnestness, and simplicity about his sentiments.

The work is in the style of Letters, which in the form of autobiography attempt to portray and describe the commencement and progress of the Christian faith and life in the experience of an individual. The author's uniform design is to show that divine grace is the sole agent of human conversion; and that, though this change is accomplished in the greatest possible variety of ways, all of them agree with each other in the principal points.

The progress of Adalbert's feelings, convictions, and conversion, afford a narrative in which besides his mental history and his aspirations there are reflections, descriptions, and allusions to such topics as interest every cultivated mind, and which agreeably and even delightfully carry the reader forward, rendering the hero of the story a personage with whom the heart deeply sympathises; thus winning by example as well as instructing by precept. The following passage belongs to that period in Adalbert's mutual history, when he is ill at ease but knows not where or how to obtain comfort.

" When I fall asleep, it is as if a demon sat before me and grinned at me, who changes himself from one dreadful form to another, and who once more presents to my confused thoughts that which is the most revolting and appalling, in order that I may take it with me into the world of dreams.

" Some time ago, the city was full of a suicide which had been committed. The individual had distinguished himself in many respects, and in
particular by considerable poetical talent. He goes to the wood, places
himself under a tree, discharges his pistol, and is no more. The populace
crowded out of the city to see the corpse, and invented a multitude of fables
concerning his being in want of money, having been unfortunate in love,
&c., as the cause of the fatal act. If a man can be but satisfied with himself, he may also be so with the want of money and the most unhappy love-
affair; but when he can no longer bear himself, he is not far from the pistol or rope.

" Some time ago, I fell asleep more quietly than usual. After the night
was past, and with the morning dawn, a greater coolness and exhaustion
had overcome me. Sweet moment, thought I: whilst a pleasing shiver
thrilled through me, and my limbs extended themselves at their ease.
Sweet moment, when the cold shiver of death shall pervade me, and my
body shall stretch itself out to take its final repose, from which we wake
no more !"

ART. XXVII.—*Jephthah, and other Poems.* By GEORGE PRYME, M. A.
          M. P. London : J. Hatchard and Son. 1838.

HERE we have beside smaller pieces a poem extending to four cantos in
heroic measure by one who is not only an M. P., but a Professor of Political Economy,—combinations which the reader will not perceive as necessary or even as very usual. To be sure, among our legislators, and our
ministers of state, there is a considerable array not only of authors but of
bards ; but from a lecturer on the principles and sources of the wealth of
nations, one does not readily expect to hear the chieftain's triumphs or
the maiden's tragedy chaunted in loftily constructed rhyme. But if he be a
senator or a disciple of Adam Smith, we like the man the better that he
wooes at intervals the muses; persuaded that where the heart is right and
tender, and fond of giving utterance to the highest and purest aspirations
of our nature, the theories of the head cannot be far wrong, or, at last,
will not do much harm. Henceforth, at any rate, we will turn with partiality to any thing which may emanate from Mr. Pryme on account of
his Jephthah.
    Jephthah is a poem of very considerable power, and is full of noble
sentiments. It consists however of description much more than of action,
and therefore labours under a defect which prevents the reader from so
deeply sympathizing with the principal characters as might otherwise
have been the result. The lines, too, are not unfrequently bald, prosaic,
and made up of the most commonplace phrases and rhymes. Still f it
be a good criterion to try a poem by its effects upon the reader, we must
pronounce the whole life-like and vivid; for it leaves a clear and frequently
forcible impression, and exactly of that which the author must have
intended to convey.
    The subject of the poem is Jephthah, not Jephthah's daughter ; the
latter having frequently been the theme of song, the former seldom or
never, in modern times, at least. Mr. Pryme rightly regards the father's
history as shadowing out a magnificent outline, although, after the manner of the Scriptural historians, the account of him in the book of Judges is
short and the touches few, This outline it has been the poet's endeavour

to fill up, by supplying minute shades and probable incidents, and by introducing many features in the life of the children of the desert as described by modern travellers, the picture being permanent and little changed by the lapse of ages: We have only further to notice, before producing a specimen, that Mr. Pryme does not follow the common translation of the Bible in regard to the sacrifice of the maiden, but one which has been supported by Dr. Randolph, late professor of Theology at Oxford, and by other interpreters. The divine just named contended, it seems, that verse thirty-one may be thus rendered: " Whatsoever cometh forth of the doors of my house to meet me shall surely be the Lord's; and I will offer to him a burnt offering," meaning thereby that she was immured so that she might devote her entire existence and thoughts to God, the daughters of Israel going " yearly to lament (*or* talk with) the daughter of Jephthah the Gileadite four days in the year." We go forward to that part of the poem, for our specimens in which Mr. Pryme paraphrases and versifies these ideas.

Jephthah's daughter and her maidens advance to greet the returning warrior and his followers, chaunting a triumphant song.

" As ceas'd the strain, her timid eye she rais'd,
Then mute and fearful on her father gaz'd;
For not the pride of triumph mark'd his brow,
But signs of anguish unperceiv'd till now;
Emotions half supprest amid the song,
That rous'd and bore his glowing thoughts along.
Yet bursts the torrent with redoubted force,
When sinks the mound that stay'd awhile its course:
So Jephthah gave his stifled feelings vent.
Clench'd his firm hand, his gather'd mantle rent,
' Low hast thou brought my now unenvied head,
And crush'd the hope that o'er mine offspring spread.
O wherefore first would thine unbidden feet
O'erstep the tent our homeward march to meet?
My hasty lip has breath'd the fatal vow;
Nor change, nor ransom, laws divine allow.
Devote to God, thy blameless life is cast,
And all our future darkens like the past.'
Gay woman mounts on Fortune's swelling tide,
Inflam'd by joy, and overborne with pride;
In giddy transport crowds redundant sail,
And steers unsteady to the favouring gale.
Yet come the storm, or sudden, or foreseen,
She meets the dark reverse with dauntless mien:
Sustains and soothes the partners of her woe,
While man's stern courage quails beneath the blow;
With patient bosom stems the threatening blast,
And calmly, firmly, struggles to the last.
So felt and acted in that trying hour
The desert's child, with more than manly power;
Her blooming cheek assum'd a pallid hue;
But calm her features, and her tears were few,
As meekly thus she said, ' Mine honour'd sire,
If urged by glory's hope, or patriot fire;

If from thy lips the fatal words have sped,
That mark my life, or rank me with the dead;
If God hath heard, and listened to thy call,
My head shall seal the price of Ammon's fall.'
　　One supplicating look to Heaven she cast,
One thought on prospects just perceiv'd and past,
And then resum'd—' This simple boon concede,
Ere yet my dreadful sentence be decreed;
Two fleeting moons for thy lost child allow,
Untouch'd, unfetter'd, by the deadly vow,
To roam o'er mountain heights and blooming vales,
Endear'd to early thought, in Gilead's tales;
There with these lov'd companions to lament
That hopeless lonely lot which fate has sent:
And summon courage for my dreary task:
' Tis all thou now canst give, or I may ask.'
　　' Go,' said her sire, his languid head he bent,
Took her cold hand, and led her to the tent."
The smaller pieces do not call for any particular remark.

ART. XXVIII.—*Southey's Poetical Works. Vol. VI.* London: Longman
　　　　　　　and Co.　1838.

THE embellishments of this volume are particularly beautiful, St. Michael's
Mount, Cornwall, and the Well of St. Keyne, being the subjects of them.
The Poems here republished are chiefly short pieces; nor was the public
previously aware that all of them were Southey's.　From a curious piece,
called " The March to Moscow," of one of these unfathered productions
when they first appeared, we quote a few verses.

　　　　The Emperor Nap he would set off
　　　　　On a summer excursion to Moscow;
　　The fields were green, and the sky was blue,
　　　　　　　Morbleu! Parbleu!
　　What a pleasant excursion to Moscow!
　　　　*　　　*　　　*　　　*

　　The Russians they stuck close to him,
　　　　All on the road from Moscow,
　　There was Tormazow and Jemalow,
　　And all the others that end in ow;
　　　Milarodovitch and Jaladovitch,
　　　　　And Karatschlowitch,
　　And all the others that end in itch;
　　　Schamscheff, Souchosaneff,
　　　　　And Schepaleff,
　　And all the others that end in eff;
　　　Wasiltschikoff, Kostomaroff,
　　　　　And Tchoglokoff,
　　And all the others that end in off;
　　　Rajeffsky and Novereffsky,
　　　　　And Rieffsky,
　　And all the others that end in effsky;
　　　Oscharoffsky and Rostoffsky,
　　And all the others that end in offsky;

And Platoff he play'd them off,
And Shouvaloff he shovell'd them off,
And Markoff he mark'd them off,
And Krosnoff he cross'd them off,
And Tuchkoff he touch'd them off,
And Boroskoff he bored them off,
And Kutousoff he cut them off,
And Parenzoff he pared them off,
And Worronzoff he worried them off,
And Doctoroff he doctor'd them off,
And Rodionoff he flogged them off,
And last of all an Admiral came,
A terrible man with a terrible name,
A name which you all know by sight very well;
But which no one can speak, and no one can spell.
They stuck close to Nap with all their might,
They were on the left and on the right,
Behind and before, and by day and by night,
He would rather parlez-vous than fight;
But he look'd white and he look'd blue,
Morbleu! Parbleu!
When parlez-vous no more would do,
For they remember'd Moscow.

And then came on the frost and snow
All on the road from Moscow,
The wind and weather he found in that hour
Cared nothing for him nor for all his power;
For him who, while Europe crouch'd under his rod,
Put his trust in his Fortune, and not in his God.
Worse and worse every day the elements grew,
The fields were so white and the sky so blue,
Sacrebleu! Ventrebleu!
What a horrible journey from Moscow.

What then thought the Emperor Nap
Upon the road from Moscow?
Why, I ween he thought it small delight
To fight all day, and to freeze all night:
And he was, besides, in a very great fright,
For a whole skin he liked to be in;
And so, not knowing what else to do,
When the fields were so white and the sky so blue,
Morbleu! Parbleu!
He stole away, I tell you true,
Upon the road from Moscow.
'T is myself, quoth he, I must mind most;
So the Devil may take the hindmost.

Too cold upon the road was he,
Too hot had he been at Moscow;
But colder and hotter he may be,
For the grave is colder than Moscovy:
And a place there is to be kept in view,
Where the fire is red and the brimstone blue,

Morbleu! Parbleu!
Which he must go to,
If the Pope say true,
If he does not in time look about him ;
Where his namesake almost
He may have for his Host,
He has reckon'd too.long without him,
If that host get him in purgatory,
He won't leave him there alone with his glory ;
But there he must stay for a very long day,
For from thence there is uo stealing away
As there was on the read from Moscow."

LITERARY AND SCIENTIFIC INTELLIGENCE.

Szentpetery's Embossed Tableau of the Battle of Arbela.—At the special request of Mr. Hielbronn we were induced to visit the Egyptian Hall,
Piccadily, to view an embossed Tableau of the battle of Arbela, which is
being exhibited for the relief of the unfortunate sufferers by the late calamitous inundation in the neighbourhood of Pest, and although notices of exhibitions do not come within the scope of our Review, the transcendant
merits of this most surprising work must claim an exception in its favour.
This Tableau is a representation on copper of the battle of Arbela, taken
from the celebrated picture of Le Brun, containing not less than two hundred figures. In the embossed Tableau the figures are in alto relievo, and
are copied with the most minute accuracy of outline, position, expression,
and every minute detail. Some of them stand forth so far from the base,
and are connected with it at such slight and almost imperceptible points,
that they seem like distant statues, it is some time before we can bring ourselves to believe that they can by any possibility have been wrought from
the original flat sheet of copper, with no other tools than a hammer and
puncheon. Yet such is the fact : and such is the life-like energy of the
multitudinous group—so eagerly do they seem to wage the mortal conflict
that we are forced to admit, that in this instance the hammer and puncheon of the embosser have achieved a decided triumph over the chisel of
the sculptor. The sheet of copper on which the whole is worked is about
three feet in length, and a foot and a half in height. This sheet the artist
first heated with charcoal in order to render it malleable, and then proceeded
to force out the figures from the back with the simple implements we have
just mentioned. He then works it from the front, compressing the figures,
and finishing the details. In this tedious process no less than ten years
were consumed. The first sheet on which he worked three years proved
unsound, and he was obliged to commence a fresh one which occupied him
seven years, and it is only by the inspection of this unfinished tableau that
an idea can be formed of the indomitable industry and perseverance of the
artist, who could thus labour on unremittingly at a single piece,
supported only by the internal consciousness of his own powers and his
determination to succeed. Szentpetery is a native of Pest, and one of the
sufferers by the late disastrous inundation. As a record of the enthusiasm
of genius and its steady perseverence in a favourite pursuit, this work
would prove highly interesting, but the execution and finishing of the
details are so perfect as to render it valuable in a far higher point of view.
We understand that 5000 guineas have been offered and refused for this
exquisite gem.

THE

MONTHLY REVIEW.

JULY, 1838.

Art. I.—*Sketches of Judaism and the Jews.* By the Rev. Alexander M'Caul, D.D., of Trinity College, Dublin. London: B. Wertheim. 1838.

The rev. author of this small volume has by various former publications acquired no inconsiderable degree of celebrity as a Hebrew scholar, and as an Annotator on the Hebrew Scriptures. His knowledge of Jewish antiquities and of modern Judaism is also extensive and minute ; and especially, as regards the present condition of the *peculiar* race, will the work before us be found instructive and curious. Whether or not the author has had any other view in its composition and publication than to convey interesting information to his readers on a subject that will always engage the attention of Christians—whether or not he has exerted himself on this occasion, having his eye directed to certain political extensions of rights that have in recent years been proposed in behalf of British Jews, does not appear, so far as we have noticed, in any profession of the sort which the book contains. But we must be allowed to state, that among the deductions which the attentive reader will make on closing the volume, one of the most forcible must be, that, seeing English Judaism is still fettered by the olden Rabbinical superstitions and intolerance—still essentially subject to Talmudic laws and numerous absurd oral traditions, which are also only harmless because the Jews dare not put them publicly forward nor act upon them, an extension of political rights to that people, even to the power of legislation, would be fraught with more peril than has been anticipated by the advocates of such extension. At any rate, if not fraught with immediate or practical evil, the liberal measure alluded to, according to Dr. M'Caul's showing, would be a violation of safe and sound political principles. We do not propose to argue for or against this view of the case, but merely to extract some of the curious information contained in these Sketches, which cannot fail to renew and enhance the interest which every reader of history and every reflecting mind are ready to bestow upon the descendants of Jacob.

Every modern writer who treats of the Jews must draw many of his most striking illustrations from those who inhabit Poland. That

dismembered country is one of the most fertile as well as characteristic gardens of Judaism. It was the policy of the kings and
government of Poland for centuries to encourage and cherish the
people in question, when in all other Christian states they were
cruelly persecuted and despised. Even at this day the Polish Jews
are, according to our author, who, we learn, has travelled in that
country, the faithful and precise representatives of what they were
nearly two thousand years ago, or in the tenth century. At the
same time he describes the Polish Jews as a well-educated and
intellectual people; the terms *well-educated* and *intellectual* requiring certain limitations which we are about to notice.

The reader of the present small volume, who may not have had
his attention drawn particularly to the singular race spoken of, may,
to use the words of our author, be truly said to know only the outside
of the Jewish nation. In England people for the most part see or
hear only of two classes—rich Jews and poor Jews. " When a rich
Jew is named, they think of the funds ; and at the mention of a
poor Jew, oranges, pencils, old clothes, &c., are generally the associated ideas." But the continental traveller makes a different
classification ; for he finds that some are called enlightened, and
some bigots, as the Gentiles speak ; or, in Jewish phraseology,
there are old-fashioned—that is, Rabbinical—and new-fashioned,
Jews.

From the dispersion to the latter end of the last century, Dr.
M'Caul says, Rabbinism prevailed universally among the Jewish
nation, with the exception of the one small sect of the Karaites ; and
he adds, that the distinguishing feature of Rabbinism is, that it
asserts the transmission of oral or traditional law of equal authority
with the written law of God, at the same time that it resolves tradition into the opinions of the present time. " And, as this oral law
is most minute in its details, and altogether immutable in its decisions, it has made the intellectual and moral state of all those who
receive it almost stationary." The rise of certain reformers, or
innovators, to be sure, has led to particular variations over those who
have become their disciples. Still the truly Rabbinical Jews are
described as bearing a striking resemblance to those of whom the
New Testament speaks. They are, " acute, subtle, disputatious,
with a profound love of learning, and an uncontrollable energy in
the pursuit of knowledge." Such, says our author, is their general
character. But the learning spoken of requires to be defined.

" It is true that they are altogether ignorant of Greek and Latin literature, and consider it a sin to learn any modern language. But a nation
which has a learned language besides the vernacular dialect, an extensive
literature in that language, and which studies that learned language
almost universally,—so that it is a rare thing to meet a Jew, however
forlorn and destitute, who cannot read it fluently, and understand it at

least a little,—such a nation must be regarded as an educated and intellectual people.

" It is true they can make no pretension to Belles Lettres. The vernacular dialect of the Polish Jews is still what was formerly the language of the whole class of German Jews, and is now called *Jewish* (Jüdisch). Half a century ago it was commonly called Jewish-German (Jüdisch-Teutsch); but, this latter term now signifies good German, printed in Jewish characters; whereas Jewish is ancient German, mixed up with Hebrew and Rabbinical; and, in Poland, with a small addition of Polish. All the theological terms are Hebrew or Rabbinical; many of the names of household implements, and not a few imprecations and terms of abuse, are Polish. It is not an uncommon thing to hear the three languages in one short sentence—as, *iach gei die Beheimos umpoiyin*, ' I am going to water the cattle.' *Beheimos* (behemoth) is Hebrew; *umpoiyin* is of Polish extraction; the rest is German. This dialect, though very free from rules of grammar, and uncertain as to its orthography, possesses a tolerably extensive literature, which forms the *lecture* of the Jewesses and *ammaratzin* or unlearned Jews. Prayers, poems, dramas, legends, commentaries, and extracts from the Rabbinical writings, have been published in this dialect. Athias also published the Old Testament complete in the Jewish character; but the language approximates so nearly to good German, that this translation has never become general in Poland. The new Testament, Pentateuch, Isaiah, Psalms, &c., have been published by the London Society in the Polish-Jewish dialect. The favourite book is R. Jacob's ' Commentary on the Pentateuch and Haphtoroth,' or weekly portions of the prophets, usually known by the title ' Tsennorennah,' or the Weiber Chumash, the women's Pentateuch. This book, which is a compilation of all that is absurd and marvellous in Rabbinical lore, furnishes the Sabbath reading for the female Jewish population; and shews, on every page, the low state of religious knowledge amongst the Rabbinical Jewesses. If the Biblical citations were taken away, it might be classed with ' Tom Thumb' or ' Jack the Giant-killer.' As it stands, it appears to the Christian reader as the most inconceivable mixture of absurdity and gravity. But, after all, though the female part of the Jewish community be neglected, the Rabbinical Jews must still be regarded as an educated people."

In support of this statement that the Jews must still be regarded as an educated people, the term *Ammaratzin*, which is taken from a Hebrew word signifying " people of the land," a designation of great reproach, may be instanced. Besides, though the females are neglected, and it be held as a grave offence for any one to teach his daughter the law, yet much attention is paid to the education of male children, one of the greatest reproaches for a Rabbinical Jew being to neglect this duty; so that as a people, the middling and lower classes of the Jews seem to have more attention paid to their peculiar education than is realized in the Christian communities of most countries. Poverty among them is hardly a bar to learning. The teachers are numerous, and their terms are very low; and a Jew, with one-quarter of the means possessed by our middling tradespeople, it is asserted, would be sure to have a private tutor. Hospitality to wandering students is universal ; and, in short, amongst the Rabbinical Jews, learning ranks higher than wealth.

When treating of the learned professions, of the prevalence of learning, and the channels into which the mind of the Rabbinical Jews are directed, we find the following clear and comprehensive sketch. The writer has been speaking of the Slaughterer, who forms one of the learned professions.

" A slaughterer must be perfectly conversant with all the circumstances which make a beast clean or unclean. For this purpose, he must study the treatises on the Sh'chitah, which contain minute details as to comparative anatomy ; nor can he exercise his art until he has been examined by a Rabbi, and has obtained a certificate of his competency. Rabbi, Melammed, Reader, and Shochet, are the learned professions amongst the Rabbinic Jews ; and the existence of these offices has in every age ensured a large number of educated men amongst them. Amongst the Jews, as well as amongst every other people, the ministers of religion have been the preservers of learning. Without them they must soon have sunk into absolute barbarism. The preservation of learning without religion is impossible. Wherever there are Jewish families, they must have a Shochet, or dispense altogether with animal food, as they dare not eat the meat slaughtered by a Gentile ; and, as the Jews are greatly scattered, it follows of course that the number of Shochtim is very great. In small congregations, they also act as reader in the Synagogue, and Rabbi. They must then possess a higher degree of learning, as the business of the Rabbi is not only to give instruction, but, with the assistance of two assessors, called judges, to settle disputes, to transact the business attendant on divorces, which are of frequent occurrence, and especially to solve cases of conscience, which are very numerous on account of the intricacy of the Rabbinic laws concerning clean and unclean food, &c.

" The mere religious necessities of the people perpetuate a certain number of learned men. But, as learning is looked upon as the most meritorious of all acts, and is, according to the Rabbinical axiom, ' equal to the fulfilment of all the other commandments,' it is not confined to the officials of the Synagogue. Many of the Jewish shopkeepers and trades-people possess a highly respectable degree of Jewish learning, and are quite at home on the subject of the controversy with Christians. Many more leave the management of the shop and all worldly business to their wives, and devote themselves exclusively to study. Many Christians will be ready to say, that all this study and diligence is much ado about nothing. The absurdities and superstitions of Rabbinism are better known than its real genius and spirit. The truth is, that, amidst all its follies and absurdities, Rabbinism possesses as many monuments of genius and intellect as any other system whatever. The Rabbinical writings are also well calculated to train and exercise the understanding. The mere circumstance that they all exist in Hebrew or Chaldee accustoms the Jewish mind at once to a learned language, and necessarily forces upon it some idea of philology. The Talmud, which may be looked upon as a vast congest of canon law, abounding with the most subtle distinctions and disputations, sharpens the intellect to the utmost. The study of the Talmud has the same effect that

the study of law generally has. But the Talmud does not monopolize the
Jewish mind. Many devote themselves to the commentaries on the Scriptures, particularly to Jarchi, Aben-Ezra, and Kimchi. Any one who has
ever looked into Rosenmüller's ' Scholia' will see that these men are not
to be despised ; that, on the contrary, for acuteness and accurate knowledge
of the Hebrew text, they have never been surpassed. Aben-Ezra's and
Kimchi's ' Exposition of the Psalms' often breathe a genuine devotional
spirit. Even when they are in the wrong, as they often are, they are sure
to instruct. Jarchi's ' Commentary on the Song of Solomon,' when compared with the attempts of modern German divines, exhibits Jewish good
sense and piety in the most favourable point of view."

Among the Rabbinic schools, however, there is one analogous to
what Christians understand by the term *free-thinkers.* These are
the readers of Maimonides. They cherish a metaphysical or
rationalist turn of mind, and are fond of the words, philosopher and
philosophy. There is also a fanatical sect, known by the name
Chasidim, or Saints, as they call themselves, Poland being its cradle and seat. They very soon attract the attention of the traveller
by their external appearance, their dress being studiously slovenly
and their features wild, in some cases even almost indicative of
insanity. Their fanaticism is extreme, the mysticism of the Cabbalistic system which they study leading them to the most absurd
opinions and practices.

" The Chasidim have separate synagogues, use the prayer-book of the
Spanish Jews, which is more Cabbalistic, and have their own Rabbies.
They reverence the Talmud less, and the Sohar more, than the other
Jews, and especially profess to strive after a perfect union with God, as
their great object. To effect this, they spend much time in contemplation ;
and, in prayer, use the most extraordinary contortions and gestures,
jumping, writhing, howling, in order to exalt their mind, and do certainly
succeed in working themselves into a state little short of phrensy. Before
their devotions, they indulge freely in the use of meat and even of ardent
spirits, to promote cheerfulness, as they regard sorrow and anxiety as
peculiar hinderances to the enjoyment of union with God. Their chief
means of edification is the spending the Sabbath-day with the Tsaddik.
On Friday afternoon and evening, before the approach of the Jewish
Sabbath, waggon-loads of Jews and Jewesses, with their children, pour
in from all the neighbourhood, from a distance of thirty, forty or more
miles. The rich bring presents and their own provisions, of which the
poor are permitted to partake. The chief entertainment is Saturday afternoon, at the meal which the Jews call the third meal, during which the
Tsaddik sagt Torah, that is, he extemporises a sort of moral-mystical-
cabbalistical discourse, which his followers receive as the dictates of immediate inspiration. For the benefit of those who are too far removed to
come on the Saturday, the Tsaddik makes journeys through his district,
when he lodges with some rich member of the sect, and is treated with all
the respect due to one who stands in immediate communication with Deity.
He then imposes penances on those whose consciences are burdened with

guilt; dispenses amulets and slips of parchment with cabbalistic sentences written on them to those who wish exemption from sickness and danger, or protection against the assaults of evil spirits; and pronounces on the sick and the barren his benediction, which is supposed to remove all infirmities, and to procure the fulfilment of every wish."

From the principles of their faith, as published by themselves, their excessive credulity and doctrinal errors may be known. One of the most extravagant tenets renders them the most subservient tools possible of their teachers; for, it is said, " the most important of all principles is unreserved devotion to the Tsaddik; never to turn aside from his precepts; to reject wisdom and science, yea, one's own understanding, and to receive only what the Tsaddik says. Even when one thinks that the Tsaddik is acting contrary to the law, he is still to believe that the Tsaddik is in the right; he must therefore reject his own understanding, and rest confidently on that of the Rabbi." This is excellent priestcraft; and, if our author's representations be correct, is not essentially different from the tenets of the generality of Rabbinical Jews—not even essentially different, as he in his last chapter endeavours to show, from the doctrines exemplified in a late Circular Letter from the Chief Rabbi of London, which has not been publicly impugned by the people over whom he presides.

As a religious system our author regards Rabbinism as partaking of good as well as of what is bad. But to say the least of it, and this is no new declaration, it must be a most burdensome code, both as respects doctrinal knowledge and daily practice. One of the most detestable features in the system regards the condition of females and the respect entertained for their mental rights. We have already noticed and read something about the education of Jewesses.

" The progress of Jewish reform has created schools for Jewish female children, both free schools for the poor, and establishments of a higher order for the wealthy. But who ever heard of a female school amongst old-fashioned Rabbinical Jews? or who ever saw a Rabbinical schoolmistress, or a Rabbinical Jewess who gained a livelihood by teaching? The female schools in London, in Germany, in Warsaw have all emanated from the power of Christian example, or the direct influence of the Government; they are not the natural offspring of Rabbinism, and consequently where this system still reigns, as in the East, and Poland generally, they are not to be found. Very many of the Jewish female children do not learn to read at all. Those that do learn are not taught by one of their own sex, but by a melammed, or a rabbi, or a tutor. In very rare instances they learn to translate Hebrew, but in general they only learn to read the words, that they may be able to repeat prayers which they do not understand. In Poland, they learn besides to read the vernacular dialect, and frequently also to write it, as they are much employed in shopkeeping, and sometimes manage all the worldly business, that the husband may give himself unreservedly to the study of the Talmud; and this last circumstance shows, if it were not abundantly attested by the high degree of mental cultivation and accomplishment commonly found amongst the Jewesses in Germany, that this want of education is not to be ascribed to any defect in the Jewish female mind, but to some external cause. The spirit of Rabbinism it is which degrades womankind, and does not suffer her to exercise the faculties which God has given. *Rabbinism lays it down as an axiom, that to study the law of God is no part of a woman's duty, and that to teach his daughters the Word of God is no part of paternal obligation.* 'Women and slaves are exempt from the study of the law.' ' A woman who learns the law has a reward, but it is not equal to the reward which the man has, *because she is not commanded to do so.* But though the woman has a reward, the wise men have commanded that no man should teach his daughter the law, for this reason, that the majority of women have not got a mind fitted for study, but pervert the words of the law on account of the poverty of their intellect. Every one who teaches his daughter the law is considered as guilty as if he taught her transgression. But this applies only to the oral law. As to the written law, he is not to teach her systematically, but if he has taught her, he is not to be considered as having taught her transgression.' *Rabbinism teaches that a woman is unfit to give legal evidence, and classes her amongst those who are incapacitated either by mental or moral deficiencies.* ' There are ten sorts of disqualification, and every one, in whom any one of them is found, is disqualified from giving evidence; and these are they—women, slaves, children, idiots, the deaf, the blind, the wicked, the despised, relations, and those interested in their testimony.' *Rabbinism excludes women from being counted as part of the Synagogue congregation. Unless there be minian, that is, a congregation of ten, there can be no public worship of God,* but the Rabbies have decided, ' that these ten must all be men, free, and adult;' ·so that if all the Jewesses in the world could be gathered into one synagogue, they would all count as nothing, and unless there were ten men present, the minister of the synagogue would not read prayers for them.

" *Rabbinism teaches, that to be a woman is as great a degradation as to be a heathen or a slave, and provides the same form of thanksgiving for deliverance from womanhood as from heathenism or slavery.* The Jew says every day in his prayers, ' Blessed art thou, O Lord, our God ! King of the universe, who hath not made me a heathen. Blessed art thou, O Lord our God ! King of the universe, who hath not made me a slave. Blessed art thou, O Lord our God ! King of the universe, who hath not made me a woman.' "

On the subject of Jewish reform, which to a certain extent has been carried in modern and even recent times, Dr. M'Caul has a good deal to say, and instances several individuals and circumstances that have been especially operative in this matter. Moses Mendelsohn at no very distant period was the means of introducing among his brethren a taste for what the old-fashioned Rabbinical Jews did and still do consider profane literature and epicurean books, as Christian books are called by them. The study of German and its most celebrated authors became popular amongst his disciples, and hence a great change, intellectual and civil, could not but be the consequence on the part of such students. Other Jews eminent for their boldness or their genius started up about the beginning of the great social and political *movement* in Europe of the last century. A Jewish periodical was even started at Königsberg about the year 1783, entitled " The Gatherer," which must be regarded as having been symptomatic of mental revolution, and as offering a new field for the exhibition of Jewish talent. It even received articles upon the abuses of Judaism, plans for reform, essays on literature, translations, &c. The appearance of several extraordinary Jews about the same period, men eminent in science and learning, aided the efforts of the Journalists. Nor among the impulses given in the same direction ought those of the French National Assembly and of Napoleon to be forgotten. But the result of all these movements at the present day, according to our author, seems not to have been so great and beneficial as has often been maintained—rationalism, as it is called, which is akin to infidelity, in so far as religion is concerned, having taken the place of Judaism, although the practical effects upon the race as citizens has been to raise them in the social scale, at the expense, however, of their nationality; and therefore Dr. M'Caul does not think that after all the gain of the sometimes highly lauded reform has been very great, looking as he, and many others do, to a greater destiny for this peculiar people than consists in mere deliverance from oppression and contumely. Even Judaism as taught in the modern Jewish catechisms, where reform is supposed to have gone farthest, does not assume an attractive appearance as painted in the volume before us. We quote some passages explanatory of our author's views on this subject.

" The first paroxysm of Jewish reform was very violent. Whilst it lasted, the Jews, as is confessed by Jost, utterly renounced the Talmud and all its observances. They thought of nothing but liberty of conscience, and breathed nothing but good-will to all mankind. Some of its effects are still visible. The reformed Jews are all outwardly, and, I doubt not, many of them in their hearts, very different from the orthodox professors of Rabbinism. But what has all the reform, that has made such a mighty noise in Germany for the last thirty years, really effected for the religious and moral improvement of the Jewish nation? Has it delivered them from the absurdities and antisocial doctrines of the Talmud? Has it helped them to make a bold and decided protest against the traditional adulterations of the pure and holy law of Moses? Has it stirred them up to put forth a frank and honest confession of their faith, exhibiting the differences between them and the old Talmudists? Not one of all these things. Jewish reform has just done as much for real improvement as the Council of Trent did for reformation. It has talked a great deal—it has done nothing. I am led to this conclusion from the perusal of some modern Jewish catechisms. I have now before me two of very considerable authority. The one is the authorized catechism for Bavaria, as appears from the title-page—' Manual of the Mosaic Religion. Compiled by Dr. Alexander Behr, under the superintendence and guidance of the Supreme Rabbi, Abraham Bing, of Wurtzburg; examined and recognised by the Rabbinate of Furth, and several rabbies of consideration. With the most gracious privilege of his Royal Majesty. Munich, 1826.' In the preface, also, it is stated that it was published by royal mandate, at the public expense; and that a royal circular was issued to all Jewish schools, commanding its introduction. The second is entitled, ' The Doctrines of the Mosaic Religion, by I. Johlson, teacher of religion at the Israelitish Congregational School, at Frankfort-on-the-Main; the third genuine and improved edition. Frankfort, A.M. 1829.' Which also appears, from the preface, to have obtained the approbation of many of the civil and ecclesiastical powers, and the thanks of the German Confederation. These catechisms, then, will tell us the principles in which the Jewish youth, of an important part of Germany, are educated; and will help us to conjecture the sentiments of the next Jewish generation. A stranger jumble of palpable inconsistency was, perhaps, never presented to the public; and the approbation of such works by public authority does not lead us to form a very high estimate of the state of Rabbinic learning amongst the Rationalist divines of Germany. These catechisms first lay down the divine authority of the Talmud; they then teach the relative duties on anti-talmudical principles; and lastly, confirm these antitalmudic doctrines by mutilated Talmudic authorities, which if taken with their context prove the contrary of that which they are cited to confirm!"

Dr. M'Caul goes on to notice particularly some of the doctrines of these catechisms to support his general assertion, which we pass over that we may come to English Judaism at the present day, which he maintains is still the religion of the Talmud; and the Talmud, he holds, was the source of all the folly, intolerance, and superstition of former Judaism. He adds, " Reforms, and rumours of reforms, have unsettled the minds of the Jews themselves, and induced many amongst them to imagine Judaism is no longer what it used to be; and thus some are led, with the most perfect good faith, to deny some of the essentials of their religion, and to attribute to it a measure of charity, and a freedom from superstition, not warranted by fact."

To show that the Talmud, however, is not even now an obsolete authority in England, he has recourse to certain sources of evidence, which are sufficiently remarkable, and, considering the difficulty of obtaining access to such documents, certainly are startling, unless explained away in the same public manner in which the writer impugns them.

In the first place, from the last catechism published in this country, our author says, that, after mentioning the five books of Moses, these words occur, " We also, from the same source, receive, as sacred and authentic, a large number of traditions not committed to writing, but transmitted by word of mouth down to later times."

The catechism goes on to say that these traditions form the
"Mishna," and next that, "in addition to this, we are guided by
the explications of the later schools of pious and learned Rabbins,
constituting what is now known by the name of the Talmud, or
Gemara." This looks very like the ancient system of Judaism.
But a document of more secret authority is described as having
fallen into Dr. M'Caul's hands that is still more illustrative and
curious. He calls it one of the Acts of the Jewish *Beth din,* or tribunal, in London. It relates to some quarrel with the Jews of
Southampton on account of an alleged violation of ceremony on the
part of the *Slaughterer* of that Jewish community, an officer, as we
have already heard, of no ordinary importance. The Slaughterer is
by name Joseph Abraham Goldman. We quote the letter referring
to this subject of the Rabbi to the Jewish congregations in England,
on which our author takes occasion to comment closely.

"' By the help of God

"' The Rav. the Gaon, the president of the tribunal of the congregations of the Church of Israel (may their Rock and Redeemer preserve
them), which are in London, and also in the congregations which are in
the country, and his righteous tribunal, hereby proclaim and make known,
that Mr. Joseph Abraham Goldman, who was formerly slaughterer and
meat-examiner in the holy congregation of Bristol, and afterwards in
Southampton, has, some months since, been convicted, both by the Rav.
the Gaon, the president of the tribunal, and also before his righteous
tribunal (may their Rock and their Redeemer preserve them), of having
broken his solemn engagement of striking of hands; and, therefore, the
said Mr. Joseph Abraham Goldman is inadmissible to give testimony or
to take an oath, and much less is he to be believed in matters of slaughtering or examining the slaughtered animals: therefore, every one who is
surnamed with the name of Israel, will take heed not to eat of his
slaughtering. Further, even the vessels of those householders who eat of
his slaughtering are unlawful, as the vessels in which carrion and torn
meat is boiled. And every one that hearkeneth to our words, upon him
shall come the blessing of good, and he shall be written and sealed to a
good life at the festial of the New Year, which is coming upon us for
good, together with every one that is written to life in Jerusalem.

"' The little one, Solomon, son of the Gaon, our teacher and our
master, Rav., Rabbi Hirsch (the memory of the righteous is blessed),
dwelling here in the aforsaid holy congregation, and its precincts.'"

Now, Dr. M'Caul argues that this document becomes particularly interesting, by being illustrative of Judaism at the present
moment in England,—presupposing, as the letter does, that the
Talmud is a book of divine authority; for in it we are told the
ceremonies of slaughtering are detailed and appointed, being, in fact,
a mysterious science which requires a licence from the Rabbi.
Mr. J. A. Goldman's infraction of the law is not explained, but the

difficulty of performing all its injunctions may be gathered from the next extract.

" Maimonides, in his treatise on the subject, defines the mode of performing the operation thus—' On which part of the animal is the slaughtering to be effected ? On the windpipe, from the edge of the uvula downwards as far as the top of the extremity of the lungs, as these parts are situated when the beast stretches out its neck to feed: this is the place of the slaughtering in the windpipe ; and all the part outside which answers to this place is called the neck. If the beast forces itself, and stretches out its neck much, or if the slaughterer force the signs, and draws them upwards, and he slaughter at the right part of the neck, but afterwards it be found that the windpipe or œsophagus is not cut at the right place, then it is a doubtful case of carrion.' In the same place he defines, that the knife or implement must have no gap in it : ' But if there be anything like a furrow in the edge of the instrument wherewith the slaughtering is effected, even though the furrow be the least possible, the slaughtering is unlawful.' But besides any flaw in the knife, there are other things which may render the slaughtering unlawful, and which are considered as the great essentials of the Rabbinic act: ' First ; if the operator makes a pause of a certain length before the act is completed. Second ; if the throat be cut at a single blow, as with a sword. Third ; if the knife enters too deep and bis hidden. Fourth; when the knife slips up or down from the right place. Fifth ; when the windpipe or the œsophagus is torn, and comes out before the act is completed.' When all these conditions of lawfulness have been satisfied, the internal structure of the animal must be examined, and the result of this examination may be to pronounce that the meat is not fit for a Jew to eat. These few out of the multitudinous decisions and definitions of the oral law may shew the necessity of having the slaughterer first examined as to his competency, and will throw some light upon the chief Rabbi's letter. The power of the Rabbi to depose a slaughterer, and the course which the chief Rabbi has actually pursued in causing his sentence to be proclaimed in all the synagogues in England, are warranted by the following passage :—' If a slaughterer, who has not had his slaughtering-knife examined before a wise man [a Rabbi], slaughters by himself, his knife must be examined. If it be found in good order, he is to be excommunicated, because he may depend upon himself another time when it has a gap in it, and yet slaughter therewith. But if it be found to have a gap, he is to be deposed from his office and excommunicated, and proclamation is to be made that all the meat which he has slaughtered is carrion.' "

Our author well remarks that the intellectual condition of a people who can submit to such doctrines and practices must be in fetters ; but this is not all, for where Jewish meat is subject to such ceremonies, and so liable to become unclean and carrion, the Jewish poor labour under excessive hardships. Their meat must be dear, and when we consider that they dare not partake of all the food provided in workhouses and hospitals, how hard must be the case of many a destitute, diseased, or aged member of the race !

Every Jew has not the benefit and privileges of being near rich and benevolent brethren in London or other large cities.

But our author does not stop here; for he maintains that, according to Talmudic law, oral declaration would not be the only severity to which the Slaughterer at Southampton would have to submit had the Rabbi and his tribunal the power to follow out their principles.

"The law is:—' That if an Israelite does not know the five things which invalidate the art of slaughtering, as we have explained, and slaughters by himself it is unlawful both for himself and others to eat of that which he has slaughtered; for this case is much the same as that of doubtful carrion, and he that eats of it a quantity equal to an olive is to be flogged with the flogging of rebellion'—that is, without measure or mercy. But with respect to the Southampton Jews there can be no doubt at all. The chief Rabbi in London, and his righteous tribunal, have officially declared, that their food is no better than carrion; and consequently they are liable, whenever the commands of the oral law can be safely executed, to be visited with the aforesaid punishment. At present, Christian laws protect the Southampton Jews from the intolerance of their own religion; and as severity cannot be brought to bear upon the offenders, this letter contains another expedient for bringing them to submission; it promises blessings and life to those other Jews who will treat their Southampton brethren as excommunicate. Twice over the letter says, 'And every one that hearkeneth to our words, upon him shall come the blessing of good, and he shall be written and sealed to a good life at the festial of the New Year, which is coming upon us for good, together with every one that is written to life in Jerusalem.' The letter here takes the Rabbinical Jews by their weak side. Every such person looks forward with fear and trembling to the New Year, for the oral law teaches that, 'As the merits and sins of a man are weighed at the hour of his death, so likewise every year, on the festival of New Year's day, the sins of every one that cometh into the world are weighed against his merits. Every one who is found righteous is sealed unto life. Every one who is found wicked is sealed unto death. But the judgment of the intermediate class is suspended until the Day of Atonement.' The principles according to which this judgment is supposed to be conducted are, that ' If a man's merits exceed his sins, he is righteous. If his sins exceed his merits, he is wicked. If they be half and half, he is a middling or intermediate person.' The consequence is, that as the New Year approaches, and especially in the month of Elul, in which the letter is dated, the Rabbinical Jews become more and more careful in observing their rites and ceremonies, that the balance of the account may not be against them. The Rabbi, however, promises them, if they will hearken to his words, that they shall receive a blessing, and be sealed to life. And this shews us at least, the estimate which the Rabbi and his righteous tribunal form of the state of the Jewish mind in England. They clearly take it for granted that the congregations to whom they wrote would be influenced by these superstitious feelings connected with the New Year—that is, they believe that the Jews of England are still under the influence of the Talmud."

It is quite clear that nothing but the Talmud or some other Jewish law, not recognised by the English code, can authorize the proceedings of the Rabbi and his tribunal in the case under consideration. What right have they to declare, for example, that Mr. Goldman is " inadmissible to give testimony or to take an oath ?" It may be said, and of course it is true, that this denunciation can only reach him as among themselves, and in the Congregation. But the very fact that such a sentence among themselves is tolerated is proof that Talmudism is powerful in England, and that it can erect a tribunal which the English constitution and its national laws never have recognised. Where then does the Judaism of this country differ from that of Poland, of Morocco, or of Palestine? It is admitted that there are many respectable and enlightened Jews in London. The Portuguese Jews have long been held in high esteem, and our author says they are now endeavouring to effect a public renunciation of some parts of Judaism. But while the Talmudic system itself remains in force through the nation, while the conduct of the Rabbi in the Southampton affair is not disputed or repudiated, what are we to think but that the other absurd superstitions and intolerant laws of oral and traditional origin would be observed as implicitly, even although greater interests and principles were at stake? Our author concludes with certain home-thrusts, which ought to be disposed of by the next advocate in the House of Commons who may undertake to plead the political rights of the Jews, as entitling them to a seat in that legislative assembly.

" If the laws respecting the slaughtering of animals, and the sentence of Rabbinic tribunals, be in force, and according to the chief Rabbi's letter they are so, then the intolerant laws respecting idolaters and Gentiles are also in force. Then all Gentiles who study in the law, or keep a Sabbath-day, are guilty of death; then it is unlawful to help a drowning idolater; it is lawful to kill an apostate Jew, either by force or by fraud, as is most convenient; there is no such thing as marriage amongst Gentiles; and, whenever the Jews have the power, it will be their duty to convert all nations by force, and to put all who refuse to the sword. It is not meant to charge any particular individual of the Jewish nation with holding these principles, but if the Talmud be true and binding, and that it is so the last Jewish catechism published in this country asserts, and the chief Rabbi's letter implies, these are the tenets and doctrines of Judaism, and hitherto the members of the Jewish persuasion have not renounced them. They still profess a religion which professes that these doctrines are divine. If their profession be sincere, then they really hold, and no doubt are prepared to act upon, these principles. If their profession be insincere, the sooner they renounce it the better. They will have more peace in their own consciences, and will contribute in no small degree to restore their nation to that position to which their origin, their talents, and the benefits conferred upon the world by their forefathers, so well entitle them."

ART. II.—*Woman's Wit; or, Love's Disguises. A Play, in Five Acts.*
By JAMES SHERIDAN KNOWLES, Author of "Virginius," "The
. Hunchback," &c. London: Moxon. 1838.

OF this new play from the pen of our finest dramatic writer of the
present age, we judge solely after a perusal in the closet, not having
had the benefit of witnessing its representation on the stage; and,
therefore, it is very probable that our opinion of it would be considerably altered or modified, were it made up from different or two-
fold advantages. As it is, we proceed to give an honest judgment
according to the best of our opportunities.

We could almost wish that Sheridan Knowles would re-write
" Woman's Wit; or, Love's Disguises:" at any rate that he would
be at the pains to prune it of some obvious blemishes that do
not seem necessary even to the present caste of the piece. And yet
it is so probable, were it to undergo any degree of remodelling, not
to say regeneration, that it would suffer in the crucible, that we must
be content and grateful for the production as it is; because, most
certainly, the beauties and excellences outweigh the amount of the
blemishes and defects, and indeed so much preponderate as must
reconcile a fastidious critic to its present shape. The drawbacks,
however, must not be overlooked by us.

The play contains two stories—two heroines and two heroes; the
heroines, be it borne in mind, attracting and concentrating the reader's
interest far more than the corresponding specimens presented of the
lords of the creation. And this, in fact, is ever the case with our
dramatist, who is pre-eminently a " Woman's man." But the two
stories do not very naturally coalesce or serve to develope or set off
one another. The one is tragical in its character, the other comical.
Now, although we have high authority for this sort of union, it is
not usual to constitute the former an underplot to the latter; and
yet such is the case in " Woman's Wit." Again, both stories, and
the two taken together, labour under strong improbabilities. We
must say that " Love's Disguises" is a misnomer; for never surely
were there such short-sighted lovers met with as the pair of heroes
already referred to, who cannot see through the thin veil assumed by
the pair of lady-loves. One thing is certain, that the reader of the
play, long before it reaches half way, apprehends what must be its
issue. To many it will be a fault not inferior to any yet noticed, that
much space is wasted and many words spent without advancing the
action of the piece, or enlarging the reader's conception of the
characters.

To find after all this, that the piece as a whole is not only tolerable but admirable, that the faults act but as specks to set off surrounding and superabundant beauties, to indicate something like
wanton power, must surely be equivalent to the highest proof in favour

of the work. And such assuredly is the triumph which Mr. Knowles has achieved. It is a triumph quite worthy of himself—of him who led the van in the endeavour to rescue the modern stage of England from the possession of puerile, effeminate, immoral, and melodramatic trash.

There is much of originality displayed in the conception of " Woman's Wit." There is novelty in the general plan, and in the several plots ; there is also novelty both in the characters and the language throughout, barring the mannerism of the author. Besides all this, there is a constant strain of fresh and vigorous thought. The author's fancy is sound, his sentiments always *wholesome*, so to speak, the expression adding the zest which raciness never fails to confer. No writer, when love is the principal or sole theme, was ever more disdainful of tawdriness, or more felicitous in striving to avoid the most distant approach to it ; for Mr. Knowles possesses the rare faculty of making the tender passion, even when described by its martyrs, and its willing, fond victims, a text for evoking ennobling declamation, or moral teaching. These few general remarks may be allowed to introduce an outline of the play itself, and certain illustrative extracts, upon which we shall offer the opinions that may suggest themselves as we go along.

Our readers will not be much misled if they fix the story some time in the reign of England's merry monarch, although we have not detected anything in itself that relates to any precise date. The scene of action is confined to the Metropolis and Greenwich,—the whole turning, as before hinted, upon the loves and fates of two young ladies. Lord Athunree is the villain of the piece ; and in the first scene we hear the following of him :—

> " He is a libertine. He hath been much
> Abroad. That dance, I will be bound, is ware
> Of his importing. Yes ; a libertine !
> A man of pleasure—in the animal
> Ignoble sense of the term—that owns no curb
> Of honour, generosity, or truth ;
> Nor hath a single grace, except the nerve—
> A contradiction which would make one question
> That valour is of itself a thing to boast of—
> To vouch the wrong he does, and stand by it !"

This is said at a ball which takes place in the house of Sir William Sutton, a right sort of old gentleman, and the uncle of Hero, " the city maid," in honour of whom the revel is given, and with whom the libertine lord is at the time dancing. A high and honourably-minded knight, Sir Valentine de Grey by name, is deeply enamoured of the wealthy and charming Hero, and she is the same in return, but secretly and under the guise of much coquetting. Lord Athunree is aware of the Knight's earnestness and purity of intention, and to chagrin him manœuvres to obtain the young lady's hand during a free dance. In fact he has long been laying siege in the same quarter, though conscious of making no progress. His dexterity, however, and the misunderstandings that he has caused on the occasion in question, are the subject of his especial boast to one of his own sort.

" *Lord Athunree.*   I did dance with her just now.
Felton.   Fair Hero ?
Lord Athunree.   Yes ; I did dance with her a free
And liberal dance—the dance of contact, else
Forbid—abandoning to the free hand
The sacred waist ! while face to face, till breath
Doth kiss with breath, and eye embraceth eye.
Your transed coil relaxing, straight'ning, round
And round in wavy measure, you entwine
Circle with circle, till the swimming brain
And panting heart in swoony lapse give o'er !
    Felton.   I know ; that foreign dance thou didst bring home.
    Lord Athunree.   The very same ; I taught it her, and first
Did dance with her to-night.
    Felton.   I had admir'd
To see you.
    Lord Athunree.   Had you not, I had admir'd
The card-room kept you.   Give you joy—you won !
But to the dance.   The evening half was out
And still he held her ear.
    Felton.   Sir Valentine ?
    Lord Athunree.   Who else ? who else that seat pre-eminent
By her fair side had held in spite of me.
I watch'd for my occasion, and it came ;
Some friend did crave a moment's audience ; ere
'Twas done, her waist was in my custody ;
Her white arm hanging from my shoulder, where
Her hand did freely couch.   ' Your game goes well !'
I whisper'd her ; ' Play boldly, and 'tis your's :
The measure this to set the outline off !
Give sway to thy rich figure !   Abandon thee
To the spirit of the dance !   Let it possess thee !
Float thee as air were footing for thee ! stud
Thy cheeks with smiles of fire, and give thine eye
The lightning's dazzling play ! fix them on mine,
That each do feed the other's, like to tongues
With converse waking converse !'
    Felton.   Well ?—I see
Thy drift !
    Lord Athunree.   Thou should'st have seen the issue on't—
While, like a pupil at a task he loves,
Whose aptitude with eager will outstrips
His master's bidding, she was twenty times

The thing I wished her!   How she rose and sank
With springy instep, while her yielding waist—
Well as her waving neck, her beauteous head—
Did show her fair and falling shoulders off!
A world she look'd and moved of passionate
Quick sense—of loveliness and joyousness—
And I, be sure, did show its reigning lord!
Nor with the measure did dominion cease;
But when her drooping lids, relaxed steps,
Disparted lips, and colour vanishing,
Gave note she must give o'er—her languid form,
Close girdled by my arm, her hand in mine,
Her cheek for pillow on my shoulder laid,
I led her to a couch, where courtesy
Of course admitted tendance!"

This was enough to offend a less sensitive and more guileful personage than Sir Valentine; so that when Hero, unconscious of having done wrong,—for, throughout the mazy dance, she had been thinking of him alone,—perceives his humour, she employs various little stratagems, such as the fair know how to use, with a view to *bring him to*; such as dropping her glove—expressing aloud her wish that she had a chair, and the like, without, however, enlisting the courteous services of her true lover, who keeps his seat, having his arms folded, and brows knitted, as if he wished " eyes could do the office of the lightning." At length the ball is at an end, and Hero and her companion Emily are retiring from it, the former wondering sadly why Sir Valentine does not see " her home," as he had done before.   But ere the subject terminates the various parties meet, and in the course of an exceedingly spirited dialogue, (the scene as a whole exhibits first-rate talents, although it does not do much to the progress of the piece in regard to incident or to action,) Hero begins to show the mettle she is made of.

>   " *Felton.*   Are you not fond of dancing, then?
>   *Sir Valentine.*   I am—
>   Innocent pastime taken innocently
>   In honest mood!—But there are natures, Sir,
>   That should eschew it—which 'tis pernicious to—
>   As wine, that 's mirth to some, to some is madness!
>   I find no fault with dancing!   'Tis an act
>   Sets beauty off, proportion, grace; when these
>   Are too set off by modesty.   For men,
>   And women more especially, of the vein
>   That 's opposite, I'd have them lookers on—
>   For their own sakes first—next for the sake of those
>   Who, what they'd blush to do, do grieve to see
>   Enacted.
>   *Felton.*   Was there any dance to-night
>   Offended you?"

" *Hero.*   Perhaps some lady, whom the gentleman
Himself did dance with, and some other noted—
    Sir Valentine.   No lady, Madam, that did dance with me.
Who yields to me her hand shall ne'er forget
Herself—at least by my o'erstepping. She
Shall find I know the honour that she does me ;
See in the freedom of the frolic measure
My reverence for her sex attending her ;
And then be handed to her seat again,
For mine own credit sake if not for her's,
By all approv'd, as gracefully come off
In partnery of honest joyance !
No lady, Madam, that did dance with me.
    Lord Athunree.   The plague repay him for the lesson he
So freely reads me—in her presence too !
    Hero.   Wilt please you name the lady gave offence ?
    Sir Valentine.   'Twere a presumptuous act for my poor tongue.
But if you know her, you must know her beauty,
Wherein I ne'er met fair to liken to her,
And that more fittingly shall name her for me.
A noble stature, stopping there where sex
Would have it reach, and bid it go no farther ;
A head of antique mould, magnificent
As may consist with softness and with sweetness ;
Features, advertisement of thoughts and moods,
Wishes and fancies, such as it beseems
To lodge with chastity and tenderness
In sumptuous palace of rich loveliness ;
And limbs of mould and act therewith consorting,
Making a paragon of symmetry !—
Gods, to such homeliness of use perverted,
As properties, to them were homeliness,
Should spurn to be applied to !"

Our readers will reasonably think that we have afforded sufficient
proofs of the excellent qualities of this first scene ; but off or on the
stage, what we have still to quote from it must carry admiration to
a higher pitch.   Think of the effect which consummate skill and
power in the art of personation will lend to the following :—

        Sir Valentine goes out, followed by Felton.
    Hero.   A most strange gentleman !—an oddity !
I took him for a man of sense,—didn't you ?
A fanciful and churlish gentleman !
Looks sour because another man looks pleased !
Lord Athunree, will see my carriage brought
Close to the door before I venture out,
If not to tax your gallantry too much ?
    Lord Athunree.   I fly to do it.   [*Goes out.*
    Hero.   Let me weep a momen
Upon your neck.—There ! I am better now,
Are my eyes red ?

Emily.   Not much.
Hero.   I will appear
To have been laughing! Laughter bringeth tears.
Most excellent!—you should have kept it tho'
For another time! I have not strength to laugh!
As 'tis, I am so weak, I laugh and cry.   *Re-enter Athunree.*
Lord Athunree, your courtesy has lost you.
A most facetious story?
    Lord Athunree.   Tell it me.
    Hero.   Tell it you! Tell it! I am dead already
With bearing it, and must not here't again,
Would I go home to night. A little plague,
To make me laugh, and know that I should cry,
For lack of very strength.—Come, let us go!
A charming ball! Fair night—most happy night?
I'll find a time to make *you* cry with laughing. [*To Emily.*
A charming night—a very charming night!"

In the second Act we are made acquainted, in some measure, with the second pair of lovers, Walsingham and Helen Mowbray; but the latter, through the base attempts of Lord Athunree and a hireling wretch, Lewson, has become degraded in Walsingham's estimation; for she has been seen issuing, in the face of day, from a roof that shelters aught but innocence, in company too with the libertine lord; and although to this same infamous house Helen has gone on a forged tale of misery, and escapes untarnished; all is done by the contrivance of that libertine, who manages to exhibit himself as her deliverer. Afterwards, when questioned, however, the villain, by innuendo and evasion, impugns her to the fullest convincing of her true lover. Upon this, disdaining to defend herself by speech, Walsingham, to his fancy, loses all trace of her, although in the guise of a stripling, named Eustace, he very often meets her and opposes her in exercise at a fencing-master's; he having it in mind to acquire such skill in handling the rapier as may some day enable him to chastise Lord Athunree, who is a very master of the art; and Eustace, we may presume, affecting the society of her former lover, and hoping by some means to disabuse him by other than a hasty disclosure, or mere disclaimers and protestations. This effect Eustace labours with great ingenuity and earnestness to produce upon Walsingham, but in vain. He mourns grievously over the fallen one, but the horrid conviction has sunk deep and is permanent. We cannot conveniently do anything like justice by extracts to the parts in which this tragical pair figure in the earlier scenes, although they are touching and effective, if one can just allow himself to overlook Walsingham's stupidity in not perceiving that Helen and Eustace are identically the same.

To return to Hero, she is determined to be *upsides* with her testy and precise lover. She thus addresses her uncle,—

" Look you, uncle !
I'll make the saucy traitor feel my power,
Or I will break my heart !   He think me fair—
I thank him !   Well-proportioned—very much
Beholden to him !   Dignified and graceful—
A man of shrewd perception !   very !—send him
On expedition of discovery !
   Sir William.   Whom mean you, Hero?
   Hero.   Whom ?—Sir Valentine !
He has made his bow !   Indeed, a gracious one—
A stately, courtly, condescending one !
Ne'er may I courtesy, if he bow not lower !
I'll bring him to his knees as a spoiled child
With uplift hands that asketh pardon, then
Command him up, and never see me more !
   Sir William.   Why, how hath this befallen ?
   Hero.   I did not dance
To please him !   No, Sir !   He is a connoisseur
In dancing !—hath a notion of his own
Of a step !   In carriage, attitude, has taste,
Dainty as palate of an epicure,
Which, if you hit not to a hair, disgust
Doth take the place of zest !   He is sick of me !
My feet the frolic measure may indulge,
But not my heart—mine eye, my cheek, my lip,
Must not be cognizant of what I do—
As wood and marble could be brought to dance,
And look like wood and marble !   I shall teach him
Another style !"

She inquires of Sir William if he will help her out in the scheme
she has concocted with a view to bring Sir Valentine to his senses,
and to humble himself before her ; and the old uncle promises to do
anything for her that may be done " in reason ;" to which Hero
replies,—

" Can do in reason !   In what reason ?   There
Are fifty kinds of reason.   There 's a fool's reason,
And a wise man's reason, and a knave's reason, and
An honest man's reason, and an infant's reason,
And reason of a grandfather—but there's
A reason 'bove them all, and that alone
Can stand me now in stead—a woman's reason !
Wilt thou be subject unto me in that ?"

The third Act is a capital one ; sentiment, situation, dialogue,
and action are excellent throughout.   Hero's stratagem is to assume the garb and character of a Quakeress, under the name of
Ruth Mapleson, and with the assistance of Clever, who becomes an
Obadiah, she succeeds beyond expectation.   She retires to her

country-house at Greenwich, to which, by Obadiah's characteristic policy and apparent simplicity, Sir Valentine is induced to repair. He is led to believe that Ruth is niece also to Sir William Sutton, that she is as beautiful as Hero, and though in every respect, as far as exterior goes, the image and even superior of that fickle and giddy one, that their minds, dispositions, and virtues are as different as day is from night,—Ruth of course being, according to Obadiah, all that Sir Valentine ever desired. We must be lavish with our extracts here. Hero enters in disguise.

> " *Hero.*   Well ?   What's your will ?
> *Sir Valentine.*   Forgive me, lady, if,
> With occupation of mine eyes, awhile
> I did forget the office of my tongue
> To give thee 'custom'd salutation.
> Still would I gaze, nor speak ; art what thou seem'st ?
> *Hero.*   What seem I, friend ?
> *Sir Valentine.*   Likeness—unlikeness !   A thing
> Most different—and yet the very same !
> What I would give averment of most strong—
> Again most strong deny !   The form of the bane,
> With the sweet virtue of the antidote !
> The rose was canker'd yesterday, to-day
> Freshness and soundness to the very core !
> Oh beauty ! that doth know its proper pride,
> And nothing deigns to ask to set it off
> Except simplicity, that offers nought,
> Yet all that's due performs ! I have not liv'd
> Till now !—I have but dealt with shows of life,
> Automatons, that do not know themselves,
> But act from causes are no part of them !
> But here is nature's mechanism—mind
> And soul—a body fitting them, informing
> With motions of their own.
> *Hero.*   Friend, art thou mad ?''

She insists that he is mad, irrational, or regardless of truth,—

> " And sooth to say, thy dress of vanity,
> Thy looks of wildness, and thy air assur'd,
> Where one who knew propriety would feel
> Disturbance—this abrupt intrusion, which
> Nor leave, nor introduction, nor acquaintance
> Doth justify—approve thee void of truth,
> Unwise, or mad !—if none of these, a man
> Of cloddish nature, base and ignorant !
> *Sir Valentine.*   Oh ! say not cloddish nature ! Say not base
> Nor ignorant ! It is the dignity
> Of man, that the bright stars do tempt his mind
> To scan the empyrean where they sit,

Plac'd infinite beyond terrestrial reach,
And scan their uses and their essences,—
High argument of his affinity
To him that made them, and the immortal light
That shall outlast this filmy shadowy sphere
Whereon they look and smile! 'Twas told to me
That thou wast perfect fair—I doubted that,
For I had found, methought, the paragon
Of beauty's wealth in woman! then 'twas said
That thou wast wise—I wish'd thee that, for still,
Tho' oft at fault, in noble house I have lodg'd
Noble inhabitant! 'twas said again
That thou wast good—then I believ'd thee wise,
For wisdom should bear goodness or no fruit!
And, good and wise, believ'd thee fairest too,
And coveted! Nor come I without leave—
Thy simple life eschewing worldly forms,
Was pledge for leave! Nor lack I introduction
That honest errand bring to vouch for me.
Nor, least of all, acquaintance—I have known thee
Since matur'd thought, my nature's fondest wish
Informing, told it loveliness of soul,
Yet more than body, both belong to woman,
And, therewith when abiding, doth make up
The highest sum that earthly happiness
Amounts to—nearest what we hope in Heaven.
  Hero. Friend, dost thou know thou talkest to a worm?"

The Quakeress discourses of worldly vanities; preaches, in this
mortal state mankind are subject to evils, diseases, and the like
tokens of infirmity and uncertainty; and that beauty is fleeting
and worthless.

 " *Sir Valentine.* Thou mean'st the beauty that but meets the eye?
  Hero. I mean the beauty thou alone dost see,
And prov'st thou only see'st. Why, what pains
Thou takest with a common piece of clay
To set it off! a fine account to turn
The bow of God to—meant for spiritual,
And not corporeal use—with divers tints
To cloth thy body! besides lading it
With the mind's produce—gems and metals—proof
Far more *without* concerns thee than *within!*
Oh! that a nature of immortal reach
Should house its aspirations in a crib
Like this poor tiny world! and, taught to look
Above the coronets of the fair stars,
Go proud with grains of dust and gossamer,
The property of things inferior to him,
As motes unto the sun! But I forget—thy errand?
 Sir Valentine. - Love!

> *Hero.*   'Tis clear, thou'rt mad !   What ! love
> Whom thou did'st never see ?"

Sir Valentine assures her he is not mad, for he maintains that he has seen the object of his present wonderment and adoration often before,—that he has talked with her, sat with her, &c. &c., meaning thereby that he has been enchained by the self-same style of beauty, " but by another worn."

> " *Hero.*   Thou hast known a maiden like me?
> *Sir Valentine.*   Yes ;
> I have lov'd a maid, most like thee—most unlike ;
> Without, as costly—but within, as poor
> To thee, as penury to affluence.
>   *Hero.* And did'st thou love and woo her for a month,
> And a defaulter thus? 'Twas grievous lack
> Of penetration.
>   *Sir Valentine.*   Nay, 'twas specious show
> That valid credit won.
>   *Hero.*   Thou art a man
> Like all thy wordly class, of shallow mind.
> Thy heart is in thine eyes : what pleaseth them
> Is sure of that.
>   *Sir Valentine.*   Nay, I had then lov'd on.
>   *Hero.*   What cur'd thy love ?
>   *Sir Valentine.*   I saw her in a dance
> Light nature show—
>   *Hero.*   A dance! Oh! I have heard
> Of such a thing. An idle pastime. What
> But folly comes of folly? Do you dance ?
>   *Sir Valentine*   I do.
>   *Hero.*   What kind of a thing is it ?   Come, shew me !
>   *Sir Valentine.*   I pray you to excuse me.
>   *Hero.*   Nay, but dance.
>   *Sir Valentine.*   'Twere out of time
> And place.
>   *Hero.* What, out of time and place, and to
> A man of gallantry, to do the thing
> A lady wishes him; and he the while
> On sufferance in her presence ! I do see
> Thou art in a grave mood, and for a man to dance,
> And look like Solomon, I must suppose
> Were more offence to seriousness, than wear
> A cap and bells. Friend, it is very clear
> Thou canst not dance, and look like a wise man—
> Yet thou didst woo a lady, thou didst say,
> And cast her off, because she did not dance
> With gravity.
>   *Sir Valentine.* She danced with lightness more
> Than lightest measure warranted. No thing

A modest woman does—say that it touches
The utmost verge of licence—but that cincture,
Of better proof than zone of adamant,
Its holy and offence-repelling fires
Doth wave around her, that the libertine,
Unwon by honour, yet is tam'd by awe!
She danc'd to gladden eyes whose burning glances
Turn thoughts of honest men on flashing swords,
On flame at stains washed out alone by blood!
The empire of her beauty giving prey
To parasites, who love for their own ends,
And by their homage shame!"

Sir Valentine does not dance, but he consents to become a convert to the simple forms and faith practised and professed by Ruth,
to assume the plain name Peter, to reduce his revenue, his mode of
living, &c., if she will but lend a favourable ear to his suit. Upon
these terms they part, she affecting to be no ways loath to the
preliminaries.

In the fourth Act we have Lord Athunree again, with his servile
agent Lewson. Their plot is now against Hero at her house in
Greenwich; the hireling is to find secret admission; his lordship is
to be on the watch, and as soon as he hears the cry of alarm, is to
run to the rescue and to make his lodging good. But as Lewson is
somewhat stupid, or rather given at times to the weakness of being
soft-hearted, it is deemed necessary to write out a few particular
instructions as to hours, positions, and movements. The first
paper on which these precise things are jotted is not sufficiently
correct; therefore Athunree keeps it and makes out another.
After this Eustace and Walsingham come across his Lordship,
when the stripling accuses his nobility of the crime of murder, and
undertakes to prove the charge at the point of the sword. A duel
is arranged for the morrow, his Lordship noting down on a piece of
paper the appointed time and place, and giving it to the opposite
party. This piece of paper is identically the same that had been
meant for the instruction of Lewson, but was corrected and copied;
and thus in a clumsy manner is the villanous plot frustrated that
might have proved far more disastrous than what had been contrived
against Helen Mowbray. It is to Helen Mowbray, in the guise of
the stripling Eustace, that the paper is handed. She had been Hero's
particular companion, and this is the only link which we can perceive that binds the two stories in the play together. She hastens
to apprise her former friend of her danger; and in so far as their
severance is concerned, a most loving and confiding stop is put
to it.

But ere coming to the winding up of the play or the denouement
of its plots, we must have another glimpse of Peter and Ruth. We
might have before mentioned that Sir Valentine took a false name,

when he first appeared before the disguised Hero, viz. that of Sir Launcelot de Vere.

> "*Hero.* Rise up! These proofs of honest passion quite
> Confound me
>   *Sir Valentine.* Hear me! O, the world! the world,
> That's made up of two hearts! That is the sun
> It moves around! There is the verdure! There
> The flower! the fruit! The spring and autumn field,
> Which in the reaping grows! the mine that, work'd,
> Accumulates in riches—ever free
> From influences of the changing stars,
> Or aught, save that which sits above them higher
> Than they above the globe!—Come! make with me
> E'en such a heavenly world.
>   *Hero.*   Beseech thee, rise!
>   *Sir Valentine.*   In hope?
>   *Hero.*   In hope!

The lover puts a variety of close questions. The last is—

>   *Sir Valentine.*   Wilt take me for thy husband?
>   *Hero.*   There's my hand—
> If no impediment forbids thee, clasp it.
>   *Sir Valentine.*   None.
>   *Hero.* Soft—I'll do't! 'Twill be a sweet revenge!   [*Aside.*
> A thought doth strike me. Thou hast loved a damsel,
> My likeness it should seem—and one know I,
> Who to the vision so resembles me,
> As doth myself, myself; nor can the ear
> That hears us, well determine which is which,
> In pitch and tone our voices so are one,
> The damsel thou affectedst, may she be—
> Her name is Hero Sutton.
>   *Sir Valentine.*   'Tis the same.
>   *Hero.* Another thought doth strike me. Is the name
> Thou gav'st to me thy real one? Alas!
> Thy colour mounteth! It is clear! Thou art
> Sir Valentine de Grey? Alas! alas!
> Your leave to be alone.
>   *Sir Valentine.*   Are you not well?
>   *Hero.* Oh, yes; I'm very well. Good e'en! Quite well!
> Well as a woman can be when she finds,
> Too late, she rashly gave her heart away
> To one, whose value for the gift will be,
> Soon as he proves 'tis his, to bid her keep it.
>   *Sir Valentine.*   To bid her keep it!
>   *Hero.*   As Hero Sutton rues!
>   *Sir Valentine.*   She never gave
> Her heart to me.
>   *Hero.*   She did! you know not when

A woman gives away her heart ! at times
She knows it not herself. Insensibly
It goes from her ! She thinks she hath it still—
If she reflects—while smoothly runs the course
Of wooing ; but if haply comes a check—
An irrecoverable—final one—
Aghast— forlorn—she stands, to find it lost,
And with it, all the world !"

Ere this scene closes, we have Sir Valentine answered in the following manner :—

> "*Sir Valentine.*   Let me hold thy hand.
> *Hero.* Never, till her, thou hast wrong'd, thou offerest
> To right.   The world return to, thou would'st quit
> It seems for me. Resume its habit : hie
> To Hero Sutton's, whom I will advise
> To look for thee to-morrow eve. Repeat
> What I have said to thee. If she denies
> What I aver, be free to come to me,
> And welcome too ! If she acknowledges,
> The hand of her, whose heart thou hast purloin'd,
> Behoves thee ask and take."

A soliloquy soon after this is worthy of Hero, and must be quoted.

> "*Enter Hero ; she goes to the window and looks out.*
> *Hero.* Whether mine eye with a new spirit sees,
> Or nature is grown lovelier, I know not;
> But ne'er, methinks, was sunset half so sweet !
> He's down, and yet his glory still appears,
> Like to the memory of a well-spent life,
> That's golden to the last, and when 'tis o'er,
> Shines in the witnesses it leaves behind.
> They say, a ruddy sunset a fair day !
> Oh ! may it be a day without a cloud,
> Which of my fate doth see the clearing up ;
> That I may quote it ever as a sign
> Of sincere fortune, often as I say
> Was ever day so bright!   How calm is all—
> How calm am I !—Would every breast I knew
> Did lodge a heart as tranquil."

We have left ourselves scarcely any room for the last Act, which must be one of great bustle and dramatic effect on the stage. Eustace, or Helen rather, though still unidentified by Walsingham, has arrived with him in the field where the duel is to be fought. Their friendship has been worked ere this to the highest pitch that can subsist between man and his sex, and he of course is to be a second in the combat.

" *Walsingham.* Shew me thy sword.
 Helen. I cannot draw it, but
My life must follow.
 Walsingham. How ?
 Helen. It is my heart—
This which I wear is nothing.   Call it steel,
'Tis steel !—a straw, it even is a straw !
Its stamina not lodging in itself,
But in the use that's made on't.
 Walsingham. This is calm,
Upon the eve of combat.
 Helen. Walsingham,
There is a kind of nature that clears up
The instant it confronts a trying thing.
In common evils, hesitates and fears ;
In ills of moment, shows sedate resolve.
 Walsingham. Why, that is woman's proper contradiction.
 Helen. It passes for't ; but sometimes 'bides in man,
Not therein less of his high caste deserving,
Tho' so resembling woman ! Think'st not so ?
 Walsingham. Assuredly.
 Helen. You see this mood is mine,
Nor was I on my guard to let it out—
'Twill lose me credit with you.   Best have pass'd
For Sir Bedoubtable any day o' the year !
You more had thought of me.
 Walsingham. No !
 Helen. You say I'm calm ?
I am so—that is, as to the issue of
This mortal meeting—for 'tis mortal !—but
I have a trouble, and—wilt thou believe me ?
'Tis touching thee !—It grieves me, Walsingham,
To leave thee an abused man behind me !
What thou didst tell me I have pondered well,
And thereon founded arguments, methinks,
More solid than I urg'd on you before.
They are here—your poor friend's legacy to you !

   [*Gives a paper.*

Stop !—you're about to speak—don't speak as yet.
If I should fall, you pledge your gentle word,
My body you will have direct convey'd
Unto the lady's I have herein named,

   [*Gives another paper.*

Deliver'd to her custody—her own ?
Nor until then, one fast'ning, fold, loop, thread
O' the vesture, thou wilt suffer be disturb'd—
No, not to search, or probe, or staunch a wound,
Or settle if indeed alive or dead,
 Or any thing !   To this, thou pledgest thee ?
 Walsingham. Dear boy, I do ?''

Walsingham contrives to get into his hands the stripling's **sword,**
and throws it into the adjoining river ; for, says he,

> " Boy, your quarrel's mine ;
> To humour thee, did I consent to play
> The second to thee. Stand aside, with broad
> And lusty breast and sinewy arm, and see
> Thy stripling form the deadly point oppose
> In the athletic villain's practis'd hand,
> Instead of grasping thee with loving force,
> Like to a doting father his boy-son,
> Or elder brother his dear younger one,
> Taking thy place, and swinging thee away !
> No, boy !   Before thy young veins part a drop
> Of their life's streams, my channel shall run dry !
>   _Helen._   Is this fair Walsingham ?
>   _Walsingham._   Yet, hear me on !
> I find I could not live without thee ! so
> Guarding thy life, I but protect my own.
> That's fair—that's rational—that's sound in nature !
> Want'st further reason ?—I will give it thee—
> Thou art like her !
>   _Helen._   Whom ?
>   _Walsingham._ Boy, hast thou read my soul—
> Have I turn'd o'er its every page to thee—
> Love, hate, hope, doubt, possession, loss, bliss, pain,
> Contentment, and despair—and in each one
> Shown thee one all-pervading cause enwrit,
> For nothing ? Whom could I compare thee to,
> But her—the heroine of my sad story ?
> Whom much thou dost resemble ! Hast thou never
> Remark'd me gazing in abstraction on thee,
> As tho'—upon perusal of thy face,
> While seem'd mine eye intent, my soul did pore
> Upon some other thing ?—I have done it oft—
> Will do it once again !   Your eyes are her's,
> In form and hue, but sunk : a darkness too,
> Not heavy, yet enough to make a cloud,
> Sits—not disparagingly tho'—'neath thine ;
> Her's were too starry brilliants, set in pearl !
> The outline of the nose is quite the same,
> But that of thine is sharper—'tis thy sex.
> The mouth is very like—oh, very like !
> But there's a touch—a somewhat deep one too—
> Of pensiveness. The cast of her's was sweetness,
> Enlocking full content. The cheek is not
> At all alike !—'tis high ; and lank below ;
> And sallow—not a dimple in't—all contrast
> To the rich flower'd and velvet lawn of her's.

But tho' thou art not she entire—thou art
Enough of her to make me love thee, boy!
With such a brother-love, as brother never,
I dare be bound, for brother felt before!
I spoke not of thy hair—it is a wood
Run wild compared to her's, and thrice as deep
I' the shade.—Yet, you are very like her!—quite
Enough to make me pour my heart's blood out,
As water for thy sake!—They are at hand!
   Helen. Then let me be at least thy sword-bearer;
And when thou need'st the steel, I'll keep the sheath
Which in thy motions would embarrass thee.
   Walsingham.   Take it, and thank thee!"

Their antagonists, Athunree and his second, Felton, come upon the ground just as Helen has got possession of Walsingham's sword. In her turn she outwits him by enjoining the opposite second to keep her friend, who is now without a weapon at bay, while she encounters the principal. We are told that in representation the scene here becomes so awakening, and is so finely and highly wrought up, that the audience are affected as if the whole were a reality,—that the multitude rise from their seats, and look as persons ready to interfere.

   " *Walsingham.*   Ha!—the boy
Has baffled and out-witted me!   [*Advances.*
   Felton.   Stand back!
I bar all interruption to the game
We are summon'd here to play.
   Walsingham.   A coward act
To draw upon a naked man!
   Felton.   My lord!
Why draw you not, and he his weapon out?
Proceed, my lord, at once.
   Lord Athunree.   Before I do,
I ask, and I must learn, in name of whom
The urchin has arraign'd and challeng'd me.
I fight not, till I know upon what cause.
   Helen.   The cause of Helen Mowbray!
   Walsingham.   Drop your hand,
And let me pass! or sure as that's a sword,
My heart is on your point!
   Lord Athunree.   Spite of thyself,
Another minute grant I thee to live.
I will not draw until I know thy name.
   Helen.   Mowbray!
   Lord Athunree.   Her brother?
   Helen.   Anything you please,
Caitiff without a parallel in crime!
   Walsingham, A brother!—Hold! Lord Athunree! Look, Sir,

A moment give I thee, to take thy choice
'Twixt murdering me, or suffering to pass !
Heaven ! do I care for life !

> [*Rushes upon Felton, and wrests the sword from
> him. At the same moment, Officers and Ser-
> vants enter.*"

Athunree's meditated plot against Hero, which had been inad-
vertently disclosed by the paper he handed to his challenger,—
Lawson also having become his betrayer, as well as the confessor
of the truth in regard to the villany practised against Helen Mowbray,—speedily, when all the parties are brought before Sir William
Sutton in his magisterial character, clears up every misunderstand-
ing and terminates the play ; a play, as we have seen, which is
brimful of beauties, that combines such sterling excellences, and
produces such powerful effects as will add new laurels to the brow of
him who has not only been the principal regenerator of our modern
drama, but who continues to be its chieftain.

Art. III.—*Milton, ou la Poesie Epique; Cours professé à L'Athenée
Royale de Paris.* Par M. Raymond de Vericour. Paris: 1838.
*Milton, or Epic Poetry; a Course of Lectures delivered at the Royal
Athenæum of Paris.* By M. Raymond de Vericour. London:
Bailliere. 1838.

One of the happy effects of the close alliance between France and
England, and the increasing approximation of the views and interests
of these two great powers, is the anxiety manifested by our neighbours to cultivate our hitherto-despised language, which sounded in
the ears of Madam de Staël like the hoarse murmur of our waves,
and to form a just appreciation of our standard works of literature
and art. Until very lately little was known in France of Shakspeare or Milton, although their celebrity was widely diffused and
readily acknowledged by the neighbouring nations. The ignorance
and self-sufficiency of French critics, and the unskilful or rather ludicrous efforts of French translators, added to the national antipathy
to every thing English, except English gold, were the main obstacles
to a proper estimation of our noblest works of fiction. The discrepancy between the tastes of the two nations, as it existed not more
than ten years ago, is thus pointedly sketched in a leading periodical
journal.

"'There is nothing in which the opinions of the French and English
differ so irreconcileably as in poetry ; and therefore, perhaps, the
critics of the one nation ought not to pass judgment on the poets
of the others. We can exchange our cotton for their wines, our
cut steel for their ormolu, and blankets for their cambrics, and
find ground for material satisfaction in the bargain ; but the prices

current of poetry are so outrageously different in the two countries, that we could not part with a scene of Shakspeare for the whole body of their dramatists ; nor would they give up one canto of Voltaire's Henriade, or the Pucelle either, for the whole of Spencer and Milton into the bargain." Happily, however, for themselves, as well as for the general interests of literature, the French critics have seen the errors of their ways : a new light has broken upon them, and they are not at all backward in proclaiming their conversion. *" Nous avons changé tout cela,"* they say to the sneering critic we have just quoted ; the veil has fallen from our eyes ; you were right, and we were wrong ; your sneers were merited, but they are no longer so : we have made acquaintance with your Shakspeare and your Milton ; the glories of your divinities have been revealed to our eyes; we are ready to prostrate ourselves, and worship and enshrine them in our temples. What would the critic, who perused the foregoing piece of flippancy, say to the following confession of faith in his divinities ?—

" The Paradise Lost possesses in the highest degree all the characteristics of elevation and sublimity. Amongst all the conceptions of the human intellect—amongst all the productions of antiquity and modern times, there is none which can bear a comparison with it, in the quality of sustained and varied sublimity."

These, we think, are terms quite comprehensive and explicit enough to satisfy the most fastidious, that the person who uses them is a firm believer in Milton ; and yet he is a Frenchman ; and what is more, a Frenchman of considerable powers of eloquence and correct literary taste.

M. Véricour, the individual to whom we allude, has been called to the task of proclaiming to his countrymen the divine attributes of our English Homer. As the apostle of a new poetic revelation to France, he delivered a series of lectures at the Athenée Royal de Paris, on the Life and Writings of Milton, which he subsequently embodied in the form of a book, and printed for general circulation. That he was deeply penetrated with the conviction of the truth of his mission, nobody who reads these pages can doubt for a moment. That his extensive reading, his familiar acquaintance with European literature, ancient as well as modern, fitted him for becoming the interpreter of the oracle is equally incontestable. The only danger seems to be, that the zeal of the new converts may hurry them into professions of enthusastic adoration, which may appear to transcend even so lofty a subject and verge into absolute idolatry.

It is curious to observe how France and England mutually influence each other in literary matters. Sometimes it happens that when the influence of a particular school begins to subside in the country of its birth, it flourishes in the utmost vigour and luxuriance in the country of its adoption ; while men of extraordinary powers of imagination, such as Shakspeare and Milton, leave behind them a luminous track of light to which all the nations of the civilized world may turn their admiring eyes, and which may become to them the beacons of new careers and new successes.

Though the delicacy and perspicuity of the French language make it excellent for conversation or business, it is not so well calculated for the loftier flights of poetry as the Spanish, the Italian or the English. Much may undoubtedly be said for the language of a Racine, a Corneille, a Voltaire; but still we are ready to maintain that the style and character of French poetry is not only very different from the style and character of English poetry, but that it is peculiar to the nation to which it belongs. Neither Italy nor England, we admit, have ever produced an author of the same stamp as Racine; and France, on the other hand, never has, and probably never will produce poets at all resembling Dante or Ariosto, Shakspeare or Milton.

On this point Keratry in his examination of the work of Emanuel Kant observes, that " the writers of Great Britain must necessarily have communicated an original character to their works, because the law allowed them to have an original character themselves : no doubt a good deal may be traced to free institutions." M. Vericour says, " it is the equality, before the law, which has powerfully contributed to give to the English poets, that general and surpassing elevation which is not to be found in the literatures of modern nations. This may appear as commonplace ; but of this be assured, that one of the most prolific sources of the sublime, that which arms the thought with energy, which imparts the greatest elevation to the sentiments, is liberty ; and it is my firm conviction, that the good old British freedom has powerfully contributed to nourish, inspire, and inflame the poets who form its glory ; and if it is the source of that superior elevation so much wanted by enlightened critics, it gives us the right to hope that the future will bring forth, among the other European nations, those noble, stately, lofty, and sublime productions which awaken the generous emotions, elevate the spirit of a people, and become the basis of its civilization. Moreover, the nation which has entombed Shakspeare in the burying-place of its kings, must assuredly be justified in its pretensions to a superior literature.

" Milton has periods that exhibit a melody to which there is nothing at all comparable in our language, and which strike the more, perhaps, in his great poem from the contrast it so frequently presents of harshness and repulsive austerity. In Milton we find all that is sublime and terrific, much that is beautiful, and sometimes, though rarely, something that is soft and delicate ; but with this, there are inelegancies which cannot fail to offend, and deformities that go near to disgust."

Delille first stripped Virgil of his toga, and dressed him according to the last Parisian fashion. Having succeeded to his satisfaction in this particular, he next attempted to force the same suit upon the reluctant Milton. There is a stateliness, a gravity, a grandeur in the language of the " Paradise Lost," with which we on this side of the channel are peculiarly struck ; and we are better pleased with the grave original, than with all the coruscations of wit which flash through the translation.

Delille, it must be confessed, had much to contend with in the intractable nature of his materials. The language is deficient in the majesty, the grace, the energy, the ductility which the language of heroic poetry should possess. It presents no opportunity of compounding, inverting, or employing peculiar or classical idioms. The French language of the thirteenth century, the language of Vellehardouin and the troubadours, now despised and forgotten, was much nearer the true language of epic poetry. Latter ages have polished down its picturesque asperities, and it has become the nerveless and emasculate domiciliary of courts. Happily the last few years have witnessed its efforts to shake off its chains and take a bolder flight.

Delille then had great difficulties to contend with in the attempt to embrace the stately and sonorous period of Milton within his puny though smooth phraseology. It was the enormous broadsword of a Paladin, crossing the delicate toasting iron of a gentleman usher. In his " Paradise Lost," we are not in Paradise, but in *Paris.* His Eve is a " charming woman," a veritable coquette, who awakes most gracefully *" en sursaut."* His translation of the line,

> " Meanwhile at table, Eve ministered naked,"

is very generally known for its absurdity, and is a fair specimen of the French graces, in which he has arrayed " the great high priest of all the nine." It runs thus :—

> " Tandis que à la table, Eve chastement nue
> Satisfaisant ensemble et le gout et la vue."

In like manner the loves of the great progenitors of the human race, are deprived of the decent colouring flung over them by Milton, and described with all the levity of the eighteenth century. Two other translations in verse followed that of Delille, one from the pen of M. Delatour de Pernes in 1813, another from Mr. Delogne D'Antroche in 1808, both inferior to Delille in harmony of versification and not remarkable for any improvement in other respects. At length Chateaubriand took up the cause of Milton in France, and gave a very respectable prose translation in 1836. It is curious to observe the Republican bard introduced to the French by three fanatic royalists ; first, Racine ; second, Delille ; and then Chateaubriand. Of course in a literal prose translation, we can only find

the *disjecti membra poetæ*—the pale reflection of the noble substance. But Mr. Chateaubriand sometimes falls into serious mistakes, as for instance, when he translates

> " Siloe's brook that flowed
> *Fast* by the oracle of God,"

" Le ruisseau de Siloe qui couloit rapidement," mistaking *fast by*
for *fast*.
　　Again,

> " Sing heavenly muse *that* on the secret top
> Of Horeb," &c.

is thus given : " Chante muse celeste sur le sommet d'Oreb ;"
where the omission of the word *that* gives quite a new meaning to
the sentence ; but this is not as bad as another translator, a M.
Pougerville, who translates

> " Unveiled her ' *peerless*' light,"
> " Devoila sa lumière *de perles*."

Chateaubriand's translation is given in the form of an essay, in
which every thing is sacrificed to the splendour of style ; the predominant failing of French writers. It was a task imposed by the
necessity of procuring a morsel of bread. This is a painful fact.
However, it is by far the most spirited translation of Milton which
has yet appeared in France.
　　We shall now proceed to give some extracts from M. de Vericour's book. We shall select his comparisons between Milton,
Dante, and Klopstock, as the most novel and instructive to the
English reader.

" The poetry which sings of the inhabitants of an invisible world, imaginary, or supposed, should be at once mysterious and picturesque. That of
Dante is deficient in the mystery, which gives eclat to a conception of the
kind. · This defect, if indeed it is a defect, is inseparable from the plan of the
Divina Commedia, which requires, as we have said, the greatest details of
description. Nevertheless this absence of a profound and sacred mystery,
may well be considered as a defect in Dante. His supernatural creations
excite our interest, but it is not that interest which is properly inherent in
supernatural creations. While contemplating the spirits and demons of the
Italian poet, you are never struck with that overwhelming awe, mingled
with astonishment, which makes you start with horror, while it fascinates
you with its majesty, as in the Paradise Lost. In the work of Dante on the
contrary, we are almost tempted to imitate the poet, we feel that we too
may interrogate his phantoms and devils without any feeling of alarm.
　　The infernal regions of Milton differ from those of every other writer :
we have shown that his devils are conceptions of extraordinary sublimity :
that they are not metaphysical beings, hideous monsters, or deformed mis-
shapen goblins, like those of Tasso and Klopstock. Those of Dante, it is
true, are superior to anything of the kind created by the ancients, and far

above what has been attempted by a crowd of moderns. But Milton alone has succeeded in imparting majesty to his Satan, in exhibiting him to us on the burning lake, his kingly brow scarred with the thunder of the Omnipotent. We must not forget, however, that Milton came three centuries and a half after Dante.

" In his poem Milton resembles by turns his personages, now the angels of light, and now the spirits of darkness. Never did poet rise to such a height to stoop to such depths. I have remarked that Milton describes the wonders of creation as God as sown them: his heaven dims the magnificence of Olympus—his hell is sublime : his pandæmonium puts the intellect of mankind to the blush. What becomes of the Prometheus of Eschylus, the Capaneus of Euripides, the Mezentius or Salmonius of Virgil, beside Satan, who retains in his whole person something of the splendour of the sun, and bears upon his brow the impress of the beauty of the skies, though it be defaced by thunder.

" The Prometheus of Eschylus comes nearest to the Satan of Milton— the same ferocity—the same invincible pride—the same hatred of domination—the same mixture of better and more generous sentiments ; but Prometheus is not sufficiently spiritual—he talks too much about chains and tortures, he is too much agitated, too much overcome, while such is the powerful energy of the Satan of the Paradise Lost, that while racked by inexpressible tortures he deliberates, disposes, and seems glorying in the thought of triumph and vengeance to come. Prometheus chained upon the rock of hate, but ever unsubdued, and braving the thunder which he sees descending upon him is a sublime image of the force and constancy of man, in a contest with misfortune and suffering and death. But what shall we say of the rebel archangel—of the leader of the infernal host—his brows circled with a burning crown, armed with his glittering sword, standing erect in haughty rivalry to the son of God, now inflamed by the genius of evil against the divine minister of the wrath of Heaven ?"

The same spirit of judicious criticism pervades the remainder of the comparison.

" Dante and Milton !—What an analogy between these two men. It is only since the end of the last century that they have attained their poetical position, and it is incontestable that the superiority and characteristic colouring of their poetry is the result of the moral qualities of these two great men, of the elevation, the nobleness of soul, in fine of those qualities of the heart which are honoured by humanity. The fires of civil war kindled the genius of these two poets : they might have seen in the passions which surrounded them, a hell upon earth with all its attendant horrors. Milton is more picturesque, more varied in his colours. Dante has a plastic power : he creates statues. If the English poet sometimes goes astray in vagueness and obscurity, the Italian by the precision of the contours formed in a hard and violent manner, sometimes falls into exaggeration. Milton opens an unlimited space to the thoughts. Dante is often more powerful and more characteristic. Like Dante, Milton was a statesman, a lover and a poet; they were both unfortunate in their political career and in their loves. Dante was driven into exile and wanted bread ; Milton survived his party. His friends perished on the scaffold, groaned in dungeons or begged their

subsistence amongst strangers.   He was marked out for the hatred of a
depraved court and an inconstant people; the finger of scorn was pointed
at him; and mediocre poets, whose morals were still lower than their talents,
carried off the favours of the court and of fortune."

The comparison between Milton and Klopstock is equally favourable to the former.

" Milton opened the way, and we have seen that never did muse take
a loftier flight than his did.   Klopstock follows Milton with a steady pace,
and even equals him at times in the selection of the principal figures, which
appear in the fore-ground of the picture.   Klopstock became the founder of
a new epic and the father of German literature.   Those who have made
the deepest study of the German language, consider the translation of the
Bible to be the form and fundamental text of classical expression in high
German (Hoch. Deutch), and not only Klopstock but many other writers of
the highest order have modelled their style upon this type.   It is worthy of
remark that in no other modern language have so many biblical phrases
and turns of expression been adopted and passed current in the ordinary
language of life.
" A god, dying by the hands of men, whom he has redeemed at the price
of his blood, the Messiah and the mystery of the Redemption, do not chill
the genius of Klopstock with a reverend dread; he seizes the harp of the
prophets and elicits from it sounds worthy of them.   Milton has sung the
fall of man, Klopstock celebrates his redemption, and as Satan plays an important part in the terrific but exquisitely drawn scenes of both these works
·(as the Deity and his angels are necessarily the chief springs)—the points
at which the poets approach each other must consequently be very numerous throughout their respective works.   There was also some similarity
in their careers,—they both threw themselves with enthusiam into Revolutions fatal to monarchy.   But while the secretary of Cromwell continued
steadfast in his principles to the hour of his death, the counsellor of the
King of Denmark made a public recantation of his.
" If Klopstock imitates Milton, if he borrows from him several of his fictions
and a great number of his personages, if he is greatly his inferior in boldness and energy, he has it must be confessed avoided some of the faults of
his model.   We do not find anything in his poem resembling the strange
and ridiculous idea of Milton of the fallen angels in order that they may
sit at their ease in the infernal council, nor any passage similar to that, so
strongly condemned by Addison, in which the defeat of the rebel angels
is related with irony and jests.
" Thus the poem of the Messiah less varied, less original, and less inflated
than the Paradise Lost, although fatiguing by reason of its mysticism and
its uniformity, is nevertheless by the unity of the inspiration, the profound
knowledge of the gospel which it displays, the religious sentiment with
which it is as it were impregnated, one of the most beautiful sacrifices which
modern poetry has offered to Christianity.   The poet of the Messiah has
found in the human nature of Jesus Christ, a veil which tempers the brilliancy of the divinity.   In his abasement he finds a means for us to elevate
ourselves to him, and in his sufferings and death he finds a source of compassion sufficient to fix upon him an interest which never flags.   We are

no longer in a world in which the father and mother of the human race are the sole beings of our own species. God himself is man; he is surrounded with men like ourselves, his disciples and friends, his worshippers and judges, his accusers and murderers—everything recalls us to ourselves by recalling us to him. We love what he loves, we hate what he hates, we are horrified at hell, and if a ray of pity penetrates into those dismal regions it is for the hapless Abbadona, carried away against his will among the rebel cohorts, unhappy because he was culpable. Klopstock often succeeds in awakening pity, he abounds in touching expressions, for to the most refined and exquisite sensibility he united a grave and religious feeling. Being a passionate lover of nature, he frequently paints it with a bold and decided pencil, and with that species of enthusiasm which is peculiar to him, but he interrogates it and describes it with an affectation which becomes downright fatiguing, and which cannot be too much blamed. Above nature, even in nature itself, he sees perpetually him who called it forth from chaos, and never does he do so, without falling into those interminable ecstasies, and without excessive transports, gratitude of and love. In his highest flights Klopstock leans upon Revelation, the fruitful source of literary beauties as well as of noble and generous sentiments. It is easy to see that he has drunk deep of the holy book, and that he has meditated on the writings and prophetical narrations of those historians of the future, who heard many ages, thrones crashing upon thrones, with a terrific sound. In the same way, the germ of all the fine things in Milton is in Genesis, but you have seen with what wonderful power of imagination he has quickened them into being. What an extraordinary magician is the poet who can draw such prodigies as the creation of Eve, and that holy bliss of our first parents, from a sublime but naked thought. Milton is a prophet who comments on Moses and on God himself. With a continuously sustained power of genius he developes his fable and imparts to it scenes which are barely hinted at in Genesis alone, the merit of being a faithful and dramatic image of human life, by stamping upon it the character of truth, of things deeply felt.

"The subject of Klopstock is, as I before observed, grave, austere and religious. It is only in Germany or England that such a subject could be handled. In the former particularly, the classic land of thought, of severe metaphysical tendency, and historical patriotism, religion is not a timid virgin who trembles at appearing in open day, who blushes at associating in national festivals, at the anniversaries of the triumphs or reverses of the country, or at its grand and imposing solemnities. There religion burns in every bosom, we find it in the narratives of the historian, in the meditations of the moralist, in the outpourings of familiar correspondence, and even in the fugitive words which have been preserved to us by tradition. It enters into all the actions of the life of man, it sustains him in his staggering pace from the cradle to the tomb."

After a rapid *exposé* of the component parts of the Messiah, M. Vericour proceeds to institute a comparison between the two poets, somewhat after this fashion:—

"The Hell and Satan of Klopstock are servilely copied from Milton: the moment the German attempts to innovate on the original, his judgment abandons him. Thus, for instance, Satan is smitten with impotency—

braved by a rebellious subject—and dethroned in public opinion by Adra-
meler, who, more terrible and more influential than his master, would destroy worlds and annihilate spirits in order that he may annihilate Satan
and reign in his place, as in that of the Eternal himself. Milton is much
more sensible in the general design of his hell and in the management of
his conspiracy. His fallen archangel is always king of hell and the soul of
revolt, as God is the soul of the world. A feeble imitation of the forms of
antiquity betrays still more the imbecility of Klopstock in the apparition of
Satan to Judas, in the figure of his father,—a fragment, however, which in
itself is very beautiful. We may notice, also, the moment when Judas
goes mad, his heart having become a hell,—where Jesus and John awake,
and repair to the Mount of Olives, where he finds his disciples asleep, and
addresses them in the words of Scripture. This is a splendid contrast
between the calm of the just man who is about to die, and the agitation of
him who is to be his murderer. In the Sanhedrim, where Caiaphas, inspired by Satan, demands the death of Jesus, we should notice the speeches
of the false sage, the hypocrite, and the madman whom we have just mentioned, to whom Klopstock has given the name of Philou. It may be that
there is not one of Milton's devils, animated with a rage more infernal than
that put forth by this demon against Christ. But the great mistake of the
German poet is in forgetting that he should not strike so hard when he
strikes for such a length of time, and that the effect of his imprecations is
in an inverse rate with their continuance.

" Satan plays a rather insignificant part in the Messiah. He often dis-
appears, but he is still present, in some measure, under the shape of Judas.
We have remarked the noble passage which shows us his despair after he
had received the price of innocent blood. He sought to annihilate even
his soul, to escape eternal torment. He adds suicide to all his other
crimes, and resuscitates in the air, with another body, as 'soon as he has
strangled himself. Klopstock punishes him after the fashion of Dante.
The traitor implores a second death with loud cries, but instead of yielding
to the prayer of fear turned to rage, they direct the eyes of the doomed
man to the splendours of the celestial world. This spectacle which makes
him feel the horrors of despair, is the prelude of his descent into the gaping
gulf of hell, which closes over him. Yet even this passage is weak and
long drawn out, compared to the moment in which the Christ of Milton, on
his car of fire, upright on the extremity of heaven, with his dread thunderbolts, hurls Satan and all his legions to the bottom of the dark abyss, which
they do not reach until after they have fallen nine days and as many nights
like flaming whirlwinds in the immense space which separates the starry
vault from the depths of the abyss. The German poet has committed
another fault in announcing twice before the fine idea of the spectacle of
the heavens unrolled to the eyes of Judas above his head, while hell is
yawning beneath his feet. There is not enough of energy in his horror at
the latter frightful abode. The writhings of the damned spirit, in all the
terrors of his crime and its punishment, called for an extraordinary colouring, in which the poet might have exhausted all the powers of his genius.
Nay, we do not even find what has been remarked after the condemnation
of a cowardly criminal, who is ferocious, though dismayed. Klopstock
shows us clearly and forcibly the clouds that gather round the culprit, but
where are the signs of celestial vengeance which should be written on his

brow? where the rolling of the dilated eye—the quivering of the lips—damnation imprinted on the features? Where is that ghostly, corpse-like, palor which overspreads the face of the condemned man before he is launched into a hideous eternity.

"The heaven of Klopstock attests the elevation of his genius; he is sometimes as fine as Milton, but he dazzles our eyes, fatigues our attention, and strikes our imagination with sterility by the profusion of his riches. From the very outset of the poem, he pours upon us planets, unnumbered globes, and paths that are bordered by a thousand suns. He finds traits of immeasurable splendour to paint his Jehovah, then all of a sudden he gives way to a luxury of details, which destroys the effect he had already produced, by imitating the majestic simplicity of Moses. In a word, spite of all the beauties that may be pointed out in the Messiah, this poem, although inspired by Milton, has nothing of the homeric fire, the lofty grandeur, of the 'Paradise Lost.' Klopstock has not sufficiently compressed the various portions of his poem; he yields to the ever recurring tension of his mysticism; he abuses dialogue, and his speeches run to an appalling length; he wants imagination to make his personages act, and his celestial and infernal creatures are far from being cast in the same mould as those of Milton. Klopstock is a patient meditative genius, with an habitual elevation of sentiment and thought. Milton calls forth the strongest emotions and makes all the cords of the human heart vibrate to his touch. We feel that the English Homer is hurried along by the tempest of an impetuous genius which bears him onward to the sphere of poetry—originality—the infinite—the sublime.

"The difficulty of his idiom arising from the artificial structure of his periods, which makes reading him a regular study, cannot be duly appreciated save by the cultivated and classical mind, which makes them, as it were, a subject of meditation. While speaking of Homer, I observed that it was necessary to ascend the summits of his genius to enjoy it fully. Neither does it suffice to read the 'Paradise Lost' once or twice: no! it must be studied—pondered on! In this way alone can we penetrate the folds of its grandeur and feel a sentiment of gratitude mingling with our admiration. We may say to those who would enrich their minds, elevate their thoughts, experience the sweetest sensations of the soul, read and re-read 'Paradise Lost,' make it your favourite study.

In conclusion we have only to state, that we have derived the highest satisfaction from the perusal of M. De Vericour's volume, constituting, as it does, a well-executed essay on epic poetry; and we sincerely hope that, for the interests of literature and the benefit of the diffusion of correct taste and a sound and judicious style of criticism, it may become as popular as it deserves to be amongst our continental neighbours.

Art. IV.—*Germany : the Spirit of her History, Literature, Social Condition, and National Economy; illustrated by reference to her Physical, Moral, and Political Statistics, and by comparison with other Countries.* By Bisset Hawkins, M.D., Oxon, F.R.S. London: Parker. 1838.

·It has never been our fortune to light upon a book in which such a multiplicity of facts, such a variety of details on every important subject, were brought together within so narrow a compass, or stated with greater clearness and perspicuity. We have here in a single volume of less than five hundred pages, a mass of information which we must have sought for through as many volumes, without having the additional advantage—even should our research prove successful—of finding it sifted, classed, and compared, so as to render it doubly valuable and immediately available.· There is not a single feature of Germany—historical, literary, social, or political—which has not been traced by Mr. Hawkins with remarkable brevity and precision. That a work which should place before our eyes the whole German empire, with all the intricacies of its petty subdivisions, was a desideratum in literature nobody who has listened to the conversations of returned tourists, or who has turned over the leaves of their printed inanities, can for a moment doubt ; and it is a matter of no small satisfaction that it has been executed in a very masterly and unpretending style. It may be said, indeed, that it is a mere compilation from other and better works, but it is a compilation judiciously executed—embracing all the most essential subjects which are necessary to give us a clear and comprehensive view of the German empire.

In England our general ideas of Germany are, that it is a romantic land covered with fine old castles and peopled by various races of bookmakers, musicians, and metaphysicians. Besides, it is the manufactory of kings and princes, exporting annually some scores of the latter and the smaller fry of barons and counts, to dazzle the eyes of the "nation of shopkeepers," with their high sounding and unpronounceable names, their red ribands and glittering stars. We laugh at their pretensions while we envy their good fortune. Noble blood is to them Fortunatus's cap ; it procures them all that the most ambitious of us islanders would aspire to, and yet we find a curious historical fact related of these high mightinesses, which might leave us at a loss to distinguish them from the descendants of a privileged " swell mob" of the middle ages. In 1215, Frederick Barbarossa exacted an oath from his nobles not to coin bad money, not to levy extraordinary tolls, and not to steal on the highway. A pretty idea of nobility, truly. An oath to coiners and highwaymen that they will neither coin nor rob is a very gentle restraint ; but taking into account the religious notions of the period, we admit that many a man would empty his neighbour's pocket without remorse, who would have shrunk from the idea of superadding perjury to a comparatively trifling offence. In the fourteenth century we find the Bavarian nobles accusing their monarch of conferring court dignities on foreigners, of chicanery towards his own nobility, to whom he was difficult of access, and of depriving them of their ancient rights of hunting. They specify instances in which the members of their own body had been seized and carried off by night, and their daughters forcibly married to foreigners. Heavy charges, certainly, and which give us a pretty fair idea of the relations which then subsisted between the monarch and his nobility. In fact, they lived in a state of open hostility ; the monarch using his endeavours to weaken the power of his nobles, the latter leaguing together and attacking their sovereign. In their endeavours to crush the power of the nobles, the kings were powerfully seconded by the knights, between whom and the lords (Herrin) the greatest enmity and jealousy prevailed. In the lesser German states feuds between noble and sovereign were things of common occurrence.

In 1520 a league of the nobles of the family of Salder was formed against the Bishop of Hildesheim. The adverse armies met at Soltau, and the nobles were defeated after a sharp and bloody contest. About the same period the Bishop of Wurzburg was murdered by some noblemen, incited by their chief, Von Grumbach, who, after a protracted resistance, was at length brought to justice. The accession of the family of Luneburg to the throne of Great Britain was favourable to the power and pretensions of the Hanoverian nobility. From that period they have been celebrated in Germany for their lofty deportment and their attachment to their order. The reason is, that they have had the government almost entirely in their own hands, which the nobles of other German states have been obliged to surrender to their princes. The nobility of Brandenburg was quite lawless and independent before the ascent of the house of Zollern to the throne. They had possessed themselves of the sovereign's domains and of the public revenue, and hence a continued contest was carried on between them for these prizes. During the reign of Joachim, the noblemen who filled offices at court amused themselves with highway robbery during the night. Von Lindenburg, the prince's favourite, was found guilty of this crime, and to the honour of the prince, his influence at court was no protection for his forfeited life. His execution served to irritate the nobles to such a degree, that one of them, Von Otterstaedt, had the audacity to write over the door of the prince's chamber—"Joachim, take care of yourself, for if you fall into our hands, we will hang you." While attempting to carry his menace into execution, Von Otterstaedt was seized, and underwent the punishment he had promised Joachim.

In 1568 we find Albert Frederick harassed and tormented into insanity by his nobles, and as they allowed him no medical relief, he remained so to the end of his life.

During the Thirty Years' War, which desolated and impoverished Germany, impoverishing the peasants, and reducing the princes to utter insignificance, the nobility alone managed to escape the deluge of misfortune which bore down the other orders of the state. In Prussia, their excesses continued unrestrained until the accession of Frederick the Great in 1640. This prince saw at once that the only remedy for these evils was to be found in a formidable standing army, and he applied himself vigorously and unremittingly to the organization and discipline of such a force, until at length he was at the head of the most effective military establishment in Christendom. The tall grenadiers of this great master of the art of war were an overmatch for the fierce and licentious nobles. He set the diet at defiance, abolished the freedom of taxation which the nobles had hitherto enjoyed, gave the peasants a legal protection against their oppression and caprice, and abolished such of their privileges as were inconsistent with good government. Thus a nobility which but a few years before had trampled upon the sovereign power became slavishly submissive to its will. Being no longer exempt from taxation, they were forced to seek distinction in the civil and military services of the state. In this new capacity their ancient chivalry broke forth in the campaigns against the Swedes and the Turks, on the Rhine and in Poland. The peace of Westphalia made this change general throughout Germany. Standing armies were everywhere introduced, and all the German governments verged towards a purer monarchy.

In addition to the monarchical tendency of the peace itself, in the seventeenth and in the early part of the eighteenth centuries, several princes mounted foreign thrones and brought their newly-acquired power to bear upon insubordination at home. The splendour of the court of Louis XIV began to be felt in the petty courts of Germany, and those nobles who before sought distinction as leaders of armed retainers moltened into silken performers in court ceremonies and pageantries of state. The French language, French manners, and French morals were introduced at all the courts beyond the Rhine. The country nobility (der Hof und der Landadel) held themselves aloof from this invasion of effeminacy. The Gallomania was of short duration. The morality of the Germans was too deeply interwoven with their national character to afford a permanent hold to French example. The latter part of the eighteenth century saw it give way, even in its strong holds, until it ultimately disappeared. Princes ascended the throne whose personal character was strong enough to introduce an effective reform. The nationality of the Germans awoke as from an unhealthy slumber. A new literature was created, and science was cultivated in a new spirit. The middle classes asserted their rights against the privileges of the nobles in a bold and determined tone. The nobility they said were alone eligible to civil and military posts, they were still in possession of monopolies, and the services exacted from their vassals were incompatible with justice and humanity. These remonstrances the nobility met with indifference and contempt, and in this relation did the two parties stand until the breaking out of the French Revolution.

The enthusiasm which was kindled throughout Germany by the first successes of the democratic party, was soon quenched in the deluge of blood which succeeded them. These saturnalia were fatal to the cause of freedom. The most upright and purest friends of emancipation from feudal thraldom, were startled at the price of blood and crime at which it was to be purchased. The nobles became the defenders of the throne, and the prince would listen to no accusation against them. But the French invasion precipitated them at once down the precipice they so much dreaded. The left bank of the Rhine was annexed to France, and the nobles of course lost all their privileges. The peace of Luneville abolished at a blow the diets in all the states which it concerned. The Rheinish confederacy were further empowered to deal as they pleased with the privileges of the nobles; a power, of which all but the King of Saxony and the Dukes of Mechlinburg thought proper to avail themselves. The religious endowments, with the single exception of those of Austria, were everywhere confiscated. The nobility were deprived of their privileges, and even rendered subject to conscription. In Prussia the necessity of making head against the invader, forced the government into the adoption of similar changes of policy. Servitude was abolished, the plebeian was allowed to purchase the estates of the noble, the latter was declared liable to conscription, and birth was declared no longer necessary for promotion in the army. After the peace of 1814, the nobility fondly hoped to recover their lost power and importance, but the middle classes had risen into importance,—to retrograde was impossible. The absolute monarch supported by his army and beloved by his people, was no longer disposed to admit the aristocracy to a share of power; and the Congress of Vienna contented itself with securing to the latter all the privileges which it could exercise without prejudice to the other classes of society, and without infringing on the Sovereign power. Their present position and numbers are thus estimated by Mr. Hawkins:

"The ordinary nobility in the different German states, is subjected to the respective sovereign powers. In no two countries is its position the same. It has almost everywhere lost its exemption from taxation, and its remaining privileges are rather forms than solid advantages. In the constitutional states, however, it takes part in the government as a legislative chamber, and in several it still continues to administer justice in minor affairs on its own domains, and to exercise the right of church-presentation,

On the whole, however, its position is rather to be ascribed to the respect which it inspires, than to the privileges to which it is legally entitled.

" The king of Prussia, and, I believe, some other German potentates, now require an university education, and certain preliminary tests from all candidates for office; this circumstance alone will probably tend to elevate the character of the German nobility, because they will be compelled to undergo a regular educational discipline, and to sustain competition; but they have also a still more difficult trial to endure in Prussia, in a struggle against increasing poverty.

" The number of noble idinviduals in Austria was estimated by Lichenstern at 475,000. But Hassel believes that this calculation falls far short of the truth. In 1785, 'the nobility of Hungary alone were estimated at 162,495; and in 1816, the male nobles of Milan were reckoned at 3,859. The number of nobles in Prussia was computed by Hassel, in 1822, at about 200,000. Spain has been estimated to possess the most numerous nobility; Poland, probably, is at least equal in this respect; Austria and Prussia follow, then Russia, then France, next Sweden, and England stands, perhaps, last; Italy is less known."

From the foregoing estimate, it appears that Germany is rich enough in all'conscience in noble blood, sufficiently so indeed to furnish a supply of that commodity to the other States of Europe. We are no longer amazed at the crowds which it sends forth to glitter for a while in our *beau monde*, like the swallows that come to revel in the sunshine of our summer. It is not our intention to follow Mr. Hawkins through his masterly chapter on the literature of Germany. In our Review of Mr. Taylor's powerful " Survey" we have already treated the subject at ample length. The various periodicals have, moreover, devoted a large portion of their columns to the work of popularizing the best productions of the several German schools, and of making the public acquainted with every point of interest connected with their writers. Those who have not had access to those sources of information, will find in the rapid sketch given in the present work all that is most deserving of attention. The exposition is clear, and the criticisms impartial and acute, for Mr. Hawkins is as judicious a critic as he is a careful and accurate statistic. As men of letters the Germans are pre-eminent. As Theologians they are not to be regarded with such cordial respect. In the cultivation of systematic geography, and of statistics, they are unrivalled. Busching, Hassel, Stein, Ritter, Crome, Meusel, Malthus, and a long array of celebrated names, have won honourable distinction in this field of science. Political philosophy and state economy have been cultivated with similar ardour, and the names of Schubert, Pœlitz, Von Rotteck and Welcker, and not a few others, have become illustrious by their success. In no country is the philosophy of legislation more sedulously investigated, and nowhere are more learned lawyers to be found, while in all that relates to the literature of their science the German medical men are confessedly the best read men in Europe. In the branches of forensic medicine, medical police and ophthalmic surgery, they 'stand at the head of their European brethren. Their superiority in theoretical pharmacy, in medical botany and dietetics, stands uncontroverted ; while the obscure and unpromising study of animal magnetism is peculiarly their own. In natural philosophy the names of Herschel, F. H .A. Von Humboldt, Gauss, Oken, Scheele, and Cuvier, who was born at Montebeliard, in the duchy of Wurtemberg, and received his education at Stutt- gard, are in the mouths of all Europe, and shed a lustre over the land of their birth. The cultivation of the arts keeps pace with the cultivation of letters. A rapid progress has been made in architec- ture ; in sculpture, Rauch and Tieck, Schadow and Ohmacht have attained considerable eminence : of Rauch and Tieck Mr. Hawkins speaks thus :—

" Christian Rauch, Professor to the Academy at Berlin, is remarkable for the truth, grace and power of his execution. His works prove him to be a man of great penetration, and, at the same time, of an imaginative mind. He possesses the secret of giving a dignified effect to modern costume. He has recently executed busts of Zelter and Schleiermacher, a colossal statue of Frederic William I., at Gumbinnen, and a monument for Franke, the founder of the orphan-asylum at Halle. Amongst his other works are an admirable little figure of Goëthe, but above all a monument to Queen Louisa of Prussia, and to Maximilian Joseph, of Bavaria.

" Christian Frederic Tieck, Professor of Sculpture to the Academy of Berlin, was born in that city in 1776. This artist has studied nature profoundly, and is well versed in classic art. His execution is singularly perfect and harmonious. His Ganymede and his Shepherd are admirable works of art, and worthy of a Grecian sculptor. He has recently execu- ted busts of the crown-princess, of Niemeyer, and of Milder the singer. Several scholars of the Berlin Academy have distinguished themselves in sculpture, as, for instance, the brothers Wichman and Rietschell." ·

The modern German school of painting springs from the year 1810. Its principal supporters are Overbeck, Cornelius, the Veits, W. Schadow and Sheffer: it addresses itself to the religious feelings of our nature, and prefers simplicity and force to ornament and grace. Cornelius is the great boast of this school. Regarding religion as the proper field of art, he made those painters whose works were especially imbued with it his peculiar study. He is established at Munich, to which city the munificent encouragement of the King of Bavaria has attracted numbers of the most eminent artists of Germany. With resources less abundant than those enjoyed by many individuals in England, this prince has done more for his small capital, and raised more noble monuments to the fine arts than any monarch of our own time. Munich is now the resort of strangers from all parts of Europe ; its artists are obtaining a wide field for exertion, and from the rank of a third rate capital it is now rising to a level with the first. In the matter of music we shall quote Mr. Hawkins's own words.

"In the cultivation of that most delightful of all fine arts, music, the Germans stand, by common consent, at the head of all the world. There the science and practice of this solace of life are carried to a perfection, and pursued to an extent, which it would be vain to seek in any other part of the globe. Those who, from old prejudices, expect to find a rival in Italy, will be grievously disappointed. In the village schools of Germany, singing is taught as a branch of education; a group of peasants, or a regiment of soldiers, will there execute choral music in a better taste than some of the professional choirs in other parts of Europe. In most of the large towns are academies, at which instrumental and vocal music are gratuitously, or almost gratuitously, taught. It forms the staple amusement of every bathing-place, of every public garden, of almost every society. Good music is sought and prized, from whatever quarter it may proceed,—not merely the composition and performance of noted names, not merely that which is new, but the truly good of all times, climes, and persons, is estimated at its just value. I shall not pause to inquire how it happens that in the more southern parts of Europe, the pretended genial soil of melody, the true musical genius is comparatively so barren, and the taste and mechanism in proportion so scanty, and so partial; but whatever may be the cause, not only is Germany the most methodical and the most learned, but she alone appears endued with the true enthusiasm, the full temperament of melody. To enumerate the great musical authors of Germany, would be to repeat a host of names familiar to all who honour sweet sounds; a small triumphant band will suffice, at the head of whom stand Handel, Gluck, Haydn, Mozart, and Weber, who have translated their art into a new language, pouring out at one moment rushing torrents of sublime eloquence, and at another gently gliding into the heart in sportive or murmuring streamlets.

"As to the instrumental performers of Germany, their names abound in the catalogue of every orchestra and concert in Europe. Of great singers she has not been so fruitful, although many such have been born of German parents established in foreign countries; and I believe that the impediment of language, and the vogue of the Italian school, have contributed to keep others in obscurity. In our own time, Sontag and Schroeder Devrient have elevated the national claims to vocal distinction. Even in the sister art of dancing, which some may, from prepossession, infer to be uncongenial to the soil, there are some most successful candidates for fame, such as Heberlé and the two Elslers; and in short, as Germany is the home of music, so also is it the only land in which, in these later and sadder days, the dance maintains its footing as a thoroughly national pastime."

In Germany as in every other country in Europe, the opera, musical farce, and splendid decorations have driven tragedy and comedy from the stage. There too, as in other countries, it is remarked that the theatre is less attended by the higher and more frequented by the lower classes. The drama, however, still maintains a firm hold, and forms an integral portion of daily existence to a large mass of the population. But the opera is in the ascendant, which Mr. Hawkins says is nowhere else so faithfully and so earnestly exhibited, and nowhere else so judiciously appreciated.

The following statistics of German publication as compared with that of France are curious and interesting.

" We perceive that the number of new publications was formerly much greater in Germany than in France, from the following comparative number of books published in the two countries.

In the Years	In France.	In Germany.	
		At Easter.	At Michaelmas.
1814	979	1490	1039
1815	1712	1777	973
1816	1851	1997	1200
1817	2126	2345	1187
1818	2431	2294	1487
1819	2441	2648	1268
1820	2465	2640	1318
1821	2617	3012	985
1822	3114	2729	1554
1823	2687	2558	1751
1824	3436	2870	1641
1825	3569	3196	1640
1826	4347	2648	2056
	33,775	32,204	18,099

50,303

In France 33,775

Balance in favour of Germany . . . 16,528

" Latterly, however, the French press appears so have gained some advance, as in 1828, when above 7000 publications are said to have been printed in France.

" Our excellent ' Foreign Quarterly Review' states, that the number of periodical works enumerated in the Leipsic catalogue for 1836, is 297. The names of 530 publishers are given in this catalogue. An Augsburg journal has lately affirmed, that on a moderate calculation, 10,000,000 of volumes are annually printed in Germany; and as every half-yearly catalogue contains the names of more than 1000 German writers, it has been assumed that there are now living in Germany, more than 50,000 persons who have perpetrated one or more books. The total value of all the books published annually, has been estimated at from 5,000,000 to 6,000,000 of dollars.

" To illustrate the increase of the book-trade during the last hundred years, we may cite the fact, that Leipsic contained in 1722 only 19 bookselling establishments, and 13 printing-offices; while in 1836 it was in possession of 116 of the former, and 22 of the latter.

" The book-trade was thirty years ago in the hands of only 300 booksellers or publishers; at present there are more than 1000. Throughout the whole Germanic Confederation, there is one bookseller to 93,000 souls, but in Austria one only in 122,222. Saxony furnishes the greatest number of new publications, next Prussia, and then Austria, but Austria is far behind in point of numbers. The number of booksellers in London has been computed, we know not how correctly, at above 800."

On the subject of religion, it is the settled conviction of Mr. Hawkins, that scepticism is making rapid strides over the whole fabric of society in Germany as well as in other countries of Europe. The tone of popular writers, the spirit in which religious matters are handled in society, and the feelings manifested towards the clergy, are some of the signs which he instances as being indicative of this result. The clergy themselves marshal the way to the precipice. Their Socinian mode of interpreting the Scriptures is laying the foundation of a popular creed of rationalism, which appears to the eyes of the orthodox Mr. Hawkins as the darkest cloud that menaces the state. The doctrines of the Rationalists were collected into systematic order by Röhr, now clerical superintendent of the grand duchy of Weimar, in his *Briefe über den Rationalismus,* and Wegschneider in his *Institutiones Theologicæ Christianæ Dogmaticæ;* from which we collect that the fundamental doctrine of rationalism is, that the mission of Christ and the whole scheme of revelation were merely intended for our instruction in certain principles, the truth of which human reason alone, without the aid of inspiration, would in process of time have been able to establish. Hence the fundamental truths of Christianity are totally slurred over or absolutely rejected. Gesenius, the celebrated Hebrew scholar, Schleiermacher and De Wette, are the most noted apostles of this doctrine of "accommodation" as it is technically termed, because it accommodates the wonders of revelation to human reason. Opposed to these are the " Supernaturalists," who maintain the necessity and reality of a revelation, while they deny the doctrine of original sin. Their opposition is not of a very decided cast, and they have given in more or less to the accommodation principle. The education of clergymen both Catholic and Protestant is conducted with the utmost care, and their sufficiency is tested by frequent examinations. The following affords a view of their comparative numbers, and their proportion to the population.

" *Prussia.* We have not been able to discover the number of the Protestant ministers. The Catholic population amounts to 4,816,813, and there are 3,200 Catholic parishes; thus there are 1,505 persons to each parish. *Saxony:* In this country there is one Lutheran minister to 1,600 inhabitants, and one Catholic minister to 432. In *Saxe Altenburg,* there is one minister to 800 inhabitants; in *Hanover,* one to 1,146 amongst the Lutherans, one to 940 in the Reformed Church, and one to 710 amongst the Catholics. In *Wurtemberg,* there is one Lutheran minister to 1,300 inhabitants, and one Catholic to 628. In Catholic *Austria,* there is one ecclesiastic to 500 inhabitants; of the Reformed Church there are 2,035 parishes, and 815 persons to each parish; of the Lutherans there are 807 parishes, and 1,400 persons to each parish; there are 50,000 Unitarians, who have 111 ministers, which is one minister to 459 individuals. In *Bavaria*, there is one minister to 1,000 inhabitants among the Catholics, and one to 914 among the Protestants.

"*Church Property in the Protestant States.* A considerable part of the church-property in Germany was seized upon by the governments when the monasteries were secularized at the Reformation; another portion, consisting of ground-rent, has, for some time, never been realized, and, finally, a part has been expended (as in Saxony,) for the establishment of schools, and on the relief of the poor. However, the little landed property belonging to each parish-church, has, for the most part, remained in the possession of the clergy, and is now the principal source of their income.

"In most livings, there is a parsonage-house, surrounded by gardens and orchards. Tithes are very common, and the value of them sometimes equals that of the church-lands. The clergyman has also certain fees, on the occasion of marriages, baptisms, burials and confirmations (these are called *Accidenzien*). Where the income from these sources is too limited, the government makes up the deficiency. In some parts, and particularly in the north of Germany, it is customary, at certain periods of the year, to make presents to the clergymen. On the whole, in Protestant Germany, the incomes of the country-clergy vary from 350 to 800 dollars; some have less than the former sum, and some as much as 1,000, 1,200, or 1,600,dollars. The value of a living often depends on the price of corn, and on the profit which the clergyman is capable of drawing from his glebe-lands. The livings in town are somewhat more valuable, varying from 450 to 1,000 dollars on an average. The two most valuable livings in Saxony are of 4,000 dollars a year, but, in both cases, this income is chiefly derived from fees.

"In no part of Germany has the church-property been better preserved from spoliation than in Hanover, where, consequently, the clergy are better paid. In Wurtemberg, the property of the church has been consolidated, and applied not only to ecclesiastical purposes, but to the establishment of schools, and to the relief of the poor. Moreover, in 1806, it was united with the royal domains, and subjected to the same administration. The lands attached to the country-churches have not, however, shared this fate, but are under the control of ecclesiastical commissioners. In Nassau, the average value of livings is from 600 to 1,800 florins, of deaneries from 1,300 to 1,800; the Protestant bishop has an income of 3,000 florins. In Prussia, the government pays out of the treasury to the support of the church, 2,326,000 dollars annually.

"*Church Property in Catholic States.* In Austria, not only are the clergy taxed in common with the lay citizens, but particular imposts are laid upon their body. The value of the church-property in this empire is 200,000,000 florins; besides a fund called the *Religious Fund*, constituted by the purchase-money of church-property (monasteries, &c.) sold by the Emperor Joseph, the annual interest of which is two and a half millions of florins. In Bavaria, the archbishop has an income of 20,000 florins, and the bishops of from 12,000 to 15,000 florins."

The greater number of Church presentations are in the hands of

Government, a fourth part only being in the hands of private individuals.

" In most Protestant states, the Catholic and the Established churches are placed upon the same footing. But as the ministers of the former persuasion are more numerous than those of the latter, and as, owing to the practise of celibacy, their wants are fewer, their incomes are generally less. On the other hand, the Catholic dignitaries are much better paid than the Protestant ones. In Rhenish Prussia, the Catholic archbishops have an annual income of 12,000 dollars, the bishops of 8,000, the deans of 1,800, or 2,000, the canons of 1,000 or 1,200. This money is now paid out of the Treasury ; the estates from which these dignitaries formerly derived their incomes having all been secularized. In Saxony, where the ruling family is of the Catholic religion, though the great mass of the population is Protestant, the clergy of the former persuasion are so well paid, as to cause great jealousy amongst those who are followers of the latter. In Hanover, and in Hesse-Cassel, the Catholic clergy are equally well paid with the Protestant, though this is not the case in Wurtemberg and Baden.

" In Austria, the Protestant clergy are provided for by their congregations, which have also to pay the *jura stolæ* to the Catholic priests. In Bavaria, the expenses of the Protestant church are defrayed by the government.

" We believe that the Jews throughout Germany are obliged, themselves, to defray the expenses of worship.

" There exist no general rules respecting the support of the clergy. Only the incomes of the higher Catholic clergy are fixed by the bull *De salute animarum*, namely, for the archbishop and prince-bishop of Breslau at 12,000 Prussian dollars; (about 1,750*l.*); for the other bishops 8,000 Prussian dollars, for the dignitaries of cathedral chapters respectively, 2,000, 1,800, 1,400 Prussian dollars ; and for canons or prebends, respectively, 1,200, 1,000 and 800 Prussian dollars, besides house-room. The incomes of all other livings, either of the Protestant or Catholic church, are very different. The clergyman receives his income either in kind or in money, It is paid in kind when it arises from a real estate belonging to his benefice, which he manages himself, or when it is rendered to him by landed proprietors. Of the same kind are tithes, rents, and other payments from land. The money-income of the clergy arises partly out of the public revenues of the crown, or of the parishes, either as a salary or compensation for appropriated lands or ground-rents, or as rents from private estates, or from endowments laid out at interest. The crown has undertaken the above-mentioned payment of the Catholic dignitaries, since their landed property had been appropriated to the public revenue. In the Trans-Rhenane part of the kingdom, where, during the French sway, the church property was seized and chiefly alienated, the crown pays a salary to the clergy, as a compensation, according to a *concordat* entered into by the French consular government with Pope Pius VII."

In the matter of education no country presents a subject of such

interesting investigation as Germany. In no country is there to be
found so ample a provision for the instruction of the people in all
sciences and arts.   Hence, there it is that the results of education
may be most advantageously weighed.   The inferences drawn by
Mr. Hawkins are not so very favourable to the predictions of our
propagandists.

"The facility with which the highest education may be obtained in
Germany, naturally introduces into the arena of life an immense proportion
of candidates for its higher prizes, too many of whom finally obtain disappointment, if not entire destitution, while not a few bury their obscure heart-
burnings in the chance pittance afforded by foreign countries, already over-
stocked with aspirants of indigenous origin.   Thus, in the course of ten
recent years, the number of Protestant clergymen has doubled in Prussia,
and the Roman Catholic priesthood has tripled; the lawyers have increased
one-fourth, but the doctors in medicine only one-seventh. At the beginning
of this period there was one lawyer in 12,600 inhabitants, at the end there
was one in 8,562; there was one doctor of medicine, at the beginning, in
27,000 souls, and at last one in 25,205.   In consequence of the increase of
students in the late years, there was recently in Prussia so many as

One student of theology in   442 inhabitants.
"   "   law in   822   "   "
"   "   medicine in 5,660 "   "

But the state in Prussia only requires—
One clergyman for . . 1,250 inhabitants.
One lawyer for   . . . 822   " "
One doctor of medicine for 3,516 " "

How many of those now employed must accordingly die or retreat, in order
to make room for the forthcoming!   In the smaller states of Germany the
prospect is still more disheartening. In the duchy of Baden, only eight
vacancies annually occur of offices in the law, enjoying a fixed salary, while
so many as forty-six candidates present themselves annually for examination;
and there are already so many as two hundred and fifty-one candidates examined and approved, and awaiting the long-deferred turn."

The Prussian system is as everybody knows the most perfect in
the world. Alluding to its operation on the mass of society, Mr.
Hawkins says,

"I am the last person to attach much weight to my own observations,
but, in default of the remarks of others, I have not succeeded in discovering
that the Prussian peasant or artisan is better informed, or more moral than
his neighbours; his manners are not superior, nor does he appear to solace
his hours of leisure more than others, with study, or books.   But the formation of character is so intimately blended in Prussia with the military
system, which converts every man into a soldier, for a certain period of his
life, that it is difficult to ascertain the respective share which is to be ascribed to the various elements which combine to mould the individual. The
most intelligent and best informed peasant in Europe has appeared to me to
be the Scotch, while the Austrian rustic is perhaps the happiest."

In the building and discipline of prisons, great improvement has taken place in Germany within the last half century. The prisons are conveniently constructed, well aired, and well regulated. The silent system is almost universally adopted and enforced by the bastinado. The latter infliction has been much complained of, but after all, it is not worse than forced labour. Mr. Hawkins gives a detailed account of the discipline and regulations peculiar to the prisons of every particular state; but to follow him in this subject, in which he seems quite at home, would be more than our limits would allow of. We shall merely notice the *labour* executed by culprits in the German prisons, as we consider it particularly deserving of attention.

" The prisoners at Munich are employed in an excellent manufactory of cloth, and as tailors and shoemakers. The cloth alone, which is of the quality worn by the higher classes, produces a revenue to the government of more than 50,000 florins yearly. The prisoners in Holstein are still, for the most part, unemployed; but not so in Schleswig, particularly at Glüdkstadt, where each prisoner is bound to do a certain quantity of work, which if he neglects he is punished; if he does more than is required, he is paid for the surplus. The prisoners are employed in spinning, carding wool, knitting stockings, weaving, making pipes for fire-engines, and sail-cloth.

" At Dresden the prisoners are employed in cleaving wood, breaking stones down to sand, and dragging coals through the town. The inhabitants can obtain the prisoners to do any sort of work for them, by paying five groschen per day to the establishment.

" At Plessenburg there is a cloth manufactory and a bakehouse in the prison. The prisoners are allowed to work a little for themselves. The managers of the prison allow culprits who have been liberated to become the superintendents of the others when at work.

" At Mannheim the employments of the prisoners are dressing hemp, weaving, knitting, making cloths, shoes, and lately, manufacturing list. The superintendents of the different kinds of works receive four hundred florins a year. Some of the prisoners are employed in making the furniture of the establishment, and others are employed by the inhabitants, at their own houses, to cleave wood. At Frieburg the prisoners are employed in stone-cutting, weaving, carpenter's-work, and as masons, shoemakers, tailors, locksmiths, and clockmakers. At Cologne, a certain number of prisoners are without occupation, those, for instance, who are condemned to a short imprisonment, debtors, and those of the untried who are not likely to remain long. Trades of all sorts are carried on by the rest of the prisoners; amongst others, lithography.

" In Austria, the daily task allotted to each prisoner is such, that the very industrious have a little time to work for themselves. The half of what the prisoner earns for himself is set apart to be given him at his liberation; the other half he can spend in buying bread, beer, or broth. In order to appreciate this privilege, we must remember that the Austrian prison has, for three days of the week, only a pound of bread for all provision.

At Naugard, the prisoner has first to pay for his support by his labour, before he receives anything extra. What he saves, is placed in the Savings'-

bank at Stettin, and should he die in confinement, it goes to his heirs. On his quitting the prison, he not only receives his extra earnings, but he is duly recommended where he is likely to obtain employment. In respect to their gains, all the prisoners are put as much as possible on the same footing; and half is at their disposal for the purchase of provisions, a little brandy, and, on Sundays, of tobacco for chewing.

"At Dresden, the sum accruing from surplus labour is never placed at the prisoner's disposal until his liberation.

"At Hamburg, the system of surplus labour has not been adopted; but a part of what the prisoners earn reverts to them.

"The other German prisons resemble more or less the above, in the arrangements they have introduced respecting the employment of prisoners."

In most of the prisons provision is made for the religious and elementary instruction of the prisoners, and a most praiseworthy care is taken of them by the respective governments after their liberation. At Hamburg it not unfrequently happens that the prisoner receives on his liberation a sum of from 200 to 300 marks as the produce of his labour. When a prisoner has conducted himself well, exertions are made to establish him honestly. In Nassau, if the prisoner's gains do not amount to a certain sum, the deficiency is supplied by the government, and care is always taken to replace him properly in the world, to prevent him from returning to his former courses. In this respect, their conduct is decidedly superior to that pursued in England, where a prisoner is turned forth upon society without any means of subsistence whatsoever, or any opportunity of earning an honest livelihood.

We come now to the social condition of Germany as expounded by Mr. Hawkins, and with this we shall close our observations on the subject. The partition of Germany into a number of small states, gives to individuals advantages of a higher degree than are enjoyed by those of any other European states. Thus the numerous states have their respective cabinet ministers, convoys, generals, and civil officers of various denominations. An office which in England is filled by a single person, gives employment to twenty in Germany. For instance, England sends out one ambassador to France, while Germany sends no less than thirteen. Then again in literature, there are thirty German universities to five British; and moreover a German university has double the number of professors of an English one, besides their Gymnasiums, Pedagogisms, and innumerable schools, with their quota of officers. Another advantage accruing from this system is, that every sovereign, how petty soever he may be, is anxious to embellish and distinguish his territory. Hence, museums, picture galleries, gardens, libraries, academies; and thus for one of such institutions in England, we shall find twenty in Germany, all open to the public; nor does it appear that the German is more heavily taxed for the procurement of such privileges than his neighbours; besides, as every palace, garden, gallery, and park is open, the money which is received from the subject is returned to him in the form of mental and bodily amusement. The gracious and cordial familiarity which prevails between the higher and lower classes is also worthy of imitation. There is no shrinking from contamination, no shuddering at impure mixture as in England. The use of the Murchaum has been severely reprehended. All that can be said is, that it disposes the mind to serenity and quiet contemplation, and is much better than gin-drinking. "The German labourer," says Mr. Hawkins, "seated at a table in a public garden, quietly smoking his pipe, listening to excellent music, and surrounded by his family, is no mean specimen of human happiness and respectability." The Germans are less the slaves of fashion and exclusiveness than any people in Europe, each considers his own means and inclinations, and pursues them without deference to others, and without offence. No one stares at a bad coat or negligent costume, and everybody is at liberty to do and dress just as he pleases. The chief gratification of the higher order in addition to the theatre, consists in a summer visit to some of the many watering-places, where they live almost entirely in public. In the smaller towns, the men of learning shut themselves up in their cabinets, and in the intenseness of their studies the extent of their acquirements and the simplicity of their manners are distinguishable at once from the rest of their European colleagues. The Cosmopolitan man of learning, says Mr Hawkins, who understands most of the European and some of the Oriental languages, while he is conversant with almost every science, is, perhaps, only to be found at the present moment in Germany. He differs from most other specimens of the same class, not only in his attainments, but in the scrupulous sanctitude— in the concientious manner in which he weighs evidence and records every minute shade of fact, and also in his impartiality and that genial love for his calling which enables him to disregard pecuniary profit, and confines his anxiety to the noble ambition of instructing his brethren, of conciliating the suffrages of the wise, and of laying the foundations of a posthumous fame, which, alas, is too rarely completed into a lasting edifice. Frankness, honesty, simplicity, modesty, and diffidence, are the chief qualities of the national character of the Germans. They are the great assertors of a truth of invaluable importance, that all are to be treated with respect, and that no superiority of rank or fortune can warrant arrogance of demeanour or pride of speech.

In addition to the general view of Germany, each of the larger states has a chapter exclusively devoted to itself. There is not a single item which may claim connexion with the statistics of each state which is not noted down with an almost tiresome precision. Thus we have the number of lodging houses, and of arrivals and departures in a given year; the number of each particular trade, profession, calling; the number of sheep, oxen, and stock of all kinds; besides revenues, population, deaths, births, marriages, and all the numerous *et cætera* that can possibly engage the attention of the compiler of statistics. We are only surprised Mr. Hawkins did not attempt to count the trees, or the farming implements in each state. It is impossible for us to give any adequate idea of this huge and compact mass of statistical information; some facts, however, there are connected with the moral condition of a country, where education is so widely diffused and so systematically conducted, which we cannot pass by without an observation.

The annual number of births in the Austrian dominions (Hungary not included) is estimated at 764,290; of marriages 167,704; and of deaths 688,763. There is one marriage annually to 130 individuals. The number of female to male births is as 1000 to 1,602. About every tenth child is illegitimate. The Bohemians are much more prolific than the inhabitants of the other provinces. Amongst them, in every eight births one is illegitimate. In the Foundling Hospital at Prague, 1,125 children were received in the year 1827. The number of marriages in the same year was six to one. In Prussia, the illegitimate births are one in twelve. The number of prostitutes in Berlin, whose names are inscribed upon the books of the police, is only 273, almost an evanescent quantity, when we compare Berlin with Paris, where the registered number amounted in 1834 to 3,816, or to London, where their name is Legion. But this apparently small number is by no means an argument in favour of the superior morality of the Berlinese, but is entirely owing to the compulsory and vexatious interference of the police. Another strange fact connected with Prussian morals is, that the law allows them a facility of divorce, of which they are not at all backward in availing themselves. The number of divorces is one in thirty-seven marriages: this is a most startling fact. In Saxony, the number of married persons is calculated at about one-third of the population, or 277,813 in round numbers; of these, 11,213 were living *separate*, and 3,798 were *divorced*. The number of illegitimate children in the same state was in 1831, one in six. The houses of correction at Spandau and Brandenburg in Prussia, contained, in 1833, 1,458 prisoners; and in 1835, 1,0134 persons were arrested in Berlin, so that one in twenty-five persons spent a portion of the year in prison. In the rural districts of Bavaria, the number of illegitimate children exceeded the number of those born in wedlock, a circumstance without parallel, even in the most dissolute cities in Europe. In Munich, the number of children born out of wedlock, almost exactly balances that born in wedlock, the illegitimates being in 1823, 998; the legitimates 1,030. In 1834, the illegitimates mustered 1,291, while the legitimates did not exceed 1339. So much for the Utopian theories of the ultimate perfectibility of

mankind. So much for the diffusion of education and the reading
of the Scripture serving as a check upon the passions. It is notorious that in Ireland, where the absence of the education that exists
in Germany is so much deplored, the number of illegitimate
children in any district is a mere fraction on the amount of population; and that in most districts it does not equal even a fraction.
Perhaps, when the Irish become as enlightened as their German
prototypes in learning, they will be equally regardless of the slender
restraints of conventional morality.

Art. V.

1. *A Treatise on the Nature, Symptoms, Causes, and Treatment of
   Insanity, with Practical Observations on Lunatic Asylums; and a
   Description of the Pauper Lunatic Asylum for the County of Mid-
   dlesex, at Hanwell, with a detailed Account of its Management.* By
   Sir W. C. Ellis, M.D. 8vo. London: Holdsworth. 1838.
2. *A Narrative of the Treatment experienced by a Gentleman during a
   State of Mental Derangement, designed to explain the Causes and the
   Nature of Insanity, and to expose the Injudicious Conduct pursued
   towards many unfortunate Sufferers under that Calamity.* 8vo. pp.
   278. London: Wilson. 1838.

MENTAL alienation in its various forms, would appear to be greatly
on the increase in this and all other civilized countries; to inquire
into the causes that originate, and the remedies that are likely to
mitigate or subdue this deplorable malady, becomes then a subject
worthy the most serious attention of the statesman or philanthropist
as well as the medical practitioner, whose professional duties require
that he be well acquainted with all the multiform derangements of
the intellect. Such being our opinion, we have thought no apology
need be offered for devoting a few pages to the subject which is
embraced in the volumes which stand at the head of this article.

Insanity, as a disease of the mental faculties, has always been a
matter of interesting investigation by reflecting men. It has been
remarked, that lunacy belongs almost exclusively to civilized man—
barbarous or savage nations being entirely exempt, or nearly so.
The Indians of North or South America we are assured by travellers
are totally free from it. There is but little insanity among the uneducated negroes of the West Indies, or of Africa. A recent
tourist among the tribes in the neighbourhood of the Cape of Good
Hope, asserts that it seldom or never occurs among that people;
our authority states that he could not make them comprehend the
meaning of the term, though they were well acquainted with the
delirium of drunkenness. In countries where the government is
despotic, where there is but little mental excitement among the mass
of the people, the intellectual faculties inactive, and the passions tor-
pid, there are but few cases of insanity. Travellers have also informed

us, that madness is an uncommon disease in Russia, though it prevails more in the large towns than among the peasantry of the country. There is but little in Spain and Portugal, though, according to Sir A. Halliday, malformations of the head, and idiocy, are common in both countries. The inhabitants of China appear to be nearly exempt from this disease. Dr. Scott, who accompanied Lord M'Carthy in his embassy to that country, heard but of a single instance. It is uncommon in Persia, Hindostan, and Turkey. Dr. Madden, in his Travels in Turkey, after remarking, that " countries where the intellect is most cultivated, there insanity is most frequent," adds, " there is no nation where madness is so rare as in Turkey, where the people of all others think the least."

The mere exitement of the passions, however, of a savage uncivilized race of men, seldom produces mental derangement, unless the brutal ferocity they manifest towards their enemies may be so considered ; but in the communities where the mass of the people have received some intellectual culture, whatever strongly affects the mind, whatever greatly excites the feelings and passions, hopes and fears, whether it be political or religious commotions and revolutions, or sudden loss or accession of fortune, disposes many to insanity. Esquirol says it was frightfully increased during the first French Revolution ; that even women strongly affected by the events of that exciting time, bore children whom the slightest cause rendered insane. The same authority also states, that during the late wars of France, the number of the insane was increased at each departure of the conscripts, either among the conscripts themselves or their parents and friends. When France was invaded by the allied army, terror multiplied the disease among the French ; and German writers make the same observation respecting its increase in Germany, when the French entered that country.

The noted South Sea bubble, when large fortunes were suddenly made and lost, when all minds were intensely agitated with hopes and fears, multiplied the inmates of madhouses. And it is a curious fact, that more were made crazy by the sudden acquisition of great wealth, than by the loss of it.

Peculiarities of insanity, or the particular delusions of the insane, are determined by the state of general intelligence, or by the kind of excitement that produced the disease. Thus during a part of the middle ages, the belief was universal that mankind were in the power of evil spirits or demons, and *demonomania* was a common form of insanity. In modern times the belief in demons, and the fear of them, has generally subsided ; but the fear of the power of government, the police, and the prison, has increased. Esquirol remarks, that in France many are now sent to the lunatic hospitals, whom the fear of the police has made crazy, that would in former times have been hung because they feared the devil. When Napo-

leon made and unmade kings and queens with great rapidity, kings
and queens increased in the French madhouses.   " So great has been
the influence of our political commotions," says Esquirol, " that I
could give the history of France from the taking of the Bastile to
the last appearance of Bonaparte, by that of the insane in the hospitals, whose delusions related to the different events of that long
period of history."

Insanity has increased as knowledge and the arts of civilized life
have advanced, and is now most prevalent in the countries most
enlightened and free.   The exact number of the insane of any country is not known, as in none have they been enumerated in such a
manner as to insure correctness.   In some countries, those only are
reckoned that are in the public institutions, or in some way supported
at the public expense.   In others, in addition to such, those that are
known to the magistrates, clergymen, or physicians of the different
districts, are also enumerated.   But in this way, many would undoubtedly be omitted, as families usually endeavour to conceal, as
long as possible, the fact that one of their number is deranged in
mind.   According to the most recent estimates, there is in France
one insane person to 1000 of the population,

Wales,	-	-	-	800
England,	-			782
Scotland,	-	-	-	574

These statements show, that insanity is very prevalent in France
and England ; yet they are, we apprehend, considerably too low.
Dr. Prichard, the most correct, and elaborate, and in our opinion the
most able writer on insanity, speaking of the number of lunatics in
France, observes : " Unfortunately no satisfactory sources of information on this subject exist, and France is much behind England
and some other countries, in all the materials for statistical researches
on the frequency of mental derangement."   He believes the estimate
for this country much too low ; and the following facts appear to
confirm his opinion.   The Quakers, or Society of Friends, have
accurate knowledge of the insane belonging to their society.   From
statements furnished by themselves, it appears there is *one* insane
person to 358 of their number.   When it is considered, that there
are but few cases of religious insanity among the Quakers, and extremely few from intemperance, and that there are no known causes
for a greater frequency of this disease with them than the other
inhabitants of England, we are forced to the conclusion, that the
returns of the number of the insane for the rest of England are too
incorrect to afford fair ground for the estimates that have been made,
while the knowledge of each other which prevails among the
Quakers, brings nearly all the cases which occur among them into
the calculation.

That the estimates for France is too small, is rendered probable
from the fact, that in other countries, where more care has insured

greater accuracy, the number of the insane has been ascertained to be considerably greater than stated to be in that country. The statistics of insanity in the Prussian Provinces on the Rhine, are more accurate than those of England or France, though the learned Dr. Jacobi thinks they are far from correct. According to this writer, there is in these provinces *one* insane person to 666 of the population.

But the most complete statistical accounts that exist of the deranged persons of any country, are those of Norway; and these exhibit *one* case of insanity to 551 of the population. Still most of the known causes of this disease prevail to even greater extent in France than in Norway, and we have no other way of accounting for the difference in the above estimate, than by supposing those of the former country to be very inaccurate.

We have no means of determining the number of the insane in Russia and other northern countries, or in Italy, Spain, and Portugal. From all we can learn on this subject, we believe the disease to be much less frequent in these countries than in France, England, Germany, and the United States. According to M. Brière, who recently visited the lunatic establishments of Italy, only *one* case of insanity is found to 4879 of the population. That there has been but little of the disease in Spain, we infer from the fact, that, but a few years since, the Hospital for Lunatics at Madrid contained but 60 patients, and that at Cadiz only 50.

In the foregoing accounts of the number of the insane, probably some idiots are included. Indeed, it is often very difficult to distinguish insanity from idiocy, as the former frequently passes into the latter, in a gradual and imperceptible manner. Thus a person may be insane one month, and the next be idiotic.

Insanity is not upon the whole a disease very dangerous to life; in France, it has been stated that the records of the medical institution for lunatics exhibit a wonderful confirmation of this assertion. Taking the entire number of the deranged in these asylums into view, it appears that fully one-half have been confined upwards of sixteen years, a vast number more than twenty years, many upwards of forty, and several beyond sixty years. The records of receptacles for the insane in this country evince nearly simil∢r results. And it is gratifying also to be able to state, that no fact relating to this disease appears better established than the general certainty of curing it in its early stage. Dr. Willis, many years ago, averred that nine out of ten cases of insanity, recovered, if placed under his care within three months from the first attack. Dr. Burrows has reported from his own experience similar consequences. Dr. Ellis, when director of the York West Riding Lunatic Asylum, stated in 1827, that of 312 patients, admitted within three months after the commencement of the insanity, 216 recovered.

Mr. Tuke, of the Retreat near York, observes, " According to the result of our experience, I should say the probability of recovery

from uncombined insanity, in recent cases, is somewhat greater than
nine to one." Several other hospitals for lunatics in England,
established within a few years, have been equally successful in curing
recent cases of insanity.

In these institutions, many no doubt are received whose madness has been caused by the immoderate use of intoxicating drinks.
Such cases are in general to be reckoned among the cases most
easily cured, for although this is not uniformly the fact, it often
happens that when the exciting cause is removed, the effect begins
to lessen, and eventually ceases. When these patients are prevented
from obtaining stimulating liquors, and are treated with sedative
remedies, they quickly show signs of amelioration and of the sub-
sidence of the disease. This may perhaps explain why, in some of
the lunatic asylums of this country, the cures of recent cases of
insanity have been more numerous than in the institutions on the
continent. Intemperance, in this country, is reported to be a frequent cause of insanity ; but, according to M. Esquirol, it is not so
in France, even among the lower classes. Among 336 lunatics in
his establishment, there were but *three* who appeared to have lost
their reason through the habit of intoxication.

More just views respecting this disease prevail than formerly :
it is no longer regarded as a disgrace, or as a disease resulting
from some criminal offence. It is now considered a physical
disorder, a disease of the brain, and one which can be as readily
cured as disease of other organs of the body. But, in order to effect
a cure, it is often necessary to remove the patient from his home,
and separate him from his relatives and former associates ; we say
it is often necessary, for undoubtedly there are cases that would not
be benefited by this course, and some that would be aggravated by
it. Quite recent cases may frequently be cured without seclusion.
Broussais refers to a great number of cures effected by active treatment alone in the commencement of the disease. On the necessity
of seclusion, M. Esquirol remarks, in a late publication, " Confinement should not be prescribed for all insane persons ; for if the delirium is partial or transitory ; if it relates only to objects of indifference, and is unaccompanied with violent passion ; if the patient
has no aversion to his home, nor to the persons with whom he lives,
and his delirium is independent of domestic habits ; if his real or
imaginary causes of excitement are not to be found in the bosom of
his family ; if the fortune or life of the patient, by retaining a large
proportion of his friends, is not compromised, and he submits to the
proper means of cure ;—in all these cases confinement may be useful,
but it is not indispensable. But if the patient, retaining a large
portion of his intellect, has a great attachment to his relations, it is
to be feared that confinement might aggravate the disease." But
such cases are much less frequent than those that require seclusion
and separation from friends and home. This renders hospitals for

the insane necessary, and we rejoice to find they are rapidly multiplying in this and all civilized countries.

Asylums for the insane are of modern origin. In fact, all public hospitals for the sick and poor may be so considered, as they originated with the Christians of the third or fourth century. But long after those suffering from other diseases were received into hospitals and provided with medical assistance, lunatics were neglected, and perished in great numbers. Some of the most furious were confined in small cells, or shut up in convents and dungeons, while others were burned as sorcerers, or as possessed of demons. Those that were tranquil were permitted their liberty, abandoned however to neglect,—to the abuse and the laughter, or to the ridiculous veneration of their fellow creatures.

But about the commencement of the seventeenth century, lunatics began to be received into the general hospitals, where they were confined in the most obscure corners of the buildings, and received no medical aid. Soon after this, in some of the large towns of France, a few separate but poorly conducted hospitals were provided for the insane, though the greater part still remained at liberty, or were confined in the general hospitals. It was not until 1792, when M. Pinel was appointed physician in chief to the Bicêtre at Paris, that correct views respecting the treatment of the insane began to prevail, and to be reduced to practice. At this institution, when M. Pinel took charge of it, were a large number of lunatics considered incurable. Many of them being very furious, were kept constantly chained. This illustrious physician, after having in vain solicited the government to allow him to unchain these maniacs, finally went in person to the authorities, and advocating with much warmth and earnestness the removal of this monstrous abuse, obtained permission to do as he pleased respecting them. Great fears were entertained for the personal safety of M. Pinel, should he undertake to unchain them. This, however, he resolved to do. The first man on whom he tried the experiment was one of the most furious, who had been in chains forty years, and had already killed one keeper by a blow with his manacles. Pinel entered his cell unattended, and offered to remove his chains and permit him to walk in the court, if he would promise to behave well and injure no one. " Yes, I promise you," said the maniac. His chains were then removed, and the keepers retired leaving the door of his cell open. " He raised himself," says the son of the celebrated Pinel, in a paper read at the Academy of Sciences, " many times from his seat, but fell again on it, for he had been in a sitting posture so long that he had lost the use of his legs. In a quarter of an hour he succeeded in maintaining his balance, and with tottering steps came to the door of his dark cell. His first look was at the sky, and he cried out enthusiastically, ' How beautiful !' During the rest of the day he was constantly in motion, walking up and down the staircases, and uttering short exclamations of delight. In the evening he returned of his own accord into his cell, where a better bed than he had been accustomed to had been prepared for him, and he slept tranquilly. During the two succeeding years which he spent at the Bicêtre, he had no return of his furious paroxysms, but even rendered himself useful, by exercising a kind of authority over the insane patients, whom he ruled in his own fashion."

In the course of a few days, Pinel released fifty-three maniacs from their chains. The result was happy beyond his hopes. Tranquillity and harmony succeeded to tumult and disorder ; and, by the aid of continued mild and judicious treatment, the most furious became calmer and more tractable, and many were restored to perfect health of body and mind. This transaction caused much sensation, not only in France, but throughout the civilized world, and created a revolution in the treatment of this unfortunate but hitherto neglected portion of our fellow creatures. To M. Pinel is unquestionably due the great credit of first employing judicious, systematic, and moral means in the cure of the insane.

At present there are in France large institutions for the reception and cure of lunatics. Among the most celebrated are the *Salpétrière* and the *Bicêtre*, and the *Maison Royale de Charenton*. The former, at the south-eastern extremity of Paris, is composed of several buildings, enclosing spacious gardens and grounds for exercise. This is for the accommodation of females only. It usually contains about 1000 lunatics. These are divided into three classes, the curable, incurable, and idiotic. M. Pariset has the medical superintendence of the curable class. The Bicêtre, about two leagues from Paris, receives only males. It usually has from 350 to 400 patients. Here are also spacious grounds for exercise, and a farm where many of the patients are employed much of the time. The Maison Royale de Charenton, a short distance from Paris, is exclusively appropriated to the reception of the insane of both sexes, and contains 600 beds. Besides these, there are others in the vicinity of Paris and in many of the large towns of France, some public and some private, but all under good regulations and well conducted.

In London, so early as 1553, lunatics were received into the Bethlem Hospital, a Royal foundation for lunatics, incorporated by Henry VIII. This hospital has been rebuilt several times, and enlarged. It is now a noble brick building, 580 feet in length, with accommodations for 400 patients. It cost about 100,000*l.*, and has an annual income of 18,000*l.* St. Luke's Hospital, another institution in London for the reception of lunatics, originated in 1732. The present building, though commenced in 1751, was not completed until 1786, at an expense of 55,000*l.* It is a solid brick edifice, 500 feet in length, and accommodates 300 patients. This hospital has an annual income of 9,000*l.*

Both these old establishments are quite defective, as they are without the useful appendage of spacious grounds and workshops, for the exercise and employment of the patients. In other parts of England, in Ireland, and Scotland there are many well-arranged and well-conducted lunatic establishments. Among the most celebrated, are the Wakefield Asylum for the West-Riding of York, and the Lancaster Asylum, in England ; the Richmond Asylum at Dublin ; and the Glasgow Lunatic Asylum in Scotland. But there are several others, more recently established, equally well conducted. Most of these institutions can accommodate from two hundred to three hundred patients. Workshops are generally attached to them, and twenty or thirty acres of land, where the patients are much of the time employed at their trades, or in agriculture. In addition to such public institutions, private ones, for the accommodation of a limited number of lunatics, are numerous. Often one such receives only those of the same sex. Some of them are fitted up with great elegance, with every thing desirable for the safety and welfare of the patients, affording to them all the advantages of a secluded private residence, with large, airy, and commodious apartments, beautiful gardens and grounds for exercise and amusement, together with experienced and careful medical superintendence.

In many of the states of the Continent, hospitals for the insane have been provided. Some of them are well, and others badly conducted. In the Netherlands, according to Halliday, much attention has been paid to the relief and comfort of the insane. At Ghent are several public establishments, and one private, for their accomodation. At Antwerp there is an excellent hospital for lunatics. It was built about thirty years since, and usually has between two hundred and three hundred patients. With this is connected the celebrated and singular establishment at Gheil, which, with perhaps some modifications, might be adopted with advantage in this country. It consists of a village, or a number of detached cottages, far removed from other habitations. These buildings are occupied by peasants of good character, who receive lunatics,—mostly those that are convalescent,—treat them with great kindness, and employ them in the cultivation of the land. Each patient is obliged to labour a certain number of hours every day when able ; and when not so employed is allowed to walk about without restraint. Scarcely any accident occurs, and very few attempt to escape. The recoveries here have been so numerous and rapid, that the fame of the institution has extended far, and many persons of distinction have been sent to it for recovery.

In Bavaria and Saxony, much has been done by government for the welfare of the insane. In Denmark and Sweden there are several lunatic hospitals. Those in the former, and especially the one at Copenhagen, merit high commendation. Many of the large

towns of Italy have one or more Asylums for lunatics. At Milan
there is a well-conducted lunatic hospital, containing near five
hundred patients, most of whom are employed in gardening and in
manufacturing clothing. At Genoa, part of the Hospitals of
Incurables is given up to the insane. About two hundred and fifty
are kept here in a wretched condition. A recent writer has the
following remarks on them :—" When we visited this establishment in 1829, though the sexes were in different wards, all varieties
and degrees of insanity were congregated together. From fifty to
one hundred were in one room, most of them chained to their
beds by their wrists and ankles. When we entered the women's
ward, the inmates were eating ; and, perhaps excited by the
entrance of strangers, their fury exceeded any thing of the kind
we ever witnessed. Mingled with the clashing of chains, were
groans, and curses, and prayers, and shouts of laughter. Every
individual appeared excited. Some came the length of the chains,
and strained every muscle to break them ; others threw at us with
their utmost strength, the little pittance they were eating ; while
others, a little less furious, beckoned to us, and besought us to look
at some coarse pictures they had drawn on the wall, or at some
rags they had fantastically put together. Throughout this vast
Pandemonium, we saw not one that appeared tranquil, or in the way
of recovery. We were told they received but little medical treatment, and were not allowed to leave their wards until death released
them."

At Florence, the average number of the insane in the *Spedale di
Bonifacio*, the hospital appropriated to them, is about three hundred. The patients are clothed alike, in white woollen dresses, and
have their apartments kept very neat. When it becomes necessary
to confine a patient, his hands are placed in a wooden case, and
bound to the abdomen by a strap around his body. Furious patients are confined in dark rooms with well-padded walls. The darkness is thought to be very serviceable in rendering them more
tranquil. The management of this institution appears to be
good. Many of the male patients are employed in gardening, or at
their trades, and the women in knitting and spinning. At Rome,
the hospital for lunatics consists of two separate buildings, one for
each sex. The number of patients is about 400. The most furious
are confined by chains. All varieties of insanity are mixed together,
and no moral measures are resorted to in their treatment. At
Naples is the celebrated Aversa, an hospital for lunatics. The
sexes are here in different buildings, above 200 in each. Great regularity prevails throughout the institution. On ringing a bell, the
patients rise, breakfast with decorum, and the more quiet are present
at religious worship. Though the advantages of this institution are
said to have been exaggerated, it is the most extensive and best
regulated hospital for the insane in Italy.

· In Germany, some of the lunatic hospitals are well conducted, and others not so. At the one in Berlin, containing 150 patients, no moral treatment appears to be adopted. There being no grounds for exercise, the patients are constantly confined to the house. At *Sonnenstein*, about four leagues from Dresden, there is a government establishment for insane patients, and the most celebrated and best conducted institution in Germany, if not in Europe. It consists of an ancient castle, situated on a hill, with extensive adjacent grounds. The number of patients is about 200; most of whom are occupied in good weather out of doors, in walking about the grounds, cultivating flowers, digging, &c. The women have a flower-garden in their department, which serves to occupy and amuse many of them; and others sew, knit, and spin. None are confined to the house; even the most furious patients are allowed to walk about with the others, with cloaks that conceal the apparatus that confines their hands. This measure is said to tranquillize them more than anything else. The whole establishment is kept extremely neat, and contains workshops, a saloon of amusement, with books, a piano, draught boards, and a billiard room. At a distance from the large building, in a lovely garden at the base of the hill, is the house for the convalescents, furnished with musical instruments, and other things for the amusement of those who are recovering.

A few miles from Bonn is another excellent hospital for lunatics, on the same plan as the one at *Sonnenstein*. It contains about 200 patients. Dr. Jacobi is the superintending physician, and resides in an adjoining house.

In the United States, hospitals exclusively for the insane are of quite recent origin. That established by the Society of Friends near Frankfort, in the vicinity of Philadelphia, in 1817, may be considered the first; though a separate building was allotted to those at the New York Hospital in 1808. But previous to this, the general hospitals of Philadelphia and New York received lunatics. Ever since the establishment of the Pennsylvania Hospital in 1752, lunatics have been received there as patients, though not until 1796 was a part of the building exclusively appropriated to them. At this time, upwards of seventy rooms were opened for their accommodation. From its establishment in 1752 until 1836, 4116 lunatics have been received, of which number 1349 have been cured, 810 have been relieved, and 548 have died.

Having taken a cursory glance at the present state of this disease throughout the civilized world, as well as made a few remarks upon its extreme unfrequency among savage or barbarous nations, and given a slight notice of the various public institutions in this country, on the continent of Europe, and in the United States, we will now proceed to investigate the merits of the works prefixed to this article; and first in respect to the one written by Sir W. Ellis, though abounding with many curious details, offers us no very

striking or enlarged views upon either the nature or treatment of
the disease; for instance, what is there in the following account
of the symptoms, but what was known to every medical practitioner
long ago.

." The first thing which we ought to examine is the state of the head:
it is there that we usually find a marked change. With very few exceptions, a considerable increase of temperature will be found in it, and it is
often much hotter than other parts of the body, which are even covered
with the clothes: when this is the case, the pulse is generally found quick,
—but this increased temperature of the head sometimes exists, even to a
great degree, without that being the case; and when the heat is not very
considerable, no variation whatever is usually to be found in the pulse:
and this rule holds good whether the case be recent or of long standing. * *
   " I could insert a catalogue of cases to show that the commencement of
insanity, and any exacerbation of it in the old cases, are attended almost
invariably (indeed I think I should be justified in saying universally) with
increased heat in the head.—In ordinary cases it extends over the entire
surface of the cranium, though in many instances particular portions of it
are of a higher temperature than the other parts.
   " The heat in the head is very generally accompanied by cold extremities. Want of sleep has been already mentioned. A cold clammy perspiration, accompanied with a peculiar fœtor, often referred to by writers
on this subject, is certainly found in many patients. It gives the skin an
appearance of having been rubbed over by some greasy substance.—
Where it is found it invariably denotes the existence of organic disease
in the brain; I do not recollect a single instance of a patient with this
symptom having recovered; and on dissection, the ventricles have uniformly been filled with a great excess of water.
   " A great want of nervous sensibility is another very frequent symptom.
To such a degree will this exist, that diseases of the most painful nature,
such as inflammation in the abdomen, in which all the viscera have, to a
certain degree, been affected, have, upon *post mortem* inspections, been
most unexpectedly discovered in those patients who neither complained
nor appeared to suffer during their lives from this cause.
   " This want of sensibility enables them to endure that, without shrinking, which in the ordinary state of the nervous system would be attended
with the most acute pain.
   " The opposite to this want of sensibility in the nerves of the five
senses, is, however, not unfrequently a symptom of insanity. Both the
optic and auditory nerves, as well as those of sensation, are frequently seen
to be painfully acute, and give rise to many expressions of extravagant
feeling, which, I believe, are really experienced by the patient, but which
cannot be understood by those to whom they are related."

As we have observed, most cases of insanity can be cured if early
and proper remedies are resorted to; among which seclusion, and
separation from friends and home, are frequently necessary.
The large establishments we have referred to in this country are

mostly well arranged, well conducted, and creditable to the wisdom and philanthropy of the age. They are not, however, in our opinion, so well adapted for the cure and the comfort of the insane as smaller ones. We are inclined to believe that government establishments would be much better, if composed of a number of buildings, situated at considerable distance from each other ; so that the insane might be properly classified, and one class never see or hear the other ; and also, where the convalescents might be entirely separated from the rest. The sexes certainly should be in different buildings, remote from each other ; and the hospital for females under the constant supervision of a lady of high character for fidelity and intelligence ; and no visitors allowed, not even the officers of the institution, without her permission and attendance. Idiots should be wholly excluded from hospitals for the insane. It is painful to behold patients, partially insane, who have received good education and been accustomed to intelligent associates, confined in the same place, and in fact classed with idiots totally destitute of mind. It cannot fail of having an injurious effect upon the former, and can be of no service whatever to the latter. The incurably insane should also be perpetually separated from the curable, and the latter never know of the former.

Too much attention cannot be given by the proper authorities to the prevention of abuses in lunatic hospitals. There are no institutions where abuses are more likely to arise ; none where they are more difficult to detect. This, the history of such institutions here and in other countries but too painfully testifies. Some patients are frequently so violent and vindictive, that it requires great command of temper in their overseers not to retaliate sometimes ; while others, instigated by appetite and passion, increased by their insanity, are perpetually on the watch to seduce those appointed to guard them from their duty. Attendants of the most unblemished moral character, and remarkable for kind disposition, for calmness and intelligence, should be procured, and well instructed in their responsible duties; and be induced by proper compensation to devote themselves perpetually to the care of the insane. Upon this subject, Sir W. Ellis has made a few just observations.

"I cannot conclude this chapter without adding a few observations on a subject which materially affects the treatment of the insane ; I mean, the medical education of those under whose care they are placed. It is perfectly inconsistent with common sense to suppose that a man shall intuitively know how to treat insanity. We have seen, that although in the greater number of cases it is attended with the same general result, yet it assumes most varied forms, and great care and discrimination are required in the treatment: indeed, it is universally acknowledged to be a most difficult and mysterious disease, and yet it is almost the only one on which the medical student receives no particular instruction. In his attendance on the hospitals he will, in all probability, have met with almost every other variety of disease which afflicts human nature; at all events, his lectures will have supplied him with some information as to their treatment. * * Indeed, except as being incidentally touched upon in the lectures on forensic medicine, it appears almost entirely neglected in the course of a medical education; and, as the subject does not form a branch of examination, the pupils naturally employ their time in those studies which will be directly available, and assist them in the obtaining their medical certificates: the result is, that professional men, in other respects well educated, commence practice almost in a state of total ignorance on the subject. This is an evil from which every individual, whatever be his rank or fortune, is liable to suffer in his own person, and in that of his friends: and a man of ingenuous mind can hardly be placed under more painful circumstances, than to find the father or mother of a family, in a state of insanity, intrusted to his care, and to feel conscious that upon him depends the restoration of the patient to reason and happiness, while his want of acquaintance with the disease renders him unfit for the task, and he knows not where to apply for advice. This is by no means an imaginary evil, it is one of frequent occurrence; and numerous are the instances, where amiable and valuable members of society are consigned for life to a perpetual banishment from their friends, in the gloom of a madhouse, solely from ignorance on the part of the medical adviser. * *

" But, in order that the insane may really be placed under the most favourable circumstances, the instruction ought not to be confined to our sex. —I do not mean that females should attend a dissecting-room, or enter upon a course of the study of medicine, but it would be most desirable that they should have an opportunity of obtaining a sound and fundamental knowledge of the various modes in which diseased action of the brain exhibits itself in the conduct, and of the dangers to be guarded against, and of the moral treatment which ought to be adopted."

In another part of the volume which appears first on our list, we have a curious notion advanced by the author in regard to the responsibility of the insane to the law; it is this:—

" In many cases, those who are really insane on some subjects, are as capable of distinguishing between right and wrong as the sane. I remember a patient, who was at work with a sharp intrument, telling me, in a fit of passion, that ' if he killed me, he knew he should not suffer for it, because he was mad.' From my knowledge of the man's disposition, I had no fear of such a catastrophe; but if violence be committed under such circumstances, is it consistent with common sense, that the man should be considered not a responsible being, because he happens to have some erroneous notions about property, and fancies that he is entitled to an estate which belongs to another? Where the act is the result of the disease, the case is perfectly different. Martin, whose mind was morbidly impressed with the notion, that it was his duty to burn York Minster, was justly acquitted on the ground of his insanity."

We leave the above extract entirely to the discretion of our readers; but wish before closing our remarks upon Sir W. Ellis's treatise, to convey a little friendly advice, and to hint to him that if the sort of reasoning here quoted, and apparent in many other portions of the work, be his common standard of thought, it is, to say the least, eminently suspicious, and if accompanied by the "medical symptoms," as he would call them, would prove conclusive of his own sanity.

The second work which we have undertaken to notice is a most singular affair; it purports to be an account of what occurred to the writer during a period of nearly three years, all which time he was in a state of mental derangement, produced through delusions of a religious nature. If such an account could be relied upon as giving a faithful history of the progress of this mental disease, it would be of the greatest value; but we are entirely of opinion that it is and must be made up from that prolific storehouse, the imagination; certainly that portion which is a relation of circumstances which occurred prior to his malady and since his recovery may be very correct, but as to the part intervening it is altogether apocryphal: let us, however, see how his insanity commenced in his own words,—

"I passed my life in the Guards quiet and unobserved. I had, as at school, three or four friends, and no very extensive general acquaintance. If I was remarkable in society for anything, it was for occasional absence of mind, and for my gravity and silence when the levity of my companions transgressed the bounds of decorum, and made light of religion, or offended against morality. I was firm also in resisting all attempts to drive me by ridicule into intemperance. In private I had severe conflict of mind upon the truth and nature of the Christian religion, accompanied with acute agony at my own inconsistency of conduct and sentiment with the principles of duty and feeling taught by Jesus and his apostles; and mingled with astonishment at the whirlpool of dissipation, and contradiction in society around me. After several years inward suffering and perplexity, question and examination, I found at last, for a time, peace, and joy, and triumph, as I imagined, in the doctrines usually styled ' evangelical.' Till then the sacrifice of Jesus Christ, instead of being a message of gladness, had always been to me one of increasing woe and shame; as a sinner, to whom it made the law more binding, the offences against the law more ungrateful —the heinousness of crime deeper, in proportion to my conception of the boundless love of Almighty God. Then I understood that the law was done away in Christ, and liberty given to the mind, so that the soul might choose gratefully what it could not be driven to by fear. In the year 1829, my conduct first became decided and extreme, through the active principle instilled by the doctrines I have named; and in the spring of the year 1830, influenced chiefly by this new principle of action, I obtained permission to sell my commission in the Guards.

" In the first place, the evangelical opinions I had embraced, containing, as I imagined, the light of everlasting truth, given me freely through the election of God the Father, for the sake of the obedience, and sacrifice of Jesus Christ, and to the end that His own glory might be made manifest, in changing a vile and weak creature into the likeness of Divine holiness,

excited in me gratitude and fear: gratitude for the gift given me, and for
that election; and fear of the wrath of God, if I disobeyed the end for
which it was given. That which had been done for me, I thought it my
duty to preach to others, and to explain the doctrines, whereby I had been
saved. Moved by these arguments, I spoke and acted in open confession
of my faith, a line of conduct not very agreeable to the army, even if called
for, and judicious. Being then in Dublin, I attached myself to a society
for reading the scriptures to the Irish poor; I attended the regimental
schools; I read the service to a detachment I commanded, as the men had
not seats provided for them in church;—I tried to establish a reading-room
for the soldiers of my battalion;—I procured religious and other books for
the sick in hospital, and being afterwards quartered in town, hearing that
two battalions of guards and the recruits, through the neglect of the Chaplain and indifference of the commanding officers, had been for a long time
upon one pretence or another without opportunity of attending divine service at all, by privately applying to a clergyman in Westminster, and to an
officer of one battalion of like sentiments to my own, we procured seats for
the men in a large chapel, belonging to the church of England. I had
obtained the like permission from a clergyman of the established church
for the other battalion, when I found that this conduct excited suspicion
and offence. Both Colonel and Chaplains showed some symptoms of
chagrin—they charged me with having sent the men to a dissenting
minister. My conduct in reading the service to the detachment I for a
time commanded near Dublin, in circulating religious books, and in other
respects, drew on me also private animadversions, although in no instance
did I transgress military discipline; in the first case, I acted only in obedience to the regulations of the army. Now, though not sure that I was
doing quite right, I felt inclined to do more:—for I outfaced slander and
cavil thus, that even if I were in the extreme, it was but fair that one should
be in the extreme in the cause of Christ, when so many were running reck-
lessly a course of gaiety and dissoluteness. But as I really esteemed my
superior officer, who was both kind, intelligent, and actively beneficent;
and as I loved good discipline, I judged it prudent to withdraw from a scene
of constant conflict with my own conscience, where I was tempted to act
unwisely, and where I might be led into quarrel with those whom I loved
and respected, through conduct I might afterwards sincerely repent of.

"In the next place, I was led by a passage in the New Testament,
exhorting the Christian to choose *liberty* rather than slavery. I conceived
this advice applicable to a situation like my own, where I was so much
confined in the liberty of speech and conversation with the private soldier,
by the strict discipline of the service. After that, I reflected on my natural
disposition, talents and acquirements. I was fond of quiet, seclusion, and
study; unused to boisterous sports, untried in situations requiring promptitude and decision. I had a long time mistrusted my courage and presence
of mind, and had feared, that, in the hour of trial, I might do discredit to
the regiment and to my own name. In 1827, in Portugal, I had seen a
bloodless campaign, excepting the assassination of one or two of the men
and outrages upon the officers, unatoned for. Though the scene was novel
and the country beautiful, my mind was fatigued by the long marches between the towns—to do nothing. I disliked idleness, accompanied by sus-

pense of mind, separation from all means of regular study, and the absence of the attractions of female society. One night we had encamped, and I came to the resolution that my life might be a very romantic one, but that it was far from being agreeable. I was cheerful and contented, and glad that we had a fine night; but I judged coolly, and with reason, that a better cause than that of kings and constitutions, the instruments after all, and the embodyings of the spirit of Satan, was required to justify the sacrifice of happiness and comfort to one, who needed not to gain his *living* by cutting his neighbour's throat."

An erroneous education, or more properly speaking a wanting of an education of the feelings and moral discipline, appears to have led the writer of the volume now under notice into those excessive religious excitements which terminated in his insanity; and while upon this subject we may be allowed to hint to the instructors of youth, in this our day of high mental excitement, the necessity of a regular and systematic education of the feelings and moral affections of their pupils, to go hand in hand with their intellectual culture. There are two different points of view under which the injurious effects of a wrong education may be considered. By too great indulgence, and a want of moral discipline, the passions acquire greater power, and a character is formed subject to caprice and to violent emotions; a predisposition to insanity is thus laid in the temper and moral affections of the individual. The exciting causes of madness have greater influence on persons of such habits, than on those whose feelings are regulated. An overstrained and premature exercise of the intellectual powers, is likewise a fault of education, which predisposes to insanity, as it does also to other diseases of the brain. These are two considerations which are of the greatest importance with respect to the welfare of families to which an hereditary constitution may belong, rendering them more liable than others to cerebral diseases. They are distinct in themselves, and each might furnish a theme for an extensive treatise, most valuable in a practical point of view. Under the first head, it would be necessary to consider the efficacy of those plans of education, of which the professed object is to form a character remarkable for sedateness, for the strict discipline of the feelings, and, as far as this is attainable, of strong passions and emotions. Such, undoubtedly, would be the kind of moral education best adapted for those who are constitutionally liable to insanity. The second remark, on the regulation of mental exercise in young persons, whose nervous systems are feebly constituted, has a more extensive bearing than on the subject of insanity. It brings forward a suggestion which is of very general interest in these times, in which mental exertion is stimulated to the utmost, and too great sacrifices are often made to the cultivation of the intellect, or even to the mere acquisition of knowledge, while the education of the moral affections is considered as a matter of secondary importance.

It is extremely difficult to determine with accuracy the cause of insanity in many cases. In examining the records of Lunatic Asylums in this country, we find intemperance in the use of intoxicating drinks mentioned as a cause. No doubt it sometimes is; but we are not without suspicion that there is some other primary and predisposing cause, that is essential to the production of insanity in the intemperate. Intemperance has long been, and is now, very prevalent in some countries where there is but little insanity; and the instances are so very numerous of long and habitual intoxication without any tendency to this disease, that our suspicion is strengthened that some other cause predisposes the brain to the disease we call insanity. Intemperance is very common among savage races of men, yet insanity is rare among them. Besides, the excessive use of intoxicating drink is not unfrequently the consequence, not the cause, of the mental derangement, and among the first symptoms of the disease. This fact has been often noticed. Still we do not doubt, that some cases are correctly attributed to intemperance; and still less we doubt, that, as a secondary cause, it is of quite frequent operation, and has much increased this disease among the labouring classes in this country. When there is an hereditary tendency to insanity, or when the brain has been much disturbed by anxiety and mental excitement, then the use of intoxicating drinks unquestionably tends to develope it; and we have no doubt that very many thus circumstanced would escape the disease, if they would entirely abstain from stimulating drinks.

But altogether the most frequent cause of insanity is hereditary predisposition. Even if one sane generation has intervened, there is not, then, a certainty the next will continue so. It is much to be feared, that if marriages are contracted in disregard of this fact, the numerous cures effected of late will but serve to increase the number of the insane in another generation. In those born of insane parents, much may be done towards preventing the development of the disease, by attention to their education, both physical and mental. " Predisposition to insanity," says M. Esquirol, " may be traced from the age of infancy; it furnishes the explanation of a multitude of caprices, irregularities, and anomalies, which, at a very early period, ought to put parents on their guard against the approach of insanity. It may furnish useful admonitions to those who preside over the education of children. It is advisable, in such cases, to give them an education tending to render the body robust, and to harden it against the ordinary causes of madness; and particularly to place them under different circumstances from those with which their parents were environed. It is thus we ought to put in practice the aphorism of Hippocrates, who advises to change the constitution of individuals, in order to prevent the diseases with which they are threatened, by the hereditary prediposition of their family."

In conclusion, we wish to state that we have noticed with much pain the great deficiency of proper medical officers in the various public institutions for the insane in England, and to call the attention of the proper authorities to so palpable and mischievous an evil; for, as we have stated elsewhere, upon proper, judicious, and enlightened attendants or the opposite, depends, the recovery of the patient, or the serious increase of the disorder.

ART. VI.—*Life and Administration of Edward, first Earl of Clarendon; with Original Correspondence and Authentic Papers, never before Published.* By T. H. LISTER, Esq. 3 Vols. London: Longman & Co. 1838.

THAT a good Life of Edward Hyde, the first Earl of Clarendon, is a desideratum in literature must be admitted by every one. His character as a statesman and an historian has been the theme of such opposite construction by the different political parties that have long divided the readers and the writers of English history, that it is scarcely possible to point out another name which offers better scope for enlightened interpretation, and demands a closer observation of impartiality at the present day, than the Apologist of Charles the First, the Chancellor of Charles the Second, and the father-in-law of the succeeding Sovereign. Clarendon not only lived and figured during the most eventful epoch in the annals of this great empire, but his celebrated History has been and continues to be the Political Bible of all who regard the First Charles in the light of a saint and a martyr, or who take high Tory ground on the great questions concerning church and state. But although such an opportunity existed for the production of a noble and original work in connexion with the name of Clarendon, we are far from thinking that Mr. Lister has shown himself equal to the performance. We admit that he has exhibited painstaking, and proofs of an earnest desire to be candid and just. While a Whig, a conservative Whig, as we take our author to be, he is a liberal construer of the character of the champion who advocated cavalier principles; and in so far he deserves to be distinguished. But the result of all this painstaking and honesty is heaviness, both in regard to bulk and style. Comparatively little of these three goodly volumes is strictly biographical; while the illustrations of the important events which characterized the age of his hero do not yet present much that is new or remarkably vivid. It does not, indeed, appear that any very minute materials exist relative to the private life of Clarendon, and what do exist have not been set in such a light by our author as the hand of genius would have done. We do not discover either in the arrangement of characteristic features, or in the reflections thence deduced, either signal power or delicacy of touch. In short, it is a very level

though laboured production, which will never occupy an elevated
rank in historical literature, either on account of the novelty or the
elegance of its contents, such as ought to have been shed around
the " illustrious Clarendon." The reader, however, if he is capable
of reflecting for himself and tracing tendencies to their results, will
from the facts adduced by Mr. Lister find the work suggestive
enough, and even from the few passages to be extracted by us will
have his mind placed in a position favourable to the exercise of important trains of thought.

Edward Hyde was born in 1609, and was the third son of a gentleman in Wilts whose family was ancient and possessions extensive.   After having studied for some time with a view to obtaining
holy orders, our hero, in consequence of the deaths of his elder
brothers, had his views directed to the bar. He entered the Middle
Temple, and afterwards rose into respectable practice. In 1640 we
find him in Parliament, before which time nothing very remarkable
in a public point of view attaches to his history. Privately, however,
before this period, his life was considerably chequered. For example,
a severe attack of ague for a long time depressed him, and afterwards
the small-pox threatened his existence. He lost his first wife before
he was twenty-one years of age, and was re-married to a daughter
of Sir Thomas Aylesbury, who was Master of Requests and of the
Mint in 1632.

Politically, Hyde at first acted as the people's advocate and
friend; but it was not long that he opposed the court, his support
on account of his assiduity, sound sense, and agreeable eloquence, as
well as distinguished abilities being covetable in any cause. It was in
relation to the Church that he first diverged from his early political
friends; and the King and Laud were not slow to extend to him
their countenance. In fact he became the secret counsellor of
Charles, and even the writer of his public papers. At length, when
republicanism triumphed, he found it necessary to consult his safety,
by escaping with the Prince of Wales to foreign parts, where he
remained in exile with royalty, in the capacity of Chancellor, but
unlike the Chancellor at home, with a poor allowance for his services.
In fact he seems to have filled a number of important offices, and to
have been an authoritative tutor to the Second Charles while abroad
and a long time after the Restoration, in as far as that facetious
and profligate monarch could be trammelled. The privations
to which the mimic court of the exile-king were subjected, and the
various distresses which Hyde had to endure, are forcibly and touch-
ingly described in the following passage :—

" In August 1652, Hyde states, in a letter to Sir Richard Browne, that
' a summ lately received at Paris for the Kinge,' ' which is all the money
he hath received since he came hither, doth not inable his cooks and back-
stayres men to goe on in provydinge his dyett; but they protest they can

undertake it no longer.' In December 1652, Hyde says, the King is ' reduced to greater distresse then you can believe or imagyne.' In June 1652, he says, in a letter to Nicholas, with respect to the distresses of the King and his adherents, ' I do not know that any man is yet dead for want of bread, which really I wonder at. I am sure the King himself owes for all he hath eaten since April; and I am not acquainted with one servant of his who hath a pistole in his pocket. Five or six of us eat together one meal a day, for a pistole a week; but all of us owe for God knows how many weeks to the poor woman that feeds us. I believe my Lord of Ormond hath not had five livres in his purse this month, and hath fewer clothes of all sorts than you have; and yet I take you to be no gallant.'

"Hyde was severely exposed not merely to the nominal distresses of pecuniary embarrassment, but to the real privations of poverty, as is apparent from many of his letters. ' At this time,' (November 9, 1652,) ' I have neither clothes nor fire to preserve me from the sharpness of the season.'

" ' I am so cold that I am scarce able to hold my pen, and have not three sous in the world to buy a faggot.' ' I have not been master of a crown these many months, am cold for want of clothes and fire, and owe for all the meat which I have eaten these three months, and to a poor woman who is no longer able to trust; and my poor family at Antwerp (which breaks my heart) is in as sad a state as I am.' It appears, too, that his official duties as Secretary in the place of Nicholas, instead of being a source of profit, caused what, in his destitute state, was a serious addition to other burdens. ' I cannot,' he says, ' avoid the constant expense of seven or eight livres the week for postage of letters, which I borrow scandalously out of my friends' pockets; or else my letters must more scandalously remain still at the post-house; and I am sure all those which concern my own private affairs would be received for ten sous a week; so that all the rest are for the King, from whom I have not received one penny since I came hither, and am put to all this charge.' In another letter, he mentions that he is reduced to want of decent clothing; and, in May 1653, tells Nicholas—' I owe so much money here, to all sorts of people, that I would not wonder if I were cast into a prison to-morrow; and if the King should remove, as I hope he will shortly have occasion to do, and not enable me to pay the debt I have contracted for his service, I must look for that portion, and starve there.' "

But these were not the only or the greatest of Hyde's causes of uneasiness; for his equanimity seems to have been severely disturbed by the jealousies and the intrigues that prevailed around him.

" ' The vexations I undergo by what I see and hear daily,' he says, in a letter to Nicholas, of May 1653, ' and the insupportable weight of envy and malice I groan under, when I behave myself (God knows) with as much care as if I were to die the next minute, does make my life so unpleasant to me, and breaks my mind, that bread and water, in any corner of the world, would give me all the joy imaginable.' ' I have,' he says, in another place, ' the good fortune to be equally disliked by those who agree in nothing else; my unpardonable crime being, that I would have the King do his business himself, and be governed by nobody; and my reason is, that by truth itself, he had more judgment and understanding, by many degrees, than many who pretend to it; and that is the only thing that breaks my heart, that he makes no more use of it.' The Queen was openly his foe : ' her displeasure,' as he himself tells us, ' grew so notorious against the Chancellor, that after he found, by degrees, that she would not speak to him, nor take any notice of him when she saw him, he forbore, at last, coming in her presence, and for many months did not see her face, though he had the honour to lodge in the same house, the palace royal, where their Majesties kept their courts.' Rupert, Buckingham, and Jermyn, almost systematically opposed him. Herbert, lately Attorney-General, created Lord Keeper through the Queen's influence, was ill-affected towards Hyde. Hyde was also obnoxious to two opposite parties, the Papists and the Presbyterians, who, irreconcileable in all besides, concurred in enmity to him.' "

Hyde's attachment to England and to Englishmen are prominent features in his life. We not only find that he maintained a constant correspondence with persons in this country during the years he was absent from it, and that indeed he formed the central point for every royalist plot, but that while he was at peace and at home, some of the most eminent men of genius that his country could produce, were amongst his frequent associates, such as Ben Johnson, Chillingworth, Selden, &c. His sympathy, however, with the people does not appear at any time to have been deep and ardent; nor do we discover evidences of his prospective wisdom having been eminent, whatever may have been his ambition, his profession of justice, his outward adherence to decencies.

We have already alluded to Hyde's authority over Charles the Second, and will quote some instances of its manner and boldness :—

" *Chan.* This business from Portugall, makes it necessary to call for the mony from France; therefore, I pray tell me, how that affayre stands, and why you do not send for the Ambassador's Secretary, and desyre him to write very earnestly aboute it.

," *King.* He expects every day for to have notice of the monyes at Havre de Grace; I will speake with him this night.

" *Chan.* Though the particular, you know, is not to be mentioned, yett ther are many thinges arysinge from this new message from Lisbone, very necessary to be well weighed; therefore you shall do well to thinke of calling your committe together. If you intende it for to-morrow morninge, you will bidd one of the secretaryes warne the rest, and that the Generall be ther.

" What do you thinke of ' Mr Mountegues being Bpp of Boloigne? it makes much noyse aboute the towne.

" *King.* I cannot tell what noise it makes; but meethinkes, if he pretends no further (which I believe he will not), that noise will dye.

" *Chan.* Trust me, it will not: I know how I trouble you; but I am a foole if that, and some thinges relating thereto, be not worthy a serious thought by your selfe.

" *King.* What are the other thinges relating to that businesse?

" *Chan.* By relatinge to that, I meane what relates to France, and your mothers comminge over, which beinge to be so soone, very many thinges are worthy your serious deliberacions, and cannot be well deliberated by others, till your selfe first weigh it and prescribe the rule.

" *King.* I understand you now, and will sett aside an afternoone for that matter. Rob. Welsh hath been with me, and his relation is just as the French man's was.

" *Chan.* You will make him give it in writinge, else you will hardly know how to proceede in it.

" *King.* It shall be done."

Here is another amusing instance :—

" *Chan.* I pray be pleased to give an aud yence to my Lᵈ Braughall, who will say many things to you of moment, and I thinke with duty enough. If you will give him leave to attend you to-morrow morning at 8 of the clocke, I will give him notice of it.

" *King.* You give appointments in a morning to others, sooner then you take them yourselfe ; but if my Lᵈ Braughall will come at 9, he shall be welcome."

Hyde was not only *de facto* prime minister under the " merry monarch," but he was for a number of years in effect monarch himself,

" *Chan.* I wish with all my hearte that we had the French money : why do you not send Fox [Sir Stephen Fox] away ?

" *King.* 'Twas you that desired that he might stay a day or two, or else he had been gone on Tewsday last ; but now he has nothing to stay for but the winde.

" *Chan.* I pray call to the Secretary to prepare a privy seale for the payment of 2000 to Sʳ J. Shaw, for so much dispursed by him, upon your order, for secrett service.

" Indeede, you are to blame, that you have not yett given your warrant to my Lord Barkshyre : I pray do not defer it.

" *King.* Is it not to make his warrant of one thousand a year, to continue for 11 years.

" *Chan.* Will you never speake to my Lord   , nor aske him the other questyon you intended about your mothers jointure ?"

He is seen to advantage in his manner of maintaining his ground before the King, when the subject was the proposal that. his wife should visit Lady Castlemaine, as told in the following paragraph :—

" He told him, that as it would reflect upon his Majesty himself, if his Chancellor was known or thought to be of dissolute and debauched manners, which would make him as incapable as unworthy to do him justice ; so it would be a blemish and taint upon him to give any countenance, or to pay more than ordinary courtesy and unavoidable civilities to persons infamous for any vice, for which, by the laws of God and man, they ought to be odious, and to be exposed to the judgment of the church and state ;

and that he would not for his own sake, and for his own dignity, to bow low a condition soever he might be reduced, stoop to such a condescension as to have the least commerce, or to make the application of a visit to any such person, for any benefit or advantage that it might bring to him. He did beseech his Majesty not to believe that he hath a prerogative to declare vice virtue, or to qualify any person who lives in a sin and avows it, against which God himself hath pronounced damnation, for the company and conversation of innocent and worthy persons: and that whatever low obedience, which was in truth gross flattery, some people might pay to what they believed would be grateful to his Majesty, they had in their hearts a perfect detestation of the persons they made address to; and that for his part he was long resolved that his wife should not be one of those courtiers; and that he would himself much less like her company, if she put herself into theirs who had not the same innocence."

But Clarendon's character does not always look so well; neither do we find him so remarkable for consistency, as for a great ostentation of magnanimity and purity. Though he could lecture Charles about his amours, and resist any proposal that would bring his wife into an intimacy with the King's mistress, he had the meanness to exert himself in such a way as tended to compromise the honour and dignity of the Queen, in reference to a similar project. Charles, in perfect keeping with his character was so gross as to present his mistress to his wife, who refused to submit a second time to the insult. But what did Clarendon do in this case? Why, as already intimated, he endeavoured to persuade her majesty to yield to her unprincipled husband's wishes. What we now quote has reference to this subject. The first passage is from the minister's private letters to Ormonde.

"The Kinge is perfectly recovered of his indisposicions in which you left him. I wish he were as free from all other. I have had, since I saw you, 3 or 4 full long conferences, with much better temper than before. I have likewise twice spoken at large with the Queene. The lady hath beene at courte, and kissed her hande, and returned that night. I cannot tell you, ther was no discomposure. I am not out of hope, and that is all I can yett say.

"All things are bad with reference to the Lady; but I think not so bad as you heare. Everybody takes her to be of the bedchamber; for she is always there, and goes abrode in the coach. But the Queene tells me that the King promised her, on condition she would use her as she doth others, that she would never live in court: yet lodgings I hear she hath. I heare of no back staires. The worst is, the King is as discomposed as ever, and looks as little after his business; which breaks my heart, and makes me and other of yr friends weary of our lives. He seeks for his satisfaction and delight in other company, which do not love him so well as you and I do. I hope it will not last always. The business of Dunkirk is like to come to nothing upon the point of payment only. We are offered 5,000,000 pistoles; we accept it; but they would pay only two in hand—the rest in two years. This wee cannot yeeld.

"Worcester House, 9 of Sept."

Mr. Lister remarks :—

"Clarendon had two interviews with the Queen, in which he attempted to show the expediency of compliance. But the warm feelings of the injured wife were proof against his prudential reasons; and the eloquent and sagacious statesman retired from the conference without success. He then besought the King, that he would let the matter rest awhile; but Charles was deaf to every voice but that of his own unworthy passions, and of the evil counsellors who pandered to them. The quarrel became more violent. 'The fire,' says Clarendon, 'flamed higher than ever. The King reproached the Queen with stubbornness, and want of duty; and she him with tyranny, and want of affection: he used threats and menaces, which he never intended to put in execution; and she talked loudly, how ill she was treated, and that she would return again to Portugal. He replied, 'she should do well first to know whether her mother would receive her; and he would give her a fit opportunity to know that, by sending to their home all the Portuguese servants; and that he would forthwith give order for the discharge of them all, since they behaved themselves so ill; for to them and their councils be imputed all her perverseness.' Clarendon, after a time, repeated his attempt at mediation—the sum of his advice to the Queen being, that she should submit cheerfully to what she could not resist. But she replied, 'that her conscience would not suffer her to consent to what she could not but suppose would be an occasion and opportunity of sin;' and Clarendon, foiled by her firmness, withdrew from the discussion, and besought the King 'that he might be no more consulted with, nor employed, in *an affair in which he had been so unsuccessful.*'"

To go back to an earlier period in Clarendon's life, and to the notice of some of his political transactions, it may be observed that although at first, after the Restoration, his administration was considerate and mild, it was not long until his real disposition was manifested. He was arrogant and pompous; but what was worse he was the abettor of oppression and tyranny. He was a notable hand at stirring up plots to afford an excuse for severe measures in behalf of the monarchy. He does not seem to stand clear of the charge of having in his lifetime countenanced schemes of assassination; nor does he appear to have been insensible to the temptations which money presented in the shape of bribes, even when coming from the French King, and when offered for the purposes of expediting a deed which was to prove injurious and disgraceful to England; witness the affair of parting with Dunkirk for a large sum which the needy Charles wanted. Nor was the King blind to Clarendon's foibles, errors, and inconsistency. Indeed he became heartily tired of his prejudices and old fashioned ways; and when he fell out of favour at court, there was no party in the state upon which he could rely. At length seventeen articles of accusation were preferred against him by the Commons, and to avoid the consequences the fallen minister withdrew to the continent, but not before penning the abject letter alluded to in the following, the intention of which was to save appearances by obtaining the royal sanction to his withdrawal.

" With a view to obtain this sanction, he addressed to the King on the 16th of November, a letter, which can scarcely be regarded by the most partial advocate as either politic or high-minded. He imputed the King's displeasure to a belief in his interference (which he strongly denied) in projecting the marriage of the Duke of Richmond to Miss Stewart,—a cause of displeasure so disgraceful, that he could not expect it to be acknowledged; and to impute it was almost an insult, even to one of Charles's character. Then, after expressions couched too much in a spirit of humility and adulation, he added, ' I do most humbly beseech your Majesty, by the memory of your father, who recommended me to you with some testimony, and by your own gracious reflection upon some one service I may have performed in my life, that hath been acceptable to you, that you will by your royal power and interposition put a stop to this severe prosecution against me; and that my concernment may give no longer interruption to the great affairs of the kingdom; but that I may spend the small remainder of my life, which cannot hold long, in some parts beyond the seas, never to return."

So much for the highmindedness of this idol of Ultra Tories, whose " History" has been lauded as an infallible and perfect record. No doubt it is unrivalled as a cabinet of portraitures of character; and for a certain appearance of fidelity and earnest and flowing truth. But in regard to the higher requisites of historical literature, not counting accuracy and fairness in the detail of facts, it is a deficient work. Clarendon's mind was not one of the foremost order. He wanted depth and grasp of comprehension. His experience was extensive, his perception of immediate interest acute. He had the show too of great morality, and loved to talk of virtue public and private as if he could not do a wrong thing. Yet after all he never took the lead in any great and decided triumph of goodness; he was but a sort of half-way goer, his most remarkable feature being, perhaps, that of artfulness without appearing to be artful.

We conclude this paper by the sketch which Mr. Lister gives of the state of manners in this country after the Chancellor's dismissal. The passage affords a good specimen of our author's research, and method of grouping anecdotes that have been carefully collected.

" Charles signalized his emancipation from Clarendon's control, by making, within a month after that Minister had retired from office, a grant of plate to Lady Castlemaine; and afterwards by an indulgence more open and unbridled in reckless extravagance and licentious pleasures. His Minister, Buckingham, encouraged in him that contempt of decency which Clarendon had been wont to reprove; and, at Buckingham's instigation, Charles installed in Lady Castlemaine's post of dishonour an actress of notorious frailty, who, in allusion to two preceding paramours of the same name, called the King her ' Charles the Third.' The few years following Clarendon's expulsion were the most glaringly profligate in that age of profligacy—the most corrupt and degraded in that reign of political degradation. Morality had fallen so low that it could scarcely obtain even the homage of the shallowest hypocrisy from those whose position, making them conspicuous, ought to have made them also mindful of the example they were setting; and the grossest crimes were sometimes pardoned if they assumed the character of frolic, Two Court favourites, the King's recent companions in an indecent revel, ' run up and down all the night, almost naked, through the streets,' and are taken into custody; ' the King takes their parts,' and a Lord Chief Justice imprisons the constable who had done his duty in apprehending them. The favourite Minister kills in a duel the husband of a woman whose paramour he is, and who assists at the combat in the disguise of a page. The King's illegitimate son Monmouth, in company with the young Duke of Albemarle and others, kills a watchman, who begs for mercy, and the King pardons all the murderers. A daring ruffian, named Blood, attempts to assassinate the Duke of Ormond, and soon afterwards to steal the regalia; Charles admits the felon to his presence—hears with amusement the boastful confession of his committed and intended crimes, and not only pardons but rewards him. The son of Ormond tells the King's Minister, before the King, that he believes him the instigator of the recent attempt to assassinate his father; and that should any such attempt succeed, he shall regard that Minister as the secret instrument, and kill him even in the King's presence. Sir John Coventry, a Member of Parliament, in the course of a debate in reply to an argument against taxing playhouses, namely, that the players were the King's servants and a part of his pleasure, asked, whether the King's pleasure lay amongst the men or the women who acted? Charles stung by Coventry's allusion to what everybody knew, sends some officers of the Guards to waylay and maim him; which they do by cutting his nose to the bone. Assuming that these facts were monstrous exceptions, and not average examples of the state of society, it may still be urged that they could not have been possible except in a period of unparalleled corruption."

ART. VII.—*The Principles of Political Economy.* By HENRY VETHAKE, LL.D. one of the Professors in the University of Pennsylvania; a Member of the American Philosophical Society, &c. Philadelphia: P. H. Nicklin and T. Johnson. 1838.

IT is not with the most distant intention of entangling ourselves in the mazes of controversy about a subject on which the most patient and laborious minds have widely differed, a subject for which some claim the dignified title of science, while others refuse to accord to it this honour, that we take up the present volume. Whatever may be the ascertained and invariable principles of political economy, they are at least only deducible by means of such a severe, abstruse, and metaphysical course of investigation and reasoning, taking only its technical terms into account, as to place it beyond the reach of a short and popular dissertation. Again, the fact that there is scarcely any one topic in the whole range of the study, which has not relations less or more numerous, and less or more delicate with others, interposes a bar to any satisfactory treatment of its many doctrines within our limits. In justice to our readers, however, who may be already acquainted with the existing state of the subject, or who may be about to enter upon its study, as well as to the learned author of the volume before us, we shall mention some of the peculiar features of the work, and quote a few specimens illustrative of the author's opinions and manner.

There is a considerable amount of novelty in the arrangement and in the matter of Dr. Vethake's book; nor can we withhold from it the character of a treatise which has both indicated the path and made progress in it by which a nearer approach to the great principles of political economy may be realised. Our author generally avoids all direct reference to preceding writers on the subject, as well as a controversial manner; on the other hand, though often adopting the doctrines of his predecessors, classifying his matter in a strictly logical form, and taking nothing for granted until he has endeavoured to establish its truth; not even passing over the introduction of any technical term without an exact definition of the meaning he attaches to it. Accordingly the work requires to be read systematically, by beginning at the beginning of it and proceeding regularly and leisurely to the end before its entire scope and pith can be understood or appreciated; thus rendering it difficult for us to do any part of it justice in the way of extract or connecting remarks. Our first extract, however, does not labour under much disadvantage from coming in an isolated shape, seeing that it constitutes the very first paragraphs in the volume. We give it as a specimen of the definitions of terms that abound in the work, and also of the strict regard which the author uniformly observes in reference to the higher moral relations of his extensive subject. Indeed, he throughout never contents himself with a pursuit merely of abstract principles, but connects every such discovery in the way which it practically bears upon the administration of public affairs, or with the transactions of private life.

"If we look around us, we shall perceive that society is so constituted, that, while only a small portion of mankind are placed by Providence in circumstances of such affluence as to render them disinclined to make any exertions, whether bodily or mental, to enlarge their means of enjoyment, most persons are engaged in producing, either what is to be directly appropriated to satisfy their own desires, or, more frequently, what is destined, by being exchanged for the products of the labour of others, to minister to the enjoyment of their fellow-men. In other words, most men are producers of *utility*, in the sense in which this word is understood in political economy. For, leaving to the moralist the decision of the question whether many objects of man's pursuit may not in reality be injurious to him, and whether be be not often making a sacrifice of higher, but future, gratification, or even sometimes subjecting himself to future suffering, that he may administer to himself perhaps a small amount only of present enjoyment, the political economist regards every thing as useful which is capable of satisfying, in any degree whatever, any of man's *actual* wants and desires. Thus spirituous liquors are said to be possessed, of utility, because they are of a nature to be objects of men's desire; which desire they evince, and afford a measure of, by the sacrifices they are willing to make in order to obtain them; and this utility is ascribed to those articles, notwithstanding that their use may, in most cases, be justly condemned, and the philanthropist, and the christian, may feel it a duty to make every proper exertion to repress the inconveniences, or mischiefs, they occasion.

"But I wish not to be misunderstood. I do not mean to insinute, or to admit, that the political economist, because he employs the word utility in reference to man as he is, and not as he ought to be, and because the *immediate* object he has in view is not the moral improvement of the species, adopts a low standard of morals, or is indifferent to such improvement. As well might the votary of any one department of science be fairly chargeable with necessarily undervaluing, and taking no interest in the progress of, any other; and the pursuits of the astronomer or chemist be condemned as vicious in their tendency, because, in observing the phenomena, and investigating the laws, of *material* nature, they take no cognizance of the categories of right and wrong. So far indeed, I may remark, is the science of political economy from leading to conclusions adverse to the best interests of mankind, and so far is it from even turning the attention of individuals, or of governments, entirely from moral to physical considerations, and teaching them to advance the happiness of society by measures wholly unconnected with morality, that I hope to make it appear to the conviction of my readers, as a legitimate deduction from the principles of the science, that there is no more efficient method of promoting the *physical* well-being of a people than to diffuse among them, as extensively as possible, the blessings of religion, of morals, and of education. It may likewise be added, that no branch of human knowledge exhibits to us more beautiful illustrations of the consistency of all truth, and of that unity of design which pervades the various provinces of creation.

"No person, after having become acquainted with the elements of our subject, will fail to perceive the desirableness, if not the necessity, of having some word to designate the idea intended to be conveyed by the term utility, as I have defined it; and if any inconveniences should result from the same term being occasionally employed in another acceptation, this will only be one of many instances of a similar kind, which are continually occurring out of the domain of the exact sciences, and which require from the student, as an essential condition to the acquisition of real knowledge, a certain perspicacity in readily perceiving the different shades of meaning of which the same forms of language admit. Whenever also an idea is considered as of sufficient importance to require it to be designated by a single term, almost the only practicable method of proceeding, in fixing upon the proper word for the purpose intended, is to select such a one as is already employed to denote some idea bearing an analogy to that which is to be expressed; for to coin an entirely new word may be regarded as wholly out of the question. The closer, too, the analogy, the better, as less violence is then done to existing usage. Now in the instance under consideration, the term utility is certainly employed very much in accordance with the meaning attached to it in common language. We speak of a bad use of an object, as well as of a good use of it; and we speak of the utility of weapons, both of offence and defence, although, if men were prevented, by the non-existence of those of the former description, from injuring one another, a considerable addition would be implied to the sum of human happiness. It seems to me, then, that it cannot reasonably be denied that the political economists are fully justified in the use they make of the term utility; while it may be allowed, that they are also called upon to be cautious how they confound this use of it with its more dignified acceptation, when it refers, not to the gratification alone of his present desires, but to man's happiness in reference to the whole of his future career."

Our author goes on to remark that certain objects are possessed of utility, though not susceptible of being appropriated,—such as the air we breathe, and, very generally, the water we drink; and all other objects besides these and the like he comprehends under the term *wealth*. Wealth, in short, is that which may be produced as well as consumed; and the production and consumption of wealth are synonymous phrases with the production and consumption of *utility*. Hence the province of political economy is to determine the laws which regulate the production, distribution, and consumption of wealth,—the practical object always being held in view, how individuals and governments ought to conduct themselves in the disposal of the wealth under their control, so as to promote in as great a degree as possible the happiness of mankind.

Taking his subject in this shape and uniformly abiding by it, we must allow to Dr. Vethake the honour of having lent it importance and dignity of a much more interesting character than is generally bestowed upon the deductions of economists. In this way, too, there being a perfect consistency in the legitimate results drawn from all sorts of truth, the hard and repulsive conclusions of merely a scientific nature are softened and warmed.

One of the most novel features in the present treatise consists in our author's comprehending not only under the definition of wealth, but likewise of capital, immaterial products, as well as those which are material. Capital, the reader is to understand, is distinguished from wealth by being that which is saved for the purpose of again producing wealth. Hence all capital is wealth, but all wealth is not capital; the useful products which are not saved, but appropriated to the gratification of the present, are merely wealth. We do not know that by any short extract the author's reasoning on the subject of *immaterial* capital can be properly understood; but as he lays great stress upon the doctrine as laid down by him, believing it not only never to have been before fully recognised, but to be essential to a correct appreciation of the intellectual and moral relations of political economy, we shall take his most concise account of his argument upon this point.

" No other test of the *increase* of wealth can possibly exist, whether it be material or immaterial, than that a greater quantity of it is produced and consumed in a given time than before. But since nothing more is intended by the *accumulation* of wealth than the increase of it, it will manifestly be proper to speak of the accumulation of immaterial products.

" Again, what is saved and appropriated as capital is not of necessity consumed slower than any other portion of wealth ; it is merely consumed by a different class of persons. We have here therefore no reason why capital should not be composed, like that portion of wealth which is not capital, in part of the products which are immaterial, as well as of those which are material. And as, in almost every instance, the *real* wages of the labourer,—which wages, when advanced to him by his employer, are a portion of the latter's capital,—consist, in a certain degree, of immaterial products, it will follow that immaterial products may be made to constitute a portion of capital.

" Perhaps, too, the analogy which has been pointed out between material and immaterial products will be more clearly apprehended by the reader, if he analyse the mode in which the former of these administers to the gratification of our desires, and compare it with that in which we derive gratification from the latter. He will not be surprised at the closeness of the analogy in question, when he perceives, as he will not fail to perceive, that, in both cases alike, the *ultimate* product is simply—*agreeable sensations.* The entire utility of the house in which we dwell, for example, arises from its adaptation to produce a series of such sensations in our minds, just as the products of the painter or the musician are adapted to do."

The argument is, that immaterial objects or products admit of being *accumulated* in the proper sense of the word. That the wages for example, which a master pays his labourer, and by which that labourer purchases a physician's advice or secures the protection of the government, form in reality a portion of the master's capital savings, or reproductive wealth. If this be so in the proper acceptation of the terms *wealth* and *immaterial*, it will not be difficult to perceive how much moral and intellectual capital may be accumulated and made rapidly to circulate, be consumed, and be reproduced. And here we may conveniently quote part of what is said in an advanced chapter of the treatise concerning the encouragement which is due to intellectual products.

" We come now to a class of producers who are very generally acknowledged to have peculiar claims to encouragement, as well from the more enlighted portion of the community, as from the government. I mean that class whose products are of an intellectual or immaterial character.

" The grounds of a distinction here are, *first*, that while almost every individual may be looked upon as estimating, with sufficient accuracy,

the relative advantages which the different descriptions of material wealth
are capable of affording him, such is far from being the fact in respect to
intellectual products.   No recondite knowledge of human nature is requisite to satisfy any reflecting mind that, without the species of encouragement now adverted to, the great body of the people, even in countries
where civilisation exists in the highest degree to which it has yet attained,
would advance very slowly, if at all, in the career of improvement.
Indeed, to me it is apparent that, but for the efforts which have been made,
and which will continue to be made, by the more enlightened portion of
society, to diffuse the blessings of education, of morals, and of religion, as
extensively as possible among their fellow-men, and made irrespective
too of any previously existing *demand* among the latter for those blessings,
mankind would degenerate into a state of hopeless barbarism.

"The *second* ground of distinction in the present case, in favour of the
intellectual products which have been mentioned, is, that every individual
of a nation, or of the great community of mankind, is interested in their
being diffused, and, to speak technically, consumed, to the greatest practicable extent.   In a country like our own especially, where the right of
suffrage is enjoyed by almost every adult male citizen, and is exercised at
comparatively short intervals, where too, in consequence, the government
is under the direct control of the people, the importance of their being an
educated, a moral, and a religious people, cannot be too strongly felt, and
acted upon."

The interest which the whole community of a nation possesses not
only in the universal prevalence of what is understood by common
education, but in the existence and encouragement of academies of
a higher order, such as colleges and universities, is manifest and
great.   Other circumstances being the same, it is well observed by
Dr. Vethake, the people generally will be benefited by the existence
of a numerous class of highly educated men, especially when, by the
direction of certain funds, the sons of persons in the middling walks
of life, and in moderate circumstances, are enabled to form a large
section of this number, and when not merely the wealthy and the
great can command the advantage.   In such a country and state of
things a taste for knowledge is sure to be created and widely
propagated through the successive gradations of society, down to the
lowest and the most ignorant ; and the consequence cannot fail to be
to elevate the character of the labourer, and thereby to augment
his command over the necessaries, the luxuries, and the immaterial
products of the country.

The doctrine which our author has laid down concerning wealth,
immaterial accumulation, and capital, enables him to dispense with
a distinction which has been very generally made between the
different kinds of labour, as if it were in certain cases productive,
and in others unproductive.   It has been very often said that all
persons engaged in agriculture, manufactures, or commerce, are
productive, while magistrates, poets, philosophers, lawyers, clergymen,
&c. are non-productive labourers; and so far the distinction is

correct, if material products alone are included in the definition of wealth, although no one can maintain that the labours of a Watt and a Bolton have not, at least indirectly, been instrumental in producing more material wealth, than the labours of many thousands of agriculturists or manufacturers. But if wealth and capital are made to comprehend as well immaterial objects as material, then every species of labour which is productive of utility, whether this utility be first, so to speak, embodied in matter, or not, will be productive, and the distinction in question be made to disappear altogether. Such are some of Dr. Vethake's deductions on the subject of labour and wealth. One of the practical and moral results from this style of reasoning deserves to find a place among our few extracts.

" It may here be mentioned that a practical and moral advantage cannot fail to result from getting rid of the distinction between the productive and unproductive labourers. Mankind, instead of being separated into two classes having occupations essentially differing, and liable on this account to an interference with each other's interests, will come to be regarded as constituting one and the same great family. The political economist, by continually associating together in his investigations every species of manual or bodily labour with that of the most refined and exalted *intellect*, cannot fail to dignify the former in his estimation; while he will, on the other hand, contribute most effectually to remove from intellectual labour the *stigma* which is ordinarily implied by designating it as unproductive. If he shall succeed in banishing from the *popular* language such phrases as ' the productive classes' and ' the unproductive classes,' he will have done more to prevent the ' workmen' of a country from esteeming themselves to be the only *useful* portion of society, than he could possibly do by reminding his readers, every time he writes the word unproductive, that his object in applying it to any individual is not to pronounce him to be unproductive of utility, but of *material* objects having utility,—not to pronounce him to be a mere consumer of the products of the labour of others, but simply to be not employed by capital, although perhaps employed in continually conferring the most extensive benefits on his fellow-men. The definitions of technical terms, which do not accord with their popular acceptation, are very apt to be forgotten even by those who have paid some attention to the science to which those terms relate : and hence it is no uncommon thing to see the popular acceptation usurp the place of the technical, even in professedly scientific treatises.

It is altogether out of the question that we should even attempt to mention the heads of the various parts and chapters into which our professor has divided his work. When we say that he has traversed the whole field of political economy,—has expatiated on the theory of value, on rents, wages, population, banking, taxation, government, &c., we have hinted enough to show the range of the treatise. No part of the work, perhaps, deserves a more careful perusal, than where the relief of pauperism is the theme, and where the reasoning goes to the support of those views which have been strongly recognised in various parts of the New Poor Law for England. His leading doctrines are, that the party relieved should never, in the case of the able-bodied, be rendered as comfortable as the independent labourer,—that if work is provided for him, it ought to be at inferior wages. His next prominent ground is, that relief administered to the physical wants of a pauper should, as far as practicable, be accompanied by an attempt to improve him religiously and morally. The following paragraphs relate to the subject we are now upon :—

" A question of great importance, and one on which political economists are not yet agreed, is now presented for our consideration. Shall the relief of pauperism be left entirely to the benevolence of private individuals, or is it a proper subject for legislative enactment? With some, the abuses of the poor-laws in England, together with the abuses in the public administration of charity which it is notorious have not unfrequently occured in our own country, have induced an opinion altogether hostile to any legislation concerning pauperism. There are others, on the other hand, who mistrust the adequacy of private charity, or of charity administrated by voluntary associations of individuals, to provide for all the cases of pauperism which may occur, of a nature to render it desirable that they should become the subjects of relief.

" Such a system of the poor-laws as is based on the principle of setting the able-bodied pauper to work, at wages lower than the ordinary rate, has the advantage, over a condition of things in which he is left, in the time of his utmost need, exclusively to the tender mercies of his fellowman, in the greater certainty of finding the assistance he requires, and at the time too when he most requires it, as well as in the greater uniformity of the assistance rendered under similar circumstances of distress;—a certainty and a uniformity, as I have shewn, not at all productive of injurious consequences to society; but on the contrary desirable, on the system of pauper relief in favour of which I have expressed myself, because of their beneficial effect, in preventing the labourers, who are from time to time thrown out of employment, from being, in consequence, depressed in their condition as much as they would otherwise be.

" The great difficulty of an efficient poor-law lies in its practical execution. It is to be hoped that, with the diffusion among the community of more enlightened views of political economy, and especially of the principles which should regulate our practice in relation to alms-giving or pauper relief, properly qualified overseers of the poor will be more readily procurable than they have hitherto been. And I am, at least, not yet prepared, without farther evidence from experience, to embrace the opinion of the impracticability of every attempt, by the action of the legislature, to relieve the destitute portion of the community, so as at the same time not to affect the public welfare injuriously by the encouragement of habits of improvidence and dependence among the labourers generally.

" One advantage of a public provision based on proper principles, for the labouring poor when thrown out of employment, seems to me to be sometimes entirely overlooked. I allude to the consequent greater willingness of the poorer classes generally to acquiesce in the inequalities of fortune which unavoidably result from the maintenance of the rights of property; rights so important, in reference to the interests of both rich and poor, to be always inviolably maintained.

"After what has been delivered concerning the destitute poor who are able and willing to work, I need not dwell on the case of the infirm, the aged, and the young, who are unable to do so. Few or none who refuse to extend a helping hand to the former class would refuse it to the latter; and a large proportion of those who earnestly object to every public provision for the able-bodied poor concede, notwithstanding, the expediency of such a provision for all others."

We wish that our author's views concerning Trades' Unions and all combinations to raise wages beyond a point at which they shall permanently remain, were weighed by the working classes everywhere fairly, and thoroughly sifted. We are sure the result of such an examination would be most salutary. He shows to our perfect conviction, if, indeed, any doubt had remained on our minds about the matter, that no permanent augmentation of the ordinary rewards of labour or rates of wages can possibly be accomplished through the instrumentality of such combinations, and that all such institutions are productive only of unmixed evil.

We have now only to add that the present volume embraces the substance of certain lectures which its author during a period of not less than fifteen years delivered in the hearing of transatlantic students, together with the result of later reflections; and that while the work reflects credit on the university to which he belongs, political economy in consequence of his treatment of the subject has put forth new claims to the character of a science, whose principles may be ascertained and elucidated to the practical wellbeing as well as the speculative exercise of mankind.

Art. VIII.

1.—*The Fan-Qui in China in* 1836-7. By T. C. Downing, Esq., M. R. C. S. Colburn.

2.—*China: its State and Prospects.* By W. H. Medhurst, of the London Missionary Society. London: Snow. 1838.

Chinese jealousy is proverbially and universally spoken of; so that any glimpses which we may obtain even of the outskirts of the empire and of the people are cordially hailed, and greedily digested. Each of the present works have furnished some of these desired and welcome glimpses, although both authors have found themselves obliged to recur for a great proportion of their matter to preceding writers. We do not find fault with this in the case of China and the Chinese; for Europe deserves to be made acquainted with such a peculiar nation; and without engrafting what is recently dis-

covered upon what is known and established, not only would anything that is really new in relation to the celestial empire be
meagre in itself, but what was old would cease.to occupy the advancing mind in the study of this host of mankind, and of their
progress in civilization. Without further preface, therefore, we
proceed to cull from the volumes before us some of the most
remarkable or novel particulars which they contain.

Mr. Downing, in his medical capacity, enjoyed some peculiar
opportunities for witnessing Chinese life. Indeed, Mr. Medhurst
is of opinion, that medical men are in an especial degree fitted to
make an impression upon this singular people, and therefore they
must command advantages to which no other foreigners can generally
lay claim. Still Mr. Downing seems to have had no other scope for
observation than that which is furnished by the usual passage from
Macao to Canton; and of this he has certainly taken the utmost
advantage; for though sometimes minute to satiety, he is always
sensible and lively. We must also remark that there is no people
in the world of whom such an extensive and accurate judgment can
be formed from a few samples as the Chinese. They possess one
literature, although they may not speak one and the same dialect.
Their institutions, opinions, and manners are uniform; so that if
we obtain access to one family, it may be said that we behold the
whole of their enormous population.

Mr. Downing gives us a graphic and picturesque description of
Chinese scenery as beheld in the neighbourhood of the Bocca Tigris,
a river which for a considerable distance maintains the breadth of
the Thames at Westminster, although it sometimes spreads out
where the banks are low, occasionally, in fact, overflowing the surrounding country. At some distance from the Tigris are long ranges
of broken and irregular hills, over the tops of which and in the in-
stertices, are seen flats of green and fruitful land. Pagodas are
planted on every remarkable eminence, the lower flats being at times
complete swamps, or when the rice is in the blade forming a large
green meadow resembling an American Prairie. Small villages and
humble roofs also stud the landscape, which are apt to suggest the
idea of English rural retreats. Our author proceeds—

" As you look around, you often notice something moving above the
paddy, and you feel some little curiosity to know what strange animal it
represents; but, after a while, you see it emerge from one of the little
creeks, and ascertain that it is the top of the mat-sail belonging to a small
boat, which has been wandering far away inland."   *   *   *   " The plot
of life thickens the further you proceed. The meagre, squalid families of
the fishermen give place to the cultivators of the soil, who appear much
more robust and healthy. Large duck-boats line the banks of the river,
and their feathered inhabitants are seen wandering among the surrounding paddy, watched and protected by their solemn masters. Males and
females of the lower orders ramble up and down in the mud with their

trowsers tucked up above the knees. As they stalk along in this manner, thrusting the leg up to the part where it is covered, into the mud, and every now and then drawing it out and putting the hand to the foot, you are at a loss to imagine what they are about. They are searching for prawns and shrimps, and other small fish, and, when they have discovered them, they seize them under the mud, between the great toe and the one next to it; and then bring them to the surface, when they are deposited in a small bag which is carried at the waist. This is one of the many instances where the foot is used with the same dexterity, and answers all the purposes of a third hand. Boats are paddled about in all directions by men employed in catching wild geese, while large junks and river craft traverse up and down, and are of every variety of colour and employment. Mixed with this motley crowd, is seen the majestic Indiaman, with the British ensign floating proudly from the peak, slowly moving under a tower of canvass, and perhaps exchanging signals with a Spaniard, a Dutchman, or an American, the upper part of which is seen over a spit of land in the reach below."

It must indeed be a motley crowd that presents itself on the face of the waters, to such an observer as our author, as the approach is made to Whampoa. Think of a people who are not so prejudiced as to consider man a terrene animal, thousands of them having been born on the water, and who regard going on shore in the light of a cruise. Boats about twenty feet long, and of a proportionable breadth, called wash-boats, swarm on all hands. They are miserably fitted up, their inhabitants, however, being good-natured smiling girls, who make their living by washing the clothes of sailors and petty officers. Other parties and persons following other callings live upon the water, in their habits resembling amphibious creatures. Thus a mother may be seen sitting at needle-work in a boat, quietly looking on, while a child of five or six years is swimming around the vessel, and another not able to walk is scrambling on all-fours about the little deck, and of course liable at every turn to fall overboard. But the danger after all is not imminent, for an air-tight or buoyant article is fastened at the back of the shoulders of the new-born infant, which it wears until able to take care of itself; so that when it chances to tumble into the watery element the mother has nothing more to do than to fish it out again.

Since we are upon the subject of amphibious beings, an extract will add to our knowledge of certain varieties belonging to a sort of floating habitation, to which some allusion in a foregoing passage has been made.

"The duck boats are certainly to be ranked among the curious singularities of the Chinese. They are large and roomy, with a broad walk extending round the covered parts a little above the surface of the water. If the Irishman may be said to give the best side of the fire to his pig because he pays the rent, surely the Chinaman may with equal propriety give the best part of his house to the accommodation of the ducks. They have the large apartments at the after part of the boat, while the man with his family exists in a miserable hovel at the head. With which society to associate, it would require some little hesitation to decide; but perhaps the ducks would have the preference. In the morning, the doors are opened, and the birds wander round the house at their pleasure. When the sun is high, large inclined planes are let down at the sides of the boat; one towards the land, and the others towards the water. Up and down these steps the feathered bipeds travel at their pleasure and take a cruise on land or water, but are prevented from proceeding too far by their anxious overseers. When it is time to retire the man gives a whistle, and at the sound every bird returns, and waddles back again into his warm, comfortable berth. When they are all on board, the stairs are hoisted to the horizontal position by means of a long bamboo lever, and everything is then made secure for the night. The proprietor of one of these boats is able to gain a livelihood by the care of these birds, which he watches with somewhat of the same kind of parental fondness as a hen over a brood of young ducklings just emerged from the shell."

·We may observe, while abiding on the Tigris, that although our author admits the battle of the Bogue, which was fought when the Andromache and Imogen forced the passage, to have been a gallant affair, he nevertheless attributes a good deal of its success to the want of skill and the neglect of the Chinese. He says, though their batteries are numerous and extensive, as well as judiciously situated, and the metal heavy, promising destruction to all who should in a hostile manner come within their reach, still the heavy guns being altogether immoveable, and fixed in the stone sockets of the ramparts, are necessarily unfitted to contend with the masters of the sea.· Besides, the Chinese are neither a warlike people nor accustomed to such sharp practice as has been more than once employed to their cost by the English.

But while the *celestials* are neither pugnacious nor brave, they may teach boastful Europeans a mastery in certain exploits which at least argue something like a philosophy, where contentment and fertility in the discovery of resources are eminently displayed. Much has been said of their industry, their methodical works, their agricultural skill, &c.; but their economy in the use of articles for food is not less remarkable. At a pinch nothing comes amiss, for they have the most accommodating stomachs imaginable. Every thing animal, from the hide to the entrails—and almost every thing vegetable, from the leaves to the roots, is made available to the support of life; and even some parts of the mineral kingdom are laid under requisition for this important purpose. Accordingly dogs afford a meal that is not regarded as undainty. Mr. Downing is minute on this subject. He states, that

" The flesh is hung up in the markets in the same manner as that of the sheep with us, and is sold by weight. The·young puppies, esteemed a delicacy in the same way as lambs are in Europe, are brought for sale in cages or baskets, carried at the ends of a bamboo on the shoulders. These little animals are very pretty, with the wool often of a beautiful white colour, and, if we could reconcile ourselves to the idea of eating their species at all, these would be the first morsels which we should feel inclined to swallow. The young ladies of the Celestial Empire make pets of the handsomer kinds of cat, so that they are often found to be in the houses of the rich. The poorer people cannot afford to keep these expensive luxuries, and, therefore, their flesh is a general article of consumption. When it is well fed, it is even considered superior to that of the dogs, and is to be seen, occasionally, upon the tables of the opulent. A small species of wild cat is sometimes caught in the southern provinces, and is brought to market as a great dainty. It is considered game, and none but the rich can afford to eat it. •Rats and mice are confined almost exclusively to the very poorest people. The former are often seen in long rows, skinned and otherwise prepared, and hung up by dozens, with a small piece of wood passed across from one hind leg to another. At Whampoa, these little animals are eagerly sought after by those in the boats, whenever they are caught on board the ships. Their bite seems to be utterly disregarded, as I have seen a rat fastened with a string tied to the hind leg, to the top of one of the covers of a boat, to form the plaything of a little boy or girl. Whenever the captive wretch had got to the end of the tether, the little urchin has taken it up with the greatest *nonchalance* by the poll of the neck, and put it into its place again. The way of catching the large water-rat is so peculiarly Chinese, that it deserves to be mentioned. These animals live in holes under the excavated banks of streams, and from thence sally forth into the water. The rat-catcher proceeds in the darkness of the night to the spot, and places one of his showy lanterns immediately before the hole. When the rat comes out to see what is the matter, he is so astonished and dazzled with the light that he becomes motionless, and then the Chinaman is enabled to capture him with ease."

We have only to remark before closing Mr. Downing's volumes and his statement regarding the uses to which the Chinese, on an emergency, devote their dogs, cats, and rats, that the first mentioned of these creatures, like their brethren in other countries, exhibit, on certain occasions, a wonderful sagacity,—that they entertain an irreconcileable ill-will towards their professional slaughterers, —and that the butchers in Canton find it necessary to carry about with them, whenever they go abroad, defensive weapons to keep off the canine breed, which are ever ready to make an attack in revenge for the wrongs done to their race, by their destroyers for the shambles. So much for an instinctive or hereditary principle.

More than a half of Mr. Medhurst's goodly octavo consists of an abridgment, a spirited one we admit, of what former authors and travellers have given to the world. The compilation, however, is interspersed with many original observations and conclusions, which are striking and appropriate. While he treats of the social, political, literary, and statistical condition and relations of the people of China, he points every portion of his information in such a manner as to bear upon their religious prospects and conversion to Christianity as becomes a writer engaged in the great missionary cause,—a cause in which he has laboured for the benefit of China, since the year 1816. Before proceeding to notice some of the facts contained in the more original part of the volume, viz., that which presents a narrative of a voyage along the north-east coast of China performed by the author in 1835,—we shall call attention to a few of the more remarkable statements, in a missionary sense, to be found in his introductory account of the general state of the country.

Mr. Medhurst inclines to receive the highest estimate that has been given of the Chinese population, rating it at 361,221,900 ; that is, the population of China Proper, besides upwards of a million for the inhabitants of Formosa, and the various tribes of Chinese Tartary, under the sway of the emperor of China. Now, as he puts it, if this be anything like an accurate calculation, if there be so many millions huddled together under one despotic monarch, amounting to one-third of the human race, bound under one heathenish spell, what a field is here for benevolent enterprise ! Well may he exclaim,

" Where shall we begin, or where can we hope to end the Herculean task ? And what proportion do our present means and efforts bear to the end in view ? Some score of individuals, is all that the churches of England and America now devote to the conversion of China—one thousand persons are thereby brought under instruction, and not more than ten converted every year. This is a very small proportion, and protracted will be the period, ere we can expect at such a rate to succeed. Could we bring one thousand individuals under instruction every day, and give them only a day's teaching each, it would take one thousand years to bring all the population of China thus under the sound of the Gospel; and if even ten of these separate thousands were every day converted to God, it would require one hundred thousand years to make all these mighty hosts savingly acquainted with divine truth. This is a startling view of the matter, but a more affecting consideration still, is, that the ranks of heathenism are increasing at a thousandfold greater ratio, than we can expect, by such a system of proselyting, to thin them. For, even allowing an increase of only one per cent. per annum, on the whole population, we shall find that they are thus adding three and a half millions, yearly, to their number; so that according to our most sanguine calculations, the heathen would multiply faster than they could be brought over to Christianity. Besides which, while we are thus aiming to rescue a few, the many are still perishing for lack of knowledge."

This is a disheartening picture, and if no relieving circumstance appeared, if no faith existed in favour of universal civilization and political freedom, no reliance on the testimony of Scriptural Prophecy, here is more than sufficient to appal the stoutest heart, and quench all the ardour of the most energetic philanthropist. But there are grounds of hope and encouragement ; and we like the manner in which our author has contrasted them with his alarming portraiture. For example, he draws some consolation from the very multitude and density of the population. He considers the people as a whole, and as we before remarked, as accustomed to one mode of thinking, and subject to the same prejudices ; so that the arguments and means of enlightenment and conversion which may be effectually applied to one person, one family, one section of the people, may be hopefully applied to the whole. Think how much may be hoped for from the single circumstance that the Chinese universally understand one mode of writing, one written language. But this is not all. What if, in the Providence of God, Christian Missionaries should come to be tolerated by a *fiat* of the government, what if a host of these indefatigable and zealous men should traverse the length and breadth of the land! Nay, to adopt the precise words of Mr. Medhurst, " it is not impossible that a remonstrance drawn up by Christian missionaries, may reach the ' dragon throne ;' or that a devoted and zealous preacher of the Gospel should be introduced to court, and plead the cause of Christianity in the imperial ear."

These, it may be said, are extravagant and unwarrantable hopes. But listen (we are not speaking to those who implicitly believe in Revelation, its promises and predictions,) and learn what really has been done. We do not go so far back as the seventh century, during which Mosheim informs us, the Nestorians established several churches in China. We come down to the Catholic mission, which commenced in the beginning of the fourteenth century, and to the successors of Xavier, a man, who after the most arduous labours for the conversion of other nations in the East, was most desirous to make an impression upon China ; for he reckoned that he had done nothing, in converting multitudes in India, while the celestial empire was unattempted. But death interrupted his personal exertions ere he was able to enter upon this enterprise. Other Catholic labourers, however, arose.

" In 1579, M. Rogier, an Italian Jesuit, arrived in China, where he was soon joined by Matthew Ricci. These devoted themselves to the study of the Chinese language, and made some proficiency in it. A dispute having arisen between the Chinese and the Portuguese, Rugiero was sent to negotiate, when he requested to be allowed to settle in Canton ; and, after some delay, he and his fellow missionary got introduced to Chaou-king-foo, then the capital city of the province. Here they were obliged to act with great caution ; as the Chinese, having heard of the conquests of the Spaniards and Portuguese, were exceedingly jealous of strangers. The affability and talents of Ricci, however, soon gained them friends. The literati admired their doctrines, so far as they agreed with Confucius, and admitted the propriety of worshipping the Lord of Heaven, but objected to the mysteries of the Christian faith ; while the prohibition of polygamy, and the vow of celibacy, were still more offensive to them. They accused the strangers of neglecting their deceased parents, and of not worshipping Confucius, while they paid too much deference to Jesus. The arguments and ridicule of their opponents, however, did not dishearten these zealous men; who, by their knowledge of the sciences, were enabled to instruct and interest the people. Converts were soon made, and a church formed, over which Ricci presided for about seven years; when he was obliged to quit the provincial city, and repair to Chaou-chow-foo, about one hundred miles to the north of Canton. Here he changed his dress, from that of a Buddhist priest, which he had formerly assumed, to that of the literati, which brought him more respect and consideration.

" Having been successful in various parts of the Canton province, he burned with a desire to preach the Gospel in the capital : and, attaching himself to the retinue of a mandarin, travelled with him to Nanking. He soon attracted attention by his discourses on science and religion, and even gained the favour of the superior authorites. Encouraged by this reception, and having received some valuable presents from Europe, he resolved to make his way to the emperor. At court, his presents were received, and his person honoured ; a house was assigned him, and he was taken into the service of the state, A.D. 1601."

Ricci having now obtained an advantageous footing, began, to diffuse his doctrines, and in a few years converted several persons of distinction; among whom was a mandarin of great talents and influence. This mandarin even defended the Christian scheme and cause in presence of the emperor. Several missionaries joined Ricci, and at Peking the number of converts daily increased. Various successes attended the efforts of these exemplary and resolute men, as well as their successors. The Christians were sometimes persecuted, sometimes encouraged and protected by the supreme power. Their knowledge in the mathematics and other branches of learning operated strongly in their favour. Some of the emperors conversed with the fathers on the subject of religion ; others felt deeply indebted to them for their skill in medicine and science. About the year 1666 the Catholic missionaries in China had much to contend against.

" About this time a learned man, named Yang Kwangseen, published a book against the missionaries. He accused them of forming a conspiracy to overturn the government; in order to which, he said, they had introduced a great number of strangers into the empire, and had secured to themselves whole hosts of adherents, who were prepared to aid them in their sinister designs. ' In teaching, continued he, ' that all mankind descended from Adam, they wish to infer that our princes came originally from Europe, and their countrymen, as the elder born, have a right to our monarchy.' And then, producing the sign of the cross, he exclaimed, ' Behold the God of the Europeans, nailed to a cross, for having attempted to make himself king of the Jews; and this is the God they invoke, to favour their design of making themselves masters of China.' These sage reasonings had the desired effect with the four regents, who ordered the missionaries to be loaded with chains, and dragged before the tribunals,

A. D. 1665. The members of these tribunals declared, ' that Schaal and his associates merited the punishment of seducers, who announce to the people a false and pernicious doctrine.' After having been threatened with death, they were set at liberty; but the venerable Schaal sunk under his trials, and died A. D. 1666, in the seventy-eighth year of his age.

" In addition to these troubles at Peking, the missionaries throughout the provinces were arrested, and three Dominicans, one Franciscan, and twenty-one Jesuits were banished to Canton. Four were still retained at court, who kept together the flock of professing Christians; until Kang-he, coming of age, found the calendar in such disorder, that he recommitted it to the hands of Verbiest, and reinstated him in his former office; thereby affording him an opportunity of promoting the interests of his church at Peking. Finding that the emperor was disposed to redress any grievances which had occurred during his minority, Verbiest presented a memorial, praying for the recal of his brethren; which, after some difficulty, was acceded to.''

In 1671, the missionaries were put in possession of their churches, but forbidden to make converts of the natives. Notwithstanding this edict, in this same year, 20,000 Chinese were baptized. The emperor of the time even studied the elements of Euclid under one of the fathers, who succeeded in his endeavour to gain the monarch's toleration for Christianity; for though he did not embrace, he desired that no one should vilify, the Gospel.

" Verbiest now rose in favour of the emperor, and accompanied him in his journeys to Tartary. The mandarins, also, encouraged by the example of the court, favoured the missionaries in all parts of the empire; and nothing seemed wanting, but an accession of labourers, to bring both China, Corea, and Tartary to the profession of Christianity : in conformity with Xavier's observation, that ' if China embraced the Gospel, all the neighbouring nations would soon demolish their idols, and adopt the Christian religion.'

" Encouraged by the openings which presented themselves, Louis XIV. king of France, resolved to send a mission to China; and having selected a number of Jesuits, well skilled in the mathematics, he sent them with honours and pensions on this important mission. Among the rest, was De Fontaney, professor of mathematics in the king's college; with Gerbillon, Bouvet, and Le Comte, afterwards celebrated for their labours in the east. They went first to Siam, and from thence proceeded, in a Chinese junk, to Ning-po, on the coast of China. The mandarins at that port received them with politeness; but the viceroy declared it unlawful for native vessels to bring Europeans to China, and threatened to send the missionaries back, and confiscate both ship and cargo, Verbiest, on hearing of this, memorialized the emperor, representing that they were men skilled in the sciences, and his brethren. To which the emperor replied, ' men of that character must not be expelled my dominions. Let them all come to my court : those who understand the mathematics, shall remain about my person : the others may dispose of themselves in the provinces, as they think fit. On the receipt of this order, the viceroy was

obliged to send those men to the capital with honour, whom he had intended to expel with disgrace."

We shall not trace, even in outline, the several fortunes which
have characterized the history of Catholic missions in China down
to this day.   It must suffice, when we state, that certain differences
which arose between themselves proved injurious to the common
cause—that even now there are many thousands of professed Catholics among the natives of the empire, (in Peking alone, says our
author, there are twenty-six thousand, over whom two French priests
preside,)—and that when the rulers do not suspect the presence of
Europeans, they are very indulgent to the native Christians,—their
jealousy being rather excited in regard to European influence and
encroachment, than the peculiarities of the Christian religion.   Indeed our author thinks that should the Catholics succeed in forming
a native clergy, competent to discharge the duties of their office,
their cause may rally; and altogether, considering his creed, Mr.
Medhurst is a liberal interpreter and narrator.   In justice to his
consistency, however, in matters of religious faith, and as is due to
those who patronise his exertions, or have any connection with
" The London Missionary Society," whose servant he is, we quote
his concluding observations with regard to the body of Christians
who have so long laboured in behalf of the Chinese.

"On the whole we may conclude, that the Romish missionaries, from
first to last, have been rather solicitous about the quantity, than the quality, of their success ; while they have displayed a spirit of timeserving
compliance with the prejudices of the heathen, and failed to exhibit
Christianity in its most inviting form to the nations.   Had they succeeded
in establishing their religion throughout China, we question whether,
from their known bigotry, they would not have presented insurmountable obstacles to the efforts of protestant labourers.   If anything earthly
could have contributed to success, they had certainly the fairest opportunity of realizing their object ; the power of numbers, the influence of
wealth, the patronage of Christian kings, the attractions of a showy worship, and high scientific attainments, all promised fair for the accomplishment of their design.   They have, however, partially failed ; and, in their
failure, read us a lesson, not to make flesh our arm, but to trust in the
living God, who worketh all things according to the counsel of his own
will.   At the same time, we are not to be discouraged by their repulse :
the laws which proscribe them, do not necessarily affect us : some of their
practices, against which the Chinese excepted, we shall not imitate ;
such as the celibacy of the clergy, and the cloistering of women ; the
interference of a foreign potentate, with the authority of the emperor,
will not be promoted by us; the Scriptures will be made the standard of
judgment, and reason and conscience alone appealed to.   Instead of beginning from the top of society, we propose commencing from the bottom ;
and aim to influence, first, the extremities, and then the heart of the
empire.   With the love of Christ for our motive, and the salvation of

souls for our end; employing Christian benevolence, and Christian intelligence, as the means; and depending simply and solely on God for his blessing, we hope and believe, that though slow, our work will be sure, and finally effectual."

We offer no opinion upon this statement, but would have those who may sneer at the idea of converting the Chinese to a belief in the Christian religion, as being most chimerical, to remember that not only what has happened may happen again, but that in so far as human efforts go, the experience, the failures, if you will, of the past, may indicate a sure and certain method of procedure for the future.

It would be wrong while upon this part of our author's work to overlook a circumstance from which he draws encouragement, but which at first sight presents nothing but grounds for despair. We have seen how he takes comfort even from the immense multitude of people that inhabit the Chinese empire, in reference to the conversion of the whole. But what shall be said to the constant and prodigious increase of the people, in the meanwhile; an increase that may be thought to proceed at a pace which no missionary exertions can ever be expected to overtake? Let our author be heard on this point.

"It has been before observed, that China, partly by additions to the number enrolled, and partly by the preponderance of births over deaths, has doubled its population several times during the last century. Such has been the rapidity and extent of the increase, that all the waste lands, within the empire, capable of cultivation, have been occupied; and the surplus population, unable to gain a subsistence at home, have been compelled to emigrate by thousands every year, to the islands and countries around. Now, the number of inhabitants is still increasing, and the Chinese in spite of their exclusive and restrictive system are bursting forth on every side, and, without our asking it, are coming in contact with Christians, and seeking shelter under European governments, where missionaries may labour unimpeded and unprohibited among them. If the same causes continue to operate, without any counteracting influence, there seems nothing to prevent the Chinese from crowding into the British possessions in Hindostan, and, under the mild and just sway of our Indian rulers, multiplying still more fast and plentifully than they have done in their own country. They have already their hundreds of thousands in Siam, and will soon occupy Birmah, Pegu, and Assam. They have long colonized the islands of the Malayan archipelago, and what should hinder them from pushing on to New Holland, where millions of acres await their assiduous and energetic cultivation; while the extensive and fertile regions of New Guinea and New Ireland lie still more contiguous to their mother country. A nation increasing as does the Chinese, cannot be long confined within narrow bounds, and restriction with them is impossible. Imperial edicts are already weak and inefficient, but will soon be flung to the winds. Hunger cannot be controlled, and necessity

knows no law. Let but another age roll by, and China double her population once more, and her very increase will break down her political
barriers, and bring her myriads in contact with the Christian world.'
Let vigorous measures be taken for the thorough instruction of the
Chinese emigrants, and, while coming adventurers get an acquaintance
with the truth, returning individuals will carry with them what they
have learned ; and thus, within and without the limits of the empire, all
will gradually be evangelized. The multiplication of their numbers,
therefore, viewed in this light, presents an encouraging aspect, and would
lead us to anticipate the period as not far distant, when China shall
stretch out her hands unto God."

It is not necessary that we should give any sketch of the progress
of Protestant missions in the East and in China. All who take an
interest in the subject will look for information elsewhere—in Mr.
Medhurst's volume among others. One great general principle
professed by the Protestants is to win their way to the confidence
of the people by deeds of benevolence and humble assiduities,—
medical efforts among the rest ; whereas the Catholics are said to
have trusted mainly to their scientific triumphs. The following
paragraphs may be added as a general account of what the Protestants have done, and of what they long to do.

" Protestant missionaries, in their attempts to operate on China, limited
their efforts, for a quarter of a century, to those parts where Europeans
generally reside, or where the British and Dutch governments afforded
protection. Considering themselves excluded from the interior of the
empire, and finding a host of Chinese emigrants in the various countries
of the Malayan archipelago, they aimed first to enlighten these, with the
hope, that if properly instructed and influenced, they would, on their
return to their native land, carry with them the Gospel they had learned,
and spread it among their countrymen. With this view, our brethren
established themselves in the various colonies around China, studied the
language, set up schools and seminaries, wrote and printed books, conversed extensively with the people, and tried to collect congregations, to
whom they might preach the word of life. Since the commencement of
their missions, they have translated the holy Scriptures, and printed two
thousand complete Bibles, ten thousand Testaments, thirty thousand separate books of Scripture, and upwards of half a million of tracts in the
Chinese language ; besides four thousand Testaments, and one hundred
and fifty thousand tracts in the languages of the Malayan archipelago,
comprising upwards of eight thousand leaves of new matter, and twenty
millions of printed pages. About ten thousand children have passed
through the mission schools ; nearly one hundred persons have been
baptized, and several native preachers raised up, one of whom has proclaimed the Gospel to his countrymen in the interior of the empire, and
endured persecution for the sake of Jesus. ' Such a result cannot but be
gratifying to the friends of missions, and on a review of it, the labourers
employed would ' thank God and take courage.'

" But all this is far more satisfying the desires of the ardent missionary, er from accomplishing the object for which he went forth. Whatever be done in the colonies, the friends of China cannot be content until some impression be made upon the mother country; and as the emigrants are but a sprinkling compared with the bulk of the population, so the converts from among the colonists bear but a small proportion to the salvation of the whole empire."

An effort was made by Mr. Medhurst in 1835 to further these great ends. After much difficulty to procure a vessel that had at the time no connection with the opium trade or any disreputable purpose, so as to compromise a missionary's character, an American brig, the Huron, was hired for several months, for the north-east coast voyage. Trade was in no respect the object of the trip, but the distribution of religious books, tracts, and portions of Scripture in the Chinese language, which had been printed at Batavia, Malacca, and Canton. A Mr. Stevens, seaman's chaplain at Whampoa, was our author's companion and coadjutor. The voyage extended from Canton to Shan-tung. A few extracts will sufficiently indicate the mode of procedure adopted by the missionaries on this occasion, their manner of reception, and the success which attended them.

"Having observed the inhabitants of Lew-kung-taou very busy, in sending off ten or a dozen boats towards the town of Wei-hae, all of them full of people, and apparently of valuables, as though they apprehended us to be marauders or desperadoes, we thought it best to undeceive them; and, notwithstanding the heavy rain, we went on shore in the afternoon. On arriving at the beach, most of the people ran up into the village, but a few of the more robust and daring, stood their ground. This was a critical moment, and the feelings of both parties were, perhaps, a little agitated. Not having set foot on this part of China before, we did not know how the natives would receive us. Much had been said about the hazard of landing at any other place except Canton; and insult, imprisonment, and death, were predicted as the consequences of such a step. The natives, on their part, did not know who or what we were; and apprehended the most fearful things, when they saw 'the fierce barbarians' coming amongst them. Stepping ashore, however, we saluted them in their own tongue, to which they cheerfully responded, and a little acquaintance with each other, soon taught both parties to lay aside their suspicions.

"After asking the name of the place, and introducing our object, we went forward, through some cultivated fields, to the village; at the entrance of which, men, women, and children stood to receive us. They returned our salutations in a cheerful manner, and led the way into a house. This was a poor, mean dwelling, half full of Barbadoes millet, which appeared to be, with them, the staff of life. One end of the chief apartment was occupied by a sort of raised platform, which served the inhabitants for table, chair, bed-place, and oven; upon this we sat down, to converse with the natives, who soon filled the house. On opening the basket of books, we found that few, if any, could read, and only one individual accepted of a volume. They were, however, very civil; and conversed familiarly, for some time. Among other things, they asked, whether our vessel was the same that had visited their island, twenty years ago, alluding to Lord Amherst's embassy; or whether we were connected with two vessels which had more recently entered their harbour, for the purpose of distributing books. They asked how many hands we had on board; and were surprised to hear, that the whole ship's company amounted to no more than fifteen persons, saying that we should never be able to get our anchor up with such a small complement of men. We invited them to come on board and see; and receiving a present of a few fresh vegetables, we returned to the ship."

The above allusion to Lord Amherst's embassy and other circumstances mentioned by Mr. Medhurst, show that the communication between one part and all others of the empire is constant and accurate.

Our author and his friend distributed their books in armfuls; sometimes the people unceremoniously helped themselves. But the general character of this eager demand requires to be explained.

"Their anxiety to obtain books, however, must not in the least be ascribed to any knowledge of, or relish for, their contents; but merely to an eager curiosity, to get possession of something that came from abroad, and an insatiable cupidity, to obtain what was to be had for nothing. After having supplied them liberally, we stood up in the midst of the threshing floor, and with a loud voice, proclaimed the news of salvation to the listening throng. We told them of God's pity to mankind, in sending his own Son to save our sinful race, and detailed to them the relation of the birth, life, death, and resurrection of our blessed Saviour; in obedience to whose command we were come, to testify the glad tidings of great joy in their ears. One man, who had listened attentively, exclaimed, 'Oh! you are come to propagate religion?' Just so, we replied, and happy will you be if you receive it.'

The mandarins were uniformly most unwilling that the missionaries should penetrate to any distance the celestial territory, although the common people did not in general side with these functionaries. Indeed, the authorities for the most part would have kept the Christians to their brig, where they were very willing to hold a confabulation; and we wonder that their obvious power was not forcibly exercised. The mandarins, however, are cowards,—

"On our arrival, we found that the mandarins had been to pay us a visit, in two junks, bringing with them about one hundred men. As there were only eight hands in the vessel, the mate was disinclined to receive them, and intimated that the captain was not on board; but they appeared so friendly, that he allowed them to come upon deck. They expressed their surprise at everything they saw, went down into the cabin, and even looked into the hold at the books and rice. The mate then fired a six-pounder, to call us on board; they were unwilling, however, that he should make the signal and begged him not to fire, lest the gun should

·burst; while one of them, a naval captain, actually made haste over the side of the vessel, in order to avoid the explosion. Finding that books were to be procured, they asked for some, and took about fifty volumes away with them. After waiting for us hours, they departed, highly pleased with what they had seen.'·

It appears that our author and his companion bore themselves with singular composure, firmness, and dignity, when a word, one might imagine, would have silenced them for ever. But the Chinese are far advanced in certain forms of civilization, and they also know too well their interest wantonly to abuse British " barbarians." Still Mr.·Medhurst was acting in known defiance of the laws of the empire, and we suspect, in similar circumstances, he would not have been so leniently dealt with in some countries nearer home.·

, " On our arrival, we were met by two native officers, who said that we must return on board, till the mandarins arrived· from the vessel, ·when they would introduce us to the general of the district. We objected, that we could not remain in the boat during the rain, and urged that the least they could do was to afford us a place of shelter. So saying, we moved on towards the custom-house, accompanied by a dense crowd, who strove on all sides to get a sight of us. Arrived at the office, we were invited to sit down, and the multitude pressed eagerly round to see the strangers. As they increased in numbers and eagerness, the police officers became exceedingly free with brooms, sticks, and whips, which they laid most profusely on the heads and shoulders of the people; hallooing and scolding, and throwing handsful of sand in their eyes, in order to keep them at a moderate distance from the building. We observed, however, that they never offered to strike or push any of the Fŭh-kĕen sailors, who seemed to carry themselves with an air of independence, and would not be turned aside from the front of the door. Seeing this, we got up and spoke to them in their own dialect, and enlarged on the doctrines of the Gospel; to which they listened attentively, and by which they were induced to receive our publications.·

" Some inferior officers gathering round, we spoke to them as long as they would listen, and employed the time as profitably as we could, while the mandarins were making arrangements for our reception.

" At length after waiting for several hours, we informed Tae-laou-yay, that unless we were speedily introduced to the general, we must return on board, as the day was fast drawing to a close, He said, that we might be introduced immediately, but he wished first to know, what ceremonies we meant to observe on seeing such a great officer. Their custom, he continued, was to kneel down, and knock the head against the ground, on coming into the presence of superiors, and he desired to be informed whether we would do the same. We told him, that we were not in the habit of prostrating ourselves before our fellow mortals, but that we were willing to pay the same deference to Chinese mandarins of high rank, as we did to our own superior officers. ' Well,' said he, ' I will speak to the general, and try to arrange that matter for you.' ' But further,' we observed, '· when the ceremony of introduction is over, we expect to be

almost to sit down in the presence of the ground, otherwise we beg leave to decline the conference.' This also,' said he, ' shall be arranged to your satisfaction;' and we, this afternoon, we proceeded to the temple, where the great officers were sitting."

We discover great acuteness and eagerness for information in the questions and answers which Mr. Medhurst records as having been elicited in the course of his conversation with the Chinese. We can only give one example.

· " Amongst other enquiries, they wished to know whence Mr. Stevens · came ; and, being told that he belonged to New England, they enquired whether there was a new, as well as an old England? which led us to observe, that there was a new, as well as old world, which was not known to the inhabitants of Europe till within the last four hundred years. After the first discovery, we added, it was soon peopled : and England, at that time, having a surplus population, multitudes emigrated, and formed the country of New England. They then asked, under what sort of government this new country was, and who was king over it ? We said, ' they had no king, but were ruled by two great assemblies, at the head of which was a president; all of them chosen by the people, and re-elected after a certain term.' They asked, ' what became of the old president, on his going out of office ?' and, on being told that he became a common man, they wondered greatly; and could not conceive how he could be restrained from exciting rebellion, and employing the power he so lately wielded, in raising up a party in his own favour. In this, they reasoned from what frequently takes place in their own country; to what might happen in other regions. With them, a man once in power, aims to be always in power, and is never content with a private station, after having held the reins of government. Hence, when an individual is deprived of the supreme authority, his antagonist never considers himself safe, till the previous ruler is put out of the world, and his whole race extirpated; lest some distant member of the fallen house, actuated by ambition or revenge, should aim at the re-establishment of the dynasty or perish in the attempt to gratify his vengeful feelings. ·They then wanted to know, whether our author had met with Mr. Stevens, and how an old Englander readily agree with a new Englander. We said that bound to each other by the peculiar tie of religion, and being actuated by liberal views, were more disposed to the promotion of a sacred object, than others,*

Such are a few of the curious and remarkable questions asked our author has... it seems...

sonable to expect that where such a commencement is realized, the
beginnings will be small. That Mr. Medhurst is an able and zealous servant in the cause cannot be doubted ; and his book furnishes
one among many instances where piety, chivalrous enterprise, knowledge, and literary skill, have all united to adorn and dignify the
character of the Christian missionary.

ART. IX.—*Homeward Bound; or, the Chase. A Tale of the Sea.*
By J. FENIMORE COOPER, Esq. 3 Vols. London : Bentley. 1838.

To produce a novel worth reading now-a-days we consider to be
one of the most considerable efforts of genius. All the requisite
talents required for this end we hold are seldom found in one
individual. The successful novelist must combine in his own person
the qualities peculiar to the poet, the philosopher, the historian and
the dramatist ; he must invent discriminately, narrate judiciously,
and give a correct portraiture of character and passion, acting in
their various scenes and producing their wonted effects. Untram-
melled by the shackles which surround the poet from the necessity he lies under of arranging his ideas in verse, the novelist is
therefore required to show a greater fidelity in his exhibitions of
nature. He must not exceed a becoming and useful exaggeration,
nor must he ever wrap his ideas in a misty cloudiness of language—
he must be distinct, graphic and true. Incidents are to be imagined
not so trifling as to create weariness, nor so extravagant as to
engender doubts as to their reality ; in fact, a novel must be a
picture of life, and the characters presented in it must have that
diversity without an excessive mixture of the wonderful which is found
in the ordinary course of things. Unity of action is essential ; the
story must have a beginning, middle, and end. A string of events
connected by no other tie than that they happened to the same
individual, which is often put forth as an historical novel, is far from
being so : we consider the most exalted name that can be given
to works of this sort is a fictitious history or memoir ; they certainly
approach not our idea of what a novel should be.

Having imagined a series of connected events, all tending to one
point and depending upon a simple action, and drawn also a group of
ideal characters, this is not all nor perhaps the most difficult portion
of the task the novelist has to accomplish. In doing this he has but
chosen the canvas and sketched in outline his intended picture. It
remains to regulate the whole, and to invest the figures with the hues
and colours of life ; to make a proper distinction of light and shade
according to the relative importance of the scenes introduced ; and
to charm the eye of the beholder with a pleasing variety, taking
particular care not to offend it by any forced or sudden contrasts.
Propriety in garb and manners must be preserved, according to the
time and place which the artist aims to present. If he goes back

to a former period, he must combine the knowledge of the antiquary with that of the historian, or the *keeping* of the work will be defective, and it will belong to the class of modern antiques. He must identify himself with the spirit of the olden time, before he can bring others into the illusion. A traveller's acquaintance with distant scenes must be attained, before he can divert his reader's imagination from the view of his native plains and hills. If he prefer remaining at home and sketching domestic scenes, he will find it hard to dignify what is common, and to excite interest without violating probability. Events and characters in humble life must be ennobled by the elevation of passion and sentiment, or invested with the soft charm of affection and quiet, or rendered lively by ridicule and humorous contrast. The monotony of rank and society, the uniform and decorous manners of the higher classes, among whom enthusiasm does not exist, must be varied by wit and disquisition, or exposed by satire. The personages must be individualized and painted at full length, so as to command the sympathy of the most careless beholder with their actions and feelings, while the novelist must leave them traits enough in common to stand as the representatives of a class. From all that we have said it may be inferred that the field which the novelist has open before him is extensive, and the effect which he may hope to produce vast. Indeed there is no mode of talent or kind of information which is not available to him, and of these materials the genuine novel writer constructs a philosophy of life, more true than any that may be gleaned from the pages of the historian. The reputation of Mr. Cooper, the well-known author of the volumes before us, is such that it would be almost a work of supererogation to make any very lengthy remarks upon his manner of writing. His style is sprightly, pointed, easy, correct, and expressive, without being too studiously guarded against the opposite faults. It is without affectation, parade, or labour. If we were to characterize a manner, which owes much of its merit to the absence of any glaring characteristic, we should perhaps say, that it is, above the style of all other writers of the day, marked with an expressive elegance. He never buries up the clearness and force of the meaning under a heap of fine words ; nor on the other hand does he think it necessary to be coarse, slovenly, or uncouth, in order to be emphatic.

The number of his works in this department of fiction is very numerous. About eighteen years have elapsed since he published "Precaution," his first work, but one of little merit, and which soon passed quietly into oblivion. "The Spy, a Tale of the Neutral Ground," came next, and at once established his reputation for ability, and excited confident expectations of his future success. Then followed, in rapid succession, "The Pioneers," "The Pilot," "The Last of the Mohicans," "Lionel Lincoln," "The Prairie," and "The Wept of Wish-ton-Wish,"—all relating to American scenes and characters. One of these, " The Pilot," and two others subsequently published, " The Red Rover," and " The Water Witch," are the fruits of several years' connexion with the American navy, and attest the writer's thorough acquaintance with the men and things of the sea. During his residence in Europe, he produced four novels of a European character, " The Bravo," " The Heiden-mauer," " The Headsman," " The Monikins," and that of which the title stands at the head of this article. These make up the full list of Mr. Cooper's novels.

It would be unjust to ascribe much of our author's success to the fact that he entered an untrodden field, and was the first to employ the copious materials for fiction afforded by the history of his native country, and the character of its early inhabitants. Endowed with considerable power of observation, a talent for lively description, and great facility in imagining incidents and weaving them together in clear and spirited narrative, he was sure of exciting curiosity and giving interest to whatever subject he touched. He has that skill in narration, the first requisite of a novelist, which, fastening the reader's attention on the issue of events immediately before him, will not allow him to observe any improbability in the plot, or incongruity in the character and actions of the agents. Take, for instance, that scene of breathless interest from " The Last of the Mohicans," the attack and defence of the island at Glenn's Falls. When we almost hear the sharp crack of the rifles, mingling with the sullen and continued roar of the cataract, and see each new expedient of the savage assailants met and foiled by the skill and activity of the scout and his Indian associates, who can pause to think on the gross improbability of the events, by which the party were betrayed into their exposed situation? It must be owned, however, that the author abuses his power. The imminent dangers and hair-breadth escapes occur too frequently, till we lose the feeling of concern and suspense, and confide too much in the courage and sagacity of the actors, for effecting their own deliverance.

Of all Mr. Cooper's novels, those relating and sketching life on the ocean find most favour with us. It is in them that he appears to be in his proper and appropriate element, and upon them we believe his reputation will ultimately depend. In these productions, he has opened a new mine of romance, accomplishing for the sea and sailors what had before been done by others for the land and landsmen; giving us real pictures of life upon the ocean, and displaying before us with a vigour which has not been equalled, the interest that attaches to a sailor's occupation; and executing in a manner hardly to be surpassed, graphic and picturesque delineations of the manners and habits of those beings who spend their lives upon the vasty deep. Man, in his sea novels, is presented before us, energetic, daring, and skilful; the sport of the waves in their wildest moments, or eluding their blind force by his ingenuity.

The contest of human skill with the angry elements, carried on upon the noble theatre of the illimitable waters, is no theme to be touched by a faltering and unskilful hand. The sublimity is in the subject, and no artificial colouring is required to heighten the effect. Simple, but picturesque strokes of description, and thorough acquaintance with the different aspects of the heavens and the ocean, with the management of a ship, and the peculiarities of sailors, are the secret of this writer's success in his maritime sketches.

We pass now to our immediate subject, " Homeward Bound." This novel is among the best of our author's sea-tales ; it contains many exciting incidents, and lively as well as vigorous sketches of life on the ocean. The pictures presented are faithful both in their grouping and separate individuality. The story consists of a detail of the adventures of the vessel " Montauk." The tale begins with a list of the crew and passengers, whose various peculiarities are in proper keeping to produce the diversified scene in which they are shortly to be the actors. This will, perhaps, suffice to explain the sort of material Mr. Cooper has worked with, and produced, as we think, a most spirited sketch of nautical manners and habits. The voyage of the packet commenced with the unsuccessful attempt of an attorney who wished to capture one Robert Davis, a passenger, who had married his bride without the consent of her guardians ; certain other passengers having sided, however, with him, his pursuer is foiled and the ship sails. But scarcely had the vessel shoved off, when it was thought that a more powerful emissary of majesty was in chase, and it was presently discovered, past all doubt, that the *Foam* was in pursuit of the liner. A desire, not to be impeded in his passage, appears to have prevailed with the captain to quicken the ship's pace, and keep a head of his pursuer, but, in the end, he had to pay dearly for this trial of skill. Perhaps before going any further into detail, it would be as well to present our readers with a sample of the work. Here is then a dialogue showing the sufferings of stewards from the inquisitiveness of passengers :—

" ' Steward,' called out Mr. Dodge, through the blinds of his state-room ; ' whereabouts, are we ?'

" ' In the British Channel, sir.'

" ' I might have guessed that myself.'

" ' So, suppose, sir ; nobody is better at guessing and divining than Mr. Dodge.'

" ' But in what part of the Channel are we, Saunders ?'

" ' About the middle, sir.'

" ' How far have we come in the night ?'

" ' From Portsmouth Roads to this place, sir.'

" Mr. Dodge was satisfied, and the steward, who would not have dared to be so explicit with any other cabin-passenger, continued coolly to mix an omelette. The next attack was made from the same room, by Sir George Templemore.

" ' Steward, my good fellow, do you happen to know whereabouts we are ?'

" ' Certainly, sir ; the land is still quite obvious.'

" ' Are we getting on cleverly ?'

" ' *Nicely*, sir ;' with a mincing emphasis on the first word, that betrayed there was a little waggery about the grave-looking mulatto.

" ' And the sloop-of-war, steward ?'

" ' Nicely too, sir.'

" There was a shuffling in the state-room, followed by a silence. The door of Mr. Sharp's room was now opened an inch or two and the following questions issued through the crevice :

" ' Is the wind favourable, steward ?'

" ' Just her character, sir.'

" ' Do you mean that the wind is favourable ?'

" ' For the Montauk, sir ; she's a persuader in this breeze.'

" ' But is she going in the direction we wish ?'

" ' If the gentleman wishes to perambulate America, it is probable he will get there with a little patience.'

" Mr. Sharp pulled-to his door, and ten minutes passed without further questions ; the steward beginning to hope the morning catechism was over, though he grumbled a wish that gentlemen would ' turn out' and take a look for themselves.—The next door that opened was that of Paul Blunt, however, who thrust his head into the cabin, with all his dark curls in the confusion of a night scene.

" ' Steward !'

" ' Sir.'

" ' How's the wind ?'

" ' Quite exhilarating, sir.'

" ' But, from what quarter ?'

" ' About south, sir.'

" ' Is there much of it ?'

" ' A prevailing breeze, sir.'

" ' And the sloop ?'

" ' She's to leeward, sir, operating along as fast as she can.'

" ' Steward !'

" ' Sir,' stepping hurriedly out of his pantry, in order to hear more distinctly.

" ' Under what sail are we ?'

" ' Topgallant sails, sir.'

" ' How's her head ?'

" ' West-south-west, sir.' "

The steward is a true sailor-and a bit of a wit ; there is a quietness and repose in his manner which give an appearance of truth and soberness to the narrative, and make us think the scene described more real than those of a similar nature found in Captain Marryatt's

novels. This author's manner is too vulgar, and his humour
far too coarse. No doubt many of his sea-views are executed
with great spirit, and the constant hurry of incidents keeps the
interest sustained throughout. But the stories are carelessly written, contain no variety of character, no plot ; and the more striking
scenes are constantly repeated, till the effect is lost. The writer
presses in too much material—we have a hurricane, a shipwreck, and
a sea-fight, every ten pages. Cooper is not so prodigal of his means.
Give him but a single gale and a lee-shore, or the topsail of a man-
of-war, appearing above the fog, and he makes the picture complete.
There are human beings too, on board the ship, and the feelings are
even painfully awakened to the alternations of hope and despair, the
rejoicings at an escape, or the last convulsive struggle with the
waters. On the other hand, Captain Marryatt sends a whole ship's
company to the bottom, and the reader cares as little about them as
he does.

But to return to the narrative of the chase. Early in the second
volume our interest is increased by the Montauk losing her masts
and being thrown out of course, by which accident she is parted from
the Foam but only to be cast upon the coast of Africa. Here they
find a Danish vessel recently wrecked with traces of murder and
piracy upon the part of the natives. The wreck, however, offers
them, by way of compensation, its masts, which the captain of the
liner with the greater part of his men proceed in quest of, leaving
a mere handful on board his own vessel ; and here commences a most
interesting part of the story :—

"For several hours, there was no other noise in the ship than the tread
of the solitary watchman. At the appointed period of the night a change
took place, and he who had watched, slept ; while he who had slept,
watched. Just as day dawned, however, Paul Blunt, who was in a deep
sleep, felt a shake at his shoulder.

"'Pardon me,' cautiously whispered Mr. Sharp : 'I fear we are about
to have a most unpleasant interruption to our solitude.'

"'Heavenly powers !—Not the Arabs ?'

"'I fear no less : but it is still too dark to be certain of the fact. If
you will rise, we can consult on the situation in which we are placed., I
beg you to be quick.'

"Paul Blunt had hastily risen on an arm, and he now passed a hand over
his brow, as if to make certain that he was awake. He had not undressed
himself, and in another moment he stood on his feet in the middle of the
state-room.

"'This is too serious to allow of mistake. We will not alarm her, then ;
we will not give any alarm, sir, until certain of the calamity.' * *

"The other drew on his coat, and in a minute both were on deck. The
day had not yet dawned, and the light was scarce sufficient to distinguish
objects even near as those on the reef, particularly when they were stationary. The rocks themselves, however, were visible in places, for the
tide was out, and most of the upper portion of the ledge was bare. The

two gentlemen moved cautiously to the bows of the vessel, and, concealed by the bulwarks, Mr. Sharp pointed out to his companion the objects that had given him the alarm.

" ' Do you see the pointed rock a little to the right of the spot where the kedge is placed?' he said, pointing in the direction that he meant, ' It is now naked, and yet I am quite certain there was an object on it, when I went below, that has since moved away.'

" ' It may have been a sea-bird; for we are so near the day, some of them are probably in motion. Was it large?'

" ' Of the size of a man's head, apparently; but this is by no means all. Here, farther to the north, I distinguished three objects in motion, wading in the water, near the point where the rocks are never bare.'

" ' They may have been herons; the bird is often found in these low latitudes, I believe. I can discover nothing.'

" ' I would to God, I may have been mistaken, though I do not think I could be so much deceived.'

" Paul Blunt caught his arm, and held it like one who listened intently.

" ' Heard you that?' he whispered hurriedly.

" ' It sounded like the clanking of iron.'

" Looking around, the other found a handspike, and, passing swiftly up the heel of the bowsprit, he stood between the night-heads. Here he bent forward, and looked intently towards the lines of chains which lay over the bulwarks, as bow-fasts. Of these chains the parts led quite near each other, in parallel lines, and as the ship's moorings were taut, they were hanging in merely a slight curve. From the rocks, or the place where the kedges were laid, to a point within thirty feet of the ship, these chains were dotted with living beings crawling cautiously upward. It was even easy, at a second look, to perceive that they were men, stealthily advancing on their hands and feet.

" Raising the handspike, Mr. Blunt struck the chains several violent blows. The effect was to cause the whole of the Arabs,—for it could be no others,—suddenly to cease advancing, and to seat themselves astride on the chains.

" ' This is fearful,' said Mr. Sharp; ' but we must die, rather than permit them to reach the ship.'

" ' We must. Stand you here, and if they advance, strike the chains. There is not an instant to lose.'

" Paul Blunt spoke hurriedly, and, giving the other the handspike, he ran down to the bitts, and commenced loosening the chains from their fastenings. The Arabs heard the clanking of the iron-rings, as he threw coil after coil on the deck, and they did not advance. Presently two parts yielded together beneath them, and then two more. These were the signals of a common retreat, and Mr. Sharp now plainly counted fifteen human forms as they scrambled back towards the reef, some hanging by their arms, some half in the water, and others lying along the chains, as best they might. Mr. Blunt having loosened the chains, so as to let their bights fall into the sea, the ship slowly drifted astern and rode by her cables. When this was done, the two young men stood together in silence on the forecastle, as if each felt that all which had just occurred was some illusion.

" ' This is indeed terrible,' exclaimed Paul Blunt. ' We have not even a 'pistol left! No means of defence,—nothing but this narrow belt of water between us and these barbarians!'"

This terrible state is ended by the dexterity of Paul Blunt, who foils the savages by the transfer of his party to the launch, which of course leaves the barbarians sole masters for a time of the Montauk. But the perils of our heroes are not all over; there is a reef which prevents the escape of the launch, and darkness overtakes them: this scene is highly appalling.

"So deep and pitchy black, indeed, had the night become, that even the land was no longer to be distinguished, and the only clews the two gentlemen had to its position were the mouldering watch-fires of the Arab camp, and the direction of the wind,

"'We will now make an attempt,' said Paul, stopping in his short walk on the sand, and examining the murky vault over head. 'Midnight is near; and by two o'clock the tide will be entirely up. It is a dark night to thread these narrow channels in, and to go out upon the ocean, too, in so frail a bark! But the alternative is worse.'

"'Would it not be better to allow the water to rise still higher? I see by these sands that it has not yet done coming in.'

"'There is not much tide in these low latitudes, and the little rise that is left may help us off a bank, should we strike one. If you will get upon the roof, I will bring in the grapnels and force the boat off.'

"Mr. Sharp complied, and in a few minutes the launch was floating slowly away from the hospitable bank of sand. Paul hauled out the jigger, a small sprit-sail, and kept it closely hauled, from being fastened to a stationary boom, and a little mast stepped quite aft, the effect of which was to press the boat against the wind. This brought the launch's head up, and it was just possible to see by close attention that they had a slight motion through the water.

"'I quit that bank of sand as one quite a tried friend,' said Paul, all the conversation now being in little more than whispers: 'when near it, I know where we are; but presently we shall be absolutely lost in this intense darkness,'

"'We have the fires of the Arabs for light-houses still.'

"'They may give us some faint notions of our position; but light like that is a very treacherous guide in so dark a night. We have little else to do but to keep an eye on the water, and to endeavour to get to windward.'* *

"While on the bank, Paul had observed that, by keeping the boat near the wind, he might stretch through one of the widest of the channels for near two miles, unless disturbed by currents, and that, when at its southern end, he should be far enough to windward to fetch the inlet, but for the banks of sand that might lie in his way. The distance had prevented his discerning any passage through the reef at the farther end of this channel; but, the boat drawing only two feet of water, he was not without hopes of being able to find one. A chasm, that was deep enough to prevent the passage of the Arabs when the tide was in, would, he thought, certainly suffice for their purpose. The progress of the boat was steady, and reasonably fast; but it was like moving in a mass of obscurity. The gentlemen watched the water a-head intently, with a view to avoid the banks, but with little success; for, as they advanced, it was merely one pile of gloom succeeding another. Fortunately the previous observation of Paul availed them, and for more than half an hour their progress was uninterrupted.

" ' They sleep in security beneath us,' said Paul, ' while we are steering almost at random. This is a strange and hazardous situation in which we are placed. The obscurity renders all the risks double.'

" ' By the watch-fires, we must have nearly crossed the bay, and I should think we are now quite near the southern reef.'

" ' I think the same; but I like not this baffling of the wind. It comes fresher at moments, but it is in puffs, and I fear there will be a shift. It is now my best pilot.'

" ' That and the fires.'

" ' The fires are treacherous always. It looks darker than ever a-head.'

" ' The wind ceased blowing altogether, and the duck of the sail fell in heavily. Almost at the same moment the launch lost its way, and Paul had time to thrust the boat-hook forward just in season to prevent its striking a rock.

" ' This is a part of the reef, then, that is never covered,' he said. ' If you will get on the rocks and hold the boat, I will endeavour to examine the place for a passage. Were we one hundred feet to the southward and westward, we should be in the open ocean, and comparatively safe.'

" Mr. Sharp complied, and Paul descended carefully on the reef, feeling his way in the intense darkness by means of the boat-hook. He was absent ten minutes, moving with great caution, as there was the danger of his falling into the sea at every step. His friend began to be uneasy, and the whole of the jeopardy of their situation presented itself vividly to his mind in that brief space of time, should accident befall their only guide. He was looking anxiously in the direction in which Paul had disappeared, when he felt a grip of his arm.

" ' Breathe even with care !' whispered Paul hurriedly. ' These rocks are covered with Arabs, who have chosen to remain on the dry parts of the reef, in readiness for their plunder in the morning. Thank Heaven ! I have found you again; for I was beginning to despair. To have called to you would have been certain capture, as eight or ten of the barbarians, are sleeping within fifty feet of us. Get on the reef with the least possible noise, and leave the rest to me.'

" As soon as Mr. Sharp was in the boat, Paul gave it a violent shove from the rocks and sprang on the reef at the same moment. This forced the launch astern, and procured a momentary safety. But the wind had shifted. It now came baffling, and in puffs from the Desert—a circumstance that brought them again to leeward.

" ' That is the commencement of the trades,' said Paul: ' they have been interrupted by the late gale, but are now returning. Were we outside the reef, our prayers could not be more kindly answered than by giving us this very wind; but here, where we are, it comes unseasonable. Ho ! this, at least, helps her !'

" A puff from the land filled the sails, and the ripple of the water at the

stern was just audible. The helm was attended to, and the boat drew
slowly from the reef and a-head.

"' We have all reason for gratitude! That danger, at least, is avoided
—Ha! the boat is aground!'

" Sure enough the launch was on the sands. They were still so near
the rocks as to require the utmost caution in their proceedings. Using
the spar with great care, the gentlemen discovered that the boat hung
astern, and there remained no choise but patience.

"' It is fortunate the Arabs have no dogs with them on the rocks; you
hear them howling incessantly in their camps.'

"' It is, truly. Think you we can ever find the inlet in this deep
obscurity?'

"' It is our only course. By following the rocks we should be certain
to discover it; but you perceive they are already out of sight, though
they cannot be thirty fathoms from us. The helm is free, and the boat
must be clear of the bottom again. This last puff has helped us.'

" Another silence succeeded, during which the launch moved slowly
onward, though whither, neither of the gentlemen could tell; but a single
fire remained in sight, and that glimmered like a dying blaze. At times
the wind came hot and arid, savouring of the Desert, and then intervals
of death-like calm would follow. Paul watched the boat narrowly, for
half an hour, turning every breath of air to the best account, though he
was absolutely ignorant of his position. The reef had not been seen again,
and three several times they grounded, the tide as often floating them off;
the course, too, had been repeatedly varied. The result was, that painful
and profound sensation of helplessness that overcomes us all when the
chain of association is broken, and reason becomes an agent less useful
than instinct.

"' The last fire is extinct,' whispered Paul. ' I fear that the day will
dawn and find us still within the reef.'

"' I see an object near us,—Can it be a high bank?'

" The wind had entirely ceased, and the boat was almost without
motion. Paul saw a darkness more intense even than common a-head of
him, and he leaned forward, naturally raising a hand before him, in
precaution. Something he touched, he knew not what; but feeling a
hard smooth surface, that he at first mistook for a rock, he raised his eyes
slowly, and discerned, by the little light that lingered in the vault of
heaven, a dim tracery that he recognized. His hand was on the quarter
of the ship!

"' 'Tis the Montauk!' he whispered breathlessly, ' and her decks must
be covered with Arabs. Hist!—do you hear nothing?'

" They listened, and smothered voices, these of the watch, mingled with
low laughter, were quite audible. This was a crisis to disturb the coolness of one less trained and steady than Paul; but he preserved his self-
possession.''

The interest of the adventure still goes on, and if it flags for a
moment, it is only to be revived with more spirit than ever by the
sudden re-appearance of the *Foam*, which ultimately overtakes the
Montauk, and the result of this affair forms the closing portion of

the third volume ; leaving a great portion of tale to be told at a future day, which Mr. Cooper has promised to do in a sequel to "Homeward Bound :" how soon it will be published we do not know, but sooner the better say we, and we think the reader will join in the exclamation with us.

In conclusion we desire to remark, that, disposed, indeed, as we are to consider that the importance of any branch of literature is to be measured by its influence on society, we regard the occasional survey of that to which we have in this article called the reader's attention, as among our most necessary duties. The time has been long past in which it was the fashion to dispute the right of fictitious compositions to any respect among well-educated, moral, and thinking people, and even a very prudent man would be looked upon as more than ordinarily severe who should be now heard arguing on the danger or worthlessness of a cleverly-written novel. We have oftentimes been necessitated to show that, in many instances, the public confidence has been abused both by authors and publishers ; but it has been our general intention to give such a view of the best novels of the day as should serve to remove any undue prejudices which might still affect their circulation. With that class, the composition of which requires but a mere passing acquaintance with the external forms of society, and which serves only to teach that which is not worth knowing, or which had better not been known, we shall wage incessant war.

Art. X.—*The Correspondence of Sir Thomas Hanmer, Bart., Speaker of the House of Commons ; with a Memoir of his Life. To which are added, Other Reliefs of a Gentleman's Family.* Edited by Sir Henry Bunbury, Bart. London: Moxon. 1838.

There exists at this moment in this country, we believe and trust, an increasing demand for authentic memoirs and the correspondence of eminent individuals, whether these be illustrative of history, human nature, or literature, at any given time. And if this be the case, it ought to be held as symptomatic of a healthier and more promising tone of feeling, judgment, and taste, than the popularity of cheap compilations and the greedy appetite for tinselled or purely fictitious publications have for years indicated. Transient excitement, highly seasoned food for the imagination, yet greatly diluted aliment for the intellect, so that much of it may be speedily and easily swallowed, never, however, to be properly digested, have been injuriously in fashion ; while an excessive fondness for variety argues that the public taste has been pampered and vitiated. And yet, if healthful amusement, vivid indications of character, or passages of life calculated to gratify curiosity and yield lessons of pointed instruction in a great variety of forms, and under exceedingly diversified conditions, be required, we counsel our readers to have recourse to such works as the present, whenever they desire profitably to obtain relief from cares or amid severe studies by means of a light sort of literature. We call the volume before us valuable as well as delightful; and were all the representatives of ancient and eminent names in the annals of Great Britain to open their muniment chests, and edit the choice contents of them in the same able and pleasant manner that Sir Henry Bunbury has here done, an amount of historical, biographical, epistolary, and antiquarian literature would become public property, the preciousness of which it is impossible to calculate. In the meanwhile, we are thankful for what we have now got, and proceed to present some specimens as well as to give some account of the volume's various contents.

These contents are of an exceedingly miscellaneous description, the only things in common between a great proportion of them being this, that, with the exception of the Memoir and the illustrative notes, the whole have been taken from the family chests of the editor, all being originals, and all having come to him from sources with which he has in some way or another a family connexion.

The personage who principally figures in the volume is, of course, Sir Thomas Hanmer, with whose family that of the editor's became closely connected by marriage in the lifetime of Sir Thomas. Both were of ancient descent; and both, we presume, have met in the editor's person as a principal branch or the stem of the genealogical tree.

The subject of the memoir was born in September 1677,—was educated at Westminster and Oxford, his reputation being that of a good classical scholar,—and when little more than twenty-one, married the widow of Charles, the first Duke of Grafton,—a lady reputed to have been a great beauty even at that time, though ten years older than the future speaker. By this marriage, his fortune and rank were greatly and favourably influenced, while his own manners, character, talents, and inheritance rendered him one of the most considerable personages of the age. He was elected to represent his native county of Flint, in the first parliament of Anne; and for many years afterwards he took a prominent part in politics as well as maintaining a distinguished position among parties. He was a Tory, his toryism evidencing itself chiefly by a uniform and strenuous endeavour to uphold the landed interest, and still more, it would appear, the ascendency of the Anglican church. He hated the Dissenters perhaps more than the Catholics, and hovered for a time between favouring the House of Stuart and the House of Hanover. He wished to be considered independent, and seems to have been far above the influence of money, though his caution and reserve, perhaps justly, may have exposed him to the charge of being a trimmer.

Of Orford and Bolingbroke, Sir Thomas cannot, from the

evidences before us, tory though he was, have entertained any very favourable or confident opinion; and though they were anxious to win him entirely to their views, merely on account, however, of his abilities and of the consideration in which he was held, yet he was reluctant to take place under them, or along with chiefs between whom there was not only no cordiality, but upon neither of whom could he depend. At length, towards the close of the Queen's reign he consented to be proposed as speaker of the House of Commons, to which eminent situation he was unanimously elected. But it is unnecessary for us to notice particularly his political career, or advert to the various party struggles and the distractions of the times; for we are anxious to pass on to certain matters possessing a literary value, as well as to quote from the correspondence some letters which on account of the celebrity of the writers or the subjects to which they relate, possess, in our estimation, particular interest. The first of these epistolary documents was addressed by a remarkable man to Sir Thomas when the latter held the speakership; and refers to the exertion made by the Queen's ministers to expel the writer of it from his seat in the House of Commons.

"FROM RICHARD STEELE TO SIR THOMAS HANMER.
March, 19th, 1713-4, *Bloomesbury-square.*

"Sir,

"The vote which passed upon me last night has, as far as common fame can do it, made me a seditious man. The whole tenour of my life and actions has been such as gave me hopes of another treatment. My friends about me tooke me down when I was going to throw away my papers, and speake what I thought most materiall for the consideration of the house on that occasion; but that is now too late to think of.

"I am pronounced a guilty man by an awfull assembly, but an assembly which cannot act in pointe of justice but in a discretionary or declarative way. They can say what they think of a thing, but I do not know whether they can go any further but by way of laying accusations before another court.

"I writ what I writ with the laws in my view, and thought myself safe as long as I had them on my side. I am sure I did what I did in order to preserve them, and they are now my refuge. It is some comfort to me that my adversaries were reduced to the lamentable shift of saying, that tho what I said were true, I should be an offender in saying it. This is a monstrous position, for hell is the only place which can be destroyed by truth. My reputation, which is dearer to me than my life, is wounded by this vote, and I know no way to heal it but by appealing to the laws of my countrey, that they may have their due effect in the protection of innocence. I therefore humbly desire proper questions may be put to bring about resolutions of this kind, to wit—

"That Mr. Steele, who is expelled this house for ——, may be prosequuted at law for his said offence, and that no non pros. or noli prosequi may be admitted in his case.

" That Mr. Steele is *or is not* capable of being re-elected into this present parliament.

" I am accused of undutifulnesse to the Queen. I hope it will appear to all the world I have not deserved that imputation. If I have, through weakness, done any thing that will support such an accusation, I know she is mercifull, and I, who have erred (if I have erred) from a good motive, shall be a proper object on which to exert that disposition in my sovereign. I desire, if I have committed any crime, to owe my safety from punishment to no other being upon earth.

" I assure you it is a painfull circumstance of my present mortification, that it robs me of the hopes of your acquaintance and friendship, which I fear it is against rules you should honour a man with, who is under the disgrace of those whome you represent. As for the rest, I ought not to be much troubled at my leaving a place wherein I was so unacceptable as not to be suffered, on the most popular subject imaginable, that of expressing my self,

S^r, y^r most obedient and
most humble servant,
R<small>ICHARD</small> S<small>TEELE</small>."

The Speaker's answer to this exhibits an acquaintance with the rules of the House, and a perspicuous statement of the principle and method of these rules; so that Sir Richard in his reply, among other things says, " You have added the authority of reason to an implicit relyance on your character in convincing."

Sir Thomas Hanmer must have kept up an extensive correspondence with many of the most notable characters of the age; for we find, in the selection before us, a great number of letters from statesmen, generals, authors, and other eminent personages. Mathew Prior often appears as a correspondent; and his letters are particularly characteristic. We go back to the year 1706 for a short specimen.

" S<small>IR</small>,

" If you can bear wth the worst poetry in the world because the author is more than any man yor servant, my present will be very acceptable. I write you no news, for that is only proper for the Post-boy and the Gazette, and remarks upon news I leave to the Observator and Review. Prose, you see, S^r, is below me, I have left method for rage, and common sence for enthusiasm. As soon as I recover from this distemper, and can think my mare a better beast than Pegasus, you will be troubled wth me. In the mean time, and ever, I am, with great truth and respect,   S^r,

" Yo^r most ob and most humble ser^t,
"M<small>AT</small>. P<small>RIOR</small>.

" I dare not presume to give my respects to my Lady Duchesse, but to Mrs. Ramsey friendship and love in great abundance, and let her take it ill if she thinks proper."

In a note, the editor says, " Sir T. Hanmer has indorsed this

letter thus : ' Mr. Prior, sent with his poem on the victory of Ra-
millies.' " Here is another from Mathew.

" SIR,

" The very reason of my not answering your letter sooner is, that I was
out of town when it arrived here, so all the excuses I can take for not coming to Euston from my attendance at the board, or my care of the plantations, will be found frivolous and scandalous; about a fortnight hence,
therefore, all fourberie apart, I will certainly mount my terrestrial steed,
and you shall see a gentle squire come pricking o'er the plain. A fortnight
hence; if Mrs. Ramsay makes the calculation, she will find that this falls
into Bartholomew-fair-time, and consequently my passion for her is very
boyling, since I can ,leave the rope-dancers' booth, my dear Betty in the
city, and pigg and pork, for her, an arbour, and a Suffolk dumplin : so pray,
Sr, desire her to be patient and discreet, and on this condition my person
is at her service. I am not master of· eloquence enough to thank you for
the kindness of your invitation, at least I will lose no merit I can have to
Mrs. Ramsay, by confessing I have a mind to come on any other acct than
that of my laying myself at her feet. I think that last sentence was
gallant.—I· have no news to tell you. The west winds have driven our
descent back, and we do not know if we shall first hear of a battle in Spain,
Italy, or Flanders. God send us success, and keep me long in your good
graces, whᵗ next and immediately under those of the above-mentioned Mrs.
Ramsay, I shall always strive to improve, as being with great truth and
respect,   Sr,
                    " Your most obᵗ and most humble serᵗ,
                                        " MAT. PRIOR."

Mrs. Ramsay seems to have been the friend and frequently the
companion of the Duchess of Grafton. Swift, in his Journal,
December, 1712, speaks of a lady, then about fifty-five, whom the
Duke of Ormond, Lord Arran, and he, one day met at dinner,
and says, " we are all very fond of her." Let us see how the
Dean himself writes to Sir Thomas in 1720.

                                        " *Dublin, Ocᵗbr* 1, 1720.
" SIR,
" There is a little affair that I engaged some friends of mine to trouble
you about, but am not perfectly informed what progress they have made.
Last Term, one Waters, a printer, was accused and tryed for printing a
pamphlet persuading the people here to wear their own manufactures exclusive of any from Englᵈ, with some complaints of the hardships they lye
under. There was nothing in the pamphlet either of Whig or Tory, or
reflecting upon any person whatsoever; but the Chancellor, afraid of losing
his office, and the Chief Justice desirous to come into it, were both vying
who should shew their zeal most to discountenance the pamphlet. The
printer was tryed with a jury of the most violent party men, who yet brought
him in not guilty, but were sent back nine times, and at last brought in a
speciall verdict, so that the man is to be tryed again next term. The Whigs
in generalle were for the pamphlet, tho' it be a weak, hasty scribble, and
generally abominated the proceeding of the Justice, particularly all the

Bishops except the late ones from Engld, the Duke of Wharton, Lord
Molesworth, and many others: Now if the Chief Justice continues his
keenness, the man may be severely punished; but the business may be
inconvenient, because I am looked on as the author; and my desire to you is
that you would please to prevayl on the Duke of Grafton, to write to the
Chief Justice to let the matter drop, which I believe his Grace would easily
do on your application, if he knew that I truly represented the matter, for
which I appeal both to the Duke of Wharton and Lord Molesworth. I have
the honour to be many years known to his Grace, and I believe him ready to
do a thing of good nature as well as justice, and for yourself I am confident
that you will be ready to give me this mark of your favor, having received so
many instances of it in former times.

"I beg you will excuse the trouble I give you, and believe me to be with
great respect,

Sr, your most obedient,

and most humble servant,

JONATH. SWIFT."

The pamphlet here referred to by the Dean, was the famous one
called a "Proposal for the universal Use of Irish Manufactures,"
to be afterwards followed by the still more famous "Drapier's
Letters." The prosecution was allowed to drop, when the Duke
of Grafton, as Lord Lieutenant, returned from England to Ireland.

Persons of less note in the republic of letters were in the habit of
cultivating the favour and countenance of Hanmer, than those
whose correspondence has been above quoted. By the time that
George the Second had ascended the throne, the stanch Tory,
after having been gradually retiring into the back scenes of the
political drama, had withdrawn entirely from public life. While this,
George, however, was Prince of Wales, and in open hostility to the
King, we find that Sir Thomas assumed a forward posture in the
House of Commons, and ably opposed the Whig government,
attaching himself heartily to the Prince. But by the time that the
Prince filled the throne, and had confirmed Walpole as his minister,
literature, domesticity, and the country seem to have engrossed the
time and attention of Sir Thomas.

Being a man of mark, possessed of great wealth and influence,
and known in the literary world to be no mean critic, he was looked
up to by the poor authors of the period, as a most desirable
patron, and was therefore "fed with soft adulation all day long."
Here is a specimen.

"Sr,
"You see it is dang'rous to be a person of candour. It draws trouble
upon you, from woh men of less Humanity and more pride are exempt. It
is this yt occasions you a second piece of Poetry. Surely a desire to please
men of worth proceeds from a better principle than vanity. If it does not,
I feel I have occasion for more humility than has fal'n to my share to with-
stand it. I confess ye crime, and am very proud to have pleas'd Sr Thomas

Hanmer. Some men are oblig'd to keep ye world at a distance to preserve themselves from contempt. If they suffer others to close with them, they immediately discover their weakness: I have therefore always judg'd a condescending nature to be a sign of a sound head and an honest heart; & I am certain I am not mistaken in this rule when I now apply it. S₋, I should be wanting to my own satisfaction, if I should not wait upon you, I will search for an opportunity to gratify it : I am too proud not to desire to have yᵉ honour of being, Sʳ

" Your most obedient and most
" Humble servant,
" WILLIAM BROOME.

" *Stuston, July* 17*ᵗʰ*, 1725."

The editor suspects with good reason that the poem which the reverend writer of this letter refers to, is that in which he lays on flattery with such a deeply-dipped brush as dashed off the following lines :—

" Unhallow'd feet o'er awful Tully tread,
And Hyde and Plato join the vulgar dead :
And all the glorious aims that can employ
The souls of mortals, must with *Hanmer* die."

The life of Sir Thomas after his retirement from the political world, was not, however, one of unmixed peace and happiness. His first wife had died only in 1723, leaving no children ; and two years afterwards when a man of fifty he took to himself another partner, who was a great deal younger than himself; and the union was anything but happy. In short, the lady eloped with her husband's own cousin, the Hon. Thomas Hervey, a hair-brained fellow, who continued to pester the staid and formal baronet in various ways, such as publishing letters to him.

Still in his solitude Hanmer found solace in literary pursuits, and in the correspondence of some of the first spirits of the age, as well as in the respect of his equals and dependants. Most of the letters addressed to him, as now published, are disfigured to be sure, by adulation; it was the vicious fashion of the age. But here is one from Bishop Berkley, bearing date August 21, 1744, which is as plain and sensible as it is kind and complimentary.

" SIR,

" As I am with particular esteem and respect your humble servant, so I heartily wish your success in the use of Tar Water may justifie the kind things you say on that subject. But since you are pleased to consult me about your taking it, I shall without further ceremony tell you what I think, how ill soever a Physician's may become one of my profession. Certainly, if I may conclude from parallel cases, there is room to entertain good hopes of yours ; both giddiness and relaxed fibres having been, to my knowledge, much relieved by tar water. The sooner you take it, so much the better. I could wish you saw it made yourself, and strongly stirred. While it stands to clarify, let it be close covered, and afterwards bottled and well corked. I find it agrees with most stomachs when stirred even five or six minutes, provided it be skimmed before bottling. You may begin with a pint a day, and proceed to a pint and a half or even a quart, as it shall agree with your stomach. And you may take this quantity either in half pint or quarter pint glasses, at proper intervals in the twenty-four hours. It may be drunk indifferently, at any season of the year. It lays under no restraint, nor obliges you to go out of your usual course of diet. Only in general I suppose, light suppers, early hours, and gentle exercise, (so as not to tire) good for all cases. With your tar water, I wish you may take no other medicines. I have had much experience of it, and can honestly say, I never knew it do harm. The ill effects of drugs show themselves soonest on the weakest persons: such are children; and I assure you that my two youngest children (when they were one three, and the other not two years old) took it, as a preservative against the small-pox, constantly for six months together without any inconvenience. Upon the whole, I apprehend no harm and much benefit in your case, and shall be very glad to find my hopes confirmed by a line from your self, which will always be received as a great favour by

> " Sir, y^r most obedient and
> most humble servant,
> " GEORGE CLOYNE."

Of Hanmer's own literary acquirements, his edition of Shakspeare forms a sufficient testimony. Dr. Johnson declares him to have been a man " eminently qualified by nature for such studies ;" and also says, " As he never writes without careful inquiry and diligent consideration, I have received all his notes, and believe that every reader will wish for more." To be sure he involved himself in a bitter quarrel with Warburton by his splendid work, and provoked that dignitary's unmeasured scurrility. Still it is a performance, which, together with others presumed to be by him, entitles him to an enviable degree of regard and consideration. The only circumstance to which we further allude on the subject of Shakspeare concerns the drawings which were made for the edition in question, viz , a contract by which the provident and cautious old politician " tethers down the artist with a notable strictness."

> " November the 28th, 1740.

" An agreement enter'd into and made this present day between Sir Thomas Hanmer, Bart., and Francis Hayman, Gent.

" 1st. The said Francis Hayman is to design and delineate a drawing to be prefix'd to each play of Shakespeare, taking the subject of such scenes as the said Sir Thomas Hanmer shall direct ; and that he shall finish the same with Indian ink in such manner as shall be fit for an engraver to work after them, and approved by the said Sir Thomas Hanmer.

" 2nd. That the said Sir Thomas Hanmer shall pay to the said Francis Hayman the sum of three guineas for each drawing, taken one with another, as soon as the whole number shall be finish'd. Upon this condition, nevertheless; and it is declared and mutually consented to, that if the whole number shall not be compleated in the manner before-mentioned by Lady Day, which shall be in the year of our Lord 1741, the said Francis Hayman shall not be entitled to receive any payment or consideration whatsoever for any part of the said work.

"THO. HANMER.
"FR. HAYMAN."

Sir Thomas died in 1746, having reached the verge of the span of life which the Psalmist accords to man as a good old age; nor did Dr. Johnson think it an unworthy office to translate from the Latin an elegant and eulogistic epitaph over him. Here is the Baronet's portrait taken from recollection.

"Of the personal appearance and manners of Sir Thomas Hanmer, in his latter days, I have heard something from a yeoman at Mildenhall, whose father was one of his tenants. His description of the great man of the village accorded well with the Montalto of Pope, and with the outward and visible signs of his character which may be gathered from other sources. My informant spoke of the baronet as a portly old gentleman, of a very stately carriage, accustomed to walk solemnly to church twice on every Sunday, followed by all his servants, and moving from his iron gates to the porch of the church between two ranks of his tenants and adherents, who stood, hat in hand, bowing reverently low, while the great man acknowledged their salutations by a few words and a dignified condescension."

Among the diversified and curious contents of the present volume, certain extracts from the Account-Book of Hanmer's first wife, Duchess of Grafton, are not the least interesting. The editor first of all tells us, that the caligraphy and orthography of this distinguished lady are not of the most perfect kind. Yet she was the only daughter of Henry Bennet, Earl of Arlington, one of the principal ministers of Charles the Second.

The Duchess ("Isabella Grafton is my name," as the cover of the Account-Book has it,) seems to have been a great frequenter of play-houses, and to have been much addicted to cards; so that though her pin-money allowance from Hanmer was £500 per annum, we surmise that additional drafts must have been resorted to, to keep up her various and in certain particulars inconsiderate expenditure. There is to "Ben the Chairman, £13," in one entry; and to "Chairmen," in another, £16. 14s. 0d., which look very like charges for evening gaieties. "To the Opera," is frequently mentioned, 10s. 9d. per. visit, and 8s. at a later period; these appearing to be the money paid at the door. She is constantly losing at cards, and large sums too, for the age and for a lady. It is fortunate that on one occasion, we observe her husband to have been the gainer from her of £7. 10s. 6d. The players are often recipients of her bounty; and the Christenings, she often patronised, appear never to have cost less than about ten guineas of what, the editor calls, self-inflicted taxation. In matters of dress she seems to have been

lavish and fanciful ; silk stockings coming very frequently into the
accounts. But what is still more to be remarked, there are for
drops of brandy a fearful frequency of entry after 1713-14. Usque-
bangh also is honoured. We suspect these drops were taken upon
the *sly ;* for one shilling and other small sums are often the charges
marked. It would, as the editor suggests, be charitable to suppose
that her Grace was a martyr to the toothache : but then it must be
borne in mind that there is no falling off in the number of outgivings
to the poor, at card-parties, and the usual occurrencies of activity and
gaiety, in juxtaposition with the *spiritual* recordings in this curious
diary. The last entry we shall mention is " For Raddell, 2s. ;" to
which the editor affixes this note—" This item, which appears frequently after 1711, is, I fear, synonymous with rouge. The coarse red
stuff with which farmers mark their sheep, is still called *raddell.*"

The next contribution we come to as produced from the Hanmer
archives is a quaint account of France, written in 1648, by another
Sir Thomas, grandfather of the Speaker. We like the account not
only because it bears the true characteristics of the age in which it
was written, but because it exhibits an accomplished, generous, and
acute English gentleman graphically sketching the state of France
in its many capacities as presented during the minority of Louis the
Fourteenth. A sketch of the young king is all that we can find
room for, from this curious and elegant document, which would fill
an ordinary foolscap octavo volume of our day.

" The ffomtaine of all honour and justice is the king, who comes to the
crowne by succession of the male line, not by any kind of election. Hee
(out of his owne regality and power) makes lawes, repeales or interprets
them, makes peace, declares warr, coynes money, grants pardons, natu-
ralises strangers, legitimates bastarde, layes what taxes and imposts hee
pleaseth, and disposeth of the money, erects courts of justice and universities, makes all governours, creates offices ; and, in a word, is absolute.

" The present monarch is Lewis, the fourteenth of that name, borne at
St. Germains en Lay, the 5th of Septembar new style, anno Dmni. 1638 ;
stiled by many A Deodatus, the king and queene having beene married 26
yeares before his birth without any issue. Hee is the son of King Lewis
the 13th, and the grandchild of King Henry the 4th, who was the first
king of the House of Bourbon, which lyne entered into the succession of
the crowne by their Salike law, as the next male lyne after the extinction
of that of Valois, in Henry the Third.

" His mother is Anne of Austria, eldest sister to Philip the Fourth, the
present King of Spaine. The tender age of this young prince will not
afford muth to bee said of his person ; no judgement can yet be made of his
inclinations, but his countenance promises as much sweetnes and goodnes
as any that ever I beheld; his complexion is pure and delicate (therein resembling his mother's side), his haire faire, his eyes black, and all his
features perfectly good and lovely ; the shape of his body is answerable, his
limbs streight and well proportioned, and strong enough.

"When hee was solely under the women's care, the Countesse of Senecy was his governesse; but now the Mareschal of Villeroy, son to the old and worthy Secretary Villesoy, is his governour, and the Abbot of Beaumont, a Dr. of the Sorbonne Colledge, and a creature of Cardinall Richlieu's, his tutor. His style in his edicts and pattents is Louis par la Grace de Dieu Roy de France, et Navarre. He signs Louys underneath, not above, as the King of England useth. His subjects, when they write to him, endorse Au Roy, and others Au Roy Tres Chrestien."

The North and the Hanmer families were allied; and the editor gives us a few extracts which are partly in prose and partly in verse from a romance entitled "Eroclea, or the Maid of Honour," written by Sir Henry North of Mildenhall, the maternal grandfather of the Speaker. This romance, which we are told fills a stout folio volume of about 640 pages, in a remarkably fine and close hand, is illustrative of greater eccentricity than the work on France by the Speaker's other predecessor; yet it is not so valuable, neither does it give evidence of such talent or culture of mind. In fact, we are told that it partakes of all the extravagances of the era, which found their way into every department—into the forms of literature as well as into religion and politics. The scene, says the editor, " is laid in Attica, in the time of Alexander the Great : there are classical names and designations in abundance, but the book consists mainly of long-drawn discussions and speculations on politics, intermingled with descriptions of masques and allegories, the ceremonials of courts, and the hunting of the stag, with elaborate designs of country seats and trim gardens, according to the fashion of the times and the taste of the writer." To the antiquary, however, and the historical student the work is by no means destitute of value ; and no doubt there are to be found in it striking fancies, original ideas, and beautiful descriptions. The pieces of poetry presented as samples, though selected, are the production of one, manifestly, who could surpass in this art scores of those who put forward claims in our times in the shape of verse. The conceits of the eccentric author's muse are graceful, as well as abundant and happily pointed. Take an example :—

> " Care-charming sleep, descend and gently glide
>   Into the temples of this sacred head,
> Let dewes of thy refreshing vapours slide
>   Into his breast; and slumber sit as lead
>   Upon his eyelids ; till it binds
>   His sences up, and his soule finds
>   Her selfe and all her facultyes at rest.
> Let no unquiet envious dreame
>   Possesse his fancy, nor once move a thought
> To stir; but drench it sweetly with the streame
>   Of thy distilling moisture ; let noe doubt
>   Perplex his mind, or make him start :

> Nor trembling feare come neare his heart ;
> Till Phœbus rises in his glory dress'd.
> But if a dreame must needs his sence invade,
> Let it be like the kisses of a bride ;
> Gentle and pleasing as a refreshing shade,
> After a scorching sun ; let musique guide
> His wandering fancy, and at his eare
> Stand centinell ; letting come neare
> Noe noise, but what hee most delights to heare.".

Sir Henry Bunbury is an honest, generous, and hearty donator to the public; for in drawing forth from his old boxes, he liberally publishes what belongs to recent as well as to remoter times. Accordingly whatever has come to him, not only as a participator in the Hanmer and the Bunbury blood, but whatever has descended in right of his lady, is laid under contribution; and thus, as well as from other sources which it is not necessary that we should particularly explain, we have a great number of Miscellaneous Letters, some of them written by celebrated individuals whose very personal appearance and manners are fresh in the recollection of the living. Pope, Young, Garrick, Goldsmith, Mrs. Jordan, Madame de Genlis, Nelson, Burke, Crabbe, Bentham, &c. &c. in this collection come agreeably before us in their unrestrained moments. We extract only one letter; it is from the author of the " Essay on Man" to the Earl of Strafford.

(*July*, 1725.)

" My Lord,

" Your Lordship will be surprised at my impudence in troubling you in yr repose and elegant retirement at Boughton. You may think I could only do so at Twit'nam. And much less could you expect disturbance from any but a living bad neighbour. Yet such, my Lord, is now yr case, that you are to be molested at once by a living and a dead one. To explain this riddle,—you may find it very inconvenient on a Sunday (your usual day of rest here) not only to be preat in upon in an evening by me, but shoulder'd in a morning at church by Sr Godfrey Kneller and his huge lady into ye bargain. A *monition* (I think they call it) from ye Drs Commons was publish'd here last Sunday, wherein that pious widow desires their leave to pull down ye tablet I set up at ye head of yr lordship's pew, to fix there a large one to Sr G. and herself, with both their figures. If yr lordship should really chance to take no great pleasure in beholding my name full before yr eyes (which I should not wonder at), yet at least (dangerous as that name is, and dreadful to all true Protestant ears), it cannot incommode you so much as a vast three-hundred-pound pile projecting out upon you, overshadowing my Lady Strafford with ye immense draperies and stone petticoats of Lady Kneller, and perhaps crushing to pieces your lordship's posterity ! This period sounds very poetical ; and yet Reeves seriously tells me, and allows me to tell yr lordship as seriously, that the main wall at yr pew will be greatly in danger of falling by ye addition of such a tomb. What I have to beg of y^r lordship as a favour is, that you will please to declare your dissent and objection, directing a few lines only in general to that effect as your commands to Mr. Pearson, proctor in the Drs Comons, and inclose it to me at Twitnam. They have appointed the *thirtieth of this month* for such of ye parish as have any objections, to show them in court, otherwise ye license will be given her. I thought fit first of all to apply to you, my Lord, who (I would fain persuade myself) will be concernd agst it, next to me; not only as the neerest neighbor to it, but as ye person I w^d hope w^d most favour me. The innovations upon all sorts of property, and ye dangers of ill precedents of all kinds, are what your lordship is a well-known opposer of : I hope you will not be so ye less though it is but the particular cause of one who so justly and so sincerely respects and honours you.

> "I am, my Lord.
> Your Lordship's most obedient
> and most oblig'd
> Humble Servant,
> A. POPE.

"My mother joins in her faithful, humble services, and in my petition for your PROTEST, a word y^r lordship is of late well acquainted with."

A Memoir of Charles Lee, the American General, who was the first-cousin of the editor's father, follows, who seems to have been a singular character, and yet a man possessed of diversified and high qualities. And lastly comes a quantity of very fine and stringent poetry by Henry Soame the editor's cousin, who died in India, in the year 1803, and is called in the Preface to the present volume, the *unfortunate*. Two short specimens of the young gentleman's poetry must conclude our extracts ; for we are confident that what we have said and already produced must satisfy our readers that the work possesses lasting attractions to the historian, the scholar, and the man of taste, as well as to all who delight in agreeable and instructive gossip. At the same time Sir Henry Bunbury has here erected a monument which his family and descendants may rightfully regard with gratitude, admiration, and reverence.

"FRAGMENT

Sour'd but untam'd in Disappointment's school,
He look'd ordain'd to ruin or to rule ;
Through his dark cluster'd ringlets, here and there
Shone ere its time a sorrow-silver'd hair ;
On his pale cheek a bitter smile there sate,
Which seem'd to mock the importance of fate;
Upon his haughty brow defiance lower'd ;
Despair was in his hollow eye embower'd :—
Still, o'er the wild expression of his face
Would beam, by starts, a momentary grace ;
Faint emanations of the God were seen
To indicate the thing he should have been.

EPITAPH

FOR HIMSELF, WRITTEN A FEW DAYS BEFORE HIS DEATH.

Ye sons of thrift, to gentle dulness dear,
Whom prudence fattens, and whom fools revere,
Jog on ! the outcast on whose grave ye gaze
Now holds your Pity—as he held your Praise.
If souls, as sages teach, immortal are,
The few he loved on earth he'll meet elsewhere.
If with the flesh they die, as some suppose,—
Go, thank your stars ye have not much to lose.

ART. XI.—*An Abridged Account of the Misfortunes of the Dauphin.*
Translated from the French, by the Hon. and Rev. C. G. PERCEVAL.
London : Fraser, 1838.

MANY of our readers will have it in recollection that nearly a twelvemonth ago a considerable sensation was created in this country by
the story of a packet of letters having fallen into wrong hands in
London ; and some of these letters having been read by a person who
had no right to do so, that he refused to give them up to the proper
owners, without acquainting the authorities, because he believed
them to reveal a dreadful conspiracy against the life and the reign
of the King of the French.   The packet came from Dresden, and
its contents spoke strongly and warmly about the *Prince*, as a person at the moment in England, meaning thereby Louis Charles
Dauphin of France, and styled Duke of Normandy. The Dauphin,
it was always given out by every French government that has
existed since the death of Louis XVI., had died in the Tower of the
Temple in June 1795, when a boy of about ten years of age ; and
his untimely end has throughout Europe and the world ever since
been a theme of tenderness and lament, while the cruelty which
caused his supposed death has met with a simultaneous and never-
ceasing torrent of execration.   However, a surmise has frequently
been entertained, and a belief extensively expressed, that the boy
escaped from his imprisonment, and that it was a substitute whom
the Revolutionary powers put forward as the deceased prince. One
of the best proofs that such a persuasion has existed, and that even
the governments of France could not give it a flat and convincing
denial, will be discovered in the fact that several persons have been
before the tribunals of that country, each alleging himself to be the
real Dauphin, although all of them have up till now been detected
as impostors.   Another claimant still exists ; it is the person now
under consideration, the same whom the packet of letters already
alluded to concerned,—which letters, by the bye, contained nothing
that could be construed into a conspiracy against the life or the
reign of the present French monarch, but only the firm conviction
and the undisguised expressions of parties, which amounted to this,

—that the Dauphin existed, that he was the person about whom they wrote, and that his prospects were brightening.

In England, we believe, very slight interest, as was to be expected, has hitherto existed on the subject of the present or the preceding claimants to the honours and the rank of the son of the "Martyr King;" nor unless the publication before us produce a sensation, or unless some future conclusive evidence appear in behalf of the person of whom we are about to say more, do we anticipate that the strange story will attract any absorbing feeling. It is quite clear, at the same time that while on the continent, and especially in France, there are many individuals who are satisfied with the claimant's pretensions, there are some even in England who have given in their assent. We need only instance the editor of the volume now on our table,—the Hon. and Rev. C. G. Perceval, Rector of Calverton, Bucks. A glance at his Preface will discover the strength of his convictions.

After expressing his deep-rooted predilections for legitimate royalty, but at the same time disavowing all political motives and designs in the present undertaking, he goes on to state that it is simply in the light of a most interesting historical question the work here translated is regarded by him. He has ever felt deeply on the subject of the French Revolution, and the sorrows and sufferings of the Royal Family of France. No portions of the tragedy, however, have shocked him more " than the treatment of the illustrious Martyr's children; especially of the young Prince, who had the misfortune of being legitimate heir to his father's crown." The feelings of abhorrence and disgust which he has experienced at the " brutal atrocities practised upon that gentle child," have only subsided " under the belief that he had passed through these tribulations, into a better state, and had been re-united, without fear of another separation, to those of whose tenderest affection he had ever been the cherished object." But he is now convinced that a much longer trial was appointed for the Dauphin; in short, but not without encountering difficulties, he is completely satisfied not only that the Duke of Bordeaux is not the legitimate heir to the French throne, but that the son of Louis XVI. is at this moment alive, nay, that the claimant of whom we are about to hear more, a person with whom the editor is acquainted, is this son. Accordingly he has been at the pains to give a translation of the original volume, published some time ago, in which the History of the " Misfortunes of the Dauphin, the son of Louis XVI." is to be found, for the benefit of the English public; and we must declare, if but a tenth of this history be true, the most extraordinary details, intrigues, injustice, and sufferings we ever heard of, will no longer astonish us. The stories about the man in the " Iron Masque," are nothing to it. Be it understood, however, that we express no opinion either one way or the other about the truth of the Pretender's

tale. Were we to do so it might not be unchangeable ; at any rate
it would not be in accordance, we imagine, with the opinion of every
one who may peruse the account before us.   Indeed its author or
authors rather, (for, besides the person calling himself the Duke of
Normandy, several other persons figure as writers in these pages,)
cannot expect that any cautious and judicious individual whatever
will give in his faith to the account without further light and
evidence.   It is over and over again asserted in the work that most
important documents and proofs are withheld till the proper time for
their production, viz. when a competent court is to try their validity
and weight ; nay, in more passages than one or two, a sort of request
that judgment be suspended till such an opportunity occurs, is made,
after which it is declared that even the present unbelieving sister of
the Dauphin, the Duchess Angoulême, will instantly be convinced
and converted.

The first part of the work consists of the Pretender's history, in
outline, of himself.   This extends to about a hundred and ten pages
of the octavo.   Then come " Documents and Reflections," which
occupy about thrice as much space ; and lastly there is a " Supplement," extending to between two and three hundred pages,—the
whole forming the most indigested and badly arranged mass we ever
met with in the form of a book on one theme.   Repetitions and
recopyings are endless ; and there is neither index nor table of
contents, nor any thing like a systematic plan to guide the mind.
Some, perhaps, may regard these circumstances as signs which no
impostor would exhibit, and as proofs only of deeply and constantly
felt truths ; others may surmise that the design is, to bewilder the
reader and poor reviewers like ourselves.   We must be allowed,
however, to state that when we find figuring in these pages and
amongst the professed advisers and agents of the Pretender, the
names of three French Advocates, besides a Confessor ; especially
when the language of the volume very often runs as that of a plural
number, *we*, it might have been expected that some regard would
have been paid to the simple artistic forms of book-making.   Surely
an Abbé and members of the French Bar might have done as much
for the person whom they profess to adore as their lawful prince, as
to have put his story into a becoming and forcible shape.   Nor
can we acquit the English editor of negligence, (it cannot be the
want of ability,) for the translation is frequently ungrammatical.
Then as to the typography, it is full of errors, in the slighter matters
of letters and sometimes words.   But this is not the worst sign of
carelessness or incompetency in correcting proof-sheets ; for there is
such a disregard of the precise and accurate use of inverted commas,
that it is often impossible to discern, without a waste of time, who
the loquitor is.   But to the volume, such as it is, intrinsically and
externally, we now solicit some attention, and accordingly begin with
the Pretender's autobiography.

Supposing his narrative to be true, and supposing that he has been subject to all the indignities which he describes, all the persecutions that have constantly tracked his steps—seventeen years of his life having, as is alleged, formed one feature in his doom, —it would be unreasonable to expect from him a narrative displaying the graces of composition, or any thing but an earnest, a straightforward, and vigorous statement of facts. We cannot say that the detail as given is generally destitute of such marks: it has sometimes the air of simple honesty. Perhaps the following, while perfectly explicit and full of plainly expressed pledges, may be deemed puerile :

" A friend to good order, I hold the factious in abhorrence. Witness to all the calamities that proud and rapacious beings have inflicted on my country, and on myself, I have judged them by their works; never shall I expect the happiness of France from those whose only design is to put themselves in the place of others; they wish for evil, because evil is the very nature and desire of their heart.

" I am the enemy of all hypocrisy, and the friend of justice and of truth ; I here, therefore, declare to all those who call themselves my friends, hoping hereafter to obtain a high office in the state, as a reward for their pretended friendship, that they deceive themselves ; for, I ask for nothing but my name and my civil inheritance. If it should be the will of Divine Providence ever to place me on the throne of my fathers, never shall hypocrisy or intrigue receive the reward due only to merit ; but I repeat, I ask for nothing but my civil inheritance, that is to say, the private property which belonged to the royal family of France, before the first revolution. No government has the right to deprive me of this inheritance. On this point, I shall have in my behalf the suffrages of all Frenchmen, because the question is a great act of national justice, and the French nation desire nothing but justice. These are my opinions, they spring from the sincerity of my heart ; I need not say that I desire to proclaim them openly. I entreat, then, all those who call themselves my friends from motives of interested policy, to withdraw themselves from me and from my affairs. I repeat it again; I will never expose the life of the least of my personal friends, for the sake of wearing a crown which is the most glorious on earth, in sight of all the world: but which cannot be so to the orphan of the Temple, Charles-Louis, Duke of Normandy."

The narrative is intended, as the writer of it himself states, to prove that the child who died in the Temple was not the son of Louis XVI. and Marie Antoinette, but that " I alone am the Duke of Normandy, the true son of the Martyr King." The writer says that he perfectly remembers as far back as the time when the royal family quitted Versailles to fix their residence in Paris : and he then goes on to describe their movements, what occurred to them and all the particulars, in an inventory-like-style, which, if true, ought to establish for him the character of having one of the most retentive memories that the prodigies in that particular have ever developed. For example,

"Of all the people who were with me in the carriage, one only is still living, it is my sister. Will she have the culpable resolution to deny this fact, which no one in the world can know except her brother ? At length, arrived at Paris, we were carried off by the people, and conducted to the Hotel-de-Ville. I ascended the stairs between my mother and Mme. Elizabeth ; these tender friends led me by the hand into a large hall, which was already full of men, many of whom were drunk ; we remained there till a late hour of the night ; and, notwithstanding the tumultuous cries of the populace, during our passage from the Hotel-de-Ville to the Tuileries, I had fallen asleep in the carriage, on my mother's lap, and I was awoke by the cry : '*My son ! my son ! they have carried him away !*' I replied '*Mamma !*' for in truth, I found myself in the hands of a stranger, who put me into the arms of a brother of *Clery, valet de chambre* to my sister, whose name was *Hannet ;* I have such a perfect recollection of this faithful servant, that I remember, as if it had happened but yesterday, that he used to amuse my sister and myself in our childhood, with the sight of a magic lantern in the evening.

"I was then *four years* old. Hannet restored me to the tender solicitude of my excellent mother, who pressed me to her bosom and covered me with kisses."

True, the Pretender says, it is no doubt very easy, with a good memory, to relate that which has been written by others, respecting what passed at the period in question. But he adds,—" all those details which have remained unknown, and have never been published, they are the touchstone for the Duchess of Angoulême if she wishes to convince herself of the truth !" This indicates confidence at least ; still the minute particulars referred to, we think, might possibly have been gathered from witnesses or still more fully from dextrous comparison and guessing. But in whatever way the truth presses, according to the Pretender's own showing, the Duchess of Angoulême is not only incredulous respecting his story, but has after numerous appeals forbidden any person to broach the subject of the writer's claims in her hearing. Samples of the Pretender's particularity will be found in what we now quote.

" The other details of this unhappy day are too well known for me to dwell upon them. The fact which I have just mentioned, proves sufficiently that I have forgotten nothing which happened in my presence ; from this day forward, my mother was constantly in tears ;—this day, which was the fore-runner of the 10th of August.

" It is clear then, that I perfectly remember the facts which I have transmitted to my sister, in proof of my identity. Amongst other questions, I have asked her, who was the person who slept in my room on the night of the 9th of August ? . . . it was my mother, who came to seek some moments of repose, and threw herself, for that purpose, on the bed of the person who sat up with me that night.

" The following day we became prisoners, for we quitted the Tuileries to go to the assembly, where we were soon shut up in a kind of prison. I had the more reason to consider it as such, because this *hole* had an iron grating : although Mme. de Tourzel, and the Princess de Lamballe, were shut up with us, it was still my tender mother who kept me in her arms, or on her lap; but the whole of this day I had eaten nothing, except a peach and a morsel of bread. I suffered still more from thirst, for the weather was very hot. Notwithstanding all the endeavours of my good mother, it was impossible to procure the least thing : at length one of our friends, it was the Minister of Justice, took us into another small room, that we might eat a rice soup and some chicken. My father, and mother, and the other persons who were with us, did not partake of our repast; my sister, even, only ate some soup : it was my good aunt, Mme. Elizabeth, who was with us, but she ate nothing. After this repast, we were taken back into the grated prison, where I soon fell asleep on the knees of my good mother. For the correctness of what I here state, I give as witnesses the Duchess of Angoulême, and the Ex-Minister of Justice, M. de Joly, who is still living."

The writer, according to his own story was at this time seven years and a half old, and the English editor will have it that memory generally extends to the age of four years. It must also be conceded that in the case of an ordinary memory, the events which the Dauphin was witness to, would make a deep impression ; but whether such precise recollections, as we now give a specimen of, could be retained, is for our readers to say:

" My mother's room and my aunt's were separated by a wainscot partition. On entering my mother's room, her bed was placed on the left, against this partition; my aunt's bed was on the right on entering her room, so that the two beds were separated only by this partition ; mine was placed at the foot of that of my good and tender mother, who awoke at the slightest movement that I made in the night, to ask if I was not ill. My sister's bed was placed in the same manner in my aunt's room, near the window in the right hand corner. A small closet in the turret, like that in my father's apartment, completed our habitation. In my mother's room there was an arm-chair, the linen of which was green and the wood painted white. I mention this arm-chair because my father used frequently to sleep in it for a short time after his dinner.

" I remained in this prison till the moment when I was delivered into the hands of Simon and his wife. Without wishing to excite the compassion of my readers or of those who will judge of my history, I shall not conceal that my cruel separation from my tender mother, my aunt and my sister, made me shed torrents of tears which the harshness of my jailers alone could force me to repress.

" This is neither the place nor the time to reveal what tyranny made me suffer in this indescribable situation of my unhappy childhood. Without succour, without hope, without friends, I was still more unhappy after the removal of Simon and his wife, who had already begun to treat me with less brutality. I was confined alone in the room, before occupied by Cléry. As I have said, this room was then quite transformed into a prison ; the door which communicated with the dining room had been removed, and it had been replaced by a sort of stove, which was lighted from the little recess that I have mentioned. The windows were so closed, that I could not see clearly. The door of the turret which opened into Cléry's apartment, and in which was the closet, had been closed : and a night table had been placed in my room, the smell of which became more and more offensive to me.

" It has been said that a turning-box had been made in the only remaining door, in which to place my food; this assertion is inaccurate ; there was indeed a wicket, but it was only opened by my jailers, when they called me, in order to ascertain that I was still there: the door in which this wicket was, had served before as the entrance to my father's room, and it was by it they entered twice a day to bring me my food. After this removal, it was no longer human voices that I heard, but the howlings of ferocious beasts, who cried out to me almost every moment : ' Capet, wolf-cub, son of a viper, come, that I may see you.' During the night, even, I was scarcely asleep, when another cerberus would open the wicket, and force me to appear before him. Worn out with these persecutions I resolved to die rather than answer.

" My prison contained myself, my bed, a chair, an oblong wooden table, underneath it a pitcher of water, and an unfurnished bedstead, which had been Cléry's. In this deplorable state no one thought of providing me with linen or other clothes, and soon devoured by vermin, and poisoned by the stench of my prison, I became seriously ill. My jailers and two municipal officers entered with some other persons, whom I did not know, and who I thought were doctors, for they questioned. me, and entreated me to speak to them, and to tell them what I wanted. I made them no answer. I had many reasons for maintaining silence ; and those reasons I have motives for not explaining here."

The manner in which the Pretender states, that he was removed from his assigned prison and the substitution of another boy, is particularly described. He says, that although there was no hope of deliverance by descending, it was contemplated and discovered that by making him ascend, and by temporally concealing him in the Tower of the Temple, the desired end might be realized. A dose of opium having been administered to him, he was lifted up.

" In this state, I saw a child which they substituted for me, in my bed, and I was laid in the basket, in which this child had been concealed, under my bed. I perceived, as if in a dream, that the child was only a wooden figure, the face of which was made to resemble mine. This substitution was effected at the moment when the guard was changed ; the one who succeeded was contented with just looking at the child to certify my presence, and it was enough for him to have been a sleeping figure, whose face was like mine ; my habitual silence contributed further to strengthen the error of my new argus. In the mean time, I had lost all consciousness, and when my senses returned, I found myself shut up in a large room, which was quite strange to me; it was the fourth story of the tower. This room was crowded with all kinds of old furniture, among which a space had been prepared for me, which communicated with a closet in the turret, where my food had been placed. All other approach was barricadoed. Before concealing me there, one of my friends, whom I shall name in the course of this history, had informed me in what manner I should be saved, on condition that I should bear all imaginable sufferings without complaining ; adding, that a single imprudent step would bring destruction on me and on my benefactors ; and he insisted above all, that when I was concealed, I should ask for nothing, and should continue to act the part of a really deaf and dumb child.

"When I awoke I recollected the injunctions of my friend, and I firmly resolved to die rather than disobey them. I ate, I slept, and I waited for my friends with patience. I saw my first deliverer, from time to time, at night, when he brought me what was necessary for me. The figure was discovered the same night; but the government thought fit to conceal my escape, which they believed to have been completed. My friends, on their part, the better to deceive the sanguinary tyrants, had sent off a child under my name, in the direction, I believe, of Strasbourg. They had even countenanced the opinion, and given information to the government, that it was I who had been sent in that direction. The government, in order entirely to conceal the truth, put in the place of the figure a child of my age who was really deaf and dumb, and doubled the ordinary guard, endeavouring thus to make it be believed that I was still there. This increase of precaution prevented my friends from completing the execution of their plan in the manner they had intended. I remained, therefore, in this vile hole, as if buried alive."

The narrative proceeds to describe many little incidents which befell the Pretender—his mode of conveyance from the Temple—the interest Mme. Beauharnois, afterwards Napoleon's wife, took in him, and a series of unexampled vicissitudes, persecutions and sufferings. Thus,—

"My misfortunes have been unparalleled : but it not being my aim to excite compassion, I here relate only a small part of them ; those circumstances alone which will form documents useful to my cause. I cannot then pass over in silence the horrible assassination of Mr. B. and the young Marie. Subsequently to this deplorable event, I was taken at sea, and brought back into France against my will; the only one of my friends who escaped my persecutors was Montmorin, and unknown to me he secretly followed my steps. Immediately after my disembarkment in France, I was put in prison. While there, two strangers, whose names are yet unknown to me, visited me, and endeavoured to persuade me to become a monk, assuring me that it was my only means of safety. I resisted their proposal; and after a long interrogatory they left me. Some time after, I was taken in the middle of the night on board a small vessel, and conveyed to a port, where armed men were waiting with a carriage to receive me. After travelling four days and four nights I was again put into prison. A poor woman apparently, but as I thought a man in the disguise of a woman, was the only person that I saw. This person waited on me. I was cruelly treated in this prison in which I remained till the end of 1803. Montmorin broke my chains, and I again recovered my liberty by the assistance of the good Josephine: she had found means to deceive her husband Napoleon with the aid of the minister Fouché. During the winter, until the commencement of 1804, my friends exerted themselves in my behalf; Pichegru was sent to the Count de Provence to consult with him respecting me. Will the world believe that this relative, deaf to the voice of nature, and listening only to the dictates of a selfish ambition, took advantage against me of the information given him by Pichegru, abused the confidence of my friends, and betrayed my last asylum."

The after scenes and series of hardships obtain the account that now we dive into.

"My bed was composed of a bundle of straw, and a woollen blanket, spread on the ground in a corner of my cold damp dungeon, which was square and vaulted. I never received any linen or clothing. The time came when I was without a shirt. My coat and trowsers were worn to shreds, and to cover myself, I was obliged to wrap my body in the blanket, gnawed through and through by the rats, who, probably, had nestled their young in it. I was nineteen years of age when I was buried in this dark dungeon, where the light of the sun or of the moon never reached me. All idea of day was effaced from my mind, as well as that of the division of time. I imagined from the worn state of my clothes, that my captivity had lasted at least half a century. I knew every step of my dungeon, and my ears readily caught the most distant sound of my gaoler's feet. With this exception, I heard no sound but that of the beating of drums, which appeared to me like the rolling of distant thunder. The space in the roof through which the air or the light might have penetrated more freely, gave me the idea of being at the extremity of a long tube, which appeared to terminate in dirty water, through which the sun might shine, or which was covered with cobwebs. The space between the walls formed a square of about twelve feet. Alone, in this hidden spot, abandoned by the whole world, I reflected with bitterness that I had no longer any friends; I considered myself as having anticipated the hour of my final interment. My hair, which I had not the means of cutting, became long and curly, my beard had grown, and when I touched my face with my hands, I could have fancied myself a wild beast. My nails were so long that they broke in bits, and I could only avoid the pain which was the consequence, by biting them with my teeth. I despaired of ever again beholding the surface of the earth, when I was one night suddenly awakened by two persons who called me by my name. I arose, wrapped in my blanket, in a pitiable state of dirt, and covered with the dust of the straw, which never having been changed, was ground to powder under me. At the appearance of extreme misery of which my whole person presented so afflicting a spectacle, my liberators exclaimed with an emotion of surprise and compassion : ' Why ! what does this mean ?' My gaoler, who was present with his lantern, made an affirmative motion of his head, saying; ' Yes, yes, it is he himself.' "

The Count de Provence comes scurvilly out, if the story be true, and is made, along with the Count d'Artois, to have been deep and earnest conspirators against the " Martyr-King's" life and throne. Be these things as they may, the Pretender says he directed his steps after his deliverance from the horrid dungeon above mentioned to Germany, and established himself in the Prussian dominions as a watchmaker. There he prospered in business, found a wife, and several children, (all of whom have right royal names,) was perse- cuted, falsely charged for deep crimes, and latterly, when the Revo- lution of the Three Days took place—having been liberated and shown himself to be a good citizen—found his way to Paris, where he began to assert his claims. These claims were not palatable to the reigning power ; and probably the strongest feature in the Pre- tender's case consists in this, that he is denied a trial, is pushed from France, although he asserts that a mass of overwhelming evidence in support of his rights are at his command—amongst others the testimony of Mme. de Rambaud, now far advanced in years, who was nurse to the Dauphin previous to the awful tragedy in the history of the Revolution, connected with the Royal family. It will be asked, why has the Pretender been so tardy in pre- ferring his claims? Take what follows as an explanation.

" ' Why,' we are again asked, ' did the Duke of Normandy wait till 1830 to bring forward his claims ?'

" If these enquirers had taken the trouble to read the documents which have already been submitted to the public, they would neither repeat this question, nor many others, which are completely answered by the facts there stated. How could the Prince have brought forward his claims, when he was dragged from dungeon to dungeon, and during the short intervals that he was at liberty, was under the necessity of keeping silence in order to preserve his life ! It is evident that he could not have taken any steps till under the reign of his uncles : and it will be proved, that, since that period, he has made a thousand ineffectual applications ; as many Royalists of the old court could testify, if they were animated with a zeal for justice, and not meanly guided by interested views. And I, who see the hand of God in every thing, cannot otherwise account for the revolution of 1830 and the causes which led to it, than by supposing it to be the result of an over- whelming influence, directing all according to the supreme will of Provi- dence. Injustice, persevered in for forty years, demanded an exemplary retribution ; this retribution has for the last six years weighed heavily upon the guilty. If political affairs had remained in the same state, in which they stood previous to July 1830, the life of the Duke of Normandy would have been spent, and probably ended in the obscurity to which the crimes of his enemies had condemned him. The establishment of a government raised on the ruins of the ancient hereditary rights, alone opened to him an approach to the bar of justice."

So many things are preferred in this volume upon the *ipse dixit* of our Pretender, that it may be right to test some of them by the ordinary marks of verisimilitude which the mind wishes and hopes to recognise in all stories where important claims and conclusions are announced. But first let us listen to some of his alleged discoveries. The following is declared to be from the letters of the Count de Provence, afterwards Louis XVIII.

" To the Duke of Fitz-James.

Versailles, May 13, 1787.

" Here is, my dear duke, the assembly of notables drawing to its close, and yet the great question has not been touched upon. You cannot doubt that the notables will not hesitate to believe from the documents which you sent them, more than six weeks ago, that *the king's children are not his own.* Those papers give the clearest proofs of the queen's guilty conduct; you are a subject too much attached to the blood of your sovereigns, not to blush at bowing before these *adulterous fruits.*

" I shall be absent, but my brother d'Artois, whose committee does not hold its sitting, will preside in my place. The fact in question once averred, it is easy to infer the consequences.

" The parliament, which dislikes the queen, will not make any great difficulty; but, if it should have the fancy to raise any, *we have the means of bringing it to reason......* In short, we must attempt the blow.

(*Signed*) LOUIS STANISLAS XAVIER."

" To the Count d'Artois.

" All that fortune could devise most fatal has been united against us for more than *eighteen months :* but it seems that she is going to relent, and to look upon us with somewhat more favour. What does it signify to us, in fact, that Condé has obtained, to our prejudice, the command of the army furnished by the King of Prussia and the Emperor. *If the blow which is preparing* is struck it *alone will be worth an army.* Sixty *mountaineers* of the Assembly, and the *English Ministry,* will remain to us; with such succours everything may be hoped for.

" ..... The reed that bends lives longer than the *oak* that breaks. You will be the *oak* in your turn, my brother, and God knows what will be the result !.;....

(*Signed*) LOUIS STANISLAS XAVIER."

" To the Count d'Artois.

" It is done, my brother, *the blow is struck !* I hold in my hand the official news of the death of the unfortunate Louis XVI, and have only time to forward it to you.

" I am informed also that his son *is dying.*

" You will not forget how *useful to the state their death* will be. Let this reflection console you; and remember that the Grand Prior, your son, is, after me, the hope and the heir of the monarchy.

(*Signed*) LOUIS STANISLAS XAVIER."

Certainly we have no historical data entitling us to think very favourably of Louis XVIII. as a moral agent, or even as an actor in the Revolution ; but it will require something more than the declaration of the Pretender's advocates, M. Gruau and the others, to induce us to believe that the above letters are anything but fabriations, especially when we find that the very next translated document runs in these terms ;—

" *George III, King of England, to the Duke of Angoulême.*
" MY COUSIN,
" I write you this letter to acquaint you that, it being our royal will and pleasure to deliver France from the oppression under which she groans, *especially since the death* of our brother and cousin, His Most Christian Majesty, as also to place one of his direct heirs upon his throne, we invest you with the command of the army which we send for this purpose, and recognize *in you alone* the right of the regency of the kingdom during the minority of Louis XVIII, son of the late king.

" That if the said child should happen to die, we will and intend that *you should reign after him, in immediate succession, without delay or division,* to the exclusion of every *pretender, direct and indirect ;* under the express condition, however, of your fulfilling the wishes of His Majesty, Louis XVI, by causing the princess Maria Theresa, his daughter, whom he destined to be your wife, to ascend with you to the throne, thus become yours.

" Being desirous to give authority to our royal decision and conduct, we proclaim before God, and in the face of all the world, that *they who conspired against the safety, power, and life of the late king, have excluded themselves from the hereditary line of succession to his crown :* interpreting thus the State Laws of France, and those of Charlemagne, which, though they render the princes of his house not amenable to the tribunals of ordinary justice, have not forbidden Princes, their peers, from becoming, by unusual means, the *organs of divine justice.*

" On which I pray God, &c.
Given at Westminster.

(*Signed*) DUNDAS."

This is too clumsy to require a dressing, and we dislike the authorities that keep company with it.

Ah! but the Pretender has something else left to support and substantiate his case ; nor can we do better than give a sample of this bright claimant's authorities and vouchers.

It so happens that the *Duke of Normandy* has a Confessor of the name of Appert, Curate of St. Arnoult ; and he assures us, in terms, like many others, exceedingly offensive in the book which the " Hon. and Rev. C. G. Perceval" translates and edits, wherein he compares the Pretender to the Saviour of mankind, that the *Duke* is the favoured child of Heaven, and has been the object of Heaven's special revelation, not once, but somewhere in the volume, it says, seventeen times. The Martin mentioned is a peasant, a gifted seer and a sort of go-between, where the corresponding parties are Heaven and Louis XVIII.

" The prince had never yet received the holy sacrament ; and how could he have done so, buried in the depths of dungeons, or kept a close prisoner ?

He ardently desired it, and Martin received an order to press the fulfilment of this duty, after which *great favours* were to be granted to the Prince. In fact, some weeks after it, the Prince beheld a first miraculous apparition. He could not persuade himself of the reality of it, notwithstanding the assurance which Martin received to that effect. It was not till after several similar apparitions, and after having received the orders of him who called himself *the Protecting Angel of France*, that he ceased to doubt. But his wavering faith deserved a severe lesson. The fourth appari·ion announced it to him, without specifying either the kind of chastisement or the motive of it, He wrote upon the subject immediately to his confessor, and he was on his way to obtain an answer, when, on the 28th of January, 1834, he was attacked and received six strokes from a dagger, but was miraculously saved, The surgeon certified that the dagger had stopped within half a line of the heart; you are aware that five of the blows were parried by a medal of our Lord and the Holy Virgin, which was pierced, and by his beads and crucifix, which were broken to pieces. But it was not long before the Prince was consoled by new apparitions which reassured him : they gave him directions, or else he received them through Martin. Sometimes the same voice spoke to him without any apparition, and it was thus that he received several orders after the seventh apparition had taken place. The first occurred on the 18th December, 1833, and the seventh on the 13th April 1834 : its object was to console him for the recent loss of an excellent priest, his friend M. Fustier, Vicar-General of Tours, and to inform him that the riot which would break out that day at Paris would have no serious consequences."

This is not the whole of the wonderful interpositions which Heaven has vouchsafed to the Duke of Normandy. Listen.

" Secret as these supernatural favours were kept, they nevertheless transpired, and were variously thought of according to men's various prejudices; when the Prince received an order to prepare himself by the communion for an extraordinary revelation. After this communion he was enjoined to attend publicly, on the 6th of July, at the parochial mass at the church of St. Eustache. There he saw the frightful ills which threaten all sovereigns, and it was enjoined him to communicate them to the Holy Father, the sovereigns generally, and especially Louis-Philippe. Some days afterwards he was to set out to go to his sister, having directed two persons to precede him, who had been pointed out to him. This was his second application to the Duchess of Angoulême, who, according to the prophecy of Martin, obstinately persisted in refusing an interview. The Prince had stopped with his family at Dresden : it was there it was told him that *the object of his journey was accomplished, and that all the intrigues would be unmasked.*

" This was in the course of August 1834. The journey occupied a month, and the result, willed by Providence, was the birth of Marie-Therese on the 15th of May 1835. This child, more favoured than her brothers and sisters, received baptism according to the Catholic rite, immediately after her birth, and had for sponsors her eldest brother and sister, who had been admitted, a few days previously, to their first communion.

" This precious family consists then of Charles-Louis, Duke of Normandy, .

and of Jane Eiaers, his wife, of whom have been born Amelia; aged sixteen years; Charles Edward, aged fifteen years; a child who died during
the last imprisonment, and since that imprisonment, Marie-Antoinette, aged
six years, Charles, aged four years, Edmund, aged two years, and Marie-
Theresa."

Precious, indeed! and that the Hon. and Rev. C. G. Perceval
has found time and inclination to edit such *precious* stuff is for him
to defend before the tribunal of common sense, and another tribunal of which we must not speak more pointedly.

Art. XII.

1.—*History and Description of the London and Birmingham Railway.*
By Peter Lecount, F. R. A. S., Civil Engineer, and Thomas
Roscoe. Illustrated with Fine Engravings. London: Tilt. 1838.

2.—*Chemins de Fer Américains; Historique de leur Construction; Prix
de Revient et Produit; Mode d'Administration adopté; Résumé de la
Législation qui les regit.* Par Guillaume-Tell Poussin.

3.—*Iron Road Book and Railway Companion, &c. &c.* By Francis
Coghlan. London: A. H. Bailey and Co.

The sedulous cultivation of those arts by which life is rendered
comfortable and respectable, has long been the distinguishing character of the English people. Foreigners bear testimony to the
energy and enterprise which mark the inhabitants of this island,
who whiten the ocean to its extremity with the sails of their ships,
and cover the land with works of art and usefulness. All this is done
by the intelligence of the community; every person performs a part
towards the grand result; the whole country is prolific of fertile
fields and well-cultivated farms, with manufactories, canals, and
excellent kept roads. Within a hundred yards of each other may be
found a rail road, a canal, and turnpike road, each of them teeming
with travel or overflowing with commerce. This mode of easy and
expeditious intercommunication knits the whole country into a
closely-compacted mass; through which, the production of commerce and of the press, the comforts of life, and the means of
knowledge are universally diffused; while the close intercourse of
pleasure or business makes all men neighbours, promotes a common
interest, and common sympathy. In a community thus connected,
a single flash of thought pervades the whole land, almost as quickly
as thought itself can fly.

How many empires have crumbled into ruins from want of that
animating impulse produced by a rapid interchange of sentiment
among their population. If, as some suppose, mankind cannot
again recede from their present advanced state of civilization, it
will certainly be from their great advantages over the ancients in an
easy and quick means of intercommunication; and, if any among the

states of the civilized world could, from this cause, claim an immortality, it is England ; and among the efforts to produce this result, we must consider the establishment of the " London and Birmingham Railway" as the most stupendous and beneficial work that has yet been accomplished.   The author of the history of this railway which is now before us, has given a few notices of the difficulties that the undertakers had to contend against, among which we extract the following :—

" In 1830 two lines were proposed ; one by Sir John Rennie, taking the Banbury and Oxford line of road, and the other by Mr. Giles, taking its course by the way of Coventry.   Companies were formed in each case, and were duly marshalled against each other, with their various staff appointments fully organised, directors, secretaries, engineers, solicitors, bankers, &c., and great were the rejoicings in Westminster Hall.

" If the battle had been waged, and if any poet could have been found capable of bringing into harmonious numbers such uncouth sounds as cuttings and embankments—blocks and sleepers—and slopes of one thousand eight hundred to one—Homer's Ghost might have trembled till all Pluto's dominions gave a simultaneous sympathising shake, like these comical clocks furnished with Hardy's ' Noddy,'* where the one cannot rejoice in a little irregular motion without the other telling tales by instantly wagging about too.   But fortunately, all parties were too wise, and they deemed it much more prudent, instead of throwing away their money in an uncertain Parliamentary contest, at once to consult, as far as possible, the interest of their several proprietaries, by selecting that line which a majority should consider the best, and thus unite the two companies into one.

" George Stephenson had, a little prior to this, been engaged by the parties who had chosen the Coventry line for the railway, and as he also gave his opinion in favour of that route, it was finally decided that the London and Birmingham Railway should go *via* Coventry, and George Stephenson and his Son were appointed engineers to the now united ' London and Birmingham Railway Company.'

" It may be thought that this period of time is passed over too lightly ; but it is best.   Why should the party feelings, the hopes and the fears, the disagreements, the quarrels, and the heart burnings of five or six years ago, be perpetuated ?   It would be in excessive bad taste, to say the least of it, and anything but amusing to the public at large ; all parties did then what all have done since, that is to say, they strained every nerve for the interests of the proprietors to the best of their ability and judgment, and who could do more ?   It may be just observed, that through the proprietors principally residing in Lancashire, and from their proximity to the Liverpool and Manchester line, being to a certain extent practical men, they were better able to take a leading part, and to judge what was

---

* " This philosophical little instrument, for which the talented Mr. Hardy received a Medal from the Society of Arts, is an inverted pendulum which moves isochronally with that of the clock on which it is put, and shews when the clock is not firmly fixed."

most advantageous; and they had heavy votes enough to oblige their judgments to be executed.

" There was this object also to be kept in view, in forming such a line as the London and Birmingham Railway, that it is a grand trunk from the metropolis towards the northern part of England, and that numerous branches would in all probability fall into it at no very distant period; that the Irish traffic would all come along it, and most probably the Scotch. It was also to be remembered, that not only the towns near the line would be benefited, but others far distant.

" The impulse to travelling which has been given from the facilities afforded by railways, and the cheapness of this mode of conveyance, has been astonishing; and will, of course, continue to improve the more they are brought into use. The increase has varied in all proportions up to the ratio on the Stockton and Darlington line, where the passengers are now eighty times as many as they were before it was in operation.

" On September the 11th, 1830, the two Companies united themselves, selecting eight persons from each as a provisional committee. Much had been done previously to this in preparing the public mind, and in endeavouring to obviate opposition, which, however, still continued very strong among those who either could not or would not see the advantages of establishing this means of communication. This has, however, perhaps worked good rather than evil; for it could only be met by the free use of the press, in order to enlighten all those who were willing to receive information on the subject of railways, and this was done to such an extent that it soon became apparent our danger would be in having too many railways instead of too few.

" In the latter end of 1830 a committee of survey was appointed to establish a regular communication with the Engineers, by way of periodical reports, and to correct errors, make improvements, confirm friends, and conciliate enemies. In October, Messrs. Stephenson and Son reported that the line, as laid down by Mr. Giles, from Islington to Chipping Barnet, South Mims, Leverstock Green, and Hemel Hempstead, was exceedingly rough, and incurred deep and extensive excavations, and that they would recommend it to leave London near Hyde Park, running almost parallel with the Edgeware Road to Watford, Hemel Hempstead, Great Berkhampstead, and Ivinghoe.

" It was also proposed to enter Birmingham on the south side by a tunnel, so as to gain a central *terminus*. Another plan was to pass up the Tame Valley from Stone Bridge, and join the Grand Junction Railway at Wednesbury, having a branch line to Birmingham; this was done with a view to the advantages of the whole line from London to Liverpool. Both companies were to have stations in Broad-street,—the Grand Junction on the north-west side, on a piece of ground of about seven and a half acres; and the London and Birmingham on the south-east side, containing about nine acres, with another station at the Bell Barn Road."

M. Poussin's work contains a list, together with an account of the various railroads in contemplation or that have been completed in the United States, from which it appears that in number they vastly exceed ours, but as to the material or manner of construction, there is not the least comparison. The Americans form their railroads in a very slight and fragile manner.

In looking into M. Poussin's work we find, that from New York to Philadelphia there either is, or will shortly be two railroads. The first of these is the Camden and Amboy railroad, constructed with a double track, and leading from the port of South Amboy, in a south-westerly direction across the State of New Jersey, a distance of sixty miles, to Camden, on the easterly bank of the Delaware, opposite to the city of Philadelphia. The passage from New York to Amboy is made by steamboat navigation, a distance of twenty-five miles through an inland passage, which separates Staten Island from the shore of New Jersey. The passage from New York to Philadelphia is made in five and a half hours.

The other line is entirely distinct from that just described. It is of about the same length, and leads from the ferry, opposite to the city of New York, through the city of Newark, and the towns of Brunswick and Trenton, directly to the city of Philadelphia. This line consists of three distinct railroads united in one line; one extending from the ferry to New Brunswick, the second from New Brunswick to Trenton, and the third from Trenton to Philadelphia. The second of these roads is not yet finished; the other two are in full operation. This route will have the advantage of passing through the principal towns of New Jersey, while the other passes directly through a very barren and desolate region.

In continuing the Atlantic line from Philadelphia to Baltimore, there will also soon be a choice of several routes. That which has been hitherto chiefly travelled, is the New Castle and Frenchtown railroad, which extends only across the peninsula from the Delaware River to Chesapeake Bay, a distance of sixteen miles, and serves as the connecting link of a chain of steamboat navigation, by which the rest of the passage is made from Philadelphia to Baltimore. The distance by the course of the steamboat from Philadelphia to New Castle is thirty-five miles, and that from Frenchtown to Baltimore nearly double, making the whole distance from Philadelphia to Baltimore a hundred and twenty miles. The time usually occupied in making the passage is from ten to eleven hours, that part of it made by the railroad occupying one hour.

There are a number of other railroads, some few of which are finished, that are intended to connect most of the cities of the northern and middle states with each other. The number of projected ones is so great, that if only half were completed, it would take a population greater than that of the whole union to be solely employed in their construction, for at least the period of one generation.

The last work at the head of this article is a very clever manual of reference for all travellers that make use of the London and Birmingham Railway in their journeys. It is written by Mr. Coghlan, a gentleman who has been some time very favourably known to the public as the author of a numerous list of exceedingly valuable guide books; which well-earned reputation, the present performance will not detract from.

ART. XIII.—*Italy: In Six Parts: With Historical and Classical Notes.* By JOHN E. READE. London: Saunders and Otley. 1838.

WOULD this Poem ever have been produced had Lord Byron never written Childe Harold? We dare not say, no; for Mr. Reade is an enthusiastic observer of whatever is beautiful or grand in nature and art, and has besides long wooed the poetic muse, and studied the poetic art with unremitting assiduity. But we are prepared to assert that after Childe Harold, "Italy" has but a poor chance to survive its author. In the first place it has much the appearance of an imitation. The same Spenserean measure is adopted, and the same objects—witness the Gladiator, and many others (a bold attempt, surely) are frequently his themes as those which attracted the power of Byron's genius. In the second place, unconsciously no doubt, and perhaps inevitably, the same thoughts and images are often seized or attenuated which the "Childe" so potently forestalled. We are sorry for this, because Mr. Reade is a person possessed of not a few of the qualities of a true poet, of the elements which constitute a poetic temperament; and because whenever, in the poem before us, he departs from the path which Byron has trod, he appears to us to exhibit more power and greater felicity every way than on other occasions. At the same time, it must be admitted that our author's verses are never otherwise than beautiful. His versification is melodious and rotund, his imagery is tastefully chosen and delicately handled, his tone of sentiment is pure, and not seldom inspiring, and by the cultivated mind and the lover of poetry very many passages and verses of this long production will be dwelt upon with satisfaction and delight—nay, what is more, the longer they are dwelt upon the greater will be the pleasure and the profit of the reader. Indeed, "Italy" being a work in which there is no connected or sustained story, but a string of imaginings and reflections, such as presented themselves to the author at the very time of his visit to the scenes and objects described, can only be properly appreciated after piece-meal, deliberate, and repeated perusal: and then, we venture to predict, that to every reader, like Sir Robert Peel, to whom the work is dedicated, capable of estimating its merits, it will afford sustained pleasure. The poem, in short, is remarkable in regard to sweetness and refinement of sentiment, but presents few claims to originality or the highest attributes of verse.

The plan of the Poem is simple enough. It follows the author, or rather, keeps pace with him as he travels from one scene and city to another, renowned on account of their natural beauties, their works of art, or the great men who have conferred immortality upon these objects; and sometimes the main current of the verse, of the descriptions, and the sentiments, is relieved by tales and episodes, in various kinds of verse. Our first specimen will be the first five stanzas of the Poem. The Apennines is the subject.

> " If thou wert aught, Time-hallowed phantom, Muse!
> Save the creation of immortal mind,
> Here, throned apart, thy temple would'st thou choose :
> Oh! never on Parnassus' heights enshrined,
> 'Mid Ida's woods, or Delphic shades reclined,

> Was a sublimer, worthier Altar thine
> Than where I stand, companion of the Wind,
> Cloud-folded on the stormy Apennine!—
> Than where I feel thee linked with Nature's life and mine.
> Else, wherefore, Vision of the Soul! wert thou
> Embodied ever from mankind apart,
> Throned on the mountain's heaven-encircled brow?
> Save that the poet felt thou wert and art   ·
> From Nature's forms created by the heart:
> The crag, the cloud, the spirit-stirring Air!
> All elements that kindred Power impart;
> Thou, who her gentler communings would'st share
> The vale, or brooklet seek, and thou shalt find her there!
> Stand—for unseen beneath a world lies shrouded:
> An upper and a nether heaven; behold
> Above—the boundless azure spreads unclouded;
> Beneath—the mists voluminous enrolled
> In wave-like ridges, fold enwrapped o'er fold:
> Now, broken, feathering up the mountain's side
> In billowy wreaths of gusty vapour rolled;
> Now, through its yawning gorges spreading wide,
> Like smoke whose eddying palls those rocky cauldrons hide;
> Upwards from their all-fathomless chasms seething
> As from the Abyss of Hell! lo, dimly seen,
> Hung round their sides the blasted pines stretch wreathing
> Their arms with a forlorn and witch-like mien;
> Above—beneath—the Quiet how serene!
> The Motion and the Silence! the bright Sun
> Casting o'er yon cloud-waves its dazzling sheen;
> A solemn Sea! still fluctuating on,
> As heaved the waves o'er earth ere yet from Chaos won.
> Lo, Life's true isthmus, thou who standest here,
> Rising between the two eternities;
> The infinite of yonder azure sphere:
> The floating Ocean of the Cloud that lies
> Beneath thee, and the world o'er canopies:
> Thou, the sole link between that earth and heaven;
> How thy grand isolation magnifies
> Thy spirit to the mighty Vision given!
> Away, each lowlier thought, each earthlier memory driven."

There is much earnestness and intensity of feeling in these, and, indeed, throughout every stanza of the Poem. Still it will be felt that the author does not rise, in spite of himself, above himself in any one burst of thought, but rather that, in spite of evident though hearty effort, he maintains merely an elegant middle flight, no part of which by a resistless mastery imprints itself distinctly and permanently upon the mind. The very plethora of words, epithets, and phrases used, sweet and musical though they be, tends to dissipate the force of the thoughts and the imagery introduced. As to the first line of the third stanza, a literary friend has pointed out to us the very obvious transference and accommodation of Byron's well-known line,

" Stop—for thy tread is on an empire's dust."
and yet, we do not for a moment suppose that Mr. Reade was conscious
of the plagiarism. If he was, it must have been after most laborious preparation; for we find the line naturally enough and even beautifully
arising out of the first stanza, out of its expression, its allusion and described situation. Extensive reading and an excessive admiration of the
best English poets will account for this and similar unconscious copyings
wherever the great creative power is wanting, such as was possessed by
men like Shakspeare, Milton, and Byron, who after all were but the servants not the absolute masters of the inspired power.

One or two specimens more will help our readers to a just appreciation
of Mr. Reade's Italy. Take him on a work of Art—the Dancing Fawn
at Florence.

" The Dancing Fawn—he cannot hide his joy,
    The pulses of delight within him bounding !
His foot pressed lightly on that music-toy,
    Now soft, now full, the answering cymbal rounding ;
How is his rapture at each note redounding !
His arms are tossed in motion, like a tree,
    When the Wind through its joyous boughs is sounding !
His face, his eyes brimful, o'erflow with glee,
His is the very life of rapture's ecstacy !"

Rome, its ruins, and its present condition are the subject of a number
of fine, impressive, and solemn stanzas—We quote one.

" Behold the skeleton—the reliques round
    Of life and mind which grasped the orb'd world !
Where Desolation, sitting on the ground,
    Her scornful lips in very mockery curled,
    In ruin hath fantastically hurled :
Lo—where the living City towers confessed :
    The cross and keys upon her flag unfurled ;
    Her power a mockery, her name a jest;
By turns, each tyrant's prey, insulted or caressed."

Mr. Reade has proved his assertion in the preface, that the whole territory of Naples is, by the Poet, unbroken, almost untrodden ground. And
it is upon this ground, as we hinted in our preliminary observations, that
he is most successful and spirited. He need not then be afraid in any
future effort to allow his Muse's genius its fullest scope and sweep over
new regions, and where no Byron has travelled or strewn amaranths
before. Hear him on the Story of Dædalus.

" Pause for awhile on yonder grassy hill,
    When, offering up the steerage of his wings,
The tale of Dædalus instructs us still :
    How beauteous those divine imaginings
Of the old time, round which fond Fancy flings
Her brightest hues to arrest the heedless mind !
How flower-like truth from buried fable springs !
Here the sad Father in his grief designed
The story of his son, in rash presumption blind :
    Thrice he essayed—and thrice the sire confessed
    The o'ermastering power of Nature as he failed !

H H 2

What need the truth implanted in each breast ?
On human wisdom the restraint entailed,
Whose glorious ambition heaven assailed ?—
To leave the baser herd behind, to prove,
Even though the wrath of man or heaven prevailed,
Its immortality, that vainly strove
To o'erleap its mortal state, and sphere itself above."

In this vigorous manner does our poet moralize and give a beautifully instructive tone to his verses, at the same time that they are classically correct in point of allusion and imagery. The Poem, indeed, admits of a long and critical review, the result of which, in candid hands, would be in no mean degree gratifying to its author; but it came at too late a period to us to receive a more lengthened notice than what we have given.

ART. XIV.—1st. *Considerations on the Vital Principle.* 2nd. *The Silkworm, and most Approved Methods of Rearing Silk.* 3rd. *Improvements on the Life-Boat.* By JOHN MURRAY. London: Effingham Wilson. 1838.

THE two first of these Pamphlets have reached second editions. The " Considerations " contain an able examination of Mr. Crosse's experiments. The scientific doctrines as well as illustrations of our author, must be dear to every one who has felt himself stunned by the dogmas of sceptics about what they call Spontaneous existence. The second publication is an improved and enlarged edition of a former work, in which not only the Natural History of the Silk-Worm is given, but the best system of rearing silk and cultivating the Mulberry in our colonies and islands is explained. The author continues to be of opinion that under circumstances of a regulated artificial temperature, such as is applied in the management of our exotic plants, the rearing of the silk-worm may be advantageously attempted and pursued in this country.

The last mentioned in the above list of Mr. Murray's publications presents another variety in his philanthropic studies. Its design is to point out certain improvements which have occurred to his mind, for the more certain preservation of human life when shipwrecked, or in danger of being shipwrecked in the vicinity of the shore, over and above those expedients which his ingenuity and perseverance in the cause of humanity have on former occasions detailed and made known on this subject to the world.

In a late article on Shipwrecks we pointed out the fearful amount of loss not only of property but of human life which the annual history of our maritime trade furnishes; and the fact is, as has been stated by others, " the loss of the mariner is a question that never enters into the calculation of commercial enterprise :" it is regarded as nothing more than an item in the tear and wear of business. The legislature has been wonderfully remiss on the subject. To be sure, expedients—Manby's amongst others—have been encouraged and employed for the purposes under consideration; but the benefit thereby realized has as yet been exceedingly limited. In these circumstances, any one who, like Mr. Murray, earnestly and assiduously devotes his attention to improvement in this pressing and momentous matter has a high claim to notice and welcome.

We do not profess ourselves competent to speak on the subject of Life-

Boats, or to balance the merits and defects which may belong to our author's proposals. It may be mentioned, however, that it is a very secure and complete apparatus which he contemplates ; one, indeed, which should render those who may enter it, he thinks, as safe as if they continued on land.

Mr. Murray has great objections to the *air boxes* that are very frequently attached to Life Boats, and mainly relied upon. But an extract will best elucidate his views about the improvements that may be effected in this serious and urgent branch of national and individual interests.

"It is not intended in this place to enter into a description of the construction of the common ' Life Boat,' or the principles on which its safety is founded; but to ' make assurance doubly sure,' I may be allowed to recommend that each seaman in the ' Life Boat' should be ' doubly armed,' being provided with Mr. Egerton Smith's ' cork jacket,' and there should be even a supply in the ' Life Boat' for the benefit of those rescued from the wreck.

" I would further recommend that the *oars* of the ' Life Boat' be severally locked to the gunwale, being confined by a loophole and nut screw, and move on a pivot axis or swivel fulcrum.

" Beside the buoyancy of the ' Life Boat' being secured by the application of cork to the gunwale and sides, by which the specific gravity of the mass is not only secured, and its floatage enhanced, it becomes also the means, inclusive of the peculiar form and construction, by which the ' Life Boat' recovers its upright position, when accidentally reversed by the waves.

" There appear to me, however, to be *other desiderata*, than those provided for ; and, which seem to enter into the idea of what purports to be a ' Life Boat,' as necessary and essential accessories :—*namely*, appendages or adjustments, by which the ' Life Boat' *may not be overturned*, for tho' a properly constructed ' Life Boat' *should* recover its original position, it *always* disconcerts the crew, and *may* also be connected with the loss of life.

" The required equilibrium, formed on the phenomena of the oscillation of the waves, I conceive, may be accomplished by *lowering the centre of gravity*, by means of which the ' Life Boat' will have a more firm hold of the sea, and the required equilibrium being adjusted and maintained, the surge will be less able to overturn it, or in other words—the ' Life Boat' will oppose a more firm resistance to its momentum or shock.

" The *second* improvement to perfect the end proposed, is to *extend* the floating surface above, by lateral float-boards, formed of plates of cork, in divided oblong squares, or segments ;—the resistance of the wave on the one side, by its upward pressure, &c., counterbalancing the force of the wave on the opposite side; action and reaction being equal, and the oscillating wave resisting as much as it is resisted. The cork-boards, which operate like lateral wings or fins, do *not rise* above the horizontal plane. The cork, being in segments, will not intercept, or interfere with, the free operation of the rowers ; and when not buoyant by the waves, they maintain a *vertical position*, and then act as *fenders* when the ' Life Boat' comes in contact with the wreck, or is accidentally driven against shelving rocks.

" By spindles moving in hollow cylinders, and loaded at their lower extremities with lead or iron, the centre of gravity may be considerably lowered ; and as these are moveable, and fall by their own weight, when in

shallow water, or when pulled on shore, the poises are forced upwards, and
the balls or conical masses of metal may be made to occupy cavities, prepared for their reception, in the keel of the ' Life Boat.' The *stems* of the
poises may *be perforated*, and, by means of pins, be *fixed*, so as to allow
the boat to float in very shallow water; or *metallic rope* might be substituted for the inelastic metallic rods. The upper orifices of the cylinders
being on a level with the gunwale, will prevent the water entering into
the boat, thro' that channel, as water, by a statical law, cannot rise above
its level or its source."

Mr. Murray appends certain observations concerning the construction
and the uses of a Shipwreck Arrow of his invention ; thus evidencing how
deeply and perseveringly he has directed his mind to the subject of losses
at sea; and furnishing proofs that he might most advantageously be employed
by government, or by any other great public body, in this field where so
much scope exists for scientific invention and humane efforts.

Art. XV.—*The Pilgrim's Progress : with a Life of the Author.* By
  Josiah Conder, Esq. Twenty-five Engravings. London : Fisher.
  1838.

The Editions of the Pilgrim's Progress are almost enumerable, but never
has any one appeared so superlatively handsome and beautiful as that which
is now before us. Talk of your Annuals and your Drawing-room books !
Here is a volume where art wedded to piety and religion may be said to
walk in her highest vocation, and to do that which Raphael would not have
deemed unworthy of his seraphic genius. We marvel how John Bunyan
would have felt had he seen himself in this imposing, exquisite, yet becoming dress. Not to speak of Mr. Melville's drawings, which, by different
hands, have been engraved according to the highest rules and models of
modern art, the letter-press is so transparently tasteful and rich, that no
Prayer-book can surpass it for the soft harmonies and appealing power of
its tone. The engravings as pictures are grand, and to be appreciated
require to be examined. Nay, the wood-cuts interspersed and woven
around leading capital letters, or pointed passages, in the allegory, are,
perhaps, the very softest and most illustrative that we ever beheld. In
fact, we strive in vain to give utterance to our estimation of this most
beautiful and adequate edition of the Pilgrim's Progress. Still, despairing
as we do, to describe the merits of its artistic and mechanical features, the
Memoir prefixed from the pen of Mr. Conder admits of transference to our
pages, and accordingly we quote a sample of it, beginning at the beginning. The biographer says—" The most popular religious book in English
literature—in which the most popular books are of a religious character—
is the production of an uneducated peasant, who worked his way out of the
lowest vice and ignorance, not by the force of his genius, so much as by
that of an impulse which quickened his genius into life, and transformed
him at once intellectually and morally. The finest specimen of well-sus-
tained allegory in any language, is the composition of this self-taught
ru t.o, who little aimed at literary celebrity in the homely parable which he
wrote to solace his prison hours, for the religious instruction of the common
people. The most admirable exposition of the elements of Christian theology
—one which is so little of a controversial or sectarian character, that it may

confessedly be read without offence by sober-minded Protestants of all per-
suasions, and yet so comprehensive, as to form the best popular body of
divinity—is the composition of an itinerant preacher, whose apostolic labours
consigned him, in the days of the Stuarts, to a twelve years' imprisonment,
in Bedford gaol, for no other crime than noncomformity. What is still
more remarkable, this work, the Odyssey of the English people—the
favourite with young and old; which the poet admires for its imaginative
beauty, and in which the artist finds the most delightful subjects for the
pencil, to the extraordinary merit of which, testimony has been borne by
critics who have had no sympathy with either the design and religious spirit
of the work, or the theological opinions interwoven with it, and who rank the
realities shadowed in the allegory with the creations of romance;—this
work—we need not name it—the Pilgrim's Progress, is, in fact, a powerful
address to the conscience; having no other object than to delineate the
successive stages of the spiritual life, and to portray the mental conflicts of
experimental piety, which, to those who have no corresponding experience,
must appear the hallucination of fanaticism. Strange that a work should
have power so to please the imagination of an indevout man, which can be
understood only by the heart in which religion has its seat;—that those
who have not the key to the cipher, should still admire the character in
which the spiritual meaning is veiled, and which experience alone can perfectly interpret."

We feel assured that the present edition of this unmatched work will
contribute to its celebrity, and be the channel of more widely experienced
results than have ever yet distinguished even its unexampled history.

ART. XVI.—*Anǵya, The Prophetess of Méwar. A Poem, in six
Cantos.* By ÉLIZABETH STEWART. London: Smith, Elder, and Co.
1838.

A MELANCHOLY passage in Oriental history, and as partly given by Colonel
Tod in his " Annals of Rajast-han," forms the theme of this poem. Little
more of it than the two first Cantos have reached us, and therefore it is
impossible to judge what may be the impression produced by the whole
when published. Of the versification and the fair writer's poetic powers,
a specimen highly creditable to her, will be'found in the opening lines.

" Beneath 'a group of cypress trees that wave,
O'er the arched entrance of a gloomy cave,
Silent she sits, and marks the purpling skies,
While evening gales and evening odours rise,
There is a scene around her which might still
The fiercest impulses of human will.
'Tis night !—but night without a shade, a cloud,
One flower of earth, one star of heaven to shroud.
On either hand, each mountain's roseate brow,
Is softly glittering in the moonbeams now :
And as their dark and dangerous steeps decline,
To fertile valleys, or the drear ravine,
The lofty cotton tree uplifts his form,
Monarch of woods, and victor of the storm,
Waves the cool plaintain, the Maduga showers,

The perfume of its gorgeous crimson flowers.
The branches of the hallowed peepul there
Tremblingly wanton in the soft clear air.
The zambak round the stately mango weaves
Its exquisitely white, and fragrant leaves."

To this sketch of scenery, one of character may be added ; in which, however, the rhythm is not faultless. The ideas as well as the language are somewhat prosaic in this latter extract.

" So passed the young years of that lonely child,
By her sweet thirst for knowledge most beguiled ;
No feebleness of her weak sex could bring,
The chain to fetter her mind's eagle wing.
In those pursuits by which the soul descries
How it has lost its region in the skies ;
And with such vividness her piercing thought,
The impress of each new instruction caught,
That her acquirements, indeed, might seem
Remembrances of some forgotten theme.
And then, benevolent Kaníya's name,
How idolized by her young heart became ;
And that stern god to whom her life was vowed,
With how much more of wondering awe she bowed
Before him—then the Bramin from his store,
To her imparted some sublimer lore—
Of how the soul when purified away
From lingering defilements of its clay,
Advancing in sublimity and love,
Should pass from glorious realm, to realm above !
And while the old man thus the hour beguiled,
Anáya lifted up her head and smiled,
And half forgot her present wayward fate,
In dreaming of that better, happier state."

ART. XVII.—*Letter to Lord Glenelg, on Negro Apprenticeship.* By JOHN INNES.

THE author of this letter made a tour through the British colonies in the West Indies in 1835, to procure, as he informs his readers, correct information for Government on the state of these settlements and possessions, and on all questions affecting their future prosperity. He also professes to have ever since exerted himself in bringing under the noble Secretary's notice, whatever was likely to aid in preparing for the unqualified freedom of the Apprentices in 1840. It is but natural, therefore, that he should attach himself to the unpopular government view of the subject. At the same time his minute acquaintance with the colonies under consideration and with the working of the Apprenticeship entitles the pamphlet to particular attention ; while his account of certain official returns, and his corrections of certain misrepresentations, go to strengthen the view of those who maintain that the interests of the apprentices as well as of the planters, together with the sanctity of national faith, can only be consulted and observed by resisting the measures advocated in Exeter Hall, and at other great popular meetings.

Art. XVIII.—*The Dramatic Works of William Shakspeare, with Remarks on his Life and Writings.* By Thomas Campbell. London: Moxon. 1838.

This large-papered and double-columned octavo which extends to about *nine hundred and sixty* pages, is to be followed by the Dramatic Works of Beaumont and Fletcher, the Introduction by Southey, and the Works of Ben Jonson, Memoir by Barry Cornwall. The letter-press is bold and clear; the text is not smothered among notes or references; while the whole in all its features is noble and massive, as one desires to behold the garb and bearing of the greatest of our dramatic princes. The price is moderate, being only *twenty shillings*; so that when taken together with the kindred works announced, a stately dramatic library will be at the command of every one, at a charge that has generally been considered moderate for any of the three separate publications.

The writers of the Memoirs and Introductory Remarks have been judiciously selected and appointed: in this respect the cast has been such as must widely recommend the large undertaking.

It is of the author of the "Pleasures of Hope," that we have now alone to speak; his Remarks, which claim attention rather on account of their liveliness and playfulness of spirit than effort to be original and profound, pleasantly guide the mind to the exhaustless treasures that follow. The anxiety which we naturally experience to become acquainted with the Bard of Avon's personal history and character, regarding which there is such a singular dearth of facts for one who has enchained the world's wonder, is finely perceived and expressed by Mr. Campbell. Still, it is not clear that a gratification of curiosity in the mere matter of biography would enhance our love or admiration of Shakspeare. Perhaps it is as well that we a e left to invest him with attributes that harmonize rather with his magic powers than with every-day reality, which, without doubt, even in his case, developed frailties and errors that might have marred the worship of posterity.

It is better, we think, that we should look for Shakspeare's life in his works than in any circumstantial memoir; nor to the searching and discerning student will the effort be found barren of delightful results. Indeed we observe that a work is on the eve of publication, called "Shakspeare's Autobiographical Poems;" and the writer of it professes to develop the Bard's character from his creations, stating that the key, simple as it may appear, unlocks every difficulty, and presents a pure and uninterrupted stream of biography. Mr. Campbell has to a certain extent adopted the same idea. He says,

"'The Tempest,' indeed, has a sort of sacredness as the last work of the mighty workman. Shakspeare, as if conscious that it would be his last, and, as if inspired to typify himself, has made its hero a natural, a dignified, and benevolent magician, who could conjure up spirits from the vasty deep, and command supernatural agency by the most seemingly natural and simple means. And this final play of our poet has magic indeed; for what can be simpler in language than the courtship of Ferdinand and Miranda, and yet what can be more magical than the sympathy with which it subdues us? Here Shakspeare himself is Prospero, or rather the superior genius who commands both Prospero and Ariel. But the time was approaching when the potent Sorcerer was to break his staff, and to bury it fathoms in the ocean—

      ' Deeper than did ever plummet sound.'

That staff has never been, and never will be, recovered."

The following passage affords another instance of the manner in which the songster of " Hope" speculates concerning the Sorcerer.

" A ' Midsummer Night's Dream' (1594.)—Addison says, ' When I look at the tombs of departed greatness, emotion of envy dies within me.' I have never been so sacrilegious as to envy Shakspeare, in the bad sense of the word, but if there can be such an emotion as sinless envy, I feel it towards him ; and if I thought that the sight of his tombstone would kill so pleasant a feeling, I should keep out of the way of it. Of all his works, the ' Midsummer Night's Dream' leaves the strongest impression on my mind, that this miserable world must have, for once at least, contained a happy man. This play is so purely delicious, so little intermixed with the painful passions from which poetry distils her sterner sweets, so fragrant with hilarity, so bland and yet so bold, that I cannot imagine Shakspeare's mind to have been in any other frame than that of healthful ecstasy when the sparks of inspiration thrilled through his brain in composing it.'

On the subject of scholarship, and its influence on poetic genius, Mr. C. speaks thus,—

" If learning could come intuitively, I have no doubt that it would enrich genius; but the toil and absorption of mind bestowed in acquiring it—the unoriginal habits of thinking—nay, the prejudices liable to accompany its acquisition—the cramping of the soul from its natural impulses and meditations—these, I apprehended, are the drawbacks on whatever advantages to inspiration may accrue from laboriously acquired erudition. It was predicted of a young man lately belonging to one of our universities, that he would certainly become a prodigy because he read sixteen hours a day. ' Ah !' but, said somebody, ' how many hours a-day does he think ?' It might have been added, ' How many hours does he feel ?' Still we have evidence that Shakspeare revelled in the fictions of antiquity, and understood its characters and moral truths. There is not a doubt that he lighted up his glorious fancy at the lamp of classical mythology :

    ' Hyperion's curls—the front of Jove himself,
     An eye like Mars, to threaten and command ;
     A station like the herald Mercury,
     New lighted on a heaven-kissing hill,'

Who can read these lines without perceiving that Shakspeare had imbibed a deeper feeling of the beauty of Pagan mythology than a thousand pedants could have imbibed in their whole lives ? How many years he was at the grammar-school has not been determined ; they may have been three, or they may have been six. At the lowest supposition he acquired some, though small Latin ; but, before we conclude that it was very small, let us recollect that Shakspeare was here the schoolboy, and not a commonplace lout. I grant that, after entering into the cares of life, it is not very probable he should have cultivated his classic acquirements. The best scholars hold their tenure of erudition on a repairing lease ; and many who have been once learned have given up their lease to avoid the trouble of repairs. The little tenement of his schoolboy learning it can scarcely be imagined that Shakspeare afterwards mended ; nevertheless, I suspect that he had much reading, how far, soever, it might fall short of erudition. There are symptoms of his having known something of French, and, if he knew any-thing of Latin, a certain requirement of Spanish and Italian was of easy access to him. Whether the latter suspicion be true or not, is it possible to conceive Shakspeare, in question of his plots, not to have been an active reader; and supposing his reading to have been desultory, it is not inex-plicable that desultory reading should have been a mighty aliment to his fancy. His mind was an alembic of sweets. The bee is not fed on fields of sugar-cane, but on the bitter herbs of the mountains; and on those mountains the most beautiful and best-tasted wild birds are better nourished that are our caged and crammed domestic fowls. I once examined the stomach of a wild bird killed in the Highlands; its feathers were splendid, and its flesh was white, firm and plump, but in its crop there was nothing but heather-bells. I had been reading the works of Burns, and could not help saying to myself—'Well, poor thing! thou seemest to me a Burns among birds, since in the wild air of nature thou couldst fatten upon heather-bells!' Shakspeare's learning, whatever it was, gave him hints as to sources from which classical information was to be drawn. The age abounded in classical translations; it also teemed with public pageants, and Allegory itself might be said to have walked the streets. He may have laughed at the absurdity of many of those pageants, but still they would refresh his fancy. Whether he read assiduously or carelessly, it should be remembered that reading was to him not of the vulgar benefit that it is to ordinary minds. Was there a spark of sense or sensibility in any author on whose works he glanced, that spark assimilated to his soul, and it belonged to it as rightfully as the light of heaven to the eye of the eagle.''

There is novelty as well as manifest justice in some of these views. We have only room to quote farther Mr. Campbell's solution of the question about Hamlet's inconsistencies, viz., " that his morbid mind is endued both with the reality and the affectation of madness. Such cases are not unknown in the history of mental aberration."

The remarks bestowed upon each play may be understood from these few specimens to have no slight share of illustrative point about them ; and we may add, the poet is often to be detected in the critic.

ART. XIX.—*A Letter to Sir James R. Carnac, Bart., on British Inter-ference with the Religious Observances of the Natives of India.* London : Allen & Co. 1838.

THE author, who seems to have had much experience in India, is very angry, especially with those persons who have designated the much-talked-of Pilgrim Tax Regulation a direct encouragement of Idolatry. Some of the facts and suggestions which he has set before us deserve careful consideration ; but we have also felt in perusing the Letter that a spirit of Special Pleading pervades it, and that the author is not always con-sistent. We have not, for instance, found his reasoning satisfactory when endeavouring to show that the withdrawing the protection of our Indian Government from the Hindoo worship, is the same thing, as respects the Hindoos, as active and direct measures intended for the suppression of their Paganism.

Art. XX..—*An Analytical and Comparative View of all Religions now extant among Mankind.* By Josiah Conder. London: Jackson and Walford. 1838.

We have heard it alleged that the only person calculated to write a history of all religions, would be one of no religion at all, neither in reality nor professedly. The observation has more of smartness in it than soundness or truth; for while it must be admitted, that there is a danger of strong prejudices operating on the mind of any man who attaches himself to any particular creed, when he comes to perform the part of a historian, interpreter, or commentator, in regard to such matters, still a person of no religious belief is sure to be a despiser and scoffer of whatever system he happens to treat, and is therefore as likely to present an erroneous and uncharitable account as will occur between those who agree upon some first principles and leading doctrines. At the same time, to go no further than the Christian world, what a lamentable diversity and rancorous opposition do exist! Whoever, therefore, like Mr. Conder, undertakes to communicate a correct view of the whole and of each creed and profession, " with their Internal Diversities," ought to be widely and deeply informed, as well as dispassionate and tolerant. To this comprehensiveness of information our author may safely lay claim; for honesty of purpose, and earnestness to do complete justice to all sects and churches, we also think, he has a right to demand credit. At the same time the strictest rules of impartiality require not of him, either in justice to his readers or himself, that he should withhold an explanation of matters of faith which his own creed recognises and upon which he reposes his everlasting hopes. That creed, we need not say to those that are to any extent acquainted with Mr. Conder's former writings, is what is understood by the term Scriptural, the peculiar doctrines of the Gospel being fully and sincerely believed in by him. But even to persons who may be of a different way of thinking, the vast mass of information crowded into this thick volume ought to recommend it strongly. It may justly be regarded as a work which has kept pace with the religious community of all shades, bringing the reader down to the present day, and planting him upon an eminence from which he may direct a mighty and momentous survey.

Art. XXI.—*A Brief Compendium of Arithmetic.* By Benjamin Snowden. London: Simpkin & Marshall. 1838.

Mr. Snowden informs us that for more than fifty years his time has been devoted to the instruction of youth. This we can well believe, for the clear, concise, and practical form of this Compendium testify as much. As an introduction to larger treatises on Arithmetic we recommend the small volume.

Art. XXII.—*Lavater's Original Maxims, &c.* By B. Werthem. Nisbet and Co. London: 1838.

This tome is almost too tiny and slender to catch the eye, especially when by the side of some of the formidable volumes which load our table. Its contents, however, are of the nature of gems which must not be estimated according to bulk, but to intrinsic quality.

ART. XXIII.—*An Opening of the Mystery of the Tabernacle.* By JOHN VIZARD. London : Crofts. 1838.

THIS is a comment on the first eight verses of the twenty-fifth chapter of Exodus, in which close biblical research, learning, and ardent piety manifest their valuable and impressive fruits. The author regards the portion of Scripture he has here expounded as forming a part of a great allegorical mystery which enfolds the most solemn and substantial truths that can engage the mind of man. The manner in which he has compared Scripture with Scripture, thence deducing much of his exposition, enables the reader to discover a mine of spiritual truth where all may have previously appeared barren, idly fanciful, or impenetrably obscure.

ART. XXIV.—*The Education of the Feelings.* London : Taylor and Walton. 1838.

THIS is a modest, well-intended, and well-executed little work. It is designed " to urge the great importance of Moral Education—to shew the bearing of a few great truths upon it—to point out the Natural Laws which the Creator has established, by which the feelings are to be trained and cultivated." The volume does not profess to contain original views on the subject of education ; for who in this age, so remarkable for enlightened, extensive, and systematic books treating of physical, mental, and moral culture can flatter himself with the idea that he has great discoveries to communicate? The object of the work is better : it is addressed to those who have not enjoyed an opportunity of studying larger and systematic treatises in this department of theoretical and practical knowledge, while from these more imposing and formidable sources it draws the best lessons plentifully. A short extract from the preface will aptly close our notice. " New works on Education are constantly ushered forth—the subject is not new to the world, but it is ever so to individuals. Every one newly invested with the office of parent, feels as fresh and vivid an interest in it as if no one had ever been educated before, and seeks eagerly for light and information. To such no apology will be necessary for giving additional testimony to truths which, if known, have not been sufficiently acted upon."

ART. XXV.—*Mrs. Wilberforce ; or, The Widow and her Orphan Family.* London : Saunders & Otley. 1838.

THE name chosen for this novel, we fear, will operate to its disadvantage, by suggesting ideas that readers will consider unnecessary and indeed unpleasant. The fiction also labours under those drawbacks which a too copious infusion of religion exhibits. The work, however, is evidently the production of one accustomed to study human character, and to indulge in earnest reflection upon the phenomena which that world of wonders is continually developing.

ART. XXVI.—*Hood's Own ; Or, Laughter from Year to Year.* No. V. London : Baily & Co. 1838.

HOOD sustains his humour admirably in this number, and in a variegated form too. Just let the heart that rejoices in pure fun turn to a piece entitled "Refusing Tithes," and author and artist will be found to combine their powers in fine style; or if a striking name afford an argument in behalf of a tale, take that of the "Great Plague," and no disappointment will be experienced even on the part of those who entertain the most favourable opinion of Mr. Hood's genius. In truth our creator of "Laughter from Year to Year" presents a phenomenon in literature; for his humour and wit are sterling as well as original and inexhaustible.

Art. XXVII.—*The Popular Encyclopædia.* Glasgow: Blackie. 1838.
The half volume before us brings this far-famed work forward to the word *Sun.* The punctuality and rapidity of the appearance of its progressing Parts when considered in connexion with the intrinsic and original merits of the Lexicon, render the improved and enlarged edition the most desirable work of the kind that is published, upon anything like a similar scale, or at a similar expense.

Art. XXVIII.—*The Practical Works of Jeremy Taylor. With a Sketch of his Life and Times.* By the Rev. George Crolly, LL.D. London: Rickerby. 1838.
The present portable, handsome, and, indeed, elegant edition of the most fervent and devotional works of one of England's most eminent divines and writers extends to eight volumes, post octavo. These volumes contain the Life of Christ, Holy Living, Holy Dying, The Golden Crown, The Worthy Communicant, Select Sermons, and The Liberty of Prophesying. In these works Taylor's copiousness, his fertility of composition, his eloquence of expression, his fervour of devotional feeling, his impressiveness and richness of thought, are universally allowed to be amazing—to have the power to melt as well as to exalt. This exemplary Prelate was certainly one of the most gifted and most sanctified of men. Not to dwell upon his mental endowments, he possessed the advantages of a comely person, and a melodious voice which were the suitable organs of a never ceasing flow of piety and pure religious ardour in thought and action. This edition will be the means of extending the influence of this great writer's choicest works, and of showing to those who may be ignorant of the treasures of divinity which our language has embodied, that unsurpassed beauty of imagery and comprehensiveness of illustration are the appropriate handmaidens of Christianity.

Art. XXIX.—*Rambles in the Pyrennees; and a Visit to San Sebastian.* By F. W. Vaux, Esq. London: Longman. 1838.
A slight, but modest and elegant narrative, detailing the particulars of a hasty tour through certain most interesting parts. The tone and temper of the author are really well calculated to induce others to visit the regions and spots which he describes, and at the same time to indicate the dispositions which an Englishman ought to cherish when he passes from his own fire-side to foreign parts. Mr. Vaux must be a desirable travelling companion; for intelligence and taste as well as activity and good humour characterize his volume.

Art. I.—*Animal Magnetism and Homœopathy.* By Edwin Lee, M.R.C.S.
London : Whittaker & Co. 1838.

It is said that when Dr. Treviranus, an eminent physician of Bremen,
visited London, Coleridge, who took a deep interest in the subject
of Animal Magnetism, anxiously inquired of the foreigner what
were the real facts relative to the phenomena of which he was
reported to have been an eye-witness. The reply is stated to have
been to the following effect,—" I have seen what I am certain I
would not have believed on your testimony, and that which I am
therefore bound to suppose you cannot believe on mine." After the
time we refer to, the subject attracted little attention in this country,
until a very recent date ; but seeing that it has been revived, and
that it is discussed with greater earnestness than ever, it may be
right that we should endeavour to let our readers have an opportunity of judging whether the Bremen Physician's answer indicated
a weak credulity, or wisdom and a philosophic tolerance. And in
this endeavour we shall avail ourselves of the statements contained
in the slender volume before us, and of some other sources of information, together with such testing criticisms and analogous cases
as may seem pertinent and fair.

But before we proceed further, it is proper that reference should
be made to Mr. Lee's competency to try the questions at issue
belonging to the mysterious subject of Animal Magnetism, since he
is the authority upon whom we chiefly rely for facts and suggestions.

Let it be borne in mind then that our author is not only learnedly
but practically acquainted with the principal medical institutions
and opinions which have obtained in France, Italy, and Germany. He has travelled much on the Continent ; he has visited
and attended the hospitals of these countries ; he is the Corresponding Member of various foreign societies, connected with medical
science ; and he has written able and satisfactory works relative to
the same branch of study. Regarding certain nervous disorders,
too, he has bestowed particular attention ; his practical experience
in this department having led to a highly approved publication. In
these circumstances, it must be evident that Mr. Lee is entitled to
more than an ordinary hearing, whenever he treats of any medical
doctrine or practice which has had its birth and has found its most

kindly soil on the Continent,—in Germany for example; and that
also when any affections, supposed to have a peculiarly intimate
relation to the nervous system, are involved, or presumed by many
to be involved, he deserves to be patiently listened to.

Mr. Lee is the only medical person in this country, we believe,
who has recently written anything like a regular work on the extraordinary subject in question. Still, as already hinted, his performance is slender in point of bulk and the number of its pages, having
at first been merely appended to his " Observations on the Medical
Institutions and Practice of France, Italy, and Germany." It was
afterwards along with an account of Homœopathy published in a
separate form for the advantage of non-professional persons; and
both accounts having in this shape met with a favourable reception,
together with the circumstance of the increased interest that has
been of late excited respecting Animal Magnetism, he has been induced to put forth a second edition of the Pamphlet, in which, however, nearly twice as much matter is condensed as was at first
deemed necessary for the author's purpose. We now proceed to
present a brief sketch of the history of Animal Magnetism, considered as a system, and to a brief exposition of its pretensions and
merits.

The historical sketch and the examination of experiments can
hardly be given in a more succinct and comprehensive manner than
has been done by Mr. Lee; but as we hope that every person who
takes an interest in the subject will peruse the work for himself, we
shall only take from it such parts as may enable us in the shortest
possible way to enforce the views which we entertain.

At the outset let us endeavour to impress upon our readers the
lesson, that an obstinate incredulity is as hostile to true philosophy
and the spirit of scientific discovery as ever superstition was, or a
facile belief in any extraordinary theory in Physics that has never
been demonstrated, never experimentally proved. At the same
time let us watch lest the thing alleged be not only novel, extraordinary, and beyond our present powers of explanation, but lest it be
altogether *opposed* to our previous knowledge of nature and facts;
let us watch, whilst it wars against received prejudices, that it do
not contradict all that has been previously ascertained scientifically
and demonstrably, according to the strictest rules of philosophical
induction, of the organization of man, and the material things external to each of us: let us be on our guard whenever we find a professor of any wonderful discovery ridiculing old-fashioned opinions,
and harping upon the evils and absurdities of bigotry,—especially
if in the very next breath he declaims about the case of the " starry
Galileo," and imagines that another martyr to popular ignorance,
error, and incredulity is at hand. But the question is, do the
Animal Magnetisers either go beyond or against the utmost stretch
and strength which science and closely observed facts have carried us?

Animal Magnetism, which as a doctrine originated in Germany, that hotbed of mysticism and extravagant theories, derived the name from the influence which the magnet has upon iron, an influence somewhat analogous to this being supposed to exist in the nervous or some undefined power of one individual over another. The doctrine was introduced into France about the middle of the last century, by an individual of the name of Mesmer; hence the term "Mesmerism," which is used synonymously with animal magnetism. Mesmerism, however, has assumed a very different and much more systematic shape since that period, although its repute has been subject to various changes down to the present period. There was a great deal of jugglery in Mesmer's process. The apartment in which he performed was fitted up in an imposing form ; he made use of magnetized apparatus and mysterious forms ; he himself, while robed in light-coloured silk, wielded a magical or magnetised rod, which he pointed to the parts he wished to affect. Nor were the desired affections denied, females and men of nervous temperament being the most illustrative patients.

The cure of certain complaints seems to have been what Mesmer contemplated by his formidable parade ; but although it affected some, on many others the process had no influence. An examination of its pretensions and merits by the Académie des Sciences and the Académie de Médecine, at length robbed the doctrine of much of its consideration. Still some of the German's disciples, after he had retired with a handsome fortune, continued to practise.

"They also employed magnetised baths, recommended the drinking magnetised water, the carrying magnetised plates of glass on the stomach, and in general their treatment was calculated to produce strong crises or convulsive actions, which they considered as a remedial process of nature, and accordingly used their endeavours to bring them on by artificial means. Certain rooms called *chambres des crises* were fitted up for the purpose ; the walls and floors being covered with mattresses and cushions, to prevent the patients, while in convulsions, from injuring themselves.

"An establishment was also formed at Strasburg, under the auspices of M. de Puysegur, one of the most zealous advocates of magnetism, which was called the *Société Harmonique des Amis Réunis.* The *chambres des crises* were abolished, and in consequence of the more gentle treatment, the violent crises seldom occurred, a state of partial sleep, or approaching to somnambulism, which was unknown to Mesmer, being the most frequent effects of this mode of magnetising ; hence the persons affected have been since termed somnambulists."

After a neglect of considerable endurance, and about twenty years ago, some physicians of eminence declared themselves believers in the powers of animal magnetism, and numerous experiments were made relating to the state of sleep or somnambulism, the phenomenon most frequently witnessed. This state is said to be induced in sus-

ceptible individuals by certain movements of the Magnetiser's
hands, called *passes*. Strict silence on all present having been
enjoined, patient and spectators, the operator went through a great
number of manœuvres, such as touching, pressing various parts of
the body, and moving the hand slowly before the face and other
regions of the sitter, up and down, transversely, &c. for hours
together.

Like all other systems true or false, that of Animal Magnetism
did not at once arrive at its utmost pitch. Perfection is not easily
attained by man. It will be admitted, however, that Mesmer's discovery made its advances at a pretty fair rate. The following points
of attainment were said to be realized before the year 1825.

" In the magnetic somnambulism the individuals are said (as in natural
somnambulism) to be insensible to external stimuli, as noises of all kinds,
pungent substances applied to the nostrils, pinching, pricking, or other
mechanical irritation of the skin; but at the same time to be able to hear
when spoken to by the magnetiser, or by persons placed by him in connexion (*en rapport*) with them, to answer his questions and to perform
various actions ordered by him. These are, however, according to the
magnetisers, merely the more common effects, and the precursors of much
more wonderful phenomena, as transference of the senses, *clairvoyance*,
or mental vision, in which, though the eyes be closed and bandaged,
objects are seen by the somnambulist, either when held before his face,
or when placed in contract with the epigastrium, occiput, or other parts;
the power of predicting events; of ascertaining the nature of diseases,
and prescribing their appropriate remedies; of knowing what is taking
place at the moment in distant parts of the world, &c.

" One magnetiser, speaking of the wonders of magnetism before the
Académie, says in reference to the absolute power of the magnetiser over
the somnambulist—' If cold, you can warm him, if warm, cool him; you
blow away his pains, and his pains vanish; you change his tears to
laughter, his sorrows to joy. Are his country, his friends absent? you
cause him to see them without seeing them yourself. You can blunt his
sensibility if he have to undergo any cruel operation. You transform
water into any liquid he desires, or which you deem useful to him—you
present an empty glass, he drinks, the movements of deglutition are performed and thirst is appeased—with nothing I have calmed his hunger,
with nothing I have served him up splendid dinners,' &c. &c."

But we have not by any means reached the climax of the *soi-
disant* science; for magnetisers found out that *passes* were not
always necessary. Looks, directed steadily and for a long time,
came to be as efficacious; nay, the will of the operator solely, even
when he was not seen by the patient, or was in another room, magnetised; although this supposed influence of the will was never
effectual at the first sitting, but after repeated practisings. In fact
the pretensions of the Mesmerians became so wonderful, and their
assertions of success were so strong in 1825, that the Académie de

. Médecine had its attention again called to the subject, and appointed a commission to examine into and report upon the experiments to be instituted. The commission pursued its investigation until 1831, when it presented a report to the Académie, containing an exposition of its labours, with the inferences deduced from them, arranged under the following heads :

1. The effects of magnetism are null in persons in health, and in some invalids.
2. They are but little apparent in others.
3. They are often produced by ennui, monotony, and the power of imagination.
4. Lastly, they are developed independently of these causes, very probably by the effect of magnetism alone.

It will be perceived from the fourth head that the commissioners countenance to a certain, an undefined extent, the doctrine in question. It will also be at once perceived, that this last admission is greatly damaged by the first and third heads ; for the opponents of magnetism attribute most of the influence, boasted of by the Mesmerians, to certain states of the nervous system as affected by disease, and other conditions and phenomena familiar in medical practice—to the powers of an excited imagination—and, in short, to other causes than any under magnetisation. It is also to be borne in mind that three of the most celebrated of the commisioners refused to sign the report. At the same time let it be recollected, that men of genius and great attainments in particular branches of science, are not always destitute of an appetite for the marvellous, when the pretended phenomena do not run counter to their own established opinions which may have brought them fame. But what is of still greater importance, the commissioners, whose good faith cannot for a moment be impugned, have published the cases upon which they rely, several of which Mr. Lee has quoted and commented upon. Here are two falling under the second and third heads, in which the effects produced were attributable to ennui, the imagination, &c., it being sufficient to place persons in situations in which they believed themselves magnetised, to be stared at wearifully by grave looking persons, and all the other mummery of these exhibitions.

"Mademoiselle L. was magnetised eleven times at the Hotel Dieu, within the period of a month. At the fourth sitting, somnolency, convulsive movements of the neck and face, with other symptoms. At the eleventh sitting her magnetiser placed himself behind her without making any signs, and without the intention of magnetising, yet she experienced more decided effects than on the preceding trials.

"An hysterical girl was magnetised several times : at each time there occurred somnolency with strong convulsive actions. Being placed one day in the same chair, in the same place, at the same hour, and in presence of the same persons, the accustomed phenomena presented them-

selves, though her magnetiser was absent. A like experiment was made
on an epileptic patient and produced a similar result."

Several cases are recorded which rendered the commissioners
doubtful of the effect of animal magnetism, and not without suspicion
of a previous understanding between the magnetisers and the somnambulists. Dupotet, a personage who has of late been figuring
in England, who takes to himself the imposing title of Baron, but
who, Mr. Lee insinuates, is only a plain M., offered to solve these
doubts, and engaged to produce at will, out of sight of the somnambulist, convulsive movements in any part of the body, by the
mere action of pointing towards the part in which the commissioners
should desire to witness these effects. The result of this and other
experiments we quote as given by our author.

" A man who had already been magnetised several times was somnambulised, and after some trials on his obedience, M. Dupotet announced
that the commissioners might produce in him any effects that they
pleased.

" M. Marc, one of the commissioners, accordingly placed himself behind the somnambulist, and made sign to M. Dupotet to produce movements in the forefinger of his right hand, and afterwards in the toes; the
somnambulist made some movements, but not in the parts indicated;
similiar movements subsequently occurred without magnetisation, and
the experiment was declared inconclusive.

" The next experiment which I shall relate, was made to exhibit before
the commissioners the faculty of mental vision, or sight with closed eyelids, on a M. Petit, in whom the results of previous trials had been very
satisfactory to the magnetisers. Somnambulism having been induced,
M. Petit was requested to select a piece of money from others held in the
hand of the magnetiser; this was done, the coin was marked and mixed
with twelve others, and the somnambulist was desired to point out the
one he had selected; he however took the wrong one. A watch was
presented to him, he mistook the hour. Other objects were also presented,
but he could never discover immediately what they were; he took them
in his hands, felt and turned them over, brought them near his eyes, and
after all, generally guessed wrong; he was able to read a few lines,
while the commissioners watched that his eyelids were closed. There is
no doubt, however, that the eyes were partially opened, as he could not
distinguish anything when a bandage was placed before them. Although
clairvoyance had been talked of by the magnetisers as a very common
phenomenon of magnetism, it was only exhibited two or three times before
the commissioners during a period of six years, and the results were
similiar to those above-mentioned.

" The following cases are given, as cures performed by magnetism.

" A law student, labouring under a paralytic affection of the limbs, was
treated by the usual means at La Charité, and at the expiration of five
months was so far recovered as to be able to get about on crutches. In
this state he was magnetised by M. Foissac. In the ninth sitting complete somnambulism was induced; he answered questions, spoke of his

disease, announced that in a month he should be able to walk about without crutches, and prescribed for himself nux vomica, sinapisms, and baths of Barèges water ; these being the remedies from which he had already derived advantage. On the day he had named, the commission repaired to La Charité, anxious to see whether his prediction would be fulfilled. On being somnambulised, the patient declared that when he awoke he should return to his bed without crutches or other support. When awakened, he asked for his crutches, but was answered that he did not require them : he arose, traversed the courts, walked up stairs, and from that day he has never used the crutches. In subsequent trials he presented the phenomena of *clairvoyance* as completely as M. Petit.

" The next case was at the time matter of great astonishment, as illustrating the extraordinary power of magnetism.

" A lady laboured under a nervous disease, which had resisted all the efforts directed against it ; she at length became oppressed with the idea that magnetism alone could cure her, and was accordingly magnetised by M. Chapelain. ' One day she went to M. Chapelain, supporting herself with difficulty on crutches ; it was pitiable to see her suffer. Armed with a benevolent will, M. Chapelain by magnetism dispersed the pains in the limbs, the sighings and gloomy thoughts with which she was affected, and restored tranquillity to this person, so cruelly agitated an instant before. " Are you well ?" he inquired. " O yes, sir, I thank you." She slept for about two hours, and on awaking walked away, carrying the crutches which had supported her on her arrival !'

" In the first of these cases it is pretty evident that the patient was already convalescent at the time the magnetic trials were made, and could most probably have walked without crutches, had he so chosen, as well at the expiration of a week as of a month. The second is one of those cases which frequently puzzles the practitioner,—of the nature of which I have offered an explanation in my work on nervous disorders, requiring for their cure an exertion of the faculty of volition, which is frequently induced by strong moral impressions. I have related one or two analogous cases suddenly cured in this way, and capable of rational explanation, without the intervention of magnetism or supernatural agency.

" I subjoin one more of the cases brought forward in proof of magnetic influence.

" A journeymen carpenter, aged twenty, subject to epileptic attacks was magnetised at the hospital of La Charité. Somnambulism was not, however, induced till after several sittings. The patient at length announced, that on a certain day, at a certain hour, he would have an attack. It accordingly took place at the time he had specified. When interrogated, while in somnambulism, respecting his disease, he declared that at the end of a year the attacks would cease ; he also mentioned the exact time at which the two following attacks would take place. These occurred at the time he predicted, and the fact of his cure only remained to be proved ; but before the expiration of the year, he was run over by a cabriolet and killed ; a circumstance which magnetism did not enable him to foresee.

" The profession will not form any very exalted opinion of the intelligence of the commissioners from the relation of these cases as illustrations of the effects produced solely by the power of magnetism. Those who have seen much of nervous diseases, are well aware analogous cases to that of the lady above-mentioned often spontaneously recover, especially after the occurence of any circumstance which forcibly strikes their imagination; and the fits of epilepsy are also frequently produced or suspended by a similar influence : this is also one of the diseases most easily feigned ; hence there would be no difficulty in predicting the period of an attack.　But had the individuals been able to foretel the occurrence of diseases which cannot be simulated, or which are less influenced by the mind—as intermittents or inflammatory affections—the commissioners might with reason have adduced such instances in proof of the magnetic power."

Really the ages of credulity, trickery, and delusion have not all fled ; and it is ridiculous were it not pitiable to know that grave and well-educated men amongst us are at this very moment lending all the monstrous absurdities in question, their earnest countenance and support, some by their positive, and many others by their suspended belief.

On the nature of the sleep pretended to be induced by the magnetisers, our author offers various important suggestions which his own experience and that of other medical practitioners render familiar.　Besides the ennui caused by monotonous and long-continued actions, he notices cases of partial sleep to which nervous and hysterical persons are subject, and during which they answer questions relating to matters on which their thoughts have been much occupied, although they remain unaffected by loud noises.　But it is said that the magnetised somnambulists are insensible to pinching and other external stimulants which ordinarily produce visible emotions and movements in the patient ; and on this circumstance great stress is laid.　We call attention to a strong case of insensibility, which has been repeatedly adduced in proof of magnetic influence.　It is that of a female on whom M. Cloquet performed the operation of amputating a cancerous breast while she was in somnambulism.　To an inquiry during the operation as to whether she experienced pain, she answered in the negative, and only complained of a tickling when the sponge was applied to the bleeding surface.　Now hear what Mr. Lee has to append to this.

" Insensibility to this extent is not unfrequently met with in various states of the nervous system—as ecstasy, mental aberration, epilepsy, &c., in which the persons have received serious wounds without appearing to feel pain.　It occasionally happens, after an injury of the head, while the patient lies in a state of coma, that he is able to answer questions, but appears insensible to the operation of trepanning the skull, or dividing the scalp.　Pinel, in his Nosographie Philosophique, mentions the case of a priest, who in a fit of mental absence, was insensible to the pain of burning.　Mr. Wardrop extirpated a tumour from the head of a young woman while she was in a state of syncope from the abstraction of blood. She was carried to her bed, and would not believe the operation had been performed till a looking-glass enabled her to verify the circumstance. I might adduce many other instances to show that the above case is not so singular as it would at first sight appear, especially to non-professional persons."

But a magnetiser, who was either really ignorant of such instances, or if not ignorant duplicit, called some sixteen months ago upon M. Oudet, a dentist and member of the Académie, concerning a lady stated to be in a state of somnambulism ; and this lady after certain prickings and the ordeal of a taper's flame applied to her finger, had a molar tooth extracted by M. Oudet, when, according to Mr. Lee's succinct account, she only drew back her head and uttered a slight cry. To us this seems not at all a wonderful state of insensibility. Not to speak of what strong moral resolution will bear, as in the case of Archbishop Cranmer when brought to the stake, there are instances where persons of very weak moral purpose and energy have endured what in ordinary cases must have been excruciating pains. How often has drunkenness induced insensibility to external stimulants and inflictions ! Persons have had, we believe, their members maimed, when thus stupified and obtused, without evincing a sense of severe pain. And will not somnambulism, ecstasies, and epilectic fits, sustain similar or greater injuries without whining ? Be this as it may, the case to which M. Oudet's attention was called, occasioned very animated discussions in the Académie on Animal Magnetism ; and Dr. Berna, who had been lecturing on the subject, sent a proposition to this learned body, offering to convince its members by their personal experience of the powers of magnetism. The proposition was accepted, and a commission was appointed, consisting of members who were theoretically both for and against Animal Magnetism. We must here introduce a long extract.

" The first meeting of the commissioners to witness the experiments took place on the 3rd of March, 1837, at the house of M. Roux, their president, where M. Berna met them, and shortly after went away in order to bring a somnambulist who waited for him in the neighbourhood. In a few minutes he returned, introducing a young girl seventeen or eighteen years of age, of a rather delicate and nervous appearance, but whose manner was unembarrased and resolved."

" The number of experiments for the evening amounted to eight; viz. 1st. Somnambulisation. 2nd. Ascertaining the existence of insensibility to pricking and tickling. 3rd. Restoration of the sensibility by the will of the magnetiser mentally expressed. 4th. Obedience to the order mentally expressed, to stop in the middle of a conversation; and, 5th, again to answer on the mental order of the magnetiser. 6th. Repetition of the same experiment, the magnetiser being separated from the somnambulist by a door. 7th. Awaking from somnambulism. 8th. In obedience to the mental order signified during somnambulism, persistance of insensibility when awakened, as also persistence of the faculty of losing or recovering sensibility, at the will of the magnetiser.

" The young girl was received by the commissioners with great kindness and affability; and, with a view to ascertain before magnetisation to what degree she was sensible to pricking in the ordinary state, her hand and neck were pricked with needles procured by M. Berna; to the inquiries of some of the commissioners, if she felt the pricking, she answered positively, that she felt nothing, nor did her face express any sign of pain. It must be remembered that she was perfectly awake, even to the acknowledgment of the magnetiser, who had not begun any part of his process. This did not agree with the proposition, as the insensibility was only to be manifested in the state of somnambulism, and subsequent to the mental injunction of the magnetiser; the commissioners were therefore somewhat surprised at this singular commencement. On further questioning, however, she admitted that she felt a little pain. After these preliminaries, M. Berna caused the somnambulist to sit near him, and appeared to contemplate her in silence, without making any of the movements termed passes. At the expiration of a minute or two, he announced that she was in somnambulism. Her eyes were then covered with a bandage, and after having again contemplated her, the magnetiser stated that she was struck with general insensibility.

" The proofs of insensibilty are of two kind : one kind rests upon the mere assertion of the individuals, upon which it is evident no reliance can be placed when there exists any motive for deceiving : the second kind are deduced from the absence of those movements or actions usually caused by painful impressions : but here must be considered both the degree of pain produced, and the firmness of the persons on whom the experiment is made. In the present case the amount of pain was not to exceed a certain point rigorously fixed by M. Berna.

" Some of the commissioners pricked the girl with needles : she did not complain of any pain, nor did her face (the upper half of which was partly covered by the bandage) show any indication of suffering. One of the commissioners, however, having pricked her under the chin more forcibly than the rest, she performed with vivacity the action of swallowing. M. Berna, who perceived it, complained of the needle having been introduced into the chin deeper than was allowed. He then informed the commissioners that he was about to paralyse, by the tacit intervention of his will, either the sensibility or the motion of any part of the somnambulist's body that was required; he, however, restricted the parts to be acted upon—1st, to the two legs; 2ndly, to the two arms; 3rdly, an arm and leg; 4thly, one arm or one leg; 5thly, to the neck, turning to the right or to the left; and 6thly, to the tongue, as far as motion was concerned; and either the whole or a part of the body as regarded sensation.

" Here, according to the injunctions of the magnetiser, the only orders that could be given to the somnambulist were—' Raise the arm'—' Raise the leg'—' Turn the head to the right or to the left'—or, ' Speak.' Thus, if when one of the commissioners said, ' Raise the left arm,' the arm were not raised, M. Berna wished it to be considered as proved that the arm was paralysed—that it was so paralysed of his tacit will, and that this was the result of animal magnetism. He also desired the commissioners, if they should not at first succeed, not to be discouraged, but to continue till they obtained the requisite effect, viz.paralysis of the part desired.

" At a second sitting, having, as he stated, placed the young girl in a state of somnambulism, M. Bouillaud required M. Berna, in writing, to paralyse the motion of the somnambulist's right arm only, and when it was done, to inform him, by closing his eyes. M. Berna, after a short period, made the sign agreed upon, which implied that his tacit will had been powerful enough to paralyse the right arm of the somnambulist's. M. Bouillaud proceeded to verify the fact, and requested the girl to move such or such limbs. When he requested her to move the right leg, she answered that she could neither move the right leg nor the right arm. Thus, although, according to the arrangement previously agreed upon, one limb only was to be paralysed, it appeared that two limbs were deprived of motion. The experiment was therefore considered to have failed, as the commissioners were not so simple as to repeat the trials till they succeeded.

" In the next experiment on the same person M. Berna proposed to the commissioners to repeat the series of experiments, viz., abolition or restitution of sensibility, either partial or total privation of restitution of movements; the faculty of hearing or not hearing a person speaking, &c. After the girl was said to be in a state of somnambulism, M. Bouillaud requested M. Berna, by writing, to deprive the somnambulist of the power of hearing him, and to touch the shoulder of another commissioner, as a sign that he had done so. He then began to converse with the somnambulist, but before the magnetiser had made the sign agreed upon, she appeared not to hear him ; but when the signal was given, she answered M. Bouillaud's questions, which was just the reverse of what ought to have happened. But the magnetiser had spoken to the commissioners about the wonderful facts of vision without the assistance of the eyes—of the famous transposition of the senses so much talked of in the annals of magnetism ; they were therefore naturally desirous to witness facts of this nature, and on the next occasion repaired to the house of M. Berna, whom they found in company with a woman about thirty years of age. After their arrival he covered her eyes with a bandage, and then stated that she was in somnambulism, and began to converse with her. It was agreed, that in this sitting there were to be two kinds of facts by which magnetism was to be tested, viz., 1st, facts, the solution of which were to be proposed to the woman said to be in somnambulism, but known to M. Berna ; and 2ndly, facts, of which the solution was also to be proposed to the subject of the experiment, but of which facts M. Berna should be ignorant. Thus, as an example of the first kind, M. Berna began by asking the woman how many persons were 'present. 'Several,' she replied, ' at least five.' This was a fact known to M. Berna, as well as to the commissioners, and also to the somnambulist herself, as her eyes were not bandaged till after their arrival. One of the commissioners was then requested by the magnetiser to write one or more words on a card. (A pack of white cards and a pack of playing cards lay on a table in the room.) The commission wrote on one of the white cards the word Pantagruel, in letters perfectly distinct, and going behind the somnambulist, placed this card against her occiput : the magnetiser was seated in front of the somnambulist, and was ignorant of the word written ; this was consequently a fact of the second kind ; that is to say, decisive in itself. The somnambulist, interrogated by the magnetiser as to what was placed at the back of her head, answered with some hesitation, that it was

something white, like a visiting card. So far there was nothing surprising.
M. Berna had, in a loud voice, requested the commissioner to take a card
and write something upon it; but she was further asked if she did not see
anything upon the card, to which she resolutely replied, ' Yes, there is
writing.'—' Is the writing large or small?'—' Pretty large,' she replied.
' What has been written?'—' Wait a moment, I do not distinguish well;
there is first an M. Yes, it is a word beginning with an M.' Such were
the first answers of the somnambulist. A plain white card was then passed
to the commissioner unknown to the magnetiser; this was substituted for
the card on which the word Pantagruel was written. The somnambulist
persisted, notwithstanding, in saying that she saw a word beginning with
an M. She subsequently added, that she saw two lines of writing, though
she could not tell what they were.

" The reporter was taking notes close to the somnambulist. The point
of the pen was distinctly heard on the paper: the somnambulist turned her
head to that side: the magnetiser asked her if she saw that gentleman.
' Yes,' she said, ' he holds in his hand something white and long.' He
then ceased writing, and passed behind the somnambulist, holding the pen
in his mouth. ' Do you see the gentleman behind?' inquired the magnetiser. ' Yes,' she replied. ' Do you see his mouth?' ' Not very well; he
has in it something white and long.' The magnetiser on this glanced with
satisfaction to the commissioners, and enjoined the reporter not to forget to
note the circumstance. After some other experiments of writing on cards,
at which the somnambulist was as much at fault as in the first instance, M.
Berna, in a loud tone, requested a commissioner to take a playing card and
place it to the occiput of the somnambulist. ' A court card?' inquired the
commissioner, ' As you please,' replied M. Berna. The commissioner,
however, instead of selecting a playing card, took a plain white one of the
same size, unknown to M. Berna, and of course to the somnambulist. He
then placed this card to her occiput. M. Berna, seated in front as before,
interrogated her. She hesitated, and at last answered that she saw a card.
On being further interrogated, she again hesitated, and then said that there
was black and red on the card. After some further efforts to induce the
somnambulist to be more explicit, the magnetiser, little satisfied with the
result of the transposition of sight to the occiput, requested the commissioner to pass the card in front of the somnambulist, close to the bandage
which covered her eyes, which was, in fact, a renunciation of the transposition of the senses, for *clairvoyance* through a bandage. The card was
quickly passed, as desired, so that M. Berna seeing the white surface of the
card, supposed that its back was turned towards himself, and the coloured
parts towards the bandage of the somnambulist. On being again questioned,
she said she now saw the card better, and then added, that she distinguished
something like a figure. M. Berna continued to question her; the somnambulist appearing to make great efforts, declared that she saw a knave.
' But which knave? there are four knaves.' She replied, ' There is black
by the side of the knave.'—' Still there are two knaves that have black on
their side.' She was again solicited by the magnetiser, and appeared to
make great efforts; at last she hit upon it—' The knave of clubs.' M.
Berna, to terminate the experiment, took the card out of the commissioner's
hand, and perceived that it was perfectly white."

Have our readers enough of this? Their answer may be *yes*, or *no;* but the commissioners had patience to witness other experiments, the results of which, however, were similar to these now described ; so that they unanimously agreed that,

" M. Berna doubtless deceived himself when he made sure of proving to the Académie, by conclusive facts, the truth of magnetism, and the elucidation by them of points of physiology and therapeutics. These facts are now known, and they are opposed to conclusions in favour of magnetism itself, and consequently they can have nothing in common, either with physiology or therapeutics.

" The commissioners will not attempt to decide whether they would have found anything more conclusive, in more numerous and varied cases furnished by other magnetisers : but one thing is certain, that if there are other magnetisers, they have not dared to come forward—they have not dared to put magnetism to the test of academical sanction or condemnation."

It must not be forgotten that in the course of the discussions in the Académie several instances of deception were brought forward, which at the time had passed current as proofs of magnetic power. Again we have recourse to Mr. Lee, whose personal and medical character will be found a sufficient voucher for the truth of that which he avers. If not, let him be answered in his own circumstantial, avowed, and calm style; and then we shall listen with patience to the magnetisers.

" M. Velpeau, in alluding to a young man who had been able to predict the periods of his epileptic attacks, and who was also said to be able to read with his eyes bandaged, says, ' I thought of looking under the bandage, which was loosely applied, and my suprise ceased. The performer of these miracles was a young law student, who had quarrelled with his friends, had no means of existence, and who entered an hospital under the pretext that he was paralytic, which was an invention. I was in the secret, and did not betray him, as it would have lost him ; although the surgeon of the hospital thought it really a paralysis, prescribed accordingly, and after uselessly trying other remedies, spoke of applying the moxa :* from that period the remedies which had been hitherto inactive performed wonders. From this hospital he went to that of La Charité, to subject himself to the experiments of magnetism.

" ' M. Georget became a zealous partisan of magnetism, after having been its opponent, and admitted its truth in his work on the nervous system : he had performed experiments, and believed them incontrovertible. M. Londe assisted at these experiments, Well, Georget carried with him to the tomb his belief in magnetism, but M. Londe has outlived him, and you have heard him declare in this assembly, that Georget and himself had been deceived, that they had been duped by some miserable creatures who have since boasted of the circumstance. However, the work exists, and

---

" * Moxa is a cylinder of ignited cotton, or other substance, applied to the skin, and by the slow action of the heat produces an ulcer.

its author is no longer here to rectify the errors it contains. In conclusion I say, that whenever the facts stated by the magnetisers to have occurred, have been inquired into, the wonderful has disappeared.'

"The following case of *clairvoyance* was a great deal talked about at the time, and has been inserted as a fact by Mr. Colquhoun in his work. ' Petronilla Leclerc, at twenty-six, admitted into the hospital of La Charité, in 1830, under the care of Dr. Fouquier, was afflicted with a cerebro-spas-modic epileptiform complaint. M. Sebire, who had the care of her, mag-netised her several times, and some remarkable phenomena were manifested. In the first sitting the somnambulist gave several marks of lucidity : some objects were presented to her, as a bottle filled with vinegar, sugar, bread, &c. which she recognised perfectly well without seeing them, as she had a bandage over her eyes. When answering the questions put to her, she turned to the opposite side and plunged her face in the pillow; without being asked, she said to the person who was holding her hand, ' You have got a head-ache,' which was true; but to try her, M. Sebire answered, that she was mistaken. ' That is singular,' replied she; ' I touched some person who had a head-ache, for I felt it,' She distinguished several persons who were present by some peculiarities in their dress.

"' The following was one of the most remarkable circumstances that occurred, The magnetiser had retired, after promising to return at half-past five o'clock, in order to awaken her. He arrived before the appointed time. The somnambulist observed, that it was not yet half-past five, to which he answered, that he had just received a letter, which obliged him to return sooner. ' O yes,' she immediately replied; ' it is that letter which you have in your pocket-book, between a blue card and a yellow one.' The fact was strictly true. M. Sebire, without saying anything, placed a watch behind her occiput, and asked her what it was o'clock by the watch ? She answered, ' Six minutes past four,' and she was right.'

" All this sounds very marvellous, and no doubt appeared conclusive to the bystander, of the truth and miraculous powers of magnetism; but un-fortunately for the magnetisers Petronilla died of phthisis, in the Salpetrière, in 1833, and repeatedly declared in the latter part of her life, to the *internes* of the hospital, that she had never experienced the least degree of somnam-bulism, and that she used to laugh in her sleeve at Georget and the others who were present at the experiments. She affirmed that she had passed with Brouillard (another somnambulist) more than one delicious evening in recounting the *mystifications* of the day, and in preparing those for the morrow. These persons also allowed themselves to be pricked and pinched without evincing pain. I am acquainted with the gentlemen to whom these avowals were made, and one of them assured me of the correctness of the above statement."

Taking leave for a time of our esteemed author,—esteemed on account of the enlightened, sober, and variously excellent qualities of his printed works,—these being the only grounds upon which we have an opportunity to form our judgment, let us also bid adieu to France and the Académie, and carry our readers to the metropolis of England.

To plain and matter-of-fact people, to those who are not in

the habit of yielding themselves up to fanaticism or charlatanism, of gulling or being gulled, but who desire to have placed before them demonstrated and unimpeachable facts in support of every new and marvellous doctrine, it will be matter of surprise to hear that there are persons in London at the hour in which we write who put faith in the absurdities and monstrosities which we have been noticing. What adds to the marvel is this, that men of acknowledged eminence in literature and science, Lords and Commons also, have lent an ear to these extravagances. Talk of the impostor who called himself a knight of Malta, the *late* Sir William Courtenay, and his deluded, ignorant, and insignificant followers, as respects wealth, rank, and influence, who, all the while may have been the tools as well as the victims of deep-scheming enemies of the state! what is to be said of the personages, some of them soon to be named, who have in a greater or less degree identified themselves with the Mesmerians,—the somnambulist-charmers,—the *clairvoyant*-speculators? But narrative will be more satisfactory than declamation.

After the revival of Animal Magnetism folly in France, and the perseverance with which its merits were obtruded upon the public, it was not to be expected that John Bull, sober-minded as he generally is, and a hater of foreign quackery, should not begin to feel some curiosity about the matter. Only a very small number of his family, however, bestowed upon M. Dupotet any attention, who as a Mesmerian missionary visited us in 1837; and the fact is, that despairing of notice and of making converts, he was about to abandon the enterprise, and to return to a more kindly soil, when certain circumstances occurred which led to a change of purpose. The Earl of Stanhope became his patron; and certain medical practitioners being solicitous to ascertain if the pretended magnetic influence could be employed as a cure in particular diseases began to attend his exhibition. The North London Hospital was selected as a theatre for experimenting, and at length two gentlemen attached to the adjoining university, Dr. Elliotson and Professor Mayo, professed themselves converts, though in unequal degrees; the former going almost the whole hog, and the latter only to the extent of believing the extraordinary effects which he had seen to be the result of the magnetiser's influence.

It is to be observed that English patients have not hitherto evinced such a susceptibility of the magnetic power, as those in France and some foreign parts; and as it is alleged by magnetisers that the proximity of moral impurity neutralizes the charm, we perhaps need not travel far to find the cause of the comparative failures in this country.

Dr. Elliotson, however, has become rather an expert operator, and has, in as far as the earlier stages of magnetising are concerned, acquitted himself to admiration. Very lately, indeed, he astonished an assembly of lookers-on, which consisted not only of certain magnates and legislators, but of literary and scientific characters. On this occasion two epileptic girls did their part with considerable accuracy.

If we understand the doctrines of magnetisers aright, it does not require learning, medical study, or any peculiar preparation to be an effective operator. Children, for example, it is said, may not only be magnetised, but an infant, by having been taught to move its hands in the necessary manner, may unconsciously do the thing. In fact the newspapers have reported that Dr. Elliotson has gravely declared, that he is "one of those who are satisfied that influence may be exerted by one animal, whether *human* or *brute*, upon another individual who is affected, being aware of the operation." We have not learned where or how he obtains proofs of his assertion.

Before leaving our London magnetisers, our readers may be amused if we copy from the Sun newspaper a detailed account of the scene witnessed in the North London Hospital, already referred to, when Dr. Elliotson was the magnetiser. While the professor was speaking,—

"Mr. Wood, who, we understood, first drew Dr. Elliotson's attention to the practicability of exercising the Mesmeric art, moved his hands behind the backs of the girls, and they fell each into a state of profound sleep. They were then pinched, violently shaken, and pulled by the arms, not by the Professor, but by several of the noblemen and gentlemen around, without manifesting the slightest degree of sensibility. But by breathing upon their hands, they were instantly awakened, when they exhibited a delirious vivacity and boldness, in remarkable contrast to their gentleness in the natural state. In the elder girl, the contrast was most striking—she sang, whistled, and jested with Dr. Elliotson and with Lords Wilton and Stanhope, with the familiarity of a playful and petted child amongst her own family, and she displayed not only great archness, but wit and humour. In the midst of her liveliest sallies, however, Dr. Elliotson, suddenly pointed the fore-finger of one hand at her forehead, and on the instant she stood immoveable as a statue, and evidently in a state of utter unconsciousness, He then pointed a finger at each upper eye-lid, and, as he raised the fingers, (several inches from her face) the lids rose also, exposing the eye-ball— and so they remained fixed, the body standing motionless. In the same manner, pointing one finger opposite the upper lip, and another opposite the chin, he moved the one finger upwards and the other downwards, with a quick movement, and the mouth opened; and she stood still, in that posture, until he breathed upon her face; when she suddenly started into consciousness, and began to dance, sing, and jest as before. * * * * She was afterwards repeatedly struck motionless, on the instant, in every variety of attitude, which, in her delirious playfulness, she might happen to assume; and this was done not only by Dr. E. himself, but frequently when he was not aware of it, and whilst she was talking to him—by a single movement of the hand, *behind her back*, by Lord Wilton, Lord Northland, and others, who seemed to enjoy the influence of their newly-discovered

Mesmeric powers. When she was seated in the chair, and thrown into
sleep, her hands lying in her lap, Dr. E. extending his arms, placed a hand
opposite each of hers, and then drawing his hands away, he raised them
upwards and inwards towards his head. Her hands followed his until she
had raised them to the level of her head, when, with a convulsive movement, she fell back in the chair, in a state of *coma*, or torpor, more profound than the previous sleep. We observed that this phenomenon followed
every experiment, in which she was caused to make any physical exertion.
When she was seated and asleep, Mr. Wood being behind her, placed his
hands near hers, and as he drew his away, hers followed them—as he
raised his, she raised hers. In the same manner, as she sat asleep, her eyes
being closed, Lord Wilton placed his left hand opposite to her right, and, as
he drew his away, hers followed, as far as her arm would extend, apparently
attracted, as a needle would follow a powerful magnet. Whilst she sat
asleep, with her body leaning forward, Mr. Wood, being still behind her,
pointed his hand to the back of her head, but at a distance of three or four
feet, and, as he retired further back, her head was raised slowly, and
moved backwards, in the direction of his hand, as far as the top rail of the
chair would allow, when she made a convulsive effort to rise, and sank into
a state of lethargy. In the same manner, when feet were pointed opposite
to hers, and withdrawn, hers followed them; and this species of attraction
was exercised upon her with the same effects by the surrounding spectators,
as well as by the medical practitioners. Numerous other experiments were
made to elicit similar phenomena, both with the patient and her sister."

We wonder when there were so many magnetic breaths, so many
magnetic hands, fingers, and toes, that the poor girl was not distracted, and almost torn to pieces, the influences, according to the
above account, being for a long time all around her. Our readers,
however, will readily perceive how fanciful was the whole of the
exhibition, and necessarily indulge in certain conjectures of their own;
so that, without detaining them on this story with any comments of
our own, let them listen to Mr. Lee's calm and conclusive estimate
of English cases. It will be observed that he speaks not from
hearsay, but from the testimony of his own eyes, and after patient, extensive, and prolonged research.

" What I have seen of these experiments leaves little doubt on my mind
that the phenomena observed are independent of any magnetic influence,
and might be reproduced without magnetisation; always provided the individuals were placed in circumstances which would lead them to suppose
themselves magnetised. Thus, at M. Dupotet's, none of the higher phenomena of magnetism are even alluded to, and the convulsive movements and
other effects follow actions made in front of the individuals; or if the magnetiser be behind them, they are aware that he is performing the *passes* upon
them. One female, after being seated, is always seized with a slight rota-
tory motion of the head, which was increased by actions directed by the
magnetiser towards her, but it also became increased, without her being
specially magnetised, and when the magnetiser was in another room. The
motion was arrested for a brief period, by the magnetiser placing his thumb

or finger on the person's forehead. On my touching her forehead, without any intention of magnetising, a like effect was produced.

"Another somnambulist, a French woman, and servant of M. Dupotet's, who is occasionally introduced at the close of the exhibition, rose repeatedly from her chair, and struggled with and even threatened to strike persons who attempted to restrain her, but was always tranquillised, and fell back into her seat, on the magnetiser taking hold of her and touching her forehead. ' On one occasion, when she rose from her seat, and the magnetiser was in the adjoining apartment, I took hold of her wrist as he had done, and, on touching her forehead, she fell back tranquillised in her chair, as on former occasions. The same person's hands were taken by the magnetiser, who repeated several times, ' Ouvrez les yeux, Julie,' which Julie, after apparently making some efforts, accordingly did. But this affords no proof that she could not open her eyes whenever she pleased, and that she did so in consequence of magnetic influence. The magnetiser declined attempting a similar result on his other somnambulists. One of these he drew from her chair towards himself by some movements of the hand, (he being seated at a little distance before her,) and she remained in a position of cataleptic rigidity till replaced in the chair; he declined, however, repeating the experiment behind the somnambulist, when she would not be aware that he was acting upon her; though, if the effect resulted from magnetic power, it must have been equally apparent.

"With respect to Rebecca and the little girl, the other capital somnambulists of the exhibition, I have no doubt that the effects observed were independent of magnetic influence, and that like effects might have been equally obtained without magnetisation. Although such cases excite a great degree of wonder in the generality of persons, and are well calculated to make converts, yet medical men, especially those who have seen much of nervous complaints, are well aware of the curious phenomena which occasionally occur in females; particularly when made objects of interest to an assembled multitude. Every medical man knows hysterical affections are aggravated, and are obstinate in proportion to the degree of attention they excite, and of sympathy manifested by relations or bystanders. Magnetisers assert that individuals, when in somnambulism, are insensible to external stimuli, and will only answer the questions of the magnetiser, or of persons placed *en rapport* with them; but this young woman called out on her ear being moderately pinched, and answered any of the questions that were proposed to her by the visitors. It is evident she had anticipated a more than usually interesting *séance*, as she repeated two or three times, ' Lord Stanhope is to be here to-day.' No effects were produced on the men subjected to magnetisation, except occasional muscular twitchings in one individual."

It is certainly lamentable that at this time of day the mummery of Animal Magnetism should be revived with greater pretensions and ardour than ever. We do not say that the propagators of the doctrine are all acting in bad faith; or that the foreign adepts have not acquired an enthusiasm,—that they have not arrived at a belief in the efficacy of the *soi-disant* science which they teach. There is so much that is flattering to human vanity in the persuasion that one can by certain manipulations, certain agencies, so disembody the soul, so free it from its cumbrous earthly tabernacle, as to allow it to escape on long voyages of discovery,—to enable the spiritual essence to become the spectator of its own operations, and the mental operations of others,—that the monstrous and preposterous nature of the doctrine may be lost sight of amid the glare of its pretensions.

There is another mode of accounting in some degree for the welcome which Animal Magnetism has obtained on the part of most of its disciples.

A common boast at the present day is this, that the public mind has become too much enlightened to repose any faith in religious superstition, in ghosts, supernatural interpositions, &c. This is the age of scientific discovery, it is proudly asserted,—the era when natural philosophy and mechanical powers have achieved a triumph. In truth, the love of the marvellous is inherent in man, and unless his intellectual powers be well disciplined, the imagination is sure to run riot in one direction or another. Natural philosophy, not religion, in these days engages the credulity of many. Science is their idol. Still the desire and love of contemplating and mastering that which is most subtle, of going beyond the world of sense, and luxuriating ourselves in thought amid agencies that are identified with what is ethereal and intangible, has rendered the subject of electricity the most enticing of any. And what a field for empiricism, for the exercise of inexplicable and mysterious fancies to disport in! The magnet however, the virtues of which are known to have an electrical character, from its curious and practical influences is the best possible agent to associate with the nervous phenomena and the mental excursions of somnambulists that could be chosen. The phrase, Animal Magnetism, adroitly mystifies and seduces; so that when well-meaning people talk or hear of its wonders, they fancy that they are conversant with beautiful and demonstrative experiments on the subject. The simple introduction of hard or learned names is not without its misleading use, and for anything we can see the foreign adepts in the departments under consideration have not shown themselves innocent of these and similar devices.

Before concluding, and while on the subject of man's inherent love of the marvellous, and of his natural and constant striving to penetrate the veil which hides futurity or distance from him, and to throw off the enchaining and blinding fabric of his organized frame, which prevents him from comprehending the manner of his soul's existence as well as the avenues to an intimate intercourse with the spirits of others, we may remark, that in all ages these yearning and vain efforts have in some one shape characterized the history of our race. We think that the Royal Touching, the delusions of the French *Convulsionnaires*, the Hohenlohe cures, the Unknown Tongues, might all be ranged under one general head with Animal

Magnetism, ranged thus not merely because they have all had their
origin in that, craving to be acquainted with mysterious influences,
but also, in so far as cures and illuminations have in each delusion
been effected, these have been accomplished through some excitement of the nervous system, or the morbid conditions of the imagination. But surely in none of the instances alluded to, can we
find such matter for wonder as in this, that when verging on the
middle of the nineteenth century, there are in the most enlightened
countries of Europe, there are in the capital of Great Britain, men
of education and acknowledged acquirements in science, who lend
their countenance and their credence to the buffooneries and charlatanism which are inseparable from the operations of the Animal
Magnetiser. One comfort is, that the doctrines of these people are
not only already too gross and absurd to be swallowed, but if left
alone they will run themselves over head and ears in folly.

ART. II.—*Colonization and Christianity; a Popular History of the
Treatment of the Natives by the Europeans, in all their Colonies.* By
WILLIAM HOWITT. London: Longman & Co. 1838.

ON late occasions we have had more than once our attention called
to the monstrous injustice and cruelties which prevail in certain
quarters of the globe under the British system of colonization;
towards the Caffres for example. It is high time that the public at
home should awake to the enormities that have stained the name
of Britons in every part of the globe where they have fixed themselves. It were enough surely that a people professing a rare degree
of attainment in Christianity and civilization were chargeable with
the neglect of the moral and immortal interests of the savage or
barbarian races among which they have so often planted themselves.
But it is not the sins of omission alone that are chargeable against
our colonists and the nation; the most flagrant acts of commission
rise in mountains above our heads and must be punished or atoned
for. It may be true that other European nations have outstripped
us in crime in their transactions with the coloured tribes of mankind; it may be true that, considering our unexampled extent and
diversity of colonial possessions, our sway is milder and our intercourse less injurious than that which neighbouring Christian powers
have established and practised in similar circumstances. Alas!
even admitting all this, we stand at a fearful distance from the
golden line of duty which the code we profess to obey has impera-
tively laid down for our guidance in every situation in dealing with
our fellow-creatures. Nor is the charge to be confined to our forefathers or to times long gone by. We boast of our light and liberality in the nineteenth century; we count our munificent acts
philanthropic enterprizes, and lay the flattering unction to our souls
that wherever the British name is known, wherever British power

is felt, there life and liberty flourish at the present day, and that the extension of our influence and our colonial system to all the benighted nations of the world would be the certain herald of peace, personal security, and moral elevation. Never was there a more preposterous egotism, never a more unwarrantable assumption. Down to our day, down to the year of Grace 1838, yea, at the very moment we write these words, the neglect, the political circumvention, the positive oppression which is chargeable against the British name, cry aloud to Heaven, and, but for the infinite mercy and forbearance of Heaven, a judgment would go out against us that would render us a byeword to posterity.

What is it ye would have? it may be asked by political economists, bold speculators, and successful traders. We answer, that we desire to see the principles which Britain as a nation, and her colonists as communities, profess to cherish and illustrate, carried into universal practice; we desire to see our countrymen recommending to Pagans and heathens the morals and the religion held out as pre-eminently excellent and conducive to happiness, by their treaties, their observance of obligations, their earnest and constant obedience of the divine law; we desire to behold that temporal prosperity which is sure to go hand in hand with a wide-spreading infection of civilization, that has never failed to attend transactions and mutual intercourse among men, where the rule of doing to others as one would wish to be done to has been faithfully observed; we desire to behold the benign principles, the steady behaviour, the glorious results, so eloquently set forth in the pages before us, fully and immediately realized.

What!—the exclamation may be on the part of some West India planter, some Cape of Good Hope functionary, some collector in Hindostan, some American lumberer, some Australian governor, or some prosperous merchant—does William Howitt expect that we are all to be saints—Christians in deed as well as by profession? We answer, William Howitt has no reason to expect any such glorious change suddenly; but this does not and ought not to prevent him from longing for its realization; it does not hinder him from labouring to hasten its birth; it does not authorize him to hold up a lower standard than the truth merely for the sake of accommodating perverted or unprincipled minds, especially when, however unwelcome that truth may be to some, it requires but to be laid plainly before the reflecting and the religious community of Great Britain to awaken an indignation and produce a cry for justice in behalf of the claims of humanity, that neither domestic legislation, foreign diplomacy, nor colonial intrigue, obduracy, or apathy shall be able to oppose. Do away with but the apathy of the British public—and to accomplish this it is only necessary to bring the truth fully and fairly before that mighty community—and the good fight is begun, the glorious victory is nigh; British possessions, traffic, and moral sway, will surpass all that was ever dreamt of by fondest enthusiasts, and our land and name will be identified with the regeneration of the world.

Great Britain is beginning to awaken from her apathy in regard to her colonial system, because the light of truth has begun to beam upon her relative to this subject. Some of the representatives of the people in Parliament have been stirring; travellers and emigrants have spoken out; the press at home is taking the matter in hand; the last, best, and greatest of the efforts of this formidable engine being the volume before us. As journalists, having the mercantile, political, and moral as well as literary advancement of our country much at heart, and identifying the condition and harmony of all these departments with the interests of civilization and their highest possible attainment with the purest and most extensive reign of Christianity, nothing can better become us than to be instrumental in propagating the facts, the inferences, and the doctrines which our author has with singular earnestness, ability, and force of eloquence laid before us. It is a noble cause in which he has embarked; no other could better become the religious, the literary character of William Howitt.

The object of the work, as stated and exhibited by our author, is to lay open to the public the most extensive and extraordinary system of crime which the world ever witnessed,—a system which has been in operation for more than three hundred years, not only under the countenance of various nations of Catholic but of Protestant Europe, England particularly, on account of her unexampled extent of possessions and intercourse. Never before has any book taken up this subject upon the comprehensive plan here adopted; never has any other author discussed the subject so plainly and philosophically. William Howitt has done his part, let others suggest remedies; he has pointed out the sores and the disease; and, having done so, our faith is strong that " in this great country there will not want either heads to plan or hands to accomplish all that is due to the rights of others, or the honour and interest of England."

After, in an introductory chapter, contrasting the profession of Christianity of European nations with their real practices towards one another, their boasting of civilization and superiority over those they please to call savages and barbarians, with their mutual, numerous, and prolonged massacres, even down to the present hour when all Europe stands armed to the teeth, no one kingdom daring to repose faith in its neighbour upon Christian principles, he proceeds to notice the circumstances that distinguished the Discovery of the New World.

" What an era of amazement was that! Worlds of vast extent and wonderful character, starting as it were into sudden creation before the eyes of growing, inquisitive, and ambitious Europe! Day after day, some news, astounding in its very infinitude of goodness, was breaking upon their excited minds; news which overturned old theories of philosophy and geography, and opened prospects for the future equally confounding by their strange magnificence! No single Paradise discovered; but countless Edens, scattered through the glittering seas of summer climes, and populous realms, stretching far and wide beneath new heavens, from pole to pole—

Another nature, and a new mankind.—*Rogers.*

" Since the day of Creation, but two events of superior influence on the destinies of the human race had occurred—the Announcement of God's Law on Sinai, and the Advent of his Son! Providence had drawn aside the veil of a mighty part of his world, and submitted the lives and happiness of millions of his creatures to the arbitrium of that European race, which now boasted of superior civilization—and far more, of being the regenerated followers of his Christ. Never was so awful a test of sincerity presented to the professors of a heavenly creed!—never was such opportunity allowed to mortal men to work in the eternal scheme of Providence! It is past! Such amplitude of the glory of goodness can never again be put at one moment into the reach of the human will. God's providence is working out its undoubted design in this magnificent revelation of

That maiden world, twin-sister to the old;—*Montgomery.*

But they who should have worked with it in the benignity and benevolence of that Saviour whose name they bore, have left to all futurity the awful spectacle of their infamy !"

The natives of America at first greeted the Europeans cordially, and as beings of a superior order to themselves. How advantageously might not these Spanish and Portuguese explorers have exemplified that while they burned to "plant the Cross," one of the great doctrines of the religion of the Gospel was, "thou shalt love thy neighbour as thyself!" But what was their conduct? Gold was their demon idol, and they steeped themselves in human blood. Still they professed themselves Christians, and were eager to convert the children of the wilderness to their speculative belief: while their hands were heavy with plundered gold and clotted with blood, they were zealous for the propagation of their faith. Has the policy and practice of other nations, of the Dutch and the English, been essentially different? And while it will be easy to show that all, Catholic and Protestant, have gone on much alike, varying, to be sure, the aspect and details of injustice and oppression according to circumstances, down to the day in which we live, is it a marvel that Christianity has made so little progress beyond Europe, during all the ages that Europe has now made herself familiar with and to the other quarters of the globe? The truth is, that, as nations, Europeans, even in the most favoured and enlightened kingdoms, have not been Christianized. Some of these nations bear the name

·of Most Sacred and Most Christian.   Wherever this religion has been established, and called that of the State, it is also true that society has been ameliorated, benign institutions have sprung up, and very many of every such community have been what they profess to be.   But just try these same nations by an unerring standard : what have they, as a whole, been and done to their neighbours ? above all, how have they systematically, perseveringly, and universally borne themselves towards the ignorant, the defenceless, the simple, or the intrepid heathen ?—part of the answer will appear from what follows.

At the very outset of European colonization, three hundred years ago, there prevailed not only in practice but in theory, woful religious errors and perversions.   The Pope, for example, supposed, and it was at the time conceded to him throughout Europe, that he had a right of dominion over all the kingdoms of the earth, and in the exercise of this right the undiscovered or lately discovered regions of the globe were by a stroke of the pen divided between the Portuguese and the Spaniards.   This was done under a preposterous assumption, and in reality to advance personal and family schemes of ambition.   But strangest of all, Europe acquiesced in the decision ; which shows not only how deaf and blind to the claims of justice and right all the nations of Christendom had grown in regard to the heathen, but how degraded and debauched public morality at home had become.   No wonder that the Right of Conquest, and such robber-phrases were framed to clothe new ideas ; but have such phrases become obsolete either in language or fulfilment ?   No, they are to this day " as smoothly trundled from our tongues," as if they were found in Holy Writ, and there recommended to our obedience.

These are some of the sentiments and views which our author introduces when entering upon the gloomy field which he so admirably traverses.   They are necessary to an explanation of the laxity of opinion and the apathy of feeling that have ever since the days of Columbus characterized Europeans in their dealings with the natives of new countries.

Our author forcibly illustrates the effect of the prevalent creed, concerning the Pope's right of bestowing new countries as he pleased, even upon Columbus, a man naturally honourable and generous.   This great navigator's discovery of one of the West India islands affords William Howitt a fit opportunity for the exercise of his fine eye in regard to landscape scenery, and his deep sympathy with the simplicities of nature and the picturesque in life.   He says,

" On discovering the island of Guanahani, one of the Bahamas, the Spaniards raised the hymn of *Te Deum.*   At sunrise they rowed towards land with colours flying, and the sound of martial music; and amid the 'crowds of wondering natives assembled on the shores and hills around, Columbus, like another Mahomet, set foot on the beach, *sword in hand,* and *followed by a crucifix,* which his followers planted in the earth, and then prostrating themselves before it, *took possession of the country* in the name of his sovereign. The inhabitants gazed in silent wonder on ceremonies so pregnant with calamity to them, but without any suspicion of their real nature. Living in a delightful climate, hidden through all the ages of their world from the other world of labour and commerce, of art and artifice, of avarice and cruelty, they appeared in the primitive and unclad simplicity of nature. The Spaniards, says Peter Martyr,—' Dryades formosissimas, aut natives fontium nymphas de quibus fabulatur antiquitas, se vidisse arbitrati sunt:'—they seemed to behold the most beautiful dryads, or native nymphs of the fountains, of whom antiquity fabled. Their forms were light and graceful, though dusky with the warm hues of the sun; their hair hung in long raven tresses on their shoulders, unlike the frizzly wool of the Africans, or was tastefully braided. Some were painted, and armed with a light bow, or a fishing spear; but their countenances were full of gentleness and kindness. Columbus himself, in one of his letters to Ferdinand and Isabella, describes the Americans and their country thus :—' This country excels all others, as far as the day surpasses the night in splendour: the natives love their neighbour as themselves; their conversation is the sweetest imaginable; their faces always smiling, and so gentle, so affectionate are they, that I swear to your highnesses there is not a better people in the world." The Spaniards indeed looked with as much amazement on the simple people, and the paradise in which they lived, as the natives did on the wonderful spectacle of European forms, faces, dress, arts, arms, and ships.—Such sweet and flowing streams; such sunny dales, scattered with flowers as gorgeous and beautiful as they were novel; trees covered with a profusion of glorious and aromatic blossoms, and beneath their shade the huts of the natives, of simple reeds or palm-leaves; the stately palms themselves, rearing their lofty heads on the hill sides; the canoes skimming over the blue waters, and birds of most resplendent plumage flying from tree to tree."

These Spaniards might chaunt a *Te Deum ;* but they were only malignant spirits, who were about to make a vast continent one wide theatre of insult, murder, and rapine. After leaving the island above described, Columbus sailed to Cuba, and thence to Hispaniola. Let us see the picture given of his reception there.

" He was visited by the cazique, Guacanahari, who was doomed first to experience the villany of the Spaniards. This excellent and kind man sent by the messengers which Columbus had despatched to wait on him, a curious mask of beaten gold, and when the vessel of Columbus was immediately afterwards wrecked in standing in to the coast, he appeared with all his people on the strand, —for the purpose of plundering and destroying them, as we might expect from *savages,* and as the Cazique would have been served had he been wrecked himself on the Spanish, or on our own coast at that time ? No! but better Christian than most of those who bore that name, he came eagerly to do the very deed enjoined by Christ and his followers,—to succour and to save. ' The prince,' says Herrera,

their own historian, ' appeared all zeal and activity at the head of his
people. He placed armed guards to keep off the press of the natives, and
to keep clear a space for the depositing of the goods as they came to land:
he sent out as many as were needful in their canoes to put themselves
under the guidance of the Spaniards, and to assist them all in their power
in the saving of their goods from the wreck. As they brought them to
land, he and his nobles received them, and set sentinels over them, not
suffering the people even to gratify that curiosity which at such a crisis
must have been very great, to examine and inspect the curious articles of
a new people: and his subjects participating in all his feelings, wept tears
of sincere distress for the sufferers, and condoled with them in their misfortune. But as if this was not enough, the next morning, when Columbus
had removed to one of his other vessels, the good Guacanaharia appeared
on board to comfort him, and to offer all that he had to repair his loss !'
  " This beautiful circumstance is moreover still more particularly related
by Columbus himself, in his letter to his sovereigns; and it was on this
occasion that he gave that character of the country and the people to
which I have just referred.   Truly had he a great right to say that ' they
loved their neighbour as themselves.' Let us see how the Spaniards and
Columbus himself followed up this sublime lesson."

  It is a matter of woful history how this and other tokens of the
friendship of the natives were recompensed. But we pass over the
sickening details, only noticing that our author severely but not
unjustly animadverts upon Principal Robertson's frequent adoption
of conventional and unchristian sentiments and terms, when characterizing the struggles between the natives and the usurpers—" But
the strangest remark of Robertson is, ' that the fatal defect of the
Peruvians was their unwarlike character.' Fatal, indeed, their
inability to contend with the Europeans proved to them ; but what
a burlesque on the religion of the Europeans—that the *peaceful*
character of an innocent people should prove fatal to them only
from—*the followers of the Prince of Peace !*"
  The conduct of the Portuguese in Brazil and in India present
nearly similar features with that of the Spaniards in the course of
their discoveries, usurpations, and exterminating as well as enslaving systems. The only green spots in these dread histories
which the heart can find to repose upon, are inseparable from the
character and exertions of Christians not only in name but in deed,
especially certain Jesuit Missionaries, who, from time to time,
planted themselves in the colonies and among the Indians.

  " The city of Salvador, in the bay of All-Saints, was founded as the seat
of government, and the Jesuits immediately began the work of civilization.
There was great need of it both amongst the Indians and their own
countrymen. ' Indeed, the fathers,' says Southey, ' had greater difficulties
to encounter in the conduct of their own countrymen than in the customs
and disposition of the natives.   During half a century, the colonization of
Brazil had been left to chance ; the colonists were almost without law and

religion. Many settlers had never either confessed or communicated since they entered the country; the ordinances of the church were neglected for want of a clergy to celebrate them, and the moral precepts had been forgotten with the ceremonies. Crimes which might easily at first have been prevented, had become habitual, and the habit was now too strong to be overcome. There were indeed individuals in whom the moral sense could be discovered, but in the majority it had been utterly destroyed. They were of that description of men over whom the fear of the gallows may have some effect; the fear of God has none. A system of concubinage was practised among them, worse than the loose polygamy of the savages. The savage had as many women as consented to become his wives—the colonist as many as he could enslave. There is an ineffaceable stigma upon the Europeans in their intercourse with those whom they treat as inferior races—there is a perpetual contradiction between their lust and their avarice. The planter will one day take a slave for his harlot, and sell her the next as a being of some lower species—a beast of labour. If she be indeed an inferior animal, what shall be said of the one action ? If she be equally with himself a human being and an immortal soul, what shall be said of the other ? Either way there is a crime committed against human nature. Nobrega and his companions refused to administer the sacraments of the church to those persons who retained native women as concubines, or men as slaves. Many were reclaimed by this resolute and Christian conduct; some, because their consciences had not been dead, but sleeping; others, for worldly fear, because they believed the Jesuits were armed with secular as well as spiritual authority. The good effect which was produced on such persons was therefore only for a season. Mighty as the Catholic religion is, avarice is mightier; and in spite of all the best and ablest men that ever the Jesuit order, so fertile of great men, has had to glory in, the practice of enslaving the natives continued.'

"Yet, according to the same authority, the country had not been entirely without priests; but they had become so brutal that Nobrega said, ' No devil had persecuted him and his brethren so greatly as they did. These wretches encouraged the colonists in their abominations, and openly maintained that it was lawful to enslave the natives, because they were beasts; and then lawful to use the women as concubines, because they were slaves. This was their public doctrine! Well might Nobrega say they did the work of the devil. They opposed the Jesuits with the utmost virulence. Their interest was at stake. They could not bear the presence of men who said mass and performed all the ceremonies of religion gratuitously.' Much less, it may be believed, who maintained the freedom of the natives."

Just observe how potent and influential is the spirit of Christianity when honestly and faithfully exemplified, even when it has to struggle amid formidable neutralizing or positively warring elements. The Jesuits, to whom reference has been made, were soon called upon to do more than follow the peaceful paths of Christianizing the natives, for they had to save the insulting and oppressing colonists from the fury of those they had so basely and cruelly wronged; and, now one of the fathers, " with his crucifix in his hand, was of more avail at the head of armies than the most able general."

The resolute resistance of the Jesuits to the avarice and vile practices of the Portuguese was sometimes crowned with success; and here we are glad to take advantage of an extract, as found in a discourse by one of the order, which so startled the people at St. Lewis to whom it was addressed, that with one accord they resolved to set their subjugated Indians free. The text was, the offer of Satan:—" All these things will I give thee, if thou wilt fall down and worship me."

" ' Things,' said he, ' are estimated at what they cost. What then did the world cost our Saviour, and what did a soul cost him? The world cost him a word—He spoke, and it was made. A soul cost Him his life, and his blood. But if the world cost only a word of God, and a soul cost the blood of God, a soul is worth more than all the world. This Christ thought, and this the devil confessed. Yet you know how cheaply we value our souls? you know at what rate we sell them? We wonder that Judas should have sold his Master and his soul for thirty pieces of silver; but how many are there who offer their own to the devil for less than fifteeen! Christians! I am not now telling you that you ought not to sell your souls, for I know that you must sell them;—I only entreat that you will sell them by weight. Weigh well what a soul is worth, and what it cost, and then sell it and welcome! But in what scales is it to be weighed? You think I shall say, In those of St. Michael the archangel, in which souls are weighed. I do not require so much. Weigh them in the devil's own balance, and I shall be satisfied! Take the devil's balance in one hand, put the whole world in one scale and a soul in the other, and you will find that your soul weighs more than the world—' All this will I give thee, if thou wilt fall down and worship me.' . . . . . . But at what a different price now does the devil purchase souls from that which he formerly offered for them? I mean in this country. The devil has not a fair in the world where they go cheaper! In the Gospel he offers all the kingdoms of the world to purchase a single soul;—he does not require so large a price to purchase all that are in Maranham. It is not necessary to offer worlds; it is not necessary to offer kingdoms, nor cities, nor towns, nor villages;—it is enough for the devil to point at a plantation, and a couple of Tapuyas, and down goes the man upon his knees to worship him! Oh what a market! A negro for a soul, and the soul the blacker of the two! The negro shall be your slave for the few days you have to live, and your soul shall be my slave through all eternity—as long as God is God! This is the bargain which the devil makes with you."

But the Spaniards and the Portuguese, some may be ready to assert, as nations had no just conceptions of the rights of mankind, and the just freedom of conscience. They were and are blind believers in the authority and pretensions of the Papal power. Protestants entertain more enlightened and benign views, and in regard to the rude and ignorant natives of the countries they have colonized, they have pursued a far worthier course, and one which the mind can dwell upon with considerable complacency. Let us see;—and first of the Dutch who commenced their career in India with a show of moderation that contrasted strongly with the conduct of the Portuguese. This leniency, however, was but a political stratagem, and employed to root out their European rivals.

" All historians have remarked with astonishment the fearful metamorphosis which the Dutch underwent in their colonies. At home they were moderate, kindly, and liberal; abroad their rapacity, perfidy, and infamous cruelty made them resemble devils rather than men. Whether contending with their European rivals, or domineering over the natives, they showed no mercy and no remorse. Their celebrated massacre of the English in Amboyna has rung through all lands and languages, and is become one of the familiar horrors of history. There is, in fact, no narrative of tortures in the annals of the Inquisition, that can surpass those which the Dutch practised on their English rivals on this occasion. The English had five factories in the island of Amboyna, and the Dutch determined to crush them. For this purpose they got up a charge of conspiracy against the English—collected them from all their stations into the town of Amboyna, and after forcing confessions of guilt from them by the most unheard-of torture, put them to death. The following specimen of the agonies which Protestants could inflict on their fellow-protestants, may give an idea of what sort of increase of religion the Reformation had brought these men.

" ' Then John Clark, who also came from Hitto, was fetched in, and soon after was heard to roar out amain. They tortured him with fire and water for two hours. The manner of his torture, as also that of Johnson's and Thomson's, was as followeth :—

" ' They first hoisted him by the hands against a large door, and there made him fast to two staples of iron, fixed on both sides at the top of the door-posts, extending his arms as wide as they could stretch them. When thus fastened, his feet, being two feet from the ground, were extended in the same manner, and made fast to the bottom of the door-trees on each side. Then they tied a cloth about the lower part of his face and neck, so close that scarce any water could pass by. That done, they poured water gently upon his head till the cloth was full up to his mouth and nostrils, and somewhat higher, so that he could not draw breath but he must swallow some, which being continually poured in softly, forced all his inward parts to come out at his nose, ears, and eyes, and often, as it were choking him, at length took away his breath, and caused him to faint away. Then they took him down in a hurry to vomit up the water, and when a little revived, tied him up again, using him as before. In this manner they served him three or four times, till his belly was as big as a tun, his cheeks like bladders, his eyes starting out beyond his forehead; yet all this he bore without confessing anything, insomuch that the fiscal and tormentors reviled him, saying he was a devil, and no man; or was enchanted, that he could bear so much: Hereupon they cut off his hair very short, supposing he had some witchcraft hidden therein. Now they hoisted him up again, and burnt him

with lighted candles under his elbows and arm-pits, in the palms of his
hands, and at the bottoms of his feet, even till the fat dropped out
on the candles.   Then they applied fresh ones; and under his arms
they burnt so deep that his inwards might be seen.'—*History of Voyages
to the East and West Indies.*

" And all this that they might rule sole kings over the delicious islands
of cloves and cinnamon, nutmegs and mace, camphor and coffee, areca
and betel, gold, pearls and precious stones; every one of them more
precious in the eyes of the thorough trader, whether he call himself
Christian or Infidel, than the blood of his brother, or the soul of
himself."

Here is a new feature in the history of modern colonization. The
thirst for gold, a greediness for hasty gains, no matter how obtained,
have been the ruling and all but universally prevailing features in
the character of Europeans in heathen lands.   With regard to the
Dutch, they have long borne a hated character for exactions and
a disregard of every honourable or humane trait in their colonial
policy.   We may be also sure that when, at the period above mentioned, their Protestant brethren, the English, were so roughly
treated, persons of another faith, of another complexion, and who
could not claim a protecting or avenging power like that of England,
would not, if standing in the way, be more tenderly handled.

With regard to the English ;—and first of their conduct in India.
Here we think our author, while justly denouncing the unchristian
system which has countenanced territorial acquisition to such an
amazing extent, has not sufficiently attended to the *set offs* which
the comparatively paternal sway of the East India Company has
introduced.   It must be admitted, that in the treatment of the
native chiefs, the Company's profession of friendship, the offer and
performance of acts of assistance in petty warfares, as much perhaps
as the threat and execution of the sword have proved disastrous to
the independence of these native powers, while the exactions to
which the great body of the population has been subjected have
ground millions, as if entirely under a wantonly oppressive yoke ;
still it appears to us that from the moment the British were settled
in India, their very existence and prosperity as a trading company
so entangled them, that territorial acquisition, and rapid aggran-
dizement in regard to political power necessarily followed, and that
the protection as well as the terror which a mastery in war threw
around them had to be invoked.   Besides, when the mind contemplates prospectively the blessings which Providence in all probability has in store through the instrumentality of the British, a
softened picture comes before us, that tends to reconcile us to much
that has been ambiguous.   At any rate the period has arrived when
England can and ought to enter upon a career which would carry
along with it, not only mighty blessings to future generations, but
offer a moral retribution for the past.   Our author relieves the dark-

ness of his general picture by alluding to the prospects which the present state of India furnishes in the following passage :—

" A new impulse is given to both commerce and agriculture. The march of improvement in the cultivation and manufacture of various productions is begun. The growth of wheat is encouraged, and even large quantities of fine flour imported thence into England. The indigo trade has become amazing by the improvement in the manipulation of that article. Sugar, coffee, opium, cotton, spices, rice, every product of this rich and varied region, will all find a greater demand, and consequently a greater perfection from culture, under these circumstances. There is, in fact, no species of vegetable production which, in this glorious country, offering in one part or another the temperature of every known climate, may not be introduced. Such is the fertility of the land under good management, that the natives often now make 26*l.* per acre of their produce. The potato is becoming as much esteemed there as it has long been in Europe and America. Tea is likely to become one of its most important articles of native growth. Our missionaries of various denominations— episcopalians, catholics, baptists, methodists, moravians, etc., are zealously labouring to spread knowledge and Christianity; and there is nothing, according to the Christian brahmin, Rammohun Roy, which the Indian people so much desire as an English education. Let that be given, and the fetters of caste must be broken at once. The press, since the great struggle in which Mr. Buckingham was driven from India for attempting its freedom, has acquired a great degree of freedom. The natives are admitted to sit on petty juries; slavery is abolished; and last, and best, education is now extensively and zealously promoted. The Company was bound by the terms of its charter in 1813 to devote 10,000*l.* annually to educating natives in the English language and English knowledge, which though but a trifling sum compared with the vast population, aided by various private schools, must have produced very beneficial effects. Bishop Heber states that on his arrival in Bengal he found that there were fifty thousand scholars, chiefly under the care of Protestant missionaries. These are the means which must eventually make British rule that blessing which it ought to have been long ago. These are the means by which we may atone, and more than atone, for all our crimes and our selfishness in India. But let us remember that we are—after the despotism of two centuries, after oceans of blood shed by us, and oceans of wealth drained by us from India, and after that blind and callous system of exaction and European exclusion which has perpetuated all the ignorance and all the atrocities of Hindu superstition, and laid the burthen of them on our own shoulders—but at this moment on the mere threshold of this better career. Let us remember that still, at this hour, Indostan is, in fact, the IRELAND OF THE EAST !"

The ameliorating influence of the arts of peaceful industry, the graciously conquering powers of even-handed justice, and of brotherly kindness, exercised by Christians over the savage, and the ferocious, are circumstances, not without exemplification. Passing by our author's sketch of the French as colonists, who have nothing to boast of, considering their limited opportunities, compared with

other European nations, we some to the English in America and to
their descendants, the present citizens of the United States. But
our readers are too familiar with the treatment which both nations
have extended to the red men of the Prairies to require any particular details in our pages, even although we had more space than is
left us for their introduction." There is one passage in the history
of America, however, which should never be forgotten by colonist,
whether they regard their temporal prosperity, the well-being of the
natives around them, or the spread of light and truth. "We refer to
the case and conduct of William Penn in his fair, open, Christian
treaty with the natives of the province which was granted to him,
and the detail should put to flight, for ever the cuckoo song that
savages in general, and the aboriginal inhabitants of America in particular, are naturally treacherous, vindictive, fonder of blood than of
peace, and beyond the reach of moral or intellectual culture.

"Arise, William Penn, and give answer! These are the very things
that in his day he heard on all hands. On all hands he was pointed at and
by which the colonies were defended : he was told that nothing but force
could secure the colonists against the red men; he was told that there was
no faith in them, and therefore no faith could be kept with them. He
believed, in the power of Christianity, and therefore he did not believe these assertions. He believed the Indians to be men, and that they
were, therefore, accessible to the language and motives of humanity.
He believed in the omnipotence of justice and good faith; and disbelieved all the sophistry by which wars and violence are maintained
by an interested generation. He resolved to try the experiment of
kindness and peace : it was a grand and a momentous trial: it was
no other than to put the truth of Christianity to test, and to learn
whether the world's philosophy or that of the Bible were the best.
It was attempted to alarm him by all kinds of bloody treachery: he
was ridiculed as an enthusiast, but he calmly cast himself on his conviction of the literal truth of the Gospel, and the result was, the
most splendid triumph in history. He demonstrated, in the face of the
world, and all its arguments and all its practice, that peace may be
maintained when men will it; and that there is no need, and therefore no excuse, for the bloodshed and the violence that are perpetually
marking the expanding boundaries of what is oddly enough termed
civilization.

"William Penn received a grant of the province to which he gave
the name of Pennsylvania, as payment for money owing to his father'
Admiral Penn, from the government. He accepted this grant, because it
secured him against any other claimant from Europe. It gave him a title
in the eyes of the Christian world; but he did not believe that it gave him
any other title. He knew in his conscience that the country was already in
the occupation of tribes of Indians, who inherited it from their ancestors
by a term of possession, which probably was unequalled by anything
which the inhabitants of Europe had to shew for their territories."

A treaty honourable and sincere on both sides was concluded amid
certain simple and solemn observances; and, continues our author,—

" There is no doubt that Penn may be declared the most perfect Christian statesman that ever lived. He had the sagacity to see that men, to be made trust-worthy, need only to be treated as men;—that the doctrines of the New Testament were to be taken literally and fully; and he had the courage and honesty, in the face of all the world's practice and maxims, to confide in Christian truth. It fully justified him. What are the cunning and the so called profound policy of the most subtle statesmen to this? This confidence, at which the statesmen of our own day would laugh as folly and simplicity, proved to be a reach of wisdom far beyond their narrow vision. But it is to be feared that the selfishness of governments is as much concerned as their short-sightedness in the clumsy and ruinous manner in which affairs between nations are managed; for what would become of armies and natives, places and pensions, if honest treatment should take place of the blow first and the word after, and of all that false logic by which aggression is made to appear necessary?

" The results of this treaty were most extraordinary. While the Friends retained the government of Pennsylvania it was governed without an army, and was never assailed by a single enemy. The Indians retained their firm attachment to them; and, more than a century afterwards, and after the government of the state had long been resumed by England, and its old martial system introduced there, when civil war broke out between the colonies and the mother country, and the Indians were instigated by the mother to use the tomahawk and the scalping-knife against the children, using,—according to her own language, which so roused the indignation of Lord Chatham,—' every means which God and Nature had put into her power,' to destroy or subdue them,—these Indians, who laid waste the settlements of the colonists with fire, and drenched them in blood, remembered the treaty with the *sons of Onas*, AND KEPT IT INVIOLATE!"

Such were some of the results of that famous treaty of which Voltaire so pointedly and happily remarked, " That it was the only one ever concluded which was not ratified by an oath, and the only one that never was broken." How unlike to Penn's, and that of the Friends of Pennsylvania, has been the general treatment of the Red Indians, and how different the consequences!—so that when the Missionaries preach to them the genuine doctrines of Christianity, the children of the desert have immediately been struck with the total discrepancy between these doctrines and the lives and practices of European professors, and have said, if these be the principles of your religion.

" ' Go and preach them to your countrymen. If they have any efficacy in them, let us see it shewn upon them. Make them good, just, and full of this love you speak of. Let them regard the rights and property of Indians. You have also a people amongst you that you have torn from their own country, and hold in slavery. Go home and give them freedom; do as your book says,—as you would be done by. When you have done that, come again, and we will listen to you.' "

We have so lately shewn the working of the English system of colonization as exemplified in South Africa, that we need not tarry at present upon this part of our author's picture, father than to state, that he, like other philanthropists makes it appear that in these regions our countrymen are widely and actively employed in the work of expulsion, moral corruption, and destruction of the original tribes.

In New Holland the system which Columbus introduced in the very first moment of discovery has, as regards the throwing off the putrid matter of our corrupt social state on a simple and unsuspecting country, so as to inoculate it with the rankness of our worst physical and moral diseases, been largely and warmly patronised. There are benefits, however, connected with this system, and which, we think, might be much more extensively produced, that has ever yet been realized, that have not been noticed in the volume before us. But to come to a conclusion, and to the islands in the Pacific, let us point out to our readers some of the effects produced when pure Christianity, and means that peacefully as well as affectionately bear upon the hearts of deeply degraded barbarians, are employed,—and when employed only by a handful of defenceless humble Missionaries.

The missionaries have presented them with that which alone they needed to insure their happiness,—Christianity; and the consequence has been, that within the last twenty years they have conveyed a cargo of idols to the depôt of the Missionary Society in London; they have become factors to furnish our vessels with provisions, and merchants to deal with us in the agricultural growth of their own country. Their language has been introduced to writing, and they have gained the knowledge of letters. They have many of them, emerged from the tyranny of the will of their chiefs into the protection of a written law, abounding with liberal and enlightened principles, and 200,000 of them are reported to have embraced Christianity.

The most beautiful thing is, that when they embraced Christianity, they embraced it in its fulness and simplicity. They had no ancient sophisms and political interests, like Europe, to induce them to accept Christianity by halves, admitting just as much as suited their selfishness, and explaining away, or abutting their eyes resolutely to the rest; they, therefore, furnished a most striking practical proof of the manner in which Christianity would be understood by the simple-hearted and the honest, and in doing this they pronounced the severest censure upon the barbarous and unchristian condition of proud Europe. 'When,' says Mr. Ellis, 'Christianity was adopted by the people, human sacrifices, infant murder, and war, entirely ceased.' Mr. Ellis and Mr. Williams agree that they also immediately gave freedom to all their slaves: They never considered the two things compatible.

Wherever Christianity has been embraced by them, the inhabitants have become actively industrious, and, to use the words of Mr. Williams, are 'very apt indeed' at learning European trades. Mr. Ellis's statement is—' There are now carpenters who hire themselves out to captains of ships to work at repairs of vessels, etc., for which they receive regular wages; and there are blacksmiths that hire themselves out to captains of ships, for the purpose of preparing iron-work required in building or repairing ships. The natives have been taught not only to construct boats, but to build vessels, and there are, perhaps, twenty (there have been as many as forty,) small vessels, of from forty to eighty or ninety tons burthen, built by the natives, navigated sometimes by Europeans, and manned by natives, all the fruit of the natives' own skill and industry. They have been taught to build neat and comfortable houses, and to cultivate the soil. They have new wants; a number of articles of clothing and commerce are necessary to their comfort, and they cultivate the soil to supply them. At one island, where I was once fifteen months without seeing a single European, excepting our own families, there were, I think, twenty-eight ships put in for provisions last year, and all obtained the supplies they wanted. Besides cultivating potatoes and yams, and raising stock, fowls, and pigs, the cultivation, the spinning and the weaving of the cotton has been introduced by missionary artizans; and there are some of the chiefs, and a number of the people, especially in one of the islands, who are now decently clothed in garments made after the European fashion, produced from cotton grown in their own gardens, spun by their own children, and woven in the islands. One of the chiefs of the island of Rarotonga, as stated by the missionaries, never wears any other dress than that woven in the island. They have been taught also to cultivate the sugar-cane, which is indigenous, and to make sugar, and some of them have large plantations, employing at times forty men. They supply the ships with this useful article, and, at some of the islands, between fifty and sixty vessels touch in a single year. The natives of the island send a considerable quantity away; I understand that one station sent as much as forty tons away last year. In November last a vessel of ninety tons burthen, built in the islands, was sent to the colony of New South Wales, laden with Tahitian-grown sugar. Besides the sugar they have been taught to cultivate, they prepare arrow-root, and they sent to England in one year, as I was informed by merchants in London, more than had been imported into this country for nearly twenty previous years. Cattle, also, have been introduced and preserved, chiefly by the missionaries: pigs, dogs, and rats were the only animals they had before, but the missionaries have introduced cattle among them. While they continued heathen, they disregarded, nay, destroyed some of those first landed among them; but since that time they have highly prized them, and by their attention to them they are now so numerous as to enable the natives to supply ships with fresh beef at the rate of threepence a pound. The islanders have also been instructed by the missionaries in the manufacture of cocoa-nut oil, of which large quantities are exported. They have been taught to cultivate tobacco, and this would have been a valuable article of commerce had not the duty in New South Wales been so high as to exclude that grown in the islands from the market. The above are some of the proofs that Christianity prepares the way for, and necessarily leads to, the civilization of those by whom it is adopted. There are now in operation among a people who, when the missionaries arrived, were destitute of a written language, seventy-eight *schools, which* contain between 12,000 and 13,000 *scholars.* The Tahitians have also a simple, explicit, and wholesome *code of laws,* as the result of their imbibing the principles of Christianity. This code of laws is printed and circulated among them, understood by all, and acknowledged by all as the supreme rule of action for all classes in their civil and social relations. The laws have been productive of great benefits."

Together with William Howitt, we entertain the most sanguine hopes in regard to any system of colonization when Christian principle and Christian exertions characterize the proceedings of Europeans, such as single-minded Missionaries have often exemplified. It is quite possible, no doubt, that men under the pretext of converting the heathen, may all the while have selfish and worldly objects in view. It is in perfect harmony with human nature that the noblest engine may be misused, and that Christianity itself may be made a cloak to the disparagement of any cause. We observe, for example, that lately in the debates in parliament relative to the colonization of New Zealand, it has been repeatedly asserted that certain individuals who have gone out to that country with the professed design of spreading the Gospel among its benighted inhabitants, have in reality contemplated large territorial acquisitions, and, indeed, established themselves most advantageously and graspingly as proprietors of land. It has also been alleged that the Society at home under whose auspices these speculators have been located in New Zealand, is unwilling to let such practices be known or examined, and that therefore the scheme of a colony authorized and regulated by parliament according to mercantile and avowedly worldly purposes, is resisted by the servants and the patrons of the missionary combinations. If all this be true it is high time that the facts should be fully exposed; but it can no more operate to the prejudice of the missionary cause, than as an instance where the best thing may be abused, and as affording one more proof that hypocrisy is not yet banished from the world.

Looking to the islands of the Pacific, behold a spectacle where men who were lately savages, are savages no longer. In many instances, no doubt, they are Christians in reality; while they have advanced far in civilization, in the arts of peaceful, profitable industry; in the very arts too that are calculated to give them any importance among nations and in the department of commerce. The view is delightful; but are there no threatening clouds? Listen—

"All this springing civilization—this young Christianity—this scene of beauty and peace, are endangered. The founders of a new and happier state, the pioneers and artificers of civilization, stand aghast at the ruin that threatens their labours,—that threatens the welfare,—nay, the very existence of the simple islanders amongst whom they have wrought such miracles of love and order. And whence arises this danger? whence comes this threatened ruin? Is some race of merciless savages about to burst in upon these interesting people and destroy them? Yes, the same irreeliminable and indomitable savages,' that have ravaged and oppressed every nation which they have conquered, 'from China to Peru.' The same savages that laid waste the West Indies; that massacred the South Americans; that have chased the North Americans to 'the far west;' that shot the Caffres for their cattle; that have covered the coasts of Africa with the blood and fires and rancorous malice of the slave wars; that have exterminated millions of Hindus by famine, and hold a hundred millions of them at this moment in the most abject condition of poverty and oppression; the same savages that are at this moment also carrying the Hill Coolies from the East—as if they had not a scale of enormities there wide enough for their capacity of cruelty—to sacrifice them in the West, on the graves of millions of murdered negroes; the same savages are come hither also. The savages of Europe, the most heartless and merciless race that ever inhabited the earth,—a race, for the range and continuance of its atrocities, without a parallel in this world. and, it may be safely believed, in any other, are busy in the South Sea Islands. A roving clan of sailors and runaway convicts have revived once more the crimes and character of the old bucaniers. They go from island to island, diffusing gin, debauchery, loathsome diseases, and murder, as freely as if they were the greatest blessings that Europe had to bestow. They are the restless and triumphant apostles of misery and destruction; and such are their achievements, that it is declared that, unless our government interpose some check to their progress, they will as completely annihilate the islanders, as the Charibs were annihilated in the West Indies."

Will not England be aroused by these and the many similar details, which William Howitt has with such fervour, beautifully conceived and enlightened philanthropy, presented in the deeply interesting and powerfully awakening volume which has now been engaging us? Yes, there is much of hope and promise in England to rejoice in the prospective vision. This very passing summer, the exertions by her sons at home, the impressions wrought upon her dependancies abroad, offer themes of gratulation and triumph. Yes, there are grounds for careering and brightening hope, for Christianity has many a heart to enshrine it in our land and to cherish its gracious activities. Without this knowledge and conviction all would be despair with the reflecting and the benevolent, because, to quote our author's conclusions,—

"There is no power but the spirit of Christianity living in the heart of the British public, which can secure justice to the millions that are crying for it from every region of the earth. It is that which must stand as the perpetual watch and guardian of humanity; and never yet has it failed. The noblest spectacle in the world is that constellation of institutions which have sprung out of this spirit of Christianity in the nation, and which are continually labouring to redress wrongs and diffuse knowledge and happiness wherever the human family extends. The ages of dreadful inflictions, and the present condition of the native tribes in our vast possessions, once known, it were a libel on the honour and faith of the nation to doubt for a moment that a new era of colonization and inter-

course with unlettered nations, has commenced; and I close this volume
of the unexampled crimes, and marvellous impolicy of Europe, with the
firm persuasion—

> " That heavenward all things tend. For all were once
>   Perfect, and all must be at length restored.
>   So God has greatly purposed; who would else
>   In his dishonoured works himself endure
>   Dishonour, and be wronged without redress.
>   Haste, then, and wheel away, a shattered world
>   Ye slow revolving seasons! We would see—
>   A sight to which our eyes are strangers yet—
>   A world that does not hate and dread His laws,
>   And suffer for its crime; would learn how fair
>   The creature is that God pronounces good,
>   How pleasant in itself what pleases Him."—*Cowper.*

ART. III.—*The History, Antiquities, Topography; and Statistics of
Eastern India.* By M. MARTIN. Vol. II. London: Allen and Co.
1888.

OWING partly to the extreme minuteness, the vast variety and
extent, the startling nature, and the striking novelty of the information, and partly to the force, the straightforwardness, and
fecundity of mind which characterize the style of Dr. Buchanan, the
original collector of this information, the present and preceding
volumes of the great work now under consideration are the most
interesting and suggestive of any publication of the kind that we
have ever perused. The portion before us extends to about *ten
hundred and fifty* octavo pages of compact print, and yet it is impossible to open it at any of its great divisions, or to glance upon
any of its chapters, without becoming so engaged as to wish to read
the whole; so that, presuming the third and concluding volume,
which will ere long appear, to be equal in point of value to either of
the earlier ones, we may safely challenge any country to produce a
fuller or more precious body of facts, one more plainly and aptly
illustrated, than that which is here collected and combined. Eastern
India to Europeans need no longer be a *terra incognita*, or an im-
perfectly-known division of the globe; although the knowledge here
afforded, while it ought to stimulate enlightened and enterprizing
minds in regard to the wants and capabilities of such an important
theatre, must comprise much that will be the source of pain and
discouragement.

A knowledge of evils in any condition is a primary step to their
cure; and we cannot but think that had the immense mass of facts
now first brought before the public from the manuscript archives
possessed by the East India Company been at an earlier date made
known to the world, gratifying fruits would have already manifested

themselves,—fruits not only identified with the progress of eastern civilization, but with the advancement of British interests.

After what we stated concerning the origin, plan, purpose, and nature of this great work in our notice of the first volume, it is unnecessary to do more on the present occasion than collect into our pages a few, a very few of the particulars to be found in some comparatively narrow space belonging to one of the several districts treated of, these being the zillahs or provinces of Bhagulpoor, Goruckpoor (northward division), and Dinajpoor.

According to the information before us, these districts are not only fertile and capable of mighty improvement in regard to soil, but the social condition of their myriads of inhabitants offers themes of arresting moment. Indeed we agree with Mr. Martin in thinking that the subjects which occupy the present volume, are to the full as valuable and interesting as those which engaged the preceding portion of the work. At any rate the narrative and descriptions improve, the reflections and illustrative matter become richer as we advance; the whole exhibiting the curious and actual framework, piecemeal and combined, of society in Eastern India.

One or two of the chapters devoted to Dinajpoor will afford ample specimens for our present citing.

Dr. Buchanan has calculated upon certain data by which he explains the population of this district, and makes it to amount to 3,000,000, being about 558 persons for each square mile. Some anomalous circumstances are connected with this multitude of inhabitants and the soil upon which they dwell. The prevailing poverty and degradation of the people, and the low as well as circumscribed degree of cultivation to which the land is subjected, need not, however, be marvelled at; but when it is stated that with such an overwhelming population, there is a general complaint of a scarcity of workmen, we may well pause and reflect. Large tracts of waste lands intimate that there is a want of farmers. This deficiency is accounted for by the extreme poverty of that class of men who have no other means than will just enable them to cultivate land that is in good condition, and from which they can receive an immediate and certain return; while the immense profit which those, who have any capital, make by lending out money to necessitous neighbours, prevents the necessary funds for the improvement of the soil from being expended in that way. Then as to the difficulty of procuring workmen, it is alleged that this arises chiefly from the want of skill and of proper implements to facilitate labour; so that the quantity which individuals can perform, is exceedingly small, and almost every individual is therefore engaged. The general inactivity and want of energy in the people must also be taken into the account; so that their condition forms a complete contrast to their physical advantages, such as the capabilities of the soil.

There are some striking facts stated in regard to the amount and progress of population in Dinajpoor, which must be valuable as data in the science of political economy. The enormous multitude of the inhabitants may be easily accounted for. We are told that there are not probably 1000 persons born in the district who are in the army, or who have left it for service of any kind, or indeed who have at all emigrated, except such as have absconded from the fear of the law, who form a numerous class. Then, according to the prevalent notions of the Mohammedans as well as Hindus in these parts, no duty seems to be more assiduously inculcated than that the women should propagate the species as fast as possible; and the lesson is cordially obeyed. To be childless at an early age is a circumstance that excites not only contempt but disgust amongst the natives. Besides, widows are allowed to live in a sort of detached marriage state, and without being excluded from society; it would, therefore, be matter of wonder that the population has not increased at a much faster rate than it has done, rather than otherwise, were it not that certain counteracting circumstances exist, which are described in the following manner :—

"There seem to be two principal means that keep the population within the bounds of subsistence, one is early marriage, and the other disease. In all the larger animals nearly resembling man, with whose manners we are well acquainted, such as the horse, ass, cow, or sheep, it has been found, that where the sexes have been allowed to unite, so soon as actuated by desire, the offspring was puny, and the operation uncertain; and I think we may safely extend the analogy to the human race. Some peculiar tribes of men in India, especially those in the western parts, and the bearers of the palanquins, are no doubt strong men; but it is not within my reach at present to form a rational conjecture concerning the reason why these differ from their countrymen. It suffices to say, that the inhabitants of Dinajpoor are a puny, weak race, and are, far from having numerous families, notwithstanding their early marriages, which on the woman's side almost always are consummated before the age of thirteen years, and on the man's very commonly before the age of sixteen. In the families of landholders it is very uncommon to trace three successive generations; and in order to preserve the succession, recourse must be had to adoption, more usually after one regular succession than after a longer period. These landholders are all married when children, and enjoy an abundant diet, comfortable dwellings, and plenty of warm clothing. It may indeed be with justice said, that the villages of Dinajpoor swarm with children. This, however, I believe, does not proceed from the prolificness of individuals, but is the natural consequence of the people being unhealthy and short lived, which of course requires a large proportion of children to the number of adults. The moralist, who with a view of checking vice, should succeed in introducing early marriages, would, I am persuaded, produce great injury. The breed of men would not only degenerate, but vice would become more predominant."

But it is disease which seems to be the grand check to the excess of population in Dinajpoor; and, to posologists, many of Dr. Buchanan's statements must be as interesting as other branches of his report are to political moralists. Fevers of the remittent kind annually sweep away multitudes; and the want of stimulating diet, and of comfortable lodging and clothing, in a great measure accounts for the prevalence of this disease. Small pox does little injury, and inoculation for this malady is pretty general. A kind of leprosy, a terrible and loathsome disease, is not uncommon, though in some other parts of Bengal it is still more prevalent. In it the skin becomes wrinkled and discoloured (a white leprosy is rare), the joints of the hands and feet drop off; it has no tendency to spontaneous cure, but continues to afflict the patient until death. It seems to be hereditary but not infectious, occupying in Bengal the place which scrofula does in the colder parts of Europe.

Before leaving the subject of population we will return for a moment to the condition of widows in the provinces under consideration; and surely if ever a hard fate was the lot of any large class of people it is that of these poor women. That many of these would rather be burned alive than submit to the contumely and oppression that awaits them after the decease of their husbands is not unaccountable.

The hardships imposed upon Hindu widows of rank will be seen from many circumstances in the statement that follows.

"They are stript of the numerous ornaments which they enjoyed while children and wives, and are not even allowed to wear a red border to their dress, while they are compelled to sleep on the ground, exposed to insects and vermin, and to act as menial servants to the rain beauties who are decked out in the ornaments of which they have been deprived. Women of a high mind often prefer the funeral pile, while many others submit with patience, especially in the families of landholders, where they have young sons totally incapable of managing their affairs; but it is not wonderful that many young women, conscious of their beauty, and thoughtless concerning its decay, scorn to submit to such harsh regulations."

That in these circumstances many widows should betake themselves to a loose life is likely enough. A rage for marriage is also easily accounted for.

But this rage is not confined to the tender sex; it infects the whole population, male and female; and hence a vast amount of that poverty which grinds to the dust the people of Dinajpoor. We are told that,—

"A man who has not money sufficient to defray the expenses of the ceremony (marriage ceremonies are enormously expensive) is everywhere willing to borrow it at any interest, and thus involves himself and offspring in difficulties, from which death alone can relieve them. In some

visions, I found that even common labourers sold their services for from
18 to 24 months, in order to raise at once a sum sufficient to enable them
to marry; and during that time the wife of course is left to provide for
herself in the best manner she can. The master, in such cases, finds the
servant in food and raiment."

"The burdens, observances, customs, and distinctions, which prevail among the Hindus, are as oppressive as ever obtained among
any people; and while still on the subject of population and marriage, some of these degrading and absurd institutions may be
strikingly illustrated. Certain orders of the Brahmans in Dinajpoor furnish examples. We are told,—

"A Kulin Brahman of Barondro cannot marry above three or four
wives, the fathers of Barondro not choosing to pay for unreasonable undertakings; for the husband always gets money with each wife, more and
more in proportion to the lowness of her birth; and he seldom gives himself any trouble about maintaining his wives and children, but leaves
these duties to the care of his father-in-law. If the family happens to
consist of sons chiefly, the maternal grandfather has great profit, because
he receives money for each at his marriage; but if there are many
daughters he has made a bad speculation; and, unless very rich, is ruined,
as he must not only sell everything, but even borrow and beg to the
utmost of his power, in order to procure them husbands. They have,
however, a greater indulgence than the lower orders; for a Kulin girl
continues marriageable at all ages, although it is considered as very disgraceful for the father to keep her long waiting; and he is even very apt
to incur still greater disgrace, by her forgetting the laws of chastity,
which these girls, brought up in the full expectation of early marriage,
are very apt to do. Husbands are, however, difficult to procure, as a
woman cannot marry a man younger than herself, and as a large proportion of the men are bought by the parents of low women. If a Barondro
Kulin marries the daughter of a Kap he is degraded to that rank; but
his sons and grandsons are more respected than usual, and are more
marriageable. A Barondro Kulin may, however, marry the daughter of
a Srotiyo without any degradation, and all the children of this marriage
are Kulins. A Kap also receives money when his son marries the
daughter of a Srotiyo, the children are elevated to the rank and Kap; but
the husband must keep his wives and children at home, and provide for
them. The Srotiyo men were thus very ill provided with women, and
so long as the rules of caste were strictly regarded, a great many of them
could not procure wives. But since the deaths of Rani Bhowani of Raj-
shahi, and of Raja Krishnochundro of Nodiya, two very pious and powerful landholders, who supported the laws of caste, these men have been
let loose, and are not ashamed to give money to procure wives, so that
the higher ranks of Kulin and Kap are defrauded both of due profit and
pleasure; for the Srotiyo fathers are not able to resist the temptation of
the money, especially as they also save what they must have given to
their betters.

"A Barhi Kulin Brahman may marry as many wives as he pleases, and some have 60; but in general they cannot procure above 8 or 10. They visit them alternately, and give themselves no sort of trouble about the maintenance of either the mothers or children.

So much for some of the deplorable features in the social condition of the people in Dinajpoor and other districts.

The food of the people is said to be in general superior to their lodging, furniture, and clothing; and in the appendix belonging to the Dinajpoor district especially, there is presented a most curious and minute account of the monthly household expenditure of families in six different ranks of life, that is well worthy the consideration of the merchant and capitalist who may be inclined to speculate in regard to a particular province in India, or who desire to obtain the utmost precision of facts whereon to found certain conclusions regarding the British empire in the East.

On the subject of food we only quote a short statement.

"Many persons," says Dr. Buchanan, "I am aware, consider that vegetable food, highly seasoned with capsicum, and water for drink, is the best diet adapted for a warm climate; but I am persuaded that they are mistaken, and have been misled by observing the sickness of newly-arrived troops or seamen, which is too often preceded by excess and intemperance. Whoever, I think, has travelled much with natives, and been witness to the weakness of their constitutions in resisting the changes of air and water, will agree with me in saying, that those who enjoy a diet which includes animal food and strong liquors in moderate quantities, are best able to resist the influence of unhealthy climates and the sudden changes of air."

We may connect this latter statement with another piece of information for the benefit of travellers in these eastern parts. For such erratic characters, it is said that there is no accommodation. One landholder, to be sure, entertains those who choose to apply; and the natives in general find people of their own caste, who will give them room in their house to sleep on the ground; and the absolute necessaries of life may commonly be procured, when there are few persons in company. But unless Europeans are travelling post from station to station, which requires relays of carriages to be placed on purpose, and is attended with an enormous expense, they must provide themselves with tents, and carry with them almost every person or thing that they require.

"A work of the present kind does not allow us to do more than speak of its general arrangement and character, and offer some few illustrative specimens under one or two distinct heads of the division of its multifarious subjects. Every branch which falls under the extensive terms, History, Topography, Antiquities, Religion, Education, &c. &c., might just as advantageously have been dwelt upon as those concerning population, marriage, and other social features, of which we have presented some specimens. One of the most

important portions of this elaborate work is that in which a circumstantial account is given of the rent, tenure, and produce of the different districts described; and now, since the proprietors of the
East India Company are dependent for their dividends on the territorial revenue of India, the management of public and private
estates becomes a matter of the deepest interest to capitalists and
speculators. To all such the necessary information will be found in
Montgomery Martin's "Eastern India;" nor do we for a moment
wonder that many old Anglo-Indians have declared that this extensive survey has presented them with a clearer view of the anatomy
of the East than anything they ever saw or heard during their
sojourn in Hindostan. Such an official survey required seven years
to complete it,—years that must have been industriously occupied,
and it was cheaply obtained at an outlay of £30,000.

Art. IV.—*A New Dictionary of the English Language.* By CHARLES
RICHARDSON. 2 Vols. 4to. London: Black, Young, and Young.
1837.

ONE of the principal excellences of a new Dictionary is to be looked
for in the completeness of the Vocabulary. As we do not propose
to give the history of English lexicography, we shall date all its improvements in this, as well as in other particulars, from the time of
the great work of Johnson, which deservedly constitutes a large
portion of his fame. Before that time, the Englishman was not provided with a Dictionary equal to the demands of a language which
had become at once so copious and so much cultivated; nor with one
sufficiently full in the collection of words. To supply this defect was
the first great difficulty that attended the labours of Johnson. "The
deficiency of dictionaries," he remarks, "was immediately apparent; and when they were exhausted, what was yet wanting must
be sought by fortuitous and unguided excursions into books, and
gleaned, as industry should find, or chance should offer it, in
the boundless chaos of a living speech. My search, however, has
been either skilful or lucky; for I have much augmented the vocabulary." He fixed, as he says himself, the works of Sir Philip
Sidney, (who died in 1586) for the boundary, beyond which he
made few excursions. He retained faithfully the language of poetry
as far back as Shakspeare and Ben Johnson, though not without sufficient cautions annexed respecting the use of many words. The
poetry of his age, no less than that of the age preceding, abjured
everything antiquated in English phraseology; and perhaps Johnson's
decisions concerning words *not used*, and *obsolete*, are not of much
value; nor have they been very scrupulously regarded. A living language is always mutable, and the English language is singularly so.
Some new words are acquired which supplant their predecessors,

and old words are sometimes revived, and again grow into favour. It is manifest, therefore, if we pass over in silence the imperfections necessarily incident to a dictionary of any language, that a responsibility must be assumed or reposed somewhere, for improving and perfecting from one time to another the vocabulary of a living language. Something of this has been attempted at different times in English; by Ash, too much in some respects, and too little in others; by Mason, in his Supplement to Johnson, not enough, and not very successfully as far as he proceeded; a little by Walker, and more by Webster; and most of all by Todd, who, we confess, wins something of our favour, by the manner in which he speaks of the English Lexicographer. "After all," says he, "what the present editor has done, he considers but as dust in the balance, when weighed against the work of Dr. Johnson."

We come now to speak more particularly of the words added by Mr. Todd to those in Johnson's Dictionary. Chalmers, in a notice prefixed to his *Abridgment*, informs us, that it contains every word in Todd's edition of Johnson, and above fourteen thousand more than were given in Johnson's Abridgment; that the whole forms the most extensive vocabulary ever published; and that, in consequence of the additions introduced by Mr. Todd, it becomes a complete glossary of the early English writers.

Johnson, indeed, in his Abridgment, omitted, we believe, at least three thousand words, which were contained in his great work. But still it must be quite an appalling fact to the common English reader, that so many thousand words are added, that were not before contained in his manual; and he will be apt to think it very marvellous, that he is able to read and understand everything in his own language, while he is furnished only with a vocabulary which is so defective. But the mystery will in a great degree vanish by a little explanation; and it will be curious to those who have not examined the subject, to see how such an unknown treasure has been acquired.

It is a fair subject of inquiry, how far back the Lexicographer should go for the materials of his work. If Chaucer is fairly entitled to the appellation of ' Father of English heroic verse,' it would seem to afford a sufficient reason for inserting his words, however antiquated, or obsolete. Though much of his poetry comes so near a dead language, that some of the poets of the last century translated portions of them into modern phrase, yet certain words and expressions of his are often revived, and contribute their share to preserve that distinction which exists between the language of poetry and the language of prose. The language of Britain, which had undergone so much revolution, seemed in the time of Chaucer to have gained little consistency in orthography or grammatical construction. Though he wrote nearly two centuries after the Norman conquest, yet so heterogeneous, in the mean time, were the materials of which the language was composed, and so little had it been cultivated, that it was a kind of wilderness, that required the hand of art to subdue it, and demanded great efforts to polish and adorn it, after it had lost much of its former rudeness. Chaucer did less than might have been expected of him towards the accomplishment of this vast work. The subjects of his poems were of a popular kind, and, like most other poets, his object also was to please. And we cannot but think, from a comparison of some of his poems with the gleanings of other writings in prose, nearly contemporaneous, that mixture of phraseology is found in his compositions, more unnatural than was required by the state of the language when he wrote, if not bordering upon affectation. Like many other poets, in attempting to shun what was trite, he appears to have fallen into some ungraceful singularities; and in avoiding vulgar diction, to have been occasionally betrayed into the use of pedantic phraseology. It is difficult, however, to form a very precise judgment in the case; for so little can be gathered from contemporary writers, that Chaucer himself is generally referred to, for ascertaining the condition of the English language at the time when he wrote. One thing, however, is sufficiently manifest, namely, that his writings contribute a portion to that old *thesaurus* of poetic phrase, which, combined with more modern diction, produces a luxuriance of style, that gives to the English language a distinguished eminence.

Another copious source of increase to the English vocabulary is the improvements and inventions in arts and sciences, the extension of commerce and the prevalence of war, and a growing intercommunity of fashion and literature among the nations of Europe. Now there can be no question, that the more general terms, such as the names of the arts and sciences, and their subdivisions, should be introduced, though it is difficult even here to preserve consistency and relative proportion. But any endeavours of the lexicographer to collect and explain all the technical terms in medicine, law, commerce, arts, and general science, would result in additions more cumbrous than useful. Some maintain that technical words are not to be considered as a part of language, and are not entitled in general to admission into a dictionary, claiming the merit of a standard. As a general rule, this is the most safe; and the exceptions must be left to the judgment of authors and compilers, who will find it sufficiently hard to satisfy themselves. Upon any plan, however, words of the kind we have mentioned must be somewhat numerous, and must increase from age to age, as long as a language shall live. Thus, to take a palpable instance, since the time of Johnson; to the word *Galvanism*, which is introduced, as it should be, by Mr. Todd, he must add, as he does, *Galvaniok*, *Galvanize*, and *Galvanometer*. Without any careful search or effort, many words of this sort must present themselves, which demand a place in a dictionary: Akin to these are the names of sects, and what pertains to sects and parties, in philosophy, and religion, and politics. Johnson was very sparing in the introduction of these even as they existed in his time; but to show what a fruitful addition they make, we need mention only a few words first inserted by Todd, which will suggest many more of a similar kind. Thus, *Pythagorean*, substantive and adjective; *Pythagorical, Pythagoric, Pythagorism*. *Arian*, substantive and adjective; *Arianism, Arianize*. *Jacobin*, substantive and adjective; *Jacobinical, Jacobinism, Jacobinize*. The few words of this kind which were introduced by Johnson, as far as we have observed, were inserted rather as common appellatives, and as expressive of the qualities of those who resembled a sect, than for the sect itself, or the founder of it; as may be seen in *Cynick, Cynical; Epicurean, Epicurism*.

We have said, that war and the military art have been among the productive causes of new words; and it is not a novel suggestion. More than a century has now passed since the authors of the Spectator reprobated the corruptions that were taking place in the English language, in consequence of the existing war with France. *Pontoons, fascines, marauder, corps, chamade, cartel*, and others, are among the words which met and successfully resisted the vollies of wit and humour which were directed against them by those authors, and acquired a place in Johnson's Dictionary. These and others of the same class, it appears, were just creeping into our language, when Addison and his coadjutors were taking cognizance of literature, and morals, and manners, in the Spectator. That such words were then uncommon, appears from what the Spectator subjoined to a letter which purported to be written by a young gentleman in the army to his father. "The father found it contained great news, but could not guess what it was. He immediately communicated it to the curate of the parish, who, upon the reading of it, being vexed to see anything which he could not understand, fell into a kind of passion, and told him that his son had sent him a letter that was neither fish, flesh, nor good red herring."

The late wars and political relations between the countries of Europe have added somewhat to the list of similar words.

A very large number of words compounded with *in, im*, and *un*, for the most part in a private sense, and some of them being mere varieties in the initial spelling, and being also interchangeable, are added to Johnson's list by Mr. Todd. Of these we believe there are not far from a thousand. There are also seventy or eighty compounded with *all*, as *all-admiring, all-approved*, &c. And if we add to them other words variously compounded, such as *high-aimed, high-swollen, slop-seller, grass-green, chair-service, dram-drinker, plain-hearted, manor-house, manor-seat*, &c. which are found throughout the book, we shall swell the catalogue of compounds to a great amount. How far such compounds are entitled to admission into a dictionary, we will not decide very peremptorily; but they scarcely deserve to be called new words, or additional words. There are many words of this kind in Johnson, and consistency seems to demand, therefore, that, as far as they are well authorized, a subsequent compiler should insert such as are not already recorded. But it is very manifest that these respond to caprice and fashion in the composition of such words; and that it is impossible for a dictionary to keep pace with the fancies of writers in their formation and use.

Another prolific source of increase to the English vocabulary is the analogical formation of words of different classes. Such is for instance as adjectives in *able*, or *ible*. There is something worthy of a passing notice in this kind of words, denominated by Horne Tooke "potential passive adjectives." This name is for the most part descriptive of their meaning. They were originally borrowed words derived from the Latin words in *bilis* through the French. But we have not been satisfied with forming those merely, which we have borrowed from the Latin; for having once found the convenience of the form, that analogical process, which is always taking place in some degree in the changes and improvements of language, has given the same form to many genuine English words; such, for instance, as the familiar terms *teachable* and *tameable*. When this method was first adopted from the Latin, it was thought necessary to translate it for the common reader into an equivalent expression. And in an old manuscript version of the New Testament, which we have seen cited, supposed to be written in the reign of Edward the Third, is found the following, among other examples of the same kind; "From henceforth, brethren, whatever things be amiable, *very*" (with the explanation annexed) "able to be loved."

All modern dictionaries, however, show us, that, being in full possession of this form, words of this kind have been multiplied as our language as occasion or convenience demanded. For instance, the following, *forgivable, deprivable, unpleadable, bewailable, devisable,* and *extirpable,* and a multitude more.

Again, words terminating in *ful,* denoting abundance or excess, constitute a considerable addition to the latter dictionaries. Among these are *abuseful, deviceful, taleful, faultful, toilful,* &c. So also those terminating in *less,* expressive of the diminution or absence of something. We have witnessed the prevalence of fashion in this class of words, and their consequent tendency to increase. In the dictionary we are examining, we find, among numerous others, *flameless, waveless, brimless, rayless, passionless, passless, lossless,* and many more.

Another class which we shall mention consists of substantives in *er,* sometimes *or,* denoting agency, such as *blackener, blandisher, caller, desolater, despoiler, desponder, fluter,* which are introduced among many others of the same kind by Mr. Todd. There are no limits to terms of this description, and a vast many pass without animadversion in conversation, and might do so in

writing, which have not found a place in any printed vocabulary, as done...
... a subsequent...

Then, again, there is that boundless catalogue of abstract nouns formed from adjectives, usually by the termination *ness*, sometimes *ty*. Words of this kind are constantly increasing, and must continue to increase. Many, it is difficult to form an estimate of the number, are added by Todd. *Inability, abstractedness, fabulousness, involuntariness, manifoldness, unqualifiedness, unsupportableness*, are a sufficient sample of the additions of these long words.

So also adverbs from adjectives by the addition of *y* or *ly* make a considerable addition; as *abstinently, bigotedly, calumniously, inheritably, unobservedly*, &c.

Again, there are additions occasioned by repeating the verb, when it is used both as a transitive and an intransitive. Johnson was not very exact in this particular, and Walker was negligent, overlooking sometimes what his predecessor had done correctly in this way. There are additions also of verbs converted from nouns, as, to *extinct, livery, quick, quip, rook*; so likewise of nouns from verbs without any change, as, *abbreviate, fluster, foreshew*; of adjectives from substantives, as, *absorbent, fiscal*; of substantives from adjectives, as *bitter, desperate, positive*.

Last and not least in this enumeration, are the active participal nouns, which are added to the vocabulary by Mr. Todd, to a great extent; such as *biting, fading, deserving, despising, ingratiating, interfering, loathing*. These additions are of questionable utility, though, if they are admitted at all, it may be done upon very slight authority. We are sure that we could furnish a large catalogue of such additions. Indeed, if we examine the nature of these words, not only in English, but in other languages, we may readily perceive how easily they perform the office of substantives, and how hopeless it is, by singling out a part of them, to do justice to the whole class.

We have thus given something like a classification of some of the principal additions made to the English vocabulary by Mr. Todd. The classification is not complete, but it is sufficiently so to account in a great degree for the fact of such a large increase of words, and to quiet much of the alarm which this increase might occasion to those who are not accustomed to speculations of this kind.

From a pretty full examination, therefore, of the work before us, we have no hesitation in congratulating the public on its appearance. One of the most considerable obstacles to an improved course of instruction in any language, is the want of a good lexicon. This being obtained, a satisfactory progress will be the natural consequence. Few labourers in the field of literature are more deserving of encouragement and commendation than lexicographers.

Nor is their occupation, as sometimes represented, one of mere drudgery. The labour, indeed, of preparing a good dictionary is great, but it is a labour combined with numerous sources of mental gratification. It should ever be remembered, that Milton, while suffering the evils of blindness, cheered his solitude by collecting materials for a Latin dictionary; and three folio volumes of authorities, are records of the recreations and pastime of a mind occupied in the splendid creations of "Paradise Lost."

ART. V,—*Hints to the Charitable, being Practical Observations on the proper Regulation of Private Charity. Intended principally for the Use of those who take an active Interest in Village Economy. By the* Hon. and Rev. S. G. OSBORNE. London: Roon. 1838.

MANY schemes in recent times have been afloat, not a few have been put to the trial, with a design to elevate the moral character, the social condition, and the comforts merely as regards the means of existence of the poor and the labouring classes. It is also an established fact, in the history of the human race, that the moment a man is conscious of being independent, that is, not to be the object of almsgiving, he not only thereafter becomes one of the productive, instead of what we called the non-productive classes of society; but he rises in the scale of intellect, and in whatever way can confer benefit and honour on himself and the community. Savings' Banks, Benefit Societies, the Poor Law Amendment Act, are instances where private as well as public exertions have been made to advance the interests of the state and the immediate condition of individuals and families, which have all been crowned with certain degrees of success. Among the measures that have been lately devised, and upon a sagacious and accurate conception of human nature (even when hampered and degraded, if you will by poverty,) as well as upon truly popular principles, is the "National Loan Fund," with the nature, the scope, and the capabilities of which every newspaper reader must be generally acquainted. We have every confidence in this enlightened scheme and institution, that it will work a revolution in a vast multitude of cases, and consequently nationally; especially where a small advance, where the command of a few pounds, will enable a tradesman, a dealer, any industrious poor man, at once to establish himself upon a footing, where something like an adequate return may be expected, and will result from his exertions. In such a case the strongest possible, because immediate and obvious, motives will be created and felt in favour of industry and economy. Previous good resolutions will be strengthened, new ones will be originated, economical advantages will be appreciated, and never afterwards, except in cases of the grossest suicidal infatuation, can such a man incur the risk of being robbed of the constant and conscious delight that is inseparable from a sense of being independent, of having a right to hold up his head among men, and of being prepared when death calls him. hence, to say, I leave not a family to be a burden to the parish.

We think that the "National Loan Fund" will, (and to a certain extent the proof has already been given,) produce upon a broad and influential scale, the mighty economical and moral benefits towards which we have glanced. It would be too much, however, to expect that the Institution will be universely applicable, or that in every instance, where it is applicable that advantage be taken of it. Obduracy, ignorance, extreme poverty, and the recklessness or helplessness and despair arising from extreme poverty's great pressure, require to be appealed to by some closer, gentler, more assiduous, and more available methods and kindnesses. Besides, as is the besetting vice, all other evils, in the social state, are most effectually assailed by direct efforts made against individual and defined points. Many philanthropists have wasted their energies by contemplating too much; by regarding every plan for ameliorating the condition of society, and of large sections of the people as unworthy of their time that had not grandeur in its front and a glorious reformation in its premises; but narrower, well, and practically directed measures are often far more fruitful of good.

In these circumstances it has been with the most cordial welcome and perfect satisfaction that we have received and read the little tract now before us; nor can it but be conducive to the benefit and satisfaction of others, when we now proceed to copy some portion of its contents, and to notice its leading principles; for thereby its circulation must be considerably enlarged, because in whatever breast real charity has taken up its abode, it is impossible that this plain, familiar and engaging exposition, (price, a trifle) will not be greedily sought after, and earnestly perused, the moment that some of its excellencies and contents are understood.

These Hints are intended principally for the use of those who take an active interest in village economy, and are calculated to be particularly applicable where there is a poor, rural population. In such cases, among farm-labourers, for example, we do not see how such an institution as the National Loan Fund can be directly of much service. We do most clearly perceive, however, that if every rural parish possessed a clergyman, a gentleman, a philanthropist like the author of the present little work, there would instantly and universally over the land be a reformation and a revolution of the most palpable and gladdening description. a well-fed, well-clothed, and a well-behaved peasantry would instantly start into being; education would be widely encouraged; and recklessness, improvidence, immorality of every other kind, would become the exception and the general rule of our landward population. It ought to be

looked upon as an anomaly in the nature of things, when farm-
servants, when country labourers, when peasants and villagers as a
great class, or as distinct classes under minor shades of condition,
are the most ignorant, the most debased in the scale of a nation's
intellectual and moral character. It is like a satire upon the pure,
the beautiful, and the abundant works of the Great Creator; it
might be construed as an argument for thinking that the turmoil,
the noisy traffic, the filth, the sickening sights, and the dense atmosphere of a city, were more congenial to man's nature, than the
earth's green, the voices and ways of its peaceful creatures, and the
invitations which rural scenery, changes, and retirement send
abroad in behalf of reflection, mental culture, and prudence. We
are not called upon, it is not for us to name or allude to the various
and complicated circumstances which have caused the forbidding
anomaly to exist in England. It is sufficient for us to remind our
readers that such is the deplorable fact, and next to assure them,
that had every parish an Osborne within it, such no longer would
be the aspect and condition of the kingdom. In the meanwhile it is
the source of no ordinary degree of satisfaction to be convinced that
our author's present little tract will, by means, partly of begetting,
partly by stimulating, speedily produce an enlightened system of
village and rural economy amongst the poor, in consequence of the
birth of many Osbornes.

The value and excellence of Mr. Osborne's Hints do not consist
in their originality, considering any one of his suggestions or statements individually: but there is originality in the combination and
arrangement, there is novelty in the measures inferred; but what is
of still greater importance, the whole, and every part separately, has
been tested by practical effects, by the author's actual experience in
management and detail,—yea, during several consecutive years. The
experiments have been conducted under his own eye, it may be
said by means of his own hand; and the results are as flattering as
they are conclusively clear.

The Hints are conveyed in the form of Letters. We cannot begin better in the way of citing, than at the beginning.

    "Dear ——,

"I do not know how I can better meet your wish 'that I would give you
an account of the clubs for the benefit of the poor that exist in the parish
with which I am connected,' than by troubling you with a few letters on
the subject, each letter referring to some one or more of the plans with
which you wish to become acquainted; my chief object being to shew you
how a given sum may be applied in charity, so as to secure the greatest
amount of benefit to the individuals relieved.

"That private charity should be properly regulated is of the highest
importance, for I firmly believe that an immense mass of evil is produced
in this country by the indiscriminate and injudicious manner in which
many persons are in the habit of relieving the wants of their poorer neigh-

neighbours." In relieving distress, we should ever seek to do so in such a manner as may tend to prevent its recurrence; we should trace it to its cause, and then apply ourselves, as far as may be, to the task of eradicating that cause.

"No one who has any knowledge of the agricultural districts will dispute the fact that a very large amount of the crime committed in them is induced by the pressure of extreme poverty; no one who has ever sought to trace the origin of this poverty, will deny that the greater proportion of it arises from habits of waste and extravagance. As the health and comfort of the body, as a whole, depends on the healthy and sound disposition of its several parts, so with a country, its well-doing, as a whole, will mainly depend upon the proper moral disposition of the various small communities of which it is composed. The man then who devotes his time to the task of raising the moral character of the parish in which he lives, acts a most useful and honourable part towards his country, and, at the same time, fulfils a duty he owes to his fellow-creatures. An experience of some years has shewn me the full value of that system of charity, which teaches the relieved that they must do much for themselves before they are entitled to expect aid from others; I know that there are persons who cry out against plans of the nature I am about to advocate, as making charity *a matter of mere cold calculation.* My understanding of the word leads me to pronounce that man as most charitable who, according to his means and station, effects the greatest quantum of good, and, therefore, I cannot but esteem that to be a foolish and weak species of benevolence which would rather give a shilling unconditionally, than upon a plan the operation of which may induce habits in the person relieved, tending to make him partially, if not wholly, independent of the aid of others. It is a poor humanity that rescues the despairing suicide from a watery grave, and then leaves him on the bank in danger of perishing by cold, or of being again driven to make the mad attempt on his own existence. A real Samaritan would see such a one to a place of shelter, and would not then leave him till every argument had been used to shew him the folly and the wickedness of the attempted act."

Indiscriminate giving of alms, of money for instance, to petitioners, is an act and a habit which cannot be separated from a host of injuries to the community and to individuals. Not to say any thing about the maldirection of funds, of that sum going to one who will make a bad use of it both to himself and as respects others, which if wisely distributed would in both ways have done positive good, see what evil the practice produces on the part of the given. Charity which, if legitimate, is twice blessed—blessing the recipient but not less the bestower, in such cases as now alluded to cannot possibly be followed by this latter reward. There can be nothing like that deliberation and reflection asserted as essential to conscious moral approbation ; there can be nothing better felt in return on the part of the giver, than release from importunity, than an easy method of satisfying a self complacency which the mere circumstance of being rich by inheritance may have enabled the giver to employ, than a cold and supercilious avoidance of a closer intimacy with per-so not so favourably situated in fickle fortune's scale, as the piece of coin was the only connecting link, or rather the insensible and obdurate barrier to all interchange of human and Christian sympathies. Nay, we believe, that there attaches to indiscriminate charity a more deceitful and deadening evil than all this. We believe that those fine sentimentalists who have gathered their moral and practical code in a certain school of romance, who luxuriate in imagination over trim cottages, simple, innocent beautiful inmates, with all the appurtenances of purling brooks, and so forth, and who through a haze of fiction regard poverty as one of the graceful and interesting feature's of the case, often sooth their souls by an indiscriminate style of giving,—not they themselves (oh! there would be pollution in the actual contact, or at least a fine dream would be put to flight) but others being made the immediate and perhaps the servile and ungracious ministers in the deed. In these and other instances, the evil consequences attendant on the work are great and far spreading; for not only is money so bestowed, for the most part, injudiciously or badly disposed of again, but the interval between the givers and receivers is enlarged, the jealousies and heart burnings between the rich and the poor are increased; there is nothing of healthy humanity on the one side, nor softening and ameliorating gratitude on the other; only another lamentable instance occurring where money is the mother and the medium of a world of evil.

Still, to use the forcible, because plain and true words of our author, on a most serious subject, regarding which error widely prevails, "to relieve the poor, to feed the hungry, to cloth the naked,—these are doubtless Christians acts;" but they will not "become less so by giving the relief under such prudential regulations, and joined to such advice as, under God's blessing, we hope may prevent the recurrence of the necessity for relief." And he proceeds to elucidate and describe his plans of procedure. His first Letter treats of the "Coal Fund;" and the subject is thus introduced:—

"Let us take the case of two parishes; for our purpose we will give them the imaginary names of Waste-penny and Save-penny. The late severe winter produced in the former parish so great an amount of misery in consequence of the poor not having provided for the purchase of fuel, that the richer classes were, I may almost say, forced to come forward with subscriptions to purchase coals for general distribution; and thus the misery of a poor population in severe weather, without means of defence against it, was for the present remedied. I will not question too narrowly the motives of all the givers: it might be, perhaps, that some gave to save their hedges, &c. nor will I go into all that was said in the cottages; some, perhaps, had argued—'they must relieve us, they cannot let us perish,' &c. &c. and upon such reasoning doubtless a great deal of improvidence does arise amongst the poor; we will be content with the fact that a heavy sum was paid by the subscribers, and at this expense the evil was remedied.

" Now some one of the subscribers was led to ask the others how was it that the poor had made no provision for the winter?—why had they not laid by money from their harvest wages for the purchase of winter fuel?—are we now to establish the principle that the poor are to be gratuitously provided with fuel every hard winter? and, for all we know, every future winter may be as severe as the last. Are we to lay it down as an acknowledged fact that the wages of our labourers are so low that they must always be dependent on the charity of the rich for fuel in the winter ? Surely this would be doing a serious injury to all parties. it would impose a heavy yearly tax on the rich, it would release the poor from their just and proper obligation to provide for the necessities of the winter out of the abundance of summer. We would wish to do something to make the winter fall light upon our poor, but we cannot always go to this extent; let us enquire what is done elsewhere. Now it so happened that a person connected with the parish of ' Save-penny' was present at this conversation; he immediately proceeds to explain to them how this difficulty is got over in that parish : we will use his own words—Instead of giving coals in my parish, the higher orders agree to subscribe a certain sum yearly to what we call our Coal Fund or Club. Every labourer of good character, whose average earnings do not exceed 13s. a week, is allowed to pay into our parson's hands 1s. weekly for twelve weeks during the summer and harvest months; for this we engage to deliver to him a sack of coals, or three bushels, every three weeks for the three winter months, being a bushel for every shilling he has paid. (The coals are delivered at his own door free of all charge for carriage.)

" ' Now the difference between the shilling paid and the actual price of the bushel of coals is made up from the subscriptions of his richer neighbours. In a hard winter such as the last (that of 1837-8) coals were very dear; we paid 17d. a bushel for them, including their delivery : the poor man thus gained 5d. on every shilling; in fact he had 5s. added to his 12s. At first it sounds a good deal to give 5s. to each family, but you must remember the yearly subscriptions of the rich are supposed to be always about the same in amount; when the amount to be depended on is once known, it is easy to make your calculations, on the supposition that coals will be at their highest price, and then all you have to do is to take care only to admit as many members as will enable you to meet your engagement with them to give a bushel for every shilling they pay, that is, twelve bushels, or four sacks, for their twelve shillings.

" ' Suppose now that in your parish you can depend upon annual subscriptions to the amount of £10; your account for this last winter would be as follows :—

Forty families paying in 12s. each £24
Subscriptions 10
                                      ————
                                      £34

Receiving twelve bushels each, or 480
    bushels, at 17d, ... £34

" ' Now bear in mind this is calculated on a very bad year, and in a very dear part of the country, so that you may safely reckon that £10 will always enable you to admit 40 members, whom you will have caused to

... best of their numberwed rings 824. We always, make our contract for the purchase and delivery as soon as possible after we know the quantity of coals that will be wanted; and as it is a ready-money transaction, we find plenty of coal-merchants ready to serve us at a fair price. In the year 1834 we only gave 13d. a bushel; now deduct for such a year, 4d. from each bushel, and you would have a balance of £8. Out of seven years that we have had a Coal Fund, we have only had to give so much as 17d. once; so that we easily accumulated a considerable balance, for our rule is never to spend the whole of the money subscribed if we can avoid it.'"

Mr. Osborne has surely good reason for congratulating himself, and saying this is a far better plan than the usual indiscriminate distribution of fuel at Christmas. An exercise of the duty of saving is begun; a system of self-support is begotten; the comfortable consciousness of independence is, in regard to one necessary of life, secured. Besides,

"We give the poor a greater interest in the proper management of their stock of fuel, for they will be much less prodigal of what they in a great degree pay for, than of that which is given them. They can look forward to the winter with one heavy care for it removed. When the winter comes, with little or any addition, the tired labourer may ever find a comfortable fire *at home* to spend his evenings by: *he is not forced to go to the beer-shop to warm himself.* The keepers of those shops know well how attractive a bait the roaring fire and high-backed bench is to the labourer returning on a winter's night from his hard day's work. ' *Just to stop and have one pint and a good warm*' is the resolution made: how is it kept? A good fire, an easy seat, liquor, and a pipe, with company, soon has a fascinating power sufficient to hold him for hours who only stepped in for a minute. The wife and children and the few sticks burning in the cottage grate at home have but little to offer to draw him from what he finds before him; and thus a habit is commenced which may end in his ruin. 'He is a fool to occupy the bench and enjoy the fire unless you drink: pint follows pint, drunkenness closes the night, and the first step in the utter destruction of a family's comfort and respectability is taken. I am convinced the coal-fire at home has kept many of our people from the fireside of the beer shop. I have not better additional proof to give you of the benefit of a Coal Fund than this; during this last most severe winter, with the exception of £8 given in coals to some of the very poor widows, &c. we were not called on to make any extra provision in the way of fuel for the poor; and this in a large parish, where the rich are ever ready to come forward."

Not many hours ago from the moment at which we now write, we have learned that the death warrant has gone forth in the House of Lords, against the Beer shops; thanks to Lord Brougham and the Duke of Wellington. But to keep to our author,—he continued his " Coal Fund" Letter by saying, that he is convinced that the poor in his parish would go on paying, in the manner they have hitherto done, even if nothing but their own money's worth of coal.

were given in the winter. Rules, that are few and simple, are added in an Appendix, for the management of such a Fund.

The second Letter refers to the " Wife's Friendly Society ;" and concerns the time of lying-in. After some sensible and feeling remarks about the child-bed of poverty, Mr. Osborne states,

" What is wanted in the cottage on these occasions may, I think, be comprised under the two heads of Actual Necessaries and Proper Comfort. It is with the former we chiefly have to deal. A midwife or medical attendant must be provided ; and there are certain articles of diet necessary for the mother and infant. The attendance of a female accoucheur is usually about half the expense of that of the regular professional man; and in some places there are women regularly instructed for the purpose, who in all common cases, are fully equal to their duty ; these are usually paid from 5s. to 7s.; the surgeon half-a-guinea. Here then is a certain pecuniary expense to be provided for. No one but the individual about to suffer can enter into all the comfort of having previously secured proper skilful help for her hour of trouble. I need scarcely say, unless the proper fee is certain to be forthcoming, there can be very little certainty of the needful attendance being secured. It is but human nature that the midwife, knocked up in the middle of the night to go some miles to a case, payment for which is quite a matter of futurity, should be apt to plead ill-disposition or other engagements,—in other words, refuse to go.

" The first thing, then, to do for your poor, is to put them in a way of securing proper skilful assistance. Leave it to their own choice whether they will have it from their own sex or ours ; they are very good judges on such matters, and when they have the means to pay are pretty sure to have the best assistance that circumstances will admit of.

" In the parish with which I am connected, it was customary some years ago, *as a matter of course*, to give to almost every poor applicant the sum of ten shillings, 'confinement-money.' An individual who with some influence at the vestry, succeeded in stopping this grant, on the ground of its being a most injudicious and uncalled-for expenditure of the poor-rate. A Society was then immediately established upon the following plan—Every labourer's wife who was thought a deserving object was, upon the recommendation of a subscriber, allowed to enter her name as a member of the ' Wife's Friendly Society ;' she then immediately commenced paying to the treasurer (the vicar's wife) the sum of 2d. weekly for one year, being a total sum of 8s. 8d., to this the Society added 2s. 10d., making in all 11s. 6d. At the time of her confinement a printed order was given her on the secretary for any sum not exceeding 10s.; this order to be given to the midwife or surgeon as payment for their attendance ; the rest of the money is given to the woman herself for the purchase of materials for gruel, &c., &c.; but it occasionally happened that a member paid her whole year without having been under *the necessity* of asking for the order ; in this case the whole 11s. 6d. is given in clothing ; it is, however, generally understood that persons are not to be recommended as members of the Society who are not pretty certain to need *the assistance* which it was founded to afford. It is not then surprising that in most cases the order is wanted before the member has paid her full year ; when this is the case, the woman applies to the lady who recommended her, who fills up a form which guarantees that she will continue to pay her weekly deposit until the whole &c. &c. has been paid. The secretary, on receiving this form properly filled up, is allowed to give the woman the full benefit of the Society. Out of above 100 cases that we have had on our books we have scarcely ever lost a farthing. From the first establishment of this club all applications to the parish for ' confinement-money ' have at once ceased.

"Now when the being in the way to increase the population of the parish was the sure road to obtain ten shillings, the poor were nearly always attended by some ignorant old woman, whose only recommendation was, that she was to be had for 4 or 5s.; they had been accustomed to think the parish " confinement-money' so surely their own that it was in general owed already for something else, so that even the old woman was not always certain of her pittance; accidents either from ignorance or inattention were by no means uncommon. Now see the difference when almost all the whole of the money to the attendant was paid by themselves, and that in a way which insured its arriving at its proper destination ; in the above 100 cases there are not, I believe, 10, in which the regular surgeon was not engaged, and I know not of one accident to mother or child; they used to demand the money of the parish as a right, they are now most grateful to be allowed to enter on the club; the order we give them is as good as money to the person receiving it; they have but to prove themselves as members of the Society, and they are able to secure the best assistance the neighbourhood affords, for the midwives or medical men know that they are sure to be remunerated, and the poor have no temptation to spend the money in any other way, for it is not in their power to do so." The plan we pursue

children as they

The remaining 18d. (if an order for 10s. has been given) will not find many luxuries : but the command of a little brown sugar and groats, will be no small solace ; while the parish described makes a rule of lending out certain bundles, which in many places, have been provided for such purposes. The Letter concludes thus:

" Having now shewn you the plan upon which we act in these cases, we may now look at the expense of supporting a Wife's Society. Each member costs the Society the sum of 2s. 10d. In any but a very large parish, if you admitted from fifteen to twenty members yearly, it would be as many as really need the assistance; a subscription of £2 18s. 8 will allow of your admitting twenty ; if you can only get £2 a year you may admit fourteen members ; and besides the comfort you will afford them, you will have induced them to save the sum of £6 0s. 10d. Remember, the comfort I speak of does not merely consist in the certainty of having proper assistance, so much as in the feeling that that assistance will be paid for in a manner that will cause no inconvenience; as the sum it will not take from the sum put by for rent, there need be no begging from overseers, the child is not ushered into the world as a pauper, it is not born under the auspices of some grudgingly paid parish attendant; with the exception of 1s. 4d. the whole 10s. comes from the parents' own savings. There are but few parishes in which, on these occasions, the poor do not, somehow or other, either from the charity of the rich or the forced contribution of the poor-rate, get as much as possible; how far better is it so to regulate the gift that its proper end is secured, whilst the receiver is taught a lesson of independence, and the advantage of laying by in time for a season which is sure to entail a certain expense.

"We have had nearly seven years' experience of the working of this Society, and have found it a most valuable one; all who really need it regularly come into it, and I can say of this, as I have before done of the Coal Fund, that I am sure, were our subscriptions done away with most of those who have ever been in it would still enter for the privilege of receiving their own money alone. I subjoin the Rules, the Form to be filled up, and the Order Ticket; of course these rules may be varied to suit the circumstances of any village."

"A 'Penny Clothing Fund' forms the subject of the third Letter.

"The plan of the Penny Fund is very simple, and may be told in a very few words; each child admitted into the Club pays one penny a week, the individual recommending it also pays one penny per week, so that at the end of the year the sum of 8s. 8d. has been amassed, which is then laid out in clothing for the child. There are numbers of individuals in every parish who, would they but take the trouble to put by this penny weekly, would scarcely miss it, and yet by so doing they would have the satisfaction of entirely clothing a child for a poor neighbour. I am sure there is no gentleman's house in which 3d. or 4d. might not be collected weekly in the servants' hall for this purpose; if the object of the Society were properly explained, many a servant would gladly put in a child. The plan we pursue is to let any persons in the parish put in as many children as they like, choosing them themselves; this gives the patrons an interest in the children and has some influence over the parents, for they will be careful lest they should by any ill conduct forfeit the esteem of those who shew this kindness to their children. Some persons put in two, others three, others again put in five or six; sixpence a week is not a ruinous tax upon a person well to do in the world, and the pleasure afforded at the end of the year in seeing six children decently clothed is an ample recompense to every benevolent mind.

"The buying of the clothing is thus managed—a linendraper attends with his shopman on a given day at the expiration of the year, with a large supply of all such articles of clothing as the poor most need for their children; the schoolroom is allotted to him as a shop for the day; in addition to the linendraper we have a person over from a neighbouring market-town, whose business it is to deal in ready-made clothing and shoes, &c. for boys; he has a room adjoining the school for his shop. Each lady (these clubs are almost always wholly supported by the female sex) appears with the children she has put in together with their parents; they are served in turn, and it is the lady's duty to see that they have their 8s. 8d. worth of goods. The children who want suits or shoes are sent into the proper department and bring back a ticket, stating what amount they have expended; they then receive the balance, if any, in whatever article of linen, &c. the parent wishes. Our club is a very large one; we this year clothed 150 children, and I am sure in the severe weather we have had, none can have regretted the having aided in so good a work. The pence are received from the children weekly, at the school; from the persons putting them in, at the end of the year. You may procure a book at Books's, 29, New Bond-street, so ruled as to enable you to keep the account of this and the Wife's Society in a manner by which you may always at once see who is in arrears.

"Now in this Club the parent has to pay one half of the value received, and that by a continued exercise of the 'laying-by' principle. Suppose a poor woman is in the Wife's Society, and has two children in the Penny Club, she is obliged to save 4d. a week, a small sum to us, but a large one to her; however she finds the benefit when the clothing-day comes, and she can take home abundance of clothing for her two children. I am quite sure it is a kinder act to put two children of a family into the Penny Club than to give the parent a blanket (the usual Christmas gift). Husband and wife both feel the want of a blanket, and every cold night is a spur to their industry to save money to buy one, but neither of them suffers when their shoeless child treads upon a stone, or big heels, for want of stockings, are broken with chilblains. I am sorry to say that, as far as my observation has carried me, the ruling principle seems to be 'that we,' i. e. husband and wife, 'must be clothed decently, as for the children, we must do as well as we can,' which means, just as little as possible. Rely on it, there is no fear for the rest of the family if you can but get the young ones clothed.

"When I see the pompous announcements in the newspapers of Christmas gifts of blankets, it always strikes me what infinite more good might be done by a little management of the money these blankets cost; if, instead of these wholesale gifts, those only were given to who cannot do anything for themselves, whilst those who can do something towards what they want were merely assisted in their efforts, twice the real good would be done.

"By clothing the children you enable many to go to school who could not otherwise go, and we make it a condition that all who are of sufficient age shall attend the Sunday school. The kindness to the children themselves is indeed great, for you secure to them that aid in the way of clothing from their parents of which otherwise they had little chance. A labouring man with a family, let him be ever so steady, requires a great deal of determination of character to enable him to put by for the little ones' winter clothing; he lives so from hand to mouth, his rent is ever so pressing a claim, his own clothes, shoes, and support so necessary, that we can scarcely be surprised that his ear is somewhat deaf to the wife's hints, 'that they must begin to think of some new clothes for the children. You will find many who will scarcely thank you for putting a child in the first year, esteeming it a great favour the next, and only anxious to get as many of their children put into the Club as they can.'"

These are the principle points in the three first Letters; the "Benefit Society," the "Loan Fund," the "Children's Endowment Society," forming the subjects of the remaining sections, are in the whole illustrated by short and simple tables, in the Appendix. We need not go through these latter portions of the work with the same particularity as has been observed respecting the former, as the detail

shall we do more than state concerning them that they are all equally feasible, and practicable in their nature, and, as lucidly explained. Part of the author's Summary of the whole, however, must not be passed over.

" DEAR ——

" I have now fulfilled my promise of affording you information with respect to the various plans for ' the amelioration of the condition of the poor," in which I have taken a part; but, before I entirely close the subject, I will sketch out an imaginary parish, in which these plans will be in force, in order that I may show you, at one view, the expense of supporting them, and their effect in leading the persons benefited to acquire habits of saving. Take for instance a country parish with a population of 500.

	£	s.	d.
The expense of a Wife's Friendly Society, enabling 14 women to provide for the ordinary expenses of their confinement, will be	1	19	8
The expense of a Penny Clothing Fund, to clothe 35 children yearly	7	11	8
The expense of a Coal Fund, providing one bushel of coals each to 60 families weekly for 12 weeks during winter, supposing coals to be even at the high price of 17d per bushel	15	0	0
Subscribed by the higher classes	£24	11	4

	£	s.	d.
The saving by the poor will be as follows:—			
The 14 women will have saved			
The 35 children will have saved		13	8
For the Coal Fund 60 families will have saved from their summer earnings	36	0	0
Saved by the poor	£49	13	0

" A Loan Fund, of which the permanent capital may be only £10, would, with proper management, circulate £50 in a year; a sum quite equal to the exigencies of a parish larger than the above.

" A Benefit Society absolutely requires nothing but the exertions necessary to form it, and a watchful eye over the adherence to its articles.

" The Endowment Society requires nothing but the agency of some benevolent individual to superintend it, and to see that the money is regularly paid into a neighbouring saving bank.

" I have no doubt that, for a sum of about £4 a year, a respectable individual might be found, in the absence of voluntary aid, who would keep the accounts and manage all the business of the above plans, the Benefit Society alone excepted; but there are few parishes in which there are not some benevolent individuals who, were the means provided, would gladly undertake the management of such institutions, expecting no reward beyond that arising from the consciousness of doing good. All that is wanted is regularity and method; with these the whole business would not occupy more than one hour weekly. We pay all our funds into the savings bank, the interest from them covering the expense of books, &c.

" By the above account you will at once readily perceive, that from a yearly subscribed sum of £24 : 11 ½ 4, you will benefit, in a judicious and useful way, 40 individuals and 60 entire families, to say nothing of the lesson you have taught them, that *weekly-saved pennies grow into yearly-saved pounds*: nay, you will have done more than this; the management of these clubs necessarily brings the labouring poor into frequent communion with the higher orders about them. This has a far greater moral effect than many would suppose : the known drunkard or gambler could expect no aid from the Loan Fund in an hour of need; the idle and profligate cannot expect to be assisted in the winter, when they are known to waste and dissipate the money they earn in the summer; a man or woman of known dishonesty can expect no encouragement, &c. &c.

" You cannot carry on these plans at all without soon becoming acquainted with the character and circumstances of nearly all your poor ; the use you may make of this knowledge I am sure I need not point out to you. I am convinced there are few things more needed in this country, than such an intercourse between the high and low as shall, easily sympathy on the one hand and obtain affection on the other. It is, in my opinion, a gross libel upon the poor to say, ' *they cannot be induced to save.*' I fear it is no libel to say ' *that sufficient pains have not been taken to teach them economy, or sufficient encouragement given to its practice.*' What is the New Poor Law but a severe and powerful engine employed to check the extravagance of the lower orders? How much better is prevention than cure: how much better would it be for the country at large if every individual who has the power and means would endeavour to lead the poor about him, by reasoning and kind persuasion, to those habits that tend to make them, except in extreme cases, independent of personal aid. Teach them to love economy by shewing its advantages, and you will not need the present severe measures to check extravagance. All the above plans, with the exception of the Benefit and Endowment Societies, were in force before the New Poor Law; and I can, I believe, with truth, allege that relief has scarcely ever been refused to an individual of this parish since the formation of our union, for none have applied who were not proper objects for it.

" Allow me now to add a few words on another branch of charity— that which consists in personal attendance on the sick and afflicted poor, from whatever cause their affliction may proceed. I should indeed be sorry to have it supposed that I wish every species of benevolence to be guided by certain fixed rules—that I seek to check the warmest and kindest feelings of our nature by a code of set forms—making every act of benevolence a matter of cold calculation : this is far from being my intention. I would have you bear in mind, that the plans we have been considering are only adapted to meet the common every-day wants of the poor, but there are other wants besides these. There are those arising from misfortune; there is the consolation needed in affliction; there are the comforts, by word and deed, which may be afforded in the hour of sickness: these and many other causes will ever afford an ample field for the exercise of Christian benevolence. But, although I should regret that the emotions of a kind heart should ever be curved by any unnecessary conditions; yet, on the other hand, I would recommend some care to be taken lest, in the excitement of a moment of sympathy, you should be led into a course of action which in a calmer moment you would condemn as imprudent. Persons in the higher ranks of life are too apt to forget the great difference that exists between their own habits and feelings and those of the lower classes. Beware lest, in your endeavour to assist persons that need, you create *fresh wants*. Many things which we are apt to consider as actual necessaries for a sick person are either positive luxuries to the poor, or at any rate neither needed nor desired by them; again, there are many accompanying circumstances about a cottage bed of sickness which are apt, at first sight, to shock us from their apparent hardship on the sufferer; for we are too much inclined to measure his feelings by our own, forgetting in how different a school those feelings have been trained."

Two observations will aptly conclude our review of the present interesting and excellent little book. The first is that without a person or persons of Mr. Osborne's character, activity, and influence, the machinery recommended will be inoperative, and perhaps injurious; the second remark is, that under the superintendence of such a philanthropist the intellectual and moral character of a parish is as sure to rise and to become conspicuous, as its condition in respect of clothing, fuel, and other exterior advantages.

ART. VI.—*Memoirs of the Musical Drama.* By GEORGE HOGARTH, Esq. Author of "Musical History, Biography, and Criticism." 8vo. 2 vols. London: Bentley. 1838.

IT is universally admitted that in no department of our literature, and also as regards the fine arts, taking each of them individually, is there such a poverty and inferiority of historical and critical works as in the case of music. Burney with all his errors in regard to dates and facts, and with all his partialities, has been by a succession of compilers servilely followed; the attractive style of his book having lent it an authority which it by no means had a right to. Hawkins, to be sure, has been at considerable pains to collect the truth as respects chronological data; but he also has been swayed by prejudices, and has, besides, left unnoticed some of the most remarkable features and circumstances regarding the history of the art in this country as well as in foreign parts. He has not, nor indeed has any writer who has preceded Mr. Hogarth, as it appears to us, comprehended, much less illustrated the relation which music in any country, wherever it has acquired a distinct character, bears to national feelings and manners. Hence the confusion, the pointless unsatisfactory nature of many of the criticisms and opinions which have obtained on the science of sweet sound; technical phraseology and distinctions, threadbare stories, and anecdotes concerning

schools, masters, and composers, filling up those pages which after
having embraced an enlarged and philosophic view of the domain of
music, of its power and purposes over the heart and soul as well as
in charming the ear, ought closely and clearly to trace the sentimental developments thence resulting as exemplified in different ages
of the world, and different conditions of society.

Mr. Hogarth, however, has not only indicated the course which
the history of music should take, but with very considerable success
has fulfilled and illustrated the plan. He has entered upon one of
the great divisions into which the science and art is generally
divided, and followed out its progress in a connected train of narrative in the several countries where in modern times it has acquired
celebrity. It is to be observed that the Musical drama is inseparable from literature, and therefore it both receives and lends illustration in regard to a field which the student of intellectual, moral,
and social attainment and refinement uniformly explores for the
surest evidences on the subject of mental culture.

But though Mr. Hogarth has shown himself to be sensible of the
scope there exists for an erudite and philosophic history of the art
of which he treats, and especially of one particular branch of it, and
though he has for the most part been able to abide by the contemplated course, this he has accomplished superficially rather than profoundly; his industry in collecting facts and anecdotes, his skill in
arrangement, and his agreeable, yea, elegant manner of detailing what
is obvious, or, it may be, proverbial, being his merits, rather than
grasp of thought, originality in discovering capabilities, or areas in
recommending modes of study and innovations, some of which from
their self-evident excellences or from the commanding judgment of
the authority might thus have become linked with his name. In
fact, we do not expect that Mr. Hogarth, with all his well-directed
devotion to the study of the science and art of music, and though in
several clever and elegant volumes, will ever have half the influence
on the English mind which the present enlightened and eloquent
Gresham Professor of Music is producing

" One other general remark respecting the execution of the volume
before us must suffice to introduce some of the observations to the
attention of our readers; it is this, that though the author has not
proved his judgment to be of the soundest character on the matter
of proportions,—certain names, eras, and countries, at times receiving at his hands a much greater or slenderer account than their
comparative merits and position seem to authorize, yet his candour,
his freedom from the prejudices of schools and sects, and the entire
absence of every thing like affectation, are recommendations that are
not more agreeable than they are rare on the part of historians and
critics.

Not only the Annals of the Italian and German, but those of the
French lyrical drama, have secured and obtained able writers; but

the opinion seems to have gone forth both abroad and at home that the English have never had composers or works which require or deserve a distinct account. It is usual to think and say that we have borrowed our opera from the Italian, and, indeed, spoiled or enfeebled that which we have borrowed by our imitations. There are some mistakes here. Our author shews, in fact, that mysteries, masques, and moralities were the parents of the musical drama; and these, it is universally known, were long in vogue in England before the mythological and allegorical performances became fashionable in Italy. Our masque was brought to perfection by Ben Jonson so far back as 1605, but the Italian opera in an exceedingly rude and imperfect form cannot be traced to an earlier date than 1594.

Dryden may be charged as having strengthened in no slight degree the prevailing and hastily adopted opinion regarding the origin of the English opera, when he says, "As the first inventors of any art or science, provided they have brought it to perfection, are, in reason, to give laws to it, so, whoever undertakes the writing of an opera, is obliged to imitate the Italians, who have not only invented, but perfected this sort of musical entertainment." But illustrious "John" is wrong in his statement of the facts, and therefore his conclusion falls to the ground. We have already seen that the Italians were not the "first inventors," but what is more, Purcell, the greatest opera composer in England, indeed the founder of the English opera, while his works consisted, as in the case of the Italians, both of music and poetry, was unlike them in this, that his dialogues were spoken not sung; and what was a still more valuable invention, and one essentially according to English character, he did not restrict himself to subjects where supernatural beings were the only actors and parties, but the feelings of mankind, the situations which human kind could sympathise with, were the fields which he delighted to traverse, enlarge, and cultivate. It ought to be matter of deep regret, however, that Purcell has found few followers of eminence in this country, and that he almost stands alone the representative of the truly English opera; for taste and worth have been sacrificed to fashion. Still England does not stand alone in this predicament.

"The Italian opera, both in England and France, receives a greater share of public support, and forms the habitual amusement of a larger portion of the community, than it seems ever to have done at any former time. In this sense of the word the Italian opera is in a flourishing state: but, viewing its situation with reference to the quality of the present productions of the Italian musical stage, it is anything but flourishing. The pre-eminence so long maintained by Rosini, whose pieces for a series of years held almost exclusive possession of the Italian stage, appears to have checked the growth of original genius, and to have rendered his successors merely his imitators; and, as usual for imitators, they have been much more successful in imitating his peculiarities of manner, and even his faults, than his beauties. They have copied, and even exaggerated, the loud and boisterous style of instrumentation adopted by him in his later works, without being able to imitate the admirable effects produced by his skill, in combination, and his thorough knowledge of the powers and properties of instruments. He was occasionally clumsy, crude, and incorrect in his harmonies, from the haste and carelessness of an impetuous temperament. They habitually combine their voices and instruments in a way which, in an earlier day, would have been held disgraceful to a tyro, from their shallow and superficial knowledge of their art. As an emphatic proof of this, it may be observed, that no Italian composer since Rossini has been able to produce a single opera overture which has been thought worthy to be transferred to the concert-room : and so much do they seem to feel their inability to stand this test of their skill as artists, that they have given up writing overtures altogether, thus depriving the opera of what has always been a beautiful and interesting feature. Such, we will venture to predict, in the light in which the fashionable Italian composers of the day—Pacini, Mercadante, Bellini, Ricci, Donizetti, and others—will be viewed before many years shall have elapsed. Their works, especially those of Bellini, contain graceful melodies ; but their airs in general are of a trivial and commonplace character, and have derived their popularity from the exquisite manner in which they are sung by the favourite performers who have just been mentioned. Concerted pieces, like those of Mozart and Rossini, in which a busy and animated dialogue is blended with beautiful combinations of harmony, and embellished by a rich and varied instrumental accompaniment, are never met with in the works of these composers ; but, in place of them, we have a succession of meagre and monotonous choruses, in which the shouts and screams of the singers are drowned by the deafening and incessant accumulation of all the noises that can be produced from the orchestra. The poetry, too, of the Italian opera is at a low ebb. After a perusal of most of the pieces which have acquired celebrity during the present century, we have not found one which is worthy of notice as a literary work. So little value is attached to the dramatic portion of a musical piece, that it is seldom thought worth while to attach to the *libretto* (as it is called) the name of its author, who is generally a hanger-on or dependent upon some musical theatre—a sort of playwright of all work, ready to manufacture to order anything that may be wanted—a person who is not only destitute of reputation and importance, but is an object of ridicule and contumely among singers, composers, and performers. Among these authors, doubtless, there are men who do not belong to this despicable class ; but none of them appear to have attained any considerable degree of literary distinction. When a modern Italian opera, whether serious or comic, is possessed of any dramatic merit,—such as *Agnese, Tancredi, La Gazza Ladra, Il Pirata, or L'Elisir d'Amore*, it has generally been taken from some foreign (chiefly French or English) drama or romance ; and its merit will be found to consist in the borrowed incidents and situations, not in the workmanship of the Italian playwright. Indeed, the present form of the Italian opera is more unfavourable to dramatic excellence than it has ever been before. The eternal introduction of noisy choruses, not, as formerly, in situations only where groups of people could be supposed to be assembled with propriety, but in almost every scene, and mingling their vociferations with the most private transactions of the characters, renders the construction of a rational drama absolutely impossible. On the modern Italian stage, in short, the music is everything, the drama nothing. The principles so philosophically developed, and so beautifully illustrated by Gluck, have fallen into oblivion: and it is only in the co-operation of a second Gluck with a second Calzabigi, that we can hope for the restoration of the Italian musical drama."

Just observe what is the result of the absurd introduction of a purely Italian mode in a country, and a school that forbid, were it merely on account of the structure of our language, the absurd and unnatural innovation.

"English recitative, instead of being founded on what may be called the natural melody of English speech, is generally made up of a tissue of musical phrases borrowed from the Italian composers; so that an English singer, delivering a piece of recitative in his own language, has the appearance of a foreigner declaiming in broken English. The same thing, though in a lesser degree, is perceptible in our English airs; which being made up of passages originally suggested by the modulations of Italian speech, are destructive of the emphasis and accent of the words to which they are united by the English composer. Similar effects are produced by the present imitation of the German music. Our composers act precisely as a painter would do, who, in painting an English landscape, instead of looking upon the scenery around him, should compose his picture by copying his rocks from Salvator Rosa, his blue distances from Poussin, his sunshine from Claude, his trees from Ruysdael, and his cattle from Cuyp. The evil has been aggravated of late years by the practice of adapting Italian, German, and French operas to the English stage; a practice which has almost put an end to the existence of English melody. Even when setting an English ballad, our composers show that their heads are full of Rossini, Spohr, Weber, or Auber. Compare their exotic productions with the genuine English strains of Purcell, Arne, Linley, Arnold, Dibdin, and Shield; and the difference is at once perceived between copying from art and copying from nature."

Among Mr. Hogarth's judicious suggestions, we like the following particularly. "The restoration of the Opera," says he, "to its place, as an important as well as a delightful branch of the drama, requires the co-operation of a musician possessed of sound views respecting the objects of his art, and capable of rendering all its resources subservient to the purposes of dramatic expression and effect, with a poet of congenial spirit, gifted with distinguished genius, and yet not afraid to commit himself by an association with a genius equal to his own." But the fact is as he states and illustrates it in the following passage :—

"In proportion as the musical part of this entertainment has acquired an ascendancy, the poetical and dramatic part has declined; a fact which our readers must have gathered from the preceding narrative. Whenever music aspires to the pre-eminence over poetry in a drama," says Metastasio,

' she destroys both that and herself.' ' Modern music,' he adds, ' has rebelled against poetry ; and neglecting true expression, and regarding all attention to words as downright slavery, has indulged herself, in spite of common sense, in every sort of caprice and extravagance; making the theatre no longer resound with any other applause than that which is given to displays of execution; with the vain inundation of which she has destroyed her own disgrace, after having first occasioned that of the mangled, disfigured, and ruined drama. Pleasures which are unable to gratify the mind, or touch the heart, are of short duration ; for though men may suffer themselves to be easily captivated by unexpected physical sensations, they do not for ever renounce the use of their reasoning faculties.' . What was the case in Italy in Metastasio's time, is the case in England, as well as in Italy, now. Sense is sacrificed to sound. Music is degraded into a gratification of the ear, instead of being regarded as a language capable of exalting the sentiment, and deepening the passion of the drama. No man of genius will suffer his poetry to be made the vehicle for unmeaning sing-song ; hence the opera is left in the hands of playwrights, and, with few exceptions, is looked upon, by people of sense and reflection, as a light and frivolous amusement, unworthy of serious notice. What can show more clearly the false position in which the opera is placed than the practice of encores? An air or duet may be a soliloquy, or a dialogue of strong pathos or deep interest ; and who, that enters ever so little into the spirit of the scene, would think of having such a soliloquy or dialogue over again ? Who would call on Macbeth to clutch a second time the air-drawn dagger, or on his sleeping wife again to show the fearful workings of remorse, in her distempered mind, because, in the one case or the other, the actor exhibited a fine piece of declamation? And yet there is hardly a tragic opera in which such absurdities do not pass current.   *   *   *

" The dramatic pieces at present set to music by our composers are generally trash ; and our composers are aware that it is so; but in self-defence, that they cannot get anything better. But neither must that good poetry runs no hazard of being degraded or destroyed in their hands, and it can hardly be doubted that they will obtain it. As to our musical performers, they will perforce become actors as well as singers, when they find that good acting as much as good singing, is essential to their success. There is no want either of dramatic talent or of musical talent in England. But it requires the co-operation of these two kinds of talent, in a degree which does not exist at present, to produce results which will be at all satisfactory to the growing taste and intelligence of the public."

It is to be regretted that our author has treated Germany so summarily compared to France on the subject of the musical drama. The former has no rival in the world, in respect of compass, variety, and grandeur ; while in the latter, if entitled to a rank among national influences, the musical drama instead of being original is the offspring and blended child of the Italian and German school. If poetry has been degraded by becoming second to music in our opera, music has been the slave of dancing in France.

ART. VII.—*Notices of the Northern Capitals of Europe.* By F. H. STANDISH, Esq. Black and Armstrong. 1838.

MR. STANDISH is an experienced traveller, and therefore notices of capitals, towns, and countries, coming from such a quarter are sure to be the vehicle of numerous recollections and reflections, the treasures of a mind that is well stored, and which it has industriously and widely accumulated. Were there no other presumption in favour of his present work than this, that it belongs not to a worn-out tract—that it treats of the Northern instead of the Southern Capitals of Europe, we should be eager to dip amongst its pages. But besides this circumstance, which indicates a proper degree of curiosity and enterprise, we have the results of actual observation delivered in an animated style, and sometimes with a degree of opinionative and sometimes regardless boldness that is queerly characteristic, and therefore amusing. For example, he says, " What little I shall please or displease by writing may be attributed to a campaign some years ago at Hamburg. Copious libations to Bacchus, combined with devotion to indulgences even more perilous in their consequences, elicited the direful vengeance of arthritic pains.' They are the unpleasing recollections of a joyous summer have never left me, and make me more than ever assured of that unwelcome truth, that there is a retributive alloy to all worldly enjoyments—

——————' Our pleasant vices
Do make them whips to scourge us.' "

But while arthritic pains and unpleasing recollections are the punishments which our author has had to endure, the result to us must be placed to the score of rewards for the time bestowed on a perusal of what he has written.

Mr. Standish states, that " My text is merely a vehicle for some notes on the paintings which may fall under my review." Many of his descriptions regard the principal collections of art in the course of his travels from the Hague to St. Petersburgh, and back by Copenhagen. We must say, however, that in spite of the spirit and ready flow of his criticisms, the least entertaining and least instructive portion of his work is that which must have cost him greatest effort, we mean where he deals in connoisseurship on works of art, and gives us a hashed-up dish of artistic slang. He is far more agreeable, and by no means so superficial and commonplace, when life, manners, scenery, and incident become his themes. We think we can show that our opinion is well founded by a few specimens taken from both sorts of notices, and this without any anxious or consecutive research among his pages. Here are certain critiques, some pictures at Amsterdam forming the subject.

" The Netscher, of ' A Lady dressing the Hair of her Son,' is equal in quality to that at the Hague, with more detail and finish; it has a force of colour I have scarcely ever seen equalled. Poel is a painter of interiors of houses, still life, and sometimes figures; but, like Kalf, occupies a low rank, and I note him only because his works are spread almost half over Europe. "Paul Potter has five pictures. I confess the famous 'Bear Hunt' does not please me; the execution of the huntsman with the cutlass, attacking the bear, is hard, and the perspective does not detach his figure and that of the animals:—it is, however, a striking painting, but horrid and cruel-looking. The 'Landscape,' by Potter, in which is seen a brown ox, grouped with a ram and an ass, near to a he-goat, and two sheep with a lamb, is much finer, or, at least, more grateful, in my opinion, to contrast plate; a woman giving suck to her child, and a man playing on a bagpipe, with a large dog, add to the variety of the scene; it is one of Potter's most agreeable paintings, and came from the collection of Mr. Vander Pot, of Rotterdam. The 'Night Watch,' by Rembrandt, known to all Europe, and commented on by Sir Joshua Reynolds, is the departure of F. B. Kok, lord of Purmerland and Ilpendam, with his suite, to shoot at a mark. There are at least twenty figures in this picture; a girl is carrying on her shoulder a white fowl, probably intended to be the prize for the successful rifleman; the names of the persons represented are written in Dutch on the top of a column. There is a great effect of light and shade in this picture; and here is discoverable the mine from whence Sir Joshua drew his tints, for there is an endless variety of colour in the picture; and almost every shade used by the English painter has been borrowed from the Dutch. After surveying attentively this and the other works of Rembrandt, I still must give the palm of merit for colour to the Sevilian painters. This may savour of obstinacy or prejudice, or perhaps both; I still cannot help yielding to the impression they convey to my feelings, and I cannot con descend to flatter prejudice by saying what I do not think."

"At Hamburg, we are informed by Mr. Standish, the arts languishly; the chief pleasures of its inhabitants being those of a sensual character. The reader must remember there was a campaign, which unpleasingly yet joyously connects the author with the last-mentioned great mercantile city; and perhaps the severity of the sweeping opinion now quoted may in some measure have had its origin in the circumstances alluded to. He farther states that even the genius of Schotel could not ensure his pictures a good sale, amongst his fellow-citizens. And then it turns out that the principal wealth in Hamburg is in the hands of the Israelites, and that what they gain they keep.

The Roxenburg Palace at Copenhagen contains a collection where the student of numismatics and other objects of antiquarian and tasteful research may be feasted.

"The Altenburg drinking-horn, supposed to be nine hundred years old, is deposited here. It is covered with brass, and worked in the Gothic fashion of elaborate and endless ornament. The famous saddle and horse accoutrements of Christian the Fourth, inlaid with pearls, and valued at 50,000l.—the ermine coronation robes—the apartment cased with paint-

iage,—the sword of Gustavus Adolphus, and, that of Charles the Twelfth, presented to Colonel Cruzer—the coronation chairs, that for the king being made of unicorn horn—the beautiful rock crystal cup, surmounted by a Cupid—and the various presents of our Queen Anne and other sovereigns to the Danish monarchs,—all these are curious and worthy of examination, by the artist and the antiquary; and, though not in the high class of historical or scientific rarities, they are all nevertheless interesting. A beautiful service of china is seen here, representing a botanical series, made for the Empress Catherine of Russia, but which her niggardly son, Paul, refused to take when ready for delivery. Adjacent to this apartment is the gallery of medals, which enjoys a general fame throughout Europe. Here is seen one coin of Suendtveskeg, father of Canute, and three of the latter king; Roman asses of a pound each, dating 600 years before Christ; specimens of the Persian tribute money to Russia, of thin, flattened shape, and oblong, about six inches long by two and a half wide, with Arabic impressions; and the largest gold piece of the mint, struck for Admiral Yule, by Christian the Fifth, being of the value of three hundred ducats."

Mr. Standish confesses that his knowledge of coins is very limited; but he has had enough of experience to prove to him to what good account the study of these enduring and easily transmitted tokens may be turned; and, in fact, declares that an English antiquarian, when surveying the Borel cabinet at Smyrna, pointed out to him a unique medal, by means of which, a people subdued by Germanicus, whom Tacitus mentions, was identified.

But it is when he gives us sketches of national manners and features that we chiefly relish our author's notices—his criticisms on art being like those of any other well-educated gentleman who has visited many of the finest galleries—merely a host of individual opinions that communicate no light to the general reader, and at most the grounds of small knowledge, we suspect, to the student of art. Here are certain general comparisons and contrasts that are striking and rapidly classified :—

" In the observations I have made on the natural products of the north, on the beauty of its scenery, and on its curiosities of art, no mention has yet been made of man or woman—of those beings without whom the loveliest land pleases not, who are the soul of animated nature, the movers and agitators of sentiment, and, in fact, the life of the world. The same degree of natural talent and vivacity is not possessed by the natives of the north as by those of the south; whether it be that Phœbus, with his rays, ripens spirits as he ripens wines, I know not, but where they do not penetrate, the human race is dull. The Russians, Swedes, Norwegians, and Danes, are all, in a greater or less degree, inferior in ready wit and ingenuity to the Italians, the Spanish, the Greeks, and the French; and this is not from want of education, but from natural sluggishness and torpidity, the effect, I suppose, of climate. The Russian boys receive the rod, and count their talent almost by the number of its strokes. A lad, after receiving five hundred stripes, said to a girl who pitied him, ' We are as familiar with this as you with leeches—we cannot do without it.' The Swedes are dull and sorry servants; the Norwegians, perhaps, worse! The Danes being more southerly, are on the same grade as the Germans, who, though excellent persons in disposition, are not reckoned the most lively in the world. Here, however, we have no assassinations, scarcely ever theft; what often happens and is believed in the south, would be incredible as told of the north. The blood which boils like the lava flood of Vesuvius in one part of Europe, is here transmitted with the purity and mildness of the mountain spring; the tempests rage and the cold pierce, but the human character is placid, temperate, and upright. The slavery to which the Russians are subject does not, as might have been supposed, impede the development of their mental energies. Every serf is sent from home for eleven months of the year, or allowed to travel; from his labour the lord draws a certain revenue, and, at the expiration of the period, he returns again to his wife, in order that the course of population from marriage may not be impeded. When rich, the term of his absence may be prolonged to an indefinite time by the payment of money. Some proprietors have never seen their serfs, and it is related that one of the latter, who had amassed great treasure, was recognised, whilst travelling, by his master, who applied to him for the loan of fifty thousand roubles, but refused to liberate him on an offer of one hundred thousand. It is the wish, I have heard, of the Emperor Nicholas and his queen, to abolish slavery in Russia, but, as the value of landed property is entirely independent on the number of slaves upon it, this would be opposed by the nobles, and if carried against their wishes, endanger the safety of the crown; for in that country, powerful as the head of government is, there exists an imperious and formidable aristocracy. The hands which strangled Paul might be found again in others to twist the sash for his successors, were their rights invaded, or their interests injured."

But to observe something like a continuous and connected route, let us start in Holland, and hear what can be said in behalf of the industry, enterprise, and perseverance of the Dutch, as compared with national characteristics of certain modern, and the undecaying evidences left by certain ancient nations.

"The arrogance of the English, the vanity of the French, the pride of the German, the superciliousness of the Italian, and the accumulated mass of all these perverse qualities—added to the legion of devils of his own— which exists in the Spaniard, must abate a little of their preponderance, when they reflect on the immense labour of the Dutch in regaining their soil from the sea, and in basing cities on the domain of ocean itself. To plant a house, they proceed as follows, where the land is marshy;—They trace the square of its dimensions, bore to the depth of seven or eight feet till they find water, pump it dry, and drive stakes round the square, by means of a weight of twelve or fourteen hundred pounds suspended from a pully; the stakes are from forty to fifty feet in length, and each requires on an average an hour and a half for driving it down. One hundred of these blocks or stakes are sufficient for a small house. The royal palace at Amsterdam took 13,695. When it is considered what immense labour the towns in Holland have required for construction, what immense sums they must have cost, and what industry the people must have possessed, to enable

them to prosper with such drawbacks on their exertions, the Pyramids of
Egypt, the Ruins of Thebes, the Palaces of Persepolis, the Hanging Gardens of Babylon, appear no longer as visionary dreams of gigantic enterprise, but as the works of man; of a being capable of conquering the
elements, of inverting the dispositions of matter, and wanting only pre-
science to be divine."

Travellers are sometimes apt to assume a superbilious bearing, at
other times to be dictatorial. Their native country and its customs are
not only made to be the rule for foreign parts and foreigners, but as
frequently to be ridiculed in the comparison. Of this affectation of
a superiority to narrow views, and this severity of father-land castigation, our author seems to be now and then guilty. He will have
it that the prudish English attach an air of mystery to their dwellings, because they surround them with trees, because the young
ladies fly round a wood at the approach of a strange carriage or a
strange person. Venetian blinds suggest to him the concealment
of a seraglio, and sundry other features and doings are set down to
prudery, which but for a perverse interpretation would be held as
the reverse of disparaging. But then in England "the whole
household retire at the front door knock or ring—the servants are
marshalled—the visitor announced—the master informed—his wife
summoned—the daughters introduced and the visit wound up by a
formal lunch, and ceremonious leave-taking." Whereas on the
Continent, "they advance to welcome the guest; the proprietor of
the domain is not on a rack of agony lest John Footman should not
present himself in his best attire, or should smell of the stable;
they are kind in their manners, and consequently easy; they do not
deal out civility by grains, for fear of giving over weight; 'being
natural, they naturally please.'" This is Mr. Standish's representation; but though we should allow it to be unexaggerated, it is a
conclusion which we think is not quite so promptly clear, that the
forms of civility and nature are all against us. At any rate our lunches
should be honoured, while every innovation which will substitute,
smiles, bows, and chatter for substantial fare, ought to be strenuously
opposed.

The Germans have praise bestowed upon them on account of
their simplicities, and of their " cleanliness of mind" as testified
by their love of flowers.

" All over Germany the natives are fond of flowers. The nursery of
Mr. Booth, a Scotchman by extraction, is famous for every variety of rose,
and at this moment for an endless variety of plants and trees, collected from
the Norwegian, Siberian, and other hyperborean regions. It is situated
at the distance of three German miles from Hamburg, in the direction of
Altona, and occupies a surface of 150 English acres. It is delightful to
see in this country the steps to the thresholds of the meanest houses, gay
with flowering plants; the small adjacent strips of land blushing with

peonies, and stock, whilst the honeysuckles and eternal creepers festoon the windows of the lowliest dwellings. There is a cleanliness of mind indicated in a taste for these embellishments, that savours of the golden age of innocence, rather than of these vitiated times. Sobriety and peace may be said to dwell where Flora reigns. In fact, after the changes of war, the devastations of revolutions, and the corrupting examples of treachery and treason attendant on unsettled politics, there is perhaps no nation in the world more pure, more sincere, and more well disposed than the German. Earnest and warm-hearted in their friendships, they love little ceremony, enthusiastic and romantic, they express themselves with the feeling that issues unadulterated from the breast: they affect no diffidence in communicating their pleasures and their griefs; they have little care to calculate the *convenience* of exercising good offices."

There is nothing very remarkable in this partiality to flowers; and, after all, we should not wonder if it were the Scotchman, Mr. Booth, who has been mainly instrumental in creating the taste in the district specified, seeing that the Scotch are celebrated as gardeners. How easy it is to fill a volume with the most decided conclusions from the slightest external intimations.

We follow our author to Finland, which is not after all a country bathed in blubber and oil. Helsinfors, for instance, is described as being a beautiful modern town, while its bay is quite a diminutive archipelago. At this place, Mr. Standish observed the custom existed which he was told prevails over Sweden, " of covering the staircase of an inn with chopped fir-sprouts, and the dining-room with festoons of green leaves." He also states for the information of future travellers that the Hotel du Nord, where he stayed, was not bad; and that " although they serve the soup in the middle of dinner, and Alpine strawberries and cream after the fish," he made a hearty meal. All over the north of Europe from the 53rd degree of latitude, spirits with cheese, caviare, or some other stimulant, is taken before the principal feed. One great want in Russia is pointed out when it is said, that the potato has not yet found general acceptation, at least amongst the lower orders. The narrative proceeds—

" I was tempted to make an excursion from Helsinfors to Abo, a distance of one hundred and fifty English miles, in order to see a part of Finland which I had heard represented as a very beautiful country. It is very beautiful, certainly, but it is a very poor one. I saw only two mansions on the road, and they were nearer to Helsinfors than to Abo; the latter town having been formerly the capital of Finland, as the other is now. You see fir, beech, and mountain-ash trees, with alder and juniper plants, clustered together very picturesquely, forming glades, and crowning mountain-tops; and you have an eternal variety of small lakes, barren scaurs, and cultivated grounds. In spite of the abundance of water, we could find no fish to eat on our road; and there was only one decent inn which was at Nyby, rather less than half way between Helsinfors and Abo. But when I speak of a good inn, my readers must not imagine that they will be received in a papered room, with sofas and tables, and a neat chimney-piece, adorned with fly-catchers in papers;—no, they will have to mount a small scaffold of steps, (for all the houses here are of wood, and built on an above-ground foundation of stone); you then enter a room which is unpainted, and the whole of the rafters stuffed with moss, to prevent the air from penetrating; the floors are clean, and you generally find a stove, which keeps the whole warm. We were visited with a good deal of rain, but the roads, which are very narrow, are maintained in beautifully neat order; and there is a Finnish law in force, that should a carriage break by the badness of the causeway, the nearest house pays for its repair. The Finland post-horses are of the size of our Shetland ponies, and, without ocular demonstration, a stranger would scarcely believe it possible for them to drag the weight and go at the pace they do, which averages seven miles an hour. We were three in a calèche, and took only two horses. The travelling here is as cheap as in Russia, costing only about three-halfpence per English mile, in English money."

The whole of Sweden is said to abound with delightful scenery, though limited in extent. The different effects of light as you wind your way among the thickets are endless. Vivid flashes through the sombre green startle and surprise, while every variety of hue is presented on a neighbouring shrub. Strawberries were the only fruit which Mr. Standish observed in the country. Now for an anecdote.

"The Swedes are a cleanly nation—they dislike the Russians, (as might naturally be supposed, since by them the whole of Finland, and other possessions, have been ravished from Sweden,) and consider them a dirty people. I will mention a fact which my readers may perhaps doubt, and I could scarcely believe had I heard it from another, and which nevertheless is quite true. On entering an inn in the Thier-Garten, I passed between several waiting girls—for house and table attendance is here performed by females, whereas at St. Petersburgh it is always the office of men—one of them turned to my servant, and said, in Swedish, 'That gentleman comes from Russia; we can tell it by the smell of his clothes.' And I have been told that a residence, even of a few days, in that country, gives a lasting odour to the garments worn there. It is asserted by some that you may scent a Croat and a Cossack regiment before you see them, but I was not aware that Russian fragrance could be so infectious, and so easily imbibed by a stranger."

The clothes of the Scottish Highlanders whose huts generally contain an atmosphere of Peat-reek, preserve the savoury scent wherever they go, and for many months after they leave their native mountains and glens.

Mr. Standish did not leave Norway untouched, the people of which he describes as being poor, and unacquainted with luxury, and yet as furnishing a richer treasury than her mistress Sweden. He farther states—

" The language is the same as the Danish, with trifling variation.
English is in general use in places of which many English know not even
the existence. The customs of antiquity are still retained in society here.
After dining with the hospitable and polite Count Wadel Jarlsberg, Viceroy of Norway, we all shook hands, and kissed those of the countess. This
ceremony is called the * Wollkommen,'—good digestion and many thanks.
I afterwards ascended the hill of Akerberg—for our repast terminated at
five o'clock—to view the town, the bay, and the distant mountains of
Christiana. The view is a very fine one, not less so than most of those
in Switzerland, where there is not snow. The sombre forests of pine and
fir give an imposing effect to the outlines of the several distances in the
ground plan, and clothe the massive bosoms of the hills.

" Loud complaints are raised against the British for imposing duties on
nine-inch Norwegian deal as high as the Russian on eleven. It is said
that hopes are entertained from Mr. P. Thompson of a more just tariff.
This, it may be imagined, is a matter of serious importance to a country
where the principal property consists in wood. I observed here a fruit
called cloudberries and ' mudberbere,' yellow when ripe, which grows in
marshes, on a bush, and has a flavour and size somewhat like the mulberry. It is grateful to the taste, and considered wholesome. In enumerating the resources of Norway, I have not stated its herring fisheries,
which are very considerable. This trade is supposed to be worth to the
country a million of dollars yearly. The small town of Fleckfeer, on the
North Sea, exports yearly 100,000 barrels.

" Amongst the peculiarities of the Norwegian legislature, in its union
with Sweden, is that of a prohibition of entry to all Jews. We who
have discussed the propriety of admitting that sect to a share in the
legislature, may be surprised at such extreme disfavour shown to the
children of Israel ; they are all considered unclean creatures, and are
damned by the Norwegians to fatten elsewhere. A solemn stipulation is,
that the Crown Prince of Sweden shall be acquainted with the Danish
language."

. We have not observed anything in our author's notices of Denmark more interesting than the following particulars in connexion
with Elsinore.

" The only objects of interest to a stranger at Elsinore, are the castle or
fortress which I have mentioned, and the garden of Marienlyst, where is
to be seen what is called the grave of Hamlet. The interior of the fortress contains nothing remarkable—the grave is a misnomer; for Hamlet
lived, reigned, and died, and was buried in Jutland. A conspiracy had
been formed against his life by his step-father and mother, as the ancient
Danish chronicles state ; he feigned imbecility of mind, being aware of
the plot laid to destroy him, formed another against them, and eventually
burned to death the whole family, by setting fire to a house in which they
were, and stopping up the doors. He afterwards reigned quietly and
respectably, and died a natural death. I may affirm that there is no
brook crowned with willows near Elsinore, where Ophelia could have
perished ; and the enthusiastic reader of Shakspeare may be relieved from
the pain her fate has inspired him with, by the conclusion of its falsity."

The grave of Hamlet, as seen in Denmark, is to the back of the mansion of Marienslust, about a stone's throw; you catch a view of the sea between a contiguous clump of trees planted in a circle, and it is noted by some scattered square stones of small size, which appear to have once served for a cenotaph, and which stand on a knoll or rising mound covered and surrounded by beech-trees. I could learn nothing of their history—they seem little respected or thought about by the inhabitants of Elsinore, but pious and romantic pilgrims have conveyed away considerable portions of them, and a few years will probably witness their total dispersion."

Such are favourable specimens of this light and lively work. To those who may contemplate a journey through the regions in which such glimpses have been taken, they will furnish hints, as regards routes, localities, and galleries of art ; in respect of the last of these objects, however, chiefly as surface notices that may enable them to arrive at safer and more weighty conclusions for themselves than those which form the staple of Mr. Standish's speculations. One thing it may be particularly wise to bear in mind, viz. that the North is recommended for winter and the South for summer-visiting and travelling.

ART. VIII.—*Man, in His Physical Structure and Adaptations.* By ROBERT MUDIE, Author of " The Heavens," " The Four Seasons," " The British Naturalist," &c. &c.   London : Orr and Co. 1838.

MAN has been the subject of innumerable books, and, no doubt, will continue a fertile theme for thousands of writers yet unborn. Directly or indirectly he may be said to be the object of all our speculations. His relation to the things and creatures around him, and to the Supreme Governor of the Universe, independently of his position in the van and at the head of all the beings which inhabit the earth, must for ever render him the grand rallying point for all philosophy. Mr. Mudie says in his preface, that " the real condition of Man can be known only from the study of the power, the wisdom, and the goodness of God, as displayed in the phenomena of nature." But, however much of truth may be in this we venture to assert that by inverting these terms a doctrine not less important and intelligible may be advanced, viz. that the power, wisdom, and goodness of the Creator can be known or judged of only or fully by us as displayed in the real condition of Man ; so true do we find it that it is next to impossible to utter any proposition of a serious character which has not our being, our interests, or our destinies, in some way deeply involved and strongly recognised.

But all important as the subject of man is to man, and necessarily universal as it is, so long as he cannot be separated from the purposes or displays of any one phenomenon which can be witnessed by our race, it is quite possible to mystify by a multitude of words, by a diffuseness of arrangement and illustration, not to speak of apparent paradoxes and inversions; such truths and facts as all may easily comprehend and act upon. We suspect that Mr. Mudie cannot on the present occasion stand exempted from this charge of verbosity and conglomeration. We suspect few will have patience even to read the volume from beginning to end, ingenious, brilliant, and eloquent though he often be ; or, at least, should any one have the perseverance to do so, we question very much if any clear conception of the author's doctrines will thence be obtained. The pertinency and the tendency of a great portion of the work, will, we fear, be dimly perceived ; while the painful conclusion will remain, that an extreme measure of self-complacency, and an air of acuteness and originality, along with truisms and abstruse metaphysics, have spoiled a hearty and generous purpose—perplexing combining with what is disagreeable to the general injury of the performance.

Mr. Mudie, we believe, has the honour of being what is understood by the phrase *self-taught* ; and a high honour it is, especially when the superiority of this kind of education has been evidenced and illustrated by so many beautiful, engaging, and useful volumes as he has written. It is manifest from his several books that he is a man of great activity, of keen and close observation, and of an earnest temperament. He is conscious of his duties and responsibility as an author, and he uniformly has the happiness and the benefit of his species before his eyes. He thinks for himself, and despises the servility of those who dare not oppose the dogmas of the schools ; nature and the Bible being his great text books. But with these text books such a mind and such habits as we have glanced at and supposed, will with far more likelihood of success employ themselves in descriptions of scenery, in the details of natural history, and in garnishing such narratives with affecting, rich, and arousing reflections, than in constructing a system of mental and moral philosophy. We really think, judging from the specimen before us, that although it be the first of a series of volumes which the author says are his favourites above all others that he has written, yet that in all probability they will be relished the least by the popular reader; while by him who has studied in academic halls, they will be deemed confused, overloaded with irrelevant or loosely connected matter, and with needless discussions, refutations, &c. Besides, the part before us is composed in one of the worst possible styles for philosophical disquisition.

We find it would be a labour not much less bulky than his volume itself in its results, were we to endeavour to set Mr. Mudie right where we think he is wrong—to show him that he often guesses when he supposes he is demonstrating—or were to undertake the task of pointing out how frequently he repeats that which is universally known, in an egotistic and peculiar style that alone confers upon the matter the appearance of ingenuity and discovery. In justice to him as well as in support of any own general observations, we shall, after letting him explain the object of the work, extract a few passages, without any particular regard to their connection s/a connection which it would not always be very easy to establish or elucidate.

" The argument for which I have endeavoured to prepare the way," says our author, " is, that the human body is organized and adapted for purposes which cannot have their complete fulfilment in the present life. This," he continues, " will lead to the consideration of Intellectual Man in a second volume; and, as the doctrine of Intellect, and its necessary consequence, Immortality, are the foundation of morality in the individual, and of good order in society, two more volumes will be required to complete the whole subject, though each of the four will, by the avoiding of the formality of system, be an entire book without the others." Or his general scheme and analysis may be taken as more fully explained in the following order :—

" We shall consider Man in four separate points of view, to the first of which we propose to confine the sequel of the present volume.

" First, *Physical Man.* Under which designation we shall consider the structure, adaptations, and senses of the body, with some hints for the culture and improvement of the last; though, in the course of doing this, we shall probably be obliged to make some short and occasional references to other parts of the general subject.

" Secondly, *Intellectual Man.* This will carry us to a much greater length than the former, because this is the part of the compound nature of Man by means of which what has been once known, or in any way expressed, is need by the individual, returns again when it is required, and often when it is not wanted, in what we call memory or suggestion.

" Thirdly, *Moral Man.* In the first and second divisions of this subject, according to the method proposed, we shall necessarily be restricted, in a great measure, to that which Man is capable of doing and knowing, without much, if any, reference to the pleasurable or the painful effects which it may have upon the individual or others; but in this division we shall have to consider the emotions, in which chiefly our happiness or our misery lie, and which have reference to those with whom we are more intimately and personally connected, as well as to ourselves.

" Fourthly, *Social Man.* Under which we shall have to consider the reciprocal duties which subsist between the individual and that society of which he forms a part, the obligations which he owes to the society of which he thus is a member. In this department it will be necessary to analyse the principles of many of our most popular subjects of conversation and attention; governments, and their influence; legislation, in its temperance and its intemperance; national churches, systems of education, and institutions of various kinds, with their real and supposed uses, and the abuses to which they are all more or less subject."

There does not appear to us, on the face of the announced purposes of the author or of his scheme, to be much promise of satisfaction. That the human body is organized and adapted for purposes which cannot have their complete fulfilment in the present life is a proposition, for instance, that will lead any reasoner upon evidence, separate from the dicta of Revelation, far beyond his depth. We anticipate, too, and indeed have before us some proofs for believing, that Mr. Mudie will involve himself in the question about the materiality and immateriality of the soul, and the arguments thence presumed to arise on the subject of immortality—topics which to say the least of them lead uniformly to repulsive, if not most inconclusive reasoning.

Our author's preliminary chapters are devoted chiefly to a consideration of the value of self-knowledge, an acquisition, which throughout a bare portion of the volume, it is endeavoured to be proved, is peculiar to man among terrestrial creatures. At the same time not a little space is wasted, we think, not only upon this point, but in an attempt to limit the application of Lord Bacon's celebrated aphorism that " knowledge is power." An example of Mr. Mudie's defining talent, and correcting propensity, and the example of a sort of mental pride, not at all agreeable in its manner, may here be introduced.

" We admit that ' knowledge is power ;' but the aphorism is expressed in terms too general for being applicable to any one practical use. We must know ' what the knowledge is,' and ' to whom' it is said to be power, otherwise the aphorism may not only be not true, but its opposite may hold, namely, that ' knowledge is weakness'—the absence or the destruction of power. As this is an elementary matter, which meets us at the threshold of our investigation, and as it is equally applicable to every species of knowledge that we can obtain or desire, whether of ourselves or of anything else, it must be carefully examined.

" Now, as to knowledge being ' power,' that is saying nothing, unless we understand what we mean by power. But there is nothing which we can call power that can be palpable to any of the senses as a separate subject of investigation. The power is a quality of some agent, and yet it is not perceptible in that agent as those qualities are to which we ascribe no power. The shape, colour, consistency, and all the common distinctions of objects which are perceptible by the senses, are not powers. No substance and no state of a substance is in itself a power; the power is shown in the change from one state to another, and unless we actually have seen a similar change take place, or are informed of it upon testimony which commands our belief, we know nothing about the power that may have been exerted in the case.

" It is true that we have a general feeling of power, as inseparably connected with everything we observe or hear of. In this sense we feel that which has *placed* things in the condition, posture, and situation in which we find them, and it is a general or short expression for an agent, and the action or effect produced by that agent. As such it is a mental feeling, and not a perception by the senses; and therefore we may conclude that no inhabitant of the earth save Man has any feeling of power, even in this very vague and general sense.

"But this general feeling is not knowledge, though it is unquestionably an element of that compound feeling which constitutes the desire of knowledge, and by doing so puts us in the way of the attainment of it. If the use of our senses is accompanied by even the faintest glimmering of thought, this feeling of power invariably takes the lead. We see the furnishings of a room, the flowers and shrubs of a garden, the streets and houses of a city, the crops on the fields, the wild plants on the waste, the waters of the sea, the clouds in the atmosphere, and the heavenly bodies in the sky; we hear sounds, we smell odours; the status of the atmosphere, the conditions of our own bodies, and the influences of our desires and fears, our exultations and depressions, all have an influence upon our feelings; and in each and all of these, and in every case that can be named or imagined, we have a feeling of power, a feeling that some agency has had and exerted, the power of producing those effects which are thus palpable to our senses or our general feeling.

"Some have denied the existence of this feeling, upon the ground that there is no object of the senses which answers to it; but this species of argument, when followed out, leads to the denial of all knowledge, and to that of all the subjects of that knowledge. Our knowledge of a thing is not the thing itself, neither has it the slightest resemblance to it, even when it is of that kind which follows instantly upon sensation. Thus our knowledge of a triangle has not three sides and three angles, whether there be the figure of a triangle before our eyes or not; and our knowledge of gunpowder would never of itself propel a cannon bullet, or blast a rock. It is the same in every other case; there is something wanting; and if we rested with the simple fact of the knowledge, the reverse of Lord Bacon's aphorism—'Knowledge is not power,'—would be the truth."

Afterwards it is asserted,—

"These observations will tend to show that the aphorism is not an absolute truth; but that knowledge is power only when it points out the power, the means of putting that power in operation, and farther shows us that we have the command of these means and the capacity for applying them. All these, then, are necessary in order to make it actual power in our hands; but they are regular steps, and each of them, considered in itself, is so much done. If we know the power, we are obviously in a better condition than if we were ignorant; and if we know the means, we are better still, because then we can know whether we have or have not the command of them; and if we have not, this knowledge may put us in the way of obtaining it at some future time. Thus, though it is only when perfect that knowledge comes up to the full encomium involved in Lord Bacon's aphorism, yet every stage and degree of it is in so far good."

Really this seems to be fighting for nought, to be a battle between words, and between certain ideas attached to them of the author's own imagining,—to be a smothering and labyrinthic process which allows of no time to breathe or to discover the point arrived at, which to the inquirer should be felt and seen as a broad platform to repose upon, and gaze from!

On the education of the body we find some striking paragraphs, though these may not be entirely free of the author's besetting sins in respect either of manner or matter.

"Is it a physical disadvantage to us, then, to be born in an age and country whose arts are so much improved, and whose resources are so developed and multiplied? Quite the reverse. This is the grand inheritance to which every Englishman is born—a far more valuable one than any legislation could by possibility confer; and not the least part of its value consists in this, that though there is a share, and a share to which no limit can be assigned, for every man that is born in the country, each individual must win his share and be worthy of it, in order that he may obtain and enjoy it. And, if there is any man who must prepare himself with more assiduity and zeal than another, it is the man whose chief dependence is upon his physical powers—upon the observation of his senses, and the application of his hands. If the task is great in this case, the encouragement is equally great; and the task never naturally and properly presents itself in such a mass at a time, as to diminish the hopes or damp the ardour of him who sets about it. It is gained by easy steps, each of which makes the labour of the one above it only half of what it was before that one was taken. Thus, if the bodily powers, whether of observation or of action, are willingly and vigorously employed, the nature of the mind is such that it will not remain idle; and such is its quickness, and the impossibility of fatiguing it, that it will educate itself, and at the same time so assist the senses that they will perceive twice as much, and the hands that they will perform twice as much, and both will accomplish their work twice as well: and not only this, but the mind can prepare the body for the work, and the work for the body, all unknown, even when the eyes are closed and the hands folded in the most balmy and refreshing sleep.

"The encouragement—the example of those who have gone before—is, however, the grand matter. We see the results in all their imposing characters, and we do not see the labour which they cost. Take the instance in anything we please—in the enjoyments, the accommodations, the ornaments, personal, domestic, local, or national, with which the country so much abounds—in the facilities of intercourse, by means of which days are condensed to hours, and degrees of longitude to miles—in time spent, and consequently expanded in the same ratio in time to enjoy—in the improved powers, by means of which a few pitchers of water and a few pennyworths of coal shall do as much more labour of force, as the strength of fifty men could accomplish in a week, or in the engine which performs by the stroke of a die in one minute what a man with a hand-tool could not do in a month. We may take our example in each or in all of these, or in a hundred others—ay, or a hundred modifications of any one of them all.

"But even in the fulness of our admiration and delight at the contemplation of these wonderful results, we must not forget that they are only results. We must not forget the sharp eye and the ten fingers, duly educated to the work; for these are the real authors of the whole. There is no occasion for undervaluing the seats of learning or the associations of learned men; but truly, for all our more substantial accommodations, personal or public, we are not very greatly indebted to them in the principle, and nothing whatever in the execution. The persons to whom we are actually indebted may have received varied portions of what we regard as common education; but one and all of them have had their real education in the workshop; and the most splendid and beneficial of them have been practical men, who have educated themselves up from the station of ordinary workmen, and who, when they began, were just as ignorant of mechanics, and made as bungling use of a tool, as we should do if we were to begin to-morrow. The workshop is the real school of experimental philosophy —the place where every hint is at once brought to the test of experience, improved if it is worthy, that is, capable of improvement, and thrown aside to give place for another and a better, if it is not. In it there are no theories doled over from week to week, or from month to month, and which, in the end, pass away like idle dreams; neither are there any dotard projectors, who go boasting all their lives of the mighty things which they are to produce, and sink to their graves in utter barrenness.

"That trains of thought are carried on in the mind, is all very well, because, without a full measure of these, the labour of the hand could not be improved; and that the results of these trains of thought, and even the steps of their progress, should be recorded in writing, and published and circulated in books, is still more commendable, because more useful, than if the train of thought is lost to the world when the thinker is laid in the dust. But truly these are nothing to that which is recorded, step by step, in real and practical results. The man who writes in the words of language, addresses himself to all who can, by the comparatively slow process of reading, make themselves masters of that language;—and science, long a cloistered monk, has not yet quite learned the every-day language of ordinary people. But he who records his thoughts in engines, or useful implements of any kind, addresses himself to the whole world, in a language which nobody can mistake, and which they who run may read, how much soever their conventional language may differ from that of him by whom the discovery and contrivance were thus written in an imperishable language, well known to all the world. Send an account of the steam-engine, and the manner of its application to the propelling of a ship through the water, to all the nations on the face of the earth, and it would not be understood by even those who were previously acquainted with the technical phrases of the English or other language in which the account was written: send a steam ship to circumnavigate the globe, and something would be known of it by even the rudest people that had curiosity enough to come and inspect it.

"But this is not all; for, in proportion as the actual and useful result—that to which the contriver gives his hand as well as his word, and thought—is more easily understood, and more readily appreciated, by those who would not understand the verbal description of the contriver, either in speech or in writing, even so it is much more comprehensible by the comparatively illiterate of his own country. The mechanical production, be it what it may, speaks directly to the senses, and through them to the minds of all who see it and feel an interest in the sight, whether they could or could not describe it in language, or even read or write."

Of the anecdotes and illustrations which Mr. Mudie's habits of reflection and his intercourse with the world have enabled him to produce by way of support of his propositions and arguments, we find some that seem to us either inept or in bad taste—while others are pithy and happy. Of this latter sort there is one derived from a visit to a London Engineer's premises, where a provincial engineer was finishing a very beautiful perspective elevation of a public work. "The lines were perfect in their form, their firmness, and their symmetry, and it seemed as if the workman was occupied in tinting an engraving by Lowry or Turrel. 'Show me your instruments,' said another engineer, who came in while we were there. A pair of old rusty compasses, with crooked legs, a bit of quill to fit upon one of them as an ink-foot, and a little iron drawing pen, as black as the lines which it had traced on the plan, were produced from an old razor case lying on the table. 'Have you no other instruments than *those?*' asked the visitor, in amazement. The other had down his brush, and holding up two well-formed and strongly-muscled hands, which we know had in former times brought beautiful forms out of the shapeless blocks with mallet and chisel, said, 'There—that's enough.'"

To illustrate the manner in which Mr. Mudie's sanguine temper and ardent style carries him away, to extravagant lengths, and to indulge in exaggerated pictures, we need only quote certain passages, regarding the hand as a wonderful instrument, and what he considers its prostitution in being devoted throughout the active periods of life, to monotonous and mechanical labour.

"Is it not a strange, a sad, a fatal prostitution, that an instrument which can fetch the most symmetrical forms, in the most graceful attitudes, out of shapeless lumps of stone, or mould them of kneaded clay,—that can animate the canvass with all but pulse and breathing,—give the state of a battle, or the story of a life, to one glance of the eye, with far more truth and effect than any verbal description, or even the actual presence of the scene itself,—that can thrill the heart by the vibration of a string, or carry the affections captive whithersoever it lists, by merely touching catgut,—is it not the most cruel, the most profligate prostitution—profligate in one of the best gifts of Heaven, that this most extraordinary and most serviceable of all instruments should be occupied, during the whole useful portion of the life of its owner, in turning the same wheel, or striking uniform blows with the same small hammer? Shall we debase this instrument by dooming it for life to perform that which could be as well done at the expenditure of one tenth the labour of a donkey, or by a falling stream, or a boiling kettle? Surely this would be doing great injustice, even in the humble and humbling mechanical view of it, to the foremost of all machines—the machine of God's own making—the one which makes all the others.

"But even this, bad as it confessedly is, is by no means the worst, either for society or for the owner of the prostituted and degraded hand." There is a mind—an immortal thinking principle—a principle capable of reading, by means of the body as its instrument or servant,—the whole of the heavens and the earth, and all the workings and wonders of human talent and industry upon the latter,—there is such a mind bound to the trundling wheel or the alternating hammer,—a wretched and miserable slave, having no enjoyment of itself, and rendering no service to the world; and so monstrous an injustice both to the one and to the other, ought not to be tolerated in a land of rational beings.

"Degrade and neglect it as we will, the immortal spirit is still the immortal spirit; it is warmed by Heaven's own ethereal fire; and all the waters of the world's oblivion cannot quench it. Cut off from the field of its proper occupation and pleasure, its restless activity is thrown wholly upon the body; but there is still no scope for it in the occupation of the body, as that which a machine can do never can require the services of a mind. Hence, when the physical occupation of the body is thus narrowed to the dull routine of a single point, upon which the labour is executed without even any simple consciousness of it, just as the feet never stumble, even in the dark, at the inequalities of a path which has been trodden a thousand times over, the mind has no occupation but about the gratification of the appetites and passions, and those, too, of the most low and grovelling description.

"Of the positive vices,—the low sensuality, the heedless and heartless life, and the frequent crimes perpetrated for the most unmeaning purposes, and on the most groundless provocations, we speak not; but we must say that, upon men in so low and lost a condition, the laws of God and man have no strength equal to even that of a cobweb. They are the most unsafe population wherewith any land can be afflicted, as they are at the mercy of every demagogue, local or general, who may wish to stir up the dregs of society, in order that he may steal through the turbid tide to the dishonest possession of that which no man would award or abet him in, if the current of society ran bright and clear. We mention no name, we assign no local habitation; but witness the unmeaning mobs, the iniquitous combinations, of weak and deluded men against their own best interests; the burnings of property; the throwing of corrosive liquids upon the person from behind corners in dark nights; the organized associations, procured and paid for out of hungry bellies, for the furtherance of that which, if accomplished to the full extent of their unmeaning madness, would only make them more hungry still. Witness this, and witness it in an enlightened nation, and an age unprecedented in improvement; and say, if you can, if there is not something sad and sickening in that which can thus degrade those around whom the means of mental and moral improvement are floating thick as the motes in the sunbeam, to this, the very lowest degree that can be named or imagined in the intellectual, the moral, and the social scale."

Such are some of the bitter fruits described as necessarily resulting from that system "which *uneducates* the physical powers of the child, in order that the man may not count for more than a small fraction of a water-wheel or a steam-engine." For our part, however, we do not here see anything to lead us either to hope for or expect the arrival of a period when there will be no handicraft industry. Were every purely mechanical operation to be performed by mechanical automata, still unvarying human drudgery would be required in the fabrication of these automata. The truth is, however, that it is impossible to point out any sort of manual labour, that either does not, to a certain extent, draw out the mind, or by its simplicity and uniformity of operations allow of that quietness and abstraction which may be advantageously filled up by mental excursions and occupation. Take the gentle employment of the sempstress, the regularity of the spinning hand and foot-domestic wheel on the one hand, and the turner or even sawyer's labours on the other, and there is no necessity for the prostitution of time or human mechanism in either case. The situation and tame drudgery of a banker's clerk put him in a much worse situation than any of those persons to whom we have alluded ; and we do not hear that these automata are remarkable personages as disturbers of the peace.

An extract which affords specimens of our author's talent at assertion, assumption, dogmatism, and inconclusiveness, may amuse if it does not much instruct our readers. Perhaps, too, something like incongruity between what has already been quoted about the education of the body, and the now asserted incapacity of the human body to acquire knowledge, as if the results of education and knowledge were essentially different, may be detected.

" We have gone at some length into the details of this—the ignorance of the senses—the merely physical parts of our compound nature, respecting even the most immediately important of our vital and sentient organs and their functions, for the purpose of showing that though the body can and does communicate information, which the mind elaborates into knowledge, yet, that the body itself does not know the information which it communicates, the subject from which it receives its impressions, or the organization by means of which those impressions are either received or communicated to the mind. In so far as the body is concerned, the feeling may be pleasurable or painful, and must indeed be the one or the other ; but beyond this it has no existence It is not anticipated before it actually takes place in the physical impression upon the sentient part, and it remains not after the physical contact is at an end. Nay, if it is not pleasurable or painful it is not felt at all ; and many have received severe wounds in the heat and excitement of battle, of which they have not been aware till admonished by the flowing blood, or by some other circumstance.

" This ought to satisfy the most determined sticklers for the possession of knowledge by the animals ; for surely, if the human body which they all allow stands foremost in the rank of organization, cannot possess knowledge,—even the knowledge of its own organs or its own existence. they would never claim a higher kind (for it is more than a degree) of capacities for beings which by their own admission are inferior. Yet, clear as is the demonstration, there is, perhaps, not one in a hundred who would not reject it as an absurd paradox; and such being the case, we need not wonder that the great body of mankind are duped into the belief of every absurdity which is so skilfully wrapt up in the mazes of language as that nothing glaringly false appears in it.

" If we say in as many words, that the dog, which, expresses delight at hearing the sound of its master's foot, which perchance greets him with a more kindly welcome than any of the human inmates of his dwelling, and which can follow after him for many miles, and find him out in a crowd of thousands, not only does not know that it has any master, but actually has no knowledge of its own existence, or of any one object in that system of nature of which it forms a part, we are liable to be disbelieved. Yet this is not only the fact, but it is a fact of which if we have not merely the faith but the demonstrative conviction, our confidence in the doctrine of immortality is shaken to its very base; and all the doctrines of morality and religion are at the mercy of the winds—our mortality is imposture, our religion is hypocrisy. If this animal, which has its day, and wholly returns to the dust, has the faculty of acquiring knowledge, what an unnecessary waste of Almighty power, what a monstrous contradiction of Infinite wisdom would it be, to confer an immortal spirit upon Man, when a dog can, do all that this spirit can do, without anything, but his mere animal organization, and do it with less teaching and more certainty than Man can possibly do! Has the Almighty Creator, through the whole of whose other works there runs such a beautiful adaptation of means to end, that every thing is done in the easiest and best manner, with the least expenditure both of materials and of power, and invariably for the good of the whole system jointly with that of the individual,—has He failed in the case of Man,—has the Creator of the heavens and the earth been found incapable of so forming a rational and immortal spirit as that it can be any benefit to its possessor which he could not have enjoyed without it, by means of his body, like the other animals?

" If this does not satisfy those religious persons who round the periods in which they essay to set forth the power, wisdom, and goodness of God, with flourishes about the knowledge and sagacity of animals, it ought at all events to silence them till they have gone to school, and learned not by ill-judged ascriptions of praise to bring the very being of their Maker into question. But it is doubtful whether it will have even this effect; for there is no mode of darkness which so stubbornly resists the light of truth, as ignorance when it puts on the mantle of religious phraseology.

" If animals could, by possibility, have knowledge, would they not employ that knowledge in the way that man employs it, in the first and least developed states of society? Would they not turn it to their aid in procuring a more abundant and easily-obtained supply of their grand necessary of life —food? And, once beginning and finding the advantage, would they not go on till we had foxes keeping poultry-yards, dogs tending their own flocks, and sheep leaving the labour of nibbling on the bare hill, and sowing turnips upon some sheltered spot? If their knowledge did not go thus far at least, *could* we call it knowledge—knowledge without a prostitution of the term? But, instead of this, the ' sagacious' dog, unless man has trained him to follow particular objects, barks and worries as readily at a burrow, while it

motion, as at a pig; and attacks the wheels of the driving carriage, even
more readily than the heels of the horses."

In fact, *education* of the body—the body's acquiring *knowledge*
—the *possession of knowledge* by the *lower animals*—are phrases
and forms of speech which are not current and are therefore apt
needlessly to startle the reader. The *training* of the body to certain
exercises and the performance of certain feats—the *skill manifested*
by the hand—the *sagacity* of the dog, are ordinary and sufficiently
clear as well as accurate styles of language ; nor do we see that our
author comes one bit nearer any contemplated principle or expected
discovery by all the wording and guarding employed in the passages
under consideration, and many others where there is as great a display of precision, correction, and novelty.

Mr. Mudie has a good deal to say in ridicule of the doctrines of
Innate Ideas, and Original Genius. In regard to the latter, all
original differences, he maintains, are purely and solely physical.
We have not found his arguments on this head satisfactory, or
calculated to suggest anything that is new. We quote a portion.

"It is the doctrine of *original genius*,—as something in which the mind
of one man differs from that of another, not only in general aptitude or
capacity, but in regard of some particular subject or class of subjects, in preference to other subjects or classes : as, we say one man has a genius for
mathematics, another for painting, a third for poetry, a fourth for music,
and so on. In short, this same genius is quite a Proteus, and may be
turned into any shape. Thus, the garrulous Frenchman, whose ordinary
powers of colloquy had failed to have any effect in drawing words from the
silent man, addressed his flattery to him in these words :—' Sir, you have
a great genius for silence.' Upon the same principle, to speak of ' a genius'
for uselessness, for folly, for vice, or for various other repulsive matters,
would be just as correct as a genius for the more estimable habits of men,
only the words in these cases are not in such good odour.

" This genius sounds all very well when we leave it perfectly general,
or keep it to the mere name of the habit ; but when we come to particulars,
it begins to put on an aspect somewhat different. If, instead of an original
genius for poetry, we were to say that a man had been composing songs,
odes, or epics, before he began to exist, or instead of one for music, that
he has had much of the same pre-existent practice on the fiddle, there are
whom we addressed ourselves would have some difficulty in maintaining
their gravity ; and yet this is what we really do express every time that we
speak of original genius, be the subject upon which that genius is displayed
what it may.

" The consideration of this as a matter of intellect, which it is usually,
if not invariably, considered as being, belongs not to the present subject ;
but as there are, in all probability, some physical differences upon which
the belief of this genius may be founded, it becomes a necessary, and far
from an uninteresting, portion of the physics of man, inasmuch as it shows,
that if we understand the body well, and teach and conduct it rightly, we
shall not only reap the reward in a physical sense, but shall get the intel-

lectual honour of possessing original genius into the bargain, as a bonus : we shall, in other words, get both a pension and a title.

"Now, if we have been in the habit of attending to the variations of our own aptitudes for observation for thought or for action, and especially if the whip of necessity has been pretty constantly and smartly applied to us, though not to such an extent as to break us down, we must have found out that there were times at which we were incapable of observing, thinking, or acting to any efficient purpose; and this when there was no specific disease of the body, no occupation of the mind, and no reverse or vicissitude of the world by which we could account for it. At other times, we must have felt the buoyancy of the ready eye, the rapid thought, and the willing hand, come upon us when we were racked by disease, perplexed in thought, or hurt and annoyed by the cares of the world. But there is not the smallest doubt that all these changes are owing to different states of the body, in respect to that quick feeling which pervades all the parts of it, and which has no necessary reference to any one particular sense."

In conclusion, we must repeat that we have not discovered grounds for thinking that Mr. Mudie has a right to indulge in the following species of self-congratulation, which occurs in his concluding paragraph, viz.—" Thus we find that man, considered only in his physical nature, is a being altogether out of place." We believe that this is neither our abiding place nor final sphere; but we desire to see other grounds, other methods of demonstration, and other evidences than those advanced in the volume before us in behalf of the doctrine, otherwise conviction will be imperfect, and perhaps contrary to an acquiescence in the great truths sought to be established.

Art. IX.—*Railroadiana. A New History of England, or Picturesque, Biographical, Historical, Legendary and Antiquarian Sketches. Descriptive of the Vicinity of the Railroads. First Series. With a Map and Illustrations.* London: Simpkin, Marshall, and Co. 1838.

We do not dislike the facetious fancy of applying the designation, "A New History of England" to this work ; for assuredly railroads and steam are destined to bring about speedily a revolution, in a variety of respects, in the social condition of the people, in our intercourse with foreigners, and in the arts of industry, and indeed in many modes of thinking and classes of opinion. Time was, when foolish battles, absurd harangues, and crooked policy were the staple which our national historians dealt in, and with which they filled page after page, and volume upon volume. Now the fashion of the day and for all time coming we hope, is to study what is the speediest and most economical rate by which to circulate the productions and the merchandise of the land, as well as of the different quarters of the world,—what is the cheapest, easiest, and pleasantest

way of diving into the most sequestered corners of the country, and
making ourselves familiar with scenes, customs, and faces, which, in
past days, it was a lifetime's theme for story and for wonder ever
to have beheld,—what is the most arrow-like line of communication
by which to be wafted a hundred or two of miles, so as to make the
inhabitants of these distant places, according to by-gone ignorance
and vulgarity, our next-door neighbours.   Such a revolution and
such improvements may well be said to change the face of the earth,
and the complexion and posture of society, and thereby beget a new
branch in literature, which, if the reader is Grecian enough, he may
denominate Railroadiana ; thus treating his ear to a euphonious
sound, and being at the same time reminded of the origin and the
novelty of the department.
   But the reader may not at once perceive how this species of literature can embrace any other topics than such as regard the speed
of conveyance, the number of passengers, and the amount or kind of
goods transmitted by the meteor-flighted steam.   How can picturesque and ancient objects, as set forth in the title page before us,
be scanned and sketched, when a glimpse is all that can be obtained
of them, when on the right and on the left an outspread and prolonged panorama will be seen only as it flies and escapes like two
stripes of canvass that unfold and are rolled up again at the rate of
some twenty miles length in the hour ? Where or how can there be
time, and, among the hastily met and hastily parted passengers,
where and how can there be opportunities for acquiring biographical sketches, or listening to historical notices of the immediate
localities ?   Then again, was there ever such an incongruity as that
which associates railroads and steam-engines with legendary lore or
romance of any kind ?
   The Introductory Remarks to Railroadiana here come to our aid
and help us to an answer to such questions and doubts.   " The
experience," we are told, " of a recent excursion on the London
and Birmingham Railway, originally suggested the idea of collecting the information contained in the following pages.   It was a fine
day in autumn, and in the few hours between the arrival of the
first and the departure of the last train, the writers sought to make
themselves acquainted with the scenery and history of Tring.   Notwithstanding it may be thought these could be compressed within
narrow limits, that time was consumed in seeking preliminary information, which might have been advantageously as well as agreeably employed in using it.   The moment came when they were
obliged to enter the Railway auxilium, or lose the last conveyance,
and they found themselves tantalized with a knowledge that they
had been occupied in gazing on what least deserved attention, while
objects of superior interest had escaped them."
   It is then taken for granted that in railroad travelling, the
" stations," as they are called, will always, (we say *generally*, or

just as convenience in regard to important interests suggests), be
fixed in the vicinity of some town of note, and that thus the public
may with certain slight helps be readily made acquainted with the
beauties and the peculiar features of our rural sections   Descriptions, narratives, and facts given in the manner of those now before
us, and gathered partly from actual observation, or in the course of
recent personal inquiry, and partly from former tourists and writers,
will consequently render good service, by enabling any passenger at
once to decide for himself, at whatever place he may be, how his
spare time can be most agreeably spent.

Such is the design of the work, which starting with the traveller
from London towards Birmingham, has in this first part furnished
sketches for fifty-six miles of the railroad line, that is, half way of
the whole. A passage in the Introduction will aptly preface the
notices and sketches to be extracted from the body of the volume.
" We find," say the writers, in reference to the general features of
the country intersected by the railroad so far as here traced, "in it
three rivers, the Colne, the Gade, and the Bulbourne, all tributaries
of the Thames ; and although the eminences which enclose these
streams are not of great elevation, nor the vales through which they
glide sufficiently depressed to afford a decided character of picturesque and romantic beauty, yet there is enough of fine scenery to
please and to gratify. Independently of the mere scenery, the
vicinity of the capital, and the salubrity of the air—(attractions not
generally neglected by the noble and the wealthy) contributed in
former days to make this district a favourite resort—thus accounting
for the growth of towns—multiplying estates in a manner unknown
in distant counties, and studding the country with the castle, the
monastery, the manor-house, or the villa, in accordance with the
wants and fashions of the times which called each into existence."

Harrow is the first station, and here the Railroadians make the
first stop. After noticing and describing what is most remarkable
in regard to the scenery and the antiquities of the place, the principal *lion* of all, the Free Grammar School, founded by John Lyon,
a farmer of the parish, becomes the subject ; Byron, among the
many distinguished personages, educated at this seminary, standing
pre-eminent in the sketch. To some of our readers the following
particulars will be new.

" On the eastern side of the church-yard there is an inscription on wood
to the memory of one ' Isaac Greentree,' upon which as the *on dit* goes,
Byron wrote *in pencil* two lines of punning poetry. We are quite willing
that he should have the credit of the authorship,—the sentiment contained
in them, being in favour of the writer, whatever his name. The spot in
question is overshadowed with limes ;—

> ' There is a time when these green trees shall fall,
> And Isaac Greentree rise above them all.'

" The original school-room, preserved with one exception, as erected in the time of the founder, is lined with oak pannels. The desks, forms, doors and floor, are of the same material, apparently of the same date. The whole is so covered with cuts and carvings of names, &c. that scarcely a spot remains free from an inscription. It would require a catalogue nearly equal to the list of the constituency of one of the Metropolitan Boroughs, to give the mere initials. We have selected one name; that of *Byron*, and present it to our readers in the form of a *fac simile* in size and shape. We should say it was characteristic of the bold, deviating turn of the individual, who it is undoubted, *carved it with his own hand*. There are none of the usual *rules* of forming letters attended to in the ' y' or the ' r'. Sir Robert Peel, on the contrary, has ' done' his name in a high capital text, of which a copy might be made for type. Close to the name of the noble ' Childe,' appears that of Col. Wildman, the gentleman-noble who destined to succeed him as the possessor of Newstead Abbey, his future residence. By the name of Sir Robert Peel, that of his own is seen. Many individuals of high celebrity have thus recorded their education at Harrow. Among them, Richard Brinsley Sheridan, the unfortunate Spencer Percival, and the present Lord Palmerston may be mentioned.

The facsimile is, in fact, a curiosity of its kind. We presume that the noble and irregular cutter of the original, distinguished himself also in the amusements which Lyon, the founder of the School, was at such pains to define and limit, viz. " driving a top, tossing a hand-ball, running, and shooting." We learn, however, that the Harrow boys, now-a-days, amongst their rudiments of learning, class *throwing of stones, demolishing windows*, and so forth, the former of the two appearing to be their favourite amusement.

It having been at Harrow that Anthony Babington was apprehended, a rather lengthened account is introduced by our Railroadians of him and his co-conspirators, their trial and execution, &c. The unity and obvious scope of the work are not very nicely observed by this sort of episode; but in such publications, neither the traveller who takes them as guides, nor the reader, inclines to be hypercritical, rather relishing diffuseness and a multiplicity of suggestions than any species of strictness that requires any regularity, or confined direction of thought. We quote the verses made by Chidiock Titchburne of himself in the Tower, the night before he suffered death; he was one of the conspirators against Elizabeth, alluded to.

> " My prime of youth is but a frost of cares,
>   My feast of joy is but a dish of pain,
> My crop of corn is but a field of tares,
>   And all my goodness is but vain hope of gain
> The day is fled, and yet I saw no sun,
>   And now I live, and now my life is done.

" 'My spring is past, and yet it hath not sprung,
The fruit is dead, and yet the leaves are green,
My youth is past, and yet I am but young,
I saw the world, and yet I was not seen,
My thread is cut, and yet, it is not spun,
And now I live, and now my life is done !
" 'I sought for death, and found it in the womb,
I look'd for life and yet it was a shade,
I trode the ground, and knew it was my tombe,
And now I dye, and now I am but made.
The glass is full, and yet my glass is run ;
And now I live, and now my life is done.' "

Watford presents in its vicinity, for description, the Church
dedicated to the Virgin Mary, with its tombs, monuments, and
inscriptions to the memory of rich or illustrious individuals. A
curious illustration is also given, to show the state of the art of
engraving in the fourteenth and fifteenth centuries, on brass plates,
inserted in their tombs. The engravings contain a goodly group,
consisting of fourteen figures,—Ralph Verney, his lady, nine boys,
and three girls. Cashiobury Park, the seat of the Earl of Essex,
furnishes the Railroadians with another interesting subject near
Watford.

At Bushy, we need not tarry ; but Hemel Hempstead must
detain us for a little.

" On stepping out of the Railway carriage at the third Station, the traveller finds himself on Box-Moor—a common, whose only embellishments
in former times were the river Gade, and the high road from London to
Aylesbury, which is part of the ancient ' Ikenild way.' Its modern improvements are the Grand Junction Canal and the Railroad, and here may
be seen the four means of communication at one view. The canal is at this
point distant forty miles from London, and whilst the boats require a day
and a half to navigate from the City Road Basin to Box-Moor, the Railroad
train travels the same distance in little more than an hour. The village at
the east end, on the canal, is called ' Two-Waters.' One of the branches of
the river Thames, which has its source at Tring, called ' Bulbourne Heath,'
falls into the Gade at this place and gives the name to the village. Certain
of the inhabitants of Hemel Hempstead have the privilege of grazing cattle
on the Moor, and a circular iron badge placed upon their door-posts indicates the inhabitant who enjoys this privilege. In summer the breeze from
the south or west brings purity and health with it, but in the winter, with
a strong touch of the east or north, there is a wind which as an old cot-
tager expressed it, ' would skin a feather.' A tolerably agreeable road of
two miles, takes you to Hemel Hempstead, and there you have not to
choose between the rival inns, ' the old and new Commercial,' for the proprietors will already have secured your patronage, by sending their own
cars or coaches down to the Station, and driving you at once into their
premises. We were fortunate enough to meet with Mr. Deacon, whose

coach is called the 'Queen Dowager,' and his inn the 'King's Arms,' the
former conveyed me safely to the latter, and right well pleased we were
with our fare during a sojourn of two days. The river Gade, on its way to
join the Thames at Dorchester in Oxfordshire, runs through the valley,
embellishing in its course the park and seat of Sir Ashley Cooper; the
former, open to visitors at all times, is reached by turning down a lane just
beyond the northern extremity of the town, and crossing the river over a
wooden bridge. From the park a view of the town is obtained, but the real
searcher after the picturesque should ascend to the exterior of the Church
tower, and the 'vale' (as the inhabitants call it) will please his eye,
although the view, except on the side towards Box-Moor, is confined.
The Church, dedicated to the Virgin Mary, is well worthy of a visit. Its
character is neatness, and its fittings are elegant and comfortable. It consists of a nave, two side aisles, and a transept, on the top of which is built a
handsome tower, with Norman-Saxon lights, the whole surmounted with a
beautiful spire of ornamented lead. At the west end is a fine door of Saxon
architecture, curiously and richly ornamented; highly adorned with fleurs-
de-lis and vine leaves alternately, fretwork, &c. The capitals are enriched
with grotesque figures. The nave is separated from the aisles by a range
of five massive columns on each side, and two half columns with sculp-
tured square capitals, which support arches with zig-zag mouldings. The
tower rests on semi-circular clustered columns, ornamented. The west
window is adorned with a representation, in stained glass, of the Good
Samaritan, a happy subject, considering it to have been chosen by the donor,
Sir Ashley Cooper. The oldest monument we could discover is placed in
the south-western corner of the Church, and is to the memory of one Robert
Albyn and his wife, who lived in the reign of Edward the Third."

At Berkhamsted it is neither scenery, church, nor antiquities that
we notice so gratefully as the story of a " Sweet Ann Page."

" Berkhamsted was of great note when the exiled Bourbons of France
sought an asylum in this country. Louis XVIII. and after him Charles
X. and family, lived at Hartwell House, about two miles from Aylesbury,
and, on their journeys to and from the metropolis, always honoured the
King's Arms with their custom, and as their numerous royal and noble visitors at Hartwell did the same, this inn has entertained in turn hearty all
the crowned heads in Europe, to the no small gratification and profit of
the worthy Mr. Page—the present landlord. Not only also is ' Miss Page,'
the landlord's accomplished daughter, to be mentioned in connection with
the King's Arms and the Regal times above alluded to, but it belongs to
the *page* of history to record, that so highly pleased was the monarch
Louis with the attentions he received, and with the superior manners of
this lady, that on her visit to Paris after his restoration, she was actually
honoured with an audience at the Tuilleries.—Miss Page has not only,
however, been thus favourably known to and respected by princes and
nobles whose day has passed, and left her possessed of a store of anecdotes
which cannot fail to amuse her present visitors; but besides these, there
were very many commercial travellers who used regularly to make the
King's Arms, at Berkhamsted, their Sunday rendezvous. Many of them
are now no more, have become heads of the houses for which they used to

journey, or, withdrawn from business altogether, are enjoying their *otium cum dignitate*. This well-managed inn, however, from the combination of the various circumstances which have been enumerated, became celebrated throughout this and the neighbouring counties; and ' mine host' and ' sweet Ann Page' were extensively known and universally respected by all classes of travellers."

The Wild Boy, Peter's history, who was found in the forest of Hertswald, near Hanover, in the year 1725, by George the First of England, while hunting, is identified with Berkhamsted. The account given by the present writers comprises all that was ever known of him, many of the facts having been collected, it is stated, from Mr. Page, of the King's Arms Inn, who was one of the pall-bearers at Peter's funeral. The *Boy* lived not only in the reign of George the First, but that of the second of the name, and part of that of George the Third.

Tring furnishes a variety of subjects for historical detail. The strong contrasts and the suggestive points in the following passage are remarkable.

"Whilst these historical details are fresh in the mind of the traveller, if he walk to the western extremity of the town, he will observe on the right hand, in a large garden enclosed by a wall, a building formed of brick and ribbed with oak, bearing unequivocal marks of age—this is no other than the *Monastery of Tring*—although now converted into the residence of a farmer, and used in this present nineteenth century as a lodging house for travellers of the working class, in which there were at the period of our visit, at least one hundred persons congregated—chiefly Railway labourers, appropriately enjoying their home-brewed ale in the very kitchen of the monks. The Dormitories and Cells may be visited by permission of the tenant. In the former there are some remains of carvings which seem originally to have represented something of the 'pomp of heraldry,' probably in commemoration of some gift or bequest which a pious life or death-bed penitence had bestowed. The chambers were lofty and vaulted, and even in decay, inspire an interest somewhat akin to awe. It has been found convenient in late years, probably, while the building was occupied as a workhouse, to ' curtail the fair proportions' of the Hall, by introducing a new floor and ceiling, and the apartment thus gained between the new floor and the original roof, is now used as a tap by the *Bankers*, as the excavators are called, who now lodge in a part of the old Priory. The kitchen has had its dimensions abated, but the original fire-place remains. What was the chapel, or part of it, is at present occupied as a stable. We in vain look for the original form of the windows of the refectory or principal Hall, as the assaults of Time had made it necessary to repair the external wall when the old window was taken out. On renewing the floor of one of the apartments, the present occupier found that a considerable number of human bodies had been there deposited. Whether the sepulchral vault of the religious establishment formerly existed on that spot, or whether the bones thus unexpectedly discovered, where the remains of victims to those crimes which history assures us were but too frequently penetrated in the ancient monasteries, can show in it no matter of conjecture. They have been left undisturbed in their resting place. The predecessor past, Mr. Beal, an intelligent farmer, and his successor, cheerfully show to the curious visitor, all that is most remarkable in their ancient dwelling; and obligingly give every information in the matter."

"Here is a companion picture to match in respect of ignorance and superstition that of the late Courtenay tragedy. Is the credulity of the year 1838 less monstrous in some parts of Kent than it was in 1751, in the neighbourhood of Tring?

"Some country people were possessed of an opinion, that an old man and woman of that town, John and Ruth Osborne, were, on account of several cattle dying of a contagion which then began, great numbers of them assembled, some on horseback, and others on foot, and went and had them proclaimed as such, in three different market towns. These unfortunate people were afterwards dragged from the vestry of the church, where they had been concealed, and so severely ducked, that the woman died on the spot, and the man a few days afterwards. Several persons were committed to custody on the verdict of the Coroner's Jury; and one, Thomas Colley (who, though a principal actor in this horrid affair, was prompted by others, and by the liquor which he had drank), was tried at the ensuing assizes for Hertfordshire, and capitally convicted. It came out at the trial, that, on the 18th of April 1751, one Nichols came to William Dell, the crier of Hemel Hempstead, and gave him a piece of paper, with four-pence, that he might cry the words written thereon, in the market-place. The words were these: '*This is to give notice that on Monday next a man and woman are to be publicly ducked at Tring in this Country for their Wicked crimes.*'

"The overseer of the parish, where these people lived, having heard this cried at Winslow, Leighton Buzzard, and Hemel Hempstead, on the several market days, and being informed that the two people were John Osborne and Ruth his wife, he sent them to the workhouse for safety. The master of the workhouse, to make still more secure, removed them, in the middle of the night of the 21st into the vestry-room of the church, thinking the sanctity of the place would have some awe upon the mob, if they came. However, on the day appointed, more than *five thousand* people were collected together at Tring, declaring their rage against Osborne and his wife as a wizard and witch: they pulled down a large wall belonging to the workhouse—(the ancient priory)—and demolished the windows and window frames. The master of the workhouse assured them they were not there; the mob would not believe him, but rushed in and searched the house, the closets, and even the boxes and trunks. They declared they would pull the house down if the victims were not produced, and some proposed setting fire to it; at last they all swore, that if Osborne and his wife were not delivered to them, they would not only burn the workhouse, but the whole town of Tring. The master being apprehensive what they would do as they had promised, at length informed them were the unhappy people were. The mob now went off in triumph, with Colley at their head. As soon as the mob entered the vestry-room, they seized Osborne and his wife, and carried them to a place called Gubblecote, about two miles off, where not finding a pond to their purpose, they carried them to Wilston Green, and put them into separate rooms in a house there; they stripped them naked, and tied them up separately in a sheet, but first they crossed the man's legs and arms, and bound his body across to his thumbs to his great toes.

"When they came to the pond, called Wilston Wear, a rope was tied under the armpits of Ruth Osborne, and two men dragged her into the pond, and through it, and Colley went into the pond, and turned her several times over and over with a stick. After they had ducked the woman, they brought her to land, and then dragged the old man in, and ducked him. Then he was set aside, and the woman ducked again as before, and Colley made the same use of his stick. Then the old man was ducked again. After which the woman was a third time ducked; and Colley went into the pond and pulled her about until the sheet wherein she was wrapped came off, and she appeared naked. She expired soon afterwards. Colley then came out of the pond, and went round collecting money for the sport he had shewn them in ducking the old witch as he called her. After the woman was dead, the mob carried John Osborne to a house, put him to bed, and laid his dead wife by his side. Ruth Osborne was seventy years of age; John was fifty-six. In consequence of these circumstances of cruelty, Colley was ordered for immediate execution, and his body was afterwards hung in chains at Gubblecote, in the parish of Tring, three miles off.

" Another instance of credulity and superstition occurred in this neighbourhood in the year 1759. At Wingrove, one Susannah Hannokes, an elderly woman, was accused by her neighbour of being a witch; for that she had *bewitched her spinning wheel*, so that she could not make it go round, and offered to make oath of it before a magistrate; on which the husband of the poor woman, in order to justify his wife, insisted upon HER BEING TRIED BY THE CHURCH BIBLE, and that the accuser should be present: she was conducted by her husband to the ordeal, attended by a great concourse of people, who flocked to the parish church to see the ceremony, where she was stripped of her clothes to her shift and under petticoat, and WEIGHED AGAINST THE BIBLE! when to the no small mortification of her accuser, SHE OUTWEIGHED IT, AND WAS HONOURABLY ACQUITTED of the charge. This account appeared in the ' London Chronicle, February 27, 1759.'"

· Of some of the gigantic undertakings to which railroads have given rise, that of cutting is not the least. For example, near Ivinghoe—

"The cross roads in this district which are some of the most untractable we have seen in all our perambulations are at length destined to undergo a change. We may imagine that instead of, as now, being obliged to visit this interesting little town by way of Tring, or to walk along the chalky banks of the Railroad for a mile and a half in a direction parallel, instead of in a straight line, to the point of destination; that a direct road will be cut to Pendley, by which, more than a mile of the distance will be saved. It was by no means a common sight, however, to witness the progress of the work on this part of the line, where there is not less than two miles of cut-

... bringing the soil to... that mechanical means of a novel character have either been resorted to for the raising of the soil to the surface. These means consist in the employment of horses to drag the workmen and their wheel-barrows of chalk up an inclined plane at an angle of not less than forty-five degrees, the operation from the bottom to the surface (a space of nearly seventy feet) occupying but a few seconds of time, the workman and vehicle being assisted in their still more rapid descent by the ... of the ... and keeping the cable, which passes over a windlass, tolerably ... From the new bridge over the direct road from Tring to Leighton the ... of this cutting, spreading east and west, and lost in distance, ... the sublime. We recommend a pause of a few minutes... ... all who can admire and appreciate the results of labour by them in ... gated numbers. We imagine that at the period of our visit, there were upwards of one thousand men employed on the two miles of cutting to which we now direct attention."

Such are samples of Railroadiana; a pleasant and well-got-up book in every respect, with the exception of some material typographical errors. A series of such volumes, following and abiding by the various lines of steam-conveyance throughout England, and the several provinces of the empire, it is quite clear, may be composed and compiled, of an instructive and agreeable character. A railroad, in fact, may become the thread to any sort of information, because interesting and touching as such lines must do every kind of scenery —coming in contact with every variety of fact in science, history, art, and literature—and being easily bended to suit the scheme of any copious and excursive writer, the whole field of thought and imagination may thus be traversed in a natural and easy style. Guide-bookmakers may take a good hint from the present publications, were it in nothing else than regards the manner of folding and placing the Map of the London and Birmingham Railway-line, and of the vicinity thereof. It is on a sheet separate entirely from the volume, but for which a pocket is cut in the inside of the left-hand board.

ART. X.

1.—*Historie of the Arrivall of Edward IV. in England and the Finall Recouerye of his Kingdomes from Henry VI.* Edited by John Bruce, Esq., F.S.A.

2.—*Memoirs of the Life and Character of Henry V. Prince of Wales and King of England.* By the Rev. J. Endell Tyler, B.D. 2 vols. 8vo. London: Bentley. 1838.

The numerous State Papers, the Biographies, and Memoirs of illustrious persons which have so rapidly multiplied upon us of late, are ... circumstances... we have had an opportunity more than some time notice, of the increasing popularity of legitimate history, and the lasting claims of authentic particulars, over the brilliancies of

fiction. We might this month enlarge the list of these truly national archives beyond the pale of publication at the head of this
paper, although there may be no other principle of union among
them, but what may be found under the head of antiquarianism,
or indicated by a name equivalent to that of royalty. We might,
for instance, have set down the "State Papers published under the
authority of His Majesty's Commission, volumes Fourth and
Fifth, which contain about 1,300 quarto pages, and relate to the
reign of Henry the Eighth ; or, to be still more precise in our intention, which particularly throw light upon the State relations
subsisting between England and Scotland between the years 1523
and 1546. The correspondence of an official and oft-times secret
character, during the period mentioned, of the Lords Wardens of
the Marches, the Council of the North, the English Ambassador at
the Scottish Court, of Henry the Fourth, James the Fourth, Queen
Margaret, Wolsey and Betoun, &c., form principal features in the
collection. One of the most interesting documents of the whole,
however, and which, besides being original, modifies a generally
received account, belongs to a date several years anterior to 1523,
viz., an English account of the sanguinary battle of Flodden, so
disastrous to Scotland, and where James the Fourth was slain.

"*Articles of the Bataill bitwix the Kinge of Scottes and the Erle of
Surrey in Branketone Feld, the 9 day of September.*

" Furst, when bothe tharmyes were within 8 myles togidres, the said
Erle sent Rugecrosse to the Kinge of Scottes, desiryng hym of bataill ;
and he answered he wold abyde hym there tyll Fryday at noone.

" The Lord Haward at 11 of the clok the said 9 day passed over the
brigge of Twysell with the vaward and artyllary ; and the said Erle
folawyng with the rerewatd, tharmy was devyded into 2 batailles, and to
either bataill 2 wynges.

" The Kinge of scottes army, was devided into 5 batailles, and every
bataill an arrowe shotte from the other, and all lyke fernes from the
Englisshe armye, in grete plumpes, parte of them quadrant, and some
pyke wise ; and were on the top of the byll, being a quarter of a myle from
the fote thereof.

" The Lord Haward caused his vaward to stale in a lytell valey, tyll the
rerewarde were joyned to oon of the wynges of his bataill, and then bothe
wardes in oon avaunced against the Scottes, and they cam down the hill,
and mette with them in good ordre, after the Almayns maner, withoute
spekyng of eny word.

" The Erles of Huntley, Arell, and Crawford, with theire host of 6000
men, cam upon the Lord Haward, and shortly their bakkes were tourned
and the most parte of theym slayne.

" The Kinge of Scottes cam with a grete puyssaunce upon my Lord of
Surrey havyng on his lyfte hand my Lord Darcy son ; whiche 2 bare all
the bronnte of the bataill ; and there the Kinge of Scottes was slayne within
a spere length from the said Erle of Surrey, and many noble men of the
Scottes slayn moo, and no prisoners taken in those 2 batailles. And in

the tyme of this bataill th Erles of Lynewes and Argyll with their pusaunce joined with Sir Edward Stanley, and they were putte to flyght.

"Edmond Howard had with hym 1000 Cheshire men, and 500 Lancashire men, and many gentilmen of York shire on the right wyng of the Lord Haward, and the Lord Chamberlain of Scotland with many Lordes dyd sette on hym, and the Chesshire and Lancasshire men never abode stroke, and few of the gentilmen of Yorkshire abode but fled. Mr Gray and Sir Humfrey Lyle be taken prisoners, and Sir Wynchard Harbotell and Maurys Barkeley slayne. And the said Edmonde Haward was thries feled, and to his relief the Lord Dacres cam with 1500 men, and put to flight all the said Scottes, and had aboute 8 score of his men slayne. In which bataill a grete nombre of Scottes were slayne."

It is farther stated, that the battle began between four and five of the afternoon, that the chase continued for three miles, there being a marvellous slaughter, and that 10,000 more of the Scotch must have been slain, if their opponents had been on horseback. After naming the number killed on each side, it is added, "The Kinge of Scottes body is brought to Berwyk. Ther is no grete man of Scotland retourned home but the Chamberlain. It is thought that fewe of them bee lefte on lyve."

The readers of Scottish and English history will remember that a report was entertained that James did not fall, or, at least, that he was not slain on Flodden Field. It was a popular and romantic version in Scotland which said that he had undertaken a pilgrimage, or was fulfilling some other religious vow; but what is not the least of the remarkable things contained among the present papers, Queen Margaret at one time either truly or pretendedly yielded to the same vulgar rumour; for the English Ambassador in 1525 writes from Scotland to Wolsey; and in reference to Queen Margaret's eagerness to be divorced from the Earl of Angus, declares,

"The Quenes Grace contynueth still at Sterling, and soweth faste for the devorce betwene Her said Grace and the said Erle of Angushe, admitting her cause to be that She was married to the said Erle, the late King of Scottes her husbande being a live, and *that the same King was alive three years after the failde of Flodden or Bronkston.*"

A great portion of the present documents illustrate the intrigue which had such admirable scope between the interests of England and France in regard to the marriage of James the Fifth. Henry of England seems not to have been the only one who for a time was solicitous that his daughter Mary should be united to the Scottish monarch; but Henry's sister, Margaret, Queen of Scots, and her party, were sufficiently peremptory in their demands regarding a marriage settlement.

"Fyrst, the Lordis of Scotland desyris mariagis betuext ye Kyngis Grace my broder dochtthyr and ye Kyng my sone his newó, and apone that desiris ye Kingis Greit Seyll, and al ye Lordis of Ingland selis, and yat to be aprewit in yer Parliament.

"In the secund, thay desyrit, he haffand hym ip mareagis, yat he be pronuncit secund persone of yat Realm, and to assyng landis, as persenis, to ye Prysuce of yat Realm, to be ansuerit to hyme.

"The thryd, ye Lordis desyris, falzeyng of this, yat, gyf it pleſit God to send Hes Grace and Prynce, that in recompens of yat he is put fra, yat he gyf ye Kyng my sone Berweyk, wyth landis that is in threype betuex Ingland and Scotland, and yat ye samyn may be ye Kyng my sone wyth ane competand sertane monys.

"Thyr is ye desyris of ye Lordis in speciall, as aperis weyl be copye be ye artykylis closit wyth in this."

What degree of sincerity on either side there might exist upon this and the other questions that arose between Henry and Scotland, it is not for us to say. We do not, however, find any reason for thinking more favourably of the licentious and remorseless King of England, of his weak contemporary on the throne of Scotland, of the haughty and magnificent Wolsey, or of any of the other principal movers in the drama, than the general tone of history and tradition has communicated. It is a painful fact, that the more closely we investigate, or see others investigate, the character of the great majority of our British monarchs, any partiality to royalty that may exist feels itself chastised, and that most unwelcome truths obtrude themselves; while ministers and statesmen generally leave behind them a testimony not more flattering to human nature. The conclusion is, that anything identical with or approaching to irresponsible power when possessed by man is almost sure to be abused; that seldom or never is there any check to despotism, selfishness, and political error save that which knowledge and liberty guard and enforce. Were we to go *seriatim* through these State Papers, the repulsive lesson would be all along corroborated and strengthened.

Let us see if the "Historie of the Arrivall of Edward IV. in England and the Finall Recouerye of his Kingdome from Henry VI.," in any respect enhances our good estimation of England's Kings. The publication which we have to glance at, is the first that has been edited on the part of the Camden Society; and although it extends to only a few small quarto pages, it is highly creditable not only to Mr. Bruce but to the institution of which he forms a member.

Mr. Bruce has made himself master of every existing or accessible historical document that bears upon the æra under review. But it occasions deep regret, though it be not a thing to be wondered at, when the paucity or the contradictory character of historical data, belonging to comparatively recent periods in our annals, come to be investigated and weighed. The present editor, for example, after enumerating the principal authorities for the narrative he publishes, says,

Upon these authorities, which in many points are most contradictory, all our subsequent chroniclers, with one exception, to be noticed hereafter, have based their statements. [...] Hall translates Polydore Vergil and Philip de Comines; Stowe [...] the Chronicle quoted by Leland; and the rest follow some one [...] some another. "The present narrative has higher claims to authority than any of those I have noticed." It was written upon the spot [...] after the events to which it relates, by some person possessed of [...] of knowledge, and it will be seen that it was adopted by Edward IV [...] an accurate relation of his achievements.".

To those who feel very curious about Yorkist testimonials in opposition to such as favour the Lancasterian faction, we recommend Mr. Bruce's authentication of the present document, and pass on to notice two or three of its several contents. It is well known that Edward threw himself upon the English coast with few followers, and when his prospects were far from certain or apparently hopeful. The fact is, that he met with formidable opposition, and was glad to disguise his utmost intent by merely at first claiming the duchy of York. When he got to this province, however, he took advantage, in a most characteristic manner, as regarded the superstitions and customs of the age, of whatever circumstances as were most likely to promote his interest and views.

" On the Saturday, the Kynge, with all his hoost, cam to a towne callid Daventre, where the Kynge, with greate devocion, hard all divine servyce upon the morne, Palme-Sonday, in the parishe churche, wher God and Seint Anne, shewyd a fayre miracle; a goode prognostique of good aventure that after shuld befall unto the Kynge by the hand of God, and medyacion of that holy matron, Seynt Anne. For, so it was that, afore that tyme, the Kynge, beinge out of his realme, in great trowble, thought, and hevines, for the infortwne and adversitie that was fallen hym, full often, and, specially upon the sea, he prayed to God, owr Lady, and Seint George, and, amonges other saynts, he specially prayed Seint Anne to helpe hym, where that he promysed, that, at the next tyme that it shuld happe, hym to se any ymage of Seint Anne, he shuld therto make his prayers, and doe his offeringe, in the honor and worshipe of that blessed Saynte. So it fell, the same Palme Sonday, the Kynge went in procession, and all the people after, in goode devotion, as the service of that daye askethe, and, when the processyon was comen into the churche, and, by order, of the service, were comen to that place where the vale shulbe drawne up afore the Roode, that all the people shall honor the Roode with the anthem, three tymes begon, in a pillar of the churche, directly aforne the place where Kynge knelyd, and devowtly honoryd the Roode, was a lytle ymage of Seint Anne, made of allebaastar, standynge fixed to the piller, closed, and clasped togethars with four borders, small, payntyd, and gowlyng rownd abowt the image, in manar of a compas, lyke as it is to see comonly, and all abowt, where as suche ymages, be wonte to be made for to be solde and set up in churches, chapells, crosses, and oratories, in many places. And this ymage was thus shett, closed, and clasped, accordynge to the rulles that, in all the churchis of England, be observyd, all ymages to be hid from Ashe Wednesday to Estarday in the morninge. And so the said ymage had bene from Ashwenesday to that tyme. And even sodaynly, at that season of the service, the boards compassynge the ymage about, were a greet crek, and a little openyd, whiche Kynge well perceyveyd, and all the people about hym. And anon, after, the bords drewe and closed togethars agayne, withowt any mans hand, or touchinge, and, as theugh it had bene a thinge done with a violence, with a gretar might it openyd, all abrod, and so the ymage stode, open and discovert, in syght of all the people there beynge. The Kynge, this seinge, thanked and honoryd God and Seint Anne, takynge it for a good signe, and token of good and prosperous aventure that God wold send hym in that he had to do, and, remembringe his promyse, he honoryd God and Seint Anne, in that same place, and gave his offrings. All thos, also, that were present and sawe this, worshippyd, and thanked God and Seint Anne there, and many offered; takyng of this signe, shewed by the power of God, good hope of theyr good spede for to come."

There is a minute detail of Falconbridge's attack upon London, which was placed in the utmost jeopardy by the attempt. Edward though victorious and in turn crushing his enemies in the various provinces, being absent and at a distance, so that he could not throw in prompt protection against the slaughter of the citizens, burnings, sackings, and devastation of every sort that then prevailed according to all the ferocity of a barbarous age. We are told,

"Over came from London freshe tydyngs to the Kynge, from the Lords, and the citizens, which, with right grete instance, moved the Kinge, in all possible haste, to approche and com to the citie, to the defence of the Quene than being in the Tower of London, my Lorde Prince, and my Ladies his doghtars, and of the Lords, and of the citie, whiche, as they all wrote, was likly to stand in the grettest ioperdy that evar they stode. In consideracion had for that gret nombar of the persones within the citie were rather disposyd to have helped to have suche mischiefe wroght than to defend it; some, for they were maliciowsly disposed, and were, in theyr harts perciall to th'Erle of Warwickes qwarell, and to the party of Henry; wherefore were many; some, for they were powre; some, mens servaunts, mens prentises, which would have bene right glade of a comon robery to th' entent they might largely have put theyr hands in riche mens cofres. Thes manar of writings moved the Kynge greatly to haste hym thetharwards; but it was behovefull, or that he came there, he were furneshed of as great, or gretar, hooste than he had had at any tyme sithe his comynge into the land; natheles, for that suche armye might nat be prepared sonne as he woulde, the sayd xiiij. day of May."

The battle of Barnet and the "fatal fight of Tewkesbury," furnish subjects for highly interesting and indeed picturesque description as given in the present "Historie;" but still the blood-thirstiness and revengeful character of the York faction are in regard to these and other occasions fully attested. In fact the assassination of Henry the Sixth in the Tower, at the instigation of Edward is scarcely acknowledged, the reader may perhaps suppose, in the following statement, guarded and bolstered though it be.

"Here it is to be remembered, that, from the tyme of Tewkesbery fielde, where Edward, called Prince, was slayne, thanne, and sonne that was taken, and slayne, and at the Kyngs wyne, all the noblemen that came from beyond the see with the sayde Edward, called Prince, and other any theyr parte-takers as many as were of eny might or puissaunce. Quene Margaret, hirself, taken, and browghte to the Kynge; and, in every part of England, where any commotion was begoone for Kynge Henry's party, anoon they were rebuked, so that it appered to every maner of the sayde partie was extincte and represed for evar, without any maner hope of agayne quikkening; utterly despaired of any maner of, hoope, or talkes. The certaintie of all whiche came to the knowledge of the sayd Henry, late called Kyng, being in the Tower of London; not havynge, afore that, knowledge of the saide matars, he toke it to so great dispite, ire, and indignation, that, of pure displeasure, and melencoly, he dyed the xxiij day of the monithe of May. Whom the Kynge dyd to be browght, to the friers prechars, at London, and there, his funerall service done, to be caried, by water, to an Abbey upon Thamys syd, xvj myles from London, called Chartsey, and there honorably enteryd."

Mr. Tyler's work comes before us in the regular form of a recent publication, of a carefully compiled history, and an elaborate memoir. He, in short, grapples with a subject where all the right requisites of the historian and the biographer may find scope. We suspect, however, that the conjectures of the antiquary rather than the resistless discoveries and satisfactory balancings afforded by the industrious investigator, where evidence is abundant though confused and often contradictory, as at first presented, are his characteristics.

Mr. Tyler's great efforts are to free Henry the Fifth's name from the charge of irregularity during his youth, to which Shakspeare has given such currency; and from what is a more serious, and, we believe, better authenticated accusation, that which says he was guilty of religious, inquisitorial persecution, such as never disgraced and stained the character of any other English monarch, unless it have been Mary of "bloody" memory, and her gross tyrannical father.

There is another feature in the history of Henry of Monmouth, which, like the last mentioned, may be said to have been according to the modes of thinking and acting which the age countenanced,— we mean a passion for war, vain conquest, unprincipled aggression, and all sorts of idle pageantry which in any way flattered for the time the barons and the monarch. Blood and treasure were alike wasted with reckless profusion. It seemed to be regarded as a sufficient cause for declaring war that the mock sovereignty of some province in France was contemplated and longed for ; it seemed to warrant all the horrors of war when unoffending Frenchmen, their fertile land, and their quiet homes were the objects of destruction! Oh! but these were chivalrous darings and exploits which brought renown to the English name! Yes, and produced a cant—a murderous phrase that France and England were natural enemies,—a phrase which never appears to have been questioned till of late. Then, think of the taxes and the half-famishing multitude at home, which such fruitless efforts occasioned, and we may come much nearer to a just estimate of the sudden but brief triumphs of our Henries and Edwards, than is to be found in romances or many publications falsely called histories.

As to the alleged mad-cap pranks of Henry's youth, Mr. Tyler's argument is that contemporary chroniclers, or annalists who succeeded the era in which Henry flourished, do not generally charge him with intemperance or immorality of any kind. He says;

"It is not because we would palliate Henry's vices, if such there be on record, or disguise his follies, or wish his irregularities to be forgotten in the vivid recollections of his conquests, that he would try 'our musical bard' by the test of rigid fact. We do so, because he is the authority on which the estimate of Henry's character, as generally entertained, is mainly founded. Mr. Southey, indeed, is speaking only of his own boyhood when he says, 'I had learned all I knew of English history from Shakspere.' But very many pass through life without laying aside or correcting those impressions which they caught at the first opening of their minds; and never have any other knowledge of the times of which his dramas speak, than what they have learned from his representations. The great Duke of Marlborough is known to have confessed that all his acquaintance with English history was derived from Shakspere: whilst not unfrequently persons of literary pursuits, who have studied our histories for themselves, are to the last under the practical influence of their earliest associations: unknown to their own minds the poet is still their instructor and guide. And this influence Shakspere exercises over the historical literature of his country, though he was born more than one hundred and sixty years after the historical date of that scene in which he first speaks of the 'royal rake's' strayings and unthriftiness; and though many new sources, not of vague tradition, but of original and undoubted record, which were closed to him, have been opened to students of the present day. It has indeed been alleged that he might have had means of information no longer available by us; that manuscripts are forgotten or lost, which bore testimony to Henry's career of wantonness. But surely such a suggestion only renders it still more imperative to examine with strict and exact scrutiny into the poet's descriptions. If these are at all countenanced by a coincidence with ascertained historical facts, we must admit them as evidence, secondary indeed, but still the best within our reach. But if they prove to be wholly untenable when tested by facts, and irreconcileable with what history places beyond doubt, we have solid grounds of rejecting them as legitimate testimonies. We must consider them either as the fascinating but aëry visions of a poet who lived after the intervention of more than a century and a half, or as inferences built by him on documents false and misleading."

When, however, Mr. Tyler proceeds to give us Henry's history during his infancy, boyhood, and youth, after all his research, we have little more than a string of favourable fancies, and fond conjectures. Assumptions are backed by sentimentalisms that possess no historical force, however amiable and charitable they may be on the part of the reverend author. Who, for instance, but an apologist or a speaker at random on the fair side, would have expressed himself in the following manner, regarding one of whose private habits so little is really known?

"To all this, Henry added that quality without which such a combination of moral excellences would not have existed, the believing obedient heart of a true christian. This last quality is not named in words by the Speaker (of the House of Commons); but his immediate reference to the grace of God and his thanks in the name of the people of England to the Almighty Saviour for having imparted these graces to their prince, appear to bring the question of his religious principles before our minds. Whilst in seeking for the solution of that question, we find other pages of history, equally genuine and authentic, which assure us that he was indeed a doubtless, a warlike, and pure Christian."

We form a much more precise opinion of Henry, from Shakespeare's pictures, and we must add, not one by any means unfavourable. Mr. Tyler is quite mistaken when he alleges that the dramatist's picture is that of a gross profligate and foul reveller in the sink of vice, in allusion to Henry's youth. It is remarkable that the poet should have created such a deep interest in the prince, had he represented him as anything worse that a somewhat hair-brained young man, whose generosities and noble feeling are ever proving themselves to hold and guide the reins of his nature. The fact is, we never think so unpleasantly or are so disappointed in regard to Hal as when, after his accession to the throne, he, popular Falstaff, frowns upon him, and in reality despotically and undeservedly punishes him. We feel indeed, that the following letter of the Prince's, quoted by our author, much more deeply and pleasingly affects his character than anything that William Shakespeare has ever narrated:—

"As to news from these parts, if you wish to hear of them, know, that we were lately informed that Owyn Glyndŵr [Owen de Glyndourdy] had assembled his forces, and those of other rebels, his adherents, in great numbers, purposing to commit inroads; and, in case of any resistance to his plans on the part of the English, to come to battle with them, and so he boasted to his own people. Wherefore we took our men, and went to a place of the said Owyn, well built, which was his chief mansion, called Saghern, where we thought we should have found him if he wished to fight, as he said. And, on our arrival there, we found no person. So we caused the whole place to be set on fire, and many other houses around it belonging to his own tenants. And then we straight to the other place of Glyndourdy, to seek the blue-dwel... ...we burnt: ...see judge in his park and the whole country round. And ...ub we remained there all that night. And certain of our people sallied forth ...and took a gentleman of high degree of that country, who was one of the said Owyn's chieftains. This person offered five hundred pounds for his ransom to save his life, and to pay that sum within two weeks. Nevertheless, that was not accepted, and he was put to death; and several of his companions, who were taken the same day, shared the same fate. We then proceeded to the commote of Edirnion in Merionethshire, and there laid waste a fine and populous country ; thence we went to Powys, and there being in Wales a want of provender for horses, we made our people carry oats with them, and we tarried there for —— days."

Allusion has already been made to Henry's persecutions unto the death of numbers who suffered for their religious belief, his own bigotry and his subservience to the priesthood lending his name an unenviable notoriety in this respect.

In proof of the uncertainty and vagueness which attach to Henry's early history, we need only mention that the place of his birth is doubtful, a wardrobe account shewing that his father resided at the Castle of Monmouth within a year of the presumed period of the Prince's birth; together with certain traditions, being the principal evidence on the subject. Here we quote some curious particulars concerning the castle now named.

" Of Monmouth Castle, the dwindling ruins are now very scanty, and in point of architecture, present nothing worthy of an antiquary's research. They are washed by the streams of the Monnow, and are embosomed in gardens and orchards, clothing the knoll on which they stand ; the aspect of the southern walls, and the rocky character of the soil admirably adapting them for the growth of the vine, and the ripening of its fruits. In the memory of some old inhabitants, who were not gathered to their fathers when the Author could first take an interest in such things, and who often amused his childhood with tales of former days, the remains of the Hall of Justice were still traceable within the narrowed pile; and the crumbling bench on which the Justices of the circuit once sate, was often usurped by the boys in their mock trials of judge and jury. Somewhat more than half a century ago, a gentleman whose garden reached to one of the last remaining towers, had reason to be thankful for a marked interposition in his behalf, of the protecting hand of Providence. He was enjoying himself on a summer's evening in an alcove built under the shelter and shade of the castle, when a gust of wind blew out the candle by his side, just at the time when he felt disposed to relinquish and rekindle his pipe. He went, consequently, with the lantern in his hand towards his house, intending to renew his evening's recreation ; but he had scarcely reached the door when the wall fell, burying his retreat, and the entire slope, with its shrubs, and flowers, and fruits, under the mass of ruin."

It is uncertain where the Prince received his education, and indeed, hardly anything but what the fertile imaginations of chronicles have bequeathed us is known of him until his father is seated on the throne, and he is created Prince of Wales. There is no reason for believing, however, that he remained in the hands of Richard, a sort of state prisoner, during the banishment of his father. At length the weak monarch, who was about to be dethroned, seems to have formed a partiality for the young man; for we read in reference to the sudden return from exile of the Prince's father,

" Either before the Earl of Salisbury's departure, or, as is the more probable, towards the last of those eighteen days through which afterwards, to the ruin of his cause, Richard wasted his time (the only time left him), in Ireland, he sent for Henry of Monmouth, and upbraided him with his father's treason. Otterbourne minutely records the conversation which is said then to have passed between them. 'Henry, my child,' said the King, ' see what your father has done to me. He has actually invaded my land as an enemy, and, as if in regular warfare, has taken captive and put to death my liege subjects without mercy and pity. Indeed, child, for you individually I am very sorry; because, for this unhappy proceeding of your father, you must perhaps be deprived of your inheritance.' To whom Henry, though a boy, replied in no boyish manner, 'In truth, my gracious king and lord, I am sincerely grieved by these tidings; and, as I conceive, you are fully assured of my innocence in this proceeding of my father.'—' I know,' replied the King, 'that the crime which your father has perpetrated does not attach at all to you, and therefore I hold you excused altogether.' "

We shall not go further into Mr. Tyler's Memoirs of Henry of Monmouth; only intimating that an examination of this new and zealous biography has not increased our romantic and favourable associations on the subject. Bolingbroke appears throughout, the crafty, subtle, and unprincipled person which general history has represented; although one or two features or facts are brought to light by our author, upon which the mind loves to dwell; and that tend to soften our opinion of a man who had a most turbulent people to govern, and a most uneasy throne to occupy. Here is a case of gratitude that is as rare as it is beautiful, when a haughty and deeply-offended personage has it in his power to be revenged.

In this year (1381) Bolingbroke's life was put into imminent peril during the insurrection headed by Wat Tiler. The rebels broke into the Tower of London, though it was defended by some brave knights and soldiers: seized and murdered the Archbishop and others; and, carrying the heads of their victims on pikes, proceeded in a state of fury to John of Gaunt's palace at the Savoy, which they utterly destroyed and burnt to the ground. Gaunt himself was in the North; but his son Bolingbroke was in the Tower of London, and owed his life to the interposition of one John Ferroux of Southwark. This is a fact not generally known to historians; and since the document which records it bears testimony to Bolingbroke's spirit of gratitude, it will not be thought out of place to allude to it here. This same John Ferrour, with Sir Thomas Blount and others, was tried in the Castle of Oxford for high treason, in the first year of Henry the Fourth. Blount and the others were condemned and executed, but to John Ferrour a free pardon, dated Monday after the Epiphany, was given; our Lord the King remembering that, in the reign of Richard the Second, during the insurrection of the counties of Essex and Kent, the said John saved the King's life in the midst of that commonalty, in a wonderful and kind manner; whence the King happily remains alive unto this day. For since every good whatever naturally and of right requires another good in return, the King of his especial grace freely pardons the said John.'"

In conclusion, while we have to repeat our praise of Mr. Tyler's industry and zeal, and our high estimation of his antiquarian knowledge, and to welcome the appearance of such valuable efforts to make the world fully acquainted with the characters of illustrious men, and the true nature of celebrated events, we must also add, that owing to the accidents of war, the ignorance or carelessness of individuals, the general want of appreciation on the part of the public, such labours as are now before us must generally prove deficient and unsatisfactory. An illustration is at hand.

"Many ancient documents (of the existence of which in past years, often not very remote, there can be no doubt,) now, unhappily for those who would bring the truth to light, are in a state of abeyance or of perdition. To mention only one example, the work of Peter Basset, who was Chamberlain to Henry the Fifth, and attended him in his wars, referred to by Goodwin, and reported to be in the library of the College of Arms, is no longer in existence; at least it has disappeared, and not a trace of it can be found there."

ART. XI.—*The Congress of Verona: comprising a Portion of Memoirs of his own Time*. By M. De Chateaubriand. In 2 vols. London: Bentley. 1838.

In every thing which M. de Chateaubriand has written, there are many things which we admire, perhaps more which we dislike, but most of all does he contribute to our amusement, and to our stock of knowledge, in regard to curious characteristics of individuals and nations. His poetic temperament, his brilliancies of fancy, are not only according to a rare species of idiosyncracy, but have as unmistakable a French air about them, as his egotism, his conceit, and his affectations. His eloquence is full of bursts, sometimes natural, sometimes artificial, but seldom otherwise than striking, on account of the variety or originality of his illustrations; and he always appears to be in earnest and sincere. But he is sparkling rather than intense, and superficial instead of being profound; while his imagination for the most part get the better of his logic; and not

... such a degree of extravagance as to nullify or
contradict the truth. Owing to these and other faults of their style,
and principles, M. de Chateaubriand's literary works would scarcely
be tolerated in any country except ... France, and even
there it is not held first-rate, unless it ... only the public
... Without inquiring particularly about the ...
... As a politician M. de C. has shown himself to be bold and
inconsistent; to be proud of his creed; and to be bold ...
But he is as romantic, as mystical, and as abstract ...
... for mental exercise, and the discovery of remedies ...
... some other great men of ardent and imaginative ...
... are straightforward and practical. In short, he ...
... whether we take him in a literary or political capacity ...
... who deals far oftener in glosses than in substantialities ...
tangibles.

The reader may take it at once for granted that ...
estimate of himself is very different from what any sober-minded ...
matter-of-fact Englishman will entertain, whether his literary or
political rank be regarded. In fact M. de C. intimates in ...
... work, that while this is the last as well as the first time that he
speaks of his political life, he anticipates that it will produce a ...
... on the European mind in regard to the merits of the Spanish
War of 1823, of which he believes and proclaims himself to have
been the instigator and author. A greater piece of self-conceit ...
self-deceit cannot easily be instanced. He had, to be sure ...
... paper and scissors or apple-pie-crust work really ...
Canning and others not deranged thwarted and spoiled, want to have
... and perpetuated miracles not only in Europe but in
America. But although his fine speculations and imaginary kingdoms, empires, and colonies have not been realised, and are destined
never to be established, he is determined that his schemes shall not
be forgotten or lost sight of, and therefore publishes that portion of
his Memoirs which he conceives will revive an interest in the French
Invasion of Spain, and in his general principles of diplomacy.

Our readers cannot expect us to go into any serious argument
upon the merits of that most unpopular campaign; or even that we
should strive to divest M. de C. of his self-complacency regarding
his active share in its promotion. A far more agreeable and interesting course will be to select some of his dissertations, discourses, and
anecdotes, in each and all of which there is something that is new or
suggestive, or at least clever and amusing. ...
These Memoirs, as already intimated, have for their main subject
the French invasion of Spain, and the Spanish war, in 1823.
Under this head the author finds himself called upon to discourse of
the laws, the history, and the character of the Spanish; and the
debates in the French Chambers, his diplomatic correspondence
and arrangements, the transactions or intrigues at Verona, of the

... consequences arising from the measures devised by the Holy Allies, ... and to satisfy ... matters which memory and imagination have ... enabled the lively panther to ... in his own style. ... uniformly ... and ... in all that is said and done. ... there it is not held that ...

Without inquiring or caring particularly about the influence and ... hands which the younger French Minister for Foreign Affairs had ... in the invasion of Spain by the Duke D'Angoulême, it is quite evi-dent that a great and indeed the principal design was to thwart Mr. Canning in his grand scheme of acknowledging the independence of the South American Colonies, and thereby to prevent England from reaping her contemplated commercial advantages. Canning marked ... and understood the spirit of the age; and he accommodated his measures in such a way as seemed to him best fitted to follow pre-vailing tendencies, simultaneously with benefiting his country. Canning and M. de C. have often been compared to one another, and by some have been supposed kindred men in regard to genius and political principle. But surely it requires no new argument and no new illustrations to convince persons who are conversant with the writings or the public career of both, that the resemblances were very few and merely accidental; whereas the differences be-tween them were as numerous and essential,—in reference to their legislative capacities and habits, for example,—as romance is dif-ferent from reality. The two, however, were similar in this, that each professed a steady and strong personal friendship for the other. From all that we have heard or read of the English statesman, he was sincere in this profession, while it now is manifest from the Memoirs before us that the Frenchman entertained the feelings of a rival, and that his jealousies were often excited. Hear how he com-ments Canning's notes and conduct:—

"Mr. Canning ventured to make, in our (that is M. de Chateaubriand's) behalf, a paltry, shameful excuse, saying that the French Government was culpable, but that it was not right to confound me with that govern-ment: this was true in a very different sense from that intended by the Speaker." His Britannic Majesty's Secretary for Foreign Affairs, in allud-ing to Mr. Brougham's speech, applied to us the comic expressions of Molière, which we have already quoted:—"Thou wouldst have it so, George Dandin!" ...

He also speaks of Canning's rivalry in the mere matter of writing diplomatic notes, saying that he warned his clerks to mind what they were about when preparing despatches for the French Minister. In another place Canning's ill-temper is alleged to be increased; and, again, the evil genius that is declared to have got possession of England is plainly enough identified with the possessor of this ill temper.

... Upon the same allegations evidently breaking faith from a mind that tempered and that felt itself unmoved, and who, a foreign, we need not expatiate; but we must blame the French diplomatist for publishing any part of the secret correspondence between him and Canning, unless the whole is laid before the world." On the very face, however, of what does appear, it is evident that we have only a garbled story; and, judging from the well known conceit of him who has thus violated the sacredness of friendship, the obligations imposed by which can surely never be severed by the deceit of either, it would be supposing a miracle were *egoïst* unfaithful to his own fame.

But Canning is not the only British Statesman whom the French minister charges with sinister views in diplomatic negotiation. Wellington and others are thought under the leadership of connection so, with a no less grave subject than that of the suppression of the slave-trade." He says, ... and that it am ....tude the importance which is attached to this great question, we cannot but admire the spirit of Christianity and its influence, past and present, in extending civilization; but at the same time, what a singular degree of perseverance has been manifested by the Cabinet of St. James's, to introduce at all Congresses, amidst questions the most pressing and interests the most urgent, this incidental and remote question of the abolition of the slave-trade! England feared that the traffic which she reluctantly renounced should fall into the hands of another nation: she wished to compel France, Spain, Portugal, and Holland, suddenly to relinquish the system of their colonies, without considering whether these nations had attained such a degree of moral preparation as would render it safe to grant liberty to the Blacks, by abandoning to the mercy of Providence the property and lives of the Whites. That which England had her other nations were called upon to do, to the detriment of their navigation and their colonial possessions. Because England, who is mistress of the East and West Indies, the Cape of Good Hope, the Isle of France, Canada, and the islands in the Mediterranean, does not want St. Domingo and the Bermudas for the sake of maintaining her fleets and her seamen, we were required to cast into the sea Pondicherri, the Isle of Bourbon, Cayenne, Martinique, and Guadaloupe—we who possess only those miserable and insulated points on the whole surface of the globe. The Marquis of Londonderry, the Duke of Wellington, the assembled populace of London in their own country—Mr. Canning, the disciple of William Pitt, and the opposer of Parliamentary Reform—the Tories, who for the space of thirty years had been adverse to the measure proposed by Wilberforce, now became enthusiastic for the emancipation of the Negroes, whilst sporting all their efforts to shackle the liberty of the Whites. Englishmen were sold for slaves in America as recently as the time of Cromwell. The secret of these inconsistencies is found in the private interests and the mercantile spirit of England. If these considerations be not borne in mind, we may incur the risk of being duped by this ardent, though late-coming philanthropy. Philanthropy is the base coin of charity." ...

&c. &c. The task being consigned to us by M. De Montmorency, we examined attentively the Duke of Wellington's memorial, and we replied to it article by article. This memorial, artfully deploring the misery of the Blacks, contended, under well-grounded complaints, three unreasonable pretensions.—1st, The right of visiting and inspecting vessels; 2d, The right of assimilating the slave-trade to piracy, in order to attack with impunity all the navies in the world; 3d, The right of interdicting the sale of merchandise produced in the European colonies cultivated by the Negroes, that is to say, the exclusive privilege of substituting for this merchandise the productions of India and Great Britain. Our answer, given in the collective name of our colleagues, was as follows. We trust that we defended the honour and interests of France."

"These suggestions and allegations are ingeniously and smartly introduced. But, however callous foreigners may be in regard to slavery and slave-traffic, English people will stare when they hear that their zeal in a great philanthropic cause is designated as pretence, and that it amounts in reality to a cunning method of advancing our commercial and maritime interests. Had M. de C. studied the British character fairly and fully, he would have discovered that the nation, whatever may have been the inconsistencies or diplomatic motives of our ministers, drove and forced these ministers to the course which they took in their foreign negotiations, and that this was done by the people in perfect accordance with the most disinterested motives of benevolence and humanity.

But before proceeding to some of the anecdotical portions of these volumes, we shall produce two striking specimens of the writer's style. The first exhibits him straining after effect by the mere use of bold and out-of-the-way images; it would be well did he never offend higher principles than those of fine taste, in such inflated extravagances. He says, "The Spaniard coveted the annihilation of the universe, but of the unpeopled universe. He was content to reign over the desolate world, like his God seated peacefully in the solitude of eternity." Now to say the least of all such flights, they should recognise truth and find in it the comparison, else there cannot be a similitude. We copy another specimen where the mere brilliancy of the antitheses, the novelty of the combinations, and the rhetorical flourishes of the language, have been sought after at the expense of every precise, distinct and informing idea. The Spanish revolution of 1822 is the theme.

"Continuing their plagiarisms from the French empire, the Spaniards borrowed the name of Sacred Battalion from the retreat of Moscow. In like manner they copied the buffooneries of the Marseillaise, the Sans Culottes, the sayings of Marat, and the diatribes of the Vieux Cordelier; but always rendering actions more vile, and language more low. They created nothing, because they did not act on the impulse of the national genius. They merely translated and acted our Revolution on the Spanish stage. Our heads without bodies, and bodies without heads, viewed from a distance, whence their horror could not be discerned, at least presented by the symmetrical arrangement of the vast country as seen in its rustic grandeur. But in the Peninsula the picture was divested of that admixture. The Spaniards passed over two centuries at one leap, in order to overtake our history, and they took their stand, with Voltaire on the one hand, and the Convention on the other. But the repressed ages returned, resumed their influence, and disturbed the order of things which violence had established. The Spanish nation was truly great in those times, when the people were independent, and the kings absolute. When the nation said, *If not, not,* and the monarch signed, *I, the King,* the two complete liberties of the democracy of *all,* and the democracy of *one,* met without jostling, and addressed each other in their own proud language; this state of things never existed in any country except Spain." to this alone.

"A great command of language, a prodigious storehouse of images, the results of much miscellaneous reading, and of favourable opportunities for observation in the high walks of life, and a never-ceasing veracity and earnestness are assuredly the inalienable property of the man who writes in the above manner. Pity it is that judgment, simplicity, and profundity have to give way to a riotous fancy, to glitter, and bombast. But we must proceed to the work of quotation, without saying much more either of the manner or the matter of the book.

Among the remarkable passages in Chateaubriand's Memoirs which his position has enabled him to record, his account of the widow of Napoleon, Maria Louisa, with whom he had an opportunity of conversing at Verona, must be cited. In as far as he is concerned, our respect for him is increased by this account, in as far as the female, disgust at filth, immorality, heartlessness, and self-degradation, is engendered. We can very readily believe the report that she bore no natural affection even for Napoleon's son; and, if eager to show her despite, she scrupled not to court the embraces of worthless men, (worthier surely than she,) and to add to the number of her offspring, as if for the purpose of reducing her first-born in the world's estimation. M. de C. says,—

"We at first declined an invitation given us by the Duchess of Parma; but her highness pressed it, and we accepted it; we found her in excellent spirits. The world had taken upon itself the task of remembering Napoleon, therefore Maria Louisa thought she need not trouble herself to think of him. We informed her that we had met her troops at Placentia, and remarked that she once possessed a much more numerous army. She replied, 'I never think of that.' She made some observations, which savoured of indifference, in reference to the king of Rome: she was then *enceinte.* Her court exhibited rather an antiquated aspect, with the exception of M. Neiperg, who was a man of elegant manners. My visit presented only two singularities—namely, that I was dining with Maria Louisa, and that the widow of Napoleon wore a pair of bracelets made of the stone of Juliet's sarcophagus. When crossing the Po, at Placentia, a single bark, newly

palace; quite desiring a sort of imperial, &c., occupied my attention. Two
or three dragoons in jackets and caps, such as are worn by the police, were
on the banks of the river, watering their horses.... This was all that remained of the glory of the man who
had melted the rocks of the Simplon, planted his standard in the capitals of
Europe, and who raised up Italy after centuries of prostration. Napoleon
revolutionised the world; filled with his name the four quarters of the
globe; sailed beyond the seas of Europe; soared to the skies, and fell and
perished at the extremity of the waves in the Atlantic....

Of Napoleon, of course, Chateaubriand's recollections and diary
furnish several striking notices. Here is a rhetorical dash, similar
to that which closes our last extracts; but the Corsican stands not
alone. " How many millions of men won with their lives the victories of Arbela, Pharsalia, and Austerlitz? Of those millions of
dead, how many survive in memory? Three: Alexander, Cæsar,
and Napoleon."

Alexander of Russia is sketched effectively, and the anecdotes
told of him are interesting in no ordinary degree. Altogether the
portrait is full of points that catch the eye. It is said,—

"Though sincere, as a man, in matters which directly concerned mankind,
Alexander was artful as a demi-Greek in what related to politics. At the
very time when he was flattering Napoleon, declaring war against the English, and pronouncing the attack on the fleet at Copenhagen—a signal act of
brigandage, one of his officers proceeded to London to convey to the Cabinet of St. James's assurances of the Czar's admiration and approval.
Accordingly, when the two Russian ships of war engaged in the blockade
of Lisbon were captured by the English, they were speedily restored to the
Czar. Bonaparte imagined that he had deceived Alexander at Erfurth,
and that he had intoxicated him with praise. One of the Generals of the
Empire wrote the following: 'We have just now made the Emperor
Alexander swallow a dose of opium; and, whilst he is sleeping, we intend
to employ ourselves elsewhere.'

"At Erfurth, a coach-house was transformed into a theatre. In front of
the orchestra, two armed-chairs were placed for the two Potentates; on the
right and left were chairs for the other monarchs; and behind were benches
for the princes. Talma, the king of the stage, performed before this audience
of kings. When he delivered the words

'L'amitié d'un grand homme est un bienfait des dieux,'

Alexander rose, pressed the hand of his grand ami, and said, 'I never felt
so forcibly the truth of these words.'

"In the eyes of Bonaparte, Alexander was then a mere fool; and he
joined his Chamberlains and Generals in laughing at him. He despised
him because he supposed him to be sincere; he admired him when he discovered his duplicity. 'He is a Greek of the lower empire,' said Napoleon,
'and we must be distrustful of him.' At Erfurth, Napoleon acted with the
bold hypocrisy of a victorious soldier; Alexander dissembled like a conquered prince. Cunning was endeavouring to dupe falsehood; the policy
of the West and the policy of the East were true to their characters."

After mentioning the prodigious extent of territory over which the son of Paul ruled, the magnificence and the magnitude of his armies, the following account and anecdotes are given.

"The man considered himself merely as an instrument in the hands of Providence, and arrogated no merit to himself. Madame de Staël complimented him on the happiness which his subjects enjoyed in being governed by him, though deprived of a constitution. Alexander replied:—'I am merely a fortunate accident.' A young man, in the streets of Paris, expressed his admiration of the emperor's demeanour even to the humblest persons. 'Is it not the duty of sovereigns to behave so?' was Alexander's answer. He declined residing in the Tuileries, recollecting that Bonaparte had been pleased to fix his quarters in the palaces of Vienna, Berlin, and Moscow. Looking up at the statue of Bonaparte on the column of the Place Vendome, he said: 'If I were elevated so high, I fear my head would be turned.' When he visited the Tuileries, he was shewn the room de la Paix. 'What use,' said he smiling, 'had Bonaparte for such an apartment?' On the day of Louis XVIII.'s entrance into Paris, Alexander stood quietly at his window, without any mark of distinction, and looked through the panes of glass to see the procession. There was sometimes a graceful gallantry in his manner, which ingratiated him in the favour of the fair sex. When visiting a lunatic hospital, he asked one of the female patients whether there were many women in the establishment who had gone mad for love. 'We have very few yet,' replied the lunatic, 'but it is to be feared that their numbers will be greatly augmented by your majesty's visit to Paris.'"

These anecdotes command our admiration, presuming them to have been the offspring of sound and serious reflection, and of a true dignity of soul. The self-possession and majesty of the man have their existences in what we next quote, supposing the passage to have received no exaggeration from the poetic temperament of the narrator.

"There was a proposition for changing the name of the bridge of Austerlitz: 'No,' said Alexander, 'it is enough that I have passed over the bridge with my army.' It was Alexander who originated the idea of the sacrifices on the Place Louis XV. An altar was raised on the spot where once a scaffold stood. Seven Muscovite priests performed the service for the dead, and the foreign troops, on their return from a review, defiled before the altar. 'Te Deum' was chanted to one of the beautiful melodies of the old Greek church. Soldiers and sovereigns knelt down to receive benediction. The memory of the French spectator involuntarily wandered back to 1793 and 1794, when even cattle refused to pass over the polluted pavement, which emitted the odour of blood. What hand had conducted to the expiatory ceremony those Tartars, many of whom inhabited sheep-skin tents at the foot of the great wall of China? Such spectacles will never be witnessed by the feeble generations succeeding the present age."

Alexander, Chateaubriand tells us, was not without his foibles.

and one instance of such weaknesses is given, viz. that of a love affair, which lasted eleven years, or, in other words, of infidelity to the empress. A daughter was the offspring of this connection, who died when on the eve of being married; a grievous bereavement, and, according to the representation before us, the immediate fore-runner of deep remorse, and a happy reconciliation.

"Alexander was on the parade, when he received intelligence of this melancholy death. He turned pale, and said,—'I am punished.' Alexander was an amiable man, and therefore he required an excuse to justify to himself his infidelity to the empress. He persuaded himself that she did not love him; that she was cold and insensible, and incapable of affection; that her husband's errors did not render her unhappy; in short, by supposing her to be without love, he believed her to be without pain, and without jealousy. But this was a mistake. Elizabeth was passionately attached to Alexander; but a natural timidity and reserve inclined her to repress her feelings. She might have said with Manzoni's 'Hermangarde,' 'Thou wert mine, and I was silent in the security of my happiness. My chaste lips could never have revealed all the transport of my heart.' Mortified by the infidelity of the woman, from whom he deserved a better return, and deeply afflicted by the death of the child who was the object of his tender affection, Alexander manifested a disposition to live on more social terms with the empress. When he discovered that he was beloved by her, his remorse increased. Their first meeting, after their estrangement, took place at Carlsrube in 1814. In the same year, the imperial couple joined each other at Vienna. Religion completed the task of repentance. But the health of Elizabeth began to decline just at the moment when she was most happy, and when her love for Alexander was increased by the admiration with which his glory inspired her. The empress, who had never been a mother, accompanied the emperor to the grave of his regretted daughter, and mingled her prayers with his."

Religious devotion, and preparation for death, were the absorbing concerns which, it is said, now occupied the Emperor. He

was sometimes seen on his knees in a churchyard during the night. When he set out on any journey, he was accustomed to say, 'every year people seem anxious to wind up their affairs with me, as if they never expected to see me again.' He often said, 'I shall perish in some obscure corner; in a wood, in a ditch, or at a road side, and I shall soon be forgotten.' On the day when he left his capital to set out on that tour which terminated his life, the tide of the Neva rose so high that it was feared it would overflow St. Petersburg. Alexander, from the upper windows of his palace, viewed the threatened disaster with dismay. A cross, banished the flood had dislodged from its place in the churchyard, was washed up in front of the palace, before the eyes of the imperial family. This mourning Calvary was regarded as a fatal presage. The czar was observed to be affected beyond measure on taking leave of his relations, prior to his departure from St. Petersburg, and when he had proceeded to a little distance on his journey, he ordered his carriage to stop, and looked back on his natal city with evident emotion."

The closing scene is thus described : " In his final moments, he ordered the blinds of his windows to be drawn up, and said, ' What a beautiful day!' as these were the last words he uttered."

To another matter we must call attention before closing our review of these Memoirs, or the anecdotes of Alexander. To prepare our readers for a treat, it is sufficient to state that in our next extract, Chateaubriand himself figures in all his personality. Oh dear! the vanity of the man is wonderful. The emperor of all the Russias, we have already seen, could humbug Napoleon ; what then must our Ex-Minister for Foreign Affairs have been in the hands of this long-headed tactician ? Let us hear,—

" The Emperor of Russia had been warned to be on his guard respecting us : he had been told that if he saw us, we should exercise over him a seduction which he would find it difficult to resist. We had been presented to him in Paris : he then supposed us to entertain *Ultra* opinions ; and as he was a *Liberal*, we naturally concluded that we could not agree except on religious points. When we met Alexander at Verona, he had become an *Ultra*, and we remained, what we had always been, a *Liberal* ; consequently, the same principles of disagreement appeared to exist, only they were now reversed. At the Congress, the Czar behaved to us with courtesy, but at the same time with reserve. We frequently met him in his promenades ; but we felt that it would seem intrusive to notice him, until he should think proper to make some sign of recognition, or address to us a word in passing by. At length he accosted us, and we walked together on the banks of the Adige. He spoke of St. Petersburg in order to avoid speaking of politics. Though M. de Montmorency had not been favourable to us, (he behaved to us according to the dictates of his high birth and his opinions,) still what he said at parting with the Emperor caused Alexander to be less afraid of us. The Countess Tolstoy, whom Alexander frequently visited, contrived to bring me into his presence. Alexander was rather deaf : we do not like to talk loud, and our indifferences to princes, is such that we did not even observe the coolness of the man, 'from whom every body else was courting a look.

" M. De Montmorency having left Verona, Alexander sent for us. We had not been together a quarter of an hour, when we found ourselves mutually agreeably to each other. We are aware that our acquaintance with that great potentate of the earth savoured too much of familiarity ; but it was the familiarity of souls, and did not imply any want of respect. The Emperor experienced that sort of surprise which we have frequently remarked on the countenances of persons who have known us only through the medium of a fanciful portrait. Absorbed by the idea of the Spanish war, and foreseeing no dangerous obstacle except British jealousy, we endeavoured to gain over Alexander, so that he might counteract the ill feeling of the Cabinet of London.

" In our different conversations, we touched upon every thing; and he listened to us without appearing to recollect his exalted station."

Chateaubriand's consistency, his Liberalism, or pure Monarchism, seeing that the *Legitimates* whom he so earnestly served, have fallen from their high estate, are matters that can now concern but few. We cannot, however, but enjoy the confusion which he makes in his eagerness after self-exaltation, in his affectation, and his fondness for uttering sentences having all the boldness of aphorisms, the point and apposition of antitheses, and the utmost figurative pomp of which his imagination and mother-tongue are master. For instance, he utters sentiments, and statements to the following effect, —it is impossible to know how to deal with kings; or to calculate in what humour to find them,—it is often necessary in diplomatic negotiations to adopt by-paths or to come to a stand-still; and a no from a sceptered fool, which may have been suggested by confessors, mistresses, or valets, may derange the wisest schemes,—the writer owed the Bourbon dynasty nothing but his fidelity and patriotism, —they distrusted him,—the French Bourbons have a traditional dislike to great names; they looked upon nobles as vassals and domestics, although they feared their ministers in council, &c., &c. Such are some of the hints which the ex-minister lets fall; to which we add a short extract without curtailment or condensation. The passage speaks of Louis XVIII.

"His majesty took a nap at the council, and he did quite right; when he was not asleep, he would tell stories. He possessed an admirable knack at mimicry; this did not amuse M. de Villèle, who wanted to stick to business. M. de Corbière would lay his snuff-box and his blue handkerchief on the table, and clap his elbows upon it; the other ministers listened in silence. We, for our part, could not help being diverted by his majesty's tales; the king was evidently delighted. When he became aware of his success, before he began a story, he sought an excuse in it, and would say with his clear, shrill voice: 'I am going to make you laugh, M. de Chateaubriand;' and accordingly we were on such occasions so natural a courtier, that we laughed as heartily as if we had received orders to do so."

There is reason to believe that the author of these assertions spoke from such a degree and extent of experience as made him particularly sensitive on the subject; and that his abstract and romantic admiration of royalty was incapable of always suppressing the vexation, which a man of humane and just principles felt, when his measures of government were opposed or baulked. Hence, independent of his peculiar faults of style, we have an obvious cause for incongruities and conflicting sentiments, the operation of which must have escaped the notice of the chivalrous and warm-natured writer.

When on the subject of ministerial influence, rencounters, and duty, we may aptly quote a specimen of such applications as sometimes are made to high officers of State.

"Men who were recommended to us, as persons animated by enthusiastic feelings and religious sentiments, honoured us with their advice. These men might possibly have been dangerous, if they had not been cowards. We received requests for interviews from certain braves, worthy of the reign of terror, who offered us their services in the way of assassination. On one occasion we were visited by a stock-jobber. Without ceremony, and without any sort of oratorial preface, he informed us that he was connected with several responsible parties; that if it were possible to communicate to him telegraphic despatches, my excellency might be a considerable gainer, without the slightest disadvantage to the public funds. We stared at this man with amazement, and then desired him to walk out at the door, if he did not prefer being thrown out at the window. He did not hesitate in making his choice; and he stared at us in his turn, as if had beheld an ozace. We rang the bell, and the gentleman took his leave with his proffered million. No doubt he thought us strangely ignorant and stupid. Who could have known of our good fortune? Had we taken advantage of it, should we now have been the less respected? The only difference is, that instead of being in straitened circumstances, we should have been in affluence; we should have had a splendid house, and should have been giving dinners. We should still have been called _monseigneur_ by courtesy, and we should have passed for a statesman."

Among our first extracts from these sparkling volumes, there were some wordy and rhapsodical opinions quoted, referring to a particular period, and to particular movements in the history of Spain. With propriety we may return to the same country, and introduce a few sketches of Spanish character. M. de C. says,

"The Spaniards are Christian Arabs: there is a degree of wildness and improvidence in their character. The mixed blood of the Cantabrian, the Carthaginian, the Roman, the Vandal, and the Moor, which flows in their veins, does not flow like other blood. They are at once active, indolent, and haughty. 'Every indolent nation,' says the author of the 'Esprit des Lois,' in speaking of the Spaniards, 'is haughty; for those who do not work consider themselves the sovereigns of those who are laborious.' The Spaniards, entertaining as they do the highest opinion of themselves, do not form the same notions of justice and injustice as we do. A transpyranean shepherd, tending his flock, enjoys the most absolute individuality. In Spain, independence destroys liberty. What are political rights to a man who attaches no value to them, and whose ideas of the blessings of life are all included in his proverb— _Oveja de basta, pasto de gracia, hijo de casa_*—to a man who, like the Bedouin, armed with his pistol, and followed by his flock, requires for his daily fare only an acorn, a fig, and olive? He thinks himself fortunate if he occasionally meet with a traveller whom he can rob and send to heaven, and is perfectly happy in being beloved by a poor shepherdess and an aged father. _'Padre viejo, y manga rota, no es deshonra.'_† The sprucely dressed _Majo_ of the Guadalquivir, with his dagger in his shepherd's crook, and his hair confined in a net, never distinguishes the thing from the person, and reduces all difference of opinion to the alternative—kill or die. This character is so profoundly stamped in the Iberian mould, that the moder-

---

* "Sheep of pure breed, free pasture, and to be one of a family."
† "An aged father and a tattered sleeve are no disgrace."

nised portion of the Spanish population; whilst they have adopted new ideas, retain, in spite of those ideas, their primitive nation feelings."

There is no less axiomatic terseness in the following passage, and a still stronger aspect of close observation. The opinions expressed seem also to point to certain lines of policy, which, could the surrounding powers agree and cordially resolve to put to a practical test, might speedily enable the nation to taste the blessings of tranquillity, so that civilization might find a congenial soil, and the people press forward to overtake their most enlightened and industrious neighbours in all the habits and the arts that adorn and enrich human life.

After having spoken strongly of the despotism of the Spanish character, according to its past and present culture, he says,

"There is allied, by a singular contrast, a disposition at once dull and comic, mild, and ostentatious. In the civil wars, when an advantage is gained, it might naturally be expected that the party gaining it would follow it up. But no such thing. The victors halt on the scene of triumph, publish rodomontades, sing songs of victory, play the guitar, and bask in the sun. The defeated party quietly retires, and acts in the same manner when its turn of triumph comes. Thus there is nothing but a succession of battles without results. If a town be not taken to-day, it will be taken to-morrow, or the day after to-morrow, or ten years hence, or never; it matters not. The hidalgos tells us that they were engaged for the space of six hundred years in expelling the Moors. They entertain too high an admiration of their own perseverance. The patience transmitted from generation to generation at length becomes merely a family shield, which protects nothing, and which serves merely as an ancient decoration to hereditary misfortunes. Decrepid Spain still fancies herself invulnerable, like the old recluse of the convent of St. Martin, near Carthagena. Gregory of Tours informs us, that the soldiers of Leuvielde found the monastery of St. Martin abandoned by all its inmates except the abbot, who, though bowed by age and misfortune, was upright in virtue and sanctity. A soldier who had raised his sword, and was about to cut off the Holy man's head, instantly fell to the ground and expired. Spanish politicians partake of the faults of Spanish warriors. In circumstances the most critical, they direct attention to insignificant measures, deliver harangues, in which they talk of doing great things, but their speeches are never followed by acts. Is this because they are stupid, or spiritless? No. It is because they are Spaniards. They are not impressed with events as other people are: they see things in a different light. They leave time to bring about results, which they never attempt to hasten by any efforts of their own. A Spaniard transmits his life to his son, without fear and without regret. The son, in his turn, pursues the same course as the father. Some centuries afterwards, the affairs which the dead have bequeathed will be terminated to the satisfaction of the living. In any other country these affairs would have been settled in a week."

But while Chateaubriand may have caught the bold and pictu-

resque points of Spanish character, we think it will be admitted that
he does not write and describe like one who was ever fit to suggest or
follow out the practical policy that would counteract and remove the
errors and hereditary evils complained of. We may also ask, can
he who writes and thinks in the manner that we have now seen, he
who, to thwart the policy of England, and one of England's most
illustrious statesmen, contemplated, proposed, and earnestly urged,
that in conjunction with the Czar, France should carry out the re-
union of the Greek and Latin churches,—should liberate Greece,—
should establish Bourbon monarchies in South America,—and
should make the Rhine the boundary of the French empire, (for
schemes no less chimerical and chivalrous were those of the minister
of Louis the Eighteenth), be ever compared to George Canning?
Does any one imagine that had the English statesman published
his political memoirs, that we should have found in them such a
predominance of fancy, such a stream of words and images, and so
little that is solid, practical, and commanding, as we have detected
in these volumes? No, for the one, in a word, has all along been a
rhapsodical projector and poetic specalatist, while the other was a
direct, decided, and intelligible performer. The genius of the
former has wasted itself politically in dreams, the latter produced
positive and definitive opinions and efforts,—the genius of the
former, when tried by the canons of literature, has employed a
rhetoric which is serious, dictatorial, high-sounding, and mystical;
while that of the other would have shot the shafts of polished satire,
or dealt in argumentation, logical, elegant, and eloquent to the dis-
comfiture or conviction, or, at least, to the comprehension of his
opponents.

Chateaubriand's Political Memoirs, his Congress of Verona, will
always testify strongly of the man, and inspire the delight and the
affection which romantic beauty, and moral excellence never fail to
command; but they will never make converts of wise men to his
style of writing or to his political projects and creed.

ART. XII.—*Narrative of an Expedition in H. M. S. Terror, undertaken
with a view to Geographical Discovery on the Arctic Shores, in the
years 1836-7.* By CAPTAIN BACK. London: Murray. 1838.

ALL the geographical knowledge which we are ever likely to obtain
of the Arctic regions, we have reason to hope will ere long be completed. Partial accounts, some months ago, were received of the
expedition undertaken by Dease and Simpson, whose preparations
and reported progress have led the British public to expect that these
adventurers will be able to fill up the blank which Back, Parry, and
others were prevented from surveying; and thus to this country will
be due the honour of resisting and overcoming some of the most
appalling obstacles that ever beset the scientific enterprise of man.

Our readers will have some recollection of our review of Captain Back's land expedition in 1833, which still left unsurveyed the Arctic shore between Regent's Inlet and Cape Turnigain. The present effort was to accomplish that by sea, which had not been completed by land. Owing, however, to the elements, to the adamantine mountains, walls, and regions of ice, to the damage done by its breaking up and its concussions, and to some injudicious arrangements at the outset, in the way of providing against the influence of cold, this last enterprise of the gallant commander of it has proved a failure, adding nothing to our geographical knowledge, and nothing in the way of discovery in the departments of natural history. If human skill, perseverance, and daring could have surmounted the difficulties and dangers encountered, and the damages sustained, Captain Back, his assistants, and crew were the men to have triumphed in the good ship Terror. But instead of brilliant scientific achievements, we have, what to many will appear no less valuable, most striking illustrations of human nature, of its development, and of the force of habit and discipline during long dark and cold months of confinement.

The frustration of the expedition was in the first place and mainly owing to the severity of the winter immediately preceding the undertaking. This severity had been so great that the ensuing summer months passed without being powerful enough to break up the work of the cold portion of the year; so that by the end of July Captain Back was checked in about 62 degrees of latitude; and before the end of August he was fast locked and imbedded in a floe off Southampton and Baffin's Islands, while within sight of land, and not far from the very spot where he was to begin operations. Having thus become part of the solid mass, admirable scope was afforded for the exercise and display, if not of British seamanship, of British exertion, ingenuity, patience, and fortitude. During some periods the ice partially opened, or the Herculean labour of sawing its edges, enabled the ship to make now and then a little progress. But all that had been accomplished in this way in the course of a week, by the action of currents and storms, would be undone in a day; and the result was, that the adventurers had to winter off Cape Comfort, entertaining the hope, however, that the ensuing summer might be propitious. But when this anxiously hoped for period arrived it was found to be absolutely necessary to return homewards, an enterprise only less formidable than such as Captain Back and his crew were willing to undertake, if the slightest hope of success had gleamed upon them.

We have already alluded to certain injudicious arrangements preparatory to the sailing of the Terror. These, however, in no shape involve the shipwrights at Chatham, but respect a new invented warming apparatus which failed. From this, perhaps, and other unascertained circumstances, both officers and men were seized with scorbutic affections, and the consequent languor in such cases. Several deaths occurred.

Of his crew, the Captain does not speak in the highest terms, although no charge is made that affects their character for obedience and unanimity to exert themselves to the utmost when danger became appalling or nerve was required. Once and only once, when the ship was going down, did the men sink under their toils. This was on their return, and when near to Lough Swilly.

"Harassed and worn out by extreme toil, the crew were no longer able to work as formerly; and though ably assisted by the officers and men of Her Majesty's service stationed along the coast, and especially by Lieutenant Murray and the officers and crew of the Wickham, yet the Terror was gradually sinking by the head; when, finding that their united efforts were unequal to keep her afloat, it was determined, as the last resource to run her ashore on a small sandy beach selected for the purpose. It was found, at low water, that upwards of twenty feet of the keel, together with ten feet of the stern-post, were driven over more than three feet and a half on one side, leaving a frightful opening astern for the free ingress of the water. The forefoot, too, was entirely gone, besides numerous bolts either loosened or broken; and when, besides this, the strained and twisted state of the ship's frame was considered, there was not one on board who did not express astonishment that we had ever floated across the Atlantic."

That Captain Back's estimate of his crew may not be mistaken, and that the value of naval discipline and habits of frank submission to wholesome regulations may be appreciated, we quote a passage that pointedly treats of these matters.

"Meantime, we were not unobservant of the habits and dispositions of the crew, hastily gathered together, and for the most part composed of people who had never before been out of a collier: some half-dozen, indeed, had served in Greenland vessels; but the laxity which is there permitted rendered them little better than the former. A few men-of-war's-men who were also on board were worth the whole together. The want of discipline and attention to personal comfort were most conspicuous; and though the *wholesome regulations* practised in his Majesty's service were most rigidly attended to in the Terror, yet such was the unsociability, though without any ill-will, that it was only by a steady and undeviating system pursued by the First Lieutenant that they were brought at all together with the feeling of messmates. At first, though nominally at the same mess, and eating at the same table, many of them would secrete their allowance, with other unmanly and unsailor-like practices. This was another proof added to the many I had already witnessed, how greatly discipline improves the mind and manners, and how much the regular service man is to be preferred for all hazardous or difficult enterprises. Reciprocity of kindnesses, a generous and self-denying disposition, a spirit of frankness, a hearty and above-board manner—these are the true characteristics of the British seaman, and the want of these is seldom compensated by other qualities. In our case, and I mention this merely to show the difference of olden and modern times, there were only three or four in the ship who could not write. All read; some recited whole pages of poetry; others sang French songs. Yet with all this, had they been left to themselves, I verily believe a more unsociable, suspicious, and uncomfortable set of people could not have been found. Oh! if the two are incompatible, give me the old Jack-tar who would stand up for his ship and give his life for his messmate."

A winter residence in the Arctic regions can never offer much variety of incident or scenery; but the position and condition of the Terror and her crew, and the excessive intensity of the weather and climate during the months of their imprisonment are barren almost to nakedness of novelty to those who have read the accounts of former adventurers in the same direction. The same grand and awful scenes, the same darkness, irksomeness, endurance, and courage; with fewer than usual of visitations of the shore, or visits by the Esquimaux, are described; nay, the wild Arctic animals seemed to have hid themselves, emigrated, or to have been cut off, so that the sporting records of the voyagers are limited to a very few exploits, a rein-deer, a bear, and some much more trifling creatures being the spoil specified. We quote a short notice of the human visitants.

"We had a second visit from the Esquimaux, with the same noisy bartering, the same cupidity, and the same unnatural readiness to exchange their children for a few needles or a saw. Esquimaux, indeed, will give any thing to procure what they desire; a laughable instance of which was afforded by a young woman who, observing that one of the officers had not much hair on his head, immediately offered to supply him with her own at the easy price of a curtain ring."

Besides the insight which the Narrative affords us of human character under trying circumstances greatly protracted, it may be generally described as containing an uninterrupted register of hardships, peril, fear, Almighty power, and Almighty protection. Early in the Narrative, and not long after encountering the regions of ice, we find these particulars,—

"We had, now, (he says) been precisely a month beset, without the option of moving in any direction but where the openings occurred, or where the whole body of the ice drifted; and this at a period admitted to be the most favourable for navigating these seas. With every thing flattering to decoy us on within twenty miles of Baffin Island, we there found ourselves suddenly stopped, and saw the ice close behind us in an unbroken line; cutting off all retreat. It will easily, therefore, be conceived, that the phenomenon which permitted even this trifling advance was hailed with exultation; and though we were soon arrested, yet three or four cracks between the floe and packed body a-head, intimated that something favourable might be expected from the returning tide. The weather, too, continued mild, and a light air blew from the west. Still, though there were occasional fluctuations in the ice during the night, September 24th came without the commnuication so eagerly anticipated. By some unaccountable caprice scarcely had the narrow opening begun to enlarge, when the ice suddenly stopped, and then, with a reaction truly alarming, pressed against the ship, so as to have her over considerably on one side to the no small risk of the part nipped, which creaked and complained bitterly; it was some hours before she righted again. It was now an object so to place the ship, that the excessive pressure, aided as it was by the spring tide, should be received equally on every part of her; and as this could not be effected without the ice saw, they were shortly made ready; and, having been fixed to large triangles formed of three high poles, were worked by means of a pulley. With one saw and some axes we were enabled to cut away a sharp piece which had already caused much annoyance, and were about removing it when the ship which had been warped there, was suddenly set by the ice against it, and in a short time crushed up the whole mass. From that moment the pressure was very great, and after midnight of September 25th, the timbers were strained so severely that there was a general creaking. Happily, it did not last, for the crack again opened out and permitted our hauling a few yards a-head, and thereby to escape being caught by an extensive floe which, after sinking all smaller pieces, had forced its way to us. The rudder had borne an amazing force with scarcely any injury, but as there was no longer any reason for exposing it, it was unhung and slung under the stern. We were nearly half way between Capes Comfort and Bylot, were in sight of each side of Frozen Strait, could clearly distinguish Cape Welsford and the dark water sky over Duke of York's Bay, were only five or six miles from the shore, which would have afforded us some shelter, and yet here we were fixed, compelled to endure the furious buffets which each successive tide brought upon us, and at the mercy of the mighty power that bound us. The temperature had varied from 18° to 23°, and the wind had drawn round to the east, though this was now become of trifling importance, as the westerly wind on which so much reliance had been placed had not even separated the floes, much less driven them from the land; and, in fact, according to our united opinions, had made no impression whatever. Deeply sensible as I was of the growing peril of our situation, with days contracting and the prospect of a speedy decrease of temperature, I now made an official demand on the officers of his majesty's ship, for their respective opinions in writing, upon the probability of any further progress being made by our own exertions in the present state towards Repulse Bay. Their unanimous conviction, from the experience of the thirty-four days in which the ship had been beset, was that any thing more, with that view, was utterly impracticable; and they recommended the adoption of certain precautions in the event of any sudden contingency obliging us to have recourse to the boats for safety. In this opinion I entirely coincided, and considering that the period had now arrived for taking a decisive step, had determined to cut a dock in a favourable part of the floe which we had quitted."

It will readily be credited that throughout the dead of winter there was not a little to try and dishearten; and that there was at least a monotony of dreariness. When Valentine's day arrived, a fond looking forward to the period of release exercised the minds of the crew.

But hope was premature; for instead of their condition becoming better, it grew worse; and on the 9th of March, while still drifting at the mercy of the surrounding masses, the ship began to be lifted up by the ice, and leakages to be discovered, occasioned by the squeezing to which she had been exposed. It was on the 16th of the month last mentioned, that,—

"Another rush drove irresistibly on the larboard quarter and stern, and forcing the ship ahead raised her up on the ice. A chaotic ruin followed! our poor and cherished courtyard, its wall and arched doors, gallery, and well-trodden paths, were rent, and in some parts ploughed up like dust. The ship was careened fully four streaks, and sprung a leak as before. Scarcely were ten minutes left us for the expression of our astonishment that anything of human build could outlive such assaults, when, at 1 A.M., another equally violent rush succeeded; and in its way towards the starboard quarter, threw up a rolling wave thirty feet high, crowned by a blue square mass of many tons, resembling the entire side of a house, which, after hanging for some time in doubtful poise on the ridge, at length fell with a crash into the hollow, in which, as in a cavern, the after part of the ship seemed imbedded. It was indeed an awful crisis, rendered more frightful from the mistiness of the night and dimness of the moon. The poor ship cracked and trembled violently; and no one could say that the next minute would not be her last, and, indeed, his own too, for with her our means of safety would probably perish. * *

"I was naturally anxious to ascertain, as far as possible, the amount of damage received; and, when inspecting the outside of the ship with the first Lieutenant and carpenter, we saw that the fore-foot was completely exposed, the ship having literally lifted up on the surface of the same ice, which had formerly, as I have said, imbedded her up to the flukes of the anchors. How far she was from the water's edge, could not be ascertained, though it was seen from the marks, that she was heaved up seven feet abaft, whilst on deck, the ascent in walking forward was considerable. The larboard side was found to be flattened and indented in such a manner, as to make it probable some injury had been sustained about the timbers near the line of flotation, in a direction six or eight feet from the main channels forward, and the quarter on the same side was bolstered up as high as the taffrail by one of the largest floe pieces, which pressed severely on one of her weakest points. These appearances with the facts of the damaged stern-post and the leaks, raised a doubt in my mind, how far the ship might be trustworthy when the ice should slacken off sufficiently to let her down to her bearings."

"In fact the Hyperborean ice, whose grasp and clench had been so much and so long regarded with dread and dislike, would have been hailed as a saviour and protecting friend, when compared to the whirl and the drifting of the loosened mountains, the plunging and crushing of conflicting icebergs. Take one scene and period as a specimen of a number of kindred occurrences:

"The detached portion, on which were two men, (a third being in the dingy, close to ....) ..... instantaneously splinted into three pieces, two of which, singularly enough, were separately occupied by the person just mentioned, who, standing steadily on the whirling and heaving ice, was violently discarded; gave a hearty cheer, while their companion, losing fast his balance from the sudden jerking of the dingy, lay stretched at full length and grasping the gunwale on each side. The cheering, however, was turned to astonishment, as they watched the ship slowly rising and heeling over to port. We on board had been surprised that no countenation occurred; and were beginning to wonder that the vessel did not recover her equilibrium, but were now startled by the conviction that she was gradually going over; and the great inclination rendering it impossible to stand on deck, every one clung on to windward as he best could, when it was we beheld the strange and appalling spectacle of what may be aptly termed a submerged berg, fixed low down with one end to the ship, and while the other, with the purchase of a long lever advantageously placed at a right angle with the keel, was slowly rising towards the surface. Meanwhile, those who happened to be below, finding every thing falling, rushed or clambered on deck, where they saw the ship on her beam-ends with the lee boats touching the water, and felt that a few moments only trembled between them and eternity. Yet in that awful crisis there was no confusion; the sails were clewed up and lowed; fresh men, fresh crews were stationed in the boats, which again were rather unhooked than lowered; the barge was hoisted out; and with a promptitude and presence of mind which I shall ever remember with admiration, the whole five were provisioned and filled with arms, ammunition, and clothing, and veered astern clear of danger. The pumps were never quitted; and though expecting that the ship might capsize, yet the question of 'Does she gain on us?' was asked, and when answered in the negative, there was still a manifestation of hope. Our fate, however, yet hung in suspense, for not in the smallest degree did the ship right: happily for us, there was a dead calm, which permitted us to examine the berg."

We cannot conclude better than by adopting what may be regarded as Captain Back's deliberate opinion of his own and the attempts of others to explore the Arctic regions and shores.

" It is not a little remarkable to reflect on the various ineffectual attempts that have been made by different commanders in modern days to fill up the small blank on the Northern charts between the bottom of and part of Regent's Inlet and Point Turnagain. Parry's and Franklin's achievements are too well known to require observation, or eulogium from me: the former could not penetrate through Fury and Hecla Strait, and the latter found it impracticable, from the damaged condition of his canoes, the want of provision, and the advanced state of the season, to proceed beyond Point Turnagain. Of Sir John Ross's eventful expedition all have heard. My own, in search of him is also before the public. Captain Lyon, in trying to reach Repulse Bay by the Welcome, was baffled by a succession of bad weather and heavy gales. And now again, I acting upon the settled experience of most of the distinguished names just mentioned, and the circumstances considered favourable, after getting nearly within sight of my port, am stopped by drift ice, at what is generally the very best period for navigating the Polar Seas; an frozen that; in October 1835, at the entrance of Fraserl Strait; and now, June 16th, am carried into Hudson's Strait, on some of the very same ice that originally begirt the ship, without having had it once in my power either to advance or retreat. In short, from north, south, east, and west, the attempt has been made; and in all equally without effect; and yet, with a tolerably open season, the whole affair is within the accomplishment of six months."

This volume is illustrated by a map and some plates from spirited drawings; and will doubtless, on account of the deep interest which the human mind takes in the history of bold undertakings, ardeous and gallant exertions, ever hereafter maintain a prominent shelf in every library of maritime literature, in every good collection of voyages and travels.

ART. XIII.

1. *Letters on the Natural History of the Insects mentioned in Shakspeare's Plays. With Incidental Notices of the Entomology of Ireland.* By ROBERT PATTERSON, Treasurer of the Natural History Society of Belfast. London: Orr & Co. 1838.

2. *Shakspeare's Autobiographical Poems. Being his Sonnets clearly developed: with his Character, drawn chiefly from his Works.* By C. ARMITAGE BROWN. London: Bohn. 1838.

THE most natural form of speech is that of dialogue. In real life the drama is earlier than the oration or the poem. Men talked together by twos and by threes, long before they had occasion to sing songs or to address senates. They invented language for the service and pleasure of every-day life, thinking of nothing further than its use in making love and managing their children and servants. When in later days society had grown, and art and refinement crept in, this homely instrument was taken up and applied to a wider purpose; it was employed to express trains of careful thought, curious inventions of fancy, the deep solitary musings of thoughtful genius, and the burning inspiration of the bard and the patriot. To this end, it of necessity somewhat changed its character; it became less colloquial, and more formal, stately, and graceful. Still more did it become so, when, instead of being spoken to the ear, it came to be written down in painful characters for the eye; when what had been "winged words" grew stationary, and instead of flying to the mind through the indolent ear, waited in grave black forms, upon a dead page, to be sought for by the inquisitive eye. Thus the active, sparkling, witty dialogue, with which man began his life on earth, passed into the prosy speech, the grave treatise, the methodical dissertation, the measured poem.

All these, being not the natural but the artificial use of a natural

instrument, were of course liable to all the infirmities of human art,
and, among others, to the special one of being heavy and tedious.
The man in conversation, who harangues instead of talking, has
departed from the primitive type of humanity, and become a bore;
and when one of his harangues, or any similar production, deprived
of the life imparted to it by the countenance, voice, and occasion,
has been made a fixture by the pen or the printing-press, the chance
is that it has grown to be tenfold more tedious, and baffles the most
patient attention. Nothing, but use, could tolerate this mechanical
method of receiving ideas. To the unaccustomed, it is but a rude,
bungling, unsatisfactory imitation of the easy and cheerful primitive
speech. A grown man, though he should master the alphabet and
the spelling-book, will hardly learn to enjoy reading. He can listen
with delight to animated conversation, he can bend an unfatigued
attention to even a profound discussion, and bear his part in it with
the readiness of a vigorous intellect; but over an oration in print,
or even an amusing tale, his mind wanders, and he falls asleep.
Custom has not rendered easy to him the unnatural process of
receiving thought through the eye, instead of the ear. Thousands,
we doubt not, who listened with enthusiasm to the recitation of old
Homer's poems, would have accounted the perusal of them on parchment, as dull as it is to the idlest sophomore of these degenerate
days.

Hence it might be expected, that written composition would seek
those forms which should most nearly resemble the primitive modes
of familiar intercourse. Accordingly we find at all times a large
tendency toward the dialogue. Even historical narrative originally,
as in the Old Testament and in the classical writers, was greatly
dramatic. The poets have especially adopted this method, and in
many instances with illustrious success. Milton, perhaps, never
excelled his own "Comus" and "Sampson"; and within the present
generation, many gifted authors have given this fashion to their
ripest and most beautiful inventions. Byron took the dramatic form,
after trying all others, and adhered to it with enthusiasm, making
it the medium of some of the noblest as well as most exceptionable
creations of his great mind.

There must be some peculiar advantages attendant on this form
of composition, or it would not thus engage the labours of the gifted,
in the face of its obvious difficulties. No doubt the associations of
romance and feeling with the drama, with its gigantic works in past
times and its fairy illusions in childhood, have done something to
effect this result. No doubt the natural interest, that pertains to
conversation, has done something. There is much in the circumstance that the reader is introduced to persons, rather than things,
to things only as they affect persons, and to persons themselves in
propriâ personâ, if it be not a bull to say so, and not in description
or narrative. He sees, hears, becomes acquainted with them; he

does not merely hear about them. The author, too, finds facilities for invention in the circumstance, that, speaking in the place of others, and not in his own person, he is compelled frequently to vary his position, to look on all matters from different points of view, and, instead of being confined to that one set of feelings, associations, and opinions which belong to himself, to express those which are suitable to many. He thus in fact multiplies himself; opens many veins of thought, and gathers innumerable suggestions of fancy, from which he would be wholly debarred if writing in monologue. The field of the drama thus becomes one of inexhaustible fertility. Imagination, personating now one and now another, looking on nature, on man, and on the incidents of the scene, first with the feelings of one party and then with those of another, gathers novelty and riches at every step of the progress.

This however implies the power of throwing aside one's identity, the poet's casting himself into the place of another. This great power of the imagination is perfectly possessed by few, and every degree of imperfection unfits for the work. Here, therefore, lies the chief impediments to success. The author is tempted at every turn to forget his assumed character and to speak in his own tongue; thus to destroy the verisimilitude by causing the persons of the scene to recite descriptions or sentiments, beautiful in themselves and well suited to the author, but inappropriate to the characters and situations. Few have the self-denial requisite to blot out some of their happiest passages, simply because they are inappropriate. Authors are, in this, too like the pretty actress, who makes herself ridiculous by the rich elegance of dress, in which she personates the part of the bar-maid, sacrificing to her own appearance the propriety of the piece.

This introduction will, perhaps, not be considered inappropriate to the subjects that we intend to embrace in this article. We shall first endeavour to show the great acquaintance Shakspeare had with natural history, and the valuable uses he made of this knowledge; and shall also try and trace, with the excellent glossary before us, the names of various species, both of the animal and vegetable kingdom, alluded to by the "Immortal Dramatist" in his plays.

We now present our readers with a slight notice of a few of the plants mentioned in Shakspeare, which we have abridged from a paper read before the Medico Botanical Society, by Mr. Rootsey, and which will exhibit the "Bard of Avon" as a most exact surveyor of the vegetable world.

"Hemlock. I was lately inquiring the particular species which the Welsh call Cegyd, and was told it differed from hemlock. Hemlock, they said, grew in gardens, like parsley; but Cegyd grew in moist hedges, with a smooth spotted stalk. Shakspeare likewise speaks of hemlock as a corn-field plant, which can be no other than the Æthusa Cynapium.

> ' Crown'd with rank fumiter and furrow weeds,
> With harlocks, hemlock, nettles, cuckoo-flowers,
> Darnel, and all the idle weeds that grow
> In our sustaining corn.'—*Lear*, act iv. sc. 4.

" In other places he is very precise in distinguishing it from *kecksies*, by which name I have always heard the Conium maculatum distinguished in Essex.

> ' Her fallow leas
> The darnel, *hemlock*, and rank fumitory
> Doth feed upon, while that the coulter rusts
> That should deracinate such savagery.
> The even mead, that erst brought sweetly forth
> The freckled cowslip, burnet, and green clover,
> Wanting the scythe, all uncorrected rank
> Conceives by idleness, and nothing teems
> But hateful docks, rough thistles, *kecksies*, burs,
> Losing both beauty and utility.'—*K. Henry V.*, act v. sc. 2.

This word *kecksies* is evidently the Welsh Cegyd, and the Latin Cicuta.

" It was the root of hemlock which was used as an ingredient in the poisonous cauldron of the Witches in *Macbeth*.

> ' The root of *hemlock* digg'd in the dark.'—Act iv. sc. 1.

" As the Conium maculatum is likely to be meant in this place, I think the Æthusa should be called by Withering's name of *lesser hemlock*.

" The etymology of the word hemlock is obscure. I consider that the word is derived from its ill smell, and consists of the aspirate H prefixed to the radix, which in Greek is Moly, from μολυω, to *moil*, or *defile*. Hence it is properly applicable to the Allium moly, and the Ligusticum Pelopponense, which latter I suppose to have been the Concion of the Greeks.

" *Fumiter*, or *Fumitory*. This double orthography of our poet illustrates the etymology of this word. It takes its name of Fumus terræ from its almost aerial lightsomeness and glaucous colour.

" *Thistle.* The world thistle seems to belong to the Dipsacus, called in English Teasle, and in Latin Carduus, from its having the shape of a heart. Wool is carded and teased by means of the Dipsacus fullonum. I suppose it takes the name of Dipsacus from its thirsty nature; for in all weathers it holds between its leaves an abundance of water.

" *Harlock, Charlock, Scharlock*, and *Scarlet*, seem to be the same word with garlick, and perhaps carrot, and originally applicable to the Sinapis arvensis, or the Allium moly, or some other plant of a more orange colour. In this neighbourhood, the name of Carlock cups is given to the Ranunculi, and perhaps the Caltha; and, after all, the Calendula may be the true plant from whence the name of scarlet is derived.

" *Nettles*, I have no doubt, receive their name from their use as a substitute for hemp in the construction of nets, and therefore the word applies to Urtica, although in this place it may be supposed as equally applicable to Lamium, or the dead nettle.

" *Cuckoo-flowers*. This name is applied to three genera, Cardamine, Lychnis, and Orchis. On asking a poor woman for the name of the Lychnis diocia alba, she said it was called Ladies' attire.

' And lady-smocks, all silver white,'
And cuckoo-buds of yellow hue.'

Love's Labour Lost, act v. sc. 2.

a name certainly preferable to that of our poet for the Cardamine pratensis, to which he evidently applies it. The orchis is called in Essex Cuckoo-flower. The woodseer, called in the New Forest Cuckoo-spit, and which, as I was informed in Sweden, the peasants consider as the cause of madness in cattle, abound upon the Lychnis and the Cardamine, and seems to indicate why they should bear the name of Cuckoo-flowers. Linnæus gives to the Ragged Robin the name of Flos cuculi, which I consider to be less entitled to it than the diocia; for I believe the latter to be Shakspeare's plant. The flowers of Cardamine are considered to be antispasmodic; but, in the New Forest, the Genista anglica is administered to children for those convulsions that accompany dentition.

" The cuckoo-*buds* of the above passage must be the Caltha palustris, and may possibly be our author's cuckoo-*flowers.*

" *Darnel* is said to be a poison which destroys the sight : its quality is narcotic, and its name I suppose to be from the same radix as the Greek δαρθάνω, *dormio.* The word ray, or in French *jurag*, seems to be the Greek αιρα, and to mean poison, as *æs æris* in Latin, whence *ærugo.*

' 'Twas full of *darnel*, do you like the taste ?'

1st *part K. H. VI.* act iii. sc. 2.

The Myrica gale seems to possess an intoxicating property, and is used sparingly for that purpose in Norway, in their drink.

" *Burnet,* in Latin *sanguisorba,* so called from its use being chiefly confined to young females, appears to me to be equivalent to the Greek word *parthenium,* a name generally applied to another plant used as an emmenagogue.

" *Cowslips.* The soporific principle of these flowers may perhaps reside in their freckles. The poet has pointed to it, in his *Midsummer Night's Dream,* with peculiar beauty and elegance :—

' The cowslips tall her pensioners be,
In their gold coats spots you see ;
Those be rubies, fairy favours :
In those freckles live their savours.
I must go seek some dewdrops here,
And hang a pearl in every cowslip's ear.'—Act ii. sc. 1.

The agreeable odour of these flowers would indicate that the virtue, if extracted by the chemist, might combine the advantages of opium with those of saffron.

" *Clover.* This, I imagine, derives its name from its leaf being cloven; it would then have the same meaning as *clubs* at cards.

" *Docks.* This herb may take its name from its penetrating into the ground. A *dog* may also be supposed to be named from the propensity of the terrier to *dig* into the earth. The genus Rumex, particularly the species of Hydrolapathum, or Aquaticus, presents us with an excellent astringent. Its affinity to the rhubarb, and the use made of the species R. acutus, would entitle it to rank high in the materia medica. The Britannica of the ancients was our common water-dock, and I am not aware that we possess a more powerful or more eligible native astringent than this plant.

" *Burs.* Woodville, in his Medical Botany, figures the Arctium lappa, which prefers a drier situation than the A. Bardana ; the latter must therefore be considered the plant of Shakspeare. The name is doubtless of the same meaning as briar, and seems to imply that it is borne away by the passing traveller, to whose clothes the flowers or the stems strongly adhere.

" *Mandrake.* There are two plants which are denominated Mandrake by our countrymen ; they have large and forked roots. Of these, the Bryonia diocia is largest, white, and hairy ; the Tamus communis is smaller, dark, and smooth. Shakspeare compares *Justice Shallow* to these roots.

' I do remember him at Clement's Inn, like a man made after supper of a cheese-paring. When he was naked, he was for all the world like a forked radish, with a head fantastically carved upon it with a knife ; he was the very genius of famine, yet lascivious as a monkey, and they called him Mandrake.'—*King Henry IV.* act iii. sc. 2.

" The etymology of the word is from its root being generally divided, and forked, like a man.

     ' Semihominis mandragorae flores.'—*Colum.*

It is also denominated Mandragon by Gerard. The English word man exists in the Latin *humanus ;* likewise in the Hebrew, and other languages. In the present instance, it is found in the Greek combined with the word *dracon,* from δερκω, *aspicio.*

" Littleton supposes the word is substituted for *andragoras,* from ανηρ, *vir,* and αγορεω, *loquor.* ' Quod humanam speciem quodam modo etiam vocem quum evellitur, si vera tradunt referat ejulans ?' To this Shakspeare adverts :—

     ' And shrieks like mandrakes torn out of the earth :
     That living mortals, hearing them, run mad.'

                Romeo and Juliet, act iv. sc. 2.

Again,

     ' Would curses kill as doth the mandrake's groan,
       I'd—' *2nd. Part King Henry VI.,* act iii. sc. 2.

From hence it appears that the plant was believed to utter a horrible and fatal shriek when dug out of the earth.

" A small forked root has been received in this country from Chinese Tartary, the name of which is Ginseng. I have always believed that the Chinese etymology of this word, was *Jin seang* (*vide* Morr. 8868), Mr. Morrison, however, in No. 8803, gives it differently ; and in part iii. p. 187, he gives it thus, *jin-san,* from *jin,* a man, and *san,* gradual ; its slow growth being supposed, according to him, to have suggested the name. I am still of opinion that the form 8803 is rather derived from 8868, or *jin-seang,* man's likeness ; and I have no doubt but it has the same meaning as the word mandrake, although the origin of the term may have been obscured by its antiquity.

" Mr. Morrison illustrates the use of this root in the following paragraph, which, as it indicates its virtue, I may be pardoned for transcribing. ' The tree Shang-tang gin-seng may be essayed by two men walking together a few miles, one having jin-san in his mouth, and the other with his mouth empty. When he who has nothing in his mouth is panting exceedingly, the other's breath will be just as usual.' This passage reminded us of Shakspeare's

> ' One poor pennyworth of *sugar-candy* to make thee long-winded.'
>
> *King Henry VI.*, act iii. sc. 3.

Thus, gin-seng appears to be chewed in the celestial empire as tobacco is with us. Loureiro shows that the Canadian root, Nin-sing, is very different in quality as well as in appearance. Galen, writing of mandrake, observes, that its virtue resides in its rind, or bark, and he considers it as cold in the highest degree. By his terms, hot and cold, we must understand the acrid and the narcotic of modern toxicologists; and those plants, the temperature of which, by the old writers, was considered as of the third and fourth degree, must merit our particular attention. The plant of Galen was the Atropa mandragora, and the Circæum of Pliny, employed by Circe in her incantations. Shakspeare alludes to it when, to imply madness, he says,

> ' I think you all have drank of *Circe's* cup.'.
>
> *C. of Errors*, act v. sc. 1.

And again,

> ' Or have we eaten of the *insane-root*,
> That takes the reason prisoner ?"
>
> *Macbeth*, act i. sc. 3.

" As the lurid Solanum Melongena, Melanzana, or Mala insana, *mad-apples*, is evidently named from its effect upon the brain, so the analogous root of the Atropa mandragora must be the insane-root of Shakspeare. It was also administered in the liquid form; for *Cleopatra* says,

> ' Ha, ha,
>
> Give me to drink *mandragora*,
> That I might sleep out this great gap of time.'
>
> *Ant. & Cl.* act i. sc. 5.

The syrup of it was likewise given as the syrup of poppy :

> ' Not poppy nor mandragora,
> Nor all the drowsy syrups of the world,
> Shall ever medicine thee to that sweet sleep
> Which thou hadst yesterday.'—*Othello*, act iii. sc. 3.

" As the hemlock and the marmaduke, so the hebenon, &c., were directed to be gathered at midnight.

> ' Thoughts black, hands up, drugs fit, and time agreeing,
> Confederate season, else no creature seeing.
> Thou mixture rank of *midnight weeds* collected,
> With Hecate's ban thrice blasted, thrice infected,
> Thy natural magic and dire property
> On wholesome life usurp immediately.'—Act iii. su. 1.
>
> (*Pours the poison into the sleeper's ears.*)

" Being a native of the countries of Circe and Medea, it was no doubt one of those which the latter collected to renovate Æson.

> ' In such a night
> Medea gathered the enchanted herbs
> That did renew old Æson.'

" The Parisian Circæa *lutetiana* is by our botanists denominated *Enchanter's*, or Enchantress's nightshade; but I generally give it the shorter name of Hagwort, and, in the manner of Pythagoras, I dedicate it to the number 2, as the Horse-chesnut and Ragwort to the numbers 7 and 13, expressive of the major and minor modes in music, and of the weeks and lunations in astronomy.

" The mandrake of Scripture, which had a remarkable smell, was evidently the flower of a different plant. In Hebrew it is *Dudaim* or *Davidaim*, as it were Flos amoris, or Flor amor; and hence probably our word Daffodils,

> ' That come before the swallow dares, and take
> The winds of March with beauty.'— *Winter's Tale*, act iv. sc. 4.

The daffodils of Milton were, however, our Crown imperials, as, lamenting the death of Lycidas, he says, alluding to the nectaries of that flower;—

> ' Bid Amaranthus all his beauties shed,
> And Daffodillies fill their cups with tears,
> To strew the laureate hearse where Lycid lies.'

" *Poppy*. Having found that our Foxglove is denominated poppies in the New Forest. A reason is given, that the flowers can be popped upon the hand. The Papaver therefore is improperly called in English by that name. The seeds of the purple Papaver are known by the name of mawseed, which indicates the proper English appellation of that plant; and this agrees with its name in the different languages that are dialects of the Teutonic, and also with the Greek *meson*, &c. Shakspeare, however, when he alludes to its entering into the composition of drowsy syrups, must have meant the Papaver somniferum.

" *Long purples*. The name of Foxglove, or Folk's-gloves, Finger-flower, or Digitalis, and Dog-fingers, as it is called in Wales, together with the magnificent spike of purple flowers borne by the Digitalis purpurea, induce me to conjecture that this plant is alluded to by our illustrious poet as long purples :

> ' There is a willow grows ascaunt the brook,
> That shows his hoar leaves in the glassy stream;
> Therewith fantastic garlands did she make
> Of crow-flowers, nettles, daisies, and long purples,
> That liberal shepherds give a grosser name,
> But our cold maids do *dead men's fingers* call them.'
>
>   *Hamlet*, act iv. sc. 7.

" The common *blue bells*, might perhaps be thought to be the garland-flower of *Ophelia*; but Lightfoot says it is the Orchis mascula, though Martyn considers that the name of Dead-men's fingers would better apply to the palmated species. Lightfoot, thinking probably that he had discovered the liberal name, may have supposed, upon this foundation alone, that the plant was an orchis. What this liberal name is in reality may be known to gentle shepherds, but by me is only supposed to be the same which Dampier has applied to a South American tree, whose flowers may perhaps resemble those of our digitalis in form, if not in colour. In Hampshire, the Lotus corniculatus is called dead men's fingers, but in the vicinity of Bristol the plant has various names; fingers and toes, devil's fingers, devil's claws, and crow-toes. The last seems to point it out as the tufted crow-toes of Milton's Lycidas. Gerard, however, in his Index, applies this name to the hyacinth, which, by Johnson, in his supplementary Appendix to his edition of Gerard, is called crow-leek.

"Gerard gives the name of

"Crow-flowers to the Lychnis floscuculi, while to another species, the diocia, he has attached that of crow-soap, which latter, in Johnson's Appendix, is made synonymus with Saponaria, or soap-wort. I think none of these were the crow-flowers of the poet. The Caltha palustris is called by that name in some parts of the country, and is much used by children in their garlands and festivities, together with the flowers of Ranunculus bulbosus and R. acris, which are called Craysies and Mayflowers. The latter term in Middlesex is given to the Iris palustris. In Essex the flowers called May are those of the Prunus spinosa, rather than the Cratægus oxyacantha. This discrepancy in our English names may be considered as a reproach to science; but the botanist, who delights in the contemplation and study of wild words as well as wild flowers, may find an ample field, or rather garden, for his erudition, in comparing the synonymes of British and European Plants, especially those whose faculties were discovered and appreciated by our experienced and benevolent ancestors, who extended their researches

　　　　　　　' To every herb that sips the dew.'

The Caltha I take to be the Mary-buds of Shakspeare.

　　　　　' And winking mary-buds begin
　　　　　　　To ope their golden eyes,
　　　　　　With every thing that pretty bin,
　　　　　　　My lady sweet arise.'—*Cymbeline*, act ii. sc. 3.

The Marygold is the Calendula.

　　　' The marygold that goes to bed with the sun,
　　　And with him rises weeping.'—*Winter's Tale*, act iv. sc. 3.

"*Hebenon.* Shakspeare ascribes the death of *Hamlet* to the juice of hebenon having been poured into his ear. As he beautifully describes the action of the poison, I transcribe the entire passage.

　　　　Ghost. ' Sleeping within mine orchard,
　　　　(My custom always of the afternoon,)
　　　　Upon my secure hour thy uncle stole,
　　　　With juice of cursed hebenon in a vial,
　　　　And in the porches of mine ears did pour
　　　　The leperous distilment; whose effect
　　　　Holds such an enmity with blood of man,
　　　　That, swift as quicksilver, it courses through
　　　　The natural gates and alleys of the body,
　　　　And, with a sudden vigour, it doth posset
　　　　And curd, like eager droppings into milk,
　　　　The thin and wholesome blood: so did it mine;
　　　　And a most instant tetter bark'd about,
　　　　Most lazar-like, with vile and loathsome crust,
　　　　All my smooth body.'—*Hamlet*, act i. sc. 5.

" The word hebenon means black, the h being a non-essential letter. Hence I conceive this plant to have been the Atropa Belladonna, which, where it is within Gloucestershire, is by the country people called, from the colour of its fruit, Inkberries. From the following passage, I think it may have been used for poisoning darts and javelins;

'Love's golden arrow at him should have fled;
And not death's ebon dart, to strike him dead.'—*Ven. and Ado.*

"I make no doubt that the name of Henbane is a corruption of hebenon, and strictly applicable to the blackberry of the Dwale, so called from its effect in making us *dull* and sullen. (Hence Solanum? *Lethale*).

'And duller shouldst thou be than the fat weed
That roots itself in ease on Lethe's wharf,
Wouldst thou not stir in this.'—*Hamlet*, act i. sc. 5.

"As for the word *nightshade*, given probably from its forming a shed for the night, this seems appropriate to the dulcamara, whose bending twigs form an arbour like the clematis. I once imagined, though I have not had an opportunity of proving it, that the nightshade possessed the property of shedding and diffusing a peculiar smell during the night, and that it derived its name accordingly. This property has furnished appellations to the lily and the lilac.

"*Heart's-ease.*—There is an interesting, and as I am informed, an ancient custom, which has descended to the present day, now existing in some parts of Wales, that, when a lady wishes to deviate from the usual practice of waiting for certain advances to be made by the other sex, she, in a graceful and elegant manner, by presenting the gentleman with a flower of the Viola tricolor, is understood to make the first overture; and thus silently, but expressively, relief is made to supersede the anxiety of mind, which is occasioned by a state of uncertainty and inquietude. Hence the name of Heart's-ease.

'Musicians, O musicians! *Heart's-ease, Heart's-ease* ! Oh,
An you will have me live, play *Heart's-ease*.'—
'Why *Heart's-ease* ?'—
'Oh, musicians, because my heart itself plays
'*My heart is full of woe!*'—*Romeo and Juliet*, act iv. sc. 5.

"The French word *pensez*, supposed to be pronounced by the flower at the moment it is presented, as if conscious of the tale it bears, is the origin of our Pansey. Nothing can be more poetical than Shakspeare's use of this all but innocent flower, in his *Midsummer Night's Dream*, from which we naturally derive another etymology, that of

'These blue-veined *violets* whereon we lean.'—*Ven. and Ad.*

'I saw, but thou couldst not,
Cupid all armed : a certain aim he took
At a fair vestal, throned by the west,
And loosed his loveshaft smartly from his bow
As it should pierce a hundred thousand hearts;
But I might see young Cupid's fiery shaft
Quench'd in the chaste beams of the watery moon,
And the imperial maiden passed on,
In maiden meditation, fancy free.
Yet mark'd I where the bolt of Cupid fell;
It fell upon a little western flower,

Before milk white, now purple with Love's wound,
And maidens call it *love in idleness.*
Fetch me that flower, the herb I show'd thee once;
The juice of it on sleeping eyelids laid,
Will make or man or woman madly dote
Upon the next live creature that it sees.

*   *   *   *

And ere I take this charm off from her sight,
(As I can take it with *another herb,*)
I'll make her render up her page to me.'—Act ii. sc. 2.

"The medical efficacy of these plants, however, as cordials, would doubtless be lost in the form of syrup, notwithstanding its sweetness; and I have chiefly alluded to them for the purpose of inquiring what was the plant intended by Shakspeare, under the name of *Dian's bud,* to counteract the charming influence of *Love in Idleness.*

'Dian's bud o'er Cupid's flower
Hath such force and blessed power.'—Act iv. sc. 1.

"Could this by possibility have been the Samolus valeraedi? My curiosity once prompted me, when walking with a farmer of my neighbourhood, to ask him if he had a name for this venerated plant, and he informed me he had only once heard it called *Kenningwort* by an Englishman, in Wales, who performed remarkable cures as an oculist by its means. He said the plant received its name from its use curing that complaint of the eye denominated the 'Kenning,' which is 'when a substance resembling a pea forms upon the candle of that organ.' Hence the Samolus, stated by Pliny to have been worshipped in this island by our ancestors, was probably this plant, and considered by them as emblematical of the efficacy of science deterging from the intellect the foul cataracts of ignorance and error. How appropriate to the purpose of the poet ! to dissipate by its agency the hallucination of love, and to dispel all overweening fondness for our most darling prejudices.

"*Yew.*—The yew seems to have taken its name from its having been employed in the construction of yokes for cattle; or perhaps, *vice versa,* the yoke, from its having been made of yew. In this latter case, the name would be derivable from the fruit, resembling in its form and in its viscous quality the yolk of an egg. Perhaps the name exists in the Greek ζυγια, our Carpinus, or true Welsh hasel, the workers of which were the original carpenters. On the Mediterranean shores, the cypress is used for coffins, because of its incorruptibility, and the tree is planted over the graves of the dead.

'Come away, come away, Death,
And in sad cypress let me be laid.'—*Twelfth Night,* act ii. sc. iv.
'Cypress black as e'er was crow.'—*Winter's Tale,* act iv. sc. 3.

"Again,

'Their sweetest shade a grove of cypress trees.'
A cypress, not a bosom hides my poor heart.'—*T. N.* a. iii.

"The true English name for the Tamcox gallica is Clifris evidently similar to cypress, derived from a Hebrew word for grave, which occurs in the name of a station in Arabia, mentioned in the Pentateuch, *Kibroth katdavak*, or the 'glutton's graves.' The word *cripe* is the English *raid*, confounded in orthography with the tree in the above passage. In the north of Europe the yew is planted for the same reason; its boughs are over the hearse, and its sprigs are introduced into the coffin. Shakspeare, in his *Twelfth Night*, directs the shroud to be stuck with it.

> 'My shroud of white, stuck all with yew,
>   Oh, prepare it.'—Act i. sc. 4.

" The chemical principle upon which depends the incorruptibility of this beautiful wood, and which renders the tree all but immortal, is probably the same with its poisonous quality, and which rendered it an important ingredient in the witch's cauldron :—

> 'Gall of goat, and slips of yew,
>   Stiver'd in the moon's eclipse.'—*Macbeth*, act iv. sc. 1.

" I understand, in some parts of England, it is the custom as soon as a person dies, to sponge the corpse over with infusion of its fresh leaves: this preserves the body from putrefaction, and preserves it for many weeks. Professor Martyn describes the case of a young lady, who was accidentally poisoned from drinking this infusion by mistake, instead of *rue* tea, as she was advised. The result was, that although dead, she retained the bloom of her countenance, so that her attendants believed her to be only in a trance: she was accordingly kept a long while uninterred, and was finally buried without any appearance of putrefaction. The importance of this wood in ancient warfare, has suggested the epithet of double-fatal, used by our author in *King Richard II.*, act iii. sc. 2.

> ' The very beadsmen learn to bend their bows
>   Of double-fatal yew against thy state.'

" Some have supposed that it was on this account so highly venerated by our ancestors, and planted by them in our churchyards ; but I consider this opinion to be unfounded. Many of the yew-trees of this country are certainly 3000 years of age, and I believe that most of those in our church-yards, which are four feet thick, and some are from eight to twelve, must be older than the introduction of Christianity into this kingdom; but the demonstration and the store of facts which corroborate and prove my position, are too copious to detail in this place.

" *Plantage—*' As true as steel as plantage to the moon.' Can this be the Alisma ? or is it one of the Lunarias or moonworts ? I suppose it is the Alisma plantago. The dedication of this herb to the moon, or Diana, from its temperature being considered cold, and from its influence upon hydrophobic patients and lunatics, and also from its seeds being emmenagogue, leads me to conjecture that this must be the species chosen by our poet as the emblem of fidelity. The word Plantago, Plantage, or Plantain, implying the similarity of the leaf in shape to the sole of the foot, may be more strictly applicable to the Plantago major, or the sweet-scented media; but the virtues of all are very imperfectly known to the scientific world. An individual who was bitten by a mad cat was not affected with the dread of water till the lapse of a long time, but she experienced a recurrence of pain and irritation *at every change of the moon*, and she was finally attacked by death, after the regular intermission of a month. I am therefore of opinion that Shakspeare was acquainted with the fact that hydrophobia is relieved by the Alisma. It might be advantageous to our excellent society, if its learned members were to institute inquiries amongst the poor people of the country relative to the properties of this and such like plants, and not reject hastily and with disdain the important knowledge to be sometimes derived from their experience. It was by such inquiries that my late immortal friend made the discovery of vaccination, which, by philosophical reasoning and induction, he rendered more and more certain as a preventive of one of the most distressing ' ills that flesh is heir to.' The more common use of ordinary plantain as an application to wounds is likewise noticed by Shakspeare."

> ' *Benvolio.* Take thou some new infection to thy eye,
> And the rank poison of the old will die.
> *Romeo.* Your plaintain leaf is excellent for that.
> *Benvolio.* For what, I pray you ?
> *Romeo.* For your broken shin.'—*Rom. and Jul.*, act i. sc. 2.

"The plant Horehound is likewise a remedy for hydrophobia, and takes its name accordingly ; the first syllable of the word being the Greek * opis*, *curo ;* and Dioscorides attests its efficacy. The true horehound is therefore the Marrubium Alyssum, or the Alyssum of Galen.

" We may likewise inquire relative to the Dog-violet, whether the Viola canina may not possess this faculty, or the Dentaria, called toothed violets, and sometimes dog's-tooth violets, or the Erythronium dens canis : called also in Hampshire, where it is abundantly wild, the dog's or hound's tooth violet.

" The name of hound's-tree, or hound's or dog's berry, given to the Cornus, would authorize a trial of this fruit likewise in this horrible complaint.

" Whether the word Madnep indicate another cure may be inquired, and whether the name apply to Heracleum Sphondylium, Heracleum Panaces, Partinaca Opopanax, or the Angelica Archangelica ?

" But, if we are to believe Pliny, we are indebted to the oracle for the discovery that the root of Cynosbatos, or Cynorrhoden, Rosa canina, or dog-rose, is a remedy for hydrophobia. It will appear, from the following extracts, that our medical roses were all known to Shakspeare, and celebrated by him, although not indeed for their therapeutic efficacy.

" Notwithstanding the best conserve is made from the fruit of the Rosa arvensis, or apple-rose, yet we must suppose that our poet, by scarlet hips, referred to the fruit of the common briar. ' The oaks bear mast, the briars scarlet hips.' *Timon*, act iv. sc. 3.

" The R. damascena is used for syrups, and the variety γ of Martyn must be the true damask-rose, so elegantly and poetically referred to in the following passages :

> ' Fair ladies mask'd are roses in the bud ;
> Dismask'd, their damask sweet commixture shews,
> Are angels veiling clouds, or roses blown.'
> *Love's L. L.* a. v. s. 2.
> ' There was a pretty redness in his lip,
> A little riper and more lusty red
> Than that mixed in his cheek : 'twas just the difference
> Betwixt the constant red and the mingled damask.'
> *As You Like It*, act iii. sc. 5.

'' I have seen roses damasked red and white,
   But no such roses see I in her cheek.'—*Sonnet* 130.
' Gloves as sweet as damask roses.'
                              —*Winter's Tale,* act iv. sc. 5,

" He also contrasts the *red* with the *white* rose, both of which contain the same medical astringent property. The white rose being rubbed on alkaline paper, instantaneously produces a very beautiful yellow colour, which may be used as a dye."

We will now turn our attention to the Animal Kingdom alluded to by Shakspeare; and in this branch of the subject we find that he depicts and dissects, without any admixture of error, the phenomena of animated nature, and with a precision truly astonishing for the age in which he lived. To illustrate his accuracy in this respect, we will extract from Mr. Patterson's work respecting the beetle.

" The beetle's hum is recorded by Crabbe among
              ——" the sounds that make
          Silence more awful."
Shakspeare has introduced it with the happiest effect into his ' Macbeth.'
              ——' Ere the bat hath flown
      His cloister'd flight; ere to the black Hecate's summons
      The Shard-borne beetle, with his drowsy hums,
      Hath rung night's yawning peal, there shall be done
      A deed of dreadful note.'—*Macbeth,* act iii. sc. ii.

" And here I may be permitted to remark, that a very slight knowledge of Natural History may occasionally assist us, in understanding the description of such authors as record what they themselves have noticed. The beetle is furnished with two large membranaceous wings, which are protected from external injury by two very hard, horny wing cases, or, as entomologists term them, elytra. The old English name was ' shard,' and this word was introduced into three of Shakspeare's plays. Thus, in his ' Antony and Cleopatra,'—
      ' They are his shards, and he their beetle ;'—act iii. sc. ii.
and in ' Cymbeline,'—
      ' Often to our comfort do we find
      The sharded beetle in a safer hold
      Than is the full wing'd eagle.'—act iii. sc. iii.
" These shards or wing cases are raised and expanded when the beetle flies, and by their concavity act like two parachutes in supporting him in the air. Hence the propriety and correctness of Shakspeare's description, the ' shard-borne beetle,' a description embodied in a single epithet. I do not mean to assert that the word shard has not other meanings ; in fact, it is employed by Hamlet in its primitive English signification—a piece of broken tile ; for the priest says of Ophelia,
      ' Shards, flints, and pebbles should be thrown on her.'—act v. sc. i.
I only deny that any of its other meanings should be used in the present instance. The one most applicable is that given by Mr. Tullet, as quoted in the notes to Ayscough's edition of Shakspeare, that ' shard-born beetle

is the beetle born in cow-dung; and that *shard expressed* dung is well known in the north of Staffordshire, where cow's shard is the word generally used for cow-dung.' But it is not so likely that Shakspeare was acquainted with the stercoraceous nidus of the insect, as that he observed the peculiarity of its flight, assisted by its expanded elytra; and if the word at the time he lived had both meanings, I hope you will acknowledge the one I have given to be the more probable. Should you, however, feel disposed to enter more fully into a question of the kind, I would refer you to a long and very interesting note published in the Zoological Journal, No. xviii. p. 147."

Our next extract from this entertaining volume shall relate to the bee and bees wax.

"Thus Cade, after having declared that he will ' make it felony to drink small beer,' and announced his intentions relative to other legislative enactments of a corresponding character, proceeds in a strain admirably illustrative of the man :—

"' Is not this a lamentable thing, that the skin of an innocent lamb should be made into parchment, and that parchment being scribbled o'er, should undo a man. Some say the bee stings; but I say' tis the bee's wax: for I did but seal once to a thing, and I was never my own man since.' "— *Second Part Henry VI.*, act iv. sc. ii.

" When Edgar had overcome the steward of Goneril, he takes from his pockets the letters confided to his charge; and as he breaks the seal, he justifies to himself the act he is committing :—

'Leave, gentle wax, and manners, blame us not;
To know our enemies' minds, we 'd rip their hearts;
Their papers are more lawful.'—*Lear*, act iv. sc. vi.

It is again mentioned, when Imogen, the fond and faithful Imogen, receives a letter from her lord Leonatus; her words are—

' Good wax, thy leave,—bleat be
Yon bees, that make these locks of counsel! Lovers
And men in dangerous bonds pray not alike;
Though forfeiters you cast in prison yet,
You clasp young Cupid's tables.'— *Cymbeline*, act iii. sc. ii.

" You are of course aware, that the sealing-wax we now employ consists of lac and resin, combined with some suitable pigment for giving it the desired colour. This lac is itself an insect product, being secreted by a species of coccus common in the East Indies. No portion of bees'-wax enters into the composition of the material now used for sealing letters; but that it may at a former period have been so used, I will not presume to deny. At present, it forms the principal ingredient of the soft and colourless wax attached to letters patent under the Great Seal, or to charters of corporations, and public documents of a similar character; but ' the lover, sighing like furnace,' never confides his sorrows to the custody of the bee's wax.

" The researches of modern times have ascertained a remarkable fact relative to the formation of this substance, namely, that it is secreted by bees different from those which attend to the feeding of the young; or, in other words, the working bees, which were formerly supposed to be all alike, may be divided into two classes,—wax workers and nurses.

" For our knowledge on this subject, we are principally indebted to the observations of a blind man,—the elder Huber, who made the study of bees the occupation and solace of many years of visual darkness. This he was enabled to do by the undiring attention of his wife, who faithfully recounted the phenomena which glass hives, variously constructed, enabled her to witness. He saw by means of her eyes, and in his experiments he was assisted by a patient investigator, M. Burnens. From Huber we learn that wax is not collected from flowers, as was formerly supposed, but is secreted by the wax-workers by means of peculiar organs, which may easily be seen, by pressing the abdomen so as to cause its distension. It is not, however, a secretion that is constantly going on; it is one which takes place only when wax is required for the construction of the comb. To supply it, the wax-workers are obliged to feed on honey, and to remain inactive, generally suspended from the top of the hive, for about twenty-four hours previous to the deposition of the wax. What we read, therefore, of the bee collecting wax and carrying it to the hive, is fabulous. The error originated in the pollen with which bees are so frequently laden, and which forms the bee bread of the community, being mistaken for two little pellets of wax, which the industrious insect was supposed to have gathered. Shakspeare, as might be expected, has adopted the universal, though incorrect, opinion of his day. In the line, therefore,

" . . . . Our thighs are pack'd with wax "—

we recognize one of those instances, where the knowledge of the present time can be contrasted advantageously with that of the past.

" The word ' honey ' is of frequent occurrence. When, in the English camp at Agincourt, King Henry the Fifth, after the just and profound reflection—

' There is some soul of goodness in things evil,
Would men observingly distil it out;'—

illustrates his meaning still further, by the observation—

' Thus we may gather honey from the weed.'—act iv. sc. i.

When Friar Lawrence is waiting in his cell for the arrival of Juliet, and is endeavouring to control the transport of the expecting Romeo, he well remarks—

' These violent delights have violent ends;'

and adds—

—— the sweetest honey
Is loathsome in his own deliciousness,
And in the taste confounds the appetite;
Therefore, love moderately.'——act ii. sc. vi.

But in general, the word is used metaphorically, not literally. Thus Norfolk, in speaking of Cardinal Wolsey, says—

—— the king hath found
Matter against him, that for ever mars
The honey of his language.'—*Henry VIII.,* act iii. sc. ii.

And in the scene where Ophelia has borne the strange and incompatible language of Hamlet, ' get thee to a nunnery,' after her first thought, which all a woman's fondness, has been given to his mental aberration—

'O! what a noble mind is here o'erthrown;'
she deplores her own condition, in the words—

'And I of ladies most abject and wretched,
That suck'd the honey of his music vows.'—act iii. sc. ii.

In the same manner the word is employed by Romeo, on his descent into
the monument where lies the 'living corse' of the 'fair Juliet.'

——'O my love! my wife!
Death, that hath suck'd the honey of thy breath,
Hath had no power yet upon thy beauty.'—act v. sc. iii.

Not content with using the word both in a literal and in a metaphysical
sense, the Poet has interwoven it into several endearing epithets, as 'honey
dew,' 'honey name,' &c.; and in 'Julius Cæsar,' the still more euphonious
expression—

'Enjoy the honey-heavy dew of slumber,'—act ii. sc. i.

"The admirable symmetry and regularity of the combs have, no doubt,
attracted your attention; but perhaps you are not aware, that their form is
almost that which a mathematician would select to combine the greatest
extent of accommodation and greatest strength, with the smallest expenditure of material. The cells are arranged so close together, and in a manner
so skilful, that no space is lost between them. The knowledge of the fact,
that there are no vacant spaces between the cells, gives increased effect to
the words of Prospero, when he replies to the imprecations of Caliban :—

——'Thou shalt be pinch'd
As thick as honey-combs : each pinch more stinging
Than bees that made 'em.'—*Tempest,* act i. sc. ii.

This passage refers to a fact in the economy of bees, which I have not yet
noticed : I mean their power of stinging. Of this fact, almost every one
has, at some time or other, had painful experience. Shakspeare says—

'Full merrily the humble bee doth sing,
Till she hath lost her honey and her sting;'—
Troilus and Cressida, act v. sc. xi.

a couplet which leads us to infer that the Poet was well aware of these
insects losing their sting, by being unable to retract it from the wound they
have inflicted.

"In the sarcasms to which Brutus and Cassius give utterance against
Antony, the same topic is thus introduced :—

'*Cas.*—The posture of your blows are yet unknown ;
But for your words, they rob the Hybla bees,
And leave them honeyless.
Ant.—Not stingless too—
Bru.—O yes, and soundless too ;
For you have stol'n their buzzing, Antony,
And very wisely threat before you sting.'—
Julius Cæsar, act v. sc. i.

"From the numerous passages in which the bee is introduced, we might
almost be warranted in supposing that this insect was a favourite with
Shakspeare. It has certainly furnished him with numerous similes, and
what is rather remarkable in a writer possessed of such varied powers of illus-

stration, he has earned it to be twice mentioned by King Henry the Fourth, in the course of one scene,—first, when meditating on the wild and riotous life pursued by the Prince; and, secondly, when he supposes that the anxiety felt by his son for the crown had caused its removal from his pillow. The first of these passages, has been already noticed; the second, I shall now quote:—

> "How quickly, nature falls into revolt,
> When gold becomes her object.
> For this, the foolish over-careful fathers
> Have broke their sleeps with thought, their brains with care,
> When, like the bee, tolling from every flower
> The virtuous sweets,
> Our thighs are pack'd with wax, our mouths with honey,
> We bring it to the hive; and, like the bees,
> Are murder'd for our pains.'—*Second Part Henry IV.*, act iv. sc. iv.

The mode in which this murder is committed, is indicated by Shakspeare in another passage. Talbot is giving vent to his surprise and vexation at the English troops being repulsed by Joan of Arc.—

> 'As bees with smoke, and doves with noisome stench,
> Are from their hives and houses driven away.'—
> *First Part Henry VI.*, act i. sc. v.

To one accustomed to look at Nature with an observant eye, the indifference manifested to her works by most individuals seems at first sight irreconcileable with that innate inquisitiveness which characterises mankind. While the poet's ear is thrilled with her soft melodies, while his imagination catches the living echo of that anthem which the morning stars hymned at creation's birth, while his soul expands as it expatiates amid this created world of wonders, and while around every sight and every sound from the vast earth and ambient air sends to his heart the choicest impulses, his brother's insensibility is to him a mystery. Every fibre in his own bosom is throbbing with delight as he looks abroad over the fair earth and variegated forms which tread its surface; joyous and stirring perceptions come thronging upon his mind, new and beautiful analogies are developing themselves to his fancy; but why is his brother unmoved? is the power of sensation palsied; or, are the heart-springs of gladness sealed up within him? No; but the spell of ignorance is upon him; he has never been initiated in the varied wonders of this magnificent world. To render this more enticing this pursuit which has been said to be "an object worthy of a good man," has in fact been the aim of Mr. Patterson. He has attempted to communicate in a pleasing form the wonders which natural history unfolds to us; and, we think, has accomplished the task he proposed to himself with considerable ability.

If the whole field of external nature, animate and inanimate, be open and free to the poet, and a great and rich storehouse from which he derives much of his wealth, unquestionably human life, the history of mankind, and especially the world within himself, are a

nor less frequent study and, ~~the theatre to which he is correct.~~ Of all men
Shakspeare was the closest ~~inspector and most faithful delineator of~~
the character of man,—his own experience, his self-dissection, no
doubt, furnishing him with the happiest and finest illustrations.
But it seems to be expecting too much, and a too literal record,
that he or any other poet should ever have set himself to autobiographical writing when exercising the powers of imagination,
especially when his surest road to excellence was to throw aside his
identity, and to cast himself into the place of another, as the case
might require. Yet the author of the second work at the head of
this article will have it, that the greatest of all poets when composing
his Sonnets was not only developing his own character, but bequeath-
ing in detail much of his personal history: he will have it, in short,
that these remarkable poems are no sonnets at all, but that they
form one continuous piece, the different portions of which cannot be
understood or justly appreciated, if taken in any other way, and
according to any other view.

Besides this alleged discovery, Mr. Brown will have it that Billy
Shakspeare was a learned as well as a travelled man; but what is
better and more, he will have it that his moral character was unimpeachable, and that in all the relations of private as well as in social
and public life, he was a model of excellence. All these things he
attempts to prove by the internal evidence found in the dramatist's
works,—ingenuity and conjecture far oftener coming to the author's
aid than facts, trustworthy testimony, or demonstration.

Mr. Brown says that Shakspeare was bred a lawyer's clerk, and
to prove this he quotes some score or two of lines, as if the Univer-
salist's words were uniformly self-descriptive or self-illustrative, and
just as if the poet of boundless observation, of the ever-creative and
modelling imagination, was a formal autobiographer. According to
this mode of interpretation, would it not be more reasonable to
assert that Shakspeare had been a Lecturer on Natural History, or
that he was a member and fellow of Botanical and Zoological
Societies? What is indeed the department in life or the branch of
knowledge to which he might not be made to belong, if such evidences are to be held conclusive? Perhaps, if he is to be identified
with any technical and distinct profession, that of a sailor, a mariner,
will appear the true and special one, for a good authority has said
that the "boatswain in the 'Tempest' delivers himself in the true
vernacular style of the forecastle,"—in a style, indeed, which, it may
be presumed, no inland man could have picked up.

But while we think that Mr. Brown is more ingenious than sound
or satisfactory, he sometimes acts the part of an original and a
sagacious critic. The following long extract affords a favourable
specimen, which the students of Shakspeare will do well to follow
out, always bearing in mind that conjecture must not be taken for

complete evidence, nor correction for perfection. Speaking of "All's Well that ends Well," our author says,

"This comedy is ascribed to the year 1598 or 9, by the chronologers, on no authority whatever. To me it appears, from its general character, an earlier work by some years. Here the third and fourth acts are chiefly at Florence. The expressions ' beside the port,' of course, means ' beside the gate,' otherwise it is a sad error; but Helena, as a pilgrim, going to the shrine of the ' great St. Jacques,' is strange enough; and such names as Escalus and Corambus are very unlike his after Italian names. *Romeo and Juliet*, an early play, contains nothing more of Italian manners than can be found in the English poem, from which it is taken, of *Romeo and Juliet*. Here we have another *Escalus*, and odd corruption, I conjecture, of Della Scala, the real prince, according to Bandello and Da Porto. As for the *Two Gentlemen of Verona*, it tends to shew more strongly than the two last mentioned, that Shakspeare, before 1597, knew not Italy as it appears he did afterwards; and that the intuitive knowledge of genius by no means belonged to him. His knowledge of the language has been denied. A question on this subject properly appertains to a consideration of the extent of his learning, of which I am about to treat; but it will be of more service in this place. Dr. Farmer thus speaks of the Italian words introduced into his plays : ' Their orthography might lead us to suspect them to be not of the writer's importation.' Whose, then, with bad orthography ? I cannot understand this suspicion; but, perhaps, it implies that the words, being inaccurately printed, were not originally correct. The art of printing was formerly far from being so exact as at present; but even now, I beg leave to say, I rarely meet with an Italian quotation in an English book that is correct ; yet I can perceive, plainly enough, from the context, the printer is alone to blame. In the same way I see, that the following passage in the *Taming of the Shrew* bears evident marks of having been correct before it was corrupted in the printing of the first folios, and that it originally stood thus :

Petruchio.—Con tutto il core ben' trovato,—may I say!—
Hortensio.—Alla nostra casa ben venuto, molto onorato signor
mio Petruchio.'

These words shew an intimate acquaintance with the mode of salutation on the meeting of two Italian gentlemen; and they are precisely such colloquial expressions as a man might well pick up in his travels through the country. My own opinion is, that Shakspeare, beyond the power of reading it, which is easily acquired, had not much knowledge of Italian ; though I believe it infinitely surpassed that of Stevens, or of Dr. Farmer, or of Dr. Johnson; that is, I believe that while they pretended to pass an unerring judgment on his Italian, they themselves must have been astonishingly ignorant of the language. Let me make good my accusation against all three. It is necessary to destroy their authority in this instance. Stevens gives this note in the *Taming of the Shrew*, '*Me pardonate.* We should read, *Mi pardonate.*' Indeed we should read no such thing, as two silly errors in two common words. Shakspeare may have written *Mi*

perdoni, or Perdonatemi; but why disturb the text further than by changing the syllable *par* into *per*? It then expresses, instead of *pardonums—
me being pardoned*, and is suitable both to the sense and the metre,

> 'Me Perdonato,—gentle master mine.'

Dr. Farmer says,—' When Pistol cheers up himself with ends of verse,'
he is only a copy of Hanniball Gonsaga, who ranted on yielding himself
a prisoner to an English captain in the Low Countries, as you may read
in an old collection of tales, called *Wits, Fits, and Fancies,*

> 'Si fortuna me tormenta,
> Il speranza me contenta.'

This is given as Italian, not that of the ignorant Pistol, nor of Shakspeare,
but of Hanniball Gonsaga; but how comes it that Dr. Farmer did not look
into the first few pages of a grammar, to teach him that the lines must have
been those?

> Se fortuna mi tormenta.
> La speranza mi contenta.

And how could he corrupt orthography (a crying sin with him) in the name
of Annibale Gonzaga? Upon this very passage Dr. Johnson has a note,
and, following the steps of Sir Thomas Hanmer, puts his foot, with uncommon profundity, in the mud. He says,—' Sir Thomas Hanmer' reads,
' Si fortune me tormenta, il sperare me contenta,' which is undoubtedly the
true reading, but, perhaps, it was intended that Pistol should corrupt it.'
Perhaps it was; but ' undoubtedly' the Doctor in his ' true reading,' containing five blunders in eight words, has carried corruption too far. There
is not much Italian in Shakspeare's works, and possibly, as I have said, he
did not know much more, though his century was very favourable to its
study. When he wrote *Hamlet*, we may presume he knew nothing
of the language, simply on account of his making Baptista the name
of a woman; an error he could otherwise have scarcely committed,
and which he corrected in a later play. The commentators having
settled, to their own satisfaction, that he was quite ignorant of Italian,
contented that his fables could not be derived from any of the *Novellieri*,
unless they had proof of a translation of the same existing in his
time. Thus they have sought everywhere for hints in English whereby
he might have formed the fable of *The Merchant of Venice*, because
that tale in the *Pecorone* was not then translated; though, for very
many reasons, it is well nigh impossible he could have taken it from
anything but that tale. If, as they confess, no published translation
existed of it in his time, then one must have been made expressly for
him, or, what is more probable, he read it in the original. To my
mind, there is further reason for believing that he read Italian. The
fable of the *Tempest* may be ascribed to his own invention, since no
similar tale is known. This I believe; yet, in my fancy, there is a
shadowing forth of it in the Milanese history; and I am not aware of
any part of that history having been translated in his time. It is true
no historical event is engrafted on the romance; but Lodovico Sforza,
ambitious to reign, resolved on the destruction of his inert nephew, the
lawful Duke Giovanni Galeazzo. Compare this with the usurpation of
Antonio over the reigning Duke, Prospero, absorbed from public affairs
in his books. But Lodovico, not daring in the city to 'set a mark so

bloody on the business.'—Prospero's words,—gave his nephew a lingering poison, and then led him away to Pavia to die. Again, there
is much in these annals of the political alliances between the courts of
Milan and Naples. Add to this, at the period of the usurpation of the
Milanese Duke Lodovico Sforza there was a Ferdinand, King of Naples,
son of Alfonzo (Shakspeare calls him Alonso); and Ferdinand's son,
though not himself, as the *Tempest*, married a princess of Milan. This is
what I mean by the shadowing forth of a romance from history. Assured
that he visited Italy, I give him, in my imagination, with some reasons on
which to rest, a direct line of travel from Venice, through Padua, Bologna,
and Florence, to Pisa. I do not say he forbore to go a little out of his way
to visit Verona, the scene of his own *Romeo and Juliet*, nor that he did
not even see Rome; but I have no grounds for such a supposition. Should
my arguments be unavailing with my readers, I have at any rate made
known his wonderful graphic skill in representing to the life Italian characters, and Italian manners and customs,—solely from books and hearsay?"

As to the Sonnets, our author says, they are not, "properly speaking," sonnets. He continues,—"a sonnet is one entire poem contained in fourteen heroic lines, of which there are but three in the
collection; the two last, and one near the last, which will be
explained." Again, "the remainder of the sonnets, so miscalled,
are poems in the sonnet-stanza. These poems are six in number;
the first five are addressed to his friend, and the sixth to his mistress." By these and some other hints our author thinks that he
has unlocked every difficulty, and directed the attention to a pure
and intelligible stream of autobiographical history. The sonnet-
stanzas are thus divided and described,—

"First Poem. Stanzas 1 to 26. To his friend, persuading him to
marry.—Second Poem. Stanzas 27 to 55. To his friend, who had robbed
the poet of his mistress, forgiving him.—Third Poem. Stanzas 56 to 77.
To his friend, complaining of his coldness, and warning him of life's decay.
—Fourth Poem. Stanzas 78 to 101. To his friend, complaining that he
prefers another poet's praises, and reproving him for faults that may injure
his character.—Fifth Poem. Stanzas 102 to 126. To his friend, excusing
himself for having been some time silent, and disclaiming the charge of inconstancy.—Sixth Poem. Stanzas 127 to 152. To his mistress, on her
infidelity.—Such should have been (had the printers in 609 received
efficient directions, and had they done their duty) the order and manner of
these poems. The attentive reader will be convinced that these divisions
are neither arbitrary nor fanciful, but inevitable. An unsought-for recommendation is, that they are thus formed into poems tolerably equal in length,
varying from twenty-two to twenty-six stanzas each."

In vindication of Shakspeare's moral and conjugal character, and
as regards an oft-repeated imputation, we are glad to have the following rational and agreeable conjectures.

"His wife was in no way alluded to when the will was first drawn out.

All his lands and personal effects, with few exceptions, appear to have been bequeathed between his two married daughters. Afterwards, interlineations were made, leaving trifling sums to his friends, or, as he calls them, his 'fellows,' Heminge, Burbage, and Condel, 'to buy them rings;' and this *item* was also interlineated,—' I give unto my wife my second best bed, bed with the furniture.' Well! there was already a sufficient provision made for the wife, which may properly be presumed, and for which tolerable evidence can be adduced, quite strong enough for the occasion. Every bequest and every condition in the will, we may imagine, were made with the wife's knowledge and consent. She, being provided for, could not but be pleased at the division of the bulk of his property between her daughters. Had the property been left out of the family, we might have imagined otherwise. But, after reading over the will, preparatory to signing, the testator thought, or it was suggested to him, that some mention of his wife ought to be made, with some memorial for her. When appealed to for her choice of a memorial, she fixed on a particular bed, which happened to be known in the house, and, consequently, must be so designated as the ' second best bed;' upon which the bequest, her own choice, was interlined. Such is my interpretation; which, of course, rests much on the probable evidence I can produce of a sufficient provision having been made for her. In the first place, it was likely she possessed property in her own right, as the daughter of a substantial yeoman; but on that it is not necessary wholly to insist. In his will everything he possessed seems specified, with the exceptions of the copyright of his works, or his share of it, and his shares in the theatre. For whose benefit were they? We cannot believe that he had disposed of his interest in the theatre when he retired to Stratford, because we have proofs to the contrary in his having written plays there and sent them to be performed at his own theatre; and, to the last, he called his partners his 'fellows,' not his *former* fellows, which he must legally have done, had they ceased to be partners. Further the conjunction of memorials, in interlineations, to his three principal partners and to the wife, looks like a shareholding connexion in his mind between them, which was to commence immediately after his death. Is it not then probable that, by a special agreement, he, and afterwards his wife, provided she outlived him, had certain shares in the theatre? The copyright also might have been prohibited by agreement, from publication, as long as either he might choose to withhold his works from the press, or his wife might live, in order to make the performance of his dramas more profitable; or until he chose, as an individual shareholder, if not as the author, to give his consent. Whether we suppose that the copyright was the property of all the shareholders, so that the publication required the consent of each individual, or that it was his own sole property during life, and afterwards his widow's for her life, we still find that her consent as shareholder, or by previous agreement, was necessary for its publication. For her own interest, as a life receiver of the yearly profits, it is not unreasonable to suppose she would not consent to the printing of the manuscripts, knowing they remained secure. But what grounds have we for believing all this, besides those already stated? A fact, I answer, to which, for such a purpose, no allusion has been made—the publication of all the plays immediately on the death of the widow in 1623. She was buried on the 8th August, and the folio was entered at Stationers' Hall on the 8th November following. Heminge and Condell were then no longer restrained, and they edited the works for their own profits. We read nothing in their *Dedication* or *Preface*; we have heard nothing of any part of the profits being for the daughters."

The subjects and the notions to which Mr. Brown invites our attention, afford room for a vast deal of speculation; but we must conclude by expressing it as our opinion, that the talent and spirit which have throughout rendered his work not only readable but interesting, might have been far more advantageously applied than in the present case; although, at the same time, it is but justice to declare, that of the thousand and one volumes of which Shakspeare has been the topic and the prompter, the one before us is neither the least ingenious, satisfactory, nor useful.

ART. XIV.

1. —*The Life of Edward Jenner, M.D.* By John Baron, M.D. London: Colburn. 1838.

2. —*Medical Portrait Gallery.* By Joseph Pettigrew, F.R.S. London: Fisher and Son. 1838.

Of all the learned professions, or those termed polite and genteel, the Medical, we believe, has furnished, considering the number of its students and practitioners the fewest subjects of popular biography. Lawyers, divines, artists, gentlemen of the army and navy, have in countless numbers been made the heroes and the themes of books; but owing, perhaps, in part, to the unceasing and uniform duties of those persons who prescribe for our bodily ills, or brandish the lancet, or dose us with drugs, and partly perhaps, to the unromantic and repulsive character of these ills and of their treatment, exciting only a professional interest, the histories of medical men seldom occupy the pens of the *littérateur*, or the ears of fashionable and studious readers. It is quite certain, however, that few of our race are allowed to remain very long unconcerned regarding the character and skill of some one of the Faculty. His visits to the sick chamber, his instrumentality in the saving of life, or services in alleviating pain, and in restoring to the blessings of health, are never forgotten, or thought of with indifference. Why then does not the history of the physician or the surgeon whose eminent services are known to thousands, and who may have essentially benefited persons dear to us, be less an object of biographical interest, than that of the warrior who has led an army to battle, where thousands have fallen and been slain? As it is by the glitter and pomp of pageantry, it is by the power of certain chivalrous and romantic associations that the mind is influenced far more than by the prosaic realities of every-day life; so that he who has been one of the most efficient instruments in behalf of humanity, who has brought comfort and happiness to multitudes of individuals and family circles, may descend to the grave ingloriously, while the scourge of his race may have his exploits trumpeted forth by posterity.

What were the merits of a Bonaparte, a Cæsar, or an Alexander, when compared with the agencies and triumphs of such men, as those, whose names and portraits, are now before us? In what country, in what age, has there clung to either of them at their decease, or afterwards, a thousandth part of the gratitude which Jenner has obtained and deserved? Why, there is not a quarter of the globe, there is scarcely a family in whole nations, there need never be an individual in this or any other country, we have reason to believe, who will not or ought not to pronounce the name with the warmth and affection due to a personal and universal benefactor. And yet what was the treatment he experienced, the opposition he encountered in his god-like career? Ridicule, misrepresentation, envy, jealousy, abuse instead of argument, were what his marvellous discovery had to stand up against; nor indeed were his opponents and impugners prompt to believe, even after facts, practice, and all but universal proof were on his side.

In the present work, Dr. Baron has traced and characterised the difficulties which Jenner had to combat in his noble enterprise for the well-being of our species, no matter of what grade in the artificial and conventional scale of life. The beggar and the prince owe him equal debts; nor is there a saint in the calendar whose memory is half so worthy of homage.

It is only from the second volume of this Life, the first having formerly appeared, that we shall now take a few passages.

Though Jenner met with the return in his own country which proverbially is that allotted to true prophets, the great, and mighty, as well the humble of other lands appreciated his merits and warmly gave expression to their grateful feelings. But still it was the lowly rather than the lofty and powerful who rewarded him most willingly and affectionately. True, when the foreign crowned heads were in England in 1814, the Emperor of Russia received him graciously, and shook hands kindly with him at parting. The Autocrat also told the Doctor that " the consciousness of having so much benefited your race must be a never-failing source of pleasure, and I am happy to think that you have received the thanks, the applause, and the gratitude of the world." Jenner's reply, though in such a presence, was characteristic and remarkable. As reported by himself, it was in these words, that " I had received the thanks and the applause, but not the gratitude of the world."

Though the potentates did not either in their individual capacity when in England, or in congress at Vienna, confer any mark of distinction on the author of vaccination, Dr. Baron tells us that some of their subjects did bear him nobly in their memory. The following characteristic testimony by the inhabitants of Brünn will amuse by its half German and half Latin style of English, whilst its spirit and truth will come home forcibly to every well-informed and well-regulated mind.

" To the Right Honourable Physician Edward Jenner, Discoverer of the Cowpock; the greatest Benefactor of Mankind; at London.

"Most Honourable Doctor,—At the most distant frontier of East Germany, in a country where the Roman's army two thousand years before triumphing; and 444 the Savages Huns under the command of Attila, and 798 the Emperor Charles, the Huns with success combating, passed, and where the Swedes under Gustav the Great 1615 have made tombly the ground of the country by the thousands of cannons, and there where even 1740 the Prussians and 1805 the French warriors victorious appeared in that remarkable country had the vaccined youth from Brünn, with the most cordial sentiment of gratitude to thee, a constant monument with thine breast-piece in the 65th year of thine age erected, even in the same time as the great English nation, by her constancy and intrepidity, rendered the liberty of the whole Europe, and as the great again Alexandre and William passed through this country. Accept generously, great man, that feeble sign of veneration and gratitude; and Heaven may conserve your life to the most remote time; and every year, in the presence of many thousand habitans, a great feast near that temple is celebrated for the discovery of vaccina. We will us estimate happy, if we can receive few ligues to prove us the sure reception of that letter. Most honourable doctor, yours most obedient servant.

            " Medicinæ Doctor Raymann, physician.
" Claviger, { first surgeon and vacciner at Vaccine Institution at Brünn.

       " Brünn in Moravia, the 20th October.

"A drawing of the ' monument,' as it is called, accompanied this letter. In the centre of the temple the bust of Jenner stands upon a pedestal, on which is the following inscription—

            " Divo Anglo
            Eduardo Jenner,
            LXV.
            Ætatis ejus Anno
            Vaccinata Brunensis
            Juventus
            MDCCCXIV."

By stringing together a few anecdotes, we will obtain an exceedingly agreeable impression of the character and the habits of Jenner.

" During his residence at Berkeley he acted frequently as a magistrate. I found him one day sitting with a brother justice in a narrow, dark, tobacco-flavoured room; listening to parish business of various sorts. The door was surrounded by a scolding, brawling mob. A fat overseer of the poor was endeavouring to moderate their noise; but they neither heeded his authority nor that of their worships. There were women swearing illegitimate children, others swearing the peace against drunken husbands, and able-bodied men demanding parish relief to make up the deficiency in their wages. The scene altogether was really noxious; and when I considered who was one of the chief actors, and the effect which the mal-administration of a well-intended statute produced, I experienced sensations which would have been altogether painful had there not been something irresistibly ludicrous in many of the minor details of the picture. He said to me, 'Is not this too bad? I am the only acting magistrate in this place, and I am really harassed to death. I want the lord-lieutenant to give me an assistant; and I have applied for my nephew, but without success.' On this visit he shewed me the hide of the cow that afforded the matter which infected Sarah Nelmes; and from which source he derived the virus that produced the disease in his first patient, Phipps. The hide hung in the coach-house, he said. 'What shall I do with it?' I replied, 'Send it to the British Museum.' The cow had been turned out to end her days peaceably at Bradstone, a farm near Berkeley."

The first effects of Jenner's discovery, on some of his sapient town folks, and their manner of treating it, may be learned from the following anecdotes.

"One lady, of no mean influence among them, met him soon after the publication of his 'Inquiry.' She accosted him in this form, and in the true Gloucestershire dialect. 'So, your book is out at last. Well, I can tell you that there be'ant a copy sold in our town; nor sha'n't neither, if I can help it.' On another occasion, the same notable dame having heard some rumours of failures in vaccination, came up to the doctor with great eagerness, and said, 'Sha'n't us have a general inoculation now?'* Both these anecdotes he used to relate in perfect good humour."

Jenner gains upon our esteem and affection as we turn the leaves of Dr. Baron's book.

"On another occasion, when travelling with him towards Rockhampton, the residence of his nephew, Dr. Davies, he observed, 'It was among these shady and tangled lanes that I first got my taste for natural history. A short time afterwards we passed Phipps, his first vaccinated patient. 'Oh! there is poor Phipps,' he exclaimed, 'I wish you could see him; he has been very unwell lately, and I am afraid he has got tubercles in the lungs. He was recently inoculated for small-pox, I believe for the twentieth time, and all without effect. At a subsequent visit, (Oct. 1818) I found lying on his table a plan of a cottage. 'Oh,' said he, 'that is for poor Phipps; you remember him: he has a miserable place to live in, I am about to give him another. He has been very ill, but is now materially better.' This cottage was built, and its little garden laid out and stocked with roses from his own shrubbery, under his personal superintendence. I may now mention some incidents of a different character. The celebrated Charles James Fox, during a residence at Cheltenham,

* "I. e. Small-pox inoculation."

had frequent intercourse with Jenner. His mind had been a good deal poisoned as to the character of cow-pox by his family physician, Moseley. In his usual playful and engaging manner, he said one day to Jenner, "Pray, Dr. Jenner, tell me of this cow-pox that we have heard so much about, what is it like?" "Why, it is exactly like the section of a pearl on a rose-leaf." This comparison, which is not less remarkable for its accuracy than for its poetic beauty, struck Mr. Fox very forcibly. He laughed heartily, and praised the simile. It has been seen that, notwithstanding the personal kindness that Dr. Jenner had with foreign states, he had next to none at home. He never succeeded in procuring an appointment for any of his relatives or friends. He mentioned that all his attempts to get a living for his nephew George had failed, though addressed to quarters where they might, without presumption, have been expected to have met with attention and success. This neglect hurt him deeply. He once said to me, "This ought to be known. You must give them 'a hard one;' and I will find an eagle's quill and whet the nib for you.' I never saw him more happy than in spending some days with Dr. Baillie at Duntisbourne, near Cirencester, in the summer of 1820. He had much recovered from the depression left by the death of Mrs. Jenner; and all the recollections of his youth, his intercourse with Mr. Hunter, together with many of the remarkable incidents which were connected with his own life, formed animating themes for conversation. The scenes around them, also, in the vicinity of the place (Cirencester) where he had first gone to school, and where he used to grope for fossils in the oolitic formation, supplied him with many associations of long-past years. I spent one of the days with them on this occasion. They passed their time in the free and unreserved interchange of their thoughts and their experience. It was cheering to see the great London physician mounted on his little white horse, riding up and down the precipitous banks in the vicinity of the house, or trotting through the green lanes, and opening the gates, just after the manner of any Cotswold squire. Nothing could exceed the relish of Baillie for the ease, and liberty, and leisure of a country life, when he first escaped from the toil, and effort, and excitement of his professional duties in London."

"Never did Lord Bacon's principles of patient and legitimate induction find a better illustrator and disciple than Dr. Jenner. This will in part appear from the able and candid summary given by the present biographer, which we now cite.

"If we look at the origin of this discovery, from its first dawning in his youthful mind at Sodbury, and trace it through its subsequent stages—his meditations at Berkeley—his suggestions to his great master, John Hunter—his conferences with his professional brethren in the country—his hopes and fears, as his inquiries and experiments encouraged or depressed his anticipations—and, at length, the triumphant conclusion of more than thirty years' reflection and study, by the successful vaccination of his first patient, Phipps, we shall find a train of preparation never exceeded in any scientific enterprise; and, in some degree, commensurate with the great results by which it has been followed. In the space of a very few years, the fruit of this patient and persevering investigation was enjoyed in every quarter of the globe; and the rapidity of its dissemination attests alike the universality of the pestilence, and the virtue of the agent by which it was in many places subdued, mitigated, extirpated. On the other side, let us remember his trials, his mortifications, the attemps to depreciate his discovery, and to check its progress, together with the personal injuries which he endured from those who affected to do him honour, and we shall find many things to counterbalance the homage and gratitude which he derived from other sources. Under all these changes, he sustained the equanimity and consistency of his character; humble when lauded and eulogised, patient and forbearing when suffering wrong; and, if it be an assured sign of a worthy and generous spirit to be amended by distinction and renown, no man ever gave stronger proofs of possessing such a spirit. Again, we have to view him in the character of a physician, exercising all the resources of a painful and anxious profession with extraordinary humanity, ability, and perseverance; cultivating his beautiful taste, for natural history and all the poetry of life, in connexion with labours so arduous and important. While interpreting nature, he enjoyed a pleasure surpassed by none of his predecessors; but he did not rest there, and might have exclaimed with the great Linnæus, *O quàm contempta res est homo: nisi supra humana se erexerit!*

But Jenner is but one of a host of scientific and philanthrophic Medicalists who have exalted and adorned human character and life in byegone and present times. There is a long list of illustrious names and histories ready for the selection of our Portrait Gallery people. We are glad, indeed, to see a high-minded, intellectual, and influential class receive for the celebration of their virtues, their talents and their triumphs, the far-renowning aids of the artist, the scholar, and the man of science: and all these are brought beautifully and efficiently forward in the publication before me.

In the present five parts we have portraits, together with biographical and critical notices, of Sir H. Halford, Albinus, Sir A. Carlisle, Haller, Ruysch, Sir Ch. M. Clarke, Akenside, Linacre, Dr. James Blundell, Caius, Morgagni, &c. The plates are finished in the finest and most elaborate style of art; they are not surpassed by any one of the many works on a similar plan that have appeared in recent times. The literary notices are conceived in an enlightened and liberal spirit by one who is extensively known to be a proficient in the branches of science of which he particularly treats. In short, while we have in this beautiful publication a popular and deeply interesting account of many great men, there is also traced in those elegant and condensed biographies the history, the progress, and prospects of Medicine itself.

To the student of the healing art, and to the practitioner, as well as to the general reader or collector of a choice library, the Medical Portrait Gallery presents much solid value besides singular attractions. A part appears every month, price three shillings, which must be pronounced cheap. We should say that the English physician or surgeon who is not a subscriber, evinces a deficiency of taste as well as an apathy in regard to professional knowledge, which ought at once to affect his practice significantly.

NOTICES.

Had this volume come to hand before the preceding article was set, the same subject in our present number had gone to press, we should have had something more to say of the book and of its author than we can now make room for. We must, however, take time to confess that Mr. Reed's representations of the extravagancies and absurdities of the Magnetizers fall considerably short of the buffoonery and charlatanism, the jargon and the folly which the *Baron's* work exhibits from beginning to end. It is idle to argue with him, or any one who indulges in such assertions as the following, when speaking of the phenomena of somnambulism, and the persons brought under magnetic influence.

"1st. They converse clearly and intelligently with all those persons with whom they are en *rapport*, or in mental relation. 2nd. They perceive the relations of external objects through some other channel than the organs of sense, through which such impressions are usually conveyed. 3rd. Their perceptions in regard to the objects of their attention are more than ordinarily acute: but the organs of the senses are closed against other impressions. 4th. They manifest a clearness or lucidity of ideas, and a temporary knowledge and intellectual activity, beyond that which they possess in their ordinary waking state. 5th. They forget, when they are awakened, everything which may have taken place during their somnambulism; but on returning into the same state, they recollect everything which occurred during their former fits."

Animal Magnetizing has not been confined, we are told to believe, either to one age or to one country. People have magnetized and been magnetized when neither party were conscious of the cause, and long before, in fact, Mesmer or the system was ever heard of. Virgil's Sibyl, if we can credit our veracious Baron, prophesied when under the magnetic chase and ecstatic somnambulism. 'Nay,

"When the Laplanders wish to know what occurs in places remote from their habitations, they send out their familiar spirits in search of intelligence; and when they have sufficiently excited their own imaginations by the sound of drums and other musical instruments, they feel a kind of intoxication, during which certain things are revealed to them which they never could have known in their natural state."

Of course the explanation is at hand.

Where assumption, assertion, and absurdity are so redundant and monstrous, it may appear impossible to go further in folly and into the ridiculous. But let us search, and perhaps beneath the lowest depths a lower still may be discovered.

"A magnetised vitreous body, which had put a somnambulist to sleep in a few seconds, was afterwards rinsed with water, and wiped with a linen cloth; on being again presented to the same magnetic subject, he fell asleep in one minute and a half. The same magnetised glass, rinsed with alcohol, produced sleep in half a minute. Another magnetised glass, rinsed with ammonia, elicited somnambulism in fifteen seconds. The same glass was plunged into fuming nitric acid. After an immersion of five minutes, it was put into a China cup with water, out of which the young somnambulist having taken it, fell immediately asleep. The same experiment was repeated with concentrated sulphuric acid, and the result was exactly the same. In all these experiments no chemical re-agent could destroy the magnetic power of the magnetised glass. Hence it follows that this power, unlike colours, electricity, and other similar fluids, does not reside merely at the surface, but that it penetrates the whole mass."

Some simple and unstained persons may derive comfort from believing that it is only a vitreous body which, among inert and inorganic substances, is susceptible of imbibing such power and influence. But be not deceived, and remain no longer ignorant, for

"A large sheet of paper, twisted and magnetised, was burnt in a *silver* plate; the carbon and cinders which remained were presented to the somnambulist, who took up as much as his hand could hold, and fell asleep in a few moments. Many cross experiments were tried with objects which were not magnetised; but no effect whatever by them was produced; but those which were magnetised being preserved with care, produced the same effects six months afterwards;—they seemed to have lost none of their magnetic power."

Might not Animal Magnetism be turned to good account by love-letter writers? To the study of such persons as believe in it, we recommend these directions:—

"On the part of the magnetiser, the most important rule he can adopt is to exert the greatest energy of volition he can command. As, when the light of the sun is transmitted through a burning-glass, even in the depth of winter, the solar rays, which previously gave little or no warmth, being concentrated, and thus brought to a focus, ignite the combustible substances exposed to them; so likewise the human mind, which is the *mirror* of the soul, by converging its rays into one focus, affects the soul brought into juxta-position with itself. I repeat, the magnetiser must will with the utmost perseverance; he must not pity when he can succour the afflicted; he need offer no vows; but let him believe in his power, and act with energy. I do not mean with violent mental excitement, for this will neutralise the effects, by absorbing the principle which ought to produce them. He should, on the contrary, enjoy perfect ease and freedom; and though he is to send to his extremities a momentum or force sufficient to raise a considerable weight, he must have nothing but his own limbs to raise. It is the excess of this momentum which strikes the patient, and produces all the magnetic phenomena."

If any of our readers have a taste for more of this offensive nonsense, let them have recourse to Baron Dupotet's duodecimo, which contains three hundred and eighty-eight pages of similar stuff, and, we warrant it, they will have a sufficiency, and to spare. We can only now say that it is matter of satisfaction to us, but by no means matter of marvel, that the nonsense of which we have been speaking has had its day amongst us—that it has nearly ceased to be a topic of conversation, or thought worthy to be laughed at; that the Council of the London University College, it is reported, have forbidden the initiated to hold their exhibitions in any place over which the authority of the establishment extends; and, what is more amusing still, that certain confessions, on the part of the somnambulists, the magnetised patients, have been threatened and to some extent made, which, we suspect, if our information be true, will cover some high and proud heads among us with ridicule, beyond any degree yet expressed or measured out.

Art. XVI.—*Romantic and Picturesque Germany.* Nos. I. and II. London: Schloss. 1838.

A work which promises to possess no ordinary degree of interest for the English reader. It has, we believe, been well received in the countries which it professes to illustrate; and this is an argument in support of its accuracy and tasteful selection. The engravings are to extend in number to no fewer than *two hundred and sixty,* by English artists, from drawings taken on the spot, traversing the length and breadth, the mountains and the valleys, of Germany; its rivers, its towns and cities, its antiquities, and whatever recommends itself on account of awakening and wonderful recollections, obtaining special notice. The letter-press has been contributed by a variety of German writers, and the English translation is furnished by Miss Henningsen.

From the specimens before us, we are enabled to state that in point of art, the work will rank with others on a similar plan which have been extremely popular in this country. In as far as a *royal octavo* scale can admit, and steel can impress, the beautiful, the picturesque, and the majestic will be represented. We cannot say that the literary portion of the first two numbers has pleased us so well as the illustrations. A sort of boarding-school sentimentality seems to have oppressed the writer, that is, of a very commonplace order. It is blown, yet feeble, and, to us, rather sickening.

Art. XVII.—*Plain Advice on the Care of the Teeth, &c.* By D. A. Cameron, Surgeon-Dentist, Glasgow. London: Tegg. 1838.

The title, besides that part which we have already copied, announces that the volume contains a popular History of the Dentist's Art, and a Chapter to Mothers on the Management of Children during the first Dentition, all which we regard as a fair and nothing more than a correct account of the work, on a subject which to every human being is more or less, sooner or later, of importance.

Art. XVIII.—*The Missionary's Farewell.* London: Snow. 1838.

Here we have the Valedictory Address to the British Churches and the Friends of Missions, (together with other notices,) of the zealous, able, and tried Apostle of the South Sea Islanders, the Rev. John Williams, previous to his recent re-departure, to re-pursue his labour of love in the same regions. The occasion which called forth the contents of this publication, the paramount interest of the subjects treated of, and the character of the parties and persons who figure in its pages, require no description or notice at our hands. The life, adventures, and triumphs of Mr. Williams himself, as given in his history of his Missionary exertions, formerly reviewed by us, confer an extraordinary value on anything that is said of or by him.

LONDON:
J. HENDERSON, 18, BANNER-SQUARE.

Lightning Source UK Ltd.
Milton Keynes UK
UKHW020217091118
331957UK00012B/1536/P